D0932788

BUILDINGS OF THE UNITED STATES

BUILDINGS *of* MARYLAND

The Society of Architectural Historians gratefully acknowledges the support of Mr. and Mrs. Roger D. Redden, whose generosity brought *Buildings of Maryland* to publication.

Initial and ongoing support for the Buildings of the United States series has come from:

National Endowment for the Humanities

Graham Foundation for Advanced Studies in the Fine Arts

National Park Service, Heritage Documentation Programs (HABS/HAER/ HALS)

Library of Congress, Prints and Photographs Division

BUILDINGS OF
MARYLAND

LISA PFUELLER DAVIDSON
and
CATHERINE C. LAVOIE

UNIVERSITY OF VIRGINIA PRESS
Charlottesville and London

University of Virginia Press
© 2022 by the Society of Architectural Historians
All rights reserved
Printed in South Korea
First published 2022

9 8 7 6 5 4 3 2 1

Library of Congress Cataloging-in-Publication Data
Names: Davidson, Lisa Pfueller, author. | Lavoie, Catherine C., author.
Title: Buildings of Maryland / Lisa Pfueller Davidson and Catherine C.
    Lavoie.
Description: Charlottesville : University of Virginia Press, 2022. | Series:
    Buildings of the United States | Includes bibliographical references and
    index.
Identifiers: LCCN 2022001413 | ISBN 9780813948041
Subjects: LCSH: Architecture—Maryland—Guidebooks. | Maryland—
    Guidebooks.
Classification: LCC NA730.M3 D38 2022 | DDC 720.9752—dc23/
    eng/20220412
LC record available at https://lccn.loc.gov/2022001413

Frontispiece: Drum Point Lighthouse (WS25), Solomons.
(Photograph by Lisa Pfueller Davidson)

❯❯ CONTENTS ❮❮

HOW TO USE THIS BOOK   ix

FOREWORD xi

ACKNOWLEDGMENTS xiii

INTRODUCTION 1

Maritime Development and the Chesapeake Culture 4
· Transportation Innovations and Trends 5 · Industrial Baltimore 8
· Black Life and Culture 10 · Residential Maryland 12 · Artisans,
Builders, and Architects 14 · Conclusion 16

WESTERN SHORE 21

St. Mary's County 23 · Charles County 30 · Calvert County 39
· Anne Arundel County 46

EASTERN SHORE 84

Cecil County 86 · Kent County 97 · Caroline County 101 · Queen
Anne's County 105 · Talbot County 110 · Dorchester County 121
· Wicomico County 130 · Somerset County 133 · Worcester
County 141

BALTIMORE CITY 150

Mount Vernon and Environs 153 · Central Business District
West 165 · Central Business District East 176 · Inner Harbor
Area 181 · Federal Hill and Locust Point 185 · East Baltimore/
Old Town/Fell's Point 188 · Southwest Baltimore 199 · Northwest
Baltimore/Bolton Hill 207 · North Charles Street and
Environs 213 · North Baltimore and Jones Falls Valley 218

CENTRAL MARYLAND 228

Howard County 230 · Baltimore County 244 · Carroll County 259
· Harford County 270

CAPITAL REGION   283

Prince George's County 285 · Montgomery County 304

WESTERN MOUNTAINS 331

Frederick County 333 · Washington County 349 · Allegany
County 359 · Garrett County 373

SELECTED BIBLIOGRAPHY 381
ILLUSTRATION CREDITS 389
INDEX 391

» HOW TO USE THIS BOOK «

In *Buildings of Maryland* the state's twenty-three counties are organized into five regional chapters according to geography and shared history, with the independent city of Baltimore covered in its own chapter. Each chapter is introduced with a short historical summary, followed by individual entries. We have arranged the counties, communities, or neighborhoods into a suggested touring order within each chapter, as shown in the maps at the beginning. The sometimes circuitous routes necessitated by the realities of bridge or road locations attempted to offer an order that still allowed for efficient travel.

Entries for individual buildings or districts are identified with a two-letter county abbreviation and number, followed by the name, with historic or alternate names in parentheses. We use the current name to aid visitors, in keeping with the standard practice of the Buildings of the United States series, but those names are subject to change over time. The primary date(s) of construction and the name of the architect or engineer (if known) appear on the next line. If a building has undergone a subsequent, substantial addition or renovation by another architect, that name follows. Next appears the address and other location information. In preparing the entries, we tried to choose representative buildings, structures, or landscapes covering a variety of themes, types, and time periods distributed across every county. By necessity, many fine examples had to be omitted from the book. Historical themes significant to Maryland are discussed in the introduction, while characteristic building types and salient issues are addressed in the sidebars.

The maps of each region, Annapolis, and Baltimore City should allow readers to readily locate each entry with the assistance of a traditional map or an electronic GPS system. Commercial businesses, churches, and public buildings are often open to visitors, and we inform you in the text if a building is now converted to a public use such as restaurant or museum. We have generally listed private properties only if visible from public rights-of-way or public waters. The few exceptions were of transcendent importance for the history of architecture in Maryland. We trust that our readers will always respect the property rights and privacy of others as they view the buildings. While every effort was made to include only extant buildings or structures, some will have been demolished or substantially altered since the book went to press.

⇒ FOREWORD ⇐

The primary objective of the Buildings of the United States (BUS) series is to identify and celebrate the rich cultural, economic, and geographic diversity of the United States of America as it is reflected in the architecture of each state. The series was founded by the Society of Architectural Historians (SAH), a nonprofit organization dedicated to the study, interpretation, and preservation of the built environment throughout the world.

The BUS series will eventually comprise more than sixty volumes documenting the built environment of every state. The idea for such a series was in the minds of the founders of SAH in the early 1940s, but it was not brought to fruition until Nikolaus Pevsner, the eminent British architectural historian who conceived and carried out the Buildings of England series, originally published between 1951 and 1974, challenged SAH to do for the United States what he had done for his country. In 2016, SAH added its first city guide to the BUS series.

The authors of each BUS volume are trained architectural and landscape historians who are thoroughly informed in the local aspects of their subjects. Although the great national and international architects of American buildings receive proper attention, outstanding local architects, as well as the buildings of skilled but often anonymous carpenter-builders, are also brought prominently into the picture. Naturally, the series cannot cover every building of merit; practical considerations dictate difficult choices in the buildings that are represented in this and other volumes. Furthermore, only buildings in existence at the time of publication are included.

For this volume on Maryland, SAH is first and foremost indebted to Gretchen and Roger D. Redden, both longtime members and supporters of SAH, who sponsored this volume. The BUS series is also grateful for the generous and ongoing support from the National Endowment for the Humanities, the Graham Foundation for Advanced Studies in the Visual Arts, the National Park Service, HABS/HAER/HALS Division, the Library of Congress, and the many individual members of SAH who have made unrestricted contributions to the series.

We thank the authors, the University of Virginia Press, the SAH Board, the BUS Editorial Advisory Committee listed at the front of this volume, Nat Case, and especially Richard Longstreth and Damie Stillman.

KAREN KINGSLEY
Editor-in-Chief
Buildings of the United States

ESTABLISH JUSTICE

⫸ ACKNOWLEDGMENTS ⫷

We begin by thanking Pauline Saliga and SAH for the opportunity to undertake the Maryland volume in the Buildings of the United States series. Although long-time Maryland residents, we gained a fuller appreciation of the great architectural variety offered by our Little America. We are most indebted to editor Karen Kingsley for her guidance and encouragement. She started us down this path through our work as co-coordinators for Classic Buildings of Maryland in SAH Archipedia, selecting the first one hundred sites. A hardy thanks to peer reviewers Damie Stillman and Richard Longstreth for their careful examination and insights and to Mark Mones at the University of Virginia Press. Special gratitude goes to Mr. and Mrs. Roger D. Redden, who generously underwrote this book.

Our employer, the National Park Service's Historic American Buildings Survey (HABS), signed on to this project through its longtime partnership with SAH and with the encouragement of former division chief Richard O'Connor. Our work benefited immensely from the talents of Heritage Documentation Programs (HDP) photographers Jarob Ortiz, Justin Scalera, James Rosenthal, Renee Bieretz, Jet Lowe, and the late Jack E. Boucher. Colleagues and associates Jamie Jacobs, Justine Christianson, Roger Reed, and Donna Ware contributed entries to the SAH Archipedia effort adapted for the book, and Chris Stevens, Christopher Marston, Todd Croteau, and Willie Graham helped with photographs, site selection, and feedback.

We are indebted to Maryland Historical Trust (MHT) staff, including the late Orlando Ridout V, who served as a friend and mentor to so many Maryland preservationists, his successor Marcia Miller, and Heather Barrett and Peter Kurtz. MHT supported numerous HABS countywide photographic surveys that informed this book. With the help of scholars James D. Dilts, Kelly L. Malloy, and Susan Pearl, MHT began an earlier process of site identification and writing of selected draft entries. MHT-funded historic site survey work has often resulted in tremendously valuable publications, in particular the work of Michael Bourne, Susan Pearl, Kirk D. Ranzetta, J. Richard Rivoire, Paul Touart, Mark Walston, Donna Ware, and Christopher Weeks.

Finally, our loving gratitude to husband Chris and son Leo Davidson, husband Tim and daughter Jill Lavoie, and sister Leslie Espino for happily allowing vacations to be co-opted by site surveys and taking road trips to photograph Maryland buildings.

LISA PFUELLER DAVIDSON AND CATHERINE C. LAVOIE

INTRODUCTION

Although Maryland is a small state, its colonial roots and diverse history and geography have produced a rich architectural heritage and earned it the moniker *America in Miniature.* Among its greatest assets are its outstanding colonial-era buildings, exemplified by the capital city of Annapolis. Equally noteworthy are those preeminent edifices of nineteenth-century Baltimore that signify the ascent of the trained architect and the city's mercantile and industrial wealth. Maryland possesses over 1,500 National Register–listed sites, including over 200 historic districts reflecting nearly four centuries of architectural development.[1] The geography of Maryland, located just south of the Mason-Dixon Line yet squarely within the Mid-Atlantic and adjacent to the nation's capital, shaped its complex sociocultural history as a border state between north and south. The architectural influence of Quakers and German immigrants related to trends to the north in Pennsylvania, while broader Southern Tidewater traditions based on early English precedents held sway on the Eastern and Western shores.

The maritime regions of the Atlantic coast and the Chesapeake Bay, and the loamy coastal plain that surrounds it, contrast with the rolling hills and fertile agricultural lands of the Piedmont Plateau that rises in a gentle slope to the Allegheny Mountains of the Appalachian range in the rugged Maryland panhandle. Maryland's relatively mild climate has sustained architectural traditions of both north and south. As said when first settled, "The Climate here in Summer time inclines to an extraordinary heat, and in Winter is very cold; but both the heat of the Summer is very much allayed by cool breezes and the cold of the winter is of short continuance so that the country is accounted sufficiently healthful, and of late agrees with English bodies."[2]

Early European settlement exemplified a contrast between enlightened religious toleration and a tobacco-centric economy based on the labor of enslaved people. Long before the First Amendment guaranteed religious freedom to all Americans, colonial proprietor and Roman Catholic Cecil Calvert, the second Lord Baltimore, enacted the *Maryland Toleration Act* of 1649 envisioned by his father, George Calvert. Although later reversed by the succeeding English monarchy, the act represented a rare outlook that set the tone for Maryland's political ideology. Although tending toward manorial, Calvert offered generous terms for land and declined to tax or enact laws without the consent of the freemen of the colony. Religious freedom attracted a range of ethnic backgrounds and beliefs for its day, encompassing En-

Tobacco farm, Southern Maryland, 1950

glish, Scots-Irish, Germans and Bohemians, Catholics, Quakers, Methodists, Lutherans, and United Brethren. This variety is reflected in Maryland's extant ecclesiastic structures, from plain-style meetinghouses to America's first Roman Catholic Cathedral (BC14).

At the same time, Maryland's early landscape was formed by a system of tobacco cultivation inextricably intertwined with slavery, including plantations first established by the Jesuits in the 1640s. Self-sufficient plantations along the many rivers and creeks that feed into the Chesapeake Bay resulted in a diffused pattern of settlement where few towns flourished. Thus Calvert directed an *Act for the Advancement of Trade* in 1683 and 1706, ambitiously designating fifty-seven 100-acre town sites as commercial centers and shipping ports, forming the basis for Maryland's first towns. Maryland prospered from a thriving maritime culture and the mid- and trans-Atlantic trade networks. Likewise, Chesapeake fishing and boatbuilding traditions were deeply ingrained in Maryland's identity. As population increased, migration continued to follow the navigable rivers farther upland.

By the mid-eighteenth century, grain production and milling began to supplant tobacco in many regions, providing new economic opportunities and facilitating inland town development. On the Eastern Shore, tobacco all but disappeared within a generation, bringing about new patterns of farming as gristmills dotted the landscape.[3] Grain production created a more stable economy, and the wealth responsible for refined Georgian brick houses, many embracing decorative patterned brickwork.

The western region of the state was not settled much before the 1740s, taking advantage of migrating Irishmen and Germans, who were also grain farmers. Market centers were built along wagon roads, forming later county seats such as Frederick and Hagerstown

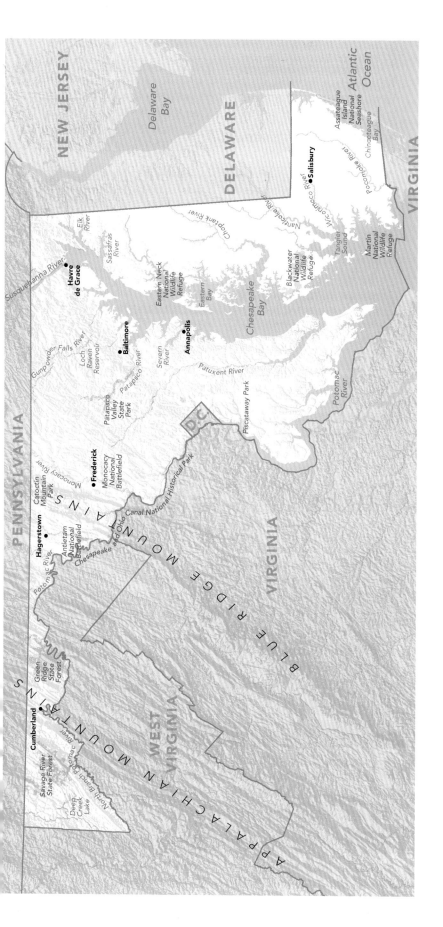

and smaller towns linked drovers and travelers to ports in Baltimore and Annapolis. Rich coal and mineral deposits were discovered on the western frontier by the early nineteenth century. At the same time, industrial development began in Baltimore, spurred by milling and manufacturing in the Patapsco River Valley and the Jones Falls.

The late nineteenth century witnessed the expansion of the federal government in Washington, which over time left an indelible mark on patterns of growth, creating residential communities accessible by commuter train or trolley. In the twentieth century federal agencies expanded into the Maryland suburbs (see **Federal Influence in Maryland,** p. <00>). This vibrant white-collar economy is responsible for Maryland's current status as one of the wealthiest states in the nation. In the twenty-first century, the sprawling Baltimore-Washington Metropolitan area dominates Maryland's economy and growth, while most other areas remain largely rural. The contrasts between east and west, rural and urban, coastal plain and mountains persist. Maryland thus provides many opportunities to examine nationally significant historical forces and their impact upon the built environment.

MARITIME DEVELOPMENT AND THE CHESAPEAKE CULTURE

As the world's largest estuary and the ideal breeding ground for an abundance of aquatic life, the Chesapeake Bay region forms a rare ecosystem. Captain John Smith, the first English explorer to the area in 1608–1609, proclaimed it "a faire Bay compassed but for the mouth with fruit and delightsome land. Within is a country that may have the prerogative over the most pleasant places of Europe, Asia, Africa or America, for large and pleasant navigable rivers. Heaven and earth never agreed better to frame a place for man's habitation."[4] A constant mainstay of Maryland's economic and leisure-time pursuits, the Bay measures approximately 200 miles in length and up to 30 miles in width, but its myriad coves and labyrinth-like marshlands comprise over 4,000 miles of meandering coastline.

Maryland's history as an English colony founded by the proprietary Calvert family begins in 1634 with the settlement at St. Mary's City on the Chesapeake's Western Shore. The numerous American Indian tribes they encountered here and on the Eastern Shore—the Accohannock, Assateague, Choptank, Delaware, Matapeake, Nanticoke, Piscataway, Pocomoke, and Shawnee peoples—are generally now recalled merely as place-names, most being driven off in the early eighteenth century. However, their settlements remain outlined in Augustine Herrman's 1670 *Map of Virginia and Maryland,* interestingly drawn from the perspective of an incoming ship.[5]

The Chesapeake Bay and its system of navigable rivers enabled the transport of tobacco, Maryland's most vital crop. They provided conduits for development that gave rise to notable port towns and

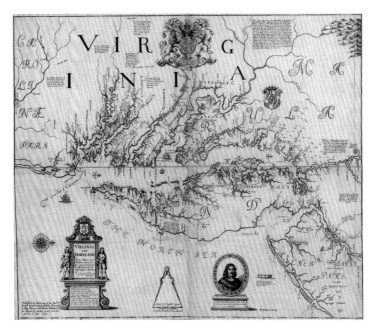

Augustine Herrman's 1670 *Map of Virginia and Maryland;* per seventeenth-century conventions, the map is oriented with the west at top, and the Chesapeake Bay inset south to north at center

communities and fostered a way of life for countless watermen. Marylanders' dependence on the Bay as a source of income, trade, and transportation was also responsible for creating a rich boatbuilding tradition (see **Maryland Wood Boatbuilding,** pp. 116–17). For a century and a half, cargoes greater in value and bulk than all the rest of the nation combined were carried on the Chesapeake.[6] During the last quarter of the nineteenth century, railroads challenged maritime dominance, and by the early twentieth century, trucking overtook maritime transport almost completely.

No longer dependent on the Bay for transportation, many of Maryland's wharfs, warehouses, and packing houses have vanished, and the wood boats particular to the region have been mostly relegated to maritime museums. Nevertheless, the landscape of the Chesapeake remains largely undisturbed from early patterns of agricultural development. Agricultural and maritime industries still form much of the basis for the local economy, known to outsiders by its bountiful produce stands and its oysters, blue crabs, rockfish, and Old Bay seasoning. Interest in the Bay has otherwise turned to recreational pursuits, attracting boaters, summer denizens, and tourists.

TRANSPORTATION INNOVATIONS AND TRENDS

As much as Maryland's history is defined by maritime travel via Chesapeake Bay small craft and Baltimore's famous transatlantic clipper ships, developments in inland transportation also gained ascendancy

Choptank oyster dredgers aboard the skipjack *Maggie Lee,* 1948

during the nineteenth century. Baltimore's geographic position as the East Coast port closest to the Midwest became key to its economic development. It inspired several pathbreaking early-nineteenth-century transportation innovations including the Chesapeake and Ohio (C&O) Canal, the National Road, and the nation's first common carrier railroad, the Baltimore and Ohio (B&O). They provided mechanisms for maximizing wealth and trade opportunities by moving coal and other materials across the Appalachian Mountains and pushed the European settlement of Maryland westward.

The engineering and construction breakthroughs of the Baltimore and Ohio Railroad are undoubtedly Maryland's most wide-reaching contribution to transportation history. The B&O was chartered on February 28, 1827, as the first U.S. railway for the commercial transportation of freight and passengers. Its early investors hoped that it could compete with the success of the Erie Canal, which opened the markets of the Midwest to New York, as well as with its local rival, the Chesapeake and Ohio Canal.[7] To succeed, the B&O pioneered new technologies and solutions for traversing the rugged landscape. The first section was completed in 1830 to Ellicott City, connecting the most influential of the Patapsco Valley mill towns to Baltimore and demonstrating the efficacy of the first U.S.-built steam-powered locomotive, *Tom Thumb.*

The C&O Canal sought to use established canal technology to move commodities such as coal and iron between the Ohio River and Washington along the Potomac River Valley more efficiently than the proposed B&O Railroad.[8] Groundbreaking ceremonies for both endeavors were held with patriotic fanfare on July 4, 1828. The canal was quickly overshadowed by the B&O and other railroads, and construction was stopped at Cumberland in 1850. Regardless, it further opened

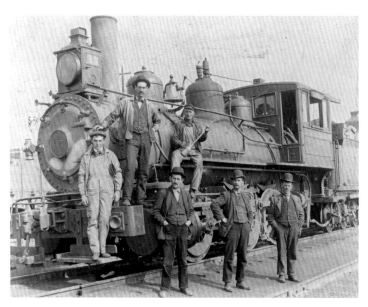

Class D B&O locomotive, built at the Mount Clare shops in 1889

the region to settlement and trade, remaining in operation until the 1920s. Maryland's Susquehanna and Tidewater Canal and Chesapeake and Delaware Canal similarly offered a short-lived challenge to the railroad while encouraging local trade. The C&O's 184.5-mile right-of-way was reborn as a recreation landscape maintained by the National Park Service through federal purchase in 1938.

Maryland's third major transportation achievement was construction of the National Road from Baltimore across western Maryland to the Ohio River. Chartered by Congress in 1806, the National Road was the first federally funded highway and an ambitious effort to encourage commercial travel. Controversy over federal funding and growing competition from the B&O Railroad and C&O Canal prompted the government to turn the National Road over to the respective states in the early 1830s. It was superseded by U.S. 40, which follows the same right-of-way in many areas and still connects the towns and villages that developed along its path.[9]

Subsequent transportation innovations shaped the state's development in ways typical of national trends. The post–Civil War expansion of railroad service to agricultural centers on the Eastern Shore and central Maryland facilitated the development of seafood- and produce-processing companies, while fueling industrial expansion in Baltimore and western Maryland. In addition to the B&O, the Western Maryland Railway, Pennsylvania Railroad, and others created a robust rail line network. Rail transportation was also harnessed to create tourism. The B&O again led the way with creation of Maryland's mountain resorts such as Deer Park and Mountain Lake Park (WM61). New railroad service also brought visitors to coastal destinations such as Chesapeake Beach and Ocean City.

Maryland's early road-building history and populated East Coast location made it well placed for the improved roads movement following the early-twentieth-century advent of bicycling and automobile travel. The first Maryland State Roads Commission was established in 1908 with the charge of bringing the state's system of largely colonial-era roads up to modern standards.[10] U.S. 1 traveling northeast to southwest and U.S. 40 traveling east to west were major local and through-travel routes in the interwar years, with U.S. 40 particularly noteworthy for early expansion into a divided highway. Commerce and recreation were supported by road improvements, such as state parks and tourist attractions along U.S. 40 in the western mountains, U.S. 301 at the Western Shore, and U.S. 13 on the Eastern Shore's Delmarva Peninsula.

Road travel was further improved by modern bridges resulting from a 1938 statewide planning effort. The natural barriers of Maryland's major waterways were finally surmounted with projects such as the Governor Harry W. Nice Bridge (1940, J. E. Greiner Company; slated for replacement) extending U.S. 301 across the Potomac River into Virginia, the Thomas J. Hatem Memorial Bridge (1938–1940, J. E. Greiner Company) carrying U.S. 40 over the Susquehanna River, and, most dramatically, the Chesapeake Bay Bridge (WS80), which opened the Eastern Shore to car-based travel via U.S. 50.[11] A new generation of road construction with the Baltimore-Washington Parkway built between 1947 and 1954 and Interstate Highways Act of 1956 further solidified Maryland's central place in East Coast automobile transportation routes, including I-95 in the 1960s (see **The I-95 Corridor,** p. 325). Areas outside of the dominant U.S. 1/I-95 corridor were also transformed by highways in this period such as the beltways around Baltimore (I-695) and Washington (I-495), the I-270 between Washington and Frederick, and additional east–west routes such as I-70 and I-68.

INDUSTRIAL BALTIMORE

Innovations in transportation directly supported the emergence of an industrial and manufacturing sector in Maryland. Prior to the Civil War, early and small-scale industrial enterprises, mostly gristmills and

Panoramic view of Baltimore's inner harbor, c. 1909

flour mills, textile mills, and iron furnaces, emerged in areas such as the Jones and Patapsco river valleys in and around Baltimore. While the railroad cities of the western mountains such as Hagerstown and Cumberland were home to important railroad shops, furniture factories, textile mills, and other businesses, Baltimore became the undisputed industrial powerhouse of Maryland by the late nineteenth century.

Already a major commercial center when Baltimore City was made independent from Baltimore County by the 1851 Maryland Constitution, the city's industrial growth continued through the mid-twentieth century with production of a wide range of items. Primary among these was steel, which dominated Baltimore's manufacturing sector, as well as the entire U.S. economy, until economic collapse in the 1970s. The massive Bethlehem Steel works at Sparrows Point, just outside the city line in Baltimore County, was the largest steel mill in the world by the 1950s, diversifying from steel rails after acquisition from the Pennsylvania Steel Company in 1916.[12] The steel and tin plate produced at Sparrows Point was transformed by other Baltimore companies into a variety of goods small and large—from cans and consumer appliances to ships, locomotives, and steel-frame bridges and buildings.

Many industrial sites highlighted here are the rare survivors that made the transition to new uses through preservation and rehabilitation. Canneries in the Canton, Fell's Point, and Locust Point neighborhoods, as well as on the Eastern Shore and Harford County, processed fruits, vegetables, seafood, and meats produced statewide.[13] One of the earliest examples, a c. 1860s oyster packing plant, now serves as the home of the Baltimore Museum of Industry (BC55), and the National Can Company (BC75) was renovated into an apartment building, while many of the other canneries that employed thousands of workers are gone.

More fortunate are the many surviving garment factory lofts and warehouses on the west side of downtown that have been converted into residential or office space. These richly detailed, architect-designed buildings, many with locally produced cast-iron fronts, are reminders of a major Baltimore industry that rivaled steelmaking in its size and scope. Another survivor is the American Brewery (BC78)

in east Baltimore now renovated into office space, while several of the Jones Falls textile mills, such as Mount Washington (BC119), Mount Vernon (BC121) and Union (BC120) are successful mixed-use projects.

These changes are indicative of the twenty-first-century economic shift away from industry in favor of service and tourism. Nowhere is that change more vivid than Baltimore's Inner Harbor (BC49), a once-gritty working waterfront now transformed into an entertainment and commercial zone. A few remnants of Baltimore's industrial past do remain around the Inner Harbor, such as the corner tower of the former Bromo-Seltzer factory (BC38) or the Shot Tower (BC62), preserved as a reminder of an earlier industrial age. However, the massive McCormick Spice Company facility on Light Street was demolished in the 1990s after the corporate offices were moved north into Baltimore County, and most of the buildings now near the Inner Harbor were built in the late twentieth and early twenty-first centuries for tourism and white-collar commerce.

While considerable architectural evidence of Baltimore's industry has been lost to deindustrialization and redevelopment, the city still boasts Maryland's richest collection of surviving factories and warehouses. The neighborhoods and institutions built by Baltimore's industrial workforce also speak to the historical importance of this sector and the city's status as a major center for skilled and unskilled workers during the heyday of European immigration. Baltimore was then a port of entry second only to New York City, as well as a beneficiary of the Great Migration of Black workers to urban centers.[14]

BLACK LIFE AND CULTURE

Despite Maryland's early dependence on a slave labor–based system of tobacco production, by 1810 its free Black population was the largest in the nation, and at the eve of the Civil War it was nearly equal to that of the enslaved.[15] Maryland's Underground Railroad network and the extent of its free Black communities is striking, and yet so was its participation in the slave trade and its post–Civil War embrace of Jim Crow restrictions. Similarly, its extraordinary stance on religious freedom is seemingly incompatible with human bondage. Why the dichotomy?

Maryland's landmark commitment to *religious* freedom helped by attracting abolitionist Quakers and Methodists who disavowed slavery and were willing to support self-sustaining free Black enclaves.[16] However, the average Maryland slaveholder owned one to three slaves, undermining Black family life and contributing to the vitality of the slave trade. Slave trafficking resulted from Maryland's position on the border between slave and free states, although proximity to the nation's capital demanded its designation as a Union state during the Civil War.

So divergent was the response to slavery that some spoke of two

Crab pickers in Hoptown section of Crisfield, c. 1950

Marylands that, like the country as a whole, broke down between north and south. The shift from tobacco to less labor-intensive grain production on the Eastern Shore and central regions significantly decreased the need for enslaved labor.[17] Meanwhile, southern counties remained entrenched in tobacco cultivation, concentrating slaveholding in four contiguous Western Shore counties: Calvert, Charles, Prince George's, and St. Mary's.[18]

The subjugation of African Americans in Maryland did not end with emancipation or through the adoption of a new state constitution in 1864, one year after the federal Emancipation Proclamation freed slaves in Confederate states, but continued through Jim Crow segregation. Statutory limitations were placed on rights to engage in certain economic activities, while law enforcement could hire out free Black people deemed vagrants and children who it argued were inadequately cared for.[19] Thus the Freedmen's Bureau—their only civil recourse—encouraged many to remain with their former owners.[20] Only about 2 percent of Black people then owned land that enabled economic independence and maintained family unity, with sharecropping or tenant farming providing the most common solution. Using the skills and community cooperation practiced during slavery, they often built log houses similar to their slave dwellings until later generations could accumulate wealth.[21] Better-off Black property owners denied access to white residential communities began forming their own by the late nineteenth century, often within commuting distance to federal jobs in Washington.

Extant plantations speak to Maryland's former slave-based economy, although few slave houses remain. As Freedman and minister James Pennington prophetically put it in 1848, due to their status as mere chattel the slave was left "without a single record to which he may appeal in vindication of his character, or honor."[22] Houses built by free Black people have fared no better, although many of the segregated, substandard row houses they once occupied in urban areas remain, particularly in Baltimore in such neighborhoods as Fell's Point, Otterbein, and Sharp-Leadenhall. Black migration to the Eastern Shore is reflected in extant food-processing company housing and in the churches and schools that formed the bedrock of communities. Also extant are a handful of meeting halls, schools, and universities. More recently, African American history is celebrated through historic sites and museums, such as those associated with Marylanders Benjamin Banneker (CM35), Frederick Douglass (WS83), and Harriet Tubman (ES65), widely recognized for their intellect, courage, and civil rights advocacy.

RESIDENTIAL MARYLAND

Although home to important commercial, institutional, and industrial structures, Maryland's houses emerge as its most distinctive contribution to a national story of architectural development. This story is told through vernacular dwellings representing diverse populations and housing for workers, along with high-style landmarks. Widely celebrated for its colonial and Federal-period houses of both the gentry and middling class, Maryland also boasts important nineteenth- and twentieth-century urban and suburban development and internationally recognized twentieth-century experiments in urban planning.

While the reconstructions at Historic St. Mary's City (WS1) show some of the earliest European house forms in Maryland, rare survivors are found on the Western and Eastern shores, notably eighteenth-century Tidewater houses with a hall-parlor plan and steeply pitched gable roof dubbed "The Chesapeake House" by scholars of the region (see **The Chesapeake House,** pp. 32–33). Chesapeake houses expanded into telescoping plans exemplified by Wyoming (CR4) also represent accumulation of wealth by the owners in agricultural and port town settings by the turn of the nineteenth century, as do the many houses enhanced by later expansions.

In central and western Maryland, the surviving early housing stock is often of brick or stone and informed by German or Quaker building traditions, such as the Hager (WM24) and Mercer Brown (ES2) houses, respectively. Rare log survivors are the Webb (ES30) and Oakley (CR48) cabins, and the James Drane House (WM65). Many more buildings in the Piedmont and Appalachian Mountain counties have original log sections incorporated into later expansions, often hidden under siding.

Maryland possesses unusually fine high-style late-eighteenth-century Georgian and early-nineteenth-century Federal houses in towns such as Frederick, Chestertown, Easton, Princess Anne, and,

"Wash Day," cleaning the marble stoops of the 2000 block of Penrose Avenue, Baltimore, c. 1945

most importantly, the state capital of Annapolis. That city's architectural ascendency began in the mid-eighteenth century with the gradual adaptation of the Georgian mode of architecture for town houses built by wealthy merchant-planters.[23] Perhaps most evocative of architectural sophistication among Maryland's landed gentry in this period are the five-part-plan houses, with a central block and side pavilions connected by hyphens (see **The Five-Part Palladian House,** pp. 54–55). Inspired by the pattern books of Andrea Palladio and the Georgian architectural taste for classical symmetry, the many outstanding five-part-plan houses in Maryland could fill their own volume.

Perhaps more typical of residential architecture in Maryland was the adoption of many popular designs, from pre–Civil War Gothic Revival and Italianate to more fanciful late-nineteenth-century Queen Anne. By the late nineteenth century, builder's guidebooks and standardized building components brought architect design to the average homebuyer, while also undermining regional building forms in favor of national trends. Mail-order houses manufactured by Aladdin, Sears Roebuck, and others further underscored this divide. In Baltimore, local builders and developers created a city, more than almost any other, whose identity is tied to the row house form.[24] For generations, Baltimore row houses were constructed at every price point and remain a ubiquitous feature of the urban landscape.

Beyond individual house design, railroad and streetcars were essential in fostering new suburban housing patterns starting in the nineteenth century. Communities of varying economic status such as Catonsville outside of Baltimore, Hyattsville, and the Black community of North Brentwood (CR20) outside of Washington offered their versions of suburban living. Most influential was Roland Park

(BC108), an early example of a comprehensively planned garden suburb now part of Baltimore City. Highly successful, it inspired the Roland Park Company to go on to develop the adjacent neighborhood of Guilford (BC110). The exclusive Washington suburb of Chevy Chase illustrates similar community planning in the same period.

During the twentieth century, Maryland's location along the highly developed Northeast corridor has made it an important market for both conventional suburban development and more experimental projects. In marked contrast to the predominantly Colonial Revival houses built in the Washington suburbs in the 1930s, Greenbelt (CR16) is an extraordinarily complete example of a "greenbelt town" planned and built by the federal government during the New Deal with an Art Deco aesthetic. During the post–World War II housing boom, developments such as Hammond Wood (CR44) offered prefabricated modernist house designs by local architect Charles M. Goodman.

Experiments in New Town planning updated the ideals embodied in Greenbelt to offer an alternative to typical suburban sprawl in the 1960s, placing Maryland on the forefront of this still uncommon approach. Most well known is developer James Rouse's planned community of Columbia New Town (CM12), one of the most successful and ambitious New Town developments in the United States. New Mark Commons (CR30) represents a mature example of New Town planning by developer Edmund Bennett with cluster planning and common open space. Equally ambitious but less fully realized was Moshe Safdie's 1970s design for Coldspring Newtown (BC115), a planned racially integrated, moderate-income neighborhood in north Baltimore.

In contrast to these more avant-garde projects, the Levitt and Sons' 1960s development of Belair at Bowie (CR13) was conventional in design and layout, but a major effort in the Washington region by arguably the most influential and well-known builders of the era. Later even traditional residential patterns became innovative again. Kentlands (CR52), designed by Duany and Plater-Zyberk (DPZ) in the 1980s, is considered the first major nonresort community in the United States to espouse the tenets of neotraditional town planning known as New Urbanism.

ARTISANS, BUILDERS, AND ARCHITECTS

In Maryland, as elsewhere, the designers and builders of the vast majority of its built environment remain unrecognized. The humble timber-frame and log buildings that made up the bulk of early construction in the Chesapeake and beyond can be best described as influenced by the building traditions of its English settlers, adapted to regional conditions (see **The Chesapeake House,** pp. 32–33), followed by other immigrant groups.[25] English persuasion persisted in Maryland, and by the mid-eighteenth century, interpretations of Renaissance classicism appeared via pattern books and immigrant artisans versed

View of Annapolis, Maryland, C. Milbourne, 1800

in the latest European trends. Fueled by the prosperity of the tobacco and maritime trades, they ushered in a period of architectural ascendancy in Annapolis and other Chesapeake towns.[26] At the same time, local artisans, builders, and informed property owners availed themselves of pattern books and builder's guides.

Perhaps Maryland's best-known immigrant artisan was English-born William Buckland, working in Annapolis. The city's affluence attracted numerous builders, carpenters, joiners, plasterers, and cabinetmakers, both transplanted and homegrown. Builders interpreted pattern-book designs to create new models particular to the Chesapeake, combining local materials, plan types, framing techniques, and architectural details while providing inspiration to the middling classes.[27]

Trained architects appeared in Maryland by the early nineteenth century, predominately in Baltimore, where the wealth had by then shifted. Two noted foreign-born architects led the movement: Benjamin Henry Latrobe from England and Maximillian Godefroy from France. Along with such protégées as Robert Mills and William F. Small, they introduced neoclassical, Greek Revival, and Gothic Revival design, and created some of the nation's first monuments. Setting a high bar, they distinguished the role of the architect from that of builder as authorities on architectural design and arbiters of good taste.

Baltimore quickly developed its own assemblage of capable local architects, many of whom began their career in the building trades or acquired skills through apprenticeship. The city's first native-born and highly skilled practitioners Robert Cary Long Sr. and Jacob Small Jr. started as carpenter-builders.[28] By the 1830s, Robert Cary Long Jr. became the city's first native-born, professionally trained architect, while Small's son, William, received training from Latrobe.

The trend toward professionalism was firmly established in Baltimore by 1850.[29] However, the city benefited from a long succession

Bird's-eye view of Baltimore, Maryland, looking south, showing the Washington Monument in foreground; lithograph and print by E. Sachse & Co., 5 N. Liberty Street, c. 1872

of architects of both backgrounds, many of whom, in turn, trained others. These included Baldwin and Pennington, Charles L. Carson, Frank E. Davis, Dixon and Dixon, George A. Frederick, Edmund G. Lind, Niernsee and Neilson, Norris G. Starkweather, Wyatt and Sperry, and John Appleton Wilson, among others. Their designs for Baltimore and the surrounding counties solidified the city's role as the state's architectural standard-bearer.

By the twentieth century, Baltimore's wealth attracted such nationally celebrated architects as McKim, Mead and White, John Russell Pope, Mies van der Rohe, Pietro Belluschi, Walter Gropius, I. M. Pei, and Moshe Safdie. Their work connects Maryland to a broad timeline of national and international architectural trends. While Maryland is not particularly well known for its modern architecture, local firms such as Charles M. Goodman, RTKL Associates, Hugh Newell Jacobson, and Keyes, Lethbridge and Condon created distinctive contemporary mid- and late-twentieth-century buildings.[30] More typical in Maryland today, however, is the use of traditional architectural forms. Maryland's preservation ethic has played a role, particularly in early historic districts such as Annapolis, where embrace of Colonial Revival motifs has continued into the twenty-first century. Unable to ignore its celebrated colonial heritage, Maryland continues to fall back on its Georgian roots.

CONCLUSION

When a federal highway project threatened the Baltimore neighborhood of Fell's Point in the late 1960s, local activists, including then–future U.S. senator Barbara Mikulski, famously organized to save the early port area, which had withstood a British siege in 1814.

One Charles Center
(BC23), Baltimore,
Ludwig Mies van der
Rohe, in 2004

Maryland's architectural past is still very visible thanks to generations of Maryland residents who have been worthy stewards of a distinguished legacy, preserving buildings from ordinary log cabins to
grand Georgian plantation houses, from modest worker row housing
to skyscrapers and factories. However, the perennial tension between
preserving history and unfettered economic development continues.

Mid-twentieth-century Baltimore was a dramatic crisis point in this
cycle, as some residents pushed back against aggressive improvement
efforts such as urban renewal and highway building in favor of preserving their city's unique historic flavor. In many ways the effort was
a success. The 1970s Baltimore Homesteading Program encouraged
rehabilitation of city-owned houses in the historic neighborhoods of
Fell's Point, Federal Hill, and Otterbein. Large-scale redevelopment of
the Inner Harbor (BC49) and Oriole Park at Camden Yards (BC79) created a popular entertainment district blending old with new economic
opportunities. However, continued widespread demolition of historic
row houses in a time of housing need, lingering effects of deindustrialization, and lack of economic and social equity continue to present
challenges to Maryland's largest city and other areas.

Bringing the story of Maryland's buildings to the present reveals
that many of the most beloved ones tend to be in conversation with
the past while still embracing creativity and community. This approach is consistent with Maryland's famed "middle temperament"
and generally conservative approach to design. Issues of climate
change and social and environmental justice characterize our current
crisis point. Stewards of Maryland's historic buildings will need to find

solutions for sea level rise threatening the state's extensive coastal areas, including Annapolis (see **Climate Change, Sea-Level Rise, and the Chesapeake Bay,** p. 119). Many communities seeking to preserve their past and meet these challenges are also historically underserved by preservation efforts. By telling the diverse stories of Maryland's built environment, *Buildings of Maryland* seeks to honor the work of earlier generations and encourage interest in the full range of buildings and places found in our "Little America."

NOTES

1. Together with the National Register sites are those listed within Maryland Inventory of Historic Properties to total over 44,000 inventoried historic sites. Of these, 75 are designated National Historic Landmarks.
2. John Speed, [Descriptions of Virginia and Mary-land] in *The Theatre of the Empire of Great Britain,* 1676, William T. Snyder Collection, Maryland State Archives, MSA SC 2111-1-3.
3. Michael Bourne, Orlando Ridout V, Paul Touart, and Donna Ware, *Architecture and Change in the Chesapeake: A Field Tour on the Eastern and Western Shores* (Newark, Del.: Vernacular Architecture Forum; Crownsville: Maryland Historical Trust, 1998), 6.
4. William W. Warner, *Beautiful Swimmers: Waterman, Crabs and the Chesapeake Bay,* 2nd ed. (Boston: Little, Brown, 1994), 11, 3–12.
5. Walter W. Ristow, "Augustine Herrman's Map of Virginia and Maryland," *Quarterly Journal of Current Acquisitions* 17, no. 4 (1960): 223–24. For his efforts, Calvert made Herrman a "free Denizen of the Province of Maryland" and gave him approximately 25,000 acres of land.
6. M. V. Brewington, *Chesapeake Bay* (New York: Bonanza Books and Cornell Maritime Press, 1953), vii.
7. James D. Dilts, *The Great Road: The Building of the Baltimore and Ohio, the Nation's First Railroad, 1828–1853* (Stanford, Calif.: Stanford University Press, 1993); John F. Stover, *History of the Baltimore and Ohio Railroad* (West Lafayette, Ind.: Purdue University Press, 1987).
8. Robert J. Kapsch, *Canals* (New York: W. W. Norton, 2004); Elizabeth Kyrtle, *Home on the Canal* (Baltimore: Johns Hopkins University Press, 1996); Harlan D. Unrau, *Historic Resource Study: Chesapeake & Ohio Canal,* prepared by Karen M. Gray (Hagerstown, Md.: U.S. Dept. of Interior, National Park Service, Chesapeake & Ohio Canal National Historical Park, 2007).
9. Karl Raitz, ed., *A Guide to the National Road* (Baltimore: Johns Hopkins University Press, 1996).
10. Maryland State Road Commission, *A History of Road Building in Maryland.* (Baltimore: State Roads Commission of Maryland, 1958), 47, 51.
11. Dixie Legler and Carol M. Highsmith, *Historic Bridges of Maryland* (Crownsville: Maryland Department of Transportation State Highway Administration and Maryland Historical Trust Press, 2002), 22.
12. Mark Reutter, *Sparrows Point: Making Steel—The Rise and Ruin of American Industrial Might* (New York: Summit Books, 1988).
13. Mary Ellen Hayward and Frank R. Shivers Jr., eds., *The Architecture of Baltimore: An Illustrated History* (Baltimore: Johns Hopkins University Press, 2004), 174–76.
14. Elizabeth Fee, Linda Shopes, and Linda Zeidman, eds., *The Baltimore Book: New Views of Local History* (Philadelphia: Temple University Press, 1991).

15. Barbara Jeanne Fields, *Slavery and Freedom on the Middle Ground: Maryland during the Nineteenth Century* (New Haven, Conn.: Yale University Press, 1987), 1, 24.

16. Kenneth L. Carroll, "Religious Influence on the Manumission of Slaves in Caroline, Dorchester, and Talbot Counties," *Maryland Historical Magazine* 56, no. 2 (1961): 182–83, 190. Whereas one in thirteen Black people were free in 1790, it was one in three by 1810. Robert J. Brugger, *Maryland, a Middle Temperament, 1634–1980* (Baltimore: Johns Hopkins University Press and Maryland Historical Society, 1988), 169.

17. Bourne, et al., *Architecture and Change,* 7.

18. Russell R. Menard, "The Maryland Slave Population, 1658 to 1730: A Demographic Profile of Blacks in Four Counties," *William and Mary Quarterly* 32, no. 1 (1975): 30. More than half of the colony's slaves lived here during the early eighteenth century.

19. Fields, *Slavery and Freedom,* 79.

20. Richard Paul Fuke, "Planters, Apprenticeship, and Forced Labor: The Black Family Under Pressure in Post-Emancipation Maryland," *Agricultural History* 62, no. 4 (Autumn 1988): 57–60.

21. George W. McDaniel, "Voices from the Past: Black Builders and Their Buildings," in *Three Centuries of Maryland Architecture: A Selection of Presentations Made at the 11th Annual Conference of the Maryland Historic Trust,* 86–87 ([Crownsville]: Maryland Historical Trust Press, 1982).

22. James W. C. Pennington, "The Fugitive Blacksmith, 1849," in *Great Slave Narratives,* selected and introduced by Arna Bontemps (Boston: Beacon Press, 1969) as cited in Edie Wallace, "Reclaiming the Forgotten History and Cultural Landscapes of African-Americans in Rural Washington County, Maryland," *Material Culture* 39, no. 1 (Spring 2007): 11.

23. Jane Wilson McWilliams, *Annapolis: City on the Severn: A History* (Baltimore and Crownsville: Johns Hopkins University Press; Crownsville: Maryland Historical Trust Press, 2011).

24. Mary Ellen Hayward and Charles Belfoure, *The Baltimore Rowhouse* (New York: Princeton Architectural Press, 2001), 2. See also Mary Ellen Hayward. "Urban Vernacular Architecture in Nineteenth-Century Baltimore," *Winterthur Portfolio* 16, no. 1 (1981): 33–63.

25. The 1798 Federal Direct Tax indicates that by that time, small mostly log houses of a single room and loft above, no larger than a 500 square foot configuration, remain dominant, and less than 10 percent were of brick with a footprint of over 1,000 square feet. Online via the Maryland State Archives: https://msa.maryland.gov/megafile/msa/speccol/sc2900 /sc2908/000001/000729/html/index.html.

26. Marcia M. Miller and Orlando Ridout V, eds., *Architecture in Annapolis: A Field Guide* (Crownsville: Vernacular Architecture Forum and Maryland Historical Trust, 1998), 12.

27. Carl Lounsbury, "The Design Process," in *The Chesapeake House: Architectural Investigation by Colonial Williamsburg,* ed. Cary Carson and Carl Lounsbury (Chapel Hill: University of North Carolina Press, 2013), 84–85.

28. Hayward and Shivers, *Architecture of Baltimore,* 87. Small's father worked as an informally trained architect as well.

29. John McGrain, "Evolution of Architectural Practice in Baltimore," Research Resources, Baltimore Architecture Foundation, https://aia baltimore.org/baltimore-architecture-foundation/resources/research -resources/evolution-of-architectural-practice-in-baltimore/.

30. Isabelle Gournay, "Context Essay—Modern Movement in Maryland (Draft)," n.d., http://mahdc.org/ma/wp-content/uploads/2017/02 /Historic-Context-Modern-Movement-in-Maryland.pdf.

WESTERN SHORE

While tobacco cultivation shaped the entire Chesapeake region both culturally and materially, it remains most evident on the Western Shore, encompassing Anne Arundel, Calvert, Charles, and St. Mary's counties. It was the first region in the state to embrace tobacco farming and the last to abandon it. From the founding of St. Mary's City in 1634 as Maryland's first permanent settlement until fairly recently, tobacco formed its economic basis. Taking advantage of loamy soil, low floodplain, and access to waterways for ease of shipment, tobacco plantations worked mostly by enslaved individuals developed along its rivers and creeks. Tobacco production was labor intensive, subject to soil depletion and fluctuating economies that conspired to keep the region decentralized and investment in its built environment cautiously restrained. The 1683 *Act for the Advancement of Trade* designated town sites, yet tobacco production was not conducive to town development. A few, such as London Town, Annapolis, and Port Tobacco, developed as centers of the trans-Atlantic tobacco trade and local commerce. By necessity, plantations were largely self-sufficient, resembling small villages; simple frame Chesapeake houses surrounded by similarly constructed dependencies and outbuildings, and the ever-present tobacco barns.

Delineated by the Chesapeake Bay to the east, the Potomac River to the west, and further apportioned by the Patuxent, Severn, and Wicomico rivers and their tributaries, the Western Shore was likewise shaped by maritime pursuits such as boatbuilding, fishing, crabbing, and oyster harvesting. Smaller wharf and watermen's communities developed, particularly with the introduction of steamboats to the region in 1817. Villages such as Lower Marlboro and Galesville thrived from the mid-nineteenth into the early twentieth centuries as centers of local commerce and light industries such as seafood packing and oyster shucking. They likewise offered employment for African American workers post-emancipation, often providing the economic means for their families and communities to subsist.

Emancipation significantly changed the landscape of the Western Shore, triggering the breakup of plantations into smaller farms. Tobacco farming was supplemented by grain, fruit, and vegetable cultivation, as the cross-gable-front farmhouse became almost as ubiquitous as the tobacco barn. With the arrival of the railroad and a better network of roadways, most of the once-active early port towns and wharf communities died out, giving way to new or newly invigorated towns, such as Leonardtown, La Plata, Hughesville, and Prince Fred-

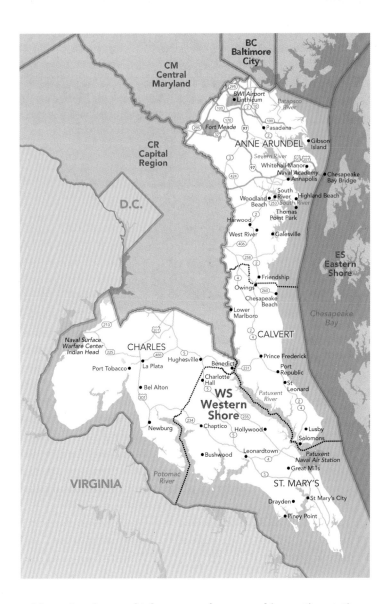

erick, centered around tobacco warehouses and inspection stations, and small-scale industries such as milling and canning.

By the early twentieth century, recreational waterfront communities were established, reached via train from Washington, and steam packer from Baltimore and further encouraged by a rise in pleasure boating. Summer camps, cottages, and rustic retreats appeared, such as Highland Beach, Sherwood Forest, and Epping Forest in Anne Arundel County and Chesapeake Beach in Calvert County. The economic depression of the 1930s undermined much of this development and put a stop to steamboat traffic. Eventually, state and local leaders realizing the value of the area's natural and historic resources worked to preserve them. Limited growth provided the opportunity for designating parks offering public access to the Chesapeake Bay wildlife sanctuaries and woodland preserves. The Maryland Archaeological Conservation Lab was built, a research and conservation facility collecting archaeological evidence of European explorers and settlers, as well as Native Americans including the Algonquin, Piscataway, Chopticoe, Secewacomoco, Yaocomico, and Patuxent tribes. Some of Maryland's earliest buildings are found here, representing types that define the architecture of the Chesapeake, as well as much of the state's preeminent Georgian architecture.

Western Shore tobacco farming all but ended beginning in 2000 with a state-sponsored Tobacco Buyout program. By then, recognition of the nation's capital as a source of jobs had sparked the development of suburban bedroom communities, a shift that started during World War II with the construction of the Naval Air Station Patuxent River in St. Mary's County. Low-density commercial sprawl has since joined the midcentury motels that line the U.S. 301 and 50 corridors. The Western Shore remains an area for retreat and leisure-time activities, yet many of its summer enclaves now appreciate a year-round population. While the vestiges of a once-thriving tobacco culture are still manifested by tobacco barns, they are now among the state's most endangered historic resources.

ST. MARY'S COUNTY
ST. MARY'S CITY

WS1 OLD MARYLAND STATE HOUSE AND HISTORIC ST. MARY'S CITY
1934, Herbert G. Crisp and James R. Edmunds Jr., and Horace Peaslee; 1974–present reconstruction. Old State House Rd.

This building is a reconstruction of the 1676 Jacobean State House that stood in St. Mary's City, the provincial capital of Maryland. Founded in 1634 as the fourth permanent English settlement in North America, St. Mary's City was no longer extant by the nineteenth century. Based upon archaeological investigations led by Herbert R. Shelton of Colonial Williamsburg, the reconstruction represents an early Maryland endeavor in historic preservation and the study of colonial life. It replicates an English postmedieval cruciform building consisting of a large first-floor assembly hall adjoining an open entrance porch and chamber above, with a matching stair tower to the rear, accessing a second-story council chamber and anteroom.

In 1966, the Historic St. Mary's City Commission was formed to preserve the archaeological evidence of the former capital and reconstruct and interpret other select buildings. St. Mary's constitutes the nation's only remaining major seventeenth-century townsite left undisturbed, containing foundations of approximately sixty seventeenth-century structures laid out in a Baroque-influenced town plan. Reconstructed earth-fast buildings include the c. 1665 Land Office, later Dutch Catholic settler Garrett Van Sweringen's inn; the Godiah Spray Tobacco Plantation house, barn, and kitchen garden; and Farthing's Ordinary.

WS2 BROME-HOWARD HOUSE AND SLAVE HOUSE
c. 1840, Vincent Camalier; 1994 moved. 18281 Rosecroft Rd.

The side-passage house was a popular residential form adopted by gentleman planters during the second quarter of the nineteenth century. It appeared during a period of widespread improvement that encompassed the construction of new houses and the expansion of older ones. Although built at one time, this house encompasses a telescoping plan reflecting the regional tradition of adding sections over time. Distinguished by its Greek Revival details, the house was built for newlyweds Susan Mackall Brome and physician John Brome. Based on similarities with other nearby houses, it was likely designed by locally prominent architect-builder Camalier. Indicative of talented craftsmen able to advance to sophisticated design work, Camalier trained at Washington's Master Carpenter's Society.

The former tobacco plantation includes a slave house, an example of the duplex quarter type that has been restored and interpreted. It was last occupied by African American caretakers, Solomon and Lily Milburn and their family, who lived here between 1930 and 1965. The buildings were moved from the site of St. Mary's City in 1994, in an effort to protect its archaeological remains.

GREAT MILLS

WS3 CECIL'S OLD MILL AND CECIL'S COUNTRY STORE
c. 1900 mill, c. 1920s store. 20864 and 20853 Indian Bridge Rd.

This group of buildings including a mill, store, house, and modest church illustrates the presence of small-scale industry in the otherwise predominantly agricultural local economy. The mill (*pictured below*), the last survivor of several situated near this location,

sits on the site of Clifton Factory (c. 1826–1900), which struggled to produce textiles as well as milling grain and wood. John T. Cecil demolished the older mill and built a two-and-a-half-story wood structure, reusing portions of the foundation, main drive shaft, and gearing. The overshot waterwheel on the northeast side was supplemented by one of the first diesel generators in the region, in 1927. Now used as a retail space, the mill still displays original equipment for milling corn and flour, as well as exterior sawmilling equipment that remained in use until 1959. The early-twentieth-century store located across the road is a quintessential example, with a one-story shed-roofed porch along the entire front of the long frame structure. Reopened as a gift store, the interior includes the original post office fixtures.

DRAYDEN

WS4 DRAYDEN AFRICAN AMERICAN SCHOOLHOUSE
c. 1890. 18287 Cherryfield Rd.

St. Mary's County maintained a racially segregated school system until 1967. African American students in grades one through seven were taught in this small frame structure from c. 1890 to 1944. It has three bays of windows on each side elevation and a single door opening at the center of its gabled front. Original diagonal beadboard sheathing has been uncovered on the interior. After use as a residence for several decades, the school has been restored as a county-operated historic site.

PINEY POINT

WS5 PINEY POINT LIGHTHOUSE

1836, John Donahoo, engineer. 44720 Lighthouse Rd.

This lighthouse at the Potomac River is representative of the first generation of Maryland lighthouses motivated by an increase in steamship travel. It replaced a lightship that had warned mariners about the dangerous shoals at Piney Point since 1821. Built by engineer and noted lighthouse designer Donahoo, the squat conical brick structure with a metal cupola top is thirty feet high and formerly housed a fifth-order Fresnel lens. It resembles other Donahoo lighthouses of the period at Cove Point (1828) in Calvert County, Concord Point (1827) in Harford County (CM78), and Turkey Point (1833) in Cecil County. He also built the adjacent brick keeper's house, which was altered from one and a half to two stories in 1884. Both structures are now part of a county park.

WS6 WARREN TOLSON COTTAGE
1910. 44910 Lighthouse Rd.

Tolson Cottage and the row of waterfront cottages to its east are the final remnants of a once-thriving summer resort. Piney Point was a popular antebellum retreat on the Potomac River, with Washington notables such as President Franklin Pierce, Daniel Webster, Henry Clay, and John C. Calhoun visiting its hotel, cottages, and wharf. In 1905, Warren Tolson, a Washingtonian who had visited as a boy purchased the property that included the twenty-five-room hotel, twenty-seven cottages, and other associated buildings. Tolson and his family resided at Piney Point every summer for thirty-eight years to run the hotel, initially living in one of the cottages on the property. In 1909 Tolson subdivided the strip of land northeast of the hotel into building lots. He built a one-and-a-half-story frame cottage with a wide porch on the end lot in 1910. Each narrow lot extended across the road to the water, allowing the property owner to erect a small gazebo or bathhouse referred to locally as "summer houses."

Today this stretch of Lighthouse Road includes a variety of early-twentieth-century frame cottages most with associated summer house structures. The two-story cottage at 44996 Lighthouse (c. 1910), has a pyramidal roof and wraparound screen porch. The shingle-clad bungalow at 45122 Lighthouse was built during the 1920s. This unique grouping along a riverfront beach is the only remnant of the former Piney Point resort, which faltered after hurricane damage in 1933 and during its final years in the 1940s served as rental housing for personnel from the new Patuxent River Naval Air Station.

LEONARDTOWN

The establishment of Leonardtown at the head of Britton's Bay in 1708 occurred after the capital was moved from St. Mary's City to Annapolis. St. Mary's City mayor Phillip Lynes laid out a hundred lots, designating one for the construction of a new courthouse. While an active port and steamboat landing, Leonardtown did not experience significant growth until the mid-nineteenth century, facilitated by railroad transport. The early twentieth century was marked by architectural improvement throughout the county, particularly within aspiring towns such as this. Centered around a town square that includes a World War I memorial, most of the buildings date to Leonardtown's later rise. Notable exceptions are the Old Jail Museum (c. 1858; 41625 Court House Drive) and Tudor Hall (c. 1760s; 41680 Tudor Place).

Of particular note is Mercantile Bank of Southern Maryland (c. 1921, Robert L. Harris, Frainie Brothers & Haigley, builder; 1966 enlarged. 41615 Park Avenue), a handsome Classical Revival building indicative of Leonardtown's early-twentieth-century prominence. Duke's Fountain Bar Restaurant (1920s; 41655 Fenwick Street) was erected by Roland Duke as the first reinforced concrete building in southern Maryland. It is distinguished by its modern stepped parapet roofline, casement windows, and painted signage.

WS7 ST. FRANCIS XAVIER ROMAN CATHOLIC CHURCH AND NEWTOWN MANOR

1731 church, 1766–1767 additions to church; 1786–1789 house; 1816 additions to both. 21370 Newtown Neck Rd.

Indicative of the early prosperity and influence of the Jesuits in Maryland, St. Francis Xavier (*pictured above*) is possibly the oldest Catholic church in the original thirteen colonies. The frame center section, a plastered barrel-vaulted basilica-plan space, has been dated via dendrochronology to 1731, but a church stood on this site as early as 1662. The Flemish bond brick vestibule and choir was added to the west end in 1766–1767, and the "confessional" on the east was added in 1816. The historically inaccurate box pews currently in the interior were added in a 1984 restoration. It is more likely an eighteenth-century Catholic church would have just had a few wood benches along the walls.

Newtown Manor, a large brick Georgian dwelling behind the church, was a residence for the Jesuits who served the parish and rode as circuit priests throughout the Western Shore. Dendrochronology indicates that the house was built in 1789, replacing a nearby 1717 structure. The gambrel roof was raised in 1816 to increase the available space. The manor house was part of a 700-acre tobacco plantation including seven outbuildings and a community of enslaved workers. The slaves included skilled workers such as James, a bricklayer who worked on construction of the manor house, and Peter and Nick, a bricklayer and carpenter for the 1816 additions. The 56 enslaved individuals at Newtown were included in the now infamous 1838 sale of over 200 enslaved workers from Jesuit plantations in Maryland to Catholic planters in Louisiana in order to financially save Georgetown University.

WS8 OCEAN HALL

c. 1719; c. 1725 alterations; c. 1910 addition. 36889 Bushwood Wharf Rd.

Dated though dendrochronology, this is one of the oldest masonry buildings in Maryland and one of the few examples of a cruck-roof formation in the country. Cruck construction originated as a medieval English building technique. At Ocean Hall, pairs of curving timbers are joined by mortise and tenon to the tie beams, crossing to either side of the ridge pole above, and the rafters supported by massive purlins. Built in an era of impermanent buildings, Ocean Hall was remarkable for its day, representing an early transition to more enduring dwellings influenced by the emerging Georgian style.

The one-and-a-half-story, single-cell-deep, central-passage house exhibits such elite early Chesapeake building traditions as Flemish-bond brick with decorative glazed headers and molded water table. The interior features an unusually tall ceiling height and generously proportioned rooms. The parlor retains its exposed post-and-beam framing, paneled walls, large fireplace, and a diverse palette of painted and grained finishes. Ocean Hall overlooks the Wicomico River, obliquely sited to face toward the no longer extant Wiccomocoe Towne, a relationship captured in a period painting that appears in the parlor overmantel. It was in fact the designation of this as a port, later known as Bushwood Wharf, that motivated merchant Gerrard Slye to erect his fine house here. A frame wing with modern kitchen was added c. 1910.

CHAPTICO

WS9 BACHELOR'S HOPE

c. 1749. 37260 Manor School Rd.

The design of this distinctive Palladian-influenced house built for William Hammersley was likely derived from English pattern books of the period. It consists of a two-story main block with a clipped hipped roof and inset loggia, flanked by tall chimneys and half-hipped roof one-story wings. It is built of Flemish-bond glazed brick on the south front and English-bond to the sides. The underside of the interior stair projects into the loggia, contributing to the openness of the great room behind it. Flanking sections comprise two rooms each with shared chimneys, with those to the front opening onto either side of the loggia. A kitchen was joined by a hyphen. The unusual design led early architectural historians to claim it as the late-seventeenth-century hunting lodge of an aristocratic family; only the c. 1705 St. Inigoes Manor (no longer extant) and the 1760s Tudor Hall, now much altered, bore resemblance to Bachelor's Hope.

HOLLYWOOD

WS10 BOND-SIMMS BARN COMPLEX
1837; 1840s; 1850s; 1895–1920. Steer Horn Neck Rd.

Located in Greenwell State Park, this barn complex is a fascinating interconnected ensemble of agricultural outbuildings largely built over the course of three decades in the mid-nineteenth century. This rare survivor of agricultural life on Maryland's Western Shore illustrates the importance of tobacco and corn cultivation. The oldest section is an earthfast log crib barn with cedar posts and roughly hewn white oak and chestnut logs V-notched together at the corners. This tobacco barn has been decisively dated to 1837 through dendrochronology corroborated by St. Mary's Orphan Court records. In the 1840s the east shed extension for hanging tobacco to dry was rebuilt.

A large earthfast tobacco barn was added immediately to the south in the 1850s with a sizable open span to allow wagons to drive in. A tobacco prize or press is located in this barn for screw compressing dried tobacco leaves into hogsheads for transportation and sale. A corn crib structure immediately west of the log barn was also built in the 1850s but received a concrete unpinning in the twentieth century. Smaller changes were made during the early twentieth century such as adding tobacco drying sheds to the sides of the corn crib and a long vehicle shed on the south side of the 1850s tobacco barn. The Bond family, owners since 1863, sold the property to Greenwell State Park in 1973.

WS11 SOTTERLEY AND SOTTERLEY SLAVE HOUSE
1703–1704; 1715 west wing; 1732 southern extension; 1762–1763 roof raised; 1768–1770 remodeled; 1840s kitchen, remodeled; 1910s restored. 44300 Sotterley Ln.

Sotterley is extremely important to the historical understanding of Chesapeake architecture, providing rare material evidence of such building practices as articulated framing, post-in-the-ground, and tilted false-plate construction. It evolved from James Bowle's single-story, hall-parlor Chesapeake house to a genteel plantation house, reflecting emerging spatial hierarchies and their corresponding rich ornamental detail, undertaken by Bowle's widow and second husband George Plater II and later generations.

The original two-room core of Sotterley, dated through dendrochronology, is one of only two surviving Maryland examples of earthfast, post-in-the-ground framing, transferred to the colony from rural England. It was an expedient means of construction, requiring little skill or financial outlay. Due to its tendency to rot, however, few remain. Sotterley is also one of three surviving examples of articulated interior framing.

Changing ideas about class and comfort are manifested at Sotterley through the addition of increasingly specialized and highly ornamental spaces. In particular was the 1768–1770 introduction of a central passage and Chippendale stair, and a formal parlor replete with crosseted overmantel with fretwork, paneling, and intricately carved shell alcoves, crafted by English-trained joiner Richard Boulton. In 1910, Sotterley underwent restoration according to the tenets of the Colonial Revival movement.

The house enjoys vistas of the Patuxent River and a landscape that includes archaeological sites, gardens, and an assemblage of outbuildings. Particularly significant is a surviving one-room, one-and-a-half story slave house, built by the 1850s. It is constructed of neatly hewn and sawn planks joined with notched corners to vertical earthfast posts. Its superiority to most slave houses likely reflected the rising value of slaves and pre-emancipation fears of dissatisfaction with their circumstances. It is one of the few publicly accessible slave quarters remaining in the United States, offering a counterpoint to genteel life in the main house.

CHARLES COUNTY
CHARLOTTE HALL

WS12 SARUM

1717; 1737, c. 1758, 1762 additions; c. 1937 remodeled; 1980s addition. 12235 Sarum Manor Dr.

Sarum, like Sotterley (WS11) is a rare survivor of Maryland's first-period domestic architecture, providing evidence of early

Chesapeake building traditions, including an innovative variation on English box-framing. Evidence also exists of a former two-story stair tower, a medieval influence seen in early colonial buildings. While most dwellings of the period were of impermanent post-in-the-ground construction, such as Sotterley (WS11), Sarum rested on brick piers, lending to its survival. Its original section manifests a modest frame, one-and-a-half-story, hall-parlor dwelling with a steeply pitched gable roof. It was dated through dendrochronology to 1717, and its rear shed addition to 1737, making it the second oldest conclusively dated building in Charles County. Flemish-bond-brick end walls with ornamental glazed headers and inset chimney were part of a c. 1758 expansion that resulted in its current saltbox configuration. A one-story brick kitchen was added in 1762. A Colonial Revival rehabilitation c. 1937 introduced reused early-period paneling in the parlor and Federal woodwork and corner cabinet in the dining room. A new addition sympathetic in material and design was made in the 1980s. Sarum encompasses a noteworthy landscape with a river view and old-growth boxwood garden. An early-twentieth-century tobacco barn speaks to the endurance of the crop in southern Maryland, while an older deteriorating barn along the riverfront is a reminder of former patterns of trade and transportation.

NEWBURG

WS13 MOUNT REPUBLICAN
c. 1792; c. 1820 wing; early-20th-century additions. 12775 Rock Point Rd.

Mount Republican is one of the grandest Federal houses in southern Maryland and an early example of the side-passage-and-double-parlor plan, popular in this region by the early nineteenth century. While the plan remained constant through the antebellum period, various stylistic details were applied over time. Distinctive elements of this house include Flemish-bond brick, diamond-pattern glazing, parapet end walls with flush paired chimneys, and ornamental cornice. Matching carriage and river-front facades feature oversized tracery fanlights. Although the architect-builder is not known, striking similarities with nearby Waverley (c. 1795; 13535 Waverley Point Road) and West Hatton (c. 1790; W. Hatton Place, Stoddard Point) suggest the work of a local master builder. A two-story service wing was added c. 1820 and a hyphen and wing c. 1900 to create the telescoping configuration indicative of the Chesapeake. Mount Republican was built as part of Theophilus Yates's tobacco plantation, overlooking the Potomac River.

WS14 SHINE INN MOTEL
1953. 11150 Crain Hwy.

The extension of U.S. 301 across the Potomac River into Virginia via the Governor Harry W. Nice Bridge in 1940 and widening into a

THE CHESAPEAKE HOUSE

Maidstone (WS35), Owings

The term "Chesapeake" has been applied to a basic house form prevalent within the Western and Eastern Shore regions from the period of early settlement through the eighteenth century. In early Maryland it appeared as a one-story-and-loft frame dwelling of either one or two rooms, with a steeply pitched gable roof. Its design and construction were based upon English vernacular building traditions adapted to suit local conditions, both material and economic. It encompassed heavy timber framing joined by mortise and tenon, with a large chimney at one or both ends. The posts of the earliest dwellings were earthfast or "post in the ground" as at Sotterley (WS11). This modest dwelling form suited the region, rich in timber. The region was poor in skilled labor,

divided highway in the mid-1950s transformed a local road into a major north–south route, inspiring construction of many motels. Built as the White House Motel, this complex is representative of roadside lodging found along U.S. 301. It includes a two-and-a-half-story central section housing the office, lobby, and restaurant with a columned porch and cupola. Two original low wings of motel rooms have entrances sheltered by an overhanging porch roof and parking spaces directly in front. As was typical for motel construction in the period, the design was economical, with minimal decoration other than an enormous free-standing sign advertising the establishment. Other surviving mid-twentieth-century motels nearby are the Bel Alton (1952; 9259 Crain Highway) and the Lafayette (1945), now the Relax Inn at 9340 Crain.

Roadside motel construction was also motivated by legalization of slot machine gambling in Charles County in 1949. In this period only Nevada and four counties in Maryland—Charles, St. Mary's, Calvert, and Anne Arundel—had legal slot machine gambling. The lively nightlife and restaurant scene with slot machines in almost every establishment earned the MD 301 corridor

however, and a simpler and more expediently built variation evolved with lighter framing members, with common rafters half-lapped and held by pegs or nails to a "false plate" resting on top of the joist ends, eliminating the need for complex mortise-and-tenon joinery. This simplified version was often referred to as the "Virginia House," although it appeared throughout the Chesapeake region.

The plan generally consisted of a multipurpose "hall" adjoining a smaller and more private "parlor." In most cases the rooms were arranged side by side, although some were placed back to back with a shared chimney, as at Maidstone (**WS35**). Space needs were supplemented by separate dependencies such as a kitchen, dairy, meat house, and slave house. Small individual buildings were more easily built, but the separation can also be attributed to factors such as climate and social segregation; heat generated by certain household

functions were thus isolated, as were nonfamily members, particularly enslaved workers. The form likewise appeared in urban areas, embraced by the working classes in houses such as Hogshead (**WS56**) into the nineteenth century.

The Chesapeake house eventually expanded to include a passage mediating between various public and private spaces. By the mid-eighteenth century a three-room-and-passage plan emerged, as at the Thomas houses Clifton and Cherry Grove (see **CR46**), followed by a four-room-and-center-passage plan, as well as a gambrel-roofed variation and more permanent brick or stone construction such as Pemberton Hall (**ES75**). Separate kitchen buildings were sometimes later attached to the main block by a hyphen as at Wyoming (**CR4**). Having served many generations, the early Chesapeake house finally fell out of favor with the emergence of the Georgian mode of architecture.

the nickname Little Vegas. A slot machine ban in 1968 brought to a

close southern Maryland's era as a gambling travel destination.

BEL ALTON

WS15 ST. THOMAS MANOR AND ST. IGNATIUS ROMAN CATHOLIC CHURCH

1741 manor; 1798 church; 1866 alterations to both. 8855 Chapel Point Rd.

Consisting of the oldest continuously occupied Jesuit residence in the United States and the oldest Catholic parish in the original thirteen colonies, this complex is of vital importance to the history of Catholicism in the United States

and of outstanding architectural significance. St. Thomas Manor was built in 1741 to house the Maryland Mission of the Society of Jesus, or the Jesuits. The parish here originated before 1640 with Father Andrew White, S.J., one of the first priests in the Maryland Colony, having arrived on the *Ark* and the *Dove* in 1634. The original four thousand acres for the manor were granted by Lord Baltimore, devout Catholic and Proprietor of the Province of Maryland, to the Jesuits in 1649. In 1794 John Carroll was ordained here as the first Roman Catholic bishop in the United States, and in 1805 three priests took their vows to the Society of Jesus, reviving the Jesuit order in the United States after decades of suppression.

St. Thomas Manor is an early example of a large-scale Georgian building in the English colonies. A pedimented pavilion frames the three center bays of the matching seven-bay principle elevations, and all the exterior walls are high-quality Flemish-bond brick. Noteworthy details include the rubbed and gauged brick keystoned flat arches over the side elevation windows and elaborate second-floor window surrounds with carved stone impost blocks on the principle facades. The current side-gable roof with bracketed eaves and the interior finishes represent repairs after an 1866 fire. However, it appears that existing layout of a center passage and a stair in the northeast corner room are original.

Now used as the rectory for St. Ignatius Church, the house is part of an attached ensemble of four buildings including a two-bay, two-story east wing that partially predates it, and to the west the remains of an earlier chapel connected to the rear facade of St. Ignatius. The church has a gable roof with bracketed eaves like the manor house and an open belfry with a pyramidal roof. The interior of the church was rebuilt after the 1866 fire and now has box pews and galleries on three sides.

PORT TOBACCO

Port Tobacco was the site of a Native American settlement of the late Woodland period, noted by English explorer Captain John Smith in 1608, prior to its establishment by European settlers in 1684. By the mid-eighteenth century the town was one of the largest and most cohesive on Maryland's Western Shore. It was an important terminus of the trans-Atlantic tobacco trade, rivaling Annapolis, Georgetown, and Alexandria as a commercial center.

Now only a handful of extant buildings face the former town square, including the 1767 Stagg Hall (WS16) and the adjacent Chimney House (c. 1766; 8440 Commerce Street), named for its impressive pent chimneys. A 1972 reconstruction of the courthouse (c. 1820; 8430 Commerce) encompasses the original, restored south wing. The Burch House (c. 1720, c. 1820, c. 1850; 8435 Commerce) manifests the hall-parlor plan typical of the period, with a later rear shed, creating a saltbox configuration. The Boswell-Compton House (c. 1820; 7280 Chapel Point Road) just beyond is an excellent example of the telescoping house form. Port Tobacco now constitutes a rare archaeological resource, with most of the eighty-some buildings that existed in its heyday marking an undisturbed site worthy of investigation.

WS16 STAGG HALL
1766–1767; 1950s reconstructed wing. 8450 Commerce St.

Stagg Hall is one of the region's most refined examples of mid-eighteenth-century domestic architecture, built for merchant John Parnham. It is the oldest and best preserved of the five remaining buildings in the once-vital early port town. It possesses such Chesapeake features as a steeply pitched gambrel roof with flared eaves and chimneys with corbeled freestanding stacks. A larger east room and off-center passage and stair hall account for its asymmetrical facade. The service wing is a replica of the original, built around the extant center chimney. Stagg Hall's exceptional interior woodwork includes paneled overmantel and wainscoting, fluted pilasters, boxed cornices, built-in cabinet, and ornamental stairway featuring turned balusters and octagonal newels.

WS17 ROSE HILL
c. 1784. 6970 Rose Hill Rd.

Rose Hill is a Georgian five-part composition noteworthy for uncommon features that set it apart from others of its type. The front and rear facades are wood frame and brick nogged, while the gable end walls, hyphens, and wings are of Flemish-bond brick. The visual impact of the main block is accentuated by its elevation above the hyphenated wings, which are flush with the south riverfront facade yet set back from the north, where they recede into the background. The south facade is further distinguished by such classically inspired elements as a central pavilion, elaborate frontispiece, and Palladian and bull's-eye windows. The interior likewise presents an unusual variation on the Georgian center-passage plan, encompassing stairways to either side that encroach upon the rear rooms, with a transverse hallway terminating at one end in a side entrance. The raised basement contained the original kitchen and (owner) physician Gustavus Richard Brown's dissecting room for the study of cadavers. The east wing functioned as a summer kitchen, while the west wing served as Brown's office. Brown was an avid horticulturalist, growing medicinal, culinary, and ornamental plants and creating the terraced lawn with formal boxwood gardens facing Port Tobacco Creek.

WS18 HABRE DE VENTURE AT THOMAS STONE NATIONAL HISTORIC SITE
c. 1773. 6655 Rose Hill Rd.

This unusual house was owned by Thomas Stone, lawyer and signer of the Declaration of Independence. Part of Thomas Stone National Historic Site since 1978, Habre de Venture has an irregular five-part plan composed of three early buildings arranged in an arc. The center main block is a Flemish-bond brick structure one and a half stories high on a raised basement with a dormered gambrel roof. The frame gambrel-roofed law office connected by a brick breeze-way to the east has one room on each level. The frame and brick kitchen wing on the west is connected by a gambrel-roofed hyphen.

A fire in 1977 destroyed the interior, roof, and second-floor walls of the main block and heavily damaged the hyphens and wings; the current house museum interior is a modern re-creation. However the original parlor paneling survives, having been collected by the Baltimore Museum of Art in 1928. The approximately 320-acre property includes a variety of outbuildings such as tenant houses, barns, and corn crib, most dating from either the second quarter of the nineteenth century or the early twentieth century.

LA PLATA

WS19 LA GRANGE
Late 1760s; 1830s remodeled. 201 Port Tobacco Rd.

La Grange represents the emergence within the Western Shore of the classically inspired Georgian plan and design aesthetic. The prominent two-story, two-room-deep, center-passage house with hyphened wing includes such high-style Georgian features as an elaborate Palladian pavilion front with pediment, triple blind-arched loggia, and fluted pilasters. At the same time, La Grange exhibits elements indicative of early Chesapeake architecture such as frame construction with brick end walls and pent chimneys. The kitchen wing was originally freestanding, and evidence suggests it may have been flanked by another dependency; it was later joined to the main block by the current hyphen. Much of the interior first-floor details indicate stylistic updates during the 1830s, while the second floor retains its original baseboards and bolection-style chair rails. It was built for physician James Craik, friend and neighbor to Gustavus Richard Brown at Rose Hill (WS17). The two properties were built at the same time and share similarities, both academically and regionally inspired.

WS20 MOUNT CARMEL MONASTERY
c. 1790; 1936–1937 restored, Philip Hubert Frohman. 5678 Mount Carmel Rd.

In the 1930s a local organization called Restorers of Mount Carmel in Maryland set about saving the house known as The Monastery, preserving an important piece of early Catholic history in Charles County. A group of four Carmelite nuns arrived at Port Tobacco in 1790 from Belgium. Mother Bernardina Matthews and her order established a chapel, school, and self-sufficient farm on the Mount Carmel property in addition to building several dwellings. By 1831 the Carmelite sisters were struggling to maintain the farm, so the remaining nuns were ordered to transfer to the convent in Baltimore, effectively abandoning the Mount Carmel property for a hundred years.

The surviving two-part wood house includes a two-story main block attached by a small hyphen to a one-story side wing. Beaded exterior sheathing dating to the 1930s restoration covers brick nogging between the structural beams at the main block. The plainness of the restored Monastery speaks to the austere life of the Carmelite nuns. Currently this historic structure sits amidst a mid-twentieth-century pilgrimage chapel and a convent for the Dicalced Carmelite nuns who returned to Mount Carmel in 1976.

BRYANTOWN

WS21 DR. SAMUEL A. MUDD HOUSE
c. 1855. 3725 Dr. Samuel Mudd Rd.

This mid-nineteenth-century frame farmhouse has been preserved as a house museum due to its association with physician Samuel Mudd, who was convicted as a co-conspirator in the Lincoln assassination for setting John Wilkes Booth's broken leg when he fled through southern Maryland. Two sections of the structure were extant in Mudd's time—a two-story, three-bay main block and a lower two-story, two-bay side wing. A third section was added in the early twentieth century to create its distinctive telescoping form, as were porches and cross gables, which have since been removed. Mudd was sentenced to prison at Fort Jefferson in the Dry Tortugas and pardoned in 1869 after his heroic efforts during a yellow fever outbreak.

WS22 HUGHESVILLE TOBACCO WAREHOUSES

c. 1940–1956. 8127–8187 Leonardtown Rd.

A remarkable row of surviving tobacco warehouses from the mid-twentieth century sits just north of Hughesville. Maryland was the last tobacco-growing state to allow loose-leaf or "open" sales where the tobacco was visible in large 50- to 150-pound baskets. This system quickly replaced the "closed" one used since the earliest tobacco-growing days where 600-pound hogshead barrels were sold via sealed bids based on samples graded by a government inspector. The first loose-leaf tobacco auctions in 1939 spurred creation of a row of unassuming industrial buildings on a narrow strip of land next to the railroad tracks in Hughesville. During the four months of the selling season from roughly April to July, this district would be teeming with tobacco farmers and buyers.

The row of warehouses includes a Quonset hut section among a variety of more conventional low-pitched gable roofs. Except for one concrete block warehouse, they all feature corrugated metal sheathing and roofs and heavy timber frame structures to reduce fire hazard. A series of loading bays along Leonardtown Road facilitated truck access. Skylights throughout the interiors allowed better visual inspection of the tobacco before bidding on the lots stacked in narrow rows. These auction houses and warehouses are some of the last surviving structures in Maryland related to tobacco sales, storage, and processing. In 2000 a Tobacco Buyout program spelled the end for already struggling tobacco farming in Maryland, and the last auction was held in 2006. Now these unusual historic structures are vacant or used as flea market spaces, and county and state officials are investigating ways to preserve and reuse them.

BENEDICT

WS23 MAXWELL HALL

c. 1768. 17388 Teaques Point Rd.

Maxwell Hall represents the once-typical four-room-plan Chesapeake dwelling of the mid- to late eighteenth century. Built by merchant George Maxwell, the plan is considered transitional, evolving from the earlier multipurpose two-room hall-parlor plan to the more sophisticated Georgian central passage. Adjoining parlors appear to the front, one slightly larger to accommodate the central entrance of the five-bay facade; to the rear is a small stair hall flanked by additional rooms. Maxwell Hall has a fully excavated cellar that housed the original kitchen and is distinguished by its gambrel roof and massive brick end chimneys with tapered shoulders and freestanding stacks, providing heated rooms at each level.

CALVERT COUNTY
SOLOMONS

WS24 CALVERT MARINE MUSEUM
1986–1989. 14200 Solomons Island Rd.

Founded in 1970 by the Calvert County Historical Society, the museum originally placed its exhibits in temporary quarters. During the 1970s the Drum Point Lighthouse, *Wm. B. Tennison* bugeye (a flat-bottomed sailboat developed in the nineteenth century for Chesapeake Bay oyster dredging), and the J. C. Lore Oyster House (WS26) were all added to the collection and management transferred to the county. The museum property includes other small craft in outdoor displays and the adjacent 1925 Solomons Schoolhouse, currently used as administrative offices. The main exhibition building opened in 1989 and was renovated in 2014.

WS25 DRUM POINT LIGHTHOUSE
1883. 14200 Solomons Island Rd.

The Drum Point Lighthouse was built in five acres of open water at the mouth of the Patuxent River by the U.S. Lighthouse Board in 1883. Receding water levels left it stranded on the beach at low tide, and it was decommissioned in 1962. In 1975 this hexagonal screw-pile lighthouse was moved to Back Creek at the Calvert Marine Museum and restored for interpretation and tours. Screw-pile lighthouses feature buildings standing on an iron frame with angled piles screwed into the seabed. The auger-like flange at the bottom of the iron piles was well-suited for anchoring the lighthouse structure into the often soft and shallow bottom of the Chesapeake Bay. The Lighthouse Board built over forty screw-pile lighthouses in the Chesapeake starting in the third quarter of the nine-

teenth century. There are now just four surviving screw-pile lighthouses in Maryland—Drum Point; Thomas Point Shoal Light Station (WS78), the only one at its original site; Hooper Strait Lighthouse, now located at Chesapeake Bay Maritime Museum (ES51); and Seven Foot Knoll Lighthouse (see BC49) now located at Baltimore's Inner Harbor. Drum Point incorporates the keeper's quarters into its structure, with four rooms on the first level surrounded by an open gallery. The second floor has two rooms located under the hexagonal roof and lit by dormer windows. The cupola is surrounded by a small open gallery and contains the light, originally a fourth-order Fresnel lens.

WS26 J. C. LORE OYSTER HOUSE
1933–1934. 14430 Solomons Island Rd.

A rare surviving seafood-packing plant, J. C. Lore illustrates Maryland's historic role as the country's leading oyster producer. By the mid-nineteenth century, overharvesting in New York and New England had resulted in a market shift to the abundant Chesapeake Bay. Improvements in canning technology and the expansion of the railroad allowed the perishable oyster to be safely transported to tables across the country. One of the largest of approximately thirty-five oyster-packing companies once located along the Patuxent River, J. C. Lore operated from 1888 to 1978, making it the longest continuously functioning packing house in the area.

Joseph Lore Sr. worked with an unknown contractor to design this facility after a hurricane damaged the original building in 1933, heralded in trade literature as "modern in every respect." Boats delivered the oysters to the waterfront receiving room, where they were loaded into wheelbarrows and deposited into rooms lined with shucking tables. The shuckers, generally European immigrant or African American women and children, extracted the oyster meat by hand and sorted it by size. Filled buckets were passed through a window to the processing room. The weights were tallied for each shucker to determine payment, and the oysters were further rinsed, canned, and held in cold storage prior to shipping. Lore's "Patuxent" oysters were made famous through the sale of canned oysters to local buyers and grocery store chains in Washington, Maryland, and Pennsylvania. Calvert County purchased the building for the Calvert Marine Museum with its closure in

1978, and it was designated a National Historic Landmark in 2001.

WS27 AVONDALE

1890 platted. Bounded by Solomons Island Rd, Langley Ln., Back Creek, and The Narrows

Solomons Island and the Avondale subdivision on the mainland comprised a regional center of seafood harvesting and processing industries, as well as boatbuilding, sport fishing, and summer recreation. In 1866 Isaac Solomon purchased a large tract of land and established an oyster cannery and boatyard. By the 1880s the commercial fleet here included several hundred locally built and maintained vessels. Directly adjacent to the growing village on Solomons Island, Avondale became the first subdivision in Calvert County, addressing growing local demand for residential building lots.

The grandest houses were built along the west and southeast side of the community, such as the picturesque Queen Anne Vail House (c. 1902; 14280 Solomons Island) built for fisherman Captain Phillip Vail and its simpler gable-front neighbor, the Abell House (c. 1910; 14286 Solomons Island). A variety of vernacular shotgun houses, I-houses, and simple frame bungalows were built on the inner blocks such as C and Calvert streets during the early twentieth century. Many were likely built as workers' residences and later used as recreational dwellings. A remarkably intact group of three one-story frame shotgun houses at 14260-62-64 Calvert seem to have been constructed at the same time. Construction of nearby Patuxent River Naval Air Station during World War II reoriented the local economy toward defense and government employment, while continued tourism and recreation maintain historic connections to the water.

LUSBY

WS28 MORGAN HILL FARM

c. 1700; c. 1836 remodeled. 1555 Wohlgemuth Hill Rd.

This is among Maryland's earliest extant houses, perched on a rise with stunning views of St. Leonard's Creek and the Patuxent River. The first section was likely built by planter Robert Day, with changes and additions by Richard Breeden and his decedents, who owned Morgan Hill from 1836 to 1949. Although remodeled in the early nineteenth century, the story-and-a-half house maintains evidence of English vernacular building traditions, including a steeply pitched gable roof, exposed interior wall and corner posts, and ceiling joists with decorative beaded edges. The house originally contained a massive central chimney, creating a small lobby entrance, reminiscent of the seventeenth-century English baffle-entry houses. The chimney was later removed in favor of gable-end chimneys with semidetached stacks typical of the Chesapeake, a central passage, and an open-string stair.

The kitchen, attached to the main block by a narrow hyphen, is a repurposed log slave house with large end chimney, one of three extant slave dwellings at Morgan Hill. Other significant eighteenth-century outbuildings reflecting its former use as a tobacco plantation include an unusually well-crafted log tobacco barn (*pictured*), log smokehouse, and corn crib.

ST. LEONARD

WS29 JEFFERSON PATTERSON PARK AND POINT FARM

7500 BCE–c. 1900 CE; 1932–1966, Gertrude Sawyer; Rose Greely and Cary Milholland Parker, landscape architects. 10515 Mackall Rd.

This 512-acre park includes a variety of archaeological and historic sites, as well as a museum, trails, picnic areas, the Morgan State University Estuarine Research Center (1994), and the Maryland Archaeological Conservation (MAC) Laboratory (1996–1998, Ayers/Saint/Gross Architects). Over thirty prehistoric sites ranging in age from 7500 BCE to contact have been identified that are characteristic of both upland and lowland utilization of the Chesapeake Bay tidewater region by Native Americans. The prehistoric sites range from simple temporary campsites to extensive shell- and fish-gathering stations. Nearly twenty historic archaeological sites including house foundations, privy pits, and wells are on the property, with the oldest dating from around 1640.

Three clusters of extant historic buildings largely relate to the twentieth-century ownership of career diplomat Jefferson Patterson. With his wife Mary Breckenridge Patterson, a pioneering filmmaker and journalist, he built Point Farm, a retreat and model farm complex, in the 1930s. Both Pattersons came from wealthy families—his father was a founder of the National Cash Register Company, and her grandfather founded B. F. Goodrich. When the couple married in 1939, Marvin (as Mary was known) was working for journalist Edward R. Murrow reporting on the war in Europe as the first female broadcaster for CBS, a career she had to leave to avoid conflict with her husband's diplomatic work.

Point Farm was realized by an all-woman design team that included architect Sawyer and landscape architects Greely and Parker, all graduates of the Cambridge School of Architecture and Landscape Architecture. Sawyer was working for Washington architect Horace Peaslee when she was hired by the Pattersons, and she opened her own office shortly after in 1934. Sawyer was an early female member of the AIA, and her career focused on residential work including many Colonial Revival renovations and additions. Her thirty-four-year association with Point Farm was her most extensive project, encompassing a master plan, twenty-six new buildings including the house and agricultural complex, renovations of two existing houses on the property, and later alterations.

Greely also worked for Peaslee before becoming the first woman architect licensed in Washington and opening her own office in 1925. She specialized in residential design integrating house and garden and was a prolific writer. Her work at Point Farm from 1933 to 1935 focused on creating the walled garden at the house and overall landscape planning. Parker continued these efforts from the late 1930s through the 1940s, refining the garden designs for the property.

An excellent late example of the American country house tradition in the early twentieth century, the main house at Point Farm is a sprawling two-and-a-half-story Colonial Revival brick manor with indoor and outdoor spaces for entertaining and formal gardens. It sits on a bluff overlooking the Patuxent River at the mouth of St. Leonard Creek. A three-car garage was incorporated into one wing of the house, with servant quarters above. Now vacant and awaiting restoration, the house includes a series of alterations by Sawyer up until 1966. The walls, terraces, and gardens around the house are in a similar state of intact neglect. The landscape includes water elements such as an octagonal fish pond in the enclosed garden at the southeast corner of the house and an in-ground swimming pool at a lower terrace with a pool house.

In addition to the house, Sawyer designed numerous agricultural buildings, most notably the farm manager's complex. Its focal point is the 1932 dairy barn with whimsical weathervanes on louvered cupolas, sited at the long end of a U-shaped yard flanked by a chicken house and granary. In 1998 the state-of-the-art Maryland Archaeology Conservation Laboratory opened next to the farm complex. Its design invoking a modern interpretation of the agricultural buildings was reviewed and approved by an elderly Sawyer. After the archaeological significance of the property was discovered in the early 1980s, Marvin Patterson began donating it to the State of Maryland. The final portion containing the main house was transferred upon her death in 2002.

PORT REPUBLIC

WS30 DAVID W. MASON HOUSE
c. 1890. 4120 Broomes Island Rd.

This is an outstanding example of a common vernacular dwelling form that appeared throughout Maryland from the mid-nineteenth though the early

twentieth centuries, enhanced with ornate detailing. The house comprises a two-story, symmetrical five-bay main block with a central cross-gable, full-width front porch, and rear service wing to create an L-shaped plan. It is distinguished, however, by its jigsawn, trefoil-pattern-trimmed cornice and porch details; gable-end bargeboards, turned and bracketed porch posts; and narrow lapped siding. It also features full-height and bay windows in the first-story facade. The rear ell extends five-bays and includes a side-facing cross gable that mimics the adjacent gable end of the main block. It is considered among the finest examples of late-nineteenth-century architecture in Calvert County.

WS31 SCIENTISTS' CLIFFS AND THE JOSEPH P. FLIPPO COMMUNITY HOUSE
1948. 2191 Cedar Rd.

This progressive bayfront community was established in 1935 by G. Flippo Gravatt and Annie E. Rathburn, a husband-and-wife team of forest pathologists for the U.S. Department of Agriculture, who conceived of it as a summer colony for scientists. The bylaws called for the construction of wood houses—many of which were built in rustic fashion from the blighted chestnut trees located on the property—and protection of such landscape features as the cliffs and ravines, trees, and other indigenous plants. Like the founder's own Chestnut Cabin and the guest quarters, Flippo's Cabin, the Community House was erected of logs milled on-site, tightly joined, and held by simple saddle notching. The low gable-roofed building features an ironstone foundation, fireplace, and chimney. Emblematic of the numerous bayside summer communities built during the first half of the twentieth century, Scientists' Cliffs now includes over two hundred mostly rustic-style houses.

PRINCE FREDERICK

WS32 LINDEN
c. 1868, c. 1907. 70 Church St.

Constructed by Henry and Georgeanna Williams, Linden sits on a bucolic site outside of the Calvert County seat of Prince Frederick. Williams practiced law in Prince Frederick and served in the state legislature while living at Linden, originally an L-shaped house with subdued Italianate details. The third owner, teacher and lawyer John B. Gray, purchased the house at auction in 1888 and is responsible for its current form. Around 1907 he had the L-shaped house transformed into one with a symmetrical plan. The addition closely matched the front gable and weatherboard siding of the original. A new porch with plain Tuscan columns stretched across the front of the house. Members of the Gray family lived at Linden until the late 1980s. Today the house and a collection of outbuildings are owned by the Calvert County Historical Society.

Lower Marlboro represents the once commonplace wharf communities that formed along the Western Shore for the shipment of tobacco and other produce from local farms. It was established in 1706 and by the mid-eighteenth century encompassed warehouses, a tavern, stores, mills, and other structures. Although much of the town was burned by the British during the War of 1812, it later rallied and by the mid-nineteenth century was once again one of the county's most bustling wharf villages. It then encompassed mills, a cannery, boatwright and blacksmith shops, and other businesses, serving steamboats for shipment of goods to Baltimore.

WS33 GRAHAME HOUSE
1750. 3825 Lower Marlboro Rd.

Little remains from the early period of Lower Marlboro, with the exception of a handful of Chesapeake houses, of which this is the finest. While displaying the same identifiable configuration, Grahame House was erected of Flemish-bond brick with decorative glazed headers, a molded-brick water table and sills, segmental-arched windows, and a steeply pitched gable roof with a rear catslide. The other two are frame, including one used for a period as a general store and post office (c. 1800; 4215 Chaneyville Road), located close to the wharf site; and another (c. 1800; 6518 Lower Marlboro Lane) that was remade c. 1860 into an ornamented cottage with front porch and large dormer.

CHESAPEAKE BEACH

WS34 CHESAPEAKE BEACH RAILWAY MUSEUM
c. 1900; 1980 restored. 4155 Mears Ave.

This station marked the terminus for the Washington and Chesapeake Beach Railway that linked Washington with the former bayside resort and amusement park. Chesapeake Beach was among the many summer communities that developed along the Western Shore around the turn of the twentieth century, becoming the premier Bay-front attraction. The station is the last intact nonresidential building in Chesapeake Beach dating from that period, which once included luxury hotels, a boardwalk, a steamboat pier with miniature railway, a casino, a dance pavilion, a roller coaster, and a carousel. Chesapeake Beach fell into decline during the Great Depression and post–World War II eras, transitioning from summer resort to year-round residential community. The railway ceased operation in 1934, and this wood station, with its overhanging hipped roof with flared eaves, wraparound porch, and square tower, was allowed to deteriorate. It was restored in 1980 and reopened as the Chesapeake Beach Railway Museum.

WS35 MAIDSTONE
1751; c. 1840. 1140 W. Chesapeake Beach Rd.

Dated through dendrochronology to 1751, Maidstone (see p. 32) is one of the earliest surviving frame houses in the region and demonstrates the influence of postmedieval English vernacular building traditions on the colonial Chesapeake house. English influence is expressed by the steeply pitched gable roof, large T-shaped end chimney, and articulated post-and-beam framing, including exposed beaded ceiling joists, sill plates, and summer beam. Indicative of the Chesapeake house, its structural framing exhibits variations on traditional English timber framing utilizing lighter members and simpler joinery. The roof includes large common rafters spiked into the ceiling joists to form trusses, secured with dovetailed collar beams.

Maidstone originally encompassed a four-room plan; a large hall adjoined a smaller heated parlor with enclosed winder stair and two smaller unheated chambers to the opposing side. The back-to-back positioning of the hall and parlor is a now-rare early plan type. It allowed the rooms to share the T-shaped chimney block, with a massive fireplace in the hall and a corner fireplace in the adjoining parlor. The two smaller chambers later became a central passage with a formal stairway, adding two rooms to the west, along with Greek Revival details. The originally separate one-and-a-half-story kitchen with a large open-hearth fireplace was later joined by a hyphen. Maidstone includes numerous tobacco barns dating from the mid-eighteenth to mid-nineteenth centuries. The house was built by yeoman farmer Lewis Lewin and since 1949 has been home to the Hicks family.

ANNE ARUNDEL COUNTY
ANNAPOLIS AND VICINITY

Annapolis is Maryland's capital and a gem of the colonial and post-Revolutionary eras, encompassing some of America's premier Georgian architecture and one of its most sophisticated early town plans. Its origins can be traced to a 1649 settlement known as Providence established by nonconformist Puritans seeking the religious freedom promised by the *Maryland Toleration Act,* issued that same year. Forming dispersed tobacco plantations, they soon migrated across the Severn River, establishing a town site, much of which was acquired by colonial proprietor Cecil Calvert to form the initial hundred-acre tract then named Anne Arundel Town. Located near the confluence of the Severn River and the Chesapeake Bay, the economy centered around maritime pursuits and shipping, including trade in Maryland's greatest commodity, tobacco. Growth was prompted in 1695 by provincial governor Francis Nicholson moving the colonial capital here from St. Mary's City.

Nicholson reenvisioned the fledgling port town; renaming it Annapolis in 1702, he overlaid its grid with a plan based upon Baroque models of seventeenth-century Europe. Unique to the colonies, it featured two prominent circles, State and Church, located at the high-point of the town plan, from which radiated diagonal streets, with a market square and other public reservations. Now recognized as one of the most important early contributions to American city planning, the scheme followed new currents in European urban planning, modifying a standard grid to create a richer urban landscape with viewsheds to the harbor. The circles were occupied by the State House (WS36) and by the Anglican Church (St. Anne's; WS60) newly established in Maryland, representing the separate spheres of church and state. Numerous brick public buildings were soon underway, scattered among an existing cityscape of one-and-a-half-story frame buildings characteristic of the Chesapeake.

The high point of the town's prosperity came under the provincial governorship of Horatio Sharpe, sent from England by Cecil Calvert. A structured governmental bureaucracy drew wealthy attorneys and politicians. Stability combined with the lucrative tobacco trade likewise attracted a citizenry of prosperous planters and merchants, artisans, craftsmen, and shopkeepers. Their wealth was transformative, manifested in the creation of increasingly more sophisticated brick-constructed houses that, like the town plan, reflected the latest European trends. By the mid-eighteenth century, the affluent looked to England, where the revival of classical architectural designs had been popularly adopted by British architects. The designs were then transferred to the colonies through pattern books and skilled immigrant craftsmen. The modest Chesapeake-styled buildings gave way to grander edifices in all but the working-class enclaves.

Annapolis's architectural ascendency took root in the 1730s and 1740s when significant transformations led to the great houses of the mid- to late eighteenth century. It began with the introduction of more sophisticated plans, two-story brick construction, and the adaptation of the Georgian mode of architecture. The 1760s through the 1780s witnessed ever more complex designs, including the introduction of the Palladian-influenced five-part-plan house, some encompassing private gardens, and the Annapolis Plan variation on the traditional center passage. Intended to rival London's best, the houses demonstrated the growing wealth of Maryland's merchants and planters.

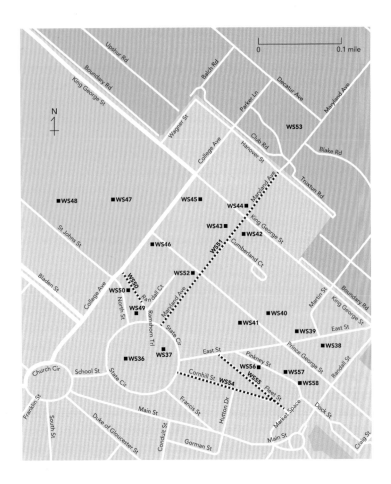

Annapolis was surpassed by Baltimore in size and importance during the post-Revolutionary era. Freed from British control over production, Baltimore benefited from industrial development, easier access to western and Caribbean markets, and the switch to more lucrative grain production and export. Annapolis remained influential as Maryland's cultural and governmental center and regional marketplace. Mid- to late-nineteenth-century growth occurred along its commercial corridors, Main Street and Maryland Avenue, spilling out to neighboring residential streets. Likewise, development within St. John's College (beginning with McDowell Hall; WS47) and the U.S. Naval Academy (WS53) contributed to the city's architectural splendor with buildings ranging from the Georgian through to Beaux-Arts and modern. Although Baltimore's eclipse was detrimental to Annapolis's economy, reduced developmental pressure facilitated the survival and integrity of the town's rich architectural heritage. Colonial Revival buildings were erected during the early twentieth century to blend within the existing built environment. In the 1950s Annapolis led the state in organizations and ordinances designed to protect its architectural landscape, including the establishment of a historic district in 1965.

WS36 MARYLAND STATE HOUSE AND STATE CIRCLE
1772–1779, Joseph Horatio Anderson; 1785–1788 dome, Joseph Clark; 1902–1905 restored, J. Appleton Wilson; annex, Baldwin and Pennington; 2007–2015 restored, Mesick, Cohen, Wilson, and Baker; and Christman Company. 100 State Cir.

This is the oldest state capitol still in active use as the seat of government and the only one to have served as the nation's capital, witnessing important events that ended the American Revolutionary War. The Continental Congress met in its Senate Chamber from November 26, 1783, to August 13, 1784, during which time George Washington appeared to resign his commission as commander-in-chief of the Continental Army. Washington's actions have been exulted as a critical step in the establishment of civil authority over military rule. On January 14, 1784, the Treaty of Paris was ratified here, officially recognizing the United States as a sovereign nation and marking the end of the war. A notable example of colonial architecture, it was designed by preeminent Maryland architect Joseph Horatio Anderson, also responsible for Whitehall (WS79). As the centerpiece of Annapolis's notable Baroque town plan, it is situated within one of two circles, at the heart of the Annapolis Historic District.

The State House was greatly praised in its day as one of the country's finest public buildings. Its exceptional classically inspired interior finishes were undertaken by noted craftsman John Rawlings, formerly of London. Its timber-framed dome was erected by Annapolis architect-builder Joseph Clark. The unusually tall dome comprises a two-stage drum and lantern with splayed pent roof and a lightning rod ornamented by a copper-sheathed carved acorn symbolizing strength.

Sadly, a renovation in 1876–1877 resulted in the removal of many interior finishes. A restoration was called for within a few decades, and at the same time, a grand annex was erected at the northwest elevation. More recently, the Old Senate Chamber was restored to the time of Washington's 1783 resignation. Bronze statues of George Washington and Molly Ridout, who witnessed the resignation from the gallery, were installed in 2014 as part of an interpretation of the event by StudioEIS of New York City. A monument to famed civil rights lawyer and Supreme Court justice Thurgood Marshall (1996, Antonio Tobias Mendez) is located on Lawyer's Mall in front of the State House's west portico. It includes a life-size bronze sculpture of

Marshall in front of a colonnade inscribed with the words "Equal Justice Under Law" facing seated bronze figures on stone benches inscribed with the names of major civil rights cases he won.

WS37 OLD TREASURY BUILDING
1735–1737, Patrick Creagh, builder. State House Grounds at East St.

In 1733 the Maryland General Assembly passed a bill allowing for the dispensing of paper currency, and by 1735 a building was under construction on the State House grounds for this purpose. Now known as the Old Treasury Building after its 1780s occupant, this one-and-a-half-story brick building is the oldest surviving public building in Maryland and the only structure besides the State House remaining on State Circle. The building's unique public function is reflected in its thick walls, heavy doors, barred windows, and masonry vaulted ceiling. However, in scale and form the Old Treasury Building also resembles a fine hall-parlor house of the period. The brick front entrance porch and a rear ell create a cruciform plan that also recalls contemporary Anglican churches. The State of Maryland undertook an extensive restoration after major cracking appeared in the ceiling vaults in 1949, an early example of state-sponsored preservation work. This restoration, led by Baltimore architects Laurence Hall Fowler and Henry Powell Hopkins, replaced Greek Revival interior features with reproduction ones thought to be more appropriate for an eighteenth-century building, but retained the original doors and hardware. Recent preservation efforts have focused on archaeology and interpreting the early history of state government in Annapolis.

WS38 WATERWITCH HOOK AND LADDER FIRE STATION NO. 1
1913; 1926, 1954 additions. 33 East St.

This fire station replaced an earlier one on the same site. Its original two-story section has a large round-arched opening for horse-drawn engines and a pair of corner towers. The east tower is topped by a tempietto sheltering the siren. In 1926 a one-story addition in matching buff-colored brick was added to the west for another vehicle bay. An elliptical-arched opening filling almost its entire facade was intended to accommodate the new motorized fire trucks. A smaller office addition was attached to the west in c. 1954. The all-volunteer Waterwitch Company served from this station until consolidation of three downtown fire stations in 1986. The building was sold to the Chesapeake Bay Foundation and thoughtfully adapted for office space and storage.

WS39 JAMES BRICE HOUSE
1767–1773. 42 East St.

Built by wealthy planter, lawyer, and politician James Brice, this is a well-documented Georgian five-part-plan house situated within an urban setting. Its clean, bold simplicity and imposing scale set it apart as one of colonial Maryland's great houses, despite the somewhat naive early interpretation of exterior classical details such as its diminutively scaled Palladian window. It is one of four five-part houses built in Annapolis, displaying distinctive building traditions of the capital city. These include its towering slab chimneys and steeply pitched gable roof, stone foundation with galleting, header-bond brick construction, and the adoption of the Annapolis Plan that first appeared in Brice's 1739 boyhood home (WS41). Thus, the best room, the large drawing room, faces the rear garden. The entrance hall from which all rooms radiate is among the largest in the city, dominated by a grand stairway. The east wing comprised the kitchen and wash house, while the west, a coach house and office.

Brice's rare and exhaustive accounts (now in the Maryland State Archives) chronicle the house's construction and early room use. They suggest he acted as his own architect, paying a small fee to an unidentified individual for "drawing the Plann," [sic] while referencing a copy of Isaac Ware's edition of Palladio purchased in 1767. The staid exterior belies the sophistication of the interior details executed by highly skilled craftsmen including plaster work by Thomas Harvey, indentured to Brice, and elegant carved chimney pieces, stair, and built-in cabinet by joiner George Foster. It remained in the family until 1874 and is currently owned by the State of Maryland, under the stewardship of Historic Annapolis, Inc.

WS40 WILLIAM PACA HOUSE

1763–1765; 1901 renovated; 1970s restored. 186 Prince George St.

This was the home of William Paca, attorney, signer of the Declaration of Independence, and a Maryland governor. Within days of his marriage to Mary Chew, Paca commenced construction of this large and imposing house that he is believed to have designed. Paca chose the newly introduced five-part plan that first appeared c. 1760 in the now much-altered Bordley-Randall House. The house included a prominent two-story rear tower, a relic of colonial architecture that distinguishes it as among the earliest of Maryland's many five-part houses. The tower provides a panoramic view of the formal garden.

Other traits characteristic of Annapolis architecture are its raised, galleted, stone foundation, facade laid in the fashionable header bond of the period, and large gable-end slab chimneys that lend greater height and prominence. The interior manifests a traditional Georgian center-passage plan with the stair to one side. The two rooms flanking the passage on the street front served as parlor and drawing room. The dining room overlooks the rear garden, with a small study behind the stair and a kitchen in the southeast wing.

Paca House was dramatically altered in 1901 with its conversion as the Carvel Hall Hotel and the addition of a massive wing extending into the garden. In the 1960s, Historic Annapolis purchased the house and the State of Maryland the formal terraced garden. Featuring rose, holly, and boxwood parterres in geometric patterns, a Chinese latticework bridge, and a summerhouse, the garden restoration was based on its appearance in the background of Charles Willson Peale's 1772 portrait of Paca. The house was opened to the public following an extensive 1970s restoration.

WS41 JOHN BRICE II HOUSE
1739; c. 1785; late 19th century.
195 Prince George St.

This house was pivotal to the development of Annapolis's domestic architecture as the first to manifest an interior layout so enthusiastically adopted by the city's well-to-do that it became known as the Annapolis Plan. It is a modification of the double-pile Georgian plan in which the central passage terminates at the most elaborately finished rooms located along the rear to take advantage of garden views and access. To one side of the front is the entrance and stair hall with a small study tucked behind the stair. The plan allowed for the discernment of public versus family space unattainable in the prevailing hall-parlor plan, marking a rise in social awareness within

polite society. Adjoining the best room intended for entertaining is a private chamber with no direct access to the entrance hall and an enclosed winder stair to the bedchamber above. The dining room adjoins the hall to the front, with a winder stair to the cellar kitchen and servant areas. Public and private spaces were further signaled through a hierarchy in molding profiles.

Also expressive of the Chesapeake region, and Annapolis in particular, are its narrow slab chimneys, gambrel roof, and paneled interior partition walls. Wealthier classes soon adopted a full two-story Georgian design mode, however the gambrel-roofed Chesapeake house continued to be built by Annapolis's artisan class into the early nineteenth century. John Brice was a member of the Governor's Council, a chief justice in the court of colonial Maryland, and twice mayor of Annapolis.

WS42 HAMMOND-HARWOOD HOUSE
1774–1780, William Buckland.
19 Maryland Ave.

Hammond-Harwood is one of the few colonial houses modeled

directly on a Palladian design and as such stands as one of the most sophisticated classically inspired dwellings in eighteenth-century America. Built for young lawyer and planter Matthias Hammond, this is also the first Maryland house entirely attributed to British master craftsman Buckland, who based his design on Italian Renaissance architect Andrea Palladio's Villa Pisani, Montagnana. Its five-part symmetrical facade with projecting central pavilion and reliance on eighteenth-century pattern books are emblematic of English classicism of the Georgian period. The five-bay main block is flanked by hyphens and two-story wings with the polygonal bays that distinguish it from similarly configured houses. The house caught the eye of Thomas Jefferson, who made two drawings of it while in Annapolis in 1783–1784, possibly inspiring his own use of such bays at Monticello. The northeast wing contains an office suite with no direct access to the main block, separating domestic from business functions, while open access was provided to the kitchen in the southwest wing.

The interior embraces the Annapolis Plan, positioning the best rooms used for entertaining on each floor to the rear of the house. A jib door located in the largest and best appointed first-floor room, used as the dining room, provides ready access to the garden while also maintaining symmetry, appearing as a window with paneled spandrel from the interior. From the exterior, it serves as the entrance, placed within a shallow pedimented pavilion articulated by pilasters. Other notable features include a richly carved frontispiece, James Gibbs–inspired bull's-eye windows, and a wealth of ornately carved interior Rococo and neoclassical woodwork.

In 1811 the house was purchased by Jeremiah Townley Chase for his daughter Frances and her husband, Richard Loockerman. It passed to their daughter Hester Loockerman Harwood, married to lawyer William Harwood, and finally to their daughters, Lucy and Hester Ann Harwood, who resided here until 1924. It was designated a National Historic Landmark in 1960.

WS43 CHASE-LLOYD HOUSE
1769–1774; 1771–1773, William Buckland; 1773–1774, William Noke. 22 Maryland Ave.

This is among Annapolis's most sophisticated and well-appointed houses and its only full three-story detached colonial-era residence. Resting on a high foundation, it extends an impressive seven bays across. It displays the symmetry and detailing indicative of Georgian architecture to embrace a tripartite facade with a central pavilion surmounted by a dentiled pediment, low-hipped roof, and slab chimneys. The elaborate entrance frontispiece is flanked by sidelights, a pattern mimicked by the tripartite window above. The interior was richly ornamented by some of colonial America's most skilled craftsmen, including Buckland's exquisitely carved wood details derived from classically inspired English Palladian design motifs. The elaborate plaster ceilings and

THE FIVE-PART PALLADIAN HOUSE

Montpelier (CR28), Laurel

Among Maryland's most distinctive domestic building forms is the five-part Palladian house, consisting of a central block flanked by hyphens and terminating wings. It first appeared in Maryland in and around Annapolis in the 1760s, embraced by the city's wealthier classes. It spread throughout the Chesapeake region, serving in rural areas as the centerpiece of a plantation or along the urban fringes as a country retreat or gentleman's farm. The five-part design was based on the work of sixteenth-century Italian Renaissance architect Andrea Palladio, who took his inspiration from classical antiquity, predominately the use of the classical orders and the emphasis on symmetry and proportion.

Palladio outlined his revival of classical design in *The Four Books of Architecture* in 1571. First pub-

cornices were executed by James Barnes and John Rawlings. Recently arrived from England in 1771, they offered plasterwork "as neat as in London."

The house is also recognized for its sophisticated plan. The most ornamental rooms are the parlor and dining room flanking the hall to the front of the house, with transverse passages separating them from the smaller, informal family sitting and dining rooms to the rear. It is the first time in Annapolis that the dining room replaced the parlor as the best finished room. The expansive central hall is bisected by an entablature with freestanding Ionic columns, beyond which is a monumental stair with a landing lit by an enormous Palladian window. It was the grandest stairway in the region, including individual articulated, seemingly unsupported steps with scrolled soffits.

Begun by Samuel Chase, a signer of the Declaration of Independence and associate justice of the U.S. Supreme Court, the house was completed by

lished in Britain in 1715–1720, his design concepts were enthusiastically adopted by British architects, launching the Anglo-Palladian movement and Georgian mode of architecture. Gaining popularity, these designs were translated into pattern books and builder's guides. By the mid-eighteenth century, Palladian-influenced design had reached the American colonies through both pattern books and immigrant architects and artisans.

The Maryland prototype corresponds with Palladio's country villa, which incorporated low-flanking arcades connecting to wings designated for agricultural use. These hyphenated wings became an integral part of the houses designed by Palladio's eighteenth-century colonial enthusiasts, best embodied by the Hammond-Harwood House (**WS42**). The form appeared most frequently in the southern colonies where it was easily adapted to the regional tradition of building separate dependencies; the wings served to isolate heat generated by functions such as food preparation.

One wing of Maryland's five-part house was thus dedicated to kitchen and service areas, while the other was used for more secluded business or family functions. Likewise, the characteristic Palladian temple-front portico, often more simply translated as a pedimented central pavilion, was an exterior articulation of the interior Georgian center-passage as at His Lordship's Kindness (**CR3**).

So popular was the five-part plan by the latter part of the eighteenth century that many earlier Georgian houses were expanded to encompass the characteristic hyphenated wings such as Tulip Hill (**WS86**) and Montpelier (**CR28**). The form persisted into the early nineteenth century, embracing Adamesque or Federal period motifs as seen in Homewood (**BC104**) and Riversdale (**CR22**). While the plan fell out of favor by the second quarter of the nineteenth century, it reappeared in Colonial Revival residences of the early twentieth century as exemplified by the Newton White House (**CR11**).

planter Edward Lloyd IV as the urban counterpart to his Wye House plantation (ES48). Lloyd hired Buckland to resume construction, undertaking the decorative details matched by few other colonial houses. It was later purchased by Judge Jeremiah Townley Chase and occupied by his nieces, including Hester Ann Chase Ridout. In 1883, she bequeathed the house to St. Anne's Episcopal Church (WS60) as a home for impoverished elderly women in recognition of the lack of social services then available.

The first-floor rooms are available for touring by appointment.

WS44 JAMES ANDREWS HOUSE
c. 1852–1858. 16 Maryland Ave.

In 1852, Irish immigrant and Main Street dry goods store owner James Andrews purchased an unimproved lot at the corner of Maryland Avenue and King George Street and erected a three-story Greek Revival town house, a relatively unusual stylistic choice in Annapolis. The house has a side passage accessed via granite stairs with wrought-iron railings and flat, stone lintels typical of Greek Revival. The use of all-stretcher pressed brick on the front facade was an early local example of this fashionable trend. A pair of parlors is located in the main block of the house, with kitchen and dining rooms in the rear ell.

WS45 OGLE HALL
1739–1742; 1775–1776 addition and renovations. 247 King George St.

Equally transformative to Annapolis's eighteenth-century architectural development as the John Brice II House (WS41) was Ogle Hall, begun the same year. Both are considered antecedents to the great houses built during Annapolis's heyday, establishing design features that came to define the city's best buildings. Ogle Hall broke from the traditional Chesapeake house to become the first full two-story, classically detailed, brick house in Annapolis. Like the Brice House, it features a variation on the Georgian center-passage plan, although embracing a transverse hall with adjoining rooms for formal entertaining. It possesses principal facades oriented to both the street and rear garden, creating the dual orientation characteristic of the Annapolis Plan. The hall is entered from the garden facade while direct entrance into the best rooms is provided by an axial, visually deceptive jib doorway on the street facade.

The house is named for Governor Samuel Ogle, who first leased it in 1747 from the heirs of original owner physician William Stephenson. In 1775–1776 the Ogles added an opulent unusual rear polygonal ballroom with some of the most ornate plaster cornices in the city. The interior finishes were updated; plaster cornices were added in the center passage, and a new stairway composed of articulated, cantilevering steps, similar to that recently built for the Chase-Lloyd House (WS43). Ogle Hall was purchased by the U.S. Naval Academy Association in 1946 for use as its Alumni House.

WS46 COMMODORE WADDELL HOUSE
1881; 1960s restored, John Wood Burch. 61 College Ave.

Commodore James Iredell Waddell was a Confederate naval officer who had graduated from the nearby U.S. Naval Academy in 1847 and lived in England during the years following the Civil War. Upon returning to Annapolis he is said to have modeled his new house on an early example of English Queen Anne he and his wife admired in Liverpool. The long brick structure has multiple cross gables topped by finials and wide eaves, but primarily horizontal lines. Perhaps most striking are the robust turned columns at the front porch and sash windows with grids of small square lights. Many interior features such as a stair hall with an elaborately carved newel post and fireplaces with decorative ceramic tile friezes are still intact. After being used as a fraternity house for St. John's College and then apartments, the Waddell House was restored to a single-family residence.

WS47 MCDOWELL HALL, ST. JOHN'S COLLEGE

1744–1746, Simon Duff, architect, Patrick Creagh, builder; 1786–1799, Joseph Clark; 1909–1910, Baldwin and Pennington. 60 College Ave.

Chartered in 1784, St. John's College is a venerable liberal arts institution known since the 1930s for its "great books" curriculum. The centerpiece of its campus is the stately Georgian McDowell Hall, which served as the original multipurpose structure and is believed to be one of the oldest continuously occupied academic buildings in the United States. McDowell Hall predates the establishment of St. John's, with initial construction starting in 1744 as an official residence for colonial governor Thomas Bladen. The ambitious plans for the house—later dubbed Bladen's Folly—were based on the publications of English architect James Gibbs and overseen by Scottish immigrant architect Duff. The double-pile, two-story structure was massive, standing nine bays wide on a raised basement. Features typical of fine Georgian design of the period include Flemish-bond brickwork with brown sandstone quoins at the front facade corners and pairs of slab-like double inte-rior chimneys on each side elevation. Funding conflicts prevented completion, and the partially constructed building sat exposed to the elements. Discussion of turning the property over to a college started as early as 1761.

In 1786, college officials hired architect Joseph Clark, currently at work completing the State House dome (WS36), to finish and modify the domestic structure for their purposes. On the exterior, Clark's main contribution was the finished roof, complete with a bell tower supported by an octagonal drum. Funding issues continued to delay finishing the project, but by 1789 two rooms were ready for use. Serving as the sole building on campus until 1835, McDowell Hall had a kitchen and dining rooms in the basement, classrooms on the first floor and part of the second floor, faculty lodging on the rest of second floor, and student dormitories in the attic. A library was located in the drum below the bell tower.

Minor changes occurred throughout the nineteenth century, with the major addition of a porch on the southwest elevation in the 1880s. Also, in 1903 a Greek Revival red Seneca sandstone porch and stair salvaged from the demolition of the State House library annex were installed on the northeast side of the building. Then in 1909 faulty wiring started a fire that substantially destroyed the interior, leaving a burnt shell. The Baltimore firm of Baldwin and Pennington had recently completed the new State House annex, and they were hired to reconstruct and restore McDowell Hall with some modifications. Repairs after another fire in 1952 and renovations in 1989 have further altered the still grand Georgian building.

WS48 FRANCIS SCOTT KEY AUDITORIUM AND MELLON HALL, ST. JOHN'S COLLEGE
1956–1958, Neutra and Alexander; 1989 addition, Ziger/Snead. St. John's St.

Dedicated on May 22, 1959, with a speech by President Dwight D. Eisenhower, Key Auditorium and Mellon Hall is an interconnected auditorium/classroom/planetarium building designed by renowned modernist architect Richard Neutra with partner Robert E. Alexander. The low-slung, flat-roofed building was a case study in Neutra's unornamented and modular architectural vocabulary. Asymmetrical massing, glass walls, large areas of unadorned brick and limestone, and exposed concrete columns all signaled the firm's modern approach. St. John's newest building represented a drastic but sympathetically scaled departure from the red brick Georgian (and Georgian Revival) buildings on campus and in the adjacent Annapolis Historic District.

In commissioning Neutra for a new multifunctional educational building, St. John's sponsored one of his best institution-

al designs and a rare East Coast commission for the Los Angeles-based architect. The complex included Key Memorial Auditorium, a six-hundred-seat performance space with a glass-walled lobby entrance. The auditorium was located at one end of Mellon Hall, an L-shaped structure with a double-loaded corridor floor plan. The two wings of Mellon Hall housed the music and science departments with spaces for classrooms, studios, and laboratories. McKeldin Planetarium, a small aluminum-sheathed domed structure with exposed aggregate concrete buttresses, is located at the other end. It is set in a shallow concrete pool (now drained), another characteristic Neutra design feature.

The roughly U-shaped footprint of the original ensemble created a sheltered courtyard facing the grassy campus quadrangle that was closed off by the addition of an administrative wing and art gallery in 1989. In spite of this alteration, Key Auditorium and Mellon Hall remain an unusual and well-preserved example of Neutra's brand of modernism in Maryland.

WS49 ALEXANDER RANDALL DUPLEX
1878–1879. 86–88 State Cir.

Prominently sited on State Circle, the Randall Duplex is an unusual example of English Queen Anne design among the colonial and more classically inspired architecture characteristic of Annapolis. Built by former U.S. congressman and Maryland attorney general Alexander Randall, the tall duplex house has mirror image plans for the two units, with each side accessed via a one-story porch at the corner. Built with brick for the basement and first-floor levels, and wood for the second and attic floors, exuberant details include fish scale shingles, pressed brick, and faux half timbering. The complex cross-hip and gable roof forms with dormers, bays, and decorative chimneys add to the liveliness of the facade.

WS50 RANDALL COURT HOUSES
1896–1903. 4, 5, and 6 Randall Ct.

A group of picturesque Shingle Style houses facing an inner courtyard illustrates the subdivision of eighteenth-century Annapolis estates in later decades. Alexander Randall had acquired a portion of the former Thomas Bordley family property around 1845, and his heirs continued to subdivide and improve the lots after his death in 1881. In 1896 a narrow pedestrian path called Randall Place was created between State Circle next to the Randall Duplex (WS49) and College Avenue, inspiring construction of 4 Randall Court. This Shingle Style cottage received well-integrated additions in 1913 and 1921. The original owner of number 4 built the complementary Arts and Crafts semidetached dwelling at numbers 5 and 6 in 1903 with the front porches facing the center of the block and the front lawn of the Bordley-Randall House.

WS51 MARYLAND AVENUE COMMERCIAL BUILDINGS
c. 1820–early 20th century. Maryland Ave., from State Cir. to the Naval Academy

Emanating from State Circle is the commercial and residential Maryland Avenue, the development of which was made possible in the nineteenth century by the division of early estates. The former brick market and meeting hall (c. 1820–1840; 79 Maryland) is perhaps the earliest, erected at the intersection with the circle, within proximity to the State House. It is distinguished by its gable-front facade framed by pilasters. A number of frame buildings with Italianate detailing were built in the 1870s and 1880s, some upgraded with new facades during the early twentieth century. An example is the former meat market and grocery store (c. 1870; 67–69 Maryland) that received a decorative cast-iron front with Adamesque motifs c. 1900. Built c. 1880 is 78 Maryland, upgraded c. 1945 with a blue glazed-tile facade with sunburst pattern and projecting marquee as an appliance store. The most imposing commercial structure is the former Masonic Temple and Opera House (WS52).

WS52 MASONIC HALL AND OPERA HOUSE
1872, Joseph M. Marshall, builder; c. 1900 renovated. 44–46 Maryland Ave.

This distinctive Italianate structure was erected for the masons by a local contractor as a combination lodge hall, opera house, and retail space. In the early years of Freemasonry, meetings were held in homes or private tavern rooms. During the late nineteenth century, laws made it possible for fraternal and benevolent societies to erect buildings and rent space that generated income to pay for their meeting rooms without being taxed as commercial landlords. The six-hundred-person, second-floor opera house provided the city's only performing arts venue, operating from 1873 to 1907. The grand opening featured a production starring Miss Laura Keene and her New York Company of Performing Artists. Rising three stories, this imposing gable-front building with dentiled pediment and heavily bracketed overhanging cornice commands a striking presence. The intact extended-bay street-front display windows date from c. 1900. The tall second-story windows denote the location of the former opera house and include elaborate drip-mold lintels with contrasting keystones incised with the Masonic symbol. The side elevation along Prince George Street is ornamented by brick pilasters and oculus windows.

WS53 U.S. NAVAL ACADEMY
1845; 1896–1910, Ernest Flagg; 1964, John Carl Warnecke and Associates. 121 Blake Rd.

In 1896 Beaux-Arts-trained New York City architect Ernest Flagg was commissioned to create a new comprehensive plan for the U.S. Naval Academy. The school for U.S. naval officers was founded in 1845 at Fort Severn and grew in a piecemeal fashion to include over 50 buildings. Flagg's design ultimately replaced all the nineteenth-century construction except for two small buildings at the main gate, the waiting room (1878) and the guard house (1881). Between 1899 and 1910, 27 buildings were constructed, including a core group of monumental French-influenced classical buildings designed by Flagg and arranged around a formal quadrangle. Despite shortfalls in the construction budget, the academy represents a remarkably fully realized example of a Beaux-Arts scheme and one of the first forays by the U.S. government into design based on those principles. It predates the transformation of the monumental core of Washington proposed by the Senate Park Commission Plan (popularly known as the McMillan Plan) in 1901, as well as redevelopment of the U.S. military academy at West Point (1902–1903, Cram, Goodhue and Ferguson).

The experience of the 1898 Spanish American War and growing awareness of the importance of naval supremacy for America's international affairs hastened the planned rebuilding. Flagg transformed the Naval Academy campus into a cohesive monumental ensemble, retained the existing mature trees, and overlaid the curvilinear paths with an axial grid. The centerpiece was the quadrangle, also called the Yard, which was designed to be open on one side with views to the Severn River.

Flagg arranged his key buildings around the other three sides of the Yard. At center facing the river, the monumental domed chapel is located at the highest point on the campus and grouped with an administration building and the superintendent's residence. The massive dormitory and mess hall for the midshipmen, Bancroft Hall, sits on the southeast side of the Yard. Colonnades connect Bancroft Hall to its flanking structures—Macdonough Hall (built as a boathouse and quickly converted into a gymnasium) and Dahlgren Hall (originally an armory). The remaining side of the Yard features the academic group of three attached buildings. Mahan Hall, designed as the library and auditorium with an impressive central tower, is flanked by two classroom buildings—Maury and Sampson halls—connected to its front corners (*pictured*). Flagg also designed a row of officers' houses placed along the perimeter wall at King George Street as a transition to the adjacent neighborhood.

Flagg's ornate buildings were initially to be executed in red brick and limestone, in deference to characteristic historic architecture of Annapolis. A politically motivated order from Congress to use New England granite as the primary building material altered the preliminary plans. Soon after construction began in 1899, both construction costs and enrollment increased dramatically, making the planned appropriations inadequate. While granite was used for several buildings in the early phases of construction, soon Flagg was pressed to revise his designs for lower costs. Terra-cotta and gray-faced brick were substituted for granite to maintain design cohesiveness. While Flagg lamented these constraints, the need for economy did inspire him to develop innovative solutions. His use of structural concrete, particularly for the framing and dome of the chapel, was widely celebrated as the most advanced use of that technology in the United States at that time.

While Flagg's buildings and master plan still define the character of the Naval Academy, there have been several later building campaigns to accommodate the growth of the institution. Between 1918 and 1924, 7 buildings were added, with another 25 structures added in 1939 to 1941. A major project to fill in Dewey Basin at the Severn River side of the Yard was initiated in 1957, adding over 50 acres to the campus. A new master plan prepared by John Carl Warnecke and Associates in 1964 was informed by Flagg's original one but called for major new construction on the fill. Michelson and Chauvenet halls were placed on a low terrace with an opening to preserve a river view from the chapel. However, Flagg's power plant and some other buildings were demolished in the process. Today the 300-plus–acre grounds include more than 200 major buildings for use by over 4,500 midshipmen.

WS54 CORNHILL STREET BUILDINGS
c. 1770 and later. Cornhill St. between State Cir. and Fleet St.

The area that comprises Cornhill and the adjacent Fleet Street (WS55) was originally set aside for the use of Governor Nicholson but was left unimproved. Recognizing the need for an area dedicated to mixed-use residential and mercantile development for the working class, in 1770 businessman Charles Wallace purchased a section extending from State Circle to the city docks. It was subdivided into twenty-eight lots laid out along two narrow roadways named after those within the affluent mercantile district in London to which it aspired. It includes surviving examples of the more modest houses built during the late colonial period for Annapolis's artisans, craftsmen, maritime tradesmen, and shopkeepers that reflect the architectural traditions of the Chesapeake, some serving as both home and workplace.

The first houses erected on Cornhill were the modest three-bay, gambrel-roofed frame house William Monroe built for himself and the neighboring five-bay brick house (c. 1770; 49 and 53 Cornhill) he built for tailor Thomas Callahan. Other colonial survivors are the two-story, six-bay, brick Brewster Tavern (1772–1773; 37–39 Cornhill) noted for its galleted stone foundation and Flemish-bond brickwork; Captain Beriah Maybury's more imposing, five-bay Kings' Arms Tavern (1771–1773; 41 Cornhill); and the two-story, side-passage Ridgely House (c. 1779; 40 Cornhill), later owned by an African American U.S. Navy sailor from 1900 to 1943.

WS55 FLEET STREET
c. 1770 and later. Fleet St. between East St. and Market Space

Along with Cornhill Street, Fleet Street also was designated for artisan and worker housing, where modest one-room and two-room houses with basement kitchens were built, such as the Christopher Hohne House (c. 1770; 45 Fleet), purchased by African American waterman Benjamin Holliday in 1886. By the latter part of the century the street was increasingly occupied by Black residents. The first African American to purchase a house (51 Fleet) here was Henry Clay in 1860, beginning the trend toward Black owners and occupants. In 1878, Black physician William Bishop built a pair of simple two-bay frame houses (1878; 46–48 Cornhill). Speculative development resulted in further division of lots along Fleet and Cornhill streets. Smaller, more densely clustered, modest, two-bay frame row houses such as 32–34, 42, 44, and 46 (c. 1858–1878) were built by whites and rented to Blacks. The Workingmen's Building and Loan Association also built rentals for working-class African Americans. Small frame houses continued to replace earlier dwellings into the turn of the twentieth century. By then, African Americans predominated on the street, only to be displaced by the rising real estate market of the 1970s and 1980s.

WS57 SHIPLAP HOUSE
c. 1715, Edward Smith; c. 1730s additions; 1817 addition and renovations; post 1957 restorations, Henry Chandlee Forman, Russel Wright. 18 Pinkney St.

WS56 HOGSHEAD
Early 19th century. 43 Pinkney St.

This is a restored example of the frame Chesapeake dwellings built in Annapolis during the colonial period. Although evidence points to a construction date during the early nineteenth century, its modest two-room plan and gambrel roof configuration are reminiscent of the dwellings that once dominated the city's architectural landscape. It speaks to the persistent use of this house form among the artisan and working classes long after Annapolis's wealthier inhabitants constructed their fine Georgian, two-story brick houses. The interior of Hogshead consists of a hall-parlor plan with the larger hall heated by a fireplace; a winder stair appears in the smaller parlor leading to two rooms above. The kitchen, with its large cooking fireplace and beehive oven, is located in the basement. Hogshead is owned by Historic Annapolis and used to interpret the life of the city's "lower and middling sort."

This is one of the earliest extant houses in Annapolis, exhibiting antiquated features such as its steeply pitched roof, robust brick end wall, and the flush "shiplap" or clapboard siding for which it is named. It was erected by sawyer and innkeeper Edward Smith and by the 1780s was being used as the Harp and Crown tavern. Its two-and-a-half-story height was uncommon among Annapolis dwellings at that time, similar in this regard only to the Charles Carroll Barrister House (c. 1724–1727; 60 College Avenue). The Shiplap House began as a two-story, frame dwelling of a single room per floor, including a cellar, the east end of the current building.

By midcentury a central passage with open stairway and adjoining room were added to the west. Shortly thereafter the brick end wall and new chimney were appended. In 1817, the west-end shed section was added and the interior upgraded with a more elaborate stairway and finishes. Its historical importance as a rare

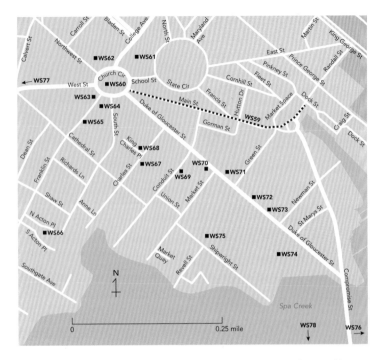

survivor of the city's early architecture was recognized in 1957, when it was acquired by the Historic Annapolis Foundation to serve as its headquarters. Separate restorations proceeded under the direction of noted historical architects Forman and Wright, and a re-created tavern room is now opened for public tours.

WS58 TOBACCO PRISE WAREHOUSE
c. 1819–1836; c. 1978 restored.
2–4 Pinkney St.

This warehouse is the only tangible reminder of the role that Annapolis played in the lucrative tobacco trade. The building was used to inspect tobacco from local plantations in compliance with a 1747 law designed to ensure the quality of Maryland's tobacco exports. The prise used to tightly pack tobacco into hogsheads once stood adjacent. A hogshead was a standard-sized wood barrel, 4 feet in length and 30 inches in diameter, that, when filled, weighed up to 1,000 pounds. The diminutive two-story, gable-front brick structure is only one-bay wide, encompassing a loading bay in the upper story. By the late nineteenth century it was adapted for retail use and was a barber shop when acquired by the State in 1968. In recognition of its historic importance, it was restored by the Historic Annapolis Foundation as an interpretative museum.

WS59 MAIN STREET BUILDINGS
Mid-18th–mid-20th centuries. Main St. between Church Cir. and the City Docks

As the prominent commercial corridor of Annapolis, Main Street has historically been the location of the city's taverns, inns, and shops, with wharves and warehouses along its waterfront terminus. Commercial

Top: Main Street Buildings (**WS59**), Maryland Inn. **Bottom left:** St. Anne's Episcopal Church (**WS60**). **Bottom right:** U.S. Post Office (**WS62**).

growth during the early to mid-nineteenth century reflected Federal and Greek Revival architectural trends, while Italianate predominated in the mid- to late nineteenth century. Many that appear to be of the latter period actually represent the transformation of earlier buildings, as pressed-brick facades and other treatments were applied. Fewer twentieth-century buildings appear, although a handful of noteworthy examples can be found.

At Main and Church Circle is the Maryland Inn (1772–1782; 16 Church; *pictured above*). Expanded to include its character-defining mansard roof in 1869–1877, it is the only Main Street building to maintain its original use. Other noteworthy buildings are the former Engine House and City Hall (1821–1822; 211 Main);

the Greek Revival gable-front Franklin and Jones General Store (c. 1840; 206 Main); and the Coffee House (1767; 195 Main), a popular gathering spot for locals and elite visitors alike. Maggio Fruit Company (c. 1920; 196–198 Main) is noted for its Craftsman-inspired multipaned leaded transom and incised parapet front.

Typical of the mid-nineteenth-century Federal-style buildings erected by free Black builders living and working in Annapolis are those of Henry Matthews (c. 1843; 176 Main) and Henry Price (c. 1820–1834; 230, 234 Main). The best of the cast-iron facade buildings lies just off Main Street at 169–171 Conduit Street (c. 1870). Earlier buildings later renovated in Italianate include 141–147, 149–153 and 155 Main, where a view of the side walls in some cases reveal the original roofline.

Still remaining are a few modest two-story, two-bay side-entrance houses (c. 1790; 109 and 111 Main) typical of those built in Annapolis well into the nineteenth century. The early surviving building at 99 Main (c. 1792–1798), distinguished by its large scale and handsome Flemish-bond brick, is one of the many shops erected in the Georgian mode to replace early warehouses destroyed in a 1790 fire. Built on the foundations of one such tobacco warehouse is a rare example of early-nineteenth-century commercial architecture (c. 1816; 77 Main) restored to its original exterior form.

On the "Market Lot" near the city docks is the Aaron L. Goodman Building (c. 1913; 100 Main), built as a department store combining classically inspired details with modern design, including a curved facade and banks of windows. Among the few extant eighteenth-century buildings is Middletown Tavern (c. 1754; 2 Market Space) erected as an "Inn for Seafaring Men." Perhaps the most notable renovation is the Stevens Hardware (c. 1880; 138–142 Dock Street), refaced c. 1940 with imitation marble and black onyx glass including a decorative frieze bearing its name.

nent of Governor Francis Nicholson's 1702 plan for Annapolis, countering a corresponding circle designated for the State House. The original church built on this site c. 1704 was the physical manifestation of a 1692 act calling for the establishment of the Church of England in Maryland. The act was a blow to the colony's Catholic proprietor who made freedom of religion a cornerstone of his provincial charter. The change influenced the 1694 decision to move the capital to Annapolis from the Catholic stronghold at St. Mary's City. The current church, a good example of architecture inspired by the Romanesque of northern Italy, is actually the third on-site, erected after a fire destroyed the second church, built in 1785–1792. Its Gothic Revival spire was added in 1865–1866. The basilica-plan interior, with a long nave and side aisles, incorporates an impressive display of exposed ceiling beams supported by large-scale ornamental brackets. Sculptor William H. Rinehart carved the stone altar and baptismal font. Tiffany stained glass windows were added in 1893 and German walnut reredos behind the altar in 1920. Its picturesque surrounding includes old-growth trees and a cemetery that dates to the mid-eighteenth century.

WS60 ST. ANNE'S EPISCOPAL CHURCH
1858–1859, J. R. Condit; 1865–1866 spire, Edmund G. Lind. 199 Duke of Gloucester St. (Church Circle)

The site of St. Anne's on Church Circle was a significant compo-

WS61 JAMES SENATE OFFICE BUILDING
1938–1939, Henry Powell Hopkins, with Laurence Hall Fowler. 110 College Ave.

The New State Office Building built in the late 1930s set the Colonial Revival tone for the rest of the state government buildings in its vicinity. Baltimore architect Hopkins, with assistance from fellow Colonial Revivalist Fowler, drew inspiration from a variety of eighteenth-century sources including the Chase-Lloyd House (WS43) and the Hammond-Harwood House (WS42) in Annapolis. This large institutional building was built on College Avenue after several other sites were considered and rejected, most notably a Randall Court site due to a preservation battle to save the Bordley-Randall House from demolition.

WS62 U.S. POST OFFICE
1901, James Knox Taylor, Supervising Architect of the U.S. Treasury; 1939 addition, Louis A. Simon, Supervising Architect of the U.S. Treasury; 2016–2019 restored, Ziger/Snead. 1 Church Cir.

When the construction contract for a new post office was announced in November 1900, one Annapolis newspaper remarked with relief that the city was to "at last have a post office building more in keeping with its dignity as the capital of an important and flourishing state." Designed under the supervision of Taylor, who led the Treasury Department's design office from 1897 to 1912, the post office is an elegantly detailed early-twentieth-century Colonial Revival design complementing its setting on historic Church Circle. The original 1901 section of the building draws inspiration from the work of English architect Christopher Wren, with a central pavilion and corners accented by stone quoins, Venetian windows with stone sills and surrounds, and other richly detailed features such as stone festoons and a central cupola supporting a gilded pineapple weathervane. The interior of the original section retains its handsome carved oak paneling, marble wainscot, and terrazzo floor. A rear addition in 1939 expanded the service ell and loading docks for automobile access. In 2019–2020 the former post office was restored and adapted for commercial use.

WS63 REYNOLDS TAVERN
c. 1747; 1906 rear ell addition. 7 Church Cir.

Original owner William Reynolds operated a tavern named the Beaver and Lac'd Hat in this two-and-a-half-story gambrel-roofed structure. Characteristic colonial Annapolis features here include internal slab chimneys and an early use of all-header brick bond. The distinctive four-brick belt course enlivens the facade by following the segmental arches of the first-floor windows. In 1812 the building was converted into a banking hall and then bank officer's residence for Farmers Bank of Maryland, the first bank in the nation to pay interest on deposits. Prominent bank officials lived in the structure until 1935. A proposal to demolish the vacant building and build a gas station mobilized prominent Annapolitans to save the former tavern. The Library Association of Annapolis occupied the property until 1974. After a restoration in the mid-1980s, Reynolds Tavern again houses a restaurant, bar, and overnight accommodations.

WS64 ANNE ARUNDEL
COUNTY COURTHOUSE
*1821–1824; 1892–1894 renovations
and additions. 8 Church Cir.*

This is Anne Arundel County's first purpose-built courthouse, erected to fulfill functions previously undertaken in the nearby statehouse. The original building is composed of a two-story main block and a three-bay-deep ell to the center rear. The interior plan comprises an entrance hall flanked by offices for the clerk of the court and register of wills, behind which was the sheriff's office and stairway, with a large courtroom in the ell. It was considered a spacious, state-of-the-art building for its time, incorporating fireproof masonry groin vaulting similar to that pioneered by Robert Mills. Deemed inadequate by the late nineteenth century, it was renovated and expanded, encompassing the Colonial Revival entrance tower with the second-floor loggia. An octagonal cupola and belfry were also added, emulating the octagonal dome of the nearby statehouse. Later flanking gable-front pavilions and the wings to the rear corners create the current H-shaped configuration.

WS65 BANNEKER-
DOUGLASS MUSEUM
(MOUNT MORIAH CHURCH)
1876; 1897 remodeled; 1984 museum. 84 Franklin St.

The African American congregation of Mount Moriah Church built this two-story brick sanctuary in 1876 less than a block from Church Circle to replace an earlier meetinghouse. This congrega-

tion had its roots in Annapolis's first African Methodist Episcopal (AME) church from the 1790s. With a modern new church, Mount Moriah could continue to be an important center of Black life in Annapolis. The gable-front form of the new building featured an auditorium-plan worship space on the second floor and offices and meeting rooms on the ground floor.

Much of the current appearance of the church is from an extensive Gothic Revival remodeling completed in 1897 to repair damage from a windstorm. In 1970 when the congregation moved to a new larger facility, Anne Arundel County acquired the church and planned to demolish it for expansion of the county courthouse. A preservation outcry ensued until a 1974 court injunction prevented demolition. The building was leased to the Maryland Commission on African American History and Culture and opened as the Banneker-Douglass Museum in 1984 with the historic sanctuary restored and a new two-and-a-half-story annex. Named for famed Maryland residents scientist Benjamin Banneker and abolitionist Frederick Douglass, it was the first museum of its kind in the state.

WS66 ACTON HALL
1772–1775; 1910 wing. 1 N. Acton Pl.

Built for John Hammond, Acton Hall differs from other gentry houses in Annapolis to embrace an uncommon three-part composition. Two-bay sections sur-

mounted by pediments adorned with elliptical windows flank a single-bay entrance section with a classical frontispiece covered by a portico. Behind the pediments can be seen a low-hipped roof with massive forward-facing interior slab chimneys that tower above. The rear facade faces Spa Creek and features a full-height demi-octagonal salon. The unusual octagonal configuration was also used by brother Matthias at the Hammond-Harwood House (WS42). The plan comprises a center passage that terminates against the elaborately ornamented salon and flanking transverse halls.

Located on Acton Cove, the site of the original city docks, the house was part of an extensive working farm. The property was subdivided in the 1880s by owner James Murray as the Murray Hill neighborhood comprised of stylish Queen Anne, Colonial Revival, Shingle, and other period houses.

WS67 JONAS GREEN HOUSE
c. 1738; late-18th-century additions.
124 Charles St.

This is the oldest dwelling on Charles Street, reflecting early Chesapeake house design as identified by its one-and-a-half-story, gambrel roof, and frame construction fortified by brick end walls. Standing in stark contrast to its mid- to late-nineteenth-century neighbors, it began with a typical hall-and-double-parlor plan that was expanded to encompass a Georgian central passage flanked by double parlors. A hyphen joins the house to a rear three-bay, gambrel-roofed kitchen, originally a separate structure as typical of the era.

Jonas and Anne Green first leased the property from Charles Carroll in 1738, at the time they were designated "Printers of the Province." They operated a printing press in a separate building on-site (no longer extant) and were well known for publishing the colonial government's proclamations, acts, and proceedings, as well as the influential *Maryland Gazette* newspaper. Anne took over after Jonas's death in 1767, operating the press until her death in 1775; this was an unusually powerful position for a woman of her time. The family continued in the printing business, publishing the newspaper until 1835. The house remained in the family until 2016.

WS68 ADAMS-KILTY HOUSE
c. 1773–1786. 131 Charles St.

The Adams-Kilty House represents Annapolis's more modestly scaled gentry-class houses mimicking the salient features of their grander neighbors. Similar to the Chase-Lloyd House (WS43), the front entrance is flanked by small windows, a pattern repeated in the tripartite arrangement of bays above. The house exhibits the fine Flemish-bond brickwork of the era to include gauged and rubbed brick jack arches and belt course. Its pyramidal roof is not common to Annapolis but appears as a compact form of the hipped roof at Acton Hall (WS66), sharing its distinctive towering front-facing slab chimneys. The interior plan is a compressed version of the Hammond-Harwood House (WS42); a central passage is flanked by modest rooms to the front, behind which is a transverse stair hall, with two unequally proportioned formal rooms facing the garden. It exhibits a cast-plaster cornice identical to that in the similarly placed dining room of the Hammond-Harwood House. The kitchen and other service spaces are located in the cellar, however, rather than in a hyphenated wing. The house was built for planter William Adams of Somerset County, who purchased the lots in 1772–1773. His lease to Thomas Brooke Hodgkins in 1786 indicates that the "brick house already erected and built" required finishing, suggesting a completion date around that time. It was purchased by William Kilty, chancellor of Maryland, in 1799.

Tilton House (c. 1760–1761; 9 Maryland Avenue) is another merchant-class residence forming a more compact variation of the city's best houses.

WS69 CHARLES ZIMMERMAN HOUSE
1893–1897. 138 Conduit St.

The Zimmerman House stands out for its exuberant Queen Anne style, one that is not well represented in Annapolis, and for the double lot that separates it from its neighbors as a fully detached residence. Indicative of Queen Anne are its irregularly massing, turrets, projecting bay, oriel window, balconette, spindled wraparound porch, and jigsawn trim. It is sided in a delightful mix of weatherboards and scalloped shingles and has a combination hipped and cross-gabled slate roof. It was erected for Charles Zimmerman, the band leader for the U.S. Naval Academy who arranged the well-known march "Anchors Away."

WS70 MAYNARD-BURGESS HOUSE
c. 1780, 1790s, c. 1838–1847, c. 1847–1858, c. 1870–1877. 163 Duke of Gloucester St.

This house presents an architectural puzzle with much to tell about the adaptation of ordinary dwellings and the life of free Black residents of Annapolis. Sections of the wood house with wrought nails and distinctive framing features are thought to represent two early construction campaigns dating to c. 1780s and the late 1790s, with the second floor added in the later period. Between 1838 and 1847 the dwelling was moved to its current site and placed on a galleted stone foundation and a new circular-sawn sill and floor joist system.

In 1847 the property was sold to John T. Maynard, a free Black man who lived here with his family, including his wife, Maria, and a daughter, both of whom he had purchased out of bondage. Evidence suggests that almost immediately following Maynard's purchase a fourth period of work commenced, representing a major reconfiguration of the main elevation from three bays to four, with doorways at each end bay in the manner of semidetached houses from the period. In the 1870s a two-story shed-roofed rear ell was added, which appears to have repurposed older materials, perhaps from a former detached kitchen. Also the door at the east bay was changed into a window, leaving the street front largely as it appears today. Maynard died in 1875, but the house remained in the family until 1914. At that time a former boarder, Willis Burgess, purchased the property, which remained in his family until 1990. Efforts to study the historic fabric of the house and conduct archaeological investigations are ongoing, with partnerships among various groups including Historic Annapolis Inc. and the City of Annapolis.

WS71 WILLIAM BUTLER HOUSE

c. 1857. 148 Duke of Gloucester St.

Builder, businessman, and possibly former enslaved person William Butler was one of the wealthiest African American men in Annapolis when he purchased this recently constructed house in 1863. The elegant three-story Italianate town house was an unusually urbane example of the type for Annapolis in this period. The brick facade is topped by a bracketed wood cornice and features three bays with tall segmental-arched openings. During his career Butler built several residential rows in Annapolis, most notably the two-story, frame grouping at 111–119 Market Street. In addition to becoming one of the wealthiest men in Annapolis of any race at the time of his death in 1892, Butler was the first Black man in Maryland to hold municipal office, serving on the Annapolis City Council from 1873 to 1875. The house remained in the Butler family until 1922, when it was sold and converted into three apartments, with a third story added onto the original two-story rear ell.

WS72 JOHN RIDOUT HOUSE
1764–1765. 120 Duke of Gloucester St.

Built for John Ridout, secretary to provincial governor Horatio Sharpe, this is one of the most sophisticated colonial houses in Annapolis. It successfully combines such emerging architectural characteristics as the Annapolis Plan and two-story brick construction with street-front and garden facades of indulgent all-header bond brick in an elegant Georgian house of grand proportion. It likewise encompasses a decorative water table and belt course, jack-arch lintels, massive slab chimneys, and unusual faux-pavilion side projections. It is elevated above a terraced garden, accessible from the drawing room via a Doric portico and from the service areas in the ground-level basement. Indicative of the Annapolis Plan and its emphasis on garden access, the elaborated rear facade includes a second-story Palladian window so generous in proportion that it pierces the roofline.

The first-floor rooms radiate from an entrance hall with an open-string stairway set off from the hall, beyond an arched opening, and flanked by small private rooms. The drawing room is the largest, overlooking the garden. The interior finishes are varied and complex, with some of the finest plaster cornices in the Chesapeake region. The cellar retains its kitchen, servants' hall, pantry, and storeroom. Adjacent is Ridout's former brick carriage house, now a residence, and his speculative town houses known as Ridout Row (WS73).

WS73 RIDOUT ROW
1773–1774. 110–114 Duke of Gloucester St.

Ridout Row is the earliest known group of row houses built with a unified facade and common plan in the Chesapeake region. It represents an attempt to introduce urban forms to Chesapeake towns and is one of only a few extant pre-Revolutionary rows. The larger central unit forms a slightly projecting pedimented pavilion to create an overall three-part composition, boasting a more elaborate Adamesque frontispiece. All three rest on a raised basement accessed by a broad window well lighting the kitchen service area. Plans are based on London's Georgian period terraced houses, locating the central stairway in a transverse passage, thereby allowing the social rooms to the rear overlooking the garden to extend the entire width. Used as the dining room, it reflects the importance then placed on dining as a social function, while its equivalent second-floor space served as the formal drawing room. The room to the street front was intended as a family parlor with the best bedchamber above. Additional bedchambers were located in the third story.

WS74 CHARLES CARROLL HOUSE

c. 1749–1751; 1773 addition; 1793–1794 renovated; 1856 renovated; 1984–2001 restored. 107 Duke of Gloucester St.

This is one of the most important buildings in Annapolis due to its early design and association with the Carrolls, one of Maryland's founding families. While altered and expanded over its more than two and a half centuries, it retains features that shed light on our understanding of colonial architecture. Charles Carroll the Settler, Lord Calvert's attorney general, helped establish Annapolis as an official port town, constructing a frame house on this site. However, it was his son, Charles Carroll of Annapolis, who appended the core of the current house in the Chesapeake tradition to encompass brick construction, gambrel roof, and the Annapolis Plan, elements just coming into vogue. A central entrance is flanked by private chambers with a pair of large rooms for entertaining to the rear overlooking the waterfront, with the kitchen and other service areas in the basement. The interior finishes constitute some of the most interesting features, including a modestly finished, period closed-string stair, floor-to-ceiling plaster paneled walls, and corner fireplaces.

The house was expanded by Charles Carroll of Carrollton, a signer of the Declaration of Independence. The roof was raised to a full two stories, removing the old-fashioned gambrel in favor of a gable roof with massive slab chimneys, and interior finishes were upgraded. The house remained in the Carroll family until 1852, when sold to the Redemptorist congregation of the Catholic Church. They added the west wing, removing the early frame house. Carroll House was restored between 1984 to 2001 and opened to the public.

WS75 UPTON SCOTT HOUSE

1762–1763, William Brown; 1968 restored. 4 Shipwright St.

This is one of the earliest of Annapolis's grand Georgian houses. It is distinguished by its indulgent use of all-header-bond brick on the front and opposing garden facades that speaks to the duality of the Annapolis Plan, low-hipped roof, and exceptional interior details. Outwardly resembling Brown's London Town Publik House (WS84), this house for Scott likewise incorporates belt courses and gauged and rubbed brick jack-arch lintels, although using glazed-header Flemish-bond brick for the side elevations. The street facade is differentiated from the rear by a central pavilion with pediment and lunette window, and ornate classical frontispiece. On the interior, a broad central entrance hall and stairway opens onto a narrow passage flanked by the best rooms overlooking the garden. Finishes consist of floor-to-ceiling cast-plaster paneled walls indicative of the city's early Georgian architecture, modillion cornices, and richly carved stairway and mantelpieces.

The house was built for physician Upton Scott, who emigrated from Ireland in 1753 at the request of Governor Horatio Sharpe. Soon-to-be Annapolis mayor Daniel Dulany called it "the best town house in America." The Sisters of Notre Dame used it as a convent from 1876 until 1968, when it was purchased by Coleman and Joan du Pont and restored. It was one of the first houses to occupy a planned garden landscape, quickly adopted for those built by William Paca (WS40), John Ridout (WS72), James Brice (WS39), and Matthias Hammond (Hammond-Harwood House; WS42).

WS76 CHANCE BOATYARD AND EASTPORT
1912–1920; 1921–1930; 1941–1942. 222 Severn Ave.

For over a century, Chance Boatyard has been the site of the construction and repair of boats ranging from small watercraft to world-class yachts and vessels for the U.S. Navy. Visible from Annapolis along the southern shore of Spa Creek is the 170 × 58–foot wood, in-water boathouse workshop erected in 1941 and now a restaurant. The oldest extant buildings are the 1915–1920 two-story brick office and attached machine shop and storeroom along Severn Avenue and the brick paint shop and adjoining machine shop, erected 1921–1930.

The boatyard is in the Eastport neighborhood, created in 1868 by the Mutual Building Association to encourage homeownership among Annapolis's working class, which by the late nineteenth century attracted a vibrant maritime industry. The boatyard was established in 1912 by Charles Chance, building and repairing boats for watermen specific to the Chesapeake fishing industry, such as bugeyes and skipjacks. During World War I operations expanded to include subchasers for the U.S. Navy, emerging as the largest boatbuilder in Annapolis. Following postwar prosperity, recreational boating took off, and Chance constructed luxury yachts.

Purchased by Annapolis Yachts in 1937, the company built their popular American Cruiser. Under the direction of naval architect Chris Nelson, during World War II, they constructed Navy patrol torpedo (PT) boats and subchasers, erecting two large boat sheds, the in-water shed, and the 307-foot steel frame and corrugated metal shed. War production required three shifts, including a crew of eight women known as the Rosie Riveters of Eastport.

With the purchase of the boat-yard in 1947, John Trumpy and Sons resumed production of such recreational boats as world-class yachts, houseboats, and cruisers. During the Korean and Vietnam wars, they constructed mine-sweepers and PT boats. Annapolis was then recognized as one of the premier boatbuilding centers on the East Coast. Operations ceased in December 1973, but the site maintains maritime functions.

WS77 GIRL SCOUT LODGE AT CAMP WOODLANDS
1952–1954, Rogers and Taliaferro; 1964, RTKL Associates. 2744 Riva Rd., approximately 5 miles west of Annapolis

Set amidst a thirty-four-acre campground with more conventional structures, this modernist interpretation of a Native American teepee combined structural ingenuity and a clever design concept. Designed by future partner Charles Lamb, the lodge was the first building by Rogers and Taliaferro to receive national attention and acclaim, launching the reputation of this prominent Maryland firm later known as RTKL Associates.

The lodge includes the teepee and an attached concrete block annex housing a kitchen and administrative space. In 1964 the annex was extended with a perpendicular section creating the current L-shaped plan. The teepee is a twelve-sided structure with low glass and wood walls topped by a large overhanging conical roof supported by tension rods and compression rings with rafter ends resting on steel shoes embedded in concrete buttresses. The standard 2 × 12 rafters used as structural members could be assembled by volunteer labor, in this instance mostly students from the Naval Academy, making construction affordable.

Approximately five feet near the top of the roof cone are sky-lights, with the metal fireplace flue forming the tip. The center of the teepee includes a unique telescoping fireplace hood and stack that allows a variety of uses integral to Girl Scout ideals, such as a communal dining hall, indoor fire circle, or other rainy-day meeting space. With a system of pulleys and counterweights the hood could be lowered near to the floor to vent campfires or raised to a height of ten feet to facilitate use of the space for dining or activities. Custom picnic tables mirroring the quadrilateral shape of each bay allow efficient use of the circular plan. The lodge received an Award for Merit from the AIA in 1954, bringing national attention to RTKL as Maryland's leading innovators in modern design.

WS78 THOMAS POINT SHOAL LIGHT STATION
1875. Chesapeake Bay at the mouth of South River, southeast of Annapolis

This is the last unaltered screw-pile cottage light station on its original site in the United States, built from a standard plan developed by the U.S. Lighthouse Service. The screw-pile type was an easy and effective method of anchoring a lighthouse in a non-stable, off-shore location such as sandy or muddy shoals. It is among the few remaining of as many as one hundred such lights built mostly along the southeastern seaboard. It features a hexagonal, frame, cottage-like structure built over a steel-frame deck that is mounted to the wrought-iron screw-pile foundation; the light is housed within a lantern atop the cottage.

Wrought-iron screw-pile technology was developed by Irish engineer Alexander Mitchell in the 1830s, improving upon a late-nineteenth-century design by Henry Whiteside for a frame structure built on wood piles. It is one of only four extant screw-pile light stations in Maryland; the others are Hooper Straight (see ES51), Drum Point (WS25), and Seven Foot Knoll (see BC49).

WS79 WHITEHALL
1764–1765, Joseph Horatio Anderson, John Rawlings, and William Buckland; c. 1769 wings. South end of Whitehall Rd., approximately 7 miles northeast of Annapolis

Built for Governor Horatio Sharpe, Whitehall is an outstanding example of Palladian architecture and one of America's finest colonial houses. Its five-part-plan was inspired by Andrea Palladio's design for a Roman Country House that appeared in Robert Morris's *Select Architecture,* published in London in 1757. The exceptionally fine interiors, the quality of which had never been witnessed in Maryland before, are attributed to English immigrant craftsmen John Rawlings and William Buckland,

who undertook the plasterwork and woodwork, respectively. In true Palladian form, Whitehall is a lofty single-story house elevated over a raised basement with distinctive river and carriage fronts. The former incorporates the first residential use of a full temple portico in America.

Whitehall began with the central block to accommodate a grand hall and flanking withdrawing rooms. The hall has a coved ceiling that rises twenty feet, and the entire room is ornamented with neoclassical and Rococo details, including window surrounds with lateral consoles, doorways with full entablatures, and festooned plasterwork. The flanking hyphened wings were not erected until 1769, when Whitehall converted from retreat to fulltime residence. The hyphens appear as closed arcaded passageways leading to pyramidal-roofed wings. Whitehall faces the Severn River, easily accessible via boat from the state capital in Annapolis.

WS80 WILLIAM PRESTON LANE JR. MEMORIAL BRIDGE (CHESAPEAKE BAY BRIDGE)
1949–1952 (eastbound span), 1969–1973 (westbound span); J. E. Greiner Company (now AECOM), engineers. U.S. 50 /301 over Chesapeake Bay.

In 1938 the State of Maryland released the transportation planning study "Maryland's Primary Bridge Program." Proposed projects included a long-desired connector between the Western and Eastern Shores, where only ferry service was available. A new automobile connection would boost the economy, particularly on the

Eastern Shore, and respond to the growing dominance of car travel. World War II delayed the bridge's construction until 1947 when Governor William Preston Lane spearheaded legislation to jump-start the project. The designer was Baltimore-based civil engineering firm J. E. Greiner Company, founded by a former B&O Railroad bridge engineer in 1908. The older, two-lane, eastbound section consists of 123 steel spans, including the central cable suspension span supported by towers 354 feet above the water. Designed to accommodate ocean-going vessels in the shipping lanes and over four miles long, it was the longest continuous overwater steel structure in the world at the time it opened. In 1973 a second parallel three-lane span opened to expand capacity and allow one-way traffic on each span. Not only are the two spans of the Chesapeake Bay Bridge the only major suspension bridges in Maryland, but their economic impact has been profound, transforming access across the Bay and allowing Eastern Shore residents to commute to Washington and Baltimore. In 2019 both major repairs to the existing spans and discussion of adding another were underway.

GIBSON ISLAND

WS81 GIBSON ISLAND BUILDINGS

1921–1922 established, Olmsted Brothers. 534 Broadwater Way.

Situated on the Chesapeake Bay north of Annapolis, Gibson Island was developed as a private planned recreational community. Baltimore judge and businessman W. Stuart Symington Jr. hired Olmsted Brothers, the premier landscape architecture firm of the day, to design what he conceived as an exclusive social club for white, non-Jewish families from Baltimore. Although the Olmsted plan was more extensive, the completed portions include a nine-hole golf course and approximately 190 private dwellings designed in a variety of fashionable modes from the 1920s through the 1950s. Many of the early property owners lived in the planned neighborhood of Roland Park (BC108) in Baltimore and were already accustomed to the type of design control exerted by the Gibson Island Land Company.

Gibson Island's most important community building was the club house designed by Parker, Thomas and Rice in 1924 and unfortunately demolished and replaced in 2015. Nearby is St. Christopher's-By-The-Sea (1928;

534 Broadwater Way), a board-and-batten nondenominational chapel originally topped by a thatched roof. The snug interior includes floor-to-ceiling paneling and exposed scissor trusses supporting the vaulted ceiling. Another noteworthy building is the Strong House (c. 1930; 635 Arylie Water Road) designed by New York City architect Alexander B. Trowbridge in a modernist vocabulary recalling the work of Frank Lloyd Wright.

PASADENA

WS82 HANCOCK'S RESOLUTION

1785; c. 1855 kitchen; c. 1900 hyphen. 2795 Bayside Beach Rd.

This late-eighteenth-century dwelling of a middling tobacco farmer was built in the Chesapeake tradition to embrace a one-and-a-half-story, gambrel-roof configuration. While containing only a single first-floor room, the house is well built of random ashlar ironstone enlivened with galleting. Galleting involved the insertion of small stones into the mortar joints to provide support for irregular stones that required thicker joints, a treatment that was decorative as well as functional. The first floor encompasses a large fireplace with paneled wall, while a boxed winder stairway lit by a small casement window provides access to two dormered chambers. A separate kitchen was erected adjacent, joined by a frame hyphen c. 1900.

The house built by Stephan Hancock on his four-hundred-acre tobacco farm remained in the family for nearly two centuries. In recognition of its importance and intact condition (still lacking electricity and indoor plumbing), it was deeded to Historic Annapolis in 1963, following the death of its last Hancock-family inhabitant. A complementary stone smokehouse and a c. 1900 board-and-batten storehouse sit adjacent.

HIGHLAND BEACH

WS83 DOUGLASS SUMMER HOUSE

1894–1895, Charles Douglass, developer. 3200 Wayman Ave.

Civil War veteran Charles Douglass, son of the famed abolitionist Frederick Douglass, established the resort town of Highland Beach in 1893, with his father's

financial backing. Tradition has it that the younger Douglass was motivated to establish this African American vacation enclave five miles south of Annapolis after he and his wife were turned away from the adjacent resort community of Bay Ridge. In 1893 he purchased forty-four acres, including five hundred feet of Chesapeake Bay beachfront, and laid out streets.

The first two cottages built were for father and son. While Charles's house was demolished in the 1950s, the two-and-a-half-story dwelling with a wrap-around porch built for Frederick Douglass remains in excellent condition. Some accounts maintain that he designed the house himself, including a second-floor balcony with views toward his birthplace on the Eastern Shore. However, the elder Douglass died in 1895 in his home in Washington before living at this summer house.

Approximately ten more cottages were built in Highland Beach by 1910, including a large nine-bedroom house for George T. Bowen, a wealthy Baltimore caterer who was formerly enslaved. The Douglass and Bowen families welcomed guests, and Highland Beach became a popular destination for those in the close-knit ranks of educated Black professionals. Famous visitors included educator Booker T. Washington, singer and actor Paul Robeson, and poet Langston Hughes. Around thirty more cottages were built between 1910 and 1930, many by distinguished Black residents of Washington such as poet Paul Laurence Dunbar and Robert and Mary Church Terrell.

After Charles Douglass's death in 1921, the remaining lots were passed to his sons Haley and Joseph, with Haley Douglass emerging as a long-serving community leader. In 1922 Highland Beach became the first incorporated African American town in Maryland, and only the second incorporated town in Anne Arundel County after Annapolis. The Douglass family remained fixtures in the community, which gradually became a year-round residential neighborhood, and continued to own the house until 1986.

WOODLAND BEACH

WS84 LONDON TOWN PUBLIK HOUSE
1758–1764, William Brown. 839 Londontown Rd.

This finely executed Georgian building is all that remains of the once-bustling colonial seaport of London Town, situated on the South River. Its orientation toward the former Scott Street reveals its prior urban context. It

was erected as an upscale tavern by local builder, cabinetmaker, and innkeeper William Brown. As an indication of its quality, it is built entirely of header-bond brick, the only known building in the Chesapeake so constructed. The facades are ornamented by a water table and belt course, and a pair of large interior slab chimneys project from the central deck of a shallow-pitched hipped roof. The principal facade is signified by a central pavilion, while secondary entrances appear to the center of the other facades, with variations in the elaboration of the brick work revealing the hierarchy of their corresponding interior spaces. An idiosyncratic floor plan encompasses four corner rooms separated by a transverse passage and a central hall with a large public room to its rear. Anne Arundel County used it as an almshouse between 1828 and 1965. It then became part of a living history museum, surrounded by public gardens and replicas of colonial buildings.

SOUTH RIVER

WS85 SOUTH RIVER CLUB
1742; 1909. South River Club-house Rd.

This unassuming one-room frame building is home to the oldest continually operating gentleman's club in the United States. It was founded by local planters, merchants, and clergymen through a 1690 land agreement from Nicholas Gassaway, whose sons John and Thomas were among its founding members. The club was established to provide a venue in an otherwise isolated location for "fellowship and fulsome discussion." Organized after similar clubs in London, weekly meetings featured game roasted in the open-hearth fireplace and secret-recipe punch. Membership remains limited to twenty-five, all the one-story-and-loft building can accommodate, and favors descendants of the original gatherers. The building still lacks electricity and indoor plumbing, although a separate kitchen was erected to the rear in 1909.

HARWOOD

WS86 TULIP HILL
1756–1762, James Trotter with John Deavour; 1789–1790 wings. 4651 Muddy Creek Rd.

Among America's finest Georgian plantation houses is Tulip Hill, the main block of which was erected for wealthy Quaker merchant-planter Samuel Galloway. It is a massively proportioned double-pile brick dwelling with an articulated hipped roof, ornamented by a signature carved tulip flower finial. A rooftop observation deck is situated between its soaring interior vaulted chimneys, affording views of the terraced gardens and the West River. The deck is ac-

cessed via a cavernous attic supported by immense queen-post trusses. The flanking hyphened wings were later added to create the five-part-plan then fashionable among Chesapeake planters. While the facade exhibits five-bay Georgian symmetry, the interior plan is imbalanced to reflect Galloway's own ideas about effective room use; the ornate drawing rooms to the north are larger than those for family use to the south. The stair includes delicate turned balusters with a repeat of the carved tulip flower motif, a symbol of the tulip poplars for which the property was named.

GALESVILLE

WS87 BENNING ROAD HISTORIC DISTRICT
1920s–1950s. 932–956 Benning Rd.

Reflective of the free Black communities that developed in pre- and post-emancipation Maryland is the former Tenthouse Creek Village along Benning Road, once home to watermen and oyster shuckers. Emancipated slaves from nearby Tulip Hill were among the first to settle in the waterfront community of Galesville. The district features housing built by the Woodfield Fish and Oyster Company (no longer extant) for their predominately African American employees between 1920 and 1950. In its heyday, the seafood-processing plant employed over a hundred workers. Most conspicuous are nine single-story, duplex units distinguished by their entrance porticos, all arranged in a neat U-shape configuration. Adjacent are dissimilar detached bungalow and vernacular one-and-a-half and two-story single-room-deep frame dwellings.

Also extant is the house built by former slave Henry Wilson (c. 1870; 862 Galesville Road), and the adjacent 1928 Hot Sox Negro League Baseball field, a cornerstone of the community. The team was formed in 1915, at the height of Negro League baseball and Jim Crow segregation. Another community landmark is the Galesville Rosenwald School (c. 1929; c. 1931 addition; c. 2003 restored; 916 Benning). It is a well-preserved example of the simple frame schoolhouses built through the philanthropic efforts of Julius Rosenwald (see Ridgeley School, CR9) to provide some parity for African American children in southern states who were denied equal education. It follows the one-teacher plan, with a second classroom added. Galesville is one of ten extant of the original twenty-three Rosenwald schools built in Anne Arundel County, rehabilitated as a community center in 2003.

WEST RIVER

WS88 CHRIST CHURCH
1867–1869. 220 Owensville Rd.

Christ Church originated as St. James-the-Less, a chapel of ease for St. James's Anglican parish. A decade later in 1862, St. James-the-Less had grown enough to become an independent new parish named Christ Church. The parishioners started construction on a replacement church in 1867, selecting a Carpenter Gothic design that closely recalls plans for parish churches published by architect Richard Upjohn in *Rural Architecture* (1852). The church is charmingly picturesque with board-and-batten siding, stained glass lancet windows, and steep shingled roof and slender bell tower. The long, narrow nave of the church is entered from the side and spanned by a wood scissor truss ceiling. An adjacent Sunday school building built in the 1930s and expanded in the 1950s continues the Carpenter Gothic theme.

FRIENDSHIP

WS89 HOLLY HILL
1698, 1713, c. 1730. 333 Friendship Rd.

Erected in three major building campaigns spanning just over a quarter century, Holly Hill encompasses the oldest surviving dwelling in Maryland, dated through dendrochronology. The story-and-a-half, frame, hall-parlor core embraces English building traditions manifested in typical Chesapeake house form. Massive internal brick end chimneys ornamented by recessed panels and a steeply pitched gable roof are indications of its English design origins. An eighteen-foot-square addition provided a central passage that mediated between public and private spheres. As a further genteel upgrade, the house was encased in Flemish-bond brick. Finally, a corresponding perpendicular brick wing was added, introducing a formal parlor, stair hall, and dining room, reserving the older section for the family's private use. The new section incorporated such refined elements as a built-in cabinet, faux-marbling, and wood paneling with four painted landscapes, including one of Holly Hill. The evolution of Holly Hill from a simple hall-parlor house to a significantly enlarged and far more sophisticated one is indicative of larger patterns of development within the Chesapeake. The original house was built by prominent Quaker merchant and planter Richard Harrison for his son Samuel, who was responsible for its later expansion.

LINTHICUM

WS90 BALTIMORE-WASHINGTON INTERNATIONAL (BWI) THURGOOD MARSHALL AIRPORT

1979, DMJM and Peterson and Brickbauer; 1997 Schaefer International Terminal, STV Group and William Nicholas Bodouva + Associates; 2001–2005, URS Corporation. 7050 Friendship Rd.

Officially opened in 1950, Maryland's largest commercial airport began as Friendship International Airport in a then-rural section of northern Anne Arundel County between Baltimore and Washington. Continuous upgrades and expansion to respond to advances in aviation ramped up in 1972–1973 after the facility was acquired by the State of Maryland and the name changed to BWI. The 1950 terminal was demolished to make way for a new larger structure.

Airport design in the 1970s, following the fashion for Brutalism, had become heavier and more fortified to accommodate increased passenger volume and security requirements. The design for BWI's new terminal is instead a skylit modular structure with exposed tubular steel trusses. The lightness contrasts with massive round piers sheathed in red glazed brick, creating a distinctive yet subdued design that could be easily expanded. In an *Architectural Record* article (December 1980), Brickbauer described the terminal as "having shed-like openness with monumental elements." The architects of the new international terminal opened in 1997 responded to the architectural vocabulary established by Peterson and Brickbauer, including a soaring atrium space and a white version of the tubular steel trusses punctuated by skylights. In 2005 the sleek new Terminal A/B was opened to expand service for major BWI carrier Southwest Airlines. That same year the airport was renamed in honor of Baltimore native Thurgood Marshall, the first African American Supreme Court justice.

EASTERN SHORE

The long eastern Chesapeake coastline stretching from Cecil County at the mouth of the Susquehanna River south to the Atlantic Ocean inlet at Worcester County is collectively known as the Eastern Shore. This region encompasses nine Maryland counties—Cecil, Kent, Caroline, Queen Anne's, Talbot, Dorchester, Wicomico, Somerset, and Worcester—occupying the sizable Maryland portion of the Delmarva Peninsula that includes Delaware and a small piece of Virginia. Rich maritime resources of fish and shellfish supported native tribes in this region for thousands of years before the arrival of the first European settlers, with rivers and creeks still bearing their tribal names. Woodland-period peoples established a variety of seasonal encampments tied to gathering, harvesting, and processing various foodstuffs, as well as more permanent villages characterized by the development of an agricultural economy supplemented by hunting and fishing.

European immigrants to the Maryland colony were attracted to the same geographically advantageous locations as Native Americans. Starting in the early seventeenth century with the expeditions of Captain John Smith to expand his holdings in Virginia, European colonists established communities along this Maryland coastline, as well as across the Chesapeake Bay on the Western Shore. Given the prominence of the Chesapeake and its many river tributaries for early transportation, commerce revolved around seventeenth- and eighteenth-century port towns, such as Charlestown, Chestertown, Easton, Cambridge, Princess Anne, and Snow Hill. Regular freight and passenger sailing ships and then steamboat service remained a primary means of transport on the Eastern Shore into the twentieth century.

Culturally and geographically part of the Tidewater region, the Eastern Shore thrived economically in the colonial era, with fertile soil for growing tobacco and other crops and ready access to the Bay's resources. Granaries and flour milling were also important endeavors after the early shift from the dominance of tobacco farming with enslaved labor to a more diversified rural economy. Less labor-intensive grain production also led to a relatively large free Black population by the early nineteenth century. Despite this shift and the presence of free Black communities, slavery-based agriculture continued to impact economic life on the Eastern Shore prior to the Civil War. Abolitionist Quakers and Methodists, allied with the free Black community and aided by the bold actions of former enslaved people such as Harriet Tubman, fueled the Underground Railroad (see ES65) across this region. While Maryland

remained with the Union during the Civil War, many white residents, especially in the counties around the Bay, were pro-slavery and sympathized with the Confederacy. Governor Thomas Hicks, from Dorchester County, embodied this complexity when he prevented secession in 1861 despite his previous support for slavery.

Industrialization arrived later to the Eastern Shore than other parts of Maryland and often took the form of processing and packaging the seafood, fruits, and vegetables abundantly produced in the region. Most railroad development occurred in the post–Civil War decades and was linked to the expansion of canneries and other industry in cities such as Elkton, Easton, Cambridge, Salisbury, and Crisfield, undertaken by a largely African American workforce. Although Eastern Shore communities have suffered from twentieth-century deindustrialization like their counterparts in other areas of the state, their quintessential blue-collar worker is the waterman, who likewise has seen difficult economic conditions in recent decades. Environmental reform has been gradually improving the conditions in the Chesapeake, but ongoing pollution problems and the impact of climate change threaten a landscape and a way of life built on crabbing, fishing, and oystering.

Historically racially segregated and generally conservative in politics and culture, the Eastern Shore embraced its separation from the rest of the state. Communities such as Smith Island off the coast of Somerset County still maintain dialects and folkways that can be traced back to the earliest English colonists. The natural beauty and remoteness attracted visitors and pleasure boaters, with many of the distinguished early manor houses surviving into the twentieth century as country estates for wealthy residents of Baltimore, Washington, and Philadelphia. For visitors of more modest means, popular resort destinations such as Betterton, Whitehaven, and Ocean City were accessible through steamboat and railroad excursions and offered a variety of amusements. The opening of the Chesapeake Bay Bridge (WS80) in 1952 connecting Eastern and Western shores transformed this region and its relationship to the rest of the state. Now easily accessible via automobile, the closer counties are viable as bedroom communities for commuters working on the other side of the Bay. Tourists flock to the Atlantic Coast, often bypassing the bayside resorts of an earlier era, aided by the extension of U.S. Route 50 all the way to Ocean City.

CECIL COUNTY
RISING SUN

ES1 EAST NOTTINGHAM FRIENDS MEETING HOUSE
1724–1744; 1810 restored. Brick Meeting House Rd.

The meetinghouse is at the heart of the Nottingham Lots, a Quaker settlement established in 1701 by Pennsylvania proprietor William Penn to lay claim to lands around the disputed border with Maryland. Penn set aside thirty-seven lots that encompassed the meetinghouse, burying ground, and individual house lots. A log meetinghouse was erected under the care of the Philadelphia Yearly Meeting, replaced by the current Flemish-bond brick section that constitutes one of the oldest Friends meetinghouses in the country. Three bays across, the central entrance is covered by the gabled hood indicative of Quaker building traditions. A fire that gutted the interior in 1744 prompted its refurbishing and enlargement by an irregularly coursed stone section that mirrors the form of the original to provide separate but equal men's and women's sections. Fire again damaged the interior in 1810, necessitating the replacement of its finishes, including the construction of the massive king post, principal-rafter roof.

ES2 MERCER BROWN HOUSE
1746; early-19th-century additions.
1270 England Creamery Rd.

This is an exemplary, positively dated example of a colonial-era southeastern Pennsylvania domestic building form that diffused into portions of northern Maryland. Indicative of Quaker Plain style architecture, it is characterized by its rare pent roof and eaves; brickwork in glazed-header, diamond- and lozenge-patterns; and datestone with owners Mercer and Hannah Brown's initials. A number of bricks are likewise inscribed with the initials of seven individuals significant to the Quaker community who assisted Mercer Brown in its construction, including clockmaker Benjamin Chandlee and cabinetmaker Hezekiah Rowles. During the early nineteenth century, a two-story frame addition was made by Amassa Churchman, the husband of Mercer's granddaughter, to whom the house had passed. A V-notched, single-story log barn built by Mercer's son in 1786 was later appended to the rear of the frame section.

The house was built on one of the Nottingham Lots that included the East Nottingham Friends Meeting House (ES1), the house of well-known Quaker minister John Churchman (1745, 1785; 115 Churchman Lane), and the William and Elizabeth Knight House (1745; 668 Little New York Road). Together they are among the most important eighteenth-century buildings in the county, known for their exceptional craftsmanship and adherence to Plain style precepts. Likewise, the adjacent village of Calvert includes among others the noteworthy Federal brick house built for Quaker merchant Elisha Kirk (c. 1810; 1212 Calvert Road) and the former Cross Keys Tavern (1744, c. 1800–1820; 1221 Calvert).

PORT DEPOSIT

Known as Creswell's Ferry until 1812, Port Deposit is located on the narrow flood plain between the Susquehanna River and steeply rising granite cliffs. Plans for a booming settlement to serve as the terminus of the Susquehanna Canal, chartered in 1783, were thwarted by the canal's construction problems and subsequent failure in 1817. However, Port Deposit's advantageous position at the northernmost navigable point on the river generated a lively trade from rafts bringing goods such as lumber, coal, iron, slate, and grain downstream to be reloaded onto ships traveling to Baltimore and farther afield. In addition, the first bridge over the Susquehanna River opened there in 1817, helping Port Deposit emerge as a major processing and manufacturing center in the nineteenth century.

The town also became widely known for its local blue gray building stone quarried from the cliffs north of town starting in the late eighteenth century. Port Deposit granite, technically a type of granite gneiss, was prized for its color, texture, and strength and became a sought-after building material throughout Maryland and beyond by the early nineteenth century. Port Deposit's historic core preserves many fine buildings, as well as sidewalks, retaining walls, terracing, and stairs, constructed with its local granite.

ES3 GERRY HOUSE
c. 1813; c. 1840s porches. 18 S. Main St.

This three-story, double-pile house is a striking example of early Port Deposit architecture with cut-stone walls. Most buildings in town have tall raised basements of local granite such as the one here, even if the floors above are brick or frame, due to frequent flooding and ice gorges that would damage weaker building material. The impressive three-story porch is supported on dressed Port Deposit granite piers with columns above and ornamental ironwork railings featuring sheaves of wheat. At 52–58 S. Main a row of four brick houses (c. 1825–1850) also features a granite raised basement for protection from river ice gorges and a practical solution to building on a granite ledge that makes digging cellars virtually impossible.

ES4 TOME CARRIAGE HOUSE
c. 1850. 80 S. Main St.

Self-made lumber millionaire and philanthropist Jacob Tome had a major impact on Port Deposit in the nineteenth century, building schools, churches, and his own sprawling house on Main Street. Known as Hytheham, the house was demolished in 1948, with its retaining walls and terracing and its carriage house extant along S. Main Street. Constructed of Port Deposit granite with a cupola and bracketed eaves, the carriage house was used as a livery stable and taxi business in later years. A gas house (c. 1850; 1200 Rowland Drive) of similar design and also built in association with Tome's house is located on the other side of the railroad tracks and now serves as a town visitor center.

Other buildings associated with Tome include Tome Memorial United Methodist Church (1872; 100 N. Main Street), built of Port Deposit granite in a Romanesque Revival mode, and Old Tome Bank (1834; 20 N. Main), converted into a school building with additions

in 1899 and more recently renovated as an apartment building. He endowed the Tome Institute, which opened in 1894 as a free public school for white students of all ages (a surviving arch is located across from 66 S. Main). Unfortunately, Tome's major legacy, the Beaux-Arts campus of the Tome School for Boys (1900–1908, Boring and Tilton, Frederick Law Olmsted), a boarding school built on the hill overlooking the town after his death in 1898, is now inaccessible with major buildings in ruins due to recent fires. After closing in 1941, the school was used as the Bainbridge Naval Training Center until 1974 and then leased to the U.S. Labor Department as a job training center in 1991. The series of stairs and landings leading from Main Street up the cliff to the Tome School are still a prominent feature of Port Deposit. They are positioned next to the Port Deposit Town Hall (64 S. Main), located in the former Tome Institute Adams Hall since 1983.

ES5 MCCLENAHAN HOUSE
1880s. 90 S. Main St.

This three-story house was built by the owners of the largest and most successful quarry in Port Deposit from the 1830s to 1914. The Queen Anne house has granite first and second floors with frame on the third and incorporates a smaller frame house at the rear from the 1840s. John McClenahan also built the large semidetached house at 60–62 S. Main in the 1880s, with one side for his son and the other for his daughter. This house is granite at its raised basement and first floor and frame covered with fashionable clapboards and shingles on the second and third floors.

PERRYVILLE

ES6 RODGERS TAVERN MUSEUM (RODGERS TAVERN)
c. 1760. 259 Broad St.

This Georgian building is the sole survivor of the early settlement of this area, facilitated by travel along the post road between Baltimore and Philadelphia. The stone tavern sits along the east bank of the Susquehanna River, near the site of the ferry established in 1695, linking what later became Perryville and Havre de Grace. Opening as the Ferry House, it was purchased in 1780 by John Rodgers. It became a favorite stopping place for such notable Revolutionary War figures as George Washington and French generals Lafayette and Rochambeau. It was purchased by the Society for the Preservation of Maryland Antiquities in 1956 and serves as a museum, telling the stories of period travelers and residents during an important chapter in American history.

CHARLESTOWN

Charlestown was established by the Maryland General Assembly in 1742 as a port town to facilitate trade within the region. It is situated on the North East River at the head of the Chesapeake Bay and was among the few places where large ships could enter. Named for colonial proprietor Charles Calvert, it was laid out by Deputy Surveyor for Cecil County John Veazey, on an ambitious plan calling for a public wharf and warehouses, town squares, courthouse, market house, church, fairgrounds, and two hundred house lots. An inspection station guaranteed Charlestown a share in the lucrative flour trade and rendered it a key port within the Chesapeake Bay's trade network and a supply depot for the Continental Army. It was likewise a popular stop along the Post Road between Philadelphia and Annapolis.

The town's potential attracted an influential citizenry and much speculation. While town managers hoped it might form the county seat, it did so only briefly, from 1782 to 1787. The town faced a setback when Elkton was selected instead. Although the fishing and fish-packing industries helped to sustain it, Charlestown's slow decline began. In the twentieth century, pleasure boating gave rise to a community of summer cottages. Today, only submerged remnants of the stone and log-cribbed wharf and a cluster of eighteenth-century houses and former taverns along the once-bustling Market Street speak to Charlestown's early history and the influence of Chesapeake culture on its economy and architecture.

ES7 PACA HOUSE
c. 1750s; later additions. 317 Market St.

Paca House reflects common building practices within the Chesapeake region, beginning as a typical one-and-a-half-story, hall-parlor frame house. It was likely built by John Paca, the father of William Paca (see WS40) of Annapolis and a Harford County landowner for use when in town on business or for speculation. It was later raised to a full two stories and expanded by a two-bay, one-room section. Not long after, it was again enlarged by a three-bay gambrel-roofed section indictive of the Chesapeake house of the last half of the eighteenth century, distinguished by its stone construction. The later front porch on the earlier section belies its true age.

ES8 INDIAN QUEEN TAVERN
c. 1740s; 1830s remodeled; 1967 restored. 322 Market St.

This former tavern is noteworthy for its articulated post-and-beam construction, brick nogging, flush, beaded shiplap siding, and unusual square, four-room plan centered around a huge chimney block. It was built by Zebulon Hollingsworth as an inn along the Post Road from Philadelphia to Baltimore. In 1804 it was purchased by Jonas Owens who also acquired the adjacent Red Lyon Tavern (ES9), working with associate, John Hasson. Hasson's widow later received the Indian Queen and her second husband, John Nelson Black, purchased the Red Lyon. Interior improvements were made in the 1830s, and during the late nineteenth century the roof was rebuilt and extended to cover a two-storied front gallery. The family retained the house until 1967, when it was restored with funding from Maryland Historical Trust and sold with a preservation easement.

ES9 RED LYON TAVERN (BLACK'S STORE)

c. 1755; c. 1830 additions; 1967 restored. 328 Market St.

The former Red Lyon Tavern is a gambrel-roof Chesapeake-styled building constructed of thick hewn poplar log planks covered with flush shiplap siding. A post-and-beam two-bay addition operated as the separate Stephen Porter Tavern. It was acquired c. 1850 by the Black family, who operated a store from the original building and a tenanted residence from the other, appending the catslide-roofed kitchen ell to the rear. A stone basement with a huge fireplace and cobblestone floor served as a winter kitchen before becoming the Blacks' stockroom. The store closed in 1896 and has since been used as a residence. It was restored in 1967.

NORTH EAST

ES10 GILPIN'S FALLS COVERED BRIDGE

1859–1860, Joseph G. Johnson, builder; 2009–2010, rehabilitated. 1199 North East Rd. over North East Creek

Maryland's streams and creeks were once traversed by dozens of wood-covered bridges, particularly along the many Susquehanna River tributaries. Local master bridge builder Joseph G. Johnson used engineer Theodore Burr's 1817 patent design for this bridge commissioned by Cecil County. Samuel Gilpin first harnessed the nearby falls of North East Creek to power his flour and sawmill in 1735. Widely popular during the era of gable-roof covered-bridge building in the nineteenth century, the Burr Arch combined multiple king post trusses with large parabolic arches to create a sturdy heavy-timber bridge design. Here a single span sits on stone abutments. Vehicular use of the bridge was discontinued in 1936; today it sits parallel to MD 272. Repairs were made to the bridge in 1932, 1959, and 1971, and a major rehabilitation in 2009–2010. At 119-feet-long, Gilpin's Falls is the longest of the six surviving covered bridges in Maryland. Jericho Covered Bridge (CM67) in Harford County also used a Burr Arch design.

ELKTON AND VICINITY

The Cecil County seat was moved from Charlestown to Elkton in 1787 to bring the center of government to a growing port town. Situated on the Elk River and the major land routes between Philadelphia and Baltimore, Elkton enjoyed early success in the flour packing that predated Baltimore's dominance in that industry. It also had a diversified manufacturing and shipping-based economy. While eclipsed by the rise of industrial Baltimore in the nineteenth century, important post–Civil War expansion in Elkton included canneries, pulp mills, machine shops, and fertilizer plants. Elkton continued to thrive into the twentieth century, with an unusual local industry. Between roughly 1913 and 1938, Maryland marriage laws allowed weddings with no waiting period or blood test, making Elkton, the first stop on trains from the north with a courthouse, the self-proclaimed Wedding Capital of the East.

ES11 CECIL COUNTY COURTHOUSE
1939–1940, Malone and Williams; 1966–1967 addition. 129 E. Main St.

By the early 1930s, Cecil County had outgrown its courthouse in part because of the paperwork generated by Elkton's popularity as a wedding location. New Deal public works funding was utilized to build this stylish modern classical replacement designed by a Salisbury firm and built about two hundred yards from the previous courthouse. Faced with random ashlar Port Deposit granite, the new courthouse attempted to combine contemporary design with local materials, to decidedly mixed reviews. In *Maryland Main and the Eastern Shore* (1942) writer Hulbert

Footner viewed the building as "hopelessly out of character with the simple, pleasant American town that surrounds it," while officials were clearly interested in making a statement of modernity. The courthouse complex was expanded into a roughly H-shaped footprint with the 1960s construction of new county buildings to the east that, with the courthouse, framed a small landscaped plaza facing Main Street. Today the courthouse provides an unexpected but attractive touch of 1930s aesthetics in downtown Elkton, which is characterized by a mix of low-scale historic buildings and generic twentieth-century infill that replaced Main Street structures destroyed in a 1947 fire. The old courthouse was demolished, but portions of its courtroom were reused in the low, mid-twentieth-century expansion of Elkton Town Hall (108–112 North Street) that also incorporates the c. 1890s fire station that formerly housed town offices on the second floor.

ES12 HISTORIC LITTLE WEDDING CHAPEL (BURBAGE-BROCK HOUSE)
c. 1820. 142 E. Main St.

By the 1920s Elkton was a hugely popular destination for eloping couples seeking a hasty wedding. A local industry sprang up offering wedding chapel services, ready-to-wear wedding bands, and honeymoon rooms at local inns and hotels. A change in the law in 1938 added a forty-eight-hour waiting period for a license, but exceptions could be made, such as for service members scheduled for overseas transport. The wedding industry remained in Elkton for many decades, but with changing laws its heyday had passed. Of the many Main Street houses with front parlors converted into wedding chapels, this three-bay two-story fieldstone house was one of the last to remain in business, closing in 2017.

ES13 CECIL BANK (ELKTON OPERA HOUSE)
1867, Dixon and Davis. 114–118 North St.

The tall three-and-a-half-story brick building with a corbeled front gable was erected as the Elkton Opera House and a meeting space for the International Order of Odd Fellows fraternal organization. Its construction immediately after the Civil War from designs by the Baltimore architecture firm Dixon and Davis signaled the prosperity of Elkton in this period. Thomas Dixon had an illustrious career spanning several different partnerships and was the architect of many public buildings, such as the Baltimore County Courthouse (CM22).

ES14 ELKTON ARMORY
1915. 100 Railroad Ave.
Elkton Armory was built, like those in Hyattsville (see CR21) and Bel Air (CM61), as part of the expansion and reorganization of the Maryland National Guard in the early twentieth century. Here the architect has not been identified; it is known that a variety of firms designed Maryland's armories. A granite-faced two-story

head house with corner towers and battlements houses offices and meeting rooms, while the drill hall is a one-story structure to the rear with stone buttresses between steel-sash windows and an arched roof. Cecil County's World War I monument, complete with Vermont marble doughboy statue, was erected in 1921 and moved to the armory's front lawn after completion of the new courthouse (ES11). In keeping with segregationist practices at the time, the names of two Black servicemen were set apart at the end of the list with the label "Colored."

ES15 FAIR HILL RACETRACK
1928–1934, William du Pont Jr. 402 Fair Hill Dr.

Now part of the Fair Hill Natural Resources Management Area in the northeastern corner of Maryland, this horse-racing complex was originally developed by du Pont Jr. as a thoroughbred training center and racing track. The viewing stands, stables, betting office, other ancillary buildings, and flat and steeplechase tracks are remarkable surviving examples of the type from the 1930s, despite some changes in recent decades. Du Pont was an avid horseman and racetrack designer who assembled nearly eight thousand acres of land in Cecil County and adjacent Chester County, Pennsylvania, for personal hunts during the late 1920s. Du Pont extended his passion for fox hunting to the steeplechase race circuit, racing his horses and designing tracks and associated facilities all along the East Coast.

The Foxcatcher National Cup, named for du Pont's racing stables, Foxcatcher Farms, debuted at Fair Hill in 1934. As completed, Fair Hill included a variety of frame buildings with board-and-batten siding such as stables, jockey weigh-in stations, betting windows, offices, as well as associated paddocks and a state-of-the-art turf racetrack that included both a flat track and a challenging steeplechase course with seventeen jumps. Since the State of Maryland acquired Fair Hill in 1975, private partners have expanded the nearby training facilities, and the Fair Hill Foundation completed major turf track renovations in 2020.

CHESAPEAKE CITY

Located near the mouth of the Bay, Chesapeake City is largely a product of the Chesapeake and Delaware Canal (see ES17), built to create a more direct route between the Delaware River and the Chesapeake Bay, thereby linking the ports of Philadelphia and Baltimore. It originated as a small settlement known as Bohemia Village, and its growth as the transfer point for goods led to its incorporation as Chesapeake City in 1850. It became a regional marketplace, with a large portion of its population working for the canal company or related maritime trades. Many of its frame buildings were constructed from the wood rafts and arks used to transport goods, recycled at Harvey Burgett's sawmill and lumberyard. Most of its historic buildings are located on the south side of the canal, along Bohemia, George, and Charles streets, and date from the 1840s through the 1870s.

The canal was purchased by the federal government in 1919 as part of its military defense network to provide a sheltered alternative to Atlantic travel. The Army Corps of Engineers straightened the canal and removed the lock, signaling the city's commercial decline by allowing ships to travel through unimpeded. Chesapeake City nevertheless maintains a vibrant historic commercial area near the waterfront.

ES16 BOHEMIA AVENUE BUILDINGS
1800–1912. Bohemia Ave., from Back Creek to 4th St.

Leading inland from Back Creek, Bohemia Avenue is Chesapeake City's principal commercial street, extending from the waterfront and former boat landing site to the south side of town. Noteworthy buildings include the imposing Franklin Hall (c. 1870; 20 Bohemia), a three-and-a-half-story, gable-front brick commercial building. It was erected by local builder Thomas Conrey to encompass offices on the upper floors and first-floor retail space used historically by hardware dealers Bowen and Boulden. Other noted retail buildings are the quintessential gable-front J. M. Reed Store (c. 1870; 100 Bohemia), a dry goods business that claimed the greatest selection in town, brought via steamboat from Baltimore and Philadelphia. Rees Hardware Store (c. 1912; 108 Bohemia) is typical of early-twentieth-century design and materials featuring a false front of pressed metal manufactured by George L. Mesker Iron Works of Evansville, Indiana. Boasting a more elaborate Mesker facade is the former grocery and general merchandise store (c. 1880; 222 Bohemia) operated by Byron Bouchelle.

Houses of note include the ornamental Brady House (1876; 104 Bohemia), embracing a cross-gable roof, bracketed crowned bays, and jigsawn porch. It was built for Henry H. Brady, who ran a fleet of tugboats, operating out of the small frame and brick-nogged office adjacent to the house. A Second Empire house (c. 1870) at number 216 was erected by builder Thomas Conrey as his own residence. Representing a common Chesapeake City dwelling form are numerous three-story, three-bay, side-hall plan houses with a distinctive upper level of half-story windows. The best preserved and oldest was built for Firman Layman (1848; 204 Bohemia), who operated the canal-front Bayard House Hotel (c. 1800; 11 Bohemia). Likewise are the houses of steamboat captains Abraham L. Colmary (c. 1848; 206 Bohemia) and John Clark (c. 1856) at number 211, and of physician William C. Karsner (c. 1884) at number 214. The finest is the 1872 house of Chesapeake and Delaware Canal executive Joseph Hedrick (301 George Street).

ES17 CHESAPEAKE
AND DELAWARE CANAL
PUMPHOUSE MUSEUM

*1854, Samuel V. Merrick and John T.
Towne. 815 Bethel Rd.*

The Merrick and Towne steam engines and the pumphouse that encases them represent an innovative nineteenth-century design and the earliest intact pumping station in the nation. It formed an integral part of the functioning of the Chesapeake and Delaware Canal, pumping water into the canal at Chesapeake City to ensure an operational water supply. The 14-mile-long canal created a direct link between the Delaware and Chesapeake bays, reducing the previous water route by 296 miles. While its planning dates to 1764, it was 1803 before Benjamin Henry Latrobe was hired as chief engineer to determine the route, 1824 when construction began, and 1829 when the first ship passed through. The irregularly coursed stone pumphouse encompasses the 39-foot-diameter lift, able to pump 20,000 gallons of water per minute into the canal from nearby Back Creek. Although it ceased operations in the early 1920s, it was designated a National Historic Landmark in 1975, one of the first engineering sites to be so recognized. It is preserved by the Army Corps of Engineers as a public museum.

WARWICK

ES18 OLD BOHEMIA
CHURCH (ST. FRANCIS
XAVIER CHURCH)

*1792; 1912 remodeled; 1825 rectory.
1445 Bohemia Church Rd.*

This church, important to the history of Roman Catholicism in America, is located on the site of a Jesuit mission begun in 1704 as the Eastern Shore counterpart to the Western Shore's St. Francis Xavier Church and Newtown Manor (WS7). It too encompassed a plantation to support mission activities while also including grist- and sawmills, a brick kiln, a wharf, and an academy that operated from 1745 to 1755, educating members of the prominent Carroll family. Extant are the brick church embellished by an entrance tower with belfry and steeple and the Georgian rectory. The name is derived from the Bohemia Manor tract on which it was established.

Bohemia Manor was part of a land grant from Lord Baltimore to Bohemian explorer, merchant, and cartographer Augustine Herrman in 1660, in payment for his mapping of the region. For a brief period, Herrman granted land for the establishment of a colony of Labadists, a communal Protestant religious organization. Herrman felt kinship with the Labadists, who like himself had immigrated from the Netherlands (some also via Dutch settlements in New York, as well as Pennsylvania). Bohemia Manor thus became a refuge for Dutch, German, Huguenot, and other northern European settlers.

KENT COUNTY
CHESTERTOWN AND VICINITY

Chestertown was established as New Town in 1706, one of six sites then designated as colonial ports of entry and the seat of the Eastern Shore's first county. Significant growth began after 1730 when the town grid was laid out. Renamed Chestertown in 1780, the port enjoyed a heyday between 1750 and 1790 as the Eastern Shore's primary shipping location for tobacco and wheat. Wealthy citizens erected the fine houses that established Chestertown's reputation as second only to Annapolis in architectural splendor. Most were built along Water Street, allowing their merchant owners a view of the wharfs and warehouses located at the terminus of High Street, the main commercial thoroughfare. These include Widehall (1769–1770; 1909 restored; 101 N. Water), Denton House (1784–1787; 1970 restored; 107 N. Water), the William Murray House (1743, 1771; 106 N. Water) and the Custom House (ES19).

As the county's governmental and commercial center, Chestertown became the focus for arts and culture, including the establishment in 1782 of Washington College (see ES22). Prominent for its location on the primary route between Philadelphia and Virginia, Chestertown offered inns and taverns, only a few of which survive, such as the White Swan Tavern (c. 1760; 231 High Street). By 1800 Chestertown was overshadowed by the port of Baltimore, yet it remained vital to the development of Maryland's Upper Eastern Shore. A building boom began in the post–Civil War era beginning with the construction of the new Italianate Kent County Courthouse (c. 1865, John A. Kennard; 103 N. Cross Street) and Court Row (c. 1850–1890; 109–117 Court), a customary row of one-story, private lawyers' offices. Growth was fueled by the arrival of the Kent County Railroad in 1872. Combined with steamboat traffic, the railroad facilitated the transport of agricultural goods as well as a canning industry. The current overlay of late-nineteenth-century buildings speaks to that era, represented by such buildings as the Second Empire Stam Hall (1886; 220 High Street), the largest and most elaborate commercial building in Chestertown. It was built for merchant and druggist Colin F. Stam to combine retail and public meeting space. Stam's own house (1877, H. M. Stuart; 114 Washington Avenue) was the first in a number of highly ornate, upper-middle-class houses built along Washington Avenue. The old town area was designated a National Historic Landmark District in 1970.

ES19 CUSTOM HOUSE
1745–1749; 1877 renovated; 1975 restored. 101 S. Water St.

This is among the finest of Chestertown's many mid- to late-eighteenth-century Georgian houses. The substantial five-bay house with partial-hipped roof was built for merchant Samuel Massey. Before it was finished, however, it was sold in 1749 to attorney and businessman Thomas Ringgold IV and his wife, Anna Maria. They added the banked rear wing that included a basement kitchen with huge cooking fireplace, cellars, and vaults. In 1772 it passed to their son Thomas Ringgold V, who operated his dry goods store and "computing house" for the neighboring customs collector from here, along with a waterfront wharf and storehouses. The house remained in the family until 1794. Following subsequent owners, Wilbur Ross Hubbard restored the house in 1975, and after his death it was transferred to Washington College, where it now houses the C. V. Starr Center for the Study of the American Experience.

ES20 CAPTAIN JAMES F. TAYLOR HOUSE
1857. 201 S. Water St.

Representing the later development of Water Street and the transition from Greek Revival to Italianate, this house is one of the most ornate mid-nineteenth-century houses in Chestertown. Greek Revival is seen in its symmetry, elaborate door surround with tripartite window above, and corner pilasters, while Italianate is manifested in its ornamental porch and low-hipped roof with bracketed overhanging eaves and cupola. The house was built for Captain James F. Taylor, who was the general agent of the Chester River Steamboat Company.

ES21 CHESTERTOWN PUBLIC SCHOOL
1901. 400 High St.

This unusually large and elaborate school building represents the county's enhanced early-twentieth-century educational system as part of a countywide consolidation program designed to improve the existing system of rural one- and two-room standardized schools. It was built for white children, while separate, smaller schoolhouses were built for Blacks. The Colonial Revival design includes Palladian windows, gambrel roof, central bell tower, and cupola. It was erected by local builder and contractor A. M. Culp, who owned and operated a lumber and buildings supply company. It now houses the offices of the county government.

ES22 MIDDLE HALL AT WASHINGTON COLLEGE
1844–1845, Elijah Reynolds. 300 Washington Ave.

Washington College, Maryland's oldest and the only private col-

lege on the Eastern Shore, was chartered in 1782 and named after George Washington with his permission and support. The original building on this site, an impressively large Georgian structure, was completed in 1789 but burned in 1827. Classes were held in various Chestertown buildings until this building was constructed. Sparsely ornamented, the Greek Revival building rises three stories and is topped by a cupola. Boarding students lived in the attic rooms, with lecture halls below. Ten years later Middle Hall was joined by East and West Halls to either side. Middle Hall is the largest of the three similar buildings that stand on a low rise at one end of the campus green and now serve as dormitories.

ES23 LAURETUM
1881, Edmund G. Lind. 954 High St.

The exuberance and eclecticism of the late Victorian era is exem-plified by Lauretum, embracing elements of Queen Anne, Eastlake, and Gothic Revival design. It invokes the picturesque components of residential and landscape architecture then fashionable and of upper-middle-class expectations for comfortable living. The house melds with its surroundings through the use of wide porches and was part of a forty-acre suburban estate conducive to the life of the gentleman farmer. It was built for Harrison W. Vickers, a Chestertown lawyer prominent in the political and civic affairs of Kent County, who served as state's attorney and in both the state and U.S. Senate.

Lauretum (Latin for Laurel Grove) is one of the few nineteenth-century residences on the Eastern Shore designed by a professional architect; Lind was one of Baltimore's most prominent and influential architects of the period. At Lauretum, he created a complex and irregularly massed building that is considered one of the Eastern Shore's most extraordinary residences. R. K. Pippins and Sons of Chestertown was the builder. Lauretum is now a bed-and-breakfast inn.

BETTERTON

ES24 EVERGREEN KNOLL
COTTAGES
c. 1940. 130 1st Ave.

The former resort town of Betterton, incorporated in 1906, sits on a bluff overlooking the Chesapeake Bay at the mouth of the Sassafras River. Steamboat lines bringing tourists from Baltimore, Philadelphia, or other cities were active on the Bay between the 1870s and 1930s, often providing links between railroad stops and Bay resorts. Betterton provided a variety of lodging from room and board offered by the wives of local fishermen in the mid-nineteenth century to over a dozen hotels as well as boardinghouses and rental cottages in the early twentieth century. Although Betterton had an amusement pier with a bowling alley, dance hall, and motion pictures, the beach was the main attraction, with superior swimming conditions because the influx of fresh water from the Upper Bay rivers discouraged the stinging nettles often found in the Lower Bay.

Betterton's larger hotels and amusement pier have been demolished or lost to fire, but many houses and cottages remain. Still available for rental are the Evergreen Knoll cottages, two rows of small frame dwellings facing each other across a common lawn leading to the water. They share a small private beach and pier. The Great Depression forced many of the steamboat lines out of business, and construction of the Chesapeake Bay Bridge (WS80), allowing easy automobile access to the Atlantic Ocean, was the final blow for the remaining passenger steamboats. The last steamboat excursion from Baltimore to Betterton sailed in 1961, and the once bustling resort is a now a quiet residential town. The Betterton Heritage Museum located in the former Most Precious Blood Catholic Church (c. 1911; 100 Main Street) offers exhibits on the town's history, including the Betterton ark, an 1886 fishing shanty.

ROCK HALL

ES25 ROCK HALL MARINE
RAILWAY
1928. 5676 S. Hawthorne Ave.

Operating for nearly a century by the Leary family, this is one of the last remaining fully functioning marine railways in the Chesapeake region. Beginning in the mid-nineteenth century, marine railways played an essential role in the repair and maintenance of the smaller-scale commer-

cial boats crucial to the regional economy. Once common along the creeks, inland bays, and sheltered harbors, marine railways are quickly vanishing, often replaced by modern lifts. This railway is located in the heart of Rock Hall Harbor, an area rich in commercial fishing and maritime history.

The railway consists of a wheeled cradle that moves along

incline rails to carry boats from the water to the yard for repair or storage. Once the boat is secured in the cradle, it is mechanically hoisted by a winch, driven by an engine located at the top of the incline. Beyond is a transfer table and rail spurs used to facilitate movement into one of four adjoining gabled wood buildings forming a continuous saw-tooth-roof structure. The business was started by George Leary, passing through the generations, and is still operated by his descendants.

The story of those who operated these boats and the town's oystering, crabbing, and fishing history is told at the nearby Rock Hall Waterman's Museum (20880 Rock Hall Avenue) housed in a period bungalow.

ES26 CAPTAIN CARTER'S FISHING SHANTY
c. 1925; 1988–1990 restored. Rock Hall Ave. at N. Main St.

This is a once-common boat type known as a fish shanty built by Chesapeake Bay watermen from the 1880s through the 1930s to provide rudimentary living accommodations and shelter from inclement weather. Before motorized vessels, watermen called upon to venture far from shore required an overnight stay. With a shanty, they could remain in a productive fishing area for the duration of a fish run or season. As typical of such boats, Carter's shanty consists of a rectangular cabin of narrow, beaded, tongue-and-groove boards and barrel-vaulted roof and set on a flat skiff-like floating platform. Purely utilitarian in nature, these shanties were built from inexpensive materials and varying specifications. As boat motors became readily available and more powerful, shanties were no longer needed. Some were adapted for use as sheds or appendages to waterfront cottages, but most have fallen victim to decay. Captain Carter's Fishing Shanty was restored by celebrated Eastern Shore waterman and boatwright Stanley F. Vansant, whose wood statue now appears alongside it.

CAROLINE COUNTY
DENTON

ES27 LAW OFFICE (PEOPLE'S NATIONAL BANK)
c. 1906. 118 Market St.

This diminutive rusticated stone bank building across from the courthouse signifies Denton's role as a commercial center for Caroline County. Denton was designated the county seat in 1790, and the first courthouse (demolished) was completed in 1797. The current courthouse is a 1966 Colonial Revival building with some remnants of the 1895 second courthouse. The richly detailed former People's National Bank stands out amidst the simple, two-story brick or concrete early-twentieth-century commercial buildings along Market Street and around the public square, although its architect is unknown. The Law Building next door (1902; 112–116 Market), at three stories the largest building in Denton's commercial district, was constructed as a Masonic lodge with commercial space on the ground floor. Both buildings are now used as law offices.

ES28 WEST DENTON WAREHOUSE AND WHARF
c. 1920; c. 1940 additions. 10215 River Landing Rd.

As the only Eastern Shore county without a major coastline, commerce and transportation via the Choptank River was especially important to Caroline County. This riverfront warehouse and wharf is a rare surviving example of the once common type. Serving various local industries including canneries and granaries, it replaced a mid-nineteenth-century warehouse on this same site. The c. 1920 warehouse is a 100 × 40–foot structure with heavy timber framing, king rod trusses, and a concrete floor. Additions to the north (40 × 20 feet) and south (40 × 40 feet), each including an office space, were added in the early 1940s when the wharfs and bulkheads in the vicinity underwent major repairs. The north addition has been removed, revealing the painted "Baugh's" sign on the gable end from former owner Baugh's Fertilizer Company. By the 1920s steamboat traffic on the upper Choptank began to wane due to damage from a 1919 flood as well as riverbank erosion and shoaling, creating navigational obstacles. Now sheathed with corrugated metal, the warehouse retains its original wood siding underneath and awaits restoration.

WILLISTON

ES29 MEMORY LANE
1864. 24700 Williston Rd.

Located in the former port village of Williston on the Choptank River, Memory Lane was built by shipping magnate Colonel John Arthur Willis as a wedding present for his daughter. Mary Virginia Willis married B. Gootee Stevens, who became president of the Denton National Bank. Willis acquired the port, known as Potters Landing, in 1847 and made his fortune from moving grain and other agricultural products on steamboats and sailing ships.

The double-pile central-hall house has fashionable Italianate decorative detail with a bracketed wraparound porch on chamfered posts, scrolled eave brackets, and an eight-sided cupola topped by a finial. In exterior detail and plan, the house resembles Design XXVII "A Small Country House for the Southern States" in A. J. Downing's influential *The Architecture of Country Houses,* first published in 1850. Downing describes this design as "a simple, rational, convenient, and economical dwelling for the southern part of the Union" and highlights the benefits of large porches and overhanging eaves in a warm climate.

HARMONY

ES30 JAMES WEBB CABIN

c. 1852; 2016 restored. 23459 Grove Rd.

This simple cabin, erected by free African American farmer James Webb, was typical of the dwellings of poor, Black (and white) families within the region during the early to mid-nineteenth century. Built of hand-hewn logs resting on a stone foundation, the cabin consists of a single room with an open-hearth brick fireplace, a loft accessed by a ladder, and a root cellar or "potato hole." Webb lived here with his father, enslaved wife Mary Ann, and their two children. As the only surviving cabin built by a free Black person in the area, it was purchased and restored by the Caroline County Historical Society. It opened in 2016 as an interpretative museum site along the Harriett Tubman Underground Railroad Byway.

PRESTON

ES31 LINCHESTER MILL

c. 1840; c. 1880, c. 1897, 1918 additions. 3390 Linchester Rd.

This is one of two surviving mills of the approximately twenty-five that once formed Caroline County's chief industry. It is also its most intact and was the last to operate, prior to its closure in 1979. The interior encompasses milling equipment spanning the course of two centuries, retaining elements of the labor-saving, grain elevator technology developed by Oliver Evans in the eighteenth century while introducing the roller mill system developed c. 1890. Although this mill was not erected until about 1840, there has been a mill here at the head of Upper Hunting Creek since the 1680s. The three-bay frame building was erected by Jacob C. Willson, with a fourth bay added by then-owner John Nichols. Lean-to sections were added as improvements in milling equipment were made; c. 1897, S. L. Webster installed the Wolf Roller machinery, and after his purchase in 1918 Frank Langrell replaced the turbines with a Fitz overshot water wheel.

The site includes the c. 1840 miller's house, a two-story, five-bay, frame I-house featuring Greek Revival corner pilasters and a small frame house for the miller's assistant. The 1879 Hog Island School, a traditional one-room, gable-front schoolhouse with bell cote, was moved to the site.

As a rare surviving mill, the building was purchased by Caroline County Historical Society in 2003 and is now a museum. Also extant is the Williston Mill and Miller's House (c. 1830; 25729 Williston Road); although the mill suffered a fire, it was restored and is also open to the public.

FEDERALSBURG

ES32 EXETER
c. 1800–1810. 408 Old Denton Rd.

This is the best-preserved turn-of-the-nineteenth-century dwelling in Caroline County and the earliest extant building in the Federalsburg area. It was erected in two sections that, although likely built within a close timeframe, represent different approaches to domestic design that reflect the changes occurring during this crucial period in the area's architectural development. It began as a simple one-and-a-half-story, two-room, central-chimney house. The new two-story, three-bay main block embraced Federal styling and a side-hall-and-parlor plan. It added a formal room for entertainment and a separate entrance and stair hall to the otherwise multipurpose early house, then relegated to kitchen and service space. The newer section is distinguished by its elaborate entrance with sidelights and shutters, transom, full pediment, reeded surround, and a punch-and-gouge-work frieze.

The early house was likely built by Abraham Lewis, a planter who purchased the Exeter tract in 1777. It was sold to James B. Robbins in 1808, who was responsible for the more upscale addition. At the same time, Robbins acquired the Exeter Mill formerly located opposite the house. Exeter is currently owned and maintained by the Federalsburg Historical Society and is open to the public.

QUEEN ANNE'S COUNTY
CENTREVILLE

ES33 QUEEN ANNE'S COUNTY COURTHOUSE

c. 1792–1794; 1876 additions, J. Crawford Neilson. 100 Courthouse Sq.

In 1782 the State Assembly voted to move the county seat of Queen Anne's County to a more central location and replace the c. 1708 courthouse building in Queenstown (1977 restored; 100 Del Rhodes Avenue). After some delay a grid of fifty-two lots around a public square was laid out along the road (now MD 213) between Chestertown and Queenstown and close to the Corsica River. Said to be the oldest Maryland county courthouse in continuous use, it was built on the public square facing Commerce Street. The original configuration was a two-story central block with a pediment and flanking lower wings. In 1876, Baltimore architect Neilson enlarged the courthouse by raising the side wings to two-stories and expanding the building to the rear. The windows, cast-iron balcony, and any surviving historic interior finishes date from Neilson's renovation, but the basic form of the late-eighteenth-century courthouse is still apparent.

ES34 CENTREVILLE TOWN HALL (QUEEN ANNE NATIONAL BANK)

1903; later addition. 101 Lawyers' Row

After a 1902 fire destroyed several blocks, a fashionable new building was constructed for the Queen Anne National Bank at the east end of Lawyers' Row. The bank moved out of their fire-damaged late-nineteenth-century two-story building at 105 Lawyers' Row, which was repaired to serve for many years as the offices of the *Centreville Observer* newspaper. The new classical bank, constructed of orange Roman bricks, has limestone accents and features round stained glass windows with the dates 1884 (founding of the bank) and 1903. The bank failed during the Great Depression, and in 1936 the building and lot were sold to the Town Commissioners of Centreville. A clock tower was added to the building's east corner at an unknown date, perhaps after conversion to the town hall.

Also noteworthy is the adjacent Centreville National Bank (1903–1904; 107 N. Commerce Street) built in the aftermath of the 1902 fire and using a similar classical approach and materials. Designed by Hill and Thompson of Newark, New Jersey, it replaced the previous 1876 bank by J. Crawford Neilson.

ES35 TUCKER HOUSE
c. 1794; later additions. 124 S. Commerce St.

One of the oldest residences in Centreville, this house is located on an original town lot purchased by James Kennard in 1792. As originally constructed, the gambrel-roofed frame dwelling was only two bays wide and two rooms deep, a popular house plan in the Tidewater during the period. Around 1815, a stair passage was added at the south gable end that extended the full depth of the house. The original "room behind room" plan with shared chimney on the north gable end was retained, with a late-nineteenth-century ell addition to the rear. The Tucker family acquired the house in 1898 and in 1968 donated it to the Queen Anne's County Historical Society for use as a house museum and offices. Also on the property is a post-and-plank meat house built in the second quarter of the nineteenth century. Wright's Chance (119 S. Commerce), another eighteenth-century gambrel-roofed house moved to a nearby lot in 1964, is also a Queen Anne's County Historical Society house museum.

ES36 HARPER HOUSE
1887–1890. 203 S. Commerce St.

Centreville's prominence was well established by the second quarter of the nineteenth century, when owners of large lots on the main thoroughfare of Commerce Street began subdividing their properties for development. The trend continued in the post–Civil War era, with buildings embracing elements of Queen Anne and Stick Style design. Among the most outstanding is this asymmetrical frame house with a central tower, multiple cross gables, and exuberant wood details built by Robert Price. Owner of Price Lumber Company, he likely viewed his ornate house as an endorsement of the benefits of wood as a building material. Along with the neighboring Jackson Collins House (c. 1887; 123 S. Commerce), Wright House (c. 1894; 201 S. Commerce), and the former Female Seminary (1876; 205 S. Commerce), they represent one of the finest assemblages of late-nineteenth-century architecture in the region.

ES37 CAPTAIN'S HOUSES
1880. 200, 204, 208, 212 Corsica St.

This ensemble of four identical frame houses was built by prominent local schooner captain John H. Ozmon to provide housing for his sailing crew and other workers. They are the oldest surviving buildings along the Centreville waterfront, reflecting the maritime trade and the transfer of agricultural goods on Maryland's Eastern Shore during the late nineteenth century. Ozmon, master of the schooner *Kent* by age twenty, ran a shipping business and by the time of his death in 1902 owned much of the Centreville Wharf area. He built as many as twenty houses, of which only these survive.

The tall, narrow, banked houses are composed of a single room per floor, with entrances to both the living space on the first floor and the rear, ground-level kitchen. A first-story porch is inset under the steeply pitched gable roof, typical of local Tidewater architecture, and single dormers to the front and rear light the half-story bedchamber.

Nearby is Ozmon's unusual brick store building (c. 1880; 114 Front Street), which is similarly banked with an elaborate porch that cantilevers over the waterfront entrance, and his cross-gabled house (1877–1880; 201 Watson Street).

CHURCH HILL

ES38 CHURCH HILL THEATRE
1929, Elwood F. Coleman; 1944 renovated. 103 Walnut St.

The crossroads town of Church Hill takes its name from the colonial parish of St. Luke's Episcopal Church (1729; 403 Main Street). It was not until the mid-nineteenth century that Church Hill began to grow as a commercial center for the surrounding agricultural communities. The current town hall (c. 1875; 324 Main) is a fine example of a combination residential/commercial building, with intact storefront windows and Eastlake decorative details. However, the most unusual survivor here is the Church Hill Theatre, built as a community hall in 1929 and used as a movie theater starting in late 1935. In addition to the meeting and theater spaces, the building contained town offices, a kitchen for community dinners, and a small retail store. After a fire in 1944, the restrained Art Deco marquee, box office, doors, and interior details were added, making this a rare example of Art Deco in a largely rural county. A nonprofit arts organization acquired the theater after it closed in the early 1980s and continues to manage it as a performing arts and educational venue.

ES39 ST. PETER'S CATHOLIC CHURCH

1823–1827; 1877 rebuilt. 5319 Ocean Gtwy.

This Gothic Revival church is a well-known landmark, situated along the busy U.S. 50 corridor, and its parish important to the history of Catholicism in Maryland. The parish was established in 1764, concurrently with St. Joseph's in Talbot County by the first permanent Catholic mission on the Eastern Shore, St. Francis Xavier, founded in Cecil County in 1704. Together they formed the "central shore" missions, and along with St. Francis Xavier in St. Mary's County (WS7), established by Jesuits in 1640 as the first Catholic settlement in the state, they represent Maryland's earliest Catholic enclaves.

A small chapel was built shortly after St. Peter's founding, replaced by the central core of the current building. Today's church is essentially a late-nineteenth-century Gothic Revival building. To increase its capacity, the roof was raised, an octagonal apse added to the north facade, and a buttressed nave and vestibule to the south, reorienting the building and creating a cruciform plan. The expanded church was embellished with such details as large rose and paired, stained glass lancet windows, scrolled exposed rafters, and bargeboards with Stick Style brackets and quatrefoil medallions.

ES40 CLOVERFIELDS

1705; many later additions. 500 Foremans Landing Rd.

As one of Maryland's oldest houses and among the first in the Chesapeake erected of brick, Cloverfields offers primary evidence of early building practices. It began as a two-story, hall-parlor house with square medieval-influenced stair tower, erected by owner Philemon Hensley, a builder and planter. Among the many remarkable components that set this house apart are its massive bent principal rafters, tilted false plate, and early use of a classically inspired cornice integral to the framing through the use of joist ends extended to form modillions. The house comprises a variety of brick bonding patterns, including an early use of common bond, and belt course and water table, stepped at the corners in the English mode. Later changes include the construction of one-story rooms flanking the tower and the introduction of a central passage (c. 1729), the raising of the new rooms to two stories (1750s), and the construction of a unified, catslide roof (c. 1761). Refinements such as Rococo mantels and plaster paneling were later introduced, along with a terraced lawn and formal gardens (1768–1769). A rear service wing was constructed in 1783–1784. A carefully researched restoration to the period of Colonel William Hemsley's ownership, c. 1784, was begun in 2017. Once completed, Cloverfields will be open to the public.

STEVENSVILLE

ES41 CHRIST CHURCH
1880. 121 E. Main St.

This is one of the most exuberant late-nineteenth-century churches on the Eastern Shore, and although built in 1880, its roots extend back to William Claiborne's Anglican settlement at Kent Point in 1632. As the first in the colony, the congregation is referred to as the cradle of the Anglican Church in Maryland. The Reverend Richard James was invited here from England to minister to a congregation eager to continue worshipping as they had in their English homeland. Claiborne immigrated via Jamestown, and much to the chagrin of Lord Calvert, settled here to claim Kent Island for the Virginia colony. Although Calvert successfully asserted his authority in 1658, political upheavals in England forced Maryland to accept Anglicanism as its official religion in 1692, with Christ Church becoming one of thirty sanctioned parishes.

The congregation moved to Stevensville to construct this church, its fifth, incorporating bricks from the foundation of the previous building as a symbolic gesture. The church exhibits a rich display of materials and textures to include novelty siding and wood shingles within a framework of chamfered rails and stiles, and a steeply pitched slate roof, lancet brick chimney, and frame bell tower with open bell cote. The soaring interior contains a combination of queen post, king post, and hammerbeam truss configurations, springing forth from oversized brackets.

ES42 CRAY HOUSE
1809; c. 1842 addition; 1976 restored. 109 Cockey's Ln.

Cray House is one of Maryland's few surviving post-and-plank buildings, a form of log construction favored by Chesapeake builders. Rather than the typical whole-log construction, wide log planks were hewn or pit-sawn to a thickness of approximately three inches, fitted together, and held with dovetail notching into corner posts. To keep the planks in alignment, they were held with vertical intermediary posts, visible on the interior. Built by John Denny, the house also represents an intact hall-parlor-plan dwelling type, built with an interior gable-end chimney and steep gable roof. Although a humble dwelling, the interior finishes included beaded partition wall, baseboard, chair rail, and architrave surrounds. New owner Mary Legg added a timber-frame section, creating a third room with an end chimney, and a gambrel roof that covered the entire house. It was purchased by Nora Cray in 1914 and conveyed by her heirs to the Kent Island Heritage Society in 1976. It was then restored as a center for local preservation activities.

WYE MILLS

ES43 WYE MILL

Late 18th century; 1840, c. 1880 renovations; 1956–1960 restored. 900 Wye Mills Rd.

This is the oldest frame gristmill on the Eastern Shore, if not in the state, reflecting an integral segment of the regional economy from the period of settlement into the twentieth century. Gristmills were first erected for local use, powered by wind or by the many rivers and streams along the Eastern Shore. As demand for wheat increased with the export trade during the late eighteenth century, so did gristmill construction. Wye Mill rests on the site of a c. 1671 mill erected by Edward Barrowclif that was owned for much of the eighteenth century by Edward Lloyd of Wye House (ES48).

The humble, one-and-a-half-story mill is of braced, heavy-timber frame construction covered with flush shiplap siding and a gable roof that exhibits innovative tilted false-plate joinery. Incorporating the pioneering milling technology developed by Oliver Evans, the mill was powered by an overshot wheel at the gable end and fed by a millrace along the banked, rear elevation. In 1840, the framing was reinforced, and again c. 1880 and in the early twentieth century, reflecting two hundred years of milling technology. Wye Mill was purchased by the state in 1953 and deeded to Preservation Maryland in 1956. It underwent a four-year restoration and is now open as a museum.

TALBOT COUNTY

EASTON

After the formation of Queen Anne's County removed land to the north, a new more centrally located seat for Talbot County was created in 1710. Another legislative act in 1788 incorporated the settlement with the name Easton, and a federal judiciary act stipulated that district court should alternate between Baltimore and Easton, setting the stage for the town's ascendance as the most prosperous and largest jurisdiction on the Eastern Shore in the early nineteenth century. Still intact Federal-period development around the courthouse square speaks to the importance of this period in Easton's history, such as the group of two-and-a-half-story Flemish-bond brick town houses (c. 1800) with delicate fanlights and carved cornices at 111–121 N. Washington Street. Arrival of the Maryland and Delaware Railroad in 1869 ushered in a period of post–Civil War economic development. Downtown Easton is oriented around the courthouse and quickly transitions from brick or frame commercial buildings to residential neighborhoods of late-nineteenth- and early-twentieth-century houses. Historic Easton Inc. was founded in 1973 to preserve the town's architecture, and shortly thereafter a historic district zoning ordinance was adopted to protect building exteriors.

ES44 TALBOT COUNTY COURTHOUSE
1794; 1898, 1958 additions. 11 N. Washington St.

The courthouse sits on a small landscaped square at the center of Easton, which was also the site of the first c. 1710 courthouse. That structure was replaced in 1794 with a five-bay, Georgian building. Expansion and renovation in 1898 added bays to either end, changed the entrance pavilion and windows, and added the current hipped roof and cupola. Additional changes over the years have expanded and altered the courthouse, particularly the 1958 additions to the rear and sides. Indicative of Maryland's split loyalties during the Civil War and ongoing racial divisions, a monument of a Confederate soldier was erected on the courthouse grounds in 1916; the county council approved a resolution in September 2021 to move the *Talbot Boys* statue from public land to a privately owned park in Virginia. A statue of famed abolitionist Frederick Douglass, born and enslaved in Talbot County, has stood prominently in front of the courthouse since 2011.

ES45 ODD FELLOWS LODGE
1879. 1 S. Washington St.

The intersection of Washington and Dover streets at the southeast corner of the courthouse square is the center of Easton's grid plan. The three-and-a-half-story Odd Fellows Lodge stands as a landmark from Easton's post–Civil War development and a key social gathering space. Built with retail space below and meeting rooms for the Miller Lodge of the International Order of Odd Fellows above, the eclectic brick building has decorated gables and chimneys facing both Washington and Dover streets.

The former Shannahan and Wrightson Hardware Company (1877–1889), nearby at 12 N. Washington, has brick from an older structure incorporated at the first story and two floors separated by rusticated sandstone belt courses above. Stone panels with the dates 1877, 1881, and 1889 on the facade, perhaps corresponding to the gradual construction of the building to its full height, are topped by a metal cornice stamped with the firm's name.

ES46 THIRD HAVEN FRIENDS MEETING HOUSE
1682–1684, John Salter, builder; 1797 addition. 405 S. Washington St.

This is the oldest positively dated building in Maryland and the oldest extant Friends meetinghouse in the country. It was erected by carpenter-builder John Salter according to specifications outlined in a surviving agreement. As built, it encompassed a cruciform plan with cross-wing entrance and stair hall to the front and a similar projection to the rear. In 1797 the building was significantly modified, removing the wings and adding a six-bay section with dual entrances for men and women, indicative of the emerging American Friends meetinghouse prototype.

Despite these modifications, Third Haven retains its original framing and roof structure, interior woodwork, facing bench, and retractable partition and has never been electrified, plumbed, or centrally heated. As a rare survivor, modified during a crucial period in the evolution of meetinghouse design in America, Third Haven is of tremendous value in understanding evolving meeting practices. It is also a well-preserved artifact of seventeenth- and eighteenth-century building traditions.

Referred to as the Great Meeting House, it sheltered the most vital Quaker meeting on the Eastern Shore, accommodating quarterly meetings that encompassed Betty's Cove, Bayside, Choptank, and Tuckahoe meetings, and the half-yearly meeting of Maryland Friends. Third Haven played a significant role in the establishment of Quakerism in the colonies, witnessing such eminent visitors as Thomas Chalkley (1698), Thomas Story (1699), John Fothergill (1722), Samuel Bownas (1728), John Woolman (1746, 1766), and Rufus Jones (1932). A new meetinghouse was erected on the property in 1880, yet the old building is still used for special meetings and those held during the summer.

ES47 RATCLIFFE MANOR

1757–1762; 1910–1935 outbuildings; 1953 kitchen addition. 7768 Ratcliff Manor Rd.

One of the most distinctive Georgian plantation houses on Maryland's Eastern Shore, Ratcliffe is situated on a small peninsula flanked by the Tred Avon River and Dixon Creek. Few Georgian houses in Talbot County can rival this one for its sophistication and integrity. Built for Henry Hollyday as the centerpiece of his thousand-acre plantation, it reflects the wealth of the merchant planters who first diversified from tobacco to more stable wheat production. Among its distinctive features are the nearly identical carriage and riverfront entrances; the former maintains it early portico with side benches, and the latter overlooks a boxwood garden and terraced landscape.

The house is recognized for its extraordinary brickwork, sophisticated wood detailing, rare and distinctive jerkinhead roof, and twelve-over-twelve windows.

A five-room Annapolis Plan provides an elegant parlor and dining room to the rear that enjoys views of the garden and riverfront, with three smaller rooms and a stair hall to the front. A brick kitchen and pantry appear to one side, joined by a hyphen to a modern kitchen addition.

Hailing from well-recognized planter families, Henry Hollyday was the son of wealthy planter James Hollyday and Sarah Covington Lloyd of Wye House (ES48). Ratcliffe remained in the family until 1902. It was then purchased by Andrew A. Hathaway, who introduced dairy farming and between 1910 and 1935 erected tenant and overseer's houses and also a gambrel-roofed dairy barn, milk house, silo, hog house, and chicken house.

COPPERVILLE

ES48 WYE HOUSE AND PLANTATION

c. 1790–1792. 26080 Bruffs Island Rd.

Located at the end of a long allée, this is one of the most important eighteenth-century plantation landscapes in the United States. Owned by Lloyd descendants for over four centuries, the post-Revolutionary main house re-

placed one dating to the seventeenth century and includes a landscape comprising a family cemetery, gardens, walks, walls, ha-ha, bowling green, and acres of formal gardens. Noteworthy for its seven-part form, the house was inspired by Palladio's Italian villas, published in Robert Morris's *Select Architecture* (1757). Wye House is representative of a transitional period, replacing comparatively heavy, ornate elements of Georgian design with lighter treatments and elongated proportions of the Federal period. The first floor follows the Annapolis Plan with the two most important rooms, the parlor and dining room, extending across the back.

As the center of a working plantation, Wye House was organized to mediate between enslaved and free-living individuals working on the property and those visiting. Famed abolitionist and statesman Frederick Douglass was enslaved here for two years, a period he recalled as crucial to his awareness of the corrupting evils of slavery. Although it is no longer extant, Douglass describes in *Narrative of the Life of Frederick Douglass, an American Slave* (1845) the "long quarter" housing slaves as a "very long, rough, low building, literally alive with slaves of all ages, conditions, and sizes," as well as numerous other "slave houses and huts."

The 1790s orangery or greenhouse, an indulgence status symbol, is the oldest extant in the United States. It is eighty-five-feet long, comprising a two-story section with a billiard room flanked by single-story wings. The brick walls are covered with rusticated stucco and include full-height Palladian windows. The so-called Captain's House also survives, likely built mid-eighteenth century as a kitchen dependency for the original house.

ST. MICHAELS

St. Michaels was established in 1778 as a speculative venture by the Liverpool merchant firm of Gildart and Gowith, under the direction of factor James Braddock, who laid out a grid of fifty-eight lots. The plan encompassed St. Mary's Square, the commercial Market (now Talbot) Street, and the harbor-facing Water Street. Although the post–Revolutionary War period proved disastrous for the company, a sheltered harbor and small affordable lots attracted craftsmen, shipwrights, carpenters, mariners, and watermen, as well as merchants and planters. Principal industries included boatbuilding, oystering, and fishing.

The town's early-nineteenth-century prosperity is manifested by several Federal-period brick houses such as shipbuilder William Merchant's house (c. 1810; 200 Mulberry Street). As a working harbor, however, simpler houses built for watermen and craftsmen prevailed, witnessing the development of prototypical forms, such as the Bruff-Mansfield House (c. 1800; 113 Green Street), a one-and-a-half-story, one-room-wide, two-room-deep frame dwelling. The house features a steeply pitched gable roof with a central dormer and a brick end chimney with a partially exposed brick firewall. The two neighboring houses are similarly configured, including the Flemish-bond brick John Harrison House (109 Green). A popular later form is the two-story, front-facing T-plan house with a two-story gallery, exemplified by the elaborate Gingerbread House (1879; 103 S. Talbot Street). It was built for James Watkins, whose name and date are incised in the foundation.

Among St. Michaels's best preserved and most interesting store buildings is the combination house, store, and office built for real estate agent James Benson (c. 1860–1870; 214 S. Talbot). The store section to the north features intact display windows, and a two-story gallery characteristic of many of the town's buildings. Other intact storefronts are seen on the former butcher shop (c. 1870), and hardware store (c. 1872) at 308 and 216 S. Talbot, respectively.

Late-nineteenth- and early-twentieth-century industries included seafood packing and canning, while steamboat traffic afforded access to markets in Baltimore and Annapolis for the lucrative oyster trade. Although the harbor now caters mostly to pleasure craft, St. Michaels's boatbuilding tradition is celebrated by the Chesapeake Bay Maritime Museum (ES51), situated in the former industrial area known as Navy Point. Due to its maritime attractions and historic architecture, the town enjoys a vibrant tourist economy.

may be part of its 1872 additions by then-owner Judge William H. Bruff. For decades, beginning in 1878, it was the home and office of physician Robert Dodson.

ES50 CHRIST EPISCOPAL CHURCH
1878, Henry M. Congdon. 301 S. Talbot St.

ES49 THE OLD INN
c. 1816. 401 S. Talbot St.

This building was erected as an inn by Wrightson Jones, who operated a shipyard. It is perhaps the first of many houses in the town to feature a two-story gallery across its facade, inset under the gabled roof. The two doorways likely relate to its function as an inn, providing access to unequally sized rooms to either side of a central hall. It remained in the Jones family until 1855 and was still being used as a hotel when sold in 1875. By the 1950s it became a restaurant.

Similar is the building (c. 1800; 101 Locust Street), erected by Joseph Harrison, also used initially as a tavern. The two-story gallery

One of the most distinctive buildings in St. Michaels is this High Victorian Gothic church. It is the fourth edifice for the Christ Episcopal Church of St. Michael Archangel parish, which dates to the 1692 establishment of the Church of England in Maryland. The congregation predates the formal development of the town, perhaps inspiring its name. Built of Port Deposit granite shipped by barge via the Chesapeake Bay, it encompasses half-timber framing with brick nogging and a buttressed central entrance tower with bell cote and spire. The lofty interior boasts a timber ceiling supported by principal rafters with through-purlins, common rafters, and king posts rising above the collar

MARYLAND WOOD BOATBUILDING

Skipjack *Kathryn*, Dogwood Harbor, Chesapeake Bay, Tilghman

Situated along the Chesapeake Bay, the world's largest estuary, Marylanders could not help but embrace boatbuilding for both commercial and recreational purposes. Responding to the singular conditions of the Chesapeake Bay and the requirements of the fishing, crabbing, and oystering industries, Maryland boatbuilders created such distinctive sailing vessels as the log canoe, brogan, bugeye, pungey, crabbing skiff, two- and three-sail bateaux, and the fishing shanty. Also originating from broadly recognized forms are the Chesapeake schooner, sloop, skipjack, and the Baltimore Clipper. While Baltimore was internationally recognized for its commercial ships, many Chesapeake boats were built by watermen for their own use, adapted to allow passage through the Bay's many shallow tributaries and coves.

The earliest Chesapeake boat is the log canoe, originating from Native American forms during the colonial era. Constructed from a single log, it was adaptable to many purposes, becoming the most conspicuous type found on the Chesapeake Bay. As large timbers became scarce, smaller logs were fastened together and planed beams. Its architect was the son of an Episcopal priest and a founder of the New York Ecclesiological Society known for his church designs, including All Saints Church (1901; 10806 Longwoods Road) in Easton.

ES51 CHESAPEAKE BAY MARITIME MUSEUM
2005, Quinn Evans Architects. 213 N. Talbot St.

Located on the former site of St. Michaels's seafood-packing industries, this complex of buildings houses the largest and most comprehensive collection of Chesapeake Bay watercraft in the nation (see **Maryland Wood Boatbuilding**, above). A freight shed built in 1888 by the Baltimore, Chesapeake, and Atlantic Railway Company was moved here in 1933 for use by the St. Michaels Packing Company as a tomato cannery. It now houses a wide-ranging assemblage of often-rare small craft specific to the Chesapeake Bay. An eighteenth-century corn crib is home to the gunning or fowl-hunting boat collection, in-

smooth. First paddled, log canoes were later rigged for sailing and outfitted with a keel. Some were expanded to include decks and small cabins for longer excursions, such as the two-mast brogan, with a sharp stem and stern that made it ideal for oyster dredging. Log-built boats later took on other forms such as the bugeye and skiff. The bugeye was specifically suited to oyster dredging, embracing a more rounded stern, cabin, and two-masted sailing rig. The name may be a reference to *buckie*, the Scottish word for "oyster." Skiffs were plank-built with a sharp bow and a flat bottom allowing them to negotiate the Bay's shallower waters.

Traditional types modified by Chesapeake boatbuilders were the two-masted schooner and the single-masted, round-bottomed sloop, the oldest sailing vessel on the Bay based upon European antecedents. An important variation on the schooner was the pungey, a longer boat with a deeper stern and taller sails. The skiff and schooner were eventually superseded by the skipjack, an enlarged skiff with a nearly flat bottom that was easier and cheaper to build, and that "skipped" across the water. It quickly became the dominant large-scale sailing vessel during the early twentieth century, now used almost exclusively for oystering. The skipjack is recognized as the official state boat of Maryland. Also particular to the Chesapeake is the fishing shanty or ark (see Captain Carter's Fishing Shanty; ES26) with a cabin that allowed fishermen overnight excursions. With the advent of motorization, local builders crafted recreational boats as well. Although many of these traditional forms are vanishing or no longer extant, significant collections are found in the Chesapeake Bay Maritime Museum (ES51), Calvert Marine Museum (WS24), and Havre de Grace Maritime Museum (100 Lafayette Street).

cluding sneak, ice, and sinkbox boats.

While these buildings display work boats, a building designed by Quinn Evans and built by Whiting Turner Contracting houses the permanent *Play on the Bay* exhibit that tells the story of recreational boating, revolutionized by the advent of fiberglass and motorized boat engines. It was built resembling a typical transverse board-and-batten barn with side shed, raised-metal gable roof, and lofty interior. An eleven-vessel floating display encompasses prime examples of such Bay boats as the rare fifty-three-foot bugeye *Edna Lockwood*. The site includes a boatbuilding and repair shop and the 1879 Hooper's Strait octagonal screw-pile lighthouse, moved here in 1966.

The museum owns several representative local houses that line its Mill Street boundary and that accommodated the first exhibitions. The museum opened in 1965 in the c. 1851 Captain Dodson House built as a three-story, two-bay brick dwelling with a decorative three-story gallery. Within the year, the exhibitions expanded into the similarly styled, neighboring Higgins House (c. 1856), and the Eagle House (1893), with a central entrance tower flanked by two-story galleries.

ES52 TILGHMAN
WATERMAN'S MUSEUM
*c. 1890–1900. 6031 Tilghman
Island Rd.*

This is the best example of a dwelling form unique to Tilghman Island and neighboring Sherwood, referred to as a W-house. It is identified by its L-shaped configuration composed of two equally sized, two-story, gable-roof sections, at the intersection of which appears a three-sided, two-story, gable-front entrance pavilion, with a porch that spans the distance between the two sections. In total, thirteen W-houses were erected, only seven of which survive, and only two remain intact. The design boasted air flow distributed throughout the house regardless of wind direction.

Originally owned by the Lee family, the house was inherited by Leona Garvin Harrison, who used it in the 1930s as an annex to her popular fishing resort known as The Elms. It was vacant when purchased by the museum in 2010 and has since been restored and opened to tell the story of the island, first inhabited by English settlers in 1656, and its maritime heritage. The other intact W-house (c. 1890; 21524 Chicken Point Road) was built for buyboat captain Alex Cooper, likely by Tilghman carpenter James Cooper.

OXFORD

Little survives from Oxford's early dominance as a port town from the 1660s through the 1760s, when it was second only to Annapolis and the designated port of entry on the Eastern Shore. The still-active ferry from Oxford to Bellevue across the Tred Avon River is thought to be the first in the country, established by Talbot County in 1683. It is located near the intersection of Morris Street and The Strand, which featured an assortment of frame residential and small-scale commercial buildings arranged on the grid recorded in a 1707 survey. A 1976 reconstruction of the seventeenth-century Oxford Custom House near the town wharf was a Bicentennial project celebrating this early history. This project coincided with the establishment of a Historic District Commission for Oxford. Despite being eclipsed in the mid-eighteenth century by ports such as Chestertown and Baltimore, Oxford continued to prosper. The arrival of the Maryland and Delaware Railroad in 1871 (after 1877 known as Delaware and Chesapeake) expanded the town and its economic base, with many residents employed in shipbuilding or over a dozen oyster-packing houses.

CLIMATE CHANGE, SEA-LEVEL RISE, AND THE CHESAPEAKE BAY

Last house on Holland Island, October 2009

In 2010 the last remaining house on Holland Island off the coast of southern Dorchester County was subsumed by the Chesapeake Bay. The former residents left long ago in 1918 when erosion and rising water levels forced the once thriving town of watermen and their families to move to the mainland. The vulnerability of the Delmarva peninsula, which has been slowly sinking since the last Ice Age, makes it a startling early warning case study in climate change sea-level rise. Scientific data indicates that troublesome flooding dismissed by some as the natural ebb and flow of water levels portends coming problems for settlement in low-lying coastal areas. Where previously it took 1,000 years for the Bay's water levels to rise three feet, they rose over a foot between 1900 and 2000, and scientists fear a rise of another two to three feet by 2100. The long Chesapeake coastline of Maryland is especially vulnerable, with places like Talbot County consisting of 600 miles of tidal shoreland, the longest in the country. Low-lying islands have slowly been swallowed by the Bay over the decades, but now rising water levels threaten landmasses such as Smith Island.

The response varies. Annapolis is trying to launch an ambitious series of flood control measures to protect its historic core, including floodgates, pumps, and seawalls. Smaller and less affluent communities face property values that are literally underwater and bide their time until relocation is possible, perhaps with government assistance. Others deny that anything extraordinary or human caused is happening, pointing to historic floods and personal experience. This view is aided by the fact that climate change–related sea level rise has been documented on the Eastern Shore since the mid-nineteenth century. Larger-scale efforts by government agencies and environmental groups such as the Chesapeake Bay Foundation take a more holistic approach to water quality and watershed management for the Bay. Reversing damage to critical sea grasses and marine life from rising water temperatures and pollution can reduce the greenhouse gas emissions driving climate change. For now this problem continues to accelerate and pose a significant threat to the communities around the Chesapeake Bay.

ES53 ROBERT MORRIS INN
c. 1750; 1875 expanded; 1961. 314 N. Morris St.

Known in the 1870s as River View House, this eighteenth-century dwelling was expanded by Albert Robins to capitalize on the growing travel trade in Oxford. The original four-room center-hall house is now encased within the 1875 structure, preserving the eighteenth-century raised pine paneling and woodwork. When expanding the inn Robins added the front porch and a third story within a mansard roof to accommodate more rooms. He named his business after one of Oxford's most prominent early citizens, Robert Morris, an Englishman who arrived in 1738 as a factor for the trading firm Cunliffe Foster and Sons and was the father of the Philadelphia banker by the same name known for financing the American Revolution.

ES54 ACADEMY HOUSE (BRATT HOUSE)
c. 1850. 205 N. Morris St.

This prominent frame structure on a high brick basement is all that survives from the Maryland Military Academy. Founded by General Tench Tilghman in the late 1840s, it was intended to be a preparatory school for the U.S. Naval Academy. The original complex of Greek Revival buildings caught fire in 1855, and only this superintendent's residence survived. The Bratt family owned this house from the 1860s until 1965.

ES55 OXFORD MEWS COMMERCIAL BLOCK
c. 1878. 103–107 S. Morris St.

The T-intersection of Market and Morris streets marks the center as Oxford's municipal and commercial area. The waterfront town park between Morris Street and the Tred Avon River at this location appears on the 1707 plat. The two-story frame commercial building at 103–107 S. Morris, constructed during Oxford's post-railroad economic boom, houses three stores with early display windows. The ensemble is unified by the original decorative parapet and an early-twentieth-century porch. The one-story gable-front former store (c. 1900) at 101 S. Morris now serves as the Oxford Museum. The brick municipal building located across Market Street (1932; 100 N. Morris) moved those functions from a now demolished building nearby. Also noteworthy is the former Oxford Bank (1916–1917; 202 S. Morris), a one-story brick classical building designed by Easton architect Frank Ross.

DORCHESTER COUNTY
CAMBRIDGE AND VICINITY

In 1684 the Maryland Assembly voted to establish a town on the south side of the Choptank River to facilitate the tobacco trade in Dorchester County, making Cambridge one of the oldest colonial cities in Maryland. Gradually the emphasis on tobacco shifted to more diversified agricultural economy. However, the use of enslaved labor and the slave trade continued until the Civil War, as did resistance via the Underground Railroad and Dorchester County's most famous resident, Harriet Tubman (see ES65). Post–Civil War growth was driven by seafood and produce processing and packaging as well as light industry, with Phillips Packing Company emerging as Cambridge's biggest employer.

Industrialization was aided by the expansion of steamboat and railroad transportation, particularly the arrival of the Dorchester and Delaware Railroad, incorporated in 1869. By the turn of the twentieth century, Cambridge was second only to Baltimore in volume of oysters shucked and canned, and more than twenty crab-picking plants

operated in the city. The loss of jobs following the closure of Phillips Packing Company (ES62) in the early 1960s contributed to the civil rights protests here between 1962 and 1967. Led by activist Gloria Richardson, Black residents of Cambridge mobilized against decades of racial discrimination and segregation in employment, housing, and education. The Maryland National Guard was deployed to occupy Cambridge during protests in 1963 and 1967, marking a difficult period in the community's history. Now bisected by U.S. 50, Cambridge retains many excellent historic buildings while trying to encourage cultural tourism related to Tubman and the nearby Blackwater Wildlife Refuge.

ES56 DORCHESTER COUNTY COURTHOUSE
1852–1854, Richard Upjohn; 1930s remodeled, William F. Stone Jr. 206 High St.

Court was being held in the Dorchester County (founded 1669) seat of Cambridge as early as 1695. A brick courthouse built during the 1770s burned in 1852, prompting city officials to commission a replacement on the same site. Richard Upjohn, the prominent New York City architect, provided plans for an Italianate building with a square tower placed asymmetrically, round-arched openings, and wide eaves with bracketed gables. Upjohn was best known for his ecclesiastical architecture, as well as a variety of mid-nineteenth-century picturesque modes. By choosing the nationally known Upjohn, Dorchester County officials signaled the economic importance of Maryland's Lower Eastern Shore in the antebellum era.

While Upjohn's design is still apparent on the exterior, extensive interior renovations took place in the twentieth century, particularly during the 1930s. These changes, which favored a Colonial Revival approach, were overseen by Baltimore architect Stone. His alterations included additions to the southeast elevation of Upjohn's original structure.

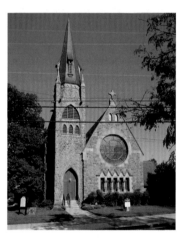

ES57 CHRIST EPISCOPAL CHURCH AND CEMETERY
1883–1884, Charles E. Cassell; 1896 addition. 601 Church St.

Across from the courthouse is the striking serpentine stone Christ Episcopal Church. This venerable congregation began as the parish church for Great Choptank Parish created in 1692 by an act of the

Provincial Assembly as one of the thirty original Church of England parishes in Maryland. The official establishment of the Anglican Church in Maryland represented a reversal of the 1649 guarantee of individual freedom of religion in the colony and followed the shift to a Protestant-led government after William and Mary assumed the English throne.

Many Maryland leaders, including five former governors, were among its worshippers and are buried in the large churchyard cemetery surrounded by a low brick wall, portions of which are from the 1790s. While burials in the cemetery date back to the seventeenth century, the current church was built in 1883 to replace a 1788 structure destroyed by fire.

With guidance from the Reverend Thomas P. Barber, rector at Christ Church from 1849 to 1892 and veteran of many building campaigns throughout Great Choptank Parish, Baltimore architect J. Crawford Neilson was consulted. Charged with guiding a new church design in keeping with the prominence of the parish, the vestry worked with Neilson and visited a variety of churches in Baltimore. Ultimately Neilson's proposed design was deemed too expensive, and another respected Baltimore architect, Charles E. Cassell, was retained.

Cassell was an experienced church architect well versed in the Ecclesiological Movement guiding Episcopalian church design in the nineteenth century. For Christ Church, Cassell offered a full expression of a cruci-

form plan, High Victorian Gothic design, with a rose window and impressive corner entrance tower topped by a spire at the nave end facing High Street. The green serpentine stone facing over granite is laid in an ashlar pattern and accented with sandstone lintels and details for a lively, polychromatic exterior.

The interior continues the ornate approach of the exterior. The nave is separated from transepts and chancel by monumental pointed arches supported on piers of clustered columns with Gothic capitals. The mahogany ceiling of the nave is supported by modified hammerbeam trusses with jig-sawn brackets. The furnishings, fixtures, and many of the stained glass windows, particularly the Tiffany Studios altar window, are original to the 1880s and continue the Gothic motifs. A matching serpentine ashlar addition at the northwest corner from 1896 contains a parish office and was built as a memorial hall named for Reverend Barber.

ES58 GOLDSBOROUGH-PHELPS HOUSE
c. 1793; later additions. 200 High St.

The residential neighborhood northwest of Christ Episcopal Church (ES57) includes some of Cambridge's finest houses, many built by the political elite or prominent businesspeople. This house is one of a few distinguished eighteenth-century structures remaining among the predominantly nineteenth- and early-twentieth-century development. Several generations of the politically active Goldsborough family owned this five-bay, center-hall brick house built for Charles Goldsborough, who served in the U.S. House of Representatives and as governor of Maryland in the early nineteenth century. The original single-pile house received a rear wing shortly after its completion. The front porch and such interior details as plaster ceiling medallions were likely added after 1832.

ES59 LEVI PHILLIPS HOUSE AND ALBANUS PHILLIPS HOUSE
1911–1912, Leon W. Crawford. 312 Mill St.
1912. 314 Mill St.

This pair of early-twentieth-century houses near the corner of Church and Mill streets is of interest for their association with the Phillips family, who were major players in establishing Cambridge as the nationally dominant center for food processing during the early twentieth century. Captain Levi Phillips, so-called from his days piloting an oyster boat, hired Wilmington, Delaware, architect Crawford to design his twenty-two-room house at 312 Mill Street in 1911. Eclectic in design, the brick house has an asymmetrical wraparound porch and Colonial Revival details. Shortly after, Phillips's younger brother, Colonel Albanus Phillips, built an even larger house next door at 314 Mill. Although not attributed to Crawford, it has a similar eclectic mix of decorative detail.

ES60 PHILLIPS HARDWARE
1910–1911, J. Benjamin Brown. 447 Race St.

In addition to founding Phillips Packing Co. in 1902, the Phillips brothers and W. Grason Winterbottom established Phillips Hardware Company in 1904. Their first store on Race St. was destroyed by the 1910 downtown fire, but they immediately rebuilt on several nearby parcels, including one owned by Brown, a local architect and builder. He designed their new three-story building with a two-tone brick facade, pressed metal cornices, and leaded glass transoms over the store windows with the initials *PHC*. In addition to retail space, both the hardware and packing company office space was in this building. Phillips Hardware is still a noteworthy commercial landmark dominating the corner of Race and Muir streets.

ES61 PINE STREET NEIGHBORHOOD
c. 1870–1930. Bounded by Pine, High, and Washington sts.

This is the largest and most cohesive African American residential neighborhood on the Eastern Shore, much of which was built as prototypical worker housing for local seafood packing companies. The community was established by free Blacks in the 1820s, centered around the newly established Waugh Chapel United Methodist Church, forming the oldest African American congregation in Cambridge. The region's large free Black population is attributed to the early shift from slave-based tobacco to less labor-intensive grain production and the impact of local abolitionist Quakers and Methodists, causing the population to rise from 77 in 1755 to nearly 3,000 by 1820. However, the extant buildings largely reflect post–Civil War Black migration, driven by jobs with the newly developed Dorchester and Delaware Railroad and the oyster- and fruit-packing industries.

The houses are mostly frame, two-story, two-bay, gable-front buildings with porches, exemplified by 605–745 Washington Street. Also appearing are four-bay, gable-front semidetached units with porches, seen together with single units at 700–728 High Street (south side). Similar owner-built examples are distinguished from company-built houses by their larger size and more ornate features, such as 518 Pine Street (c. 1900) with its original bracketed porch and entrance with transom and sidelights, merchant Daniel O. Seward's brick house (c. 1890; 635 High Street; *pictured*), and local butcher Cyrus St. Clair Jr.'s eclectic house (c. 1888; 423 High). Black-owned businesses included J. F. Henry's house and store (c. 1890; 518 Muir Street) and the mansard-roofed Hayes Drug store (c. 1880; 622 Pine). The Waugh Chapel United Methodist (rebuilt 2008; 425 High) and Bethel African Methodist Episcopal (1879, 1903; 623 Pine) churches reflect the influence of the Methodists and form anchors for the community.

ES62 PHILLIPS PACKING CO., PLANT F
c. 1920s. 411A Dorchester Ave.

Partners Levi and Albanus Phillips and W. Grason Winterbottom founded Phillips Packing Company in 1902 with a single plant and grew to national prominence in the food processing and packing industry, supplying oysters, fruit, and vegetables. Most of their extensive manufacturing facilities have been demolished, but Plant F, the remaining factory, is currently undergoing a mixed-use rehabilitation. Phillips Packing purchased the brick former furniture factory in 1930 and used it to can vegetables such as tomatoes, lima beans, and sweet and white potatoes. Government contracts to supply C and K rations to the military during World Wars I and II kept Phillips Packing busy. Admiral Richard Byrd also carried Phillips products on his Antarctic expeditions in the 1930s, largely due to his friendship with Albanus Phillips, a colorful character who modeled himself on Theodore Roosevelt.

Packing Plant F was sold to Consolidated Foods in 1957 and closed completely in the early 1960s. The next generation of the

Phillips family shifted the business into seafood restaurants and crab products still available today. The redevelopment plans for "The Packing House" have been developed by the Eastern Shore Land Conservancy and Cross Street Partners (formerly historic preservation development company Struever Bros. Eccles and Rouse). They intend to highlight local food and products and eventually include a new green space dubbed Cannery Park. Another surviving piece of the once extensive Phillips complex is the former office for Plant B, a c. 1930 Colonial Revival building located nearby at 16 Washington Street.

ES63 STANLEY INSTITUTE MUSEUM (ROCK SCHOOL)
c. 1875. 2400 MD 16

This quintessential one-room schoolhouse is the oldest and most intact building erected specifically for the education of African American children in Dorchester County. It was part of a post–Civil War Reconstruction initiative in response to state legislation passed in 1872. Typical of rural schoolhouses, it is a simple rectangular, gable-front frame building with a front vestibule. The school started in 1867 when a smaller structure was moved to this site for use as both a school and meeting place for a newly formed African American Methodist congregation, who then built Christ Rock United Methodist Church (ES64) across the street. Based on the combined use of timber-frame construction and factory-made building components, it is likely that parts of the earlier building were repurposed. Built as Colored School No. 3, it became known as Stanley Institute, named for the Reverend Ezekiel Stanley, a founder and president of the first board of trustees. The school was used continuously until 1966. It was restored and opened as a museum in 2007, interpreting the history of African American education in the county.

ES64 CHRIST ROCK UNITED METHODIST CHURCH
1875; 1889, 1910–1911 additions. 2403 Rock Dr.

The church was erected concurrent with the Stanley Institute (ES63) by its African American congregation, many of whom migrated to this area after the Civil War. Like several rural churches across the Eastern Shore, the design was influenced by a catalog of architectural patterns published by the Methodist Board of Church Extension. A vernacular expression of Gothic Revival, it was built of hewn and sawn lumber as a simple, gable-front building with a central entrance. A six-foot rear extension and the current interior finishes were made in 1889. In 1910–1911, the corner entrance tower was built and the original doorway replaced by a large colored-glass lancet window. A Sunday school room with choir loft above added to the rear includes a mix of reused bays that contribute to its unique character. The church is the oldest of four extant post–Civil War Black churches built on the Lower Eastern Shore.

ES65 HARRIET TUBMAN UNDERGROUND RAILROAD VISITOR CENTER

2017, GWWO Architects. 4860 Golden Hill Rd.

After her escape to Philadelphia in 1849, Harriet Tubman, born Araminta Ross and enslaved in Dorchester County, boldly ferried enslaved people to freedom as a conductor on the Underground Railroad. During the Civil War she continued her work as a spy, scout, and nurse and became a prominent abolitionist and suffragist. The Maryland Park Service and National Park Service joined forces in the early 2010s to create a historical park commemorating Tubman's life and work on the Eastern Shore. Few historic structures remain directly related to Tubman, but the marshy landscape of the park, adjacent to Blackwater Wildlife Refuge, evokes her experiences and those of other nineteenth-century residents. In 2021 archaeologists located the site of a cabin likely owned by Tubman's father, Benjamin Ross, on land recently added to the refuge. This rare find was immediately celebrated as a tangible link to a place where Tubman spent formative young adult years, from roughly 1839 to 1844.

Opened in 2017, the Visitor Center for the new park was designed by the Baltimore firm GWWO Architects, who also designed the visitor center for Fort McHenry National Monument (BC57) in Baltimore. Here the concept is titled "The View North," to recall the journey north to freedom from slavery. The building takes the abstracted form of a row of gable-roofed structures, frankly contemporary but intended to signify the various barns or safehouses on the Underground Railroad. The large sections house administrative offices to one side and exhibit and visitor spaces to the other, with an opening to the north and the "legacy garden" at the middle. The low glass and steel connecting hyphens also offer views of the surrounding landscape.

ES66 NAUSE-WAIWASH LONGHOUSE (TRINITY METHODIST EPISCOPAL CHURCH)

1894. 4201 Maple Dam Rd.

Built as Trinity Methodist Episcopal Church and later used by the Hughes African American Methodist congregation from 1955 to 1998, the church now serves as the nontraditional longhouse of the Nause-Waiwash Native American tribe. The Nause-Waiwash are the descendants of the Nanticoke, Choptank, and Pocomoke Indians who were the original inhabitants of this area of Dorchester County. The tribes were officially recognized by the colonial government in a 1720 treaty, but by midcentury the treaty was dissolved and the tribes were forced to flee into the marshes. Although this building bears no resemblance to the traditional longhouse, as seen in a replica built on the site of Handsell at Indiantown (ES70), it serves as a permanent location for tribal ceremonies and gatherings. The plain meetinghouse is a rectangular, gabled-front building with a double-door entrance with transom and a rear shed-roofed apse.

ES67 BUCKTOWN STORE

c. 1860. 4303 Bucktown Rd.

Bucktown Store is known as the site of one of Harriet Tubman's first acts of resistance in 1835, when she refused to help an overseer tie up another enslaved person. A heavy weight thrown by the overseer struck her in the head and nearly killed her. This incident caused Tubman to have seizures for the rest of her life and is often cited as evidence of her strength and determination. This carefully restored one-story store was likely built c. 1860, replacing an earlier iteration of the store where the famous incident took place. It is a rare surviving example of a mid-nineteenth-century rural general store in the state.

VIENNA

ES68 JAMES K. LEWIS WHARF HOUSE (OLD CUSTOM HOUSE)

c. 1825–1845. Water St. at Church Sts.

This building serves as a reminder of Vienna's early maritime commerce, built as the private wharf house or office for merchant James K. Lewis. Vienna was named one of Dorchester County's ports of entry in 1706, although this building dates to a post–Revolutionary era construction boom driven by the emergent grain trade. The town once had a federal customhouse that operated from 1791 to 1866, along with a tobacco inspection station established in 1747, but neither is extant. Only this private office remains of the buildings that once facilitated the town's lucrative maritime trade.

The diminutive, gable-front frame building is banked along the waterfront, with an entrance into a brick storage cellar facing the Nanticoke River and an office entrance at street level. A large board-and-batten door with strap hinges, and small openings to either side wall covered with iron bars provided a secure location for valuable goods (a post-shipment granary formerly stood adjacent). The office interior is finished with plaster, and a ladder stair provides access to an unfinished storage loft.

Lewis's adjacent residence (1861; 100 Church Street) is one of the earliest and most noted Italianate houses in the county. It is built of pressed brick with fine mortar joints and is three stories in height, with distinctive half-story windows in the upper level and a low-hipped roof. A frame back building dates to c. 1840.

ES69 HURST BROTHERS SERVICE STATION
1927. 303 Race St.

This was one of the first purpose-built automobile service stations on the Eastern Shore, erected on the site of the Creighton blacksmith and wagon shop, ushering in a new era in transportation. It was built for brothers A. Milby and J. Lloyd Hurst and operated by the family into the 1970s. It contained a lunch counter and sold hunting and fishing licenses, becoming a popular local meeting spot. Typical of service stations of the era, it is a rectangular frame building with a hipped roof extending to form a drive-through canopy to shelter the gas pumps and has a double-door entrance flanked by display windows. It was purchased by the town commissioners and since 2002 has served as a local history museum.

ES70 HANDSELL AND INDIANTOWN
c. 1770; 1837 rebuilt; 2015–2020 restored. 4835 Vienna Rhodesdale Rd.

Handsell represents the dwellings of affluent settlers to Dorchester County, located near the confluence of the Nanticoke River and Chicone Creek and the site of an early Native American village. The well-crafted brick facade of this Georgian manor house has been preserved, although the house was rebuilt in a more vernacular tradition following a fire likely set by raiding British privateers c. 1780. The early house was a full two stories with a shallow front pavilion, set on a raised basement that housed the kitchen and had a central-passage, double-pile plan. It was built for English-born gentleman-merchant and member of the Maryland Assembly Henry Steele and his wife, Ann Billings Steele, daughter of an Oxford merchant. Handsell was left in ruins, with the facade and sections of the side walls remaining, until purchased by John Shehee and rebuilt in 1837, a date ascertained through dendrochronology. The rebuilt house is only a single-pile, with the repaired section marked by common-bond brickwork. By c. 1850 the house was tenanted, and c. 1930 it once again was abandoned.

The Handsell tract was patented in 1665 to Thomas Taylor, a military officer and Indian trader licensed to maintain the interests of its Nanticoke and Chicone tribe inhabitants. Although recognized by the colonial government in 1720, their claim was later revoked, the tribes were relocated, and the property was sold. The area, however, is still referred to as Indiantown. To honor their early occupation near the waterways that bear their names, an authentic replica of a native longhouse (*pictured*) was constructed in 2014 by the Nanticoke Historic Preservation Commission, also undertaking Handsell's restoration.

WICOMICO COUNTY
SALISBURY AND VICINITY

ES71 WICOMICO COUNTY COURTHOUSE

1878, E. M. Butz; 1936 addition, Malone and Williams; 1974–1975; mid-1990s additions. 101 N. Division St.

Wicomico County was created in 1867 from the partition of Somerset and Worcester counties. The design of its new courthouse, built a decade later, embraced High Victorian Gothic, then fashionable in Salisbury. Much of downtown Salisbury was destroyed by a fire in 1860 and the Civil War delayed rebuilding. In the 1870s, dredging to improve the Wicomico River channel to Salisbury and railroad construc-tion transformed the county seat into the most important transportation hub on the Lower Eastern Shore with a thriving trade in lumber, produce, grain, and other commodities.

When the new courthouse was completed in 1878, it was the largest and most elaborately decorated building in Salisbury. Architect Butz of western Pennsylvania designed several courthouses in this period with a similar eclectic approach; W. V. Hughes was the builder. The courthouse's polychromatic brick facade has stone and brick banded arches over the windows and patterned brick with black accents in the eaves and belt courses. Most striking are the two corner towers with steep mansard slate roofs; the taller northwest tower features a clock. The courthouse survived another disastrous downtown fire in 1886, after which the late-nineteenth-century building boom continued.

As Salisbury continued to grow into the largest city on the Eastern Shore, more space was needed for government functions. In 1936 a large addition was built to the courthouse's rear. Funded with New Deal public works monies, the three-story brick addition on a tall limestone basement is ornamented with stone pilasters and Art Deco bas-reliefs. It was the work of the local firm of Malone and Williams, who designed a similar courthouse a few years later in Cecil County (ES11). Further large additions in the mid-1970s and mid-1990s do not encroach on the earlier sections.

ES72 FAITH COMMUNITY CHURCH (ASBURY UNITED METHODIST CHURCH)
1887–1888, Jackson C. Gott; 1928 addition. 225 N. Division St.

This Romanesque-influenced structure was built as the Asbury United Methodist Church for one of the earliest Methodist congregations in Wicomico County, established in 1778. Methodism spread to the Eastern Shore in 1772 in an effort to challenge the Church of England, and by 1778 Methodist societies had formed in Salisbury and Quantico. Initially meetings were held in members' houses; a frame meetinghouse was built c. 1801, replaced in 1856. The current building was erected

after the second church was destroyed in the city fire of 1886. Executed in Port Deposit granite, the auditorium-style sanctuary is laid out on a diagonal axis, aligning the pulpit with the corner entrance tower. The sanctuary is lit by a colored-glass lantern that sits atop the pyramidal slate roof. The congregation was named for noted evangelist minister Francis Asbury, a missionary from England in 1771, who became the bishop of the Methodist Episcopal Church. By the 1950s, the congregation had outgrown the building, selling it to Faith Community.

ES73 POPLAR HILL
c. 1795–1805. 117 Elizabeth St.

A rare survivor of early Salisbury, Poplar Hill is one of the largest and most finely detailed Federal houses on the Eastern Shore. It was begun by Levin Hardy, a local merchant formerly of Newport, Rhode Island, on the 357-acre farm he purchased in 1795. Before the house could be completed, however, Hardy died, and the task fell to physician John Huston, who purchased it in 1805. While Poplar Hill's sophisticated styling has been attributed to Hardy's urbane Newport roots, it may have been influenced by the noted gable-front Chanceford (ES97).

Poplar Hill's exceptional detailing includes an elaborate frontispiece and Palladian windows to the front and rear. The plan encompasses a broad central passage and stair hall, bisected by an ornately carved elliptical arch. The dining room, the largest room, and a back hall to an adjoining service wing occupy the east side, with a parlor and private family chamber to the west. The farm was subdivided post–Civil War to form part of the upscale Newtown (ES74) suburban community that now surrounds it. The house is owned by the City of Salisbury and operates as a house museum.

ES74 NEWTOWN HISTORIC DISTRICT

Mid-19th–early 20th century. Encompassing Division, Broad, and Williams sts.

Newtown is one of Salisbury's earliest and most exclusive suburbs. Development began around the turn of the nineteenth century with the division of a 75-acre tract known as Haynie's Settlement, referred to as New Town by the 1820s. Growth began in earnest after the Civil War and the arrival of the railroad, and that coupled with the industrialization of the 1880s through the 1920s sparked population growth and housing demand. Salisbury was then one of the most prosperous towns on the peninsula, and nowhere is it more evident than in Newtown, with large houses in a range of revival styles. Representative examples include the Greek Revival– and Italianate-influenced house (c. 1850; 325 N. Division Street) built for phy-

sician Cathell Humphreys and his wife Isabella Huston of Poplar Hill (ES73) and the similarly styled Park Hall (1856; 115 Broad Street) built for his brother, Humphrey Humphreys. Also notable are the Queen Anne Gillis-Grier House (1887–1888; 401 N. Division) and the late Second Empire house (1897–1898; 200 E. William Street) built for Thomas Cooper, editor of the *Salisbury Advertiser.*

ES75 PEMBERTON HALL

1741. 5561 Plantation Ln.

Pemberton Hall is an exceptional, early gambrel-roofed Chesapeake house and the oldest house in Salisbury. It exhibits decorative Flemish-bond brickwork with glazed headers and a commodious three-room plan, a variation on the pervasive hall-parlor plan to include a separate dining room, reflecting the emerging importance of dining within polite society. Quality finishes set it apart from others of its era, including an expansive hall with exposed joists, paneled walls with pilasters, and built-in cupboard. The hall adjoins back-to-back dining and warming rooms, each with a corner fireplace. A separate "cook house" built in 1785 was later joined by a hyphen (reconstructed).

Pemberton Hall was erected at the head of the Wicomico River, where its owner, planter and shipping merchant Isaac Handy, operated a commercial landing. The house stayed in the Handy family until 1835 and remained largely unchanged into the twentieth century. By midcentury, however, it had fallen into disrepair, and in 1963 the Pemberton Hall Foundation was formed to save it. Having been restored, it is now the centerpiece of a county park and open to the public.

WHITEHAVEN

ES76 WHITEHAVEN HOTEL

c. 1810–1815; c. 1883 additions.
2685 Whitehaven Rd.

Once a busy port on the Wicomico River, Whitehaven is now a quiet residential village of primarily late-nineteenth-century houses. The ferry here was established in 1688 and still transports patrons the short distance across the Wicomico. The only remaining commercial establishment in town is the Whitehaven Hotel located next to the ferry landing.

An early-eighteenth-century hall-and-parlor house is encased within the late-nineteenth-century expansion with a mansard roof providing additional lodging space. The shift to automobile travel and dredging the river up to Salisbury ended Whitehaven's heyday, and the hotel closed in the 1940s. After years as a private residence, the hotel was restored in the 1990s and is now a bed-and-breakfast. Although the cannery and other commercial structures in Whitehaven are gone, other landmarks include the Whitehaven Schoolhouse (c. 1886; 1908; 100 Church Street) and Whitehaven United Methodist Church (1892; 108 Church), as well as the late-nineteenth-century houses along River Street.

SOMERSET COUNTY
PRINCESS ANNE AND VICINITY

The establishment of Princess Anne was authorized by the Maryland General Assembly in 1733, in response to local citizens eager to form a commercial center at the head of the Manokin River. The town began with 25 acres of David Brown's Beckford tract, laid out in a grid of 30 lots. Representing an area of the Lower Eastern Shore unsurpassed in wealth and influence, Princess Anne was designated the seat of Somerset County in 1742. Growth escalated with post-Revolutionary increases in the demand for grain, the region's staple crop. The period is represented by several Federal-style buildings, none finer than Beckford (ES82) and Teackle Mansion (ES78). The earliest extant commercial building is the Washington Hotel (1797–1798; 1838 addition;

11784 Somerset Avenue), begun when Zadock Long added a "billiard house" to an existing dwelling and opened it as a tavern. His son Edward H. C. Long "rebuilt and repaired" the tavern, leasing it to various keepers, before it was reimagined by new owners as the Washington Hotel in 1856.

In the post–Civil War era, the arrival of the Eastern Shore Railroad encouraged the development of a flour-milling complex and a cannery, while offering work to emancipated persons. The prosperity of that era is exhibited by the large number of Queen Anne, Italianate, and Colonial Revival houses, such as the Charles H. Hayman House (1898; 30491 Princess William), and by early-twentieth-century civic buildings such as the new courthouse (ES77). Commercial buildings date primarily between 1880 and 1910, the most elaborate being the brick Cohn Store Building (c. 1908; 11760 Somerset Avenue) with its bold granite cornice and round-arched windows.

ES77 SOMERSET COUNTY COURTHOUSE
1904–1905, Frank E. and Henry R. Davis. 30512 Prince William St.

The Colonial Revival brick courthouse is the third in Princess Anne, replacing an 1833 gable-front building. Its classical design harkens back to the county's eighteenth-century heyday, as did other civic-minded buildings of the period, including the Bank of Somerset (1903; 11732 Somerset Avenue) and Peoples Bank of

Somerset (c. 1907; 30513 Prince William). The courthouse is distinguished by shallow central pedimented pavilions to the front and Somerset Avenue side, and by contrasting granite Ionic-columned portico, jack-arch keystone lintels, stringcourse, and dentiled cornice. Its architects, Frank and Henry Davis, were from Baltimore, while contractor W. P. Pusey and Sons hailed from Snow Hill.

ES78 TEACKLE MANSION
1802–1805; 1818–1819 hyphens and wings; 1996 restored. 11736 Mansion St.

This is a refined Federal interpretation of the Maryland five-part-plan house, built by Littleton D. Teackle, a merchant who exchanged local grain for imported coffee, cocoa, and sugar and served as first president of the Bank of Somerset and in the Maryland House of Delegates from 1824 to 1836. His house was the largest in Princess Anne, rivaling the finest on the Eastern Shore. The gable-front main block and wings and the exquisite Federal detailing were likely inspired by Wye House (ES48). In 1814, the wings were extended to form hyphens connecting to new wings. Interestingly, the shed roofs of the hyphens appear as two stories to the front only while the parapets of the wings mimic the gable front of the main block. The interior features ornamental plaster details and axial and radial symmetry created by false apertures such as the windows in the partition wall that also provide borrowed light from the parlor.

Teackle Mansion is prominently situated at the terminus of Prince William Street, facing downtown. Now owned by the Somerset County Historical Society, it was restored in 1996 and opened to the public. Nearby is the surviving of two gable-front houses (c. 1805; 30466 Prince William Street), built to accommodate free and enslaved servants.

ES79 SETH D. VENABLES HOUSE (SIMPLICITY)
c. 1853. 11748 Mansion St.

Local house carpenter Seth Venables built a number of Federal and Greek Revival houses in Princess Anne likely inspired by nearby Teackle Mansion (ES78), although relatively staid in design. Known appropriately as Simplicity is this two-story, three-bay, side hall-and-parlor frame dwelling he built for himself and his family. Francis Barnes House (1853–1854; 30449 Prince William Street) is perhaps the most elaborate of Venables's documented designs, combining elements of Greek Revival and Italianate modes embellished with lively details. The William Lecates House (c. 1852; 30459 Prince William) provides an excellent example of Venables's Greek Revival designs, featuring a two-story portico. The earliest is the Judge Levin T. H. Irvin house (c. 1850; 30480 Prince William), a gable-front dwelling with corner pilasters and a side-hall plan, a design similar to the house Venables built for Joseph B. Brinkley (c. 1856–1857) at 11619 Somerset Avenue.

ES80 LITTLETON LONG HOUSE
c. 1830. 11696 Church St.

Built for local merchant Littleton Long, this is the most intact and well executed of numerous gable-front Federal-period houses in town. The symmetrical three-bay facade with pedimented gable front with a circular window mirrors the main block of Teackle Mansion (ES78), although of frame construction. Like Teackle Mansion, the plan of Long's house encompasses a transverse hall with a stair to one end, twin parlors to the rear, and a two-story service wing. A simplified version of Long's house is seen in one of the few extant antebellum commercial buildings in town that he built as his store (c. 1848; 11787 Somerset Avenue).

ES81 GLEBE HOUSE
1784–1785, William Bowland, builder; 1970s restored. Market Ln., on unnamed street at rear of motel

Glebe House is significant both as a regionally specific, eighteenth-century domestic building form and for its association with the Anglican Church of Maryland. Used by middling Chesapeake planters, the form is identified by its one-and-a-half-story height, steeply pitched gable roof, four-room configuration, and Flemish-bond brick end walls. The four-room plan encompasses an entrance and stair hall with an unheated room behind it, with two unequally sized adjoining rooms to the other side, using the shared chimney to create corner fireplaces. Further distinguishing the house are its fine finishes, including a two-run open stair with heavy turned balusters and raised-panel hearth walls.

The house is significant historically as the only designated "glebe house" on the Lower Eastern Shore, built for the support of the local Anglican priest. It sits near the edge of town, no longer maintaining its plantation landscape. Early documents record its specifications and identify its builder as William Bowland. It was sold in the post–Revolutionary War era and held by private owners thereafter. It was abandoned when acquired by the Somerset County Historical Society and restored in the 1970s.

ES82 BECKFORD
c. 1830. 11700 Mansion St.

Prominently sited on the western edge of Princess Anne, Beckford was built for John Dennis, who served in the Maryland House of Delegates and from 1797 to 1805 in the U.S. House of Representatives. This house is indicative of the shift from Georgian to Federal design starting to appear around the state. Although five-bays wide and three-bays deep with robust proportions, Beckford features slender chimneys and finely detailed ornamentation rather than the thick moldings characteristic of the late eighteenth century. Shallow plaster panels at the belt course between the first and second floor are similar to those seen at the Teackle Mansion (ES78), built around the same time.

Inside, the first floor is divided into five rooms, three across the front, with a stair hall at the center, and the two principal rooms at the rear. The finest molded plaster decorations and mantels decorated with neoclassical urns and swags, likely imported from Philadelphia, appear in these parlors. The architectural sophistication and fine craftmanship of Beckford illustrate the prominence of the Dennis family and Princess Anne's growing importance as a port on the Manokin River at the turn of the nineteenth century.

ES83 COTTMAN HOUSE
c. 1884. 11695 Beckford Ave.

This two-story frame house built for Isaac and Priscilla Cottman offers an example of nineteenth-century African American home ownership in Princess Anne. It was renovated by the Somerset Historical Trust starting in 2006 as a rental property and sold to private owners in 2019. The Trust raised the house onto brick piers and added a one-story rear ell. Next door at 11685 and at 11679 Beckford are the two remaining of five matching c. 1870 tenant houses formerly on this block. They each had a two-story one-bay section joined at the side to a one-and-a-half-story section, with the house standing on brick piers and the side gable roofs covered with sheet tin.

ES84 METROPOLITAN UNITED METHODIST CHURCH
1886. 30522 Dr. William P. Hytche Blvd.

The trustees of John Wesley Methodist Episcopal Church purchased this lot, the former site of Somerset County's eighteenth-century jail, in 1884. The Reverend Joseph R. Waters required a more centrally located and larger church for his growing African American congregation, which had been founded in 1841 on a rural site outside of town. The cornerstone was laid in 1886 for this Gothic Revival brick church that features a tall bell tower at the front-gabled entrance. The tower is topped by a pyramidal roof and the belfry openings are decorated with original spindlework.

ES85 UNIVERSITY OF MARYLAND EASTERN SHORE

1886 founded; 1938–1954 campus reconstructed, E. Wilson Booth; later additions. 1 Backbone Rd.

Now a campus in the state university system, the University of Maryland Eastern Shore has a long history as a privately established HBCU (historically black college and university). In 1886, the same year his new church, the Metropolitan United Methodist Church (ES84) was built, the Reverend Joseph R. Waters helped found Princess Anne Academy. The Delaware Conference of the Methodist Church and the Centenary Bible Institute of Baltimore worked together to create an institution of higher learning, mainly to train Black ministers. In 1890, the federal government ruled that Maryland, along with states to the south, would forfeit Morrill Act land-grant college funding if they did not make provisions to accommodate Black students. In order to avoid integrating the existing land-grant school in College Park (CR25), officials negotiated with Princess Anne Academy to provide a land-grant curriculum to African American students and designated the school the Eastern Branch of the Maryland Agricultural College.

Despite this agreement, the college remained private until 1926, and then from 1926 to 1936 it was administered by Morgan College, the Centenary Biblical Institute school outside of Baltimore (now Morgan State University; see BC111). Finally, in 1936, administrative control was transferred to the Board of Regents of the University of Maryland, setting the stage for a slow process of rebuilding what was then called Maryland State College.

Today the historic core of the sprawling campus is the grouping of Colonial Revival buildings, most built between 1938 and 1954, arranged in a quadrangle around a wide lawn lined with paths and mature trees. With buildings designed by Salisbury architect E. Wilson Booth over a sixteen-year period, this ensemble created a grand setting for the college in the tradition of Beaux-Arts campus planning. These buildings replaced frame ones to meet the design and construction standards adopted by the State of Maryland for its university system in the mid-twentieth century. University President Harry Clifton Byrd was brutally frank that his motivation for seeking New Deal funding for the Princess Anne campus was to avoid admitting Black students to College Park. Just a few years before, in 1935, the University of Maryland was forced to admit Donald Gaines Murray to its law school after a successful lawsuit brought by Charles Hamilton Houston and a young Thurgood Marshall.

Major rebuilding was funded by the Works Progress Administration (WPA) and first saw the completion of Bird Hall (1938–1940) and J. T. Williams Hall (1938–1940, formerly the main administration building, Maryland Hall) on the southwest end of the quadrangle. Somerset Hall (1940), next to Bird Hall along the lawn, was a massive men's dormitory and was joined to Harford Hall (1940) behind it by a one-story brick colonnade. Next is Wilson Hall, a temple-front building with a monumental Doric portico also built in 1940 to house the Department of English, Modern Languages, and Education. Additional buildings around the lawn were built after World War II, such as Frederick Douglass Library (1969). Trigg Hall, on a tall basement with a full Ionic portico, was built in 1954 at the other end of the quadrangle lawn to house the Department of Agricultural Science, and Waters Dining Hall (1950) was constructed on the west side of the lawn across from Somerset Hall. Carver Hall Science Building (1972) filled the remaining open space on the east side of the lawn after full recognition as University of Maryland Eastern Shore in 1970. Continued expansion of the campus in recent decades has added new groupings of buildings around quadrangles to the west and north.

ES86 WATERLOO
c. 1750–1760; early 19th century; 1959 additions. 28822 Mt. Vernon Rd.

Waterloo is one of five pre–Revolutionary War houses that represent the height of architectural achievement on the Eastern Shore. According to architectural historian Paul Touart, few Somerset County planters of the mid-eighteenth century aspired to such ostentatious architectural statements as Waterloo's owner, Henry Waggaman, one of the county's wealthiest planters and a member of the Provincial Assembly of Maryland. Like others in the region, Waggaman likely grew a combination of tobacco, corn, and wheat utilizing enslaved labor. Waterloo exhibits exceptional brickwork, including glazed checkerboard and diaper patterns, highlighted by contrasting stone quoining. Rather than adopt the traditional center-passage plan, Waggaman chose a four-room plan manifested in a two-and-a-half-story, pedimented gable-front main block, the first of its kind in the area. A stair hall with an unusual three-flight twisted-baluster stair sits to the front of a large parlor, with adjoining rooms with corner fireplaces to the other side. A hyphen and kitchen wing were added later.

Waterloo was owned by several prominent local families during the nineteenth century before it was purchased by the county for use as an almshouse, from 1864 to 1948. Once again a private residence, the flanking hyphen and bedroom wing were added in 1959. None of the plantation-era outbuildings remain, although the office of physician Littleton Handy, who owned Waterloo briefly during the 1850s, is extant. It may have been Handy who first called the property Waterloo.

ES87 ALMODINGTON

c. 1750; c. 1785, mid-20th-century additions. 10373 Locust Point Rd.

This is one of Somerset County's most elaborate mid-eighteenth-century plantation houses and a distinguished representative of the area's rich decorative brick-work. Almodington includes glazed headers and checker-board patterns, as well as gauged brick segmental lintels with alternating glazed bricks and ornamental belt courses. It likewise boasts rare plaster cove cornices, original twelve-over-twelve sash windows, and a pediment-ed, Ionic-columned Georgian porch.

Situated on the Manokin River, the house was built for John Elzey II on the Almodington tract patented for his grandfather, John Elzey in 1663. This area, known as Manokin Hundred, and neighboring Monie and Great Annemessex hundreds had the largest number of brick dwellings and those over a thousand square feet than anywhere else in Somerset County. Almodington represents the emergence of the brick, two-story, single-pile, center-passage house, superseding the frame, one-and-a-half-story, hall-and-parlor-plan dwellings of previous generations. Such houses foretold of the development of even more complex, double-pile Georgian houses, such as Ratcliffe Manor (ES47).

CRISFIELD

ES88 WARD BROTHERS WORKSHOP

c. 1900, c. 1960s. 3199 Sackertown Rd.

Occupying a marshy lot outside of Crisfield, this building was the workshop of Lemuel Ward Jr. and Steve Ward, famed as the fathers of twentieth-century decorative wildlife carving in the United States. The brothers were barbers by trade and began carving in the folk tradition of wood hunting decoys by 1918. They started incorporating more lifelike features into their work, and by the 1930s their decoys were widely renowned. After a national award in 1948, they began expanding their interest in purely decorative wildlife carving, garnering national attention for this work in the 1950s and 1960s. They lived their entire lives at this property, in an adjacent c. 1880 house built by their father, which was demolished in 2013. The workshop consists of three frame structures that were combined in the early 1960s. The original two-room section at the north was the first shop. When the brothers gave up barbering to pursue decoy carving full-time, they moved their father's c. 1900 barbershop back from the road and attached it to the workshop. They then added a lean-to structure on the south to serve as a painting studio and unified the three parts behind a false front. The Crisfield Heritage Foundation now offers tours of the workshop. In addition, many examples of their work are on display at Salisbury University's Ward Museum of Waterfowl Art (1991, Davis, Bowen and Friedel; 909 S. Schumaker Drive).

WORCESTER COUNTY
POCOMOKE CITY

With its deep-water river port and railroad connections, Pocomoke City developed in the late nineteenth century into a thriving economic center for Worcester County and the lower Delmarva Peninsula. A small settlement in earlier decades, it was incorporated as Newtown in 1865. Around this time the ferry crossing of the Pocomoke River was replaced by a bridge providing a connection to neighboring Somerset County. It was after reincorporation as Pocomoke City in 1878 that expansion began in earnest, with many residents employed in the local shipyards, canneries, or lumber mills. The town center experienced devastating fires in 1888 and 1922, prompting rebuilding of many two- and three-story commercial buildings along Market Street in brick or stone. After the later fire, Market Street was widened to better align with the new steel and concrete bascule movable bridge (1920, J. E. Greiner Company) over the Pocomoke River. Because of these fires, Pocomoke City's commercial core has a noteworthy assortment of early-twentieth-century buildings while the residential neighborhoods offer a full complement of late-nineteenth- and twentieth-century house types ranging from the grand houses of mill owners and merchants to the tenant houses built for workers.

ES89 DELMARVA DISCOVERY CENTER (DUNCAN BROTHERS GARAGE)
c. 1922; 2009 renovated. 2 Market St.

Pocomoke City is situated beside U.S. 13, a north–south route along the Delmarva Peninsula first planned in 1925. The early-twentieth-century nationwide movement for improved roads received increased urgency with the burgeoning popularity of the automobile. This period also saw a shift to trucks instead of steamboats for transporting local produce and seafood to market. Duncan Brothers Garage was built at the foot of the new bridge shortly after its completion to serve this clientele. This L-shaped Colonial Revival building was renovated to house the Delmarva Discovery Center, a natural and cultural history museum. An intact Colonial Revival Atlantic Red Star gas station (c. 1922) is located on the same lot as the Discovery Center.

ES90 MAR-VA THEATER
1927; 1937 interior renovated. 103 Market St.

Frank Bartlett, owner of Berlin's Globe Theater (c. 1917; 12 Broad Street, now a restaurant), purchased several lots on Market Street after the 1922 fire. Originally opened as a vaudeville and silent movie theater in 1927, the Mar-Va began showing talkies in the 1930s, around the same time it received an extensive Art Deco interior renovation. The theater was designed for racially segregated seating in the balcony including a separate entrance for Black patrons on the north end of the facade, and separate ticket booth, lavatory, and later concession stand on the upper floor. The theater closed in 1993, failing into disrepair. Purchased by a community group in 2003, the theater was renovated and reopened as a performing arts center and movie theater in 2009, making it with Church Hill Theatre (ES38) one of the few surviving and functioning historic theaters on the Eastern Shore.

ES91 COSTEN HOUSE
c. 1876. 206 Market St.

This house is a fine example of the factory-produced wood architectural decoration popular in the late nineteenth century and manufactured in Pocomoke City's steam-powered lumber, shingle, and planing mills. The jigsawn brackets and vergeboards and turned porch posts enliven a rather conservative center-hall I-house and give it a fashionable Italianate veneer. Physician Isaac Costen and his wife, Olivia Adams Costen, purchased the house shortly after its construction. Costen also served in the Maryland General Assembly starting in 1881 and as the first mayor of Pocomoke City in 1888. Local preservationists with the Spirit of Newtown Committee acquired the house when it was threatened with demolition in the 1970s and helped turn it into a city-owned house museum.

SNOW HILL

Throughout its history, Snow Hill, located alongside the Pocomoke River that feeds into the Chesapeake Bay, has enjoyed a relative prosperity manifested in its architectural cityscape. First recognized by Native Americans for its wealth of natural resources, the town site drew English settlers as early as the 1640s. When the Maryland Assembly passed the Act for the Advancement of Trade in 1683 to establish five new towns in the region, Snow Hill's advantageous location earned it a place. It thrived as a shipping port for goods extending trade to the Eastern Seaboard and the West Indies, prompting its designation as county seat in 1742. The town was named for a district in London, the site of a major water conduit.

The late-nineteenth-century decline in the Eastern Shore's maritime trade, as other modes of transport took its place, only provided new opportunities for Snow Hill when the railroad arrived in 1870. It was then that such industries as lumber and food processing opened along the banks of the Pocomoke River. Although those too have now gone, Snow Hill maintains integrity and vibrancy.

ES92 WORCESTER COUNTY COURTHOUSE
1894–1895, Jackson C. Gott; later additions. 1 W. Market St.

The red-brick Colonial Revival courthouse, distinguished by a central tower with clock and octagonal lantern, is the county's third. A fire destroyed much of the downtown yet provided an opportunity for revitalization, beginning with this building. Gott's mix of colonial motifs include pedimented pavilions defined by Ionic pilasters, Doric portico, and round-arched windows with upper tracery. Later additions occupy the former courthouse square to the sides and rear of the building, leaving only the facade intact.

ES93 CORDDRY LUMBER WAREHOUSE
1924. 312 N. Washington St.

This is the last of the industrial buildings once found along the banks of the Pocomoke River in Snow Hill. It was built as a warehouse for the W. D. Corddry and Sons Lumber Company, reflecting Snow Hill's industrial growth during the late nineteenth and early twentieth centuries. The frame warehouse is distinguished by a rooftop monitor and extant interior platform elevator. At the same time that Corddry built his warehouse, he erected a house (1924; 114 W. Market Street) that combines Colonial Revival with Craftsman motifs.

The warehouse sits immediately adjacent to the Snow Hill Bridge (1932; J. E. Greiner Company), a steel and concrete, single-span bascule bridge with pedestrian sidewalk, classical tender's house, and ornamental lampposts. The bridge was part of a larger initiative during the 1920s and 1930s to replace outmoded bridges, accommodating the switch from steamboat to truck transport. On the other side of the bridge are the remnants of a former concrete cannery building.

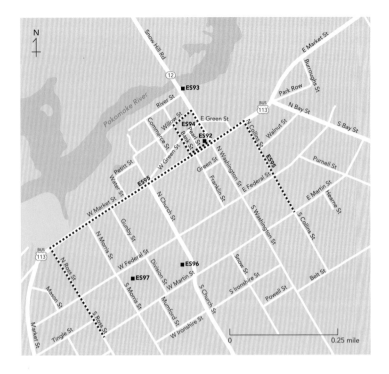

ES94 SNOW HILL BUSINESS DISTRICT

1894–1920s. Bounded roughly by W. Market, Bank, Willow, and N. Washington sts.

Snow Hill's commercial buildings date mostly from the turn of the twentieth century, following an 1893 fire that devastated the downtown. They are of brick construction, two to three stories in the eclectic styles of the period, with brick or bracketed wood cornices, corbeled brickwork, and parapet rooflines. Of particular note is the former Charles B. Timmons Furniture Store (c. 1900; 300 N. Washington), distinguished by its clipped corner with oriel window, entrance fanlight, and original storefront. The pressed brick Sturgis Building (c. 1894; 106 W Market) features a metal cornice with fan-shaped crest and arched entrance alcove. The pressed-brick Commercial National Bank (1897; 105 Pearl Street) is distinguished by its entrance with a short pyramidal spire and stained glass windows. The three-story Masonic Lodge building (c. 1894; 109–111 Pearl Street) is one of the largest, featuring a modillioned cornice ornamented with Colonial Revival detailing; it originally housed an A&P Grocery Store with lodge rooms above. The former Goodman's clothing store (1893; 110 Green Street) is set off by its buff brick, molded brick medallions, and a decorative metal cornice.

ES95 SNOW HILL RESIDENTIAL AREA

c. 1820–1880s. Bounded by Market, Collins, Martin, and Ross sts.

Southwest of downtown are the single-family houses of the town's professionals and business owners, ranging from formal, early Federal and Greek Revival houses to the more free-form romantic styles of the later nineteenth century, many influenced by local building traditions. Representative examples include the George Washington Purnell Smith House (c. 1860) at 201 E. Market Street. Gothic Revival details enliven this traditional two-story house, built for a local attorney, that was named Maples following 1890 renovations. Other fine Gothic Revival houses followed, such as those for druggist Peter D. Cottingham (c. 1873; 101 N. Church Street), physician George W. Bishop (c. 1872; 103 S. Church), and George S. Payne (c. 1860; 301 W. Federal Street).

A mansard roof with Gothic details distinguishes the eclectic Hargis House (1887; 101 S. Church). Many earlier Federal and Georgian houses were updated to include Gothic detailing, including the John S. Aydelotte House (c. 1840; c. 1880 remodeled) at 104 E. Market and the Payne House (c. 1830; c. 1870 remodeled) at 116 W. Market. Representing a regional form characterized by a two-story front gallery, created from an extension of the principal gable roof, are the William H. Farrow House (c. 1820; 300 W. Federal), also with a telescoping two-story service wing, and the Samuel Richardson House (c. 1840; 300 W. Green Street).

ES96 GOVERNOR JOHN WALTER SMITH HOUSE
1889, Jackson C. Gott. 104 S. Church St.

This is the grandest of many Queen Anne houses in Snow Hill and one of the few attributable to a noted architect. The unrestrained rambling design with its multiple gables, wraparound porch, and towers embraces an equally sophisticated interior plan of lavishly decorated rooms, a vast entrance and stair hall, reception room, parlor, library, dining room, and service wing. It was built for John Walter Smith, whose businesses spanned lumber, transportation, banking, and agriculture, while his political career included service in the U.S. House of Representatives (1899–1900), two terms as Maryland governor (1900–1908), and three terms in the U.S. Senate (1908–1920).

ES97 CHANCEFORD
c. 1792. 209 W. Federal St.

Chanceford is Snow Hill's earliest and most refined residence, an example of the pedimented gablefront Federal house. Built as the city was emerging as the center of trade and commerce for the Lower Eastern Shore, Chanceford's elegance foretold of Snow Hill's 1800–1860 rise to prominence, as one of the few extant structures remaining from the eighteenth century. It was erected for James Rownd Morris, a wealthy landowner and politically prominent member of Lower Eastern Shore society. Its design was likely influenced by the newly erected and much-admired Wye House (ES48), the home of the prominent Lloyd family.

Built of stuccoed brick, the main block exhibits a double-pile, transverse-hall plan, connected by a hyphen to a rear two-story wing that included a formal dining room and kitchen with a cellar cooking fireplace. The exceptional interior woodwork encompasses intricately carved punch-and-gougework cornices and mantels, crosseted doorway and window frames, and wainscoting framed by pilasters, differing in each room. In 1801, the house was purchased by Judge William Whittington who referred to it as Ingleside, and it remained in the family until 1874. It was John Warner Station who owned it during the first half of the twentieth century and dubbed it Chanceford. Its gable-front design set the tone for many others to follow, in particular the Ann Jenkins House (c. 1840; 106 E. Market Street), with a more typically positioned service wing to one side.

BERLIN

ES98 ATLANTIC HOTEL
1895; 1980s, 2009 renovations. 2 N. Main St.

The centerpiece of Berlin's thriving downtown commercial district is the Atlantic Hotel. Berlin emerged as an important commercial center for upper Worcester County in the early nineteenth century due to its location at a stagecoach stop on the Philadelphia post road. The arrival of the railroad after the Civil War made Berlin a key junction on the Lower Eastern Shore. The town hosted a steady stream of visitors on their way to Ocean City as well as traveling salesmen (drummers), visiting the many stores and businesses. The Atlantic Hotel, then operating in a c. 1845 structure, had a livery stable on the property so drummers could arrange local transportation to make their sales rounds. A fire in 1895 destroyed this building and the entire commercial core of Berlin.

The hotel's owner, Horace Harmonson, rebuilt and reopened within six months. His new Atlantic Hotel was a three-story brick building with a cast-iron cornice and full-width, one-story porch. Harmonson operated the hotel until the 1930s. Berlin's fortunes suffered during the Great Depression, and although the Atlantic Hotel remained open, the town found it was increasingly difficult to compete with the popularity of Ocean City, particularly after World War II.

In the 1980s, a group of residents banded together to save and renovate the hotel, also launching a renaissance for Berlin. Today Berlin's center is defined by the rows of red brick commercial buildings mainly from the post-fire reconstruction, now restored. On many blocks, they share a continuous metal awning sheltering the sidewalk. The former Exchange and Savings Bank (c. 1902; 1 S. Main) and former First National Bank (c. 1905; 3 S. Main) provide visual variety to the streetscape with towers and finials enlivening their one-story forms. The Atlantic Hotel continues to be a keystone of Berlin's resurgent popularity for tourism.

Maryland's primary seaside resort sits on a barrier island lying be-tween the Atlantic Ocean and the Sinepuxent Bay that until the late nineteenth century was largely deserted. Ocean City's first hotel opened in 1875, spurring early growth facilitated by a rail line from Berlin in 1881. The Trimper family built two hotels in the 1890s and in the succeeding decades installed the first amusement park rides. The boardwalk and original city pier were started by hotel owners, in 1902 and 1906, respectively. Early extant boardwalk hotels include the rebuilt Atlantic (1926; 401 Baltimore Avenue), the Lankford (1924; 807 Atlantic), and the Majestic (1925; 613 Atlantic).

Boardinghouses appeared, often run by the wives of fishermen and lifesaving station employees, such as the Tarry-A-While (1897; 108 Dorchester Street) and the Jefferson (c. 1903; 3 Dorchester Street). Individual and multi-unit cottages and bungalows were built during the early twentieth century. Most were raised on piers, clad in wood shingles, and offering front porches catching the ocean breeze, such as 505–507, the Rosemont at 509, and 511 Baltimore. Extant Colonial Revival houses, now seemingly out of sync with their surroundings, include the Esham House at 707, the shingled house at 711, and the George Vickers House at 800 Baltimore. Small apartment buildings were constructed for longer stays, such as Crop Ayre (608 N. Balti-more). The Gothic Revival St. Paul's By the Sea (1900; 302 Baltimore) and other churches contributed to early references to Ocean City as the Ladies Resort.

A post–World War II boom and the 1952 construction of the Ches-apeake Bay Bridge (WS80) ushered in increased development, the re-placement of many old buildings, and the advent of the motor lodge. Few single-family houses were built during this period, with the exception of the atypical International Style Joseph Edward Collins House (1949; 710 Baltimore). In the 1980s and 1990s more early struc-tures gave way to luxury hotels and condominiums, commanding the beachfront with balconied rooms providing views of the ocean, such as the colorful Hyatt Place (1 16th Street) by Fisher Architecture of Salisbury. Still, many noteworthy buildings speaking to the earlier seaside town remain and are as illustrative of Ocean City ethos as Thrashers french fries, Dolles Candyland, and Dumser's Dairyland ice cream.

ES99 U.S. LIFESAVING STATION MUSEUM AND GUARDHOUSE
1878–1891; 1934. 813 Atlantic Ave.

This is Maryland's only surviving U.S. lifesaving station, and one of Ocean City's earliest buildings. Its prototypical one-and-a-half-story, frame, gable-front form with ocean-facing double doors to provide easy access for a life-saving boat was developed by ser-

Top left: U.S. Lifesaving Station Museum and Guardhouse (**ES99**). **Top right:** Henry's (Colored) Hotel (**ES100**). **Bottom:** Sea Breeze Inn (Sea Breeze Motel; ES101).

vice architect J. L. Parkinson. The current main section was erected in 1891 as a separate building providing accommodation for the keeper and his crew, later joined by a hyphen. The U.S. Lifesaving Service was superseded by the U.S. Coast Guard in 1915, which continued to use the building until 1962. The adjacent watchtower was erected in 1934–1935, after the devastating hurricane of 1933. Both were moved to the current site and rehabilitated as a maritime museum, opening in 1977.

ES100 HENRY'S (COLORED) HOTEL
c. 1890. S. Baltimore Ave. at S. Division St.

This is one of the few remaining late-nineteenth-century buildings in Ocean City and among the small number that catered to African American tourists. Ocean City was strictly segregated, open to Black visitors only during postseason "Colored Excursion Days." Henry's offered lodging to Black tourists as well as entertainers performing at the nearby Pier Ballroom. Its well-known guests included Cab Calloway, Duke Ellington, Count Basie, and Willie Harmon. The two-story, L-shaped shingled building with wraparound porch was built by Worcester County landowner Granville Stokes and owned by African American businessman Charles Henry and family from 1926 to 1953. It was purchased by Pearl Bonner in 1954 but no longer caters to visitors.

ES101 SEA BREEZE INN (SEA BREEZE MOTEL)
c. 1970. 201 N. Baltimore Ave.

This quintessential seaside motor lodge represents the 1960s and 1970s development within Ocean City, typified by units with individual entrances and access to a front carpark. Built in its elongated form to resemble a ship, Sea Breeze Motel's open exterior walkways hastened access while also providing a place from which to catch a breeze, hence inspiring its name. Many such motor lodges were built here, beginning with the 1956 Santa Maria Motel (now gone), although few remain. Extant are the former Sun Tan Motel (207 N. Baltimore) that encompasses flanking buildings facing a parking area and the similarly styled Madison Beach Motel (9 N. Baltimore) that includes a separate bungalow-style office building.

ES102 WALKER COTTAGE
c. 1910. 611 N. Baltimore Ave.

This shingled bungalow is a remarkable survivor of early-twentieth-century Ocean City, retaining its large lot as well as the integrity of its original design. It was built for William Walker of Washington, who referred to it as Romarletta. The summer cottage features a pyramidal roof with front dormer and an inviting wraparound porch. It remained in the Walker family until 1950. Today, it is one of a number of bungalows that now appear incongruously among the flashy, large-scale hotels that dominate Baltimore Avenue.

BALTIMORE CITY

Baltimore is known as a quirky, gritty place through its most famous popular cultural works such as the writings of iconoclastic journalist H. L. Mencken, the oeuvre of proudly transgressive filmmaker John Waters, and the groundbreaking television series *The Wire*. The rich architectural heritage of Maryland's largest city also offers compelling stories crucial to understanding the forces driving state and national history. Baltimore was shaped by both racial segregation and the development of ethnic immigrant enclaves that stood in stark contrast to the neighborhoods of the elite. Both fiercely unique, yet profoundly representative, Charm City looms large as historically one of the most important cities in the United States and the unofficial capital of Maryland.

Baltimore's emergence as an industrial and financial powerhouse and primary commercial and cultural engine for the state of Maryland seemed unlikely when the legislature issued a town charter in 1729. Baltimore Town included just sixty lots on the north side of the Patapsco River, and for nearly three decades development was limited. It was the rise of flour milling and export in the 1750s that awakened the great potential of Baltimore's geographic position as the East Coast deepwater port closest to the Midwest. When Baltimore City (now including neighboring Jones Town and Fell's Point) officially incorporated in 1797, it had already matured enough to have public works such as a market, some paved streets, streetlights, and a dredged shipping channel.

The population grew to 80,000 by 1830, making Baltimore the second largest city in the United States, with significant immigrant populations from Germany, Ireland, Scotland, France, and Haiti. The Haitian immigrants joined the largest free Black community in the country and before emancipation in 1864 coexisted with enslaved workers both in households and in the skilled trades such as shipbuilding. Baltimore began to eclipse Annapolis as the most important city in Maryland and take its place among other East Coast urban centers such as Philadelphia, Boston, and New York. Baltimore became an important center for industry and manufacturing as varied as cotton textiles, seafood and vegetable canning, fertilizer, steelmaking, shipbuilding, railroads, ready-made clothing, brewing, and pharmaceuticals. In addition to its international port and location along the National Road, Baltimore became the center of major transportation innovations through the Baltimore and Ohio Railroad, founded in 1828.

The accumulated wealth of the late eighteenth and early nineteenth century created a cultural and aesthetic awakening in Baltimore. A new generation of European immigrant and home-grown archi-

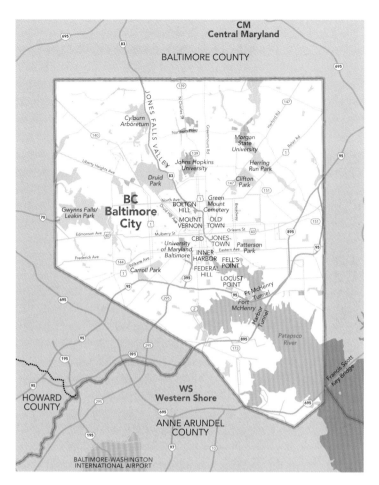

CM
Central Maryland

BALTIMORE COUNTY

JONES FALLS VALLEY

Cylburn
Arboretum

Morgan
State
University

Johns Hopkins
University

Herring
Run Park

Druid
Park

Clifton
Park

BC
Baltimore
City

Gwynns Falls/
Leakin Park

North Ave.
BOLTON
HILL

Green
Mount
Cemetery

MOUNT
VERNON

OLD
TOWN

Edmonson Ave

Mulberry St

CBD

JONES-
TOWN

University
of Maryland,
Baltimore

INNER
HARBOR

Eastern Ave.

Patterson
Park

Frederick Ave

FELL'S
POINT

Carroll Park

FEDERAL
HILL

LOCUST
POINT

Ft. McHenry
Tunnel

Fort
McHenry

Harbor Tunnel

Patapsco
River

HOWARD
COUNTY

WS
Western Shore

Francis Scott Key Bridge

ANNE ARUNDEL
COUNTY

BALTIMORE-WASHINGTON
INTERNATIONAL AIRPORT

tects designed grand town houses and institutional and civic buildings, including some of the nation's first monuments, that employed the latest European styles and up-to-date construction technologies such as structural and ornamental wrought and cast iron. Baltimore's commercial and financial success also inspired local philanthropists who established world-class institutions of arts and culture, medicine and science, and education and social welfare throughout the nineteenth century. These efforts included Peale's Baltimore Museum (BC48), Davidge Hall (BC39), the music school and library at the Peabody Institute (BC7), the Enoch Pratt Free Library (BC15), and the Walters Art Museum (BC6). Perhaps most impressive was the largesse of merchant Johns Hopkins, who established both the hospital (BC77) and the university (see BC105) that transformed medical and educational practices in the United States in the late nineteenth century.

In terms of ordinary residential life, few cities are so closely identified with row housing as Baltimore. Row houses available at every price point, made affordable by a system of ground rents, created high homeownership rates for the citizens of Baltimore. Row housing appeared in every stylistic mode with fierce competition among speculative builders, resulting in rich ornamental details and other amenities. In the twentieth century the row house was also a focus of

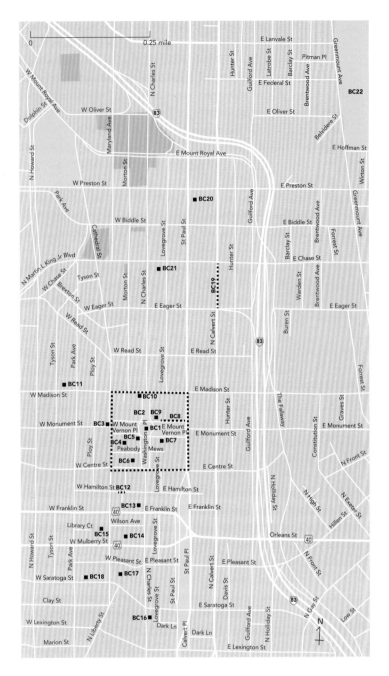

revitalization efforts, including the city's path-breaking Homesteading Program that preserved many of the oldest neighborhoods.

In 1888 Baltimore expanded from ten to thirty square miles through annexation, and new residential development was supported by expansion of the horse-drawn railway lines into electric streetcar companies. Baltimore was poised for further success as the sixth largest city in the United States, with over a half million in population in 1900. A disastrous fire destroyed most of the downtown commercial district in 1904, but it inspired rapid rebuilding using the latest construction methods and design modes.

Immigration continued to soar, with Baltimore second only to New York as a port of entry for those seeking a new life in the United States. Another annexation in 1918 increased the city's size to almost ninety square miles, now encompassing large areas with a more suburban character. Led by the Baltimore Municipal Art Society founded in 1899, Baltimore embraced City Beautiful movement–inspired civic improvements such as the Baltimore City park plan (1904, Olmsted Brothers). More prosaic, but arguably more critical, early-twentieth-century efforts created an extensive sewer system, stricter fire codes, and a comprehensive zoning ordinance adopted in 1923.

After struggling through the Great Depression like many urban centers, Baltimore industry roared back into production for World War II. Accelerated suburbanization after the war started a population decline that began to erode the city's economic base and exacerbated the inequalities of Jim Crow segregation for Black citizens in a struggling city. Officials seeking bold action embraced federal highway construction and urban renewal. While some of the most potentially damaging projects were thwarted by local activists, new highways such as those along the Jones Falls, across Locust Point, and through West Baltimore hurt already fragile working-class neighborhoods, particularly African American ones already crowded due to housing discrimination. Redevelopment of the central business district and the Inner Harbor did successfully harness comprehensive planning to reinvent these areas as part of an expanded service/tourism-based economy. Today Baltimore continues to embody all the complexity of a major postindustrial city while still trying to extend its legacy of progress to all its citizens. Yet with an amazing stock of historic buildings and tightknit neighborhoods embracing their distinctive identities, Baltimore has great potential for a second renaissance.

MOUNT VERNON AND ENVIRONS

BC1 WASHINGTON MONUMENT
1815–1829, Robert Mills. 699 N. Charles St.

This massive Doric column was the first significant monument in America and the first in memory of Revolutionary War hero and first president George Washington, one of the most revered and memorialized personages in American history. While the U.S. Congress advocated for a monu-

ment before his passing, it was not until 1848 that the obelisk in Washington was begun. The task was instead undertaken first by the citizens of Baltimore. The column contains a stair to a viewing platform crowned by a statue of General Washington to obtain a height of 178 feet. It is mounted on a tall stone plinth where a gallery displays Washington memorabilia. The monument is built of locally quarried stone by Baltimore contractors Towson and Steuart, and the statue was created by Italian sculptor Enrico Causici.

Robert Mills capitalized upon his status as the nation's first native-born and -trained architect to secure the commission, yet his design is evocative of European models—most notably, Roman emperor Trajan's Column (113 CE) in Rome and the Vendôme Column (1810) in Paris. Concurrent with the Battle Monument (BC40), the two earned Baltimore the title of Monumental City and sparked a rash of monument and statuary building that lasted for over a century. The statue depicts Washington with his outstretched hand presenting the scrolled document resigning his military commission, an event that occurred in the State House (WS1) in Annapolis, hence Maryland's greatest claim to historical events surrounding the nation's first president.

BC2 MOUNT VERNON PLACE

1829–1836, Robert Mills; 1875–1876, Frederick Law Olmsted; 1917–1924, Carrère and Hastings. Charles St. bounded by St. Paul, Cathedral, W. Madison, and W. Centre sts.

Mount Vernon Place is one of the best conceived and executed city planning projects of the nineteenth century. Begun as the site of Baltimore's monument to George Washington (BC1), Mount Vernon Place became a fashionable urban park, residential neighborhood, and the centerpiece of the city's arts and culture district. The site, selected for its dramatic views, originated as Colonel John Eager Howard's Belvidere estate. City managers optimistically projected Baltimore's expansion, extending Charles Street to the site. Mills laid out the current configuration of squares on north–south and east–west axes, named respectively Washington Place and Mount Vernon Place in honor of Washington and his Virginia home. In 1875, Frederick Law Olmsted's Boston firm reconfigured Mills's rectilinear classical design to create a more curvilinear and picturesque landscape, turning lawns into sculpture gardens. In 1917, a redesign by Carrère and Hastings of New York followed City Beautiful ideals of symmetry, uniformity, and axial alignment.

Along the perimeter of Mount Vernon Place is some of the city's finest architecture, ranging from Greek Revival to Beaux-Arts classical and designed by such noted architects as Niernsee and Neilson, Edmund G. Lind, Stanford White, John Russell Pope, and Delano and Aldrich, beginning in the 1840s. The opulent residences were joined in the twentieth century by fashionable apartment buildings and hotels. The Peabody Institute (BC7), begun in 1858, was the first to distinguish

Mount Vernon Place as an area of arts and culture, followed by the Walters Art Museum (BC6) in 1909.

BC3 DECATUR MILLER ROW HOUSE
1852, Niernsee and Neilson. 700 Cathedral St.

This house represents Niernsee and Neilson's initial foray into the use of the Italianate, newly emerged on the Baltimore scene. Built for tobacco merchant Decatur Miller, its design was inspired by the Italian palazzo to include a piano nobile plan with the principal entertaining rooms elevated above a rusticated ground floor resembling the recently completed Waverley Terrace (BC88). The house was among the first in the city to embrace cast-iron details, manufactured by Bartlett, Hayward and Company, as well as the use of a full brownstone facade. Brownstone then appeared in other fashionable houses, including two additional palazzos by Niernsee and Neilson (1855; 10–12 E. Monument Street).

BC4 GARRETT-JACOBS HOUSE
1884–1893, McKim, Mead and White; c. 1905; 1909–1913 additions, John Russell Pope. 7–11 W. Mount Vernon Pl.

The most imposing town house on Mount Vernon Place was built for Robert Garrett, president of the Baltimore and Ohio (B&O) Railroad. Its plan was so massive that a court battle ensued to prevent its construction, arguing that its Renaissance Revival style, while appropriate for New York City, was not in keeping with conservative Baltimore. The vestibule alone measures 20 × 24 feet and adjoins a portico that projects onto the sidewalk. Its lavish interior décor is among the grandest in Baltimore. Garrett's widow and her second husband, physician Henry Jacobs, added a large ballroom in 1905, later enhancing the gallery space, and eventually incorporating the adjoining house. In the 1940s, the house was used by various organizations and is currently owned by the Engineers Club of Baltimore. It remains the largest town house ever built in Baltimore.

BC5 HACKERMAN HOUSE (THOMAS-JENCKS-GLADDING HOUSE)
1849–1851, Niernsee and Neilson; 1892 renovations and addition, Charles Platt; 1989–1991 renovation, James R. Grieves Associates. 1 W. Mount Vernon Pl.

This imposing Greek Revival house was among the first erected along Mount Vernon Place, setting the tone for this exclusive neighborhood. Built for physician J. Hanson Thomas, it was touted by the *Baltimore Sun* as "one of the

most elegant and princely speci-
mens of architectural taste and
mechanical skills" in the city. The
twenty-two-room mansion encompasses a sixty-foot-long parlor, Gothic Revival dining room,
and Elizabethan-styled library.
The Jencks family purchased

the house in 1892, adding a rear
conservatory and a Tiffany dome
above the staircase. It was purchased by the Hackerman family
in 1985 and donated to the city; it
houses the Walters Art Museum's
(BC6) Asian Art collection.

BC6 WALTERS ART MUSEUM

*1905–1909, Delano and Aldrich;
1974 addition, Shepley, Bullfinch,
Richardson and Abbott; 1998–2001
addition, Kallmann, McKinnell and
Wood. 600 N. Charles St.*

The Walters is one of the architectural and cultural anchors
of Mount Vernon Place. It is the
legacy of philanthropist Henry
Walters and his son William T.
Walters, originating as their extensive personal collections of
art and artifacts from around the
globe. Emulating an Italian palazzo, the ashlar limestone building
rises from a ground level of rusticated granite with blind windows
with iron grilles contributing to
its solid aura. The galleries are
arranged around the sky-lit arcaded interior courtyard or Great
Hall inspired by the seventeenth-

century Collegio dei Gesuiti built
for the Jesuits in Genoa, Italy.

The elder Walters began opening his house at 5 W. Mount Vernon Place for public viewings of
his collection in 1874. In 1905,
he hired designers and craftsmen to New York's elite to create a purpose-built structure for
his burgeoning collection. Four
period rooms—Gothic, Francis I,
Louis XIV, and Louis XVI—were
the work of L. Marcotte and Company, and Durand et Compagnie
of Paris created the reproduction
furnishings. The museum opened
in 1909, and upon his death in
1931 Henry Walters bequeathed
his house, museum building, and
collection to the city.

A contrasting Brutalist poured-
concrete annex was erected in
1974; its high plinth-like foun-

dation and incised horizontal patterns mimic the lines of the original building. A glass atrium entrance lobby with suspended stair was added at the juncture of the two parts.

BC7 PEABODY INSTITUTE
1858–1861 conservatory; 1875–1878 library, Edmund G. Lind, J. Crawford Neilson, consulting architect. 1 E. Mount Vernon Pl.

A gift to the city from philanthropist George Peabody, the institute that bears his name was built as a cultural center offering a free public library, conservatory of music, art gallery, and lecture hall. It is noteworthy for its Renaissance Revival design and innovative building technology, representing a collaboration between English immigrant architect Lind and Baltimore architect Neilson. Its stylish facade was paired with structural iron supplied by local manufacturers Bartlett, Robbins and Company, with wrought-iron beams from the Phoenix Iron Company of Pennsylvania and iron roof trusses from the Kellogg Bridge Company of Buffalo. Providing both economy and efficiency of design, the delicate cast- and wrought-iron frame permits grand open spaces and a pleasing environment for the valuable book collection. Referred to as the Cathedral of Books, the spectacular gilded ironwork comprises six stories of alcove book stacks (*pictured above*).

BC8 BROWNSTONE ROW
1853–1854, Michael Roche, Louis L. Long. 18–28 E. Mount Vernon Pl.

This row of six large, elegant houses is an example of both speculative housing intended for elite Baltimoreans and a superlative use of brownstone, then a popular material for high-end antebellum town houses within the city. Designed and begun by builder-contractor Roche, the row was ultimately completed by local architect Long. The interior room arrangement followed Baltimore convention to contain a ground-floor formal dining room with the other entertaining rooms above. Placing the dining room adjacent to the kitchen differed from the New York plan whereby double parlors and a formal dining room all occupied the principal story. Brownstone Row constituted some of the largest, most opulent houses then available in Baltimore.

BC9 MOUNT VERNON PLACE UNITED METHODIST CHURCH
1872, Dixon and Carson. 10 E. Mount Vernon Pl.

Of all the fine buildings surrounding Mount Vernon Square, this High Victorian Gothic church is one of the showiest, competing visually with the adjacent Washington Monument (BC1). Its asymmetrical towers, rose window, pointed relieving arch, and sculptured finials are enhanced by the use of polychrome materials such as green serpentine stone walls and red and buff sandstone trim. A triple entranceway features charming details of carved flora and fauna. On the basilica-plan interior slender cast-iron columns support carved wood pointed-arch trusses. Architects Dixon and Carson formed their successful partnership while this church was under construction.

Thomas Dixon, the elder architect, designed several High Victorian Gothic churches for East Coast cities, but this one stands as one of his most noteworthy designs.

BC10 GRAHAM-HUGHES HOUSE
1888, George Archer. 718 Washington Pl.

This eclectic house, with its rock-face ashlar marble facades, is among the most distinctive in Mount Vernon Place. Archer was known for his designs for Gothic Revival churches, later buildings for The John Hopkins Hospital (BC77), and various period revival residences of which this is considered his masterpiece. It sits at the intersection with W. Madison Street, projecting two bold and highly decorative facades radiating from its prominent round corner tower. It was built for George and Sarah Graham, later passing to their daughter Isabella and her husband Thomas Hughes, for nearly ninety years of family occupancy.

BC11 FIRST AND FRANKLIN PRESBYTERIAN CHURCH (FIRST PRESBYTERIAN CHURCH) AND MANSE
1854–1859, Norris G. Starkweather; 1873–1874 spire, Edmund G. Lind. 200–210 W. Madison St.

Eager to make a statement with a new uptown edifice, the congregation of First Presbyterian called Starkweather from Philadelphia to design a Gothic Revival church, the most lavish the city had witnessed. Exemplifying the English Gothic Perpendicular

Style of the late Middle Ages is its steeply pitched roofline and parapets, piercing central tower, and flanking octagonal turrets. Faced in a warm brown New Brunswick sandstone, the church exudes adornment. Its dizzying height is achieved through structural iron manufactured by the Patapsco Bridge and Ironworks and a spire designed by Starkweather's former chief draftsman Lind.

The complementary Manse was also designed by Starkweather and constructed concurrently for the church's Reverend John Chester Backus as his private residence (purchased by the congregation in 1923). The congregation merged with Franklin Street Presbyterian Church in 1873 to become First and Franklin Presbyterian Church.

BC12 HAMILTON STREET ROW HOUSES
c. 1819, Robert Cary Long Sr. 12–18 W. Hamilton St.

Intended for a sophisticated clientele is this early example of multi-unit row houses, designed by this celebrated local architect. With staid neoclassical detailing and a piano nobile plan elevating the principal rooms over a low ground-floor entrance level, the row houses appear almost modern-day. Built of Flemish-bond brick with contrasting white marble details, they encompass five stories, including a basement kitchen and finished attic. Of note are the tripartite windows, entrances with sidelights separated by jambs capped with molding to resemble slender unassuming Doric columns, and,

emblematic of Baltimore's early row houses, a single dormer lighting the attic story. Long resided in one of the units himself.

BC13 FIRST UNITARIAN CHURCH
1818, Maximilian Godefroy; 1893 remodeled, Joseph Evans Sperry. 1 W. Franklin St.

This is one of the most monumental of America's early neoclassical buildings and the greatest of Godefroy's extant works. French born and trained, Godefroy was among the luminaries of Baltimore's early-nineteenth-century architectural community of professionally trained immigrant architects who brought the latest in European design and engineering concepts to an America in search of its own cultural identity. Like the Basilica of the Assumption (BC14) built concurrently, it represents a significant break from traditional religious architecture. It embodies the root elements of early neoclassicism in a rational composition featuring a play of geometric shapes in a typically restrained manner. The building's bold cube-like form is surmounted by a hemispheric dome, with a pedimented portico supported by slim Tuscan columns and the triple-arch motif considered a particularly French interpretation. A stucco finish contributes to its austere appearance, with embellishment confined to the terra-cotta *Angel of Trust* sculpture appearing in the tympanum. It is a replica by Henry Bergel of the original created by Antonio Capellano, who was also responsible for realizing Godefroy's design for the Battle Monument (BC40).

The interior features a huge semicircular coffered dome, supported by arches and engaged pilasters. Poor acoustics led to a remodeling in 1893, partitioning the arches into side aisles and masking the curved chancel. A Tiffany stained glass elliptical transom was added in 1904. The church is significant historically as the site of Dr. William Ellery Channing's celebrated 1819 "Baltimore Sermon" where he espoused for the first time the fundamental principles of American Unitarian thought.

BC14 BASILICA OF THE ASSUMPTION

1805–1821, Benjamin Henry Latrobe; 1879 addition, John R. Niernsee; 1888 addition, E. Francis Baldwin; 2006 restored, John G. Waite Associates. 409 Cathedral St.

This was the first Roman Catholic Cathedral in the United States and is considered among Latrobe's masterworks. The celebrated gneiss stone structure was one of the most provocative and influential buildings of its day due to a pathbreaking neoclassical design that includes a temple-front hexastyle portico, domes, and bold, clean detailing. It was the first church to break with the English-inspired Wren-Gibbs prototype that dominated eighteenth-century American religious architecture and to be equal to the finest contemporary buildings of Europe. Here, Latrobe successfully married Catholic liturgical traditions with the bold rational geometry of the neoclassical style.

Its construction was envisioned by Father John Carroll, vicar general of the Roman Catholic Church in the United States and its first bishop. Thus, Baltimore is considered the birthplace of the Roman Catholic hierarchy in this country. Although Maryland was founded by the Carroll family as a haven for persecuted Catholics, for nearly a century prior to the American Revolution and the adoption of a new Constitution, Catholics were not free to worship openly. Bishop Carroll intended the Basilica to celebrate their resurgence, with a splendid church.

The impressive, light-filled interior was transformed from a Greek to a Latin cross by an added bay in the nave, with a massive central dome at its crossing. A complex system of interrelated vaults surrounds the great rotunda and dome inspired by those of sixteenth-century French architect Philibert Delorme. Vaulted interior spaces demonstrate Latrobe's innovative skill at engineering as well as design; no other American church of its day was completely vaulted in masonry. The towers and portico, believed to be part of Latrobe's original design, were completed in 1831–1837 and 1863, respectively. The sacristy wing, designed by Niernsee, was finally added in 1879 and expanded by Baldwin in 1888. The Basilica was designated a National Historic Landmark in 1971 and was restored in 2006 to include the reinstallation of Latrobe's clear glass windows and skylights while incorporating modern systems.

BC15 ENOCH PRATT FREE LIBRARY CENTRAL BUILDING
1930–1933, Clyde N. Friz, with Tilton and Githens. 400–420 Cathedral St.

In 1933 Baltimore's new central library opened in a limestone-sheathed building decorated with stylized classical motifs. Merchant and philanthropist Enoch Pratt established the city's free library system in 1882 with four neighborhood branches and the first central building designed by Charles L. Carson (1886; demolished). Not only was the new central building larger and more fashionable, but it benefited from the expertise of Edward Tilton, a New York City architect who made a specialty of library design during the early twentieth century.

Like the Carnegie-funded libraries proliferating nationally, Baltimore's library system embraced Progressive library design and operations, including an open floor plan and open stacks for lending collections available to all residents. The street-level entrance and display windows along Cathedral Street recalled a department store welcoming all patrons inside to browse. The Children's Room entrance on Mulberry Street signaled a new commitment to serving young readers. Following the terms of Pratt's bequest, the library system was one of the few public institutions in the city available to all, regardless of race. The library reopened in 2020 after a major renovation that included sensitive restoration of its elegant Art Deco features.

BC16 ST. PAUL'S EPISCOPAL CHURCH

1854–1856, Richard Upjohn. 233 N. Charles St.

The design of St. Paul's is based on Italian Romanesque churches, unusual for both Baltimore and Upjohn, one of the foremost practitioners of Gothic Revival. Upjohn was inspired by his recent travels through Rome. The basilica plan, the result of constrains imposed by the remains of the previous church gutted by fire, is expressed externally by a central-gable front with an arcaded loggia flanked by towers. Bas-relief panels by Italian sculptor Antonio Capellano on the facade, also remnants of the prior building, depict Moses holding the Ten Commandments and Christ breaking bread at the Last Supper.

The original dark interior was enlivened in 1903 by moving the black walnut chancel reredos to the rear of the church and replacing it with one by Tiffany, and by installing a large chancel window designed by Helen Maitland Armstrong. St. Paul's occupies the site of the first church erected in 1731, then marking the outer reaches of the city. The church housed the first of three Episcopal parishes established under the 1692 Act of Maryland Assembly to form the "mother church" of the local Episcopal congregations.

BC17 ST. PAUL'S EPISCOPAL CHURCH RECTORY

1789–1791; c. 1829 kitchen, 1830s wing. 24 W. Saratoga St.

Curiously perched on a lawn raised above street level, this is a rare remnant of Baltimore's late-eighteenth-century development.

It was constructed for the rector of St. Paul's Episcopal Church (BC16), financed through public lottery and the donation of a lot by John Eager Howard. It remains a fine example of late Georgian architecture characterized by its symmetrical facade, central pavilion, classical entrance, and Palladian window. The extensive nine-bay facade belies its narrow single-pile plan, with an unusual pentagonal stair hall projecting from the rear. The wing to the east, erected c. 1829, housed the kitchen, while the flanking west wing was built in the 1830s to include tripartite windows characteristic of that period. After being rented to outside groups for many years, the rectory was renovated and reoccupied by the parish in 2019.

BC18 ST. ALPHONSUS CHURCH

1842, Robert Cary Long Jr. 114–120 W. Saratoga St.

This German Catholic Church is a landmark of early Gothic Revival architecture and the masterwork of Baltimore architect Long Jr. His admiration for English architect and proponent of Gothic design A. W. N. Pugin is evident in his work and in his belief that Gothic and Greek were the only styles worth emulating. This was Long's first Gothic Revival church and first major commission. Executed in the English Perpendicular mode, its towering height and overall stability was achieved through an early use of structural cast iron. The symmetrical brick building, originally painted in imitation of stone, features a crenellated parapet pierced by

Left: Belvidere Terrace (BC19). **Top right:** Ross Winans House (BC20). **Bottom right:** Green Mount Cemetery (BC22), gatehouse.

buttresses topped with finials and telescoping central tower, and ogee windows replete with drip moldings and delicate tracery. The exterior, however, appears austere when compared with the soaring, richly ornamented interior with slim clustered marbleized columns supporting elaborate fan vaults, full-height stained glass windows, stenciled ornamentation, and high altar. It was commissioned by German and Austrian Roman Catholic Redemptorist fathers who came to Baltimore to minister to a growing working-class congregation.

BC19 BELVIDERE TERRACE

1879–1882, Wilson and Wilson; Wyatt and Sperry. 1000 block N. Calvert St.

One of the most admired row house blocks in Baltimore, Belvidere Terrace represents an early and exuberant use of Queen Anne architecture. Completed first, the east side was designed by local architects John Appleton Wilson and his partner and cousin, William T. Wilson. The former is credited with introducing the picturesque Queen Anne style to Baltimore, with one of his first designs for the Catherine McKim House (1879; 1037 N. Calvert). McKim then hired them to design the adjacent grouping of fifteen unified row houses.

Once those row houses were completed, the family hired Wyatt and Sperry to design an even more eclectic grouping of twenty-two row houses along the west side of Calvert Street. While they differ in design from the previous units, they maintain the overall form and scale, adopting many of the same materials and architectural motifs. Together, Belvidere Terrace represents the best of Baltimore's late-nineteenth-century eclecticism, exhibiting a riot of forms and textures to include pressed and molded brick and foliated spandrels in terracotta with contrasting marble, granite, and pressed-metal details, ornamental gables, Romanesque arches, and multipaned windows.

BC20 ROSS WINANS HOUSE
1882, Stanford White of McKim,
Mead and White. 1217 St. Paul St.

Baltimore millionaire Ross R.
Winans (grandson and namesake
to railroad pioneer Ross Winans)
inherited the wealth his family
amassed through railroad ventures
with the B&O and in Russia. He
hired White to design his fashionable house on St. Paul Street when
this area was one of Baltimore's
wealthiest neighborhoods. Work
on the Winans House overlapped
with the design of White's other
Baltimore landmark, Lovely Lane
Methodist Church (BC102). The
forty-six-room house has a pictur-
esquely eclectic exterior executed in brick and brownstone with
touches of both Richardsonian Romanesque and French Renaissance
Revival architectural modes influential at the time. The lavish interiors, many of which still survive,
were appointed with carved oak,
teak, and mahogany paneling, Tiffany Studios tiles, leaded glass, par-
quet floors, and other fine decoration. Starting in 1928, the Winans
House hosted a variety of nonresidential uses, including funeral parlor, girls' preparatory school, and
doctor's office. After a restoration
in 2005, the Winans House continues to serve as offices.

BC21 BELVEDERE HOTEL
1902–1903, Parker and Thomas.
1 E. Chase St.

One of the early works in Baltimore designed by the prolific firm
of Parker and Thomas, this modern skyscraper hotel was a prime
example of contemporary trends
in hotel design also seen in New
York, Philadelphia, and Washington. As described by *Architectural*
Record in March 1905, the Belvedere was one of a new generation
of hotels "in a different class architecturally from any similar buildings which have preceded them."
The Belvedere featured a fashionable Beaux-Arts classical design,
as well as the latest in structural
and systems technology.

Located between the uptown
train stations and the central business district, the Belvedere moved
large-scale commercial development well north of downtown
into the Mount Vernon neighborhood and became a gathering
place for Baltimore's social elite.
The hotel featured approximately
300 guestrooms and bathrooms, a
twelfth-floor ballroom and banquet halls, and a dining room, tearoom and other rooms for entertainment on the first and second
floors. The kitchen, laundry, and
mechanical rooms were located in
the basement and subbasement.
Today the Belvedere houses condominiums, several restaurants,
small offices, and retail businesses, and the medieval-styled bar
room later dubbed the Owl Bar.
A parking garage and small retail
mall was added to the building's
rear in 1978.

BC22 GREEN MOUNT
CEMETERY
1838–1839, Benjamin Henry
Latrobe Jr.; 1840–1846 gatehouse,
Robert Cary Long Jr.; 1851 chapel,
Niernsee and Neilson; 1929 mauso-
leum, Buckler and Fenhagen. 1501
Greenmount Ave.

This is among America's earliest
rural cemeteries, created from
a landscape design by engineer
Latrobe overlaid on tobacco
merchant Robert Oliver's former country estate by the same

name. It was inspired by Mount Auburn Cemetery (1831) in Cambridge, Massachusetts, which launched a rural cemetery movement in America that quickly spread to other progressive urban areas. Characterized by their picturesque landscaping and artistic commemorative memorials, rural cemeteries were first established in response to overcrowded urban burial grounds and increased industrialization that imposed pressures on urban sanitation. Located on the urban fringes, rural cemeteries also provided urban dwellers a bucolic retreat. With their meandering paths and lush plantings, they offered a prototype for the American park movement begun in the mid-nineteenth century with Fairmount Park (1855) in Philadelphia and Central Park (1858) in New York City.

Green Mount consists of sixty-eight acres of picturesque landscaped grounds and funerary art surrounded by high stone walls, now located within the heart of east Baltimore. Its rolling hills and high elevation provide splendid vistas of the cityscape and is shaded by old-growth trees. Due to its exceptionally fine memorials and statuary, Green Mount can be seen as an outdoor sculpture garden that includes works by noted artists Hans Schuler, W. H. Rinehart, and Edward Berge, and with early gravestones and vaults by well-known local stonecutters Frederick Baughman and T. Horatio Bevan.

Among its significant structures is the Gothic Revival five-part gatehouse (*pictured on p. 163*), a central portal with towers and single-story hyphens that connect to a flanking office and waiting room. The octagonal, cut-stone chapel features a spire that rises 102 feet, flying buttresses, pinnacles, lancet bays, and a porte-cochere. It replaced Robert Oliver's house, initially used for that purpose. The superintendent and caretaker cottages, designed in the same mode, were likely built then as well. In 1929, a Classical Revival mausoleum ornamented with Art Deco and Egyptian motifs was erected. Among the many worthies buried at Green Mount are eight Maryland governors and seven city mayors; philanthropists Johns Hopkins, Enoch Pratt, Henry and William Walters, and Moses Sheppard; and industrialists Robert Garrett, Arunah Abell, Ross Winans, Alex Brown, and Robert Oliver.

CENTRAL BUSINESS DISTRICT WEST

BC23 ONE CHARLES CENTER
1962, Ludwig Mies van der Rohe. 100 N. Charles St.

One Charles Center (*see p. 17*) was the first phase of Baltimore's postwar efforts to address a shrinking downtown tax base with a bold urban renewal project. The twenty-three-story aluminum and glass tower was designed by renowned

architect Mies van der Rohe in the spare and elegant version of avant-garde modernism he made famous. The twenty-two-acre Charles Center site contained nineteenth- and early-twentieth-century buildings considered blighted because of declining use for wholesale and light manufacturing. The project proposed cutting through the street grid and placing modern office towers and a hotel around a central plaza. Six teams submitted proposals for a speculative office building to launch the development. The promise of a signature Mies tower for downtown Baltimore won the site for Metropolitan Structures, a Chicago-based development firm.

The T-shaped office tower has an anodized aluminum and glass curtain wall hung on a reinforced concrete structural system, as demonstrated by the glass lobby walls recessed under the piers. The tower and its plaza sit on a tall concrete podium (originally faced with travertine) containing a parking garage and retail spaces. A central elevator and service core gave each floor an open plan for maximum flexibility.

One Charles Center was later joined by other pieces of the complex including a pair of residential towers at Two Charles Center (1965–1969, Conklin and Rossant), the Morris A. Mechanic Theater (1967, John Johansen; 2015 demolished), a bold Brutalist structure, and Charles Center South (1975, RTKL Associates), a hexagonal tower of black granite and glass.

While the award-winning Charles Center brought national attention to the revitalization efforts in Baltimore, it suffered from the same problems as many visionary modernist projects. Incomplete realization of the master plan and a dramatic break with the existing urban landscape meant that Charles Center never quite became the hoped-for catalyst of a fully revitalized downtown. It can, however, be credited with creating momentum and a model of urban planning that informed the Inner Harbor redevelopment effort.

BC24 SUN LIFE BUILDING
1970, Peterson and Brickbauer,
with Emery Roth and Sons. 20
S. Charles St.

Sited on a large plaza at the southeast corner of the Charles Center (see BC23) redevelopment area, Sun Life embodies the planning principles and International Style vocabulary of Baltimore's signature commercial district urban renewal project. The steel frame rests on just four main steel beams set in bedrock. Granite facing between the ribbon windows and at the top and bottom of the fourteen-story tower give Sun Life's facade strong horizontal lines. The same design team designed the nearby Mercantile Bank and Trust Building (1969–1975; 111 W. Baltimore Street) with complementary, but different, fine materials and careful proportions.

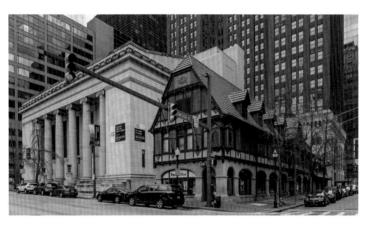

BC25 HANSA HAUS
1911, Parker, Thomas and Rice. 11
S. Charles St.

The Savings Bank of Baltimore commissioned one of the city's most illustrious firms to design an office for their German tenant Albert Schumacher and Co. The large German immigrant community in the city supported a thriving passenger and freight business between Bremen, Germany, and Baltimore. As agents for the North German Lloyd Steamship Company, company officials requested a unique building possibly modeled on a medieval courthouse in Halbertstadt, Germany.

The two-and-a-half-story, brick and stucco building with decorative half-timbering was named Hansa Haus after the medieval Hanseatic League, a trade confederation of German city-states. The steep jerkinhead roof frames a gable facing Charles Street that includes a tile panel depicting a ship under full sail. Originally the exterior walls were decorated with the coats of arms of the Hanseatic League cities. Still, it is remarkable that Hansa Haus has survived both economic pressures and anti-German sentiment during World Wars I and II and remains largely intact and in use as retail and office space.

BC26 SAVINGS BANK OF BALTIMORE
1905–1907, Parker and Thomas.
1 E. Baltimore St.

This so-called Temple of Thrift (*pictured with* BC25) built of ashlar Beaver Dam marble was modeled after Greek temples. Taking advantage of its corner location and to impress potential customers, the bank includes two facades, with a classical portico to the front and an inset colonnade on the side, both with full-height fluted Ionic columns. Contrasting with its imposing classical details, decorative cast-iron window grilles provide a notable modern touch. The Savings Bank of Baltimore was established in 1818 by a group of the city's wealthiest citizens to provide a safe repository for the savings of the less affluent yet "worthy poor" as a means of encouraging thrift. This building was the bank's second home, erected after the first was destroyed in the 1904 fire. The classical design was selected by the bank's directors to express security, strength, and dignity.

BC27 LORD BALTIMORE HOTEL
1928, William L. Stoddart. 20 W. Baltimore St.

When opened in 1928, this was the largest hotel ever built in the state of Maryland and a prime example of up-to-date hotel construction. New York City architect Stoddart specialized in hotel architecture, having worked early in his career for George B. Post and Sons, the firm largely responsible for creating the early-twentieth-century urban hotel building type. The scale and form of the urban hotel had shifted from a single tower such as the Belvedere Hotel (BC21) to multitower forms rising from a base several stories high. Advances in structural engineering allowed ballrooms and other large spaces to be located on the lower floors, such as the second-floor ballroom at the Lord Baltimore. This arrangement was now considered preferable to moving large groups up and down on elevators to ballrooms on the top floor.

Stoddart designed hotels and commercial buildings for many smaller cities, mainly in the South, but the Lord Baltimore stands out as one of his largest projects. This twenty-three-story structure has a U-shaped plan for the guest-room floors with a decorative mansard roof tower crowning the center, creating a distinctive profile on the Baltimore skyline. The inventive combination of stylized Renaissance Revival and classical motifs was highly fashionable in hotel design of the late 1920s. Operated by the Radisson chain for many decades, the Lord Baltimore was renovated in 2014 and is now independently operated.

BC28 BREWERS' EXCHANGE
1896, Joseph Evans Sperry. 20 Park Ave.

This elegant three-story Beaux-Arts classical building was designed by a leading Baltimore architect for the ale and beer brewers' guild of Baltimore. Baltimore was a national center of the brewing industry, largely due to the imported expertise of its German immigrants. The Brewers' Exchange both offered a venue to negotiate prices for brewing-related commodities and securities and became a striking symbol of the accomplishments of the local industry. At this midpoint in Sperry's prolific career he was the sole partner in his firm. The richly decorated terra-cotta facade was fabricated by the New York Architectural Terra-Cotta Company.

BC29 HUTZLER'S DEPARTMENT STORE

1888, Baldwin and Pennington; 1931–1932, 1941 additions, James R. Edmunds Jr. 210–234 N. Howard St.

Built in an eclectic Romanesque Revival style, this was Baltimore's first purpose-built department store in what subsequently became the fashionable retail center of the city, now an uncommon survivor of late-nineteenth-century department store design. It was built for the German-Jewish Hutzler brothers, who referred to their grand new store as the Palace Building. The striking design features pressed-metal polygonal bays, Moorish arched entrance, pediment ornamented by the Goddess of Justice intertwined with the "Hutzler's Brothers" name, and stone foliage and arabesque carvings, heads, and rustication. The interior contains a double atrium with two sky-lit courts modeled after the exclusive Bon Marché in Paris. Hutzler's marked the final transition from specialty shop to dry-goods store to department store, ushered in by urbanization, cheap mechanized production of ready-made goods, and delivery of goods by railway, coupled with streetcar lines providing customers easy access to downtown.

A five-story Art Deco section by Edmunds was later appended, and a new street-level facade of the same polished black granite was applied to the original building to tie the parts together. It was one of the few department stores to expand during the Depression era, further extended by the planned, five-story Hutzler's Tower. Built of variegated brick forming vertical bands of windows, columns, and pilasters, it has a black granite street facade punctuated by large plate-glass display windows and Art Moderne entrances with sleek revolving doors. Hutzlers ceased operations in 1990, and the buildings now sit vacant.

BC30 STEWART'S DEPARTMENT STORE (POSNER BUILDING)

1899, Charles E. Cassell. 226–232 W. Lexington St.

The success of the Hutzlers Brothers' department store sparked the development of others including the equally impressive Renaissance Revival building erected directly across the street for Elias and Samuel Posner. It was sold in 1904 to Louis Stewart, becoming the flagship building for the local Stewart's Department Store chain. The richly ornamented, white brick and terra-cotta building has two principal facades to take advantage of its corner location, each with a central pedimented entrance pavilion flanked by large display windows, featuring Ionic and Corinthian columns, garlands, and lion's heads. The building demonstrates how appealing architectural motifs were as much a part of department store design as street-front display windows and open floor plans, luring customers with the company's good taste and distinguishing them from their competitors. The building is among Cassell's best works, hailed in its day as "one of the largest and handsomest business structures in the city."

BC31 G. KRUG AND SON IRONWORKS AND MUSEUM
1810; last-quarter-19th-century additions. 415 W. Saratoga St.

Standing alone and seemingly out of step with its surroundings is a rare surviving early Baltimore ironworks recognized as the oldest continually operating blacksmith shop in the nation. Begun by blacksmith Augustus Schwatka, operations expanded under Gustav Krug to include architectural wrought and cast iron. Krug began working here in 1858, reestablishing the business as G. Krug and Son by 1871. This intriguing three-part brick industrial building now houses both an operating custom metal works manufactory and a museum reflecting Baltimore's role in the development of architectural iron. They produced ornamental fences, railings, doors, locks, and such found on landmarks throughout the city including The Johns Hopkins Hospital (BC77), the Mercantile Safe Deposit and Trust Building (BC44), and the Baltimore Zoo.

The two-and-a-half-story, common-bond brick, Georgian-influenced section housed the original business, later repurposing the adjacent four-story, Flemish-bond brick residential building. The two sections are united by painted signage. A more decorative rear addition introduces round-arched windows separated by pilasters and a double-door entrance with a hoist for the egress of materials and finished products. Built as part of a post–Civil War expansion, it reflects the move from hand-made to steam-powered, machine-made processes to increase production and lower costs. While more modern technologies are currently employed, the business is still operated by the Krug family.

BC32 PASCAULT ROW
c. 1819, attributed to William F. Small; 1978 rehabilitated. 651–665 W. Lexington St.

Along with Hamilton Street Row Houses (BC12), this is the only other extant example of the multi-unit row houses designed by noted architects and master builders in Baltimore during the post–War of 1812 era. This row of stylish late-Federal period terraced houses designed by Latrobe-protégé Small was erected by master builder Rezin Wight for merchant and French émigré Louis Pascault. The period witnessed the arrival of noted architects from Europe and other prominent American cities, where the use of classically inspired architecture was already established. They motivated the design and construction of impressively sized and stylishly detailed individual town houses and multi-unit rows such as this, capitalizing on the city's growing prosperity.

Pascault Row exhibits Adam-esque design manifested in its understated elegance, signature stone oval motif panel, and frontispiece of slender engaged Tus-

Top: Lord Baltimore Hotel (**BC27**). **Middle left (above):** G. Krug and Son Ironworks and Museum (**BC31**). **Middle right (above):** Hutzler's Department Store (**BC29**). **Middle (below):** Brewers' Exchange (**BC28**). **Bottom left:** Hippodrome Theater at the France-Merrick Performing Arts Center (**BC33**). **Bottom right**: Abell Building (**BC35**).

can columns. Later altered to accommodate storefronts as the neighborhood became more commercial, the row was endangered when purchased by the University of Maryland in 1978. The facades were then restored, and the interiors rehabilitated for use as student housing.

BC33 HIPPODROME THEATER AT THE FRANCE-MERRICK PERFORMING ARTS CENTER
1914, Thomas Lamb; 2002–2004 renovated, Hardy Holzman Pfeiffer Associates, Schamu Machowski + Patterson. 12 N. Eutaw St.

Scottish-born architect Lamb was the preeminent theater specialist in the country, designing movie palaces and vaudeville theaters in dozens of major cities through his New York City–based firm during the early twentieth century. In Baltimore he designed a combination motion picture/vaudeville theater for pioneering movie theater promoters Pearce and Scheck that opened on November 23, 1914. As an impressive addition to Baltimore's entertainment district with a richly ornamental facade of terra-cotta and patterned brick, the Hippodrome was promoted as the "largest playhouse South of Philadelphia." Performances at the Hippodrome featured vaudeville acts, short movies, and a house orchestra into the 1950s, thereafter switching to movies only.

The Hippodrome was the last operating downtown movie theater in Baltimore when it was shuttered in 1989. The France-Merrick Foundation spearheaded redevelopment efforts creating a theater complex incorporating a whole city block. The larger space incorporated into the restored theater would address the limitations of the original shallow stage and include the shells of two former bank buildings to the north. The Hippodrome Theater reopened in 2004 with a recreated terra-cotta cornice and signage.

BC34 BALTIMORE EQUITABLE SOCIETY (EUTAW SAVINGS BANK OF BALTIMORE)
1857, Joseph F. Kemp. 21 N. Eutaw St.

This elegant Renaissance Revival building in painted brownstone reflects the importance of the finance industry in Baltimore and the city's role as a national center for manufacturing and shipping. It is also perhaps the oldest building in the Central Business District to survive the 1904 fire. Moreover, it represents an era when banks erected single-purpose structures meant to evoke security and prosperity through the use of dignified, classically inspired architectural motifs. It was erected by builders Gardner and Matthews for the Eutaw Savings Bank, established in 1847, as the company's first purpose-built structure.

By 1887, the company had outgrown this building and had built a new one opposite, at 20 N. Eutaw, designed by Charles L. Carson. This larger and more elaborate brownstone building, in a similar yet more finely articulated Renaissance Revival style, was an indication of the company's growing prosperity. The original building was then sold to the

Baltimore Equitable Society, one of the nation's first and largest fire insurance companies, established in 1794. The "fire mark" depicting clasped hands appeared on the facades of buildings, indicating the protection bestowed to policyholders and alerting firefighters. The bank relocated to a multipurpose structure in 2003, finally following a national trend disregarded for decades by most of Baltimore's financial institutions, which favored remaining in their purpose-built structures as emblematic of their long-standing service to the community.

BC35 ABELL BUILDING
c. 1878, George A. Frederick. 329–335 W. Baltimore St.

Perhaps surprisingly, some of the most exuberant late-nineteenth-century buildings in Baltimore are the vertical manufactories and warehouses of the Loft District, and none better than the Italianate-influenced Abell Building. The attention to detail applied to these industrial buildings is noteworthy, reflecting their design by some of Baltimore's best architects of the period. Considered among Frederick's most successful works, the polychromatic building combines pressed brick, decorative corbeling, and terra-cotta, with lintels, Corinthian columns, and imposts in contrasting stone and marble. Likewise, it encompasses the city's most extensive ornamental cast-iron street-level facade, manufactured by Bartlett, Robbins and Company of Baltimore. The Abell served as one of the city's many vertical manufactories, producing ready-made clothing

at a rate second only to New York City. Considered the best extant loft structure in the district, the building reflects Baltimore's rise as a national industrial leader, from about 1870 to 1915. Others include the Inner Harbor Lofts I, formerly the Heiser (1886), the Rosenfeld (1905), and the Strauss (1887) buildings at 32–42 S. Paca Street that together form a microcosm of industrial loft design as it appeared in Baltimore, reflecting Richardsonian Romanesque, High Victorian Gothic, and Beaux-Arts classical styles.

BC36 ROMBRO BUILDING
1881, Jackson C. Gott. 22–24 S. Howard St.

This is among the most highly embellished late-nineteenth-century industrial building in the area, exhibiting the influence of Néo-Grec with its squared geometry, robust fluted columns, and bold incised floral motif details. Nearly every inch of the building not consumed by floor-to-ceiling sash windows is represented by ornamental brick and terra-cotta and a decorative cast-iron storefront manufactured by the Variety Iron Works of Baltimore. Within its brick framework appear a tripartite arrangement of windows separated by slender Corinthian columns in contrasting stone. Although built for the Johnson Brothers, investment bankers, it is named for long-time owner-occupant Morris Rombro, whose name appears in the upper parapet. Rombro's shirt-making manufactory operated here from 1919 until 1958. As with many such industrial buildings, it has been adapted for reuse as apartments.

BC37 ALBERTI, BRINK AND COMPANY AND ASA BUILDINGS
c. 1867, George H. Johnson; 1889. 318–322 W. Baltimore St.

This Renaissance Revival building exhibits the oldest and most distinctive of Baltimore's few extant, full-scale decorative cast-iron facades. It was the work of Johnson, one of the nation's leading designers of cast-iron architecture and an innovator in fireproof construction, and Bartlett, Robbins and Company of Baltimore, one of the nation's foremost architectural ironworks. The production of cast-iron facades in the United States began in the mid-nineteenth century as a cheaper and more easily produced alternative to stone as both ornamental and structural building components. They remained popular until the turn of the twentieth century when replaced by structural steel that provided greater strength albeit without ornamentation. This building is distinctive in its use of twisted Venetian Gothic and Corinthian columns and floor-to-ceiling round-arched windows. It was constructed for Alberti, Brink and Company, fancy goods importers; used by garment manufacturers during the twentieth century; and more recently renovated as housing.

The adjacent ASA Building (1889; 318 Baltimore) is an unusually eclectic and ornate commercial structure that combines brick, brownstone, terra-cotta, and metal. A pressed-metal oriel window rises three stories, stressing the building's verticality while brandishing Sullivanesque spandrels in organic foliated patterns. Terracotta is used to create playful animal heads, masks, solar disk motifs, and intertwining leaves and vines. The monogram *ASA* in the parapet is for original owner Arunah S. Abell, an industrialist and founder of *The Sun* as a "penny paper" in 1837.

BC38 BROMO SELTZER ARTS TOWER (EMERSON BROMO-SELTZER TOWER)
1911, Joseph Evans Sperry. 312–318 W. Lombard St.

The signature structure of Baltimore's historic skyline is actually a remnant of the former Emerson Drug headquarters and laboratory that was demolished by the City of Baltimore in the late 1960s. It was built by Captain Isaac E. Emerson, inventor of the Bromo-Seltzer headache/indigestion remedy and founder of the Emerson Drug Company. Emerson's flair for self-promotion and local boosterism extended to his company headquarters, which featured a fifteen-story campanile modeled on the Palazzo Vecchio in Florence, Italy.

Part of an otherwise conventional building, this dramatically tall corner tower served as a bold advertisement for the company's most successful product. Its clock was purported to be the largest four-dial gravity-driven nonchiming clock in the world, with faces twenty-four-feet in diameter displaying the words "Bromo Seltzer." Until structural concerns required its removal in 1936, the top of the crenellated tower featured an illuminated fifty-one-foot high rotating steel Bromo-Seltzer bottle visible for miles. Since 2008 the tower has housed a series of artists' studios and exhibit space, with tours available of the clockworks and a collection of Bromo Seltzer and Maryland glass bottles. The clock underwent a major restoration in 2015–2017 to return it to its original gravity-driven operation.

BC39 DAVIDGE HALL
1812, Robert Cary Long Sr. 655 W. Baltimore St.

Built of painted handmade brick for the College of Medicine of Maryland, this is the oldest anatomical theater in the nation and one of Baltimore's earliest neoclassical buildings. It features a massive pedimented portico, Delorme dome, and rotunda reminiscent of the Pantheon in Rome. The building is named for physician John Beale Davidge, the college's founder and first dean, who offered lectures on anatomy and physiology, teaching through the path-breaking dissection of human cadavers. The building speaks to the changing nature of medical study in the early nineteenth century when dissection was recognized as the best means for gaining practical knowledge of the workings of the human body.

Modeled after contemporary examples in both the United States and Europe, Davidge Hall combined classroom, library, and laboratory space with two stacked lecture halls. Chemical Hall's first-floor amphitheater features tiers of benches around a central viewing area. Anatomical Hall above is surmounted by the dome, punctuated by circular skylights with an oculus at its apex and an ornamental plaster ceiling. Only three other anatomical theaters were erected in the nation prior to this (Pennsylvania Hospital, 1796; the University of Pennsylvania, 1805–1806; and Dartmouth College, 1811), none of which survives. It was designated a National Historic Landmark in 1997.

CENTRAL BUSINESS DISTRICT EAST

BC40 BATTLE MONUMENT

1815–1825, Maximilian Godefroy. Monument Sq., N. Calvert St., between E. Fayette and E. Lexington sts.

Designed to commemorate the thirty-nine Baltimoreans who died during the War of 1812 British attack on Baltimore on September 12–14, 1814, this is the earliest significant war memorial in the nation. It was constructed concurrent with the Washington Monument (BC1), inducing President John Quincy Adams to proclaim Baltimore the Monumental City. The success of the monument's design, combining neoclassical with Egyptian motifs, is demonstrated by its use as the city's official emblem. As a French immigrant Godefroy was likely influenced by the popularity of the latter style in France, sparked by Napoleon's expedition to Egypt in 1798–1799.

The thirty-nine-foot-high marble monument encompasses a base resembling an Egyptian cenotaph, a column carved in the form of a Roman fasces, and an allegorical statue of Lady Baltimore. The eighteen rusticated marble layers of its base symbolize the states within the union at that time. False doors enhance its tomb-like appearance, suggesting Egyptian themes of dignity and eternity, with black marble inscriptions guarded by griffins, the symbol of immortality. The cords that bind the fasces, the Roman symbol for unity, bear the names of the thirty-nine dead. Lady Baltimore wears a victory crown and holds in one hand a laurel wreath, a symbol of glory, and in the other, a rudder, a symbol of navigation or stability. The figures were crafted by Italian sculptor Antonio Capellano. It is situated in Monument Square, fronting the Baltimore City Courthouse (BC41).

BC41 CLARENCE M. MITCHELL JR. COURTHOUSE (BALTIMORE CITY COURTHOUSE)

1894–1901, Wyatt and Nolting. 100 N. Calvert St.

Baltimore conducted a nationwide design competition for a new courthouse, which attracted entries from such prominent ar-

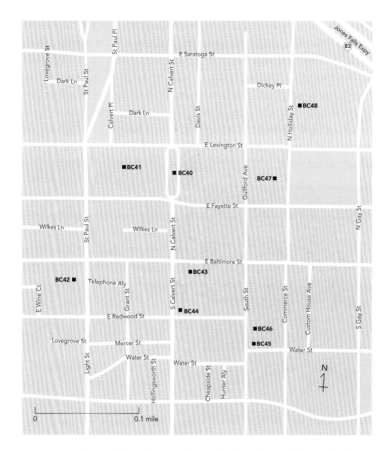

chitects as Daniel Burnham and Carrère and Hastings. Beaux-Arts classicism was emerging as the design idiom for major public buildings, particularly just after the World's Columbian Exposition of 1893 in Chicago. Local architects Wyatt and Nolting won the blind competition with a design creatively combining Greek, Roman, and Renaissance Revival details. The courthouse fills the entire block on the west side of Monument Square facing the Battle Monument (BC40). Its imposing facade features a tripartite composition of a tall rusticated granite base, white marble upper stories punctuated by a monumental Ionic colonnade at the center, and a balustraded cornice. The Beaux-Arts ideal of cooperation between the arts extended to the interior, with a rich decorative program of murals, sculptures, marble staircases, and other features. Painter John La Farge contributed *The Lawgivers,* a mural depicting a gathering of Moses, Emperor Justinian, Mohammad, and Confucius, four leaders of the world's major religions.

The U.S. Post Office and Courthouse (1930–1932, James A. Wetmore, Supervising Architect of the U.S. Treasury) stands on the east side of Monument Square. Its classical design was intended to be a companion piece to the city courthouse when it replaced an earlier Richardsonian Romanesque building from 1890.

To the courthouse's north is Preston Gardens (1914–1919), a four-block linear terraced greenspace that mitigates a difficult ground level change along St. Paul Street. Embodying City Beautiful ideas, the park was designed by landscape architect Thomas Hastings. It features a central grand stairway set against a brick retaining wall leading to curving paired stairways that reach the upper promenade.

BC42 BANK OF AMERICA (BALTIMORE TRUST BUILDING)
1924–1929, Taylor and Fisher, Smith and May; Girard Engineering.
10 Light St.

When completed, at thirty-four stories (509 feet), this was the tallest office building in the country south of New York City, and it is still one of the most prominent and engaging features of the Baltimore skyline. A collaboration of architects and engineers, it is the city's only setback skyscraper and an excellent example of Art Deco. The building was erected of local brick on a framework of structural steel with an elaborate first-story facade, cornice, and exuberant stylized Art Deco details in Indiana limestone. The latter encompass a playful mix of sun-

burst, zigzag, and other geometric patterns interspersed with representations of indigenous wildlife such as the eagle, owl, and crab, designed by Austrian-born Louis Fentner of New York. In the banking hall, murals by Griffith Baily Coale and McGill Mackall depict important events in Maryland and Baltimore history. They are among other artistic representations of the city's progress and industry, embracing themes such as medicine, textiles, shipping, manufacturing, and the railroads.

BC43 ONE SOUTH CALVERT BUILDING (CONTINENTAL TRUST BUILDING)
1899–1901, Daniel H. Burnham.
201–207 E. Baltimore St.

This is the only structure in Baltimore designed by an architect associated with the Chicago School of architecture, pioneers of the iconic skyscraper. The building utilizes iron- and steel-frame construction married with other fireproof materials such as brick, stone, and terra-cotta, sheathed in classically inspired architectural motifs. Indeed, the Continental Trust Building is one of the few to survive the 1904 Baltimore Fire. Although the interior was burned, the shell remained intact, providing one of the first tests of fireproof construction. Known for their aesthetics, Burnham and his contemporaries treated skyscrapers as a three-part composition, the design equivalent of the base, shaft, and capital of the classical column, as exemplified here. The building likewise takes advantage of the structural stability of iron and steel and plate glass to increase the glazed area.

BC44 MERCANTILE SAFE DEPOSIT AND TRUST BUILDING
1885–1886; c. 1899 addition, Wyatt and Sperry. 200 E. Redwood St.

This building was a milestone in the work of Wyatt and Sperry, and the design of which Wyatt is said to have been most proud. It exhibits such hallmark features of Richardsonian Romanesque as massive masonry walls, punctuated by oversized round-arched and flat-banded windows, and lights divided by colonnettes. Likewise, terra-cotta is used to form quoins, lintels, and relief panels cast in intricate foliated patterns and those symbolic of its commercial function, such as the head of Mercury, the god of commerce. Local manufacturers provided much of the building material including bricks and terra-cotta from Russell Burns and Company, structural iron and heating apparatus by Hayward, Bartlett and Company, and ironwork by G. Krug and Son (BC31).

The Mercantile Trust Company is also significant to the commercial history of Baltimore and post–Civil War era financial practice as one of the first to offer "department store" banking, allowing customers to borrow and save from a single institution. Its substantial Romanesque design was used to convey a sense of impenetrability, and it was in fact one of the few buildings to withstand the 1904 Baltimore fire. It was rehabilitated by Helm Foundation in 2012, operating as the Chesapeake Shakespeare Company theater.

BC45 CANTON HOUSE
1923, Smith and May. 300 Water St.

The Colonial Revival Canton House was designed as the headquarters for the Canton Company, first established in 1828. One of Baltimore's largest corporations, Canton was a real estate development, import-export, and manufacturing enterprise that contributed significantly to the rise of the city as a world-class industrial and commercial center. Its myriad operations were located in the waterfront community created and named for the company. Then-president Walter B. Brooks selected Colonial Revival for Canton House to reflect the architecture of the period in which the company was first developed, thereby signifying its long-standing legacy. Built of Flemish-bond brick above a first floor of ashlar limestone, Canton House is elegant in its austerity. The narrow South Street facade approximates a Federal-period town house while the elongated Water Street side with parapet end wall is evocative of early-nineteenth-century commercial architecture.

BC46 FURNESS HOUSE
1917, Edward H. Glidden. 19–21 South St.

Unusual for Baltimore, this striking brick building was erected for the noted Furness Withy and Company steamship enterprise of Great Britain, drawing from the Adamesque architectural tradition native to that country. It was designed by local architect Glidden, known for upscale commercial structures and apartment buildings. Furness House displays refined classically inspired design beginning with an understated limestone-faced ground level with a recessed entrance flanked by tripartite windows. The principal rooms above are manifested on the exterior by an elaborate central pavilion framed by fluted limestone pilasters, dentiled pediment, and a grand Palladian window. Appearing in *The American Architect* in February 1919, Furness House reflects the importance of Baltimore to the international shipping trade of the nineteenth and early twentieth centuries.

BC47 BALTIMORE CITY HALL
1867–1875, George A. Frederick. 100 Holliday St.

One of the earliest and most intact examples of Second Empire government architecture, this monumental building is in a style that dominated American public architecture from the end of the Civil War until around 1880. Its success was demonstrated by its featured appearance in *Harper's Weekly* on May 1, 1869. Frederick's design was likely developed from published sources of Italian Renaissance plates combined with mid-nineteenth-century French books featuring the mansard roof to create an American interpretation of French Renaissance motifs. The building features a central block with four corner pavilions and tall mansard with dormers. A circular tower rising from the center of the building features an iron dome supporting a gilded roof lantern. Inside, an impressive grand stair hall and rotunda are rich in Renaissance ornament derived from classical architecture.

BC48 PEALE CENTER FOR BALTIMORE HISTORY AND ARCHITECTURE (PEALE'S BALTIMORE MUSEUM)
1814, Robert Cary Long Sr.; 1829 renovated, William F. Small; 1930–1931 restored, John Scarff. 225 N. Holliday St.

This neoclassical building was the first in the country designed specifically for use as a museum. It was undertaken under the direction of Rembrandt Peale, the son of renowned painter and naturalist Charles Willson Peale and an accomplished artist in his own right. Peale intended the building to serve as both museum and art gallery, containing such curiosities as a mastodon skeleton, stuffed birds, and Egyptian mummies, as well as Peale family paintings. It was part of Baltimore's post–War of 1812 era rise as a city of arts and culture that included noted works of architecture, monuments, and cultural and scientific institutions.

With no prior design models, Long adopted a traditional five-bay Georgian house scheme. The central bay was expanded to create a monumental stone section laid against the Flemish-bond brick facade, encompassing a recessed entrance, tall round-arched windows lighting the primary exhibition gallery, and pediment with sculptural relief. The building included such innovations as a heating system designed by Robert Mills.

The museum closed in 1829, and following a renovation by William F. Small, reopened as the Baltimore City Hall. From 1878 to 1889, it became part of Baltimore's Colored School system; known as Male and Female Colored School Number 1, it housed one of the city's first grammar schools and the first Black high school in the state. By 1906 the building was abandoned and threatened with demolition. However, public outcry led to its eventual restoration in 1930–1931 under the direction of John Scarff. The building recently was returned to use as a museum, known as the Peale Center for Baltimore History and Architecture.

INNER HARBOR AREA

BC49 INNER HARBOR REDEVELOPMENT
1970s–present. Bounded by Light, E. Pratt, and President sts. and the Patapsco River

The Inner Harbor of Baltimore's deepwater port on the Patapsco River was transformed in the 1970s and 1980s from a gritty mix of industrial and commercial uses into a tourist and entertainment destination. Postwar proposals for aggressive interstate highway construction would have

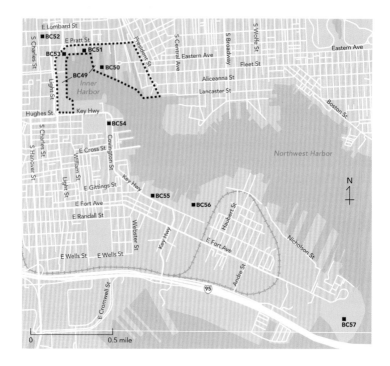

run a bridge across the Inner Harbor to link I-95 to the Jones Falls Expressway and an East–West Expressway along the north side. Public outcry ensued, and early efforts were launched to reclaim land around the Inner Harbor for public use. The Inner Harbor Master Plan of 1964 was a direct outgrowth of the early success of Charles Center (see BC23), and its implementation was overseen by a new city agency created in 1965, Charles Center–Inner Harbor Management. Through this mechanism, city planners enforced design guidelines and arranged the massing of buildings around the Inner Harbor to foreground lower, more sculptural structures framed from behind by mid-rise buildings and tall towers. By the 1970s parks, a brick promenade along the water, and a few key commercial projects such as the United States Fidelity and Guaranty (USF&G) Life Insurance Company's forty-story tower (now the Transamerica Tower; BC52) and the World Trade Center (BC51) were in place.

The original idea was to reclaim the waterfront for Baltimore residents—few people conceived that Baltimore could attract large numbers of visitors. Attitudes began to change with the popularity of the visiting tall ships during the 1976 Bicentennial celebration and the opening of the Maryland Science Center (1971–1975, Edward Durell Stone; 601 Light Street). Also important was the docking of the 1854 sloop-of-war the USS *Constellation* as a permanent attraction, thought to be the original 1797 frigate with modifications. However, it was developer James Rouse's controversial Harborplace (BC53) festival marketplace project that provided a catalyst for the final transformation of the Inner Harbor into a tourist destination. The National Aquarium (BC50) and Baltimore Hyatt Regency (A. Epstein and Sons and RTKL Associates; 300 Light) followed shortly thereafter, both opening in 1981.

Today predominately late-twentieth-century construction around the Inner Harbor is accompanied by a few historic survivors. Maritime history is represented by the USS *Constellation* and other attractions managed by Historic Ships of Baltimore, including the Seven Foot Knoll Lighthouse (1855). Relocated to Pier 5 from the mouth of the Patapsco River in 1988, it is a screw-pile lighthouse typical of the Chesapeake Bay. Another nod to the history of the Inner Harbor includes preservation of the Pratt Street Power Plant (1900–1909, Baldwin and Pennington; 601 E. Pratt Street) as a mixed-use project. Standing in dramatic contrast across the slip on Pier 5, the tent-like fiberglass-reinforced Teflon roof of the Columbus Center (1995, Eberhard Zeidler; 701 E. Pratt) houses event space and a technology incubator now owned by the University System of Maryland. A small glass-walled pavilion with a swooping roofline was added to the park on the west edge of the Inner Harbor in 2004, bringing the architectural ensemble up to the twenty-first century and serving tourists as the Baltimore Visitor Center (2004, Design Collective; 401 Light).

More recent development of hotels and other commercial structures to the east is a testament to the Inner Harbor's continued success as a tourist and convention draw. The transformation of a working harbor into an entertainment district signaled the reinvention of Baltimore to a regional and national audience while, for better or worse, embodying shifts from production to consumption as a catalyst for the American economy.

BC50 BALTIMORE NATIONAL AQUARIUM

1981, Peter Chermayeff for Cambridge Seven Associates; 2002–2005, Bobby C. Poole, with Chermayeff, Sollogub and Poole. Piers 3 and 4, 501 E. Pratt St.

The aquarium stands as the sculptural centerpiece of the Inner Harbor and an example of Baltimore's national influence in urban redevelopment during the 1980s. Designed by an interdisciplinary firm that first reimagined the aquarium building type for Boston's New England Aquarium, this project inspired an international burst of aquarium construction with its bold, sculptural exterior and innovative exhibits. Visitors move on a one-way path through seven levels from the bottom of the Atlantic Ocean to a rainforest canopy under the glass pyramid roof. The dramatic roof profile and position projecting into the harbor compliments the aquarium's status as a blockbuster education and entertainment attraction drawing millions of visitors. Chermayeff's firm also designed the Glass Pavilion north addition that opened in 2005 and added another dramatically angled roof line to the Aquarium's profile.

Top: Baltimore National Aquarium (BC50). **Bottom:** Harborplace at Inner Harbor (BC53).

BC51 WORLD TRADE CENTER
1973–1977, I. M. Pei and Partners. 401 E. Pratt St.

Built by the State of Maryland to spur redevelopment of the Inner Harbor, the World Trade Center is a pentagonal concrete and glass tower twenty-eight stories high that originally housed the Maryland Port Administration. The tower is elevated on concrete piers that straddle the promenade along the water's edge, with one pier emerging from the Inner Harbor itself. The slim tower added a vertical element to the new Baltimore skyline, similar to the USF&G Building (BC52). Long ribbons of windows and a public observation deck on the twenty-seventh floor provide panoramic views of the harbor.

BC52 TRANSAMERICA TOWER (UNITED STATES FIDELITY AND GUARANTY [USF&G] BUILDING, LEGG MASON BUILDING)
1973, Vlastimil Koubek. 100 Light St.

Rapid construction of this forty-story skyscraper launched the Inner Harbor redevelopment effort and marked the transition between that area and the Central Business District. Intended as a signature building and a new consolidated corporate headquarters for USF&G Life Insurance, the tall, slender tower clad in Spanish pink granite sits boldly perched on its own raised plaza encompassing a city block. The fine materials continued on the interiors, which featured extensive use of English brown oak and rosewood. Now called Transamerica Tower, it retains its title as the tallest building in Maryland.

BC53 HARBORPLACE AT INNER HARBOR
1979–1980, Rouse Company, developer; Benjamin Thompson, architect. 301 Light St. and 201 E. Pratt St.

While efforts to reshape the Inner Harbor into a modern commercial district had been underway for years, it was the opening of

Harborplace in 1980 that transformed this former industrial landscape into a tourist destination. Developer James Rouse initiated the "festival marketplace" concept at Faneuil Hall/Quincy Market in Boston before bringing this successful urban redevelopment strategy to his home state of Maryland. With Harborplace, Rouse was seen as an urban savior, appearing on the cover of *Time* magazine in 1981 with the headline "Cities are Fun!" Arranged perpendicularly, each long two-story pavilion has inner and outer retail arcades, with spaces for stores, market stalls, cafés, and restaurants. While architecturally Harborplace resembles any number of the suburban shopping centers developed by Rouse and others, it also recalled the older urban market forms and represented a pathbreaking willingness to invest in inner city redevelopment at a low point in urban living.

Here the existing Baltimore public markets were bypassed to create a reimagined market experience in entirely new buildings. The space at the corner of Light and E. Pratt Streets between the two pavilions became a public plaza and amphitheater that facilitated circulation between the business district and the waterfront. Rouse's vision for festival marketplaces rather idealistically included local retailers re-creating the small-scale capitalism he viewed as the heart of urban life. Initially Harborplace did house some local businesses, but this popular destination quickly became dominated by national chains.

Thompson and Rouse went on to build more festival marketplaces, including South Street Seaport in New York City and Riverwalk in New Orleans. While these projects initially proved to be quite successful, the tenants tended to be major national chains and the overall atmosphere much like the suburban mall. Even as accusations of inauthenticity and questionable benefit to local business dogged Harborplace and other festival marketplaces, they were widely recognized as effective late-twentieth-century downtown redevelopment tools. Sold by the Rouse Company in 2003, Harborplace continues to draw Inner Harbor tourists.

FEDERAL HILL AND LOCUST POINT

BC54 AMERICAN VISIONARY ART MUSEUM (AVAM)

1993–1995, Rebecca Swanston and Alex Castro; 2004, Diane Cho. 800 Key Hwy.

Located at the base of Federal Hill, the AVAM extends the playful artistic vocabulary of its collections to a signature building. The campus includes the 1913 offices of the Baltimore Copper Paint Company, two historic whiskey warehouses, and an outdoor sculpture garden. Described by architect Castro as deliberately nonorthogonal, the museum incorporates the curved brick wall of the former office into its sculptural form, a reuse particularly appropriate for an institution dedicated to outsider art including many works using found objects. A mosaic apprenticeship program for at-risk youth begun in 2000 covered the curved wall with shards of recycled glass, mirror, and china. In 2004 the adjacent whiskey barrel warehouses were adaptively reused and added to the complex as the Rouse Visionary Center. The museum also sponsors a cross-city kinetic sculpture race each year that celebrates the quirky and creative in Baltimore.

BC55 BALTIMORE MUSEUM OF INDUSTRY (S. B. PLATT AND CO. OYSTER PACKING)
1865, 1900 addition. 1415 Key Hwy.

The former complex of the S. B. Platt Company represents one of the earliest surviving examples of a major Maryland industry. Chesapeake Bay oysters were a prized commodity, and canneries devoted to processing and shipping this valuable product proliferated in Baltimore neighborhoods with convenient water and rail access. Many plants expanded into canning fruits and vegetables during the warm months when seafood processing was discontinued. Platt started in 1865 in a two-story brick office/processing building with a one-story workroom ell on the rear. In 1900 a two-story brick addition with ground-level doors was added to move products more easily for shipping. Harbor access at the rear of the complex allowed boats to deliver oysters or produce directly to cleaning sheds. The museum now showcases the original cannery building as well as exhibits on other Baltimore industries. Outdoor displays include a restored 1942 whirly crane from the Bethlehem Steel Fairfield shipyard and the 1906 steam tugboat *Baltimore,* built by the Skinner Shipbuilding Company of Baltimore.

BC56 DOMINO SUGAR FACTORY
1921, Charles T. Main. 1100 Key Hwy. East

The massive neon "Domino Sugars" sign on the roof of this refining plant is arguably one of Baltimore's most recognizable icons and a symbol of this city's historic importance in the sugar-processing industry. Built by the American Sugar Refining Company in one campaign and extending to the harbor on pilings, this sprawling plant was one of the largest sugar refineries in the United States for many decades. It featured a state-of-the-art pressure filtration system for purifying the liquefied sugar that allowed faster production with less labor than older gravity-fed systems. The complex comprises sixteen structures, including four reinforced-concrete processing buildings, offices, warehouses, and ancillary buildings. Currently the refinery continues to process about seven million pounds of sugar a day with about six hundred employees. An LED replica of the original neon sign was installed in 2021.

Top left: American Visionary Art Museum (AVAM; BC54). **Bottom left:** Fort McHenry National Monument and Historic Shrine (BC57). **Right:** Domino Sugar Factory (BC56).

BC57 FORT MCHENRY NATIONAL MONUMENT AND HISTORIC SHRINE
1798–1802; many later modifications. 2400 E. Fort Ave.

The nighttime bombardment of Fort McHenry by the British Navy on September 13–14, 1814, inspired lawyer Francis Scott Key to write the poem that would become the lyrics for the U.S. national anthem. Now a unit of the National Park Service (NPS), Fort McHenry preserves and interprets the original late-eighteenth-century five-bastioned fortification, barracks, officers' quarters, and powder magazine, including buildings and defensive features added later in the nineteenth century. As its importance for coastal defense waned, the fort continued to be used as a garrison until 1912, a hospital during World War I, and a Coast Guard training facility during World War II.

The 1914 centennial of the War of 1812 bombardment raised awareness of the fort's history, and by 1925 it was a national battlefield park under the management of the War Department. In 1933 Fort McHenry and all the battlefield parks were transferred to the National Park Service. Despite modifications and various restoration efforts over the decades, the original brick and earth pentagonal star fort and parade ground configuration is one of the finest examples of early coastal fortifications in the United States.

A contemporary visitor center designed by GWWO Architects of Baltimore opened in 2011 and replaced the one built during the mid-twentieth century NPS improvement program known as Mission 66. Designed with curved walls to reference an abstract flag, the new visitor center's exterior contrasts zinc sheathing in some areas with red brick repurposed from fort restoration work. On the interior, an introductory film culminates with the uncovering of a window wall revealing the fort flying a reproduction of the Star Spangled Banner Flag, continuing a tradition started with the previous visitor center.

EAST BALTIMORE/OLD TOWN/FELL'S POINT

BC58 HOMESTEAD ROW HOUSES

c. 1830; 1970s renovated. 600 block of Stirling St.

This row of the ubiquitous two-and-a-half-story Baltimore row house was among the first to be renovated under the city's path-breaking 1970s Homesteading project aimed at the revitalization of abandoned city-owned houses. Under the program, any one of five thousand vacant houses could be purchased for $1 by a new owner willing to commit to its renovation. The highly successful program is credited with the resurgence of such older areas of the city suffering from deterioration and suburban flight as Federal Hill, Fell's Point (see BC66), and Otterbein (BC81). This was the most common row house form to appear in Baltimore from the 1790s through the mid-nineteenth century. The units are grouped in pairs with sally ports between units for access to the backyards from an otherwise impenetrable row. They originally provided housing for workers in Old Town's early manufacturing district.

BC59 THE MCKIM CENTER (THE MCKIM FREE SCHOOL)

1833–1835, William F. Small and William K. Howard. 1120 E. Baltimore St.

Built through an endowment from Quaker cotton merchant John McKim, this is among the first and most archaeologically correct examples of the Greek Temple form in Baltimore. The design for the granite building with its monolithic Doric columns was derived from the Temple of Athena and Hephaestus in Athens and the north wing of the Acropolis's Propylaea. Small and Howard likely referred to James Stuart and Nicholas Revett's influential publication *Antiquities of Athens* of 1762. As symbolic of a nation founded on democratic principles, the Greek Temple was deemed an appropriate model for Baltimore's first school directed toward free public education. The realization of John McKim's vision for the education of indigent immigrant

youth, it became the model for the city's Public School buildings No. 1 through No. 4 (no longer extant). In the post–Civil War era, it was supplanted by the public school system, becoming the city's first free kindergarten. In 1945, in partnership with the Society of Friends, it was adapted for reuse as the McKim Community Center featuring youth training, athletic programs, and community outreach.

BC60 OLD TOWN FRIENDS MEETING HOUSE (AISQUITH STREET MEETING HOUSE)
1781, George Matthews; 1967 restored, Francis H. Jencks. 1201 E. Fayette St. at Aisquith St.

Among the oldest religious buildings in the city, the meeting-house reflects both the diversity of religious groups represented in Maryland and Friends' influential role in Baltimore's early development. Although Maryland was established as a Catholic colony, there were more Quakers in the state by the turn of the nineteenth century. The meetinghouse was attended by some of Baltimore's most prominent businessmen and philanthropists including hospital founders Johns Hopkins and Moses Sheppard; first president of the B&O Railroad Philip Thomas; John McKim, industrialist and founder of the McKim Free School; members of the Ellicott family, founders of Ellicott's Mills; and industrialists and abolitionists Elisha Tyson and son Isaac. Altered from an English plan to conform to the prototype developed by American

Friends with separate but equally sized rooms for men and women during the late eighteenth century, Old Town highlights an important period of transition. Vacated in the 1920s, it was restored in 1967 and reopened as part of the Peale Museum system, leased to the McKim Center to provide programing for the underprivileged youth of the community.

BC61 JEWISH MUSEUM OF MARYLAND (LLOYD STREET AND B'NAI ISRAEL SYNAGOGUES)
1845, Robert Cary Long Jr.; 1860 extension, William H. Reasin. 11 Lloyd St.
1876, Henry Burck; 27–35 Lloyd St.

The Lloyd Street synagogue (*pictured above*), a Greek Revival temple-front building, was the first purpose-built synagogue in Maryland, erected for the original Baltimore Hebrew Congregation from which all others sprang forth, and the third-oldest synagogue in the country. It is distinguished by its massive portico of fluted Doric columns and a stained glass window depicting the Star of David, the first appearance on the exterior of an American synagogue. As dictated by Jewish tradition, the interior includes flanking balconies for women, and in the basement are

ritual baths and ovens for baking Passover bread. The east end was later extended thirty feet.

In 1891, the congregation built another synagogue, selling this building in 1905 to the Jewish Guardians of the Sacred Heritage. By the 1950s, the congregation had dwindled, and the building was threatened with demolition. In response, the Jewish Historical Society was formed; the synagogue was restored and in 1960 was rededicated as the Jewish Museum of Maryland, interpreting the Jewish experience in America with the emphasis on Maryland. The museum utilizes both this and the neighboring B'nai Israel synagogue built for the Chizuk Amuno Congregation, or Defenders of the Faith, a High Victorian Gothic building with Romanesque and Moorish touches.

BC62 BALTIMORE SHOT TOWER (PHOENIX SHOT TOWER)
1828. 800 E. Fayette St.

When the old Phoenix Shot Tower in the Jonestown neighborhood was threatened with demolition in 1921, the citizens of Baltimore rallied to save this rare industrial artifact. The tapered and crenellated brick tower rose to a height of 215 feet, making it the tallest structure in the United States for nearly two decades after its completion in 1828. The height was a purely functional response to lead drop shot production methods based on Englishman William Watts's 1782 patent. Molten lead was dropped from the top of the tower through a perforated metal plate, or colander, with holes sized according to the shot type desired (mainly for small game hunting). The round drops that naturally formed on the descent were collected and cooled in a water tank at the bottom, and then sorted, polished, and packed in twenty-five-pound sacks.

A fire in 1882 destroyed the tower's interior, which was rebuilt, and shot production continued until 1892, when newer methods prevailed. The tower's purchase by concerned citizens and transfer to the city represents one of the first examples of historic preservation in Baltimore. It was restored in 1928 and opened to visitors as a scenic overlook. Now leased and operated by Carroll Museums and situated within a park, this National Historic Landmark needs repairs and safety upgrades to again allow visitor access.

BC63 CARROLL MANSION (CATON HOUSE)
c. 1811. 800 E. Lombard St.

Touted in its day as the finest house in Baltimore, this remains one of the city's best examples of Federal period architecture. It was designated a National Historic Landmark as the last residence of Charles Carroll of Carrollton, a signer of the Declaration of Independence. It stands in the former Jonestown, Baltimore Town's earliest neighborhood, erected for wealthy merchant Henry Wilson. Although its architect is not known, it has been speculated it was William F. Small.

In 1821, it was acquired by Carroll for his daughter Mary and her husband, merchant banker Richard Caton. In later life, Carroll left Doughoregan Manor (CM10) each year to spend the winter months here, making it his permanent residence from 1827 until his death in 1832. While imposing, the design of the house is elegantly restrained; it is constructed of Flemish-bond brick with a central pavilion and a gable roof with interior slab chimneys. It rises three-and-a-half stories to encompass a ground level with a counting room where Caton received his business associates (originally with its own exterior entrance, since infilled) and an open elliptical staircase that rises the full height of the house. The elevated second floor contained the primary entertaining rooms with bedchambers above. The house was bought by the City in 1914 as part of the centennial commemoration of the 1814 Battle of Baltimore during the War of 1812 (followed by its purchase of the nearby c. 1793 Star-Spangled Flag House at 844 Pratt Street in 1929). The Carroll Mansion opened in 1918 as Baltimore's first vocational school, becoming its first recreation center in 1929 and a New Deal–era settlement house in 1935. It was restored and opened as a house museum in 1967.

BC64 LEWIS MUSEUM OF MARYLAND AFRICAN AMERICAN HISTORY
2005, RTKL Associates, with Freelon Group. 830 E. Pratt St.

Opened in 2005 with funding from the foundation created by philanthropist Reginald F. Lewis, the museum highlights African American history and culture in Maryland and beyond. Reviewing the new museum for the *Baltimore Sun,* Edward Gunts praised "its use of architectural symbolism—through colors, forms, and materials—to create a building that avoids cliches but is undeniably African-American in spirit." During planning, the possibility of reusing an existing building or designing something with overt African symbolism were both rejected in favor of a more abstract new design. Baltimore firm RTKL Associates, longtime leaders in local modernist design, and the Freelon Group of Durham, North Carolina, used the colors black, red, ivory, and gold, referencing both the Maryland flag and diversity of African heritage, to enliven the simple yet bold exterior volumes of the museum. Particularly prominent is the full-height angled red wall at the Pratt Street entrance atrium,

intended to symbolize the abrupt change in status quo of Africans being forcibly taken to North America.

BC65 EASTERN AVENUE PUMPING STATION
1910–1911, Henry Brauns. 751 Eastern Ave.

Opened in 1912 as a key piece of Baltimore's new sewerage system, the pumping station's location granted easy access by rail or barge for coal delivery to power its three large Corliss engines. The grand Classical Revival building with orange brick walls accented by granite and sandstone presented a fashionable public face masking its prosaic function. In 1960 the Corliss engines and exterior coal conveyors were removed for smaller electric turbines, and the smokestack was shortened. The pumping station continues to serve its original purpose while efforts have launched recently to revive the Public Works Museum that operated in a portion of the building from 1982 to 2010.

BC66 FELL'S POINT HISTORIC DISTRICT
c. 1726 established; 1761 town plan, Edward Fell. Bounded roughly by the Patapsco River and Castle, Gough, and Caroline sts.

Developed separately from early Baltimore Town is Fell's Point, a once thriving port town annexed in 1773 to become the epicenter of the city's eighteenth- and nineteenth-century maritime and shipping industries. Fell's Point dates to its c. 1726 settlement by English Quakers Edward and William Fell, and it was here that William, a ship carpenter, established the area's first shipyard. A gridded town plan concentrated around the waterfront was laid out in 1761 by William's son Edward and his wife Ann. Possessing the deepest harbor, Fell's Point was key to Baltimore's rise as an important industrial center, including the manufacture of its sailing schooners and the famed Baltimore clipper. Baltimore's shipping industry declined in the 1830s with the development of canals and railroads. Steam-powered industries replaced shipbuilding, including machine shops and iron foundries, oyster-packing plants, and canneries. Fell's Point includes some of Baltimore's earliest buildings, encompassing a fine array of late-eighteenth- and nineteenth-century row houses representing many of the city's quintessential forms, as well as commercial and industrial structures and warehouses that reflect the important role it played in Baltimore's economic development.

BC67 THE INN AT HENDERSON'S WHARF AND BELT'S LANDING CONDOMINIUMS (HENDERSON'S WHARF B&O RAILROAD TOBACCO WAREHOUSE AND BELT'S WHARF WAREHOUSE)

1897, E. Francis Baldwin; c. 1870; 1991 renovated. 1000 and 936 Fell St.

Adjoining one another are the former warehouses for the Baltimore and Ohio Railroad and Belt's Wharf, among the last remnants of the national shipping network that operated in Baltimore from the post–Civil War era to about 1930. The former was designed by Baldwin as official architect for the B&O. This handsome brick building (*pictured above*) was used as a tobacco bailing and storage facility during a period when Maryland was the third-largest producer of tobacco in the country. Tobacco from the southern Tidewater region was shipped to the wharf, sorted, and packed into hogsheads before being sent to market. The massively scaled and finely detailed building rises six stories, with huge ground-level arched openings covered by paired iron doors, a reminder of its days as a stronghold for lucrative tobacco shipments. The warehouse was redeveloped as a hotel and condominiums.

Adjoining it is the older Belt's Wharf Warehouse, the last such facility to operate in Fell's Point. Established in 1845, Belt's Wharf was the terminal warehouse for a shipping fleet operated by Baltimore merchant C. Morton Stewart. Concealing earlier sections, the current building consists of a decorative brick facade featuring round-arched ground level openings with recessed entrances and unusually ornamental facades featuring pilasters with corbeled brick capitals set within a similarly styled cornice. The large second-floor arched openings were originally used as loading bays. The warehouse was redeveloped as condominiums in 1984–1991, part of the larger transition of such buildings for residential use.

BC68 CAPTAIN STEELE HOUSE
c. 1788. 931 Fell St.

This is one of Baltimore's last surviving intact Georgian houses, built for prominent merchant Jesse Hollingsworth and later purchased by Captain John Steele. Urban dwellings of its size and sophistication were fairly uncommon at the time of its construction, and most that did exist were erected in the Old Town area near the Inner Harbor and have long since disappeared. The house is an elegant, three-and-a-half-story, three-bay, side-passage dwelling erected with Flemish-bond brick, distinguished by its stylish detailing. Located near the wharf along a largely commercial street, the building stands out among its neighbors, reflecting the lifestyles of the merchant class in Fell's Point during the late eighteenth century.

BC69 ROBERT LONG HOUSE
c. 1765; later additions. 812 S. Ann St.

Believed to be the only surviving colonial-period building in Fell's Point, this house was built for Robert Long, who purchased lot no. 144 of the Fell family's newly created town plan. Its design reflects the architectural character of the southeastern Pennsylvania region from which Long originated, exemplified by the distinctive pent roof over the first-story bays. Falling into neglect by 1969, it was scheduled for demolition, but it was saved by the Society for the Preservation of Federal Hill and Fell's Point and purchased in 1975 for use as its headquarters. The house was restored and now interprets the life of a Fell's Point merchant of the eighteenth century.

BC70 FELL'S POINT RECREATIONAL PIER
1914, Theodore Wells Pietsch; 2017 rehabilitated. 1715 Thames St.

The pier functioned as both a social center for the local, largely immigrant community and as one of the East Coast's largest ports of entry for the shipping trade. Modeled after the public piers that appeared in British seaside towns, it included a dance hall and other spaces for social and educational gatherings. With ferry service between it and Locust Point across the river, the pier served as a point of passage for immigrants newly processed at the Locust Point Immigration Station. And as part of a working pier, it housed the offices of the harbormaster. The building combines elements of Georgian Revival and Beaux-

Arts classicism, encompassing a great hall manifest on the exterior facade by full-height arched windows behind an arcade of Doric columns. The rusticated ground level's wide entrance portal facilitates both pedestrian and vehicular access to the pier. Left vacant for many years, the building's transformation into a boutique hotel was completed in early 2017. The ballroom once occupied by immigrants is now an opulent banquet hall.

BC71 BOND STREET WHARF BUILDING
2002, RTKL Associates. 901 S. Bond St.

Designed by a prominent Maryland architectural firm, this industrial-scaled building was intended to create unconventional workspace to attract IT companies as part of a "Digital Harbor" campaign. It was built on the site of the former Terminal Warehouse (1900) that burned in 1992. The contemporary design is in keeping with the warehouse buildings that appeared along the Fell's Point waterfront during the nineteenth century, a few of which remain, such as the adjacent Brown's Wharf Warehouses (1822, 1868; 1621 Thames Street). Like its predecessors, the Bond Street Wharf building employs varying window types and sizes, belt courses, and other architectural features to lessen the impact of its grand scale and to blend with the surrounding commercial buildings. Perhaps its most distinctive feature is the broad multicolored painted banner that reflects the painted signage that historically appeared on warehouses and other commercial buildings throughout the city. To the west side is an open courtyard and welcoming greenspace that overlooks the harbor and faces the distinctive Levering and Company Coffee Warehouse (c. 1846; 1401 Thames Street), with its parapet-gable end facade, loading bays, and rounded corners.

BC72 SHAKESPEARE STREET ROW HOUSES
1790s. 1628–1632 Shakespeare St.

Typical of the row houses that were home to average Baltimoreans from the late eighteenth century through the 1840s was

Top left: Douglass Place (BC73). **Bottom left:** National Can Company (BC75). **Right:** Patterson Park Observatory (BC76).

the two-story design with a single dormer and either two or three bays across. They appeared on side streets and alleys, depending on size, providing housing to workers, artisans, shopkeepers, and those involved in the maritime trade. Early examples such as this row of three exhibit such Federal detailing as Flemish-bond brick with stone jack-arch lintels, entrance with transom, corbeled cornice, and slab chimney. Most were two rooms deep (although the more modest examples were only a single room) with no hall and a tight winder stair between the two rooms; only the larger three-bay-wide examples included a side hall. The earliest were of frame construction, only a few of which survive, such as 809 S. Bond Street.

BC73 DOUGLASS PLACE
c. 1892–1893. 516–524 S. Dallas St.

This group of five modest row houses was built by prominent abolitionist and activist Frederick Douglass as an investment property. Their location in a narrow alley illustrates the use of these spaces for worker housing in Baltimore before this practice was outlawed in the early twentieth century. Each house is two-stories high and two bays wide on a raised basement, with a one-story ell at the rear. While small, the houses were up-to-date with vernacular Italianate features such as sheet metal cornices with brackets and segmental-arched door and window openings. In typical Baltimore fashion, the houses front directly on the sidewalk with a brick stoop leading to the doorway.

BC74 SHIP CAULKERS' HOUSES
c. 1797. 604, 612–614 S. Wolfe St.

The double house at 612–614 and the single at 604 are rare survivors of a once common eighteenth-century dwelling form inhabited by Baltimore's working class. Of frame construction with partial brick nogging, the units are only a story-and-a-half in height and two-bays wide, measuring a modest 12 × 16 feet. They consisted of a single room with a fireplace and winder stair in one corner that led to a loft above, lit by a single dormer window. As frame structures, they predate the city's 1799 ordinance that prohibited the construction of such residences, then determined to be a fire hazard. According to city directories, they were occupied during the 1830s through the 1850s by African American freedmen and their families; the men were typically employed as ship caulkers working in the yards located just a few blocks away. The double house is quickly deteriorating, while the single house has been restored.

BC75 NATIONAL CAN COMPANY
c. 1880; c. 1900; 1934–1939 renovated. 801 S. Wolfe St.

This Art Deco cannery, rehabilitated as apartments, reflects the important role that Baltimore played during the late nineteenth and early twentieth centuries as the center of the canning industry in America, and in the 1930s as the can-making center of the world. Its dominance is attributed to Baltimore's extensive transportation network combined with ready access to Maryland's produce and fishing industries. Factories in Fell's Point, Canton, and southeast Baltimore manufactured both cans and canned foodstuff. The National Can Company encompasses two buildings erected for the oyster-packing industry, now set behind a modern facade. Can making began here in 1909 with the John Boyle Can Company. Purchased by the Metal Package Corporation in 1920, the company focused exclusively on the production of cans and decorative metal containers. It was acquired by National Can Company in 1935, and the plant was refurbished to include the current Art Deco facade, one of Baltimore's few such industrial buildings.

BC76 PATTERSON PARK OBSERVATORY
1891–1892, Charles H. Latrobe. E. Lombard St at Patterson Park.

Architect Charles Latrobe, third generation of the family to design buildings in Baltimore, used his experience as a bridge designer and civil engineer to design this fanciful observatory with a prefabricated iron superstructure on a granite base. The four-story octagonal observatory is topped by a conical roof and has projecting balconies at each level reminiscent of a Chinese pagoda. It served to enhance Patterson Park's greatest natural asset—its hilltop view of the harbor and the Chesapeake Bay. The park was incrementally expanded starting in 1860 from a small 1827 promenade popular in this densely developed residential area of east Baltimore. While it is smaller than Druid Hill Park (BC101) in northwest Baltimore, the improvements to Patterson Park exhibited the same picturesque English-inspired design and civic-minded goals, with an increased emphasis on athletics in the early twentieth century.

BC77 THE JOHNS HOPKINS HOSPITAL
1877–1889, John Shaw Billings and Cabot and Chandler. 601 N. Broadway

One of the leading research and teaching hospitals in the United

States was founded through the generosity of Baltimore philanthropist Johns Hopkins, who left the other half of his fortune to create Johns Hopkins University (see BC105). In his 1873 letter directing the work of the hospital trustees, Hopkins requested "a Hospital, which shall, in construction and arrangement, compare favorably with any other institution of like character in this country or in Europe." To accomplish this goal, advice was sought from five doctors who could offer thoughts on best practices for hospital design. In this period modern medicine was still in its infancy and purpose-built hospitals rare. The trustees presumed they would build the most current hospital form recently imported from Europe—a pavilion plan hospital with a central administration building and separate ward buildings connected by corridors.

Army doctor Billings proposed a main building flanked on either side by a ward building, with over a dozen pavilion wards to the rear of the fourteen-acre site connected by low corridors. Today only the Administration Building, with its grand rotunda, and two former "pay ward" buildings to either side remain as remarkable survivors of nineteenth-century hospital design among a greatly expanded twentieth- and twenty-first-century medical complex. Designed by the Boston firm of Cabot and Chandler, these structures are a tour de force, of decorative detailing in pressed brick, terra-cotta, and Cheat River blue stone, topped by a lively copper-sheathed roofline.

BC78 THE HARRY AND JEANETTE WEINBERG BUILDING (AMERICAN BREWERY)
1887, Charles Stoll; 2009 rehabilitated, Cho Benn Holback + Associates. 1701 N. Gay St.

Baltimore has a long brewing history thanks to its large German immigrant population, with twenty-nine breweries supplying beer to local taverns by 1850. Technological changes and increasing demand for beer resulted in the establishment of large-scale operations such as American Brewery. The brewery was founded in 1863 by John Frederick Wiessner, who immigrated from Germany in 1853. In 1886, Wiessner's expansions included this eclectic building, an imposing five-story brick and stone structure with an iron frame and a central tower with a mansard roof. As was typical of the time, the interior was laid out for gravity-flow processing, with malt storage in the tower and state-of-the-art Linde ice machines for artificial refrigeration. In 2009 the building underwent an award-winning rehabilitation for use as nonprofit offices.

BC79 ORIOLE PARK AT CAMDEN YARDS

1989–1992, Joseph Spear for HOK Sport; RTKL Associates, planner. 333 W. Camden St.

Opened in 1992 as the home of the American League Baltimore Orioles and the first baseball-only Major League Baseball (MLB) stadium built in decades, Camden Yards had a profound influence on stadium design in the United States. It ushered in a new retro design approach inspired by vintage baseball stadiums while it also embraced its historic setting. The ballpark garnered widespread praise from fans, players, and architectural critics for its revival of baseball tradition, integration into the urban fabric, and stunning views of the Baltimore skyline.

Prior to construction of Oriole Park at Camden Yards, the Orioles played at Memorial Stadium (1922, Pleasants Pennington and Albert W. Lewis; demolished 2001), one of the first multipurpose stadiums of the mid-twentieth century. HOK Sport, a subsidiary of the firm Hellmuth, Obata and Kassabaum, initially considered various sites outside the city for a conventional multipurpose stadium replacement. Then the Orioles organization asked for a more traditional, baseball-only facility in downtown Baltimore, with the site at the Camden Station B&O Railroad yards ultimately inspiring a more creative and successful solution. Modern amenities such as skyboxes were combined with traditional baseball experiences such as an asymmetrical structure housing a grass field in an urban setting. The upper decks were supported on steel trusses instead of concrete, creating a visually lighter structure that recalled historic ballparks. The massive, four-block-long B&O warehouse (1898–1905, E. Francis Baldwin) at Camden Yards was renovated to house the Orioles' offices and served as a unique backdrop for right field.

Oriole Park's success directly inspired construction of a host of new retro-style ballparks in urban settings, with HOK Sport dominating this specialized de-

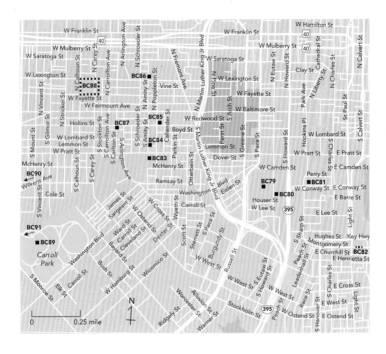

sign field. Now nearly every MLB team plays in a baseball-only park built between 1995 and 2015. The Camden Yards location of both Oriole Park and the stadium for the National Football League Ravens franchise (1996–1998, HOK Sport; 1101 Russell Street) expanded the adjacent Inner Harbor tourist and entertainment zone.

BC80 CAMDEN STATION

1857, 1865–1867 wings; Niernsee and Neilson; 2019 restored, Cho Wilkes Benn. 301 W. Camden St.

This imposing building, a full block in length, was designed by Niernsee and Neilson and overseen by B&O supervising architect Joseph Kemp. It replaced the B&O's Mount Clare Station as the company's principal terminal, relocating closer to downtown and the Inner Harbor while also creating offices for the company's executive staff. Intended to rival the great passenger train stations

of London, Camden Station is a richly ornamented Italianate building featuring a gable-front central section with a grand tower with astronomical clock and wings surmounted by cupolas. Elaborate cast-iron window pediments and traceries, fluted columns, and entrance loggia were produced by the local Hayward and Bartlett Company.

The Italianate style had newly emerged on the Baltimore architectural scene and was one in which Niernsee and Neilson were early proponents. Its exuberant design and expansive footprint reflect the success of the B&O, then expanding its operations. The main block was completed first, with the planned 180-foot central tower and wings following. The station was purchased by the Maryland Stadium Authority for the construction of Oriole Park (BC79) after passenger service was discontinued in 1986 and restored.

BC81 OLD OTTERBEIN
EVANGELICAL UNITED
BRETHREN CHURCH
AND THE OTTERBEIN
NEIGHBORHOOD
*1784–1785, Jacob Small Sr.; 1839
remodeled. 112 W. Conway St.*

Among Baltimore's few surviving eighteenth-century religious buildings, Old Otterbein reflects the religious toleration that attracted a wide range of faiths to the city during its early history. It is also a reminder of the vibrant German community that once surrounded it. The elegant Georgian church was erected of brick using a Flemish-bond pattern for the two street-facing facades. It features a square telescoping entrance tower with an octagonal cupola and round-arched clearglass windows with tracery, characteristics of English architect Christopher Wren's seventeenth-century church architecture. An entrance vestibule was later installed to one side, as was the projecting rear apse.

The church is named for pastor Reverend Philip Wilhelm Otterbein, who came from Germany in 1752 as a missionary to the Germans of Pennsylvania, settling in Baltimore in 1774. Breaking from the Lutheran Church, Old Otterbein became the "mother church" of a new sect, the United Brethren in Christ founded by Otterbein and former Mennonite Martin Boehm, in 1800. Otterbein was buried in the churchyard following his death in 1813, and a monument was erected on the hundredth anniversary. The United Brethren was joined with the Evangelical United Brethren Church in 1946.

The immediate surroundings have been redeveloped with new row houses and the Baltimore Convention Center; however the remains of the Otterbein community lie a block south, bounded by Barre, Hanover, Lee, Hill, and Sharp streets. Situated near the harbor, it is one of the city's oldest residential neighborhoods, originally home to a largely German population that also included merchants, industrialists, and workers of varying nationalities involved in maritime trades.

By the late nineteenth century, Otterbein was inhabited by a mostly poor African American population, and by the 1960s it was threatened with demolition under the guise of urban renewal. It was spared with pressure from preservationists, and the row houses were renovated as one of the city's most successful Homesteading projects. Prototypical forms such as the early two-and-a-half-story with dormer, two-story-plus-attic, and three-story Italianate represent a microcosm of Baltimore's nineteenth-century row house development, as does the adjacent Federal Hill neighborhood.

BC82 "HALF-HOUSE" ROW
HOUSES
c. 1835. 102–116 E. Montgomery St.

These are among the smallest row houses in Baltimore, composed of only the front half of the two-story, gable-roof-with-dormer type, as demonstrated by their original front-facing shed roofs. With only a single room per floor, half-houses were generally built as rentals for those at the lowest income level. This row of eight houses is organized in staggered pairs appearing at an angle to the street to provide greater privacy. While they have since received rear additions to complete the gabled roof configuration, side profiles clearly indicate the ghost of the original form. They are part of a historically African American section known as the Sharp-Leadenhall neighborhood that was established in the 1790s by freed slaves and German immigrants. These row houses were sold to freed craftsmen, including carpenters and blacksmiths. The neighborhood became home to the first school for African Americans in Baltimore (1802, no longer extant) at 112 Sharp Street.

BC83 BALTIMORE AND OHIO TRANSPORTATION MUSEUM (B&O MT. CLARE STATION AND RAILROAD SHOPS)
1851; 1883 Passenger Car Shop and 1891 Print Shop Annex, E. Francis Baldwin. 901 W. Pratt St.

The B&O Museum encompasses what remains of the oldest and most fully integrated railroad manufacturing complex in the United States, if not the world. Established in 1829 as the B&O Mount Clare Station and Railroad Shops, it is recognized as the birthplace of American railroading. It was the site of such innovations in railroading technology as the American steam locomotive pioneered by Ross Winans and Phineas Davis and the first iron railroad bridges in groundbreaking designs by Wendel Bollman. At its height the B&O shops produced everything from steam locomotives, freight and passenger cars, and bridges to hardware and building components used throughout the system. The first long-distance passenger and freight railroad service in the world left here for its initial run along the thirteen-mile line to Ellicott City (see CM6) on May 22, 1830.

The shops began in 1829–1830 as a carriage repair shed and stable (the first cars were pulled by horses). A forge and a machine shop were added in 1833, and by 1834 the first steam-powered locomotives were under production. After the Civil War a foundry, blacksmith shop, and office building were added. At its 1920s height, the shops stretched ten city blocks, turning out an average of eighteen new or rebuilt locomotives per week, with a workforce of about three thousand. The last steam locomotive was manufactured here in 1948, and on July 4, 1953, the 125th anniversary of the laying of the cornerstone of the original tract, the B&O Railroad Museum opened. It comprises one of the most significant collections of historic railroad equipment and artifacts in the world, recognized as a National Historic Landmark in 1961.

Three extant structures comprising the museum are the polygonal Mount Clare Station, Queen Anne library and print shop annex, and the passenger car shop. The latter is a unique twenty-two-sided brick building with clerestory and domed cupola that serviced railroad cars and engines. It was then the largest polygonal building in the world, measuring 240 feet in diameter and featuring a central turntable on which to move the cars. The museum includes rides aboard the Mile One Express train.

BC84 IRISH RAILROAD WORKERS MUSEUM (ROW HOUSES)
1848, Charles Shipley, builder. 912–920 Lemmon St.

These dwellings represent the typical two-bay, two-story-and-attic row houses built for working-class Baltimoreans during the mid- to late nineteenth century. The row was erected by noted local builder Shipley as housing for the largely Irish workers at B&O Railroad's Mt. Clare yards. Evolved from a former two-and-a-half-story type, the new attic story with its low-pitched gable roof and half-story windows provided more usable space. The small windows, derived from the frieze-band windows appearing in the Greek Revival houses built for more affluent citizens, the round-arched lintels, and corbeled brick cornice speak to the attention to detail given to even modest rows, where one existed at every price point,

and competition among builders was fierce.

Home ownership in Baltimore was made affordable by the ground-rent system, charging a nominal annual rental fee for the land, as opposed to outright purchase. This modest row also reflects the city's housing hierarchy whereby the small houses such as these were relegated to alleyways. Only 10 feet, 9 inches wide, they are two rooms deep with a tightly winding stairway between, originally including a single-story frame kitchen to the rear. This group now forms the Irish Railroad Workers Museum as part of the B&O Railroad Museum district, providing insight into the lives of immigrant working-class Baltimore.

BC85 CARTER MEMORIAL CHURCH (ST. PETER THE APOSTLE CHURCH)
1843–1844, Robert Cary Long Jr.; 1849, 1868 additions. 13 S. Poppleton St.

This church was built as a missionary church for the large population of Irish Catholics who settled in this neighborhood to work in the nearby B&O Railroad yards. Designed as a Greek Revival temple, it was modeled after the classical Athenian structure known as the Theseum. The red brick church features a massive hexastyle front, with fluted Doric columns, triglyph- and metope-patterned molded-brick frieze, and cornice with guttae ornament. The church was a cornerstone of the community, expanding to include a rectory (c. 1849), also designed by Long; a convent (c. 1860); girls' school (1869); and the House of Mercy (1869) for distressed women and girls. The rear chancel was extended and the semicircular apse added later. Stained glass windows (1898–1912) were created by the Mayer Studio in Munich. This was the first of four landmark religious buildings by Long, including the similar Lloyd Street Synagogue (BC61), built the following year.

BC86 EDGAR ALLAN POE HOUSE AND THE POE HOMES
c. 1825. 203 Amity St.

This was the Baltimore home of the renowned author, editor, and literary critic best remembered for his macabre short stories. Poe lived here between 1832 and 1835, a crucial period in his career when he turned from poetry to acclaimed short stories. It also represents an intact example of Baltimore's quintessential two-and-a-half-story-with-dormer row house form. It is the only house in the Poppleton neighborhood, once occupied by railroad workers, to survive a 1938 slum clearance project. It was saved by the Edgar Allan Poe Society and opened as a museum in 1949. Poe died in Baltimore under mysterious circumstances in 1849; his grave is located in the Burying Ground of Westminster Hall (Presbyterian Church; W. Fayette and N. Green Streets).

The house now stands among the Poe Homes, the first public housing project in Baltimore, created as segregated housing for African Americans, opening in 1940. The project was modeled after those initiated by the Federal Housing Division of the Public Works Administration. The two- and three-story modernistic brick buildings include a distinctive first-story pent, tripartite windows, and panels of patterned brick, arranged around an open court. It is noteworthy as an initial attempt to address the need for decent, affordable housing for the city's poor Black population. The neighborhood is currently undergoing a second wave of redevelopment. Known as Center/West, the contemporary-designed, mixed-use project by Gensler for La Cité Development provides market-rate and affordable housing units and retail space.

BC87 HOLLINS MARKET
1864, George A. Frederick. 26 S. Arlington Ave.

This Italianate building is the only intact nineteenth-century market house in Baltimore. It was one of eleven municipal market houses operating in the city during their late-nineteenth- and early-twentieth-century heyday, and one of the few that incorporated both a market and civic meeting hall.

Baltimore has a long tradition of public market houses that began with the first in 1763, providing a venue for local farmers offering fresh produce and other foodstuffs. Although the preferred plan was for an open shed-like structure, a few market houses such as Hollins included a second-floor hall that in its day was the only available space for traveling shows, balls, and public receptions. It replaced a typical shed form (similar to the rear addition) built in 1838 to serve the working-class community that developed around the B&O Railroad shops.

BC88 WAVERLEY TERRACE AND FRANKLIN SQUARE

c. 1850, Thomas Dixon, and Charles Shipley, builder. 100 block of N. Carey St. and Franklin Sq.

Waverley Terrace (*pictured above*) is significant for its sophisticated design and location within Franklin Square, one of Baltimore's earliest residential enclaves planned around an urban park. This exceptional grouping constituted the first Italianate row houses in the city. It was built for speculative developers James and Samuel Canby, who designated the park square as an amenity to entice buyers. Built on a grand scale and forming a unified composition, the four-story row houses are fashioned after the Italian Renaissance palazzo to embrace a piano nobile plan. The facades encompass a rusticated ground story in brownstone, with plastered walls painted to resemble the same. The principal floor is distinguished by full-height French windows with heavy bracketed window heads and ornamental iron balcony. Inside, this floor had forty-foot-deep double parlors separated by ornamental columns.

Franklin Square was a response to urban reformers lamenting the lack of healthy, verdant environments as block upon block of dense row house development was taking shape. The row houses set the tone for the neighborhood, which soon became one of the city's best addresses. They are now co-op apartments comprising eight units per house. In 1854, Dixon designed six side-hall plan, full brownstone Italianate row houses to the south side of Franklin Square (1313–1323 W. Fayette Street) known as Canby Place.

BC89 MOUNT CLARE

1756–1760, Patrick Creagh (?), 1767–1768 additions; 1906 wings, Wyatt and Nolting; 1903 landscape, Olmsted Brothers. 1500 Washington Blvd.

The country home and plantation of Charles Carroll (known as the Barrister to distinguish him from the other Charles Carroll), and his wife Margaret Tilghman, this is the only remaining of numerous extravagant colonial-era retreats that once skirted the city. The Georgian house encompasses an opposing five-bay river-facing facade with a central pedimented pavilion and a three-bay carriage facade to which was added a distinctive entrance portico with upper chamber and Palladian window. A kitchen dependency to one side was then matched by an office to the other, both joined to the house by hyphens. The resulting five-part house form had recently appeared in Carroll's home city of Annapolis, as had the polygonal bays on the dependencies and a transverse hall plan with the primary rooms to the rear, facing the river. Such features lend support for its attribution to Annapolis builder Patrick Creagh.

The property was first utilized for recreational purposes in 1870 when leased to the West Baltimore Scheutzen Association as a clubhouse and pleasure grounds. The dilapidated hyphenated wings were removed in 1871. In 1890, Mt. Clare was purchased by the City, and a landscape plan was developed by Olmsted Brothers in 1903. As part of its restoration, the hyphenated wings were rebuilt in 1908, and in 1917 the house opened as a museum, including a rare collection of paintings, furniture, and decorative arts. The former grounds are now Carroll Park.

more. A protracted, planar block of fifty two-story, two-bay-wide red brick row houses flanked by corner stores creates an impressive unified street front. Adding to its visual impact, the block appears as a face-off between two quintessential Baltimore housing forms, these red brick houses with contrasting white marble basement, lintels, and front stoop and similar units faced with Formstone, across the street.

White marble steps and other details are an identifying feature of Baltimore's row housing. Locally quarried Beaver Dam marble added a level of distinction that became a source of pride for many lower- to middle-income homeowners. Formstone, on the other hand, is a faux stone veneer that was developed in Baltimore in 1937 by L. Albert Knight (it is similar to a product first developed in Columbus, Ohio, in 1929). Touted as maintenance free, energy efficient, and fireproof, Formstone was applied as a resurfacing material to untold numbers of the city's row houses. While at the time it was viewed as an upgrade due to its resemblance to more expensive stone, it has since been criticized as undermining historic character, resulting in costly removals. Nonetheless, Formstone has long been a recognizable component of Baltimore's row house landscape.

BC90 WILKENS AVENUE ROW HOUSES

1912, Walter Westphal, builder. 2600 block of Wilkens Ave.

The row of houses along the south side of this block, built by large-scale developer Walter Westphal, is touted as the longest in Balti-

BC91 CARROLLTON VIADUCT

1829, James Lloyd. Across Gwynn's Falls

The first stone masonry railroad bridge built in the United States, this 297-foot-long viaduct carried the earliest section of the B&O

track across Gwynn's Falls on the way to Ellicott's Mills. The finely dressed ashlar stonework includes an arch 80 feet in diameter spanning the water and a smaller arch between two of the buttresses to accommodate a wagon road.

Gwynn Falls Trail, accessible from Washington Boulevard, uses the former wagon road right-of-way under the viaduct, which still carries modern rail traffic like its larger counterpart, Thomas Viaduct (CM15)

NORTHWEST BALTIMORE/ BOLTON HILL

BC92 PENNSYLVANIA STATION
1910–1911, Kenneth M. Murchison Jr. 1525 N. Charles St.

The Pennsylvania Railroad replaced its 1886 Baltimore station with this impressive new Beaux-Arts classical structure designed by New York City architect Murchison. A cast-iron marquee on the first story runs the full width of the building. Centrally located north of downtown and surrounded by several residential neighborhoods and institutions of higher education such as the Maryland Institute College of Art (BC96), Penn Station's design and siting reflected City Beautiful civic improvement ideals. A remarkably complete Rookwood Pottery ceramic tile installation is still extant on the interior, as are three stained glass domes. Although historically Penn Station never quite functioned as a true Union Station for Baltimore, in spite of early inclusion of Western Mary-

land Railway service, it is now the main hub for Amtrak service and various commuter rail lines.

BC93 UNIVERSITY OF BALTIMORE, JOHN AND FRANCES ANGELOS LAW CENTER
2010–2013, Behnisch Architekten and Ayers/Saint/Gross. 1401 N. Charles St.

Founded in 1925 as a private institution to provide evening classes in business and law, the University of Baltimore became public in 1975 and part of the University System of Maryland in 1988. The most recent addition to its urban campus is the Angelos Law Center opened in 2013. Its design by the German firm Behnisch Architekten in partnership with Baltimore firm Ayers/Saint/Gross was selected in 2008 through an international competition for a landmark new building for the law school. Incorporating green roofs, rainwater capture, and other in-

novations in sustainable design, the Angelos Center rises twelve stories around a central atrium. Its mirrored glass and steel facade is enlivened by stacked, block-like forms sheathed in a variety of irregular fenestration patterns, creating a unique, contemporary landmark in central Baltimore. The Student Center opened in 2006 (Murphy and Dittenhaufer; 21 W. Mount Royal Avenue) is another noteworthy contemporary building on campus, with the curving, zinc-coated copper sheathed form at the top enclosing a two-hundred-seat theater.

in 1982. Belluschi worked with the Boston firm Jung/Brannen to design the boldly sculptural building set within a large plaza. The Meyerhoff was a late work for the prolific modernist, who designed several important buildings in Maryland over his long career, including the Church of the Redeemer (BC114) and College Center at Goucher College (CM26). The oval shape of the main auditorium is expressed by the brick-sheathed cylinder rising from the center of the structure. Sloping metal roofs cover the lobby area at the front of the building, and a

BC94 JOSEPH MEYERHOFF SYMPHONY HALL

1978–1982, Pietro Belluschi, with Jung/Brannen Associates. 1212 Cathedral St.

Meyerhoff Symphony Hall provided a new home for the Baltimore Symphony Orchestra (BSO)

projecting oval form houses the backstage areas. The Meyerhoff's earth tone and brick red color palette reflects its late-1970s period, with fine wood finishes throughout the interior of the auditorium. In the 1990s, RTKL Associates renovated the acoustics systems.

BC95 MOUNT ROYAL B&O STATION

1894–1896, Baldwin and Pennington; mid-1960s renovated, Cochran, Stephenson and Donkervoet. 1400 Cathedral St.

Sited below the surrounding grade at the Howard Street tunnel cut opening, the B&O's third passenger station in Baltimore brought enhanced service to the Bolton Hill neighborhood.

Its Romanesque Revival exterior of rusticated Maryland granite with Indiana limestone trim features a 150-foot-tall clock tower at the center. The unusual surviving original iron train shed directly behind the station is also impressive in scale. After rail service was discontinued in 1961, the Maryland Institute College of Art (BC96) acquired and renovated the station, retaining much of the original interior, including marble columns, mosaic tile floors, and wood wainscoting. The successful adaptive use has been heralded as an early example of this preservation approach in a period when many U.S. architectural landmarks were being demolished.

BC96 MAIN BUILDING, MARYLAND INSTITUTE COLLEGE OF ART (MICA)

1908, Pell and Corbett. 1300 W. Mount Royal Ave.

MICA is one of the oldest art colleges in the country, founded as the Maryland Institute for the Promotion of the Mechanic Arts in 1826. For many decades the school was housed over the Centre Market until it was destroyed in the 1904 downtown fire, launching plans for a new purpose-built structure located uptown near the Bolton Hill neighborhood. New York City architects Pell and Corbett designed a new Renaissance Revival palazzo for MICA that was partially funded by industrialist and philanthropist Andrew Carnegie. In addition to a library and studios for pottery, metalworking, wood carving, drafting, and textile design, the new building featured galleries and exhibition rooms serving as Baltimore's only publicly accessible art museum at the time. MICA continues to expand and modernize, adding the sleek and angular glass form of the Brown Center (2003, Charles Brickbauer and Ziger/Snead) to house its digital arts programs and student housing, galleries, and exhibit space in the colorful glass cylinder of The Gateway (2006–2008, RTKL Associates).

BC97 BOLTON SQUARE COMMONS
1967–1968, Hugh Newell Jacobson. 200 block of W. Lafayette Ave., 1400 blocks of Jordan and Mason sts.

This welcoming enclave of mid-century modern attached houses was designed as part of a larger city-sponsored redevelopment of the Bolton Hill neighborhood. Bolton Hill had long been known for its fine nineteenth-century brick Italianate and Romanesque Revival row houses. By the 1950s, however, the neighborhood had suffered a long decline with blocks of row houses abandoned. The Baltimore Urban Renewal and Housing Agency demolished several blocks including Jordan and Mason streets, holding a design competition for up-to-date replacement housing. Jacobson's winning design encompasses thirty-five units with private gardens that center on a common green space. The Bolton Square row houses maintain the scale, varying heights, and red brick facades of the neighborhood's old-

er row houses yet provide a fresh new face. The minimalist modern facades feature horizontal bands of floor-to-ceiling bays and alternating flat and gabled roofs separated by parapet fire walls. They are arranged in a slightly staggered, arching pattern with green setbacks to the front and walled gardens and the commons to the rear. The result is a private verdant setting within an otherwise harried urban environment. In 1969 Bolton Square received the American Institute of Architects' coveted Honor Award for Excellence in Architecture.

BC98 PRINCE HALL GRAND LODGE (EUTAW PLACE TEMPLE)
1892, Joseph Evans Sperry. 1301–1305 Eutaw Pl.

Originally built as a synagogue for the Oheb Shalom Reform congregation, Eutaw Place Temple served a German Jewish immigrant community in the Bolton Hill neighborhood. It was the second grand Renaissance Revival synagogue built in the vicinity just after Baltimore Hebrew Congregation Synagogue opened a few blocks away (1890–1891, Charles L. Carson; now Berea Temple Seventh-Day Adventist). In this period upper-class members of the Jewish community were moving uptown from East Baltimore, away from newer Eastern European and Russian Jewish immigrants. This change was facilitated by the development of streetcar lines and new residential construction around Druid Hill Park.

Sperry designed an impressive building sheathed in rusticated white Beaver Dam marble from Baltimore County. Synagogue history holds that the design was modeled on the Great Synagogue of Florence, Italy. A grand red tile dome sits on a tall copper drum at the center, with smaller matching domes on the corner towers at the entrance. The Moorish-inspired interior accommodated approximately two thousand worshippers in a bright open space with a second-floor balcony around three sides. In 1960 the property was sold to the Prince Hall Grand Lodge, Maryland's premier African American Masonic Lodge, which counted Supreme Court Justice Thurgood Marshall and musician Eubie Blake among its members.

BC99 ORCHARD STREET UNITED METHODIST CHURCH
1882, Frank E. Davis; 1990s restored. 512 Orchard St.

One of the oldest churches in Baltimore built by an African American congregation, Orchard Street Methodist was founded by former enslaved person Trueman Pratt in 1837. Growth of the free Black community in the neighborhood during the aftermath of the Civil War created the need for a new and larger sanctuary. Baltimore architect Davis designed a handsome red brick Romanesque-influenced church with barrel-

vaulted interior supported by exposed carved trusses and ornate Corinthian columns. First known as Metropolitan United Methodist, the church served as a center of Black life in segregated West Baltimore. The fate of the church was uncertain after the congregation moved out in 1972, and vandals and fire damaged the building. By the 1990s the church was restored by the Greater Baltimore Urban League, and it continues to serve its surrounding neighborhood.

BC100 ST. MARY'S SEMINARY CHAPEL
1806–1808, Maximilian Godefroy; 1967–1968 restored, Alexander Cochran. 600 N. Paca St.

This was the first building in Baltimore—and, in fact, the country—influenced by Gothic architecture, and the city's first work by noted French-born architect Maximilian Godefroy. It was erected as the chapel for the nation's first seminary, established in 1791 by French priests from St. Sulpice in Paris, invited here by Bishop John Carroll. Godefroy had only recently immigrated to take a position as professor of civil and military architecture and fine arts at the seminary. The chapel lacks some of the most exuberant elements associated with Gothic Revival. However, it was the first in the country to link Gothic design to ecclesiastical architecture, becoming a model for similar Baltimore churches such as Zion Lutheran (1807–1808; 400 E. Lexington Street). The interior consists of a nave flanked by side aisles, transepts, a semicircular apse, and a plaster ceiling simulating ribbed vaulting. In 1971, the chapel was designated a National Historic Landmark. It sits within St. Mary's Park behind the Mother Seton House.

BC101 DRUID HILL PARK

1860 established, Howard Daniels, landscape architect, Augustus Faul, landscape architect and civil engineer, George A. Frederick, architect. Bounded by Druid Park and Swann drs., Reisterstown Rd., and Jones Falls Expwy. (I-83)

Baltimore was in the forefront of mid-nineteenth-century park development when its City Park Commission was formed by Mayor Thomas Swann in 1858. By 1860 the city agreed to purchase Druid Hill, the Rogers family's five-hundred-acre estate located approximately two miles north of the harbor. Druid Hill Park became the third major urban park in the country, representing the same civic ideals about nature and recreation as its New York City contemporary, Central Park. Landscape architect Daniels designed a winding network of carriage roads, footpaths, and bridle paths with scenic clearings in the picturesque English landscape tradition, with the assistance of Faul, who took over for Daniels following his death in 1863. Faul developed the park's first comprehensive plan in 1870, building on Daniels's earlier work. Newly accessible via streetcar lines, the hilltop picnic groves, woods, and landscaped hills of the park were immediately popular with the citizens of Baltimore. In 1863 to 1864 Rogers's c. 1801 house was renovated as an Italianate park pavilion, primarily by adding wide porches on four sides while various amenities and structures were added over the decades. The park also ensured protection for a new drinking water reservoir serving the city; Druid Lake was completed in 1871 and employed an innovative earthen dam.

Between 1863 and 1895 the Park Commission built trolley stations, a superintendent's house, entrance gates, greenhouses, and more, designed by its architect George A. Frederick. These structures are a catalog of exotic revival styles including Moorish, Asian, Stick, and Italianate. The Latrobe Pavilion (originally the Rotunda Station) is a charming example executed in Moorish Revival, as is the eclectically Chinese Pavilion (both 1864). Frederick also designed the Maryland Building for the 1876 Centennial Exhibition in Philadelphia in a fashionable Stick Style. After the exhibition, the building was dismantled and reassembled in Druid Hill Park, making it one of the few surviving structures from this event. It now serves as an education center for the Maryland Zoo. The Zoological Park was established in 1876 and gradually expanded with a number of early-twentieth-century buildings.

The conservatory and botanic gardens (now Howard P. Rawlings Conservatory and Botanic Gardens of Baltimore; *pictured*) were constructed after designs by Frederick in 1888. It is currently the second-oldest steel frame and glass building in the United States still in use. A major renovation and expansion in 2004 converted the production greenhouses from 1901 into displays for three different biomes. Early-twentieth-century renovations and improvements in Druid Hill Park, many adding athletic facilities or accommodating automobile access, were informed by the 1904 comprehensive parks plan for Baltimore prepared by the Olmsted Brothers firm. Earlier de facto racial segregation was codified in the early twentieth century by construction of separate athletic facilities for Black and white patrons, such as tennis courts, baseball diamonds, and pools. These Jim Crow practices, which continued until 1956, inspired important civil rights protests for Black Baltimoreans centered around fair access to Druid Hill Park.

NORTH CHARLES STREET AND ENVIRONS

BC102 LOVELY LANE METHODIST CHURCH
1884–1887, McKim, Mead and White. 2200 St. Paul St.

Built as First Methodist Episcopal Church, Lovely Lane is considered the "mother church" of American Methodism. Its tall rusticated granite bell tower, modeled on the twelfth-century church of Santa Maria, Abbey of Romposa, near Ravenna, Italy, creates a

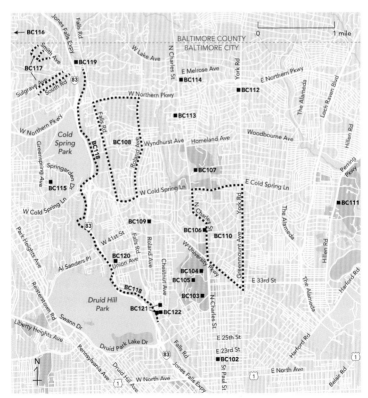

striking appearance along St. Paul Street. Largely unornamented on the exterior, White's inventive interpretation of Romanesque architecture has a lively facade created by rusticated blocks of gray Port Deposit granite. In addition to the massive corner tower, deep porches with round-arched arcades and a varied roofline add to its dynamic and massive appearance. Curved walls at the east and west of the large central block correspond to the elliptical sanctuary inside, an acoustically advantageous feature possibly attributed to Pastor John F. Goucher and the congregation's emphasis on choral music. The shallow elliptical dome over the sanctuary is decorated with the night sky executed in blue and gold.

BC103 BALTIMORE MUSEUM OF ART

1927–1929, 1933 addition, John Russell Pope; 1982, 1994 additions, Bower, Lewis and Thrower. 10 Art Museum Dr.

This was the first museum designed by Pope, one of America's premiere interpreters of classically inspired architecture. Like other Beaux-Arts-trained architects, Pope believed monumental architecture to be the highest form of art. Over the course of his career he designed memorial forms ranging from mausoleums to national monuments and institutions of art and science. Here, Pope developed a symmetrical, biaxial plan featuring a central portico, with interior galleries interspersed with quiet open spaces, a plan that would inform his museum designs thereafter. Borrowing from Roman motifs, the museum maintains Pope's severity, employing broad expanses of limestone walls broken by niches, recessed panels, and pedimented porticoes, similar to Pope's concurrent University Baptist Church (1925–1928) and Temple of the Scottish Rite (1928), at 3501 and 3800 N. Charles, respectively. While evocative of the architecture of antiquity, it reflects Pope's own brand of classicism specific to the modern American experience. It was erected during the heyday of museum building in America, from 1870 to 1940.

The building constituted the first purpose-built home for the collection previously housed in the Mount Vernon Place residence of its Garrett family benefactors. Following the museum's success, Pope was asked to prepare designs for the expansion of the Metropolitan Museum of Art in New York City and the Tate Gallery and British Museum in London. By the 1930s Pope was considered America's leading museum architect, culminating his career with the National Gallery of Art in Washington.

Pope also designed the first of three major additions, repeating the fundamental characteristics of the original building while introducing an interior court. The next two were built appropriately contemporary to the modern art housed within. The Bower, Lewis and Thrower additions provide a stark contrast to Pope's earlier work, embracing modern materials, abstract forms, and an outdoor patio and sculpture garden.

On the property is the last remnant of Robert Goodloe Harper's Oakland estate, a spring house or dairy designed by Benjamin Henry Latrobe, c. 1812, one of the two remaining Latrobe buildings in Baltimore. Modeled after the Temple of Ilissus in Athens, this delightfully pretentious dependency takes the form of a Greek Temple in miniature, featuring a pedimented portico supported by Ionic columns. It was moved here in 1932 to enable its preservation based on a design by architects Pope and Laurence Hall Fowler.

BC104 HOMEWOOD

1801–1806, Charles Carroll Jr., owner/architect; Robert and William Edwards, master carpenters. 3400 N. Charles St.

Homewood is significant for its association with the prominent Carroll family and as one of the nation's most refined country houses of the Federal period. The property was gifted by Charles Carroll of Carrollton to his son Charles Carroll Jr. upon his marriage to Harriet Chew of Philadelphia. Intended as a seasonal country retreat, its construction was likewise financed by Carroll Sr., and although the allowance was generous, Charles Jr. spent three times the initial proposal, a fact reflected in the exceptional quality and craftsmanship. Carroll likely acted as his own "gentleman architect" relying on pattern books of the period, such as William Pain's *The Practical Builder,* first printed in America in 1797. The house's highly skilled master carpenters, Robert and William Edwards, and bricklayer Michael Keplinger likely helped with design concepts as well. Homewood is a five-part Palladian plan embracing elements of Federal or Adamesque design to include such delicately refined details as the three-part windows, elaborate doorway entablature, and delicate interior plasterwork. Homewood is now a house museum and the showpiece of Johns Hopkins University Homewood campus (BC105). Homewood was the only one of several suburban villas that surrounded Baltimore to survive intact.

BC105 GILMAN HALL– HOMEWOOD CAMPUS, JOHNS HOPKINS UNIVERSITY

1913–1915, Parker, Thomas and Rice; 2007–2010 renovated, Kliment Hasbland. Bowman Dr.

In 1902 after Johns Hopkins University president Daniel C. Gilman proposed moving the school to a new campus in a more rural setting, benefactors donated a large site along North Charles Street that included Homewood (BC104). After a competition in 1904, the winning campus master plan by Parker and Thomas took inspiration from contemporary trends in Beaux-Arts campus design as well as the historic Carroll family house and colonial architectural traditions. The Georgian Revival university buildings were symmetrically arranged around a quadrangle, connected by low brick arcades and designed with motifs recalling Georgian architecture.

After some delays acquiring the funds to begin construction, the architects (now Parker, Thomas and Rice) revised their master plan, adding Gilman Hall to the west end of the quadrangle as a focal point for the campus. A circular drive at N. Charles Street on the east linked Homewood with the edge of the new quadrangle. Gilman Hall's main facade blends enlarged features of both Homewood and Independence Hall in Philadelphia, namely a classical portico and a central bell tower. Gilman became a symbol for the university and firmly established the Georgian Revival design idiom for Homewood campus construction.

The design of Gilman Hall also reflected the research-based educational philosophy pioneered in the United States by Johns Hopkins University. The humanities and social science department classrooms and offices were arranged around a library reading room and stacks. Each department also had access to a dedicated stacks area for its subject matter. The large size of Gilman Hall was masked by building it into a hillside so only two stories and the bell tower were visible from the quad while two additional stories were accessible from the rear. Georgian Revival science and engineering department buildings with laboratories added to the Homewood campus's original ensemble of academic buildings. Also built 1913 to 1915, these buildings were designed by other prominent firms such as Carrère and Hastings (Chemistry), Joseph Evans Sperry (Mechanical and Electrical Engineering), Wyatt and Nolting (Physics), and Walter Cook and Winthrop A. Welch (Geology).

In 2010 the New York City firm Kliment Halsband completed a major renovation of Gilman Hall. The inaccessible open light well at the core of the building was enclosed with an atrium to create new gathering areas, and library stacks that were largely empty since construction of a new library at the east end of the quadrangle in 1964 were converted into offices and other spaces.

BC106 HIGHFIELD HOUSE
1962–1964, Ludwig Mies van der Rohe. 4000 N. Charles St.

After completing One Charles Center (BC23), the renowned modernist designed Highfield House, an elegant apartment building in his signature modern idiom. The fifteen-story tower slab has a reinforced concrete structure sheathed with a sleek glass and steel curtain wall. Highfield House's sophisticated design extended to the garage, plaza, and pool integrated into the site, providing popular suburban amenities with refined urban living. The glass-enclosed two-story lobby is recessed and centered under the main structural block, with terrazzo floors, original furnishings, and marble-sheathed walls around the elevator core. Still a successful residential building, this is one of only two Mies buildings in Maryland.

BC107 EVERGREEN HOUSE

1857–1858, John W. Hogg, builder; mid-1880s, Charles L. Carson; 1922–1942, Laurence Hall Fowler. 4545 N. Charles St.

Primarily associated with the Garrett family of B&O Railroad fame and wealth, Evergreen House was renovated and expanded multiple times by Baltimore's finest architects. The original construction of an Italianate villa for William Broadbent in 1857–1858 is attributed to builder Hogg. The house changed hands several times until it was purchased by T. Harrison Garrett and his wife Alice Whitridge Garrett in 1878. The Garretts' major renovation and expansion campaign in the mid-1880s was overseen by Carson, including nearly doubling the size of the house with the porte-cochere wing and gymnasium.

When the next generation of the Garrett family inherited the property in 1920, Evergreen was an impressive ensemble of a house with forty-eight rooms and fifty acres of gardens. Diplomat John Work Garrett and his wife Alice Warder Garrett sought to update the entire house according to modern taste and sensibilities. Architect Fowler spent a large portion of his career helping the Garretts modify the fussy eclecticism of earlier generations into an elegant early-twentieth-century country house.

Starting with converting the second story of the north wing into a theater and redoing a billiard room and bowling alley into museum space, Fowler's changes also accommodated the artistic interests of the younger Garretts. The couple were accomplished collectors—the new space would house John Garrett's Chinese porcelain and Japanese netsuke (small carved ornaments worn as part of traditional Japanese dress)—and Alice Garrett both performed and hosted visiting artists in her theater. Fowler also worked with her to transform the gardens with the addition of a piazza and formal Italian-style plantings and features. Other noteworthy changes included the theater interior by Russian émigré theater stage and costume designer Léon Baskt. Baskt's work here is characterized by bold colors and geometric forms inspired by Russian folk art. Miguel Covarrubius, the Mexican artist and illustrator, was commissioned to paint scenes of John Work Garrett's diplomatic career in the New Library designed by Fowler in 1932. The house has been jointly managed by The Johns Hopkins University and the Evergreen House Foundation since 1952 and is open for regular house museum tours and events.

NORTH BALTIMORE AND JONES FALLS VALLEY

BC108 ROLAND PARK

1891, George Kessler, landscape architect; 1897, Olmsted Brothers, landscape architects. Bounded roughly by Falls Rd., W. Northern Pkwy., Roland Ave., W. Cold Spring Ln., and Stony Run

This bucolic Baltimore neighborhood is an early and highly influential example of a comprehensively planned garden suburb. The Roland Park Company, led for decades by developer Edwin Bouton, weathered initially sluggish sales during the economic downturns of the 1890s to become synonymous with upscale "suburban" development. The first phase of Roland Park's development, Plat 1, was laid out by Kansas City landscape architect Kessler in 1891. He established the core landscape characteristics of Roland Park including curving streets following the natural hilly topography, attractive vistas, and large building lots.

Perhaps more important and influential than the naturalistic landscape were the deed restrictions the Roland Park Company attached to all lot sales in order to control use and architectural quality. Deed restrictions included a minimum house cost of $3,000, minimum setbacks of thirty feet, and required fees for street and other maintenance. Bouton explored adding racially restrictive covenants to Roland Park deeds as early as 1893 but was discouraged by the lawyers he consulted. The company instead practiced de facto racial exclusion. A few houses were built by the company to inspire lot sales in the 1890s, but generally lot owners hired their own architects or chose designs from popular pattern books. The houses built in Plat 1 east of Roland Avenue reflected the eclectic suburban houses popular in the 1890s, including Queen Anne and Shingle Style. The minimum cost essentially served as both a social and design restriction for the neighborhood that quickly became a popular alternative to more congested genteel Baltimore neighborhoods such as Mount Vernon Square. A variety of amenities was also instrumental in the success. The Lake Roland elevated line opened in 1893, providing efficient public transit between Roland Park and downtown. The Roland Park Company built a Tudor Revival shopping center (1894, Wyatt and Nolting; *pictured*), one of the first in the country, to provide commercial services in a handsome building. The Baltimore County Club (1898, Wyatt and Nolting) and the Roland Park Country Day School (1894) completed the self-contained community that proved very attractive to Roland Park residents.

Plat 2 expanding Roland Park west of Roland Avenue was first proposed in 1897 and opened in 1901. The deed restrictions and basic site planning were continued, now with even larger lots and grander houses. The minimum house cost requirement evolved into a requirement that house plans be approved by the Roland Park Company. Frederick Law Olmsted Jr., heir to the most prominent landscape architecture firm in the United States, worked on this and future additions to Roland Park through 1910. The houses of Roland Park continued to display a variety of fashionable eclectic modes including Shingle Style, Tudor Revival, Colonial Revival, and Arts and Crafts.

The Roland Park Company went on to develop several adjacent neighborhoods with Olmsted plans such as Guilford (BC110), begun in 1913, and Homeland in 1924. Starting with Guilford, the company included restrictive covenants legally forbidding Black or Jewish ownership. Annexed by the City of Baltimore in 1918, Roland Park remained one of the most successful planned garden suburbs in the United States and the inspiration for many prominent early-twentieth-century projects such as the Country Club District in Kansas City, Missouri.

BC109 CONCRETE ROW HOUSES
1905, Edward L. Palmer. 835–843 W. University Pkwy.

Inspired by postmedieval rural English cottages popular in the Arts and Crafts movement of the late nineteenth and early twentieth centuries is this grouping of five row houses. They were designed when Palmer was making a name for himself as architect for the Roland Park Company. The Old World styling belies the innovations that these houses represent, an early use of poured-in-place reinforced concrete that did not appear again in Baltimore for another sixty years with the Mechanic Theater (no longer extant). The design is also credited with introducing the popular "Daylight" row house plan to Baltimore, a two-room-wide and two-room-deep plan boasting a window in every room, and a front porch or sunroom. Indeed, these delightful painted concrete houses with rough-sawn timber details, red tile roofs, clipped gables, and overhanging bracketed eaves included front covered porches and attached rear "summer houses."

Palmer designed similar semi-detached units or "group homes" centered on a common green space in Edgevale Park (1911; 500–609 Edgevale and 4–14 Englewood roads), inspired by the cottage designs of English architect Charles F. A. Voysey.

BC110 GUILFORD
1913–1950; Edward H. Bouton, Frederick Law Olmsted Jr., and Edward L. Palmer. Bounded by University Pkwy., N. Charles St., York Rd., and Cold Spring Ln.

Guilford was developed by a division of the Roland Park Company as Baltimore's premier residential suburb, named for the country estate that preceded it. The comprehensively planned community encompassed a landscape plan developed by Olmsted Jr. to include winding streets, sidewalks, lush landscaping, three communal parks, and ten smaller private parks reached by rear gardens. Main thoroughfares run north and south, while secondary roadways curve to follow the site's natural topography, a characteristic important to the Olmsted design philosophy. The plan likewise included such up-to-date infrastructure as sewage and water systems, gas lines, and buried electrical and telephone lines. The architectural tone of the neighborhood was set by Palmer, the company's chief architect from 1907 to 1920, who designed early

"show houses." Palmer and Bouton traveled to Europe in 1911 to study the domestic architecture and gather ideas that would contribute to the character of the community, encompassing a variety of revival styles. Along with partner William D. Lamdin, Palmer designed over 150 such houses in Guilford, including examples of Italian Renaissance Revival (1914; 4014 Greenway), Jacobean Revival (1913; 4001 Greenway), Colonial Revival (1914; 4100 Greenway), Classical Revival (1914; 3701 Charles Street), English Arts and Crafts (1914; 3911 Juniper Street), and French Renaissance Revival (1916; 16 Charlcote Place) styles. Palmer also designed Tudor Revival houses (1913) on Bretton Place and Chancery Square along the community's eastern border.

Examples of other noted architects and their work include Laurence Hall Fowler (1914; 205 Wendover Road), Edward H. Glidden (1922; 8 Bishop's Road), Mottu and White (1914; 4402 Greenway), Howard Sill (1927; 204 E. Highfield Road), Bayard Turnbull (1922; 4101 and 4105 Greenway), Guy Lowell (1922; 8 Charlcote Place), and John Russell Pope (1914; 15 Charlcote Place).

BC111 UNIVERSITY MEMORIAL CHAPEL, MORGAN STATE UNIVERSITY
1941, Albert I. Cassell. 4307 Hillen Rd.

Founded as the Centenary Biblical Institute by the Baltimore Conference of the Methodist Episcopal Church in 1867 and renamed Morgan College in 1890, Morgan

State moved to its current campus in northeast Baltimore in 1917, with assistance from the Carnegie Foundation. Carnegie Hall (1919, Edward Tilton) became the first purpose-built college building on the campus of this HBCU (historically black college and university), sited at the east of what would become the main academic quadrangle. Starting with Carnegie Hall, all of the early buildings on the campus were constructed with locally quarried stone using Georgian Revival forms and decorative motifs.

Morgan State became a public institution in 1939, as the University of Maryland was seeking ways to expand opportunities for Black students while keeping its College Park campus racially segregated. At this time the first student center and chapel for Morgan State was built after designs by noted African American architect Cassell. He designed institutional buildings for many clients, including Howard University in Washington, where he was on the faculty. The chapel continues the local stone facades of the main quadrangle, here with a subdued Collegiate Gothic approach. Recent construction on the campus has embraced contemporary design such as the glass and steel pavilion of the Earl S. Richardson Library (2008, Sasaki) with areas of smoothly dressed stone to harmonize with the historic buildings. A campus extension to the west across Hillen Road includes the Earl G. Graves School of Business and Management (2015, Ayers/Saint/Gross, with Kohn Pederson Fox) and Martin D. Jenkins Hall

Behavioral and Social Sciences Center (2017, HOK), both dramatic steel and glass structures with sculptural forms.

BC112 SENATOR THEATER
1939, John J. Zink. 5904 York Rd.

The finest movie theater surviving in Baltimore, and the entire state of Maryland, is this Art Deco gem in the Govans neighborhood of north Baltimore. Designed by prolific regional theater architect Zink for the Durkee chain, the Senator rivaled the downtown movie palaces of the period. Its stepped cylinder front facade is adorned with neon backlit glass block and neon signage while Vitrolite panels and aluminum bands add further Art Deco flare. While some details have been changed, most notably the addition of three smaller screening rooms in 2013, the interior of the Senator is also remarkably intact, with original terrazzo floor and murals in the lobby, wood veneer, aluminum wall coverings, and stylized floral wall motifs in the main theater. The 2013 renovations also included a reproduction of the original lobby chandelier and restoration of historic features.

BC113 CATHEDRAL OF
MARY OUR QUEEN
*1954–1959, Maginnis, Walsh and
Kennedy. 5200 N. Charles St.*

This post–World War II modern
Gothic Roman Catholic cathedral is both contemporary and
indicative of local architectural
conservatism. Designed by prolific Roman Catholic church architects Maginnis, Walsh and
Kennedy of Boston, it has a Latin cross plan with a central entrance flanked by towers. While
the form and plan are traditional, down to the load-bearing masonry construction, side aisles,
and buttresses, the angular lines,
stylized sculptural program, and
smooth random ashlar limestone
walls firmly place its design in
the mid-twentieth century. The
massive sanctuary seats 1,900
worshippers and serves as the
co-cathedral with the downtown
Basilica of the Assumption (BC14)
for the Archdiocese of Baltimore,
the first in the United States.

BC114 CHURCH OF THE
REDEEMER
*1954–1958, Pietro Belluschi, with
Rogers, Taliaferro and Lamb. 5603
N. Charles St.*

When this Episcopal congregation decided to expand, they
hired internationally renowned
architect Belluschi to design a
new modernist church and two
large support buildings of offices
and classrooms. The nine-acre site
already included an 1858 Gothic
Revival chapel, a rectory, and
a 1928 parish hall. Completed in
1958, Belluschi's design was one of
the earliest examples of nontraditional church architecture in the
region and an influential example
of progressive mid-twentieth-
century ecclesiastical building.
His careful approach included
using local materials and responding to existing historic buildings,
while utilizing the contemporary architectural vocabulary of
modernism. Maryland architects
Rogers, Taliaferro and Lamb su-
pervised construction and provided sophisticated site planning
that incorporated the modern
buildings with the historic ones.
Known as RTKL Associates since
1961, this partnership with Belluschi helped establish their national reputation.

Belluschi's design scheme
linked a new sanctuary, an administration building, and an
education building to the historic chapel and parish hall by a series of loggias. The loggias create
six courtyards designed by Baltimore landscape architect Edward B. Baetjer, which provide
spaces for contemplation and reflect Belluschi's interest in traditional Japanese architecture. The
loggia columns and the low walls
of Belluschi's church are sheathed
with the same stone as the historic chapel, which was obtained
from the demolished rectory and
reopening the original quarry.
The steeply pitched cross gable on

hipped roof of the church matches the form of the historic chapel while creating a dramatic sculptural profile for the new sanctuary that suggests traditional Japanese *irimoya* roof forms.

Church of the Redeemer is also an early example of a communal rather than hierarchical interior plan for ecclesiastical architecture. The white marble altar was pulled out from a traditional position against the wall to reflect recent liturgical reforms turning the celebrant to face the congregation. The cruciform plan recalls historic church forms while the interior materials such as exposed pointed-arch roof supports composed of laminated strips of Douglas fir communicate a spare and elegant modernism.

BC115 COLDSPRING NEWTOWN
1972–1977, Moshe Safdie. 4800 Tamarind Rd.

Coldspring Newtown was an ambitious, but only partially realized effort to create a planned neighborhood on a large undeveloped plot of land between Jones Falls Valley and the working-class Black neighborhood of Park Heights. The lofty goal was to create a racially integrated, moderate-income community that would bring middle-class residents back to the city at a time of increased out-migration to the suburbs. Working with a development firm from Boston, the city brought in Israeli Canadian architect Moshe Safdie, celebrated for his Habitat '67 project at the Montreal Exposition. An admirer of Le Corbusier, Safdie proposed 3,800 housing units clustered around common landscaped open space with separate pedestrian and automobile circulation.

The hilly and wooded conditions of the site inspired relatively high-density residential groupings, updating the principles of early-twentieth-century Garden City planning with a 1970s aesthetic that included exposed concrete and irregular house forms. Coldspring Newtown's "deck houses" grouped attached units in staggered rows over parking garages covered by concrete terraces. Red brick paths, steps, ramps, benches, and planters created human scale and visual interest along the pedestrian-friendly terraces.

Even with heavy public subsidy, units sold slowly, and the project floundered under high construction costs. Only phase one was completed (about 225 units) and the planned high-rise apartments and retail went unbuilt after government priorities changed. Later development on the site was executed in a more conventional suburban fashion, and the original vision for the project was officially canceled in 1994. Even with its truncated realization, Coldspring Newtown represents an important contribution to international planning ideals, and many long-time residents enjoy its thoughtful and innovative design.

BC116 TEMPLE OHEB SHALOM
1958–1960, Walter Gropius and Sheldon Leavitt; 2002 renovated, Levin/Brown Architects. 7310 Park Heights Ave.

In 1953, this congregation decided to leave its 1892 sanctuary (BC98) in the Bolton Hill neighborhood to build a new synagogue in far northwest Baltimore. More suburban in character, the Pikesville area attracted new residential construction and a number of important Jewish institutions in the post–World War II period. World-renowned German architect and Bauhaus School founder Gropius worked in association with architect Sheldon Leavitt and TAC (The Architects Collaborative) to create a dramatically modern synagogue and school complex for the German Reform congregation's evolving needs, his only religious commission. The sanctuary at the front of the complex has a bold volumetric form with four tall concrete barrel vaults and connecting slabs spanning the 83 × 90–foot sanctuary. On the front elevation the vaults mimic the shape of ancient tablets of law. The design included glass mosaic murals in the entrance lobby by Hungarian immigrant artist Gyorgy Kepes.

The school and administration structures to the rear and side have a more subdued but still frankly modern flat-roofed steel, glass, and concrete construction, with the same orange brick in-fill employed at the vaults. The multifunctional, family-oriented complex and large lot with lawns and parking signified the postwar shift to a suburban synagogue type. When Levin/Brown Architects renovated the temple in 2002, they reversed Gropius's unusual arrangement of having the floor ascend toward the bema, or raised platform for Torah reading during services, and altered the connection between the sanctuary and social hall that could originally be opened for overflow seating during high holidays.

BC117 MOUNT WASHINGTON RESIDENTIAL AREA BUILDINGS
c. 1850s–1880s. 1700–2000 blocks of South Rd. and Sulgrave Ave.; and bounded by Thornbury, Dixon, and Kenway rds., and Maywood Ave.

The Mount Washington residential area was first developed by George Gelbach Jr. and the Reverend Elias Heiner as a summer retreat of villas befitting its lush setting among the wooded hills and meandering streams of the Jones Falls. Although built in the shadows of Mount Washington Cotton Mill (BC119), the community was intended for middle- and upper-class Baltimoreans seeking a "healthy, retired, and respectable country residence" accessible via the Baltimore and Susquehanna Railroad's northern line. Gelbach and Heiner built such houses as the Second Empire Laboriere (1856; 1705 South).

Gelbach and Heiner also founded the former Mount Washington Female College (1855, Thomas Dixon; 5801 Smith Avenue) that has a three-story brick octagonal building reminiscent of the work of Orson S. Fowler.

Other developers followed, and the summer retreat blossomed into a year-round community. In the 1860s and 1870s brothers Thomas and James Dixon developed the adjacent area dubbed Dixon Hill, considered Baltimore's first planned suburb. Thomas Dixon had the advantage of owning a lumber company, providing a wide range of wood materials to build and ornament the community's Gothic Revival, Queen Anne, and Stick Style villas. They designed and built thirty-five houses, including their own Gothic Revival cottages (c. 1870; 1813 and 1815 Thornbury Road). They are also responsible for the exceptional Carpenter Gothic Mount Washington Presbyterian Church (1878; 1801 Thornbury).

Nearby are the Swiss Chalet–inspired villas at 5600, 5602, 5603, 5604, and 5607 Roxbury Place built c. 1870 by developer John Graham, who partnered with John Nichols to form the Cottage Building Association.

BC118 JONES FALLS VALLEY MILLS

1810; later additions and alterations. Jones Falls Valley from Smith Ave. to Wyman Park Dr.

The steep drop of Jones Falls supported important water-powered industries starting with gristmills and then textile mills. Numerous mills producing cotton duck, a heavy canvas used for sails, tents, bags, or clothing, were built into the steep ravines of the valley. By the late nineteenth century Baltimore mills were producing 80 percent of the world's cotton duck and supplying the sails for Baltimore's robust shipbuilding industry. Company-owned worker housing was located nearby, often perched on the hillsides along narrow, winding streets and now part of neighborhoods such as Hampden, Woodberry, and Mount Washington. The mills were paternalistic operations with the villages maintaining a homogenous, largely white population well into the twentieth century. Baltimore's surviving mill villages still have a remarkably isolated feeling in spite of the nearby rushing traffic of the Jones Falls Expressway (U.S. 83) built in 1956.

BC119 MOUNT WASHINGTON MILL

1810; 1847, 1850 additions. 1340 Smith Ave.

Founded as Washington Cotton Factory, this mill is located just inside the city line along Jones Falls. Its original design was modeled on Slater Mill in Rhode Island and featured a long, narrow, three-and-a-half-story building of stone with a gable roof. One of the generation of early mills inspired by President Thomas Jefferson's 1807 embargo on British goods, it is currently perhaps the oldest extant textile mill outside of Rhode Island. The complex was changed and added to over the years, including the 1847 brick addition on the east end of the original mill and a one-story brick dye house and machine shop built in 1850.

In 1853 William E. Hooper and Sons, the leading manufacturers of cotton sail cloth in the country, added this complex to its group of seven Jones Falls mills. Another even larger consolidation in 1899 added Hooper's mills to the Mount Vernon Woodberry Cotton Duck Company. After World War I most production of cotton duck moved to mills in the South. Maryland Bolt and Nut Company purchased the mill and operated here until the late 1980s. During the 1990s several buildings in the historic complex were preserved and incorporated into a shopping center.

BC120 UNION MILL (DRUID MILL)
1866; 1872 addition. 1600 Union Ave.

Owner Horatio Gambrill built the first section of Druid Mill in 1866, a long two-story stone building with an Italianate tower. Another one-story building added in 1872 doubled the size of the operation, with weaving located in the newer structure. It used coal-generated steam power from the very beginning, leading the post–Civil War change among the Jones Falls mills.

In 1892 the complex became Mount Vernon Mill No. 4, before being added to the Mount Vernon Woodberry Cotton Duck Company consolidation in 1899. In 1917 Poole and Hunt purchased the property for manufacture of washing machines and other appliances. After a variety of owners between 1935 and 2009, Hamel Builders converted the nineteenth-century mill buildings and boiler plant, now renamed Union Mill, into offices for nonprofits, low-cost housing for teachers and city employees, and small shops.

BC121 MOUNT VERNON MILLS NO. 1, 2, AND 3
c. 1850, 1853, 1873. 3000 Falls Rd. and 3000 Chestnut Ave.

Mount Vernon Mill was a major cotton textile producer in the Jones Falls Valley, starting with Mill No. 1, located in a converted flour mill, in 1850. Capacity was expanded by construction of Mill No. 2 in 1853 and Mill No. 3 in 1873 nearby on Chestnut Avenue. After severe damage from a fire in 1873, Mill No. 1 was entirely rebuilt in brick with a square end tower and decorative corbeling. Mount Vernon was the last textile mill operating in Baltimore when it closed in 1972. Mills No. 2 and 3 were renovated into offices and galleries in 1987, while No. 1 became apartments, offices, and restaurants in 2013. The still extant mill worker's neighborhood of Stone Hill (BC122) is located above the Mount Vernon Mills. These small stone company houses were sold to the workers after a strike in the 1920s.

BC122 ELISHA TYSON
HOUSE AND STONE HILL
c. 1811. 732 Pacific St.

This handsome stone house was built as the summer residence of Quaker industrialist and abolitionist Elisha Tyson adjacent to his Laurel Flouring Mill. Erected c. 1790, Tyson's mill launched the industrial development of this area of the Jones Falls, accessed by the new Falls Turnpike that Tyson helped establish in 1805. Tyson is recognized as an important advocate for African American civil rights as a founder of the Maryland Society for the Abolition of Slavery (1789) and Baltimore's first permanent school for Blacks, the African Academy (1797), and through the establishment of safe houses along the Underground Railroad.

His house is a vernacular interpretation of Federal architecture built of rough-cut, randomly coursed local granite, parged under the front porch, with a servant's quarter wing. The mill and house were purchased c. 1840 and redeveloped as Mount Vernon Mills (BC121). Although the mill burned in 1843 and was replaced with spinning mills, Tyson's house was retained for the mill superintendent.

Stone semidetached millworkers' housing, known as Stone Hill, was then built around the Tyson House. Lining the one- to two-block-long Pacific, Puritan, Bay, and Field streets, they are two-bays per unit with shared, single-story rear kitchen wings served by alleys. While typical of the unit types built by paternalistic millowners, these are somewhat more refined by their stone construction, raised basements, front porches, and details such as quoining, brick-end lintels, and doorway transoms.

CENTRAL MARYLAND

The region defined here as central Maryland offers a study in geographic contrasts, from the rocky hills along the Susquehanna, Patapsco, and Patuxent rivers to rolling Piedmont farmland to the flat coastal plain of the western shore of the Upper Chesapeake. It includes the counties that ring the city of Baltimore: Howard, Baltimore, Carroll, and Harford. Thus, the development of this region shares many early historic influences with its urban core. European settlers attempted to extend the enslaved-labor-dependent tobacco-growing economy of the Tidewater region, with mixed success. River ports such as Elkridge Landing, created by the Maryland Assembly in 1733, later experienced the limitations of transport in shallow waters, particularly in competition with the deep-water ports of Baltimore or Havre de Grace at the mouth of the Susquehanna. Waterways such as the Patapsco and Jones Falls turned out to be more suited to early efforts in grain milling as well as iron and textile production at sites such as Elkridge Furnace (CM14), and the textile mills of Oella (CM34) and Savage (CM18).

Numerous merchant mills were established in this region to take advantage of flour export trade through the port of Baltimore, including survivors such as Jerusalem Mill (CM66), Rockland Mill (see CM39), McKinstry's Mill (CM55), and Union Mill (CM43). The pioneers were the Ellicott brothers, who established Ellicott's Mills in 1772 just as the state was beginning to introduce crop diversification, turning from tobacco to grain production. As the state's earliest and most prosperous mill town, Ellicott's Mills—renamed Ellicott City in 1867—provided the model for best practices that was later utilized to create a significant milling industry in Baltimore.

Limited river navigation also inspired important early transportation initiatives in building turnpikes, canals such as the Susquehanna and Tidewater that connected the port at Havre de Grace with agricultural markets in central Pennsylvania, and of course, railroads. In the turn-of-the-twentieth-century heyday of rail transport, central Maryland was crisscrossed by numerous freight and passenger lines traveling to additional markets for farm produce and manufactured goods. The early innovations of the Baltimore and Ohio Railroad linked the growing towns of the Patapsco River valley such as Ellicott City and Sykesville with Baltimore, and eventually points west, as well as offering the first railroad service south to Washington. The Western Maryland Railway traversed the northern part of central Maryland, connecting Owings Mills and Baltimore with Westminster and Union Bridge; this portion was completed by 1862, and the link to

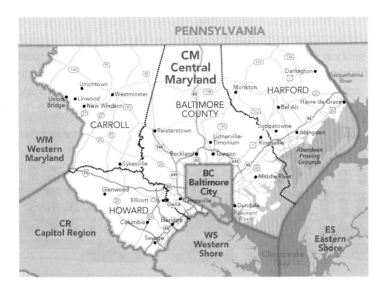

Hagerstown was finished ten years later. By the 1880s the Maryland and Pennsylvania (Ma&Pa) created an important north–south route that connected Baltimore with York, Pennsylvania, through the Baltimore County seat of Towson and the Harford County seat of Bel Air. In addition to freight transport, the growth of railroads shaped residential development for both year-round and summer houses in communities surrounding Baltimore such as Catonsville, Lawyers Hill, Ellicott City, and Sykesville. The picturesque landscapes of Harford and northern Baltimore counties were particularly attractive as retreats for wealthy citizens from Baltimore and Philadelphia, with estates designed by architects from those same cities.

Central Maryland also contained thriving stone quarries, which provided building materials sought after throughout the region and beyond. Local stone both characterized vernacular building traditions, particularly those of the German, Welsh, and Quaker communities sharing a cultural hearth with Pennsylvania to the north, and enriched the work of area architects on major private and public structures. Varieties of granite gneiss found in Sykesville, Ellicott City, around the town of Granite, or just across the Susquehanna River in Port Deposit offered durable and handsome building materials. Peach Bottom slate quarried by Welsh immigrant miners in Whiteford-Cardiff in upper Harford County and across the border in Pennsylvania was prized for its strength and fade-resistance. Cockeysville marble, also known as Beaver Dam marble, from Baltimore County adorns the Washington Monument and the front stoop of row houses throughout Baltimore.

The twentieth century in central Maryland has been characterized by industrial and suburban development along what is now the I-95 corridor and east to the Chesapeake. Much of the industrial development has been driven by the growth of the so-called military-industrial complex during both world wars. The massive Aberdeen Proving Ground and Edgewood Arsenal were founded in 1917 for development and testing of ordnance and chemical weapons, respectively. The combined facilities now occupy the majority of Harford County's Chesapeake coastline. The town of Dundalk was a planned community built during World War I by the U.S. Shipping Board Emergency Fleet Corporation to support the massive Bethlehem Steel production facilities at Sparrows Point. During World War II, Middle River became a defense boom town in Baltimore County thanks to the rapid growth of the Glenn L. Martin Aircraft Company (CM28).

Residential development accompanied these industrial expansions and, more significantly, accommodated the flight of white residents out of Baltimore City into the surrounding counties. James Rouse's celebrated Columbia New Town (CM12) sought to avoid the social and cultural negatives of unplanned suburban sprawl. While a major accomplishment, Columbia remained an exception to residential and commercial development in central Maryland.

HOWARD COUNTY
ELLICOTT CITY

Central to the development of Howard County and emblematic of its distinctive architectural traditions is Ellicott City, Maryland's first and most successful mill town. Founded in 1772 by the Ellicott brothers as Ellicott's Mills, it became the epicenter of a regional flour-milling industry within the Patapsco River Valley, the importance of which cannot be overstated. Ellicott's Mills helped to encourage crop diversification, while providing the model for best practices within the milling industry. The Ellicotts, Quakers who migrated from southeastern Pennsylvania, where milling was already deeply entrenched, developed a large-scale grain-milling complex and associated industries through a system of vertical integration and the construction of the Baltimore and Frederick Turnpike to the port of Baltimore. The Baltimore and Ohio (B&O) Railroad's first destination was Ellicott's Mills, arriving in 1831. The town continued to grow and prosper throughout the nineteenth century as a mill town, commercial and governmental center, transportation hub, and summer retreat. Its importance was recognized in 1839 by its designation as the seat of the Howard District of Anne Arundel County and finally of Howard County, in 1851.

Ellicott City is also known for its varied topography and handsome stone buildings. The town is shaped by the steep, rocky terrain and by the confluence of the Patapsco River and its tributaries. Buildings range from worker housing to hotels, municipal and commercial buildings, and the B&O Railroad Station. The use of locally quarried granite is the most distinguishing feature of the architectural landscape. While influenced by the Georgian and Greek revivals, they are defined less by style than by their skillfully laid, random ashlar

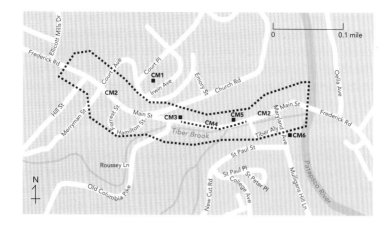

stonework, including quoining, monolithic lintels, and fine mortar joints. The original mill was lost to floods, but a flour mill still sits on its site, a distinctive modern structure built of steel and concrete, brick and glass (1917; 27 Frederick Road). Some early buildings stand near the mill, including the George Ellicott House (1789; 24 Frederick) and the Ellicott's Mills operator's house (c. 1789; 8000 Main Street). To the west lies the civic center surrounding the Howard County Courthouse (CM1) and the residential district, and to the northeast, the former mill village of Oella (CM34).

CM1 HOWARD COUNTY COURTHOUSE

1840–1843, Charles Timanus Jr.; 1842, Samuel Harris; 1938, Buckler and Fenhagen. 8360 Court Ave.

Overlooking the town is the handsome Greek Revival gable-front courthouse. Its construction was prompted by the 1839 designation of the Howard District of Anne Arundel County. It was built of ashlar granite by contractor and stonemason Timanus, who honed his design skills through a previous collaboration with noted Baltimore architect Robert Cary Long Jr. on the Patapsco Female Institute of 1837 (now a preserved ruin at 3655 Church Road). Samuel Harris, "architect and measurer of buildings," was hired in June 1842 to oversee the final phases of construction. The courthouse is distinguished by its boldly expressed stone details and domed octagonal lantern, indicative of its civic function.

The courthouse received a substantial addition encompassing a preexisting house constructed for transplanted Baltimore attorney Edwin P. Hayden. A second addition reoriented the courthouse, happily maintaining the original front. Both additions are sensitive to the older building, erected of granite and incorporating the distinctive pediment motif.

Across from the courthouse is Lawyers' Row, a grouping of small frame, late-nineteenth-century gable-front buildings erected as offices for local attorneys. The oldest and most intact is the Henry Wootton Law Office (c. 1869; 8351 Court).

Howard County Jail (1851; 1 Emory Street), like the adjacent courthouse, was also built of local granite by Charles Timanus Jr. to meet the demands placed on Ellicott City as the newly designated county seat. It was significantly enlarged by the current Gothic Revival- and Italianate-influenced main building (1878) designed by Scottish-born civil engineer John Laing. It features a central gabled pavilion and is surmounted by a lantern similar to that of the courthouse.

CM2 ELLICOTT CITY COMMERCIAL BUILDINGS
1810s–1940s. 8000–8300 blocks of Main St.

The heart of Ellicott City is the Main Street corridor along the old Frederick Turnpike. Most buildings date to the town's heyday that began in the 1830s, sparked by the arrival of the B&O Railroad and the distribution of the Ellicott brothers' landholdings. Stone merchant-class single houses appear alongside multi-unit working-class housing, retail shops with residences above, and the former hotels that ac-

commodated travelers along the turnpike and tourists arriving by rail. The city's prosperity is exhibited by three banks designed by Baltimore architects. An iconic element of the town's skyline is the cupola of the old Ellicott City Firehouse (1889; 3829 Church Road; *pictured on p. 235*). As chain department stores emerged, two such local establishments were built: Taylor's (1924; 8197 Main), and Caplan's (1926; 8125 Main) both built of buff brick with parapet roof lines, and large display windows. Similarly styled was the Ellicott City Motor service garage and showroom (1921; 8289 Main). The Federal Emergency Administration built the Colonial Revival firehouse (1938–1939, Hubert G. Jory; 8390 Main); and U.S. Post Office (1940–1941; 8267 Main) with murals depicting Ellicott City by Peter DeAnna.

CM3 HOWARD HOUSE HOTEL
c. 1850; 8202–8208 Main St.

This is the grandest of Ellicott City's former hotels, reflecting its growing reputation as a summer retreat. The Second Empire building is distinguished by its stone construction, mansard roof, and front galleries. The others, also of stone construction, include the Ellicott's (Old) Patapsco Hotel (c. 1810; 8044–8046 Main), purchased in 1846 by the Granite Manufacturing Company to house workers in their nearby textile mill, and investor Andrew McLaughlin's Railroad Hotel (c. 1840; 8030–8034 Main), which encompassed eighteen guestrooms, each with a fireplace.

CM4 HOUSES ON MAIN STREET
c. 1835–1840. 8066–8198 Main St.

The Samuel Powell House (c. 1835; 8198 Main) is the grandest and oldest of the stone merchant-class single houses along Main Street. Powell erected it on a lot acquired from Samuel Ellicott in 1835, a period marking the end of first-generation Ellicott ownership. Also noteworthy is the four-bay, stone single house (c. 1840) at 8081 Main. At 8180–8182 Main, the Alexander Walker House (c. 1835) is one of a number of granite multifamily buildings. Walker lived in one unit while renting the other. The three-story units had a ground-floor kitchen with the parlor elevated above.

Other multi-unit dwellings include 8126–8132 Main, later purchased by the Odd Fellows, and one built by investor Andrew McLaughlin (c. 1837) at 8066–8070 Main. McLaughlin also built the shop-house (c. 1837) at 8066–8068 Main. For many years it was owned by the Hunts, a brother-sister team who operated a general store and millinery in the two shops, respectively. Note the pilastered residential entrance.

Nearby at 3752–3736 Old Columbia Pike, the semidetached stone workers' houses (c. 1844), known as Tonge Row after English owner Ann Tonge, are typical of housing provided within mill towns.

CM5 OLD PATAPSCO NATIONAL BANK OF MARYLAND
1905, T. Buckler Ghequiere. 8098 Main St.

This bank by Baltimore architect Ghequiere is built of Flemish-bond brick with glazed headers and contrasting stone quoining, lintels, and cornice, and an oversized entrance pediment. Ghequiere's work in Ellicott City followed in the footsteps of his uncle, Robert Cary Long Jr., who designed Mount Ida (c. 1833; 3691 Sarah's Lane) and the Patapsco Female Institute (see CM1). This bank replaced the first purpose-built bank (1887) designed by Charles E. Cassell; the Queen Anne–influenced building still sits adjacent at 8090 Main. A third bank, built by the rival Washington Trust Company (1906; 8137 Main), a white marble and terra-cotta Beaux-Arts classical building, was designed by Mottu and White.

CM6 BALTIMORE AND OHIO ELLICOTT CITY STATION MUSEUM (B&O RAILROAD STATION)
1830–1831, Jacob Small Jr., with John McCartney; 1885 freight house, E. Francis Baldwin. 2711 Maryland Ave.

The Baltimore and Ohio (B&O) was the first railroad in the nation to offer freight and passenger service, with Ellicott City as the terminus of the original thirteen-mile line. The station is the oldest in the country, built of granite from the Ellicotts' quarry. Designed by Small, it was built by McCartney, an engineer from Ohio then hired by the company to erect the Thomas Viaduct (CM15). The stone is skillfully laid in a rich, random ashlar pattern, ranging from huge blocks and quoins to tiny galleting, with ultra-thin mortar joints. It is banked into the hillside with the ticketing office, waiting room,

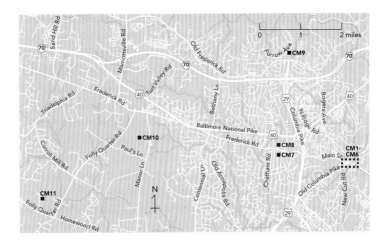

and track platform on the second level, and storage area for goods prior to transport on the first. At the south end is the car house and rail spur that brought cars through the large arched entrance. Adding a late-nineteenth-century flourish is the decorative brick freight house with bracketed eaves, built in response to increased passenger use as patrons clamored for the thrill of riding the "iron horse." Baltimoreans traveled here via train during summer months as Ellicott City became a summer retreat. The station was designated a National Historic Landmark in 1968 and now houses a railroad museum.

CM7 MACALPINE

1868; 1877 additions and renovations, William Gerwig. 3621 MacAlpine Rd.

MacAlpine is representative of the country houses built by more affluent county residents in the post–Civil War era to embrace fashionable architectural design and modern amenities. James Mackubin, an Ellicott City attorney, had the house built for himself and his wife, Comfort Dor-

sey. It was updated and expanded about a decade later to accommodate their growing family; the renovations included a mansard roof, front porch with porte-cochere, and gable-front service wing. New amenities included a hot-air furnace, attic water tank, bathroom, laundry and clothes room, and servant call bells. Gerwig was a Catonsville house carpenter who by 1882 advertised as an architect and builder. For the design of this house he likely referred to one of the many pattern books or design catalogs of the period.

CM8 ST. JOHN'S EPISCOPAL CHURCH

1859–1861, Norris G. Starkweather; 1886 belfry; 1968–1974 renovation and expansion, Cochran, Stevenson and Donkervoet. 9120 Frederick Rd.

This Ellicott City congregation was formed in 1821 as a chapel of ease for Queen Caroline Parish. In October 1859 the church vestry approved new church plans and specifications provided by Starkweather. He had moved his architectural practice from Philadelphia to Baltimore earlier in the

Top left: Ellicott City Commercial Buildings (**CM2**), Ellicott City Firehouse. **Top right:** Baltimore and Ohio Ellicott City Station Museum (B&O Railroad Station; **CM6**). **Bottom left:** St. John's Episcopal Church (**CM8**). **Bottom right:** Carrollton Hall (Folly Quarter; **CM11**).

decade to work on the Gothic Revival First Presbyterian Church (BC11) in that city. For St. John's, he selected Romanesque for the design, which represented a move away from the Ecclesiological movement's strict adherence to Gothic for church architecture during the 1840s and 1850s.

The church was partially built on the foundations of the original church, and its original configuration was a six-bay stone structure with a stone tower and spire at the east corner of the facade. The smaller stone tower at the west corner was finished with a wood belfry in 1886. The church was renovated and lengthened by three bays to the north after a study was conducted by the Baltimore firm of Cochran,

Stevenson, and Donkervoet in 1968. The gallery and vestibule at the south end of the sanctuary were doubled in depth. The interior features an exposed wood truss at each bay supported on a scrolled bracket, and the ceiling is sheathed with boards that cover the common rafters. In addition to churches, Starkweather designed several grand Italianate villas during this period, including nearby Elmonte (CM9).

CM9 ELMONTE
c. 1858, Norris G. Starkweather.
9095 Furrow Ave.

This Italianate villa was built for Sally Dorsey of the prominent Dorsey family of Howard County as part of a gentlewoman's farm. The villa became a sought-after form for genteel farmers such as the Dorseys anxious to showcase their refined taste. By embracing the form, Dorsey acknowledged her awareness of the latest trends in both picturesque architectural and landscape design. Elmonte is constructed of indigenous, random-laid ashlar granite and comprises a central main block with a bracketed hipped roof with cupola, a projecting parlor, a sweeping veranda, and a setback service wing.

CM10 DOUGHOREGAN MANOR

c. 1739–1740; c. 1762–1764 additions; c. 1832 additions. End of Manor Ln.

The family seat of the influential Carroll family of Maryland, Doughoregan Manor, began in 1702 with a seven-thousand-acre land grant from colonial proprietor Cecil Calvert to his attorney general Charles Carroll, who became the wealthiest man in Maryland. The house today is a sprawling three-hundred-foot-long, five-part Georgian residence of brick with a rough-cast finish, tetrastyle Doric porticoes front and rear, and an octagonal cupola, built as the centerpiece of a sprawling, slave-operated tobacco plantation. The main block began as a one-and-a-half-story dwelling with a gambrel roof characteristic of the Chesapeake house, flanked by detached kitchen and chapel buildings that later were joined by hyphens. The chapel was built when Catholic worship was prohibited, and for many years the family opened it to the local community for Sunday services. Additions and renovations made in the 1830s by grandson Charles Carroll V included the Greek Revival flourishes.

The manor encompasses an extensive array of outbuildings, many in stone, including a Gothic Revival cottage-style gatehouse (c. 1860; 3120 Manor Lane). Doughoregan Manor was designated a National Historic Landmark for its association with its third owner, Charles Carroll of Carrollton, the only Catholic signer of the Declaration of Independence. The house remains in the family.

CM11 CARROLLTON HALL (FOLLY QUARTER)

1831–1832, William F. Small. 12280 Folly Quarter Rd.

This neoclassical house is among Small's finest, indicative of the work of his mentor, Benjamin Henry Latrobe. It was commissioned by Charles Carroll of Carrollton for his granddaughter Emily MacTavish and built on his Doughoregan Manor estate (CM10) of locally quarried ashlar granite. Like Latrobe, Small favored Greek- and Roman-inspired architecture, demonstrated here by elegant restraint and classical proportions, flush tripartite windows set within arched recesses, and monumentally scaled tetrastyle Greek porticos. The staid exterior belies the sophistication, grand scale, and complexity of the interior. Its central passage with groin-vaulted ceiling is as broad as the adjoining rooms; parlors for entertaining are on one side, and a private library and parlor that flank an open-well stair are on the other. The second floor contains a twenty-four-foot-square gallery with an eight-light oculus domed ceiling. Small emulated Latrobe's Rational House plan, placing the dining room in relationship to the service stair and basement kitchen. It is now owned by the Franciscan Friars.

COLUMBIA

CM12 COLUMBIA NEW TOWN

1963–c. 1990, James Rouse, developer. Bounded by MD 108, MD 100, I-95, and MD 32, and bisected by U.S. 29

Located midway between Baltimore and Washington, Columbia is one of the most successful and innovative New Towns built in the United States during the second half of the twentieth century, and the most ambitious of Rouse's many ventures. Responding to the suburban sprawl following World War II, progressive large-scale developers pursued New Towns as a marketable solution to the social and environmental ills associated with conventional suburban planning, such as racial and socioeconomic homogeneity, overreliance on the automobile, and a lack of green space. Columbia and Reston, its contemporaneous counterpart in northern Virginia, were among the most publicized New Town experiments nationwide.

Rouse got his start in mortgage banking in the 1930s, establishing The Rouse Company in 1954 to become one of the country's largest and most influential commercial developers and an early pioneer of enclosed shopping malls and later "festival marketplaces" such as Harborplace (BC53) in Baltimore. He began planning Columbia in 1962, amassing approximately fourteen thousand acres within the year. Rouse assembled a professional team to develop a master plan, ranging from architects, landscape architects, and engineers to sociologists, housing economists, and health and education specialists to create an overall concept for Columbia that aimed to "provide the best possible environment for the growth of people."

The plan encompassed ten "villages," each containing residential neighborhoods and commercial, educational, and recreational facilities, arrayed around a town center. The villages included green space, pedestrian-friendly paths, and a variety of housing types to accommodate every income level. Curvilinear roadways, coordinated signage, and public art contribute to the aesthetic distinctiveness and sense of community. Columbia's cultural center is formed by the Merriweather Post Pavilion and nearby Lake Kittamaqundi with its lakefront promenades, cafés, and the *People Tree* sculpture (*pictured*). The pavilion (1967) and the lakefront former Rouse Company headquarters building (1969) at 10475 and 10275 Little Patuxent Parkway, respectively, represent architect Frank Gehry's first major commissions. Adjacent is Columbia Mall, the commercial and retail center, which opened in 1971. Construction at Columbia began in 1966, and Rouse officially dedicated the village of Wilde Lake in 1967. The final village, River Hill, was begun in 1990. Columbia remains one of the area's most desirable places to live, and in many ways a bedroom community for nearby urban centers.

CM13 OAKLAND MANOR
1810–1811, Abraham Larew; 1988 restored. 5430 Vantage Point Rd.

Among the most sophisticated early-nineteenth-century houses in Howard County is this three-part, rough-cast stone neoclassical dwelling designed and built for Charles Sterrett Ridgely, land developer and politician. It was later purchased by Baltimore merchant Robert Oliver for his son, Thomas Oliver, who accumulated an estate of over a thousand acres. In 1838 the buildings were described as "of the most costly, substantial and elegant kind." Measuring 110 feet in length with stone walls 26 inches thick, the first floor then comprised a large hall, six rooms, and two pantries and incorporated central heat, a rare luxury in its day.

One of the most extensive estates in the county, Oakland included outbuildings, tenanted farmsteads, a mill complex, and a manufacturing village (still extant is Oakland Mills Blacksmith House and Shop; 5471 Old Columbia Road). An on-site quarry supplied the stone to build the house and other buildings such as the extant cross-gable-roofed washhouse. Oakland was one of many farm complexes that gave way to the development of Columbia (CM12), although happily this house was spared. Restored, it was opened to the public in 1988.

ELKRIDGE

CM14 ELKRIDGE FURNACE COMPLEX
c. 1835–1873. 5741–5745 Furnace Ave.

Six buildings remain of the once bustling Elkridge Furnace ironmaking endeavor, which originated in the mid-eighteenth century. The discovery of iron ore in the Patapsco River Valley made ironmaking one of the first industries in the area, with furnaces using water from the Patapsco to cool their bellows and run machinery. Colonial-era iron production diversified the economy of the struggling tobacco port of Elkridge Landing while still utilizing the enslaved labor and small-scale settlement patterns of the region. This operation was founded c. 1755 by Caleb Dorsey Jr., who also operated Dorsey's Forge farther north along the Patapsco. Around 1815, Elkridge Furnace was acquired by the entrepreneurial Ellicott family after changing hands many times in the preceding decades. They expanded the capacity, with Elkridge Furnace producing sixteen thousand tons of pig iron in 1826.

Most of the remaining structures likely were built in the 1830s by the Ellicotts. These include a c. 1835 two-and-a-half-story, side passage owner's house, which boasts fine brickwork and refined details inside and out reflecting the transition from Federal to Greek Revival. The two-story kitchen wing to the rear appears to be part of the original construction.

Abutting the owner's house to the east lies the company store and dormitory. The primary elevation was originally that facing the Patapsco River rather than the one oriented to the street. Likely built during the second quarter of the nineteenth century, the company store is the most intact example of a building erected for this purpose in the state. Even more remarkable are two small, one-story dovetail plank outbuildings that sit west of the owner's house on stone foundations. Possibly used as housing for either free or enslaved furnace workers, these structures represent rare survivors of a once common but ephemeral form of construction.

A wood manager's house (c. 1835) sits directly across the street at 5730 Furnace Avenue. While smaller and plainer in finish than the owner's house, the decorative details reflect a shared building period and stylistic approach. Also nearby at 5735 Race Road is a recently restored two-story brick semidetached house built for furnace workers in the mid-nineteenth century.

The furnace continued to change hands frequently; it was sold to its final owner, the Great Falls Iron Company, in 1858. At this time the complex included a dozen more buildings along Furnace Avenue, likely worker housing. The Patapsco River flooded in 1868 and again in 1873, destroying the furnace and ending iron production at this site. Robert H. Brown acquired the property in 1887 and was probably responsible for the late-nineteenth-century alterations to the owner's house. Today, that house, the store, and the semidetached workers' house have been restored under a lease agreement with the State of Maryland for use as the Elkridge Furnace Inn restaurant and event venue.

CM15 THOMAS VIADUCT
1833–1835, John McCartney, builder, Benjamin Henry Latrobe Jr., engineer. Across the Patapsco River between Relay and Elkridge Landing

Virtually unchanged since its 1835 completion, this viaduct on the Washington branch of the Baltimore and Ohio Railroad (B&O) was the first multispan

masonry railroad bridge erected in the United States and the first built on a curving alignment. Benjamin Henry Latrobe Jr., an engineer with the B&O and son and namesake of the famed architect, designed the massive viaduct, which had to be high enough to avoid flooding of the Patapsco River while also accommodating a 4-degree curve.

To do so, he laid out the piers on radial lines, resulting in a wedge shape with wider sides facing the outside curve of the viaduct. The 612-foot-long viaduct (704 feet including the approaches) has 8 elliptical arches with pilasters between them. The viaduct rises 59 feet from the water level to the base of the cast-iron decorative rail and has a 26-foot-wide deck that accommodates a double track and a 4-foot-wide pedestrian walkway. It is built of 63,000 tons of rough-dressed granite ashlar obtained from nearby quarries on the Patapsco River set in cement mortar.

Officially named for Philip E. Thomas, the first president of the railroad (1827–1836), the viaduct was nicknamed Latrobe's Folly because of public doubts that it would even be able to support its own weight. Now a National Historic Landmark and a National Historical Civil Engineering Landmark, it has defied all expectations, remaining in service to the present. Its smaller predecessor, the Carrollton Viaduct (BC91) located over Gwynn's Falls in Baltimore, also shares this distinction.

CM16 BELMONT MANOR AND HISTORIC PARK (BELMONT)
c. 1760; c. 1789 kitchen; 1917 additions. 6555 Belmont Woods Rd.

The oldest extant house associated with the prominent Dorsey family, Belmont is distinguished by Chesapeake-influenced architectural elements including a one-and-a-half-story configuration, clipped gable roof with paired end chimneys, and interior wood paneling. The main block was erected for Caleb Dorsey Jr. on property passed down through generations and with money generated by the Elkridge Furnace (CM14) he established in 1755. Built of Flemish-bond brick and measuring 50 × 24 feet, Dorsey's house was an imposing dwelling for its day. The hyphens and wings were configured c. 1798, and the rough-cast facing then fashionable applied c. 1815. The house was brought into the modern era in 1917, adding a new kitchen wing and expanding the hyphens. The property encompasses terracing, boxwood gardens, and outbuildings including a c. 1850 stone bank barn. Now owned by Howard County, Belmont is used as an event venue.

CM17 LAWYERS HILL
Early 19th to early 20th century. Lawyers Hill Rd. and Old Lawyers Hill Rd.

This enclave was developed as an early railroad suburb, with the commute to Baltimore made feasible by the extension of the B&O over the Patapsco River Valley via the Thomas Viaduct (CM15). Waning industrial production in the area motivated major landowning families such as the Dorseys and the Ellicotts to sell property to city residents seeking a healthful retreat. By 1873, regular passenger service to Baltimore supported a lively summer community. Dubbed Lawyers Hill for its many prominent attorney residents, the neighborhood features over two dozen houses on large wooded lots set in rolling topography. Most of the houses were built between the mid-nineteenth and early twentieth centuries in various

fashionable architectural modes. Many are wood, and although sizable, they have an informal massing in keeping with the atmosphere of a suburban retreat.

While long driveways and setbacks make some of the houses inaccessible to public viewing, several representative examples are visible from the road. The Elkridge Assembly Rooms (*pictured*) at 6090 Lawyers Hill Road is a Shingle Style community hall built in 1871 on land donated by lawyer George Washington Dobbin, one of the first residents and a founder of the Baltimore Bar Association. The house known as Armagh was built by Dobbin for his son Robert at 6204 Lawyers Hill in 1860. Although altered with a "Georgian" entrance in the 1960s, Armagh still has a classic Italianate appearance. Maycroft (6060 Old Lawyers Hill) is a quintessential Queen Anne house with an asymmetrical form, fish scale shingle sheathing, and a stylized Palladian window. Dobbin's daughter Susan Mayer built this house in 1881 with her husband Charles, who served as general counsel for the B&O.

Later houses tended to be smaller, as families continued to subdivide lots. A classic two-story foursquare dwelling with shingle siding was built at 6170 Lawyers Hill in 1910. Little Hill House at 6053 Old Lawyers Hill is a Colonial Revival hall-and-parlor house designed by Philadelphia architect R. Brognard Okie in 1916. It received a sympathetic wing addition in 1945. Okie also designed Lift-A-Latch (1914; 6176 Lawyers Hill) another Colonial Revival cottage nestled into the hillside back from the road. Despite the shift from railroad commuting to automobile, particularly with the construction of I-95 through its western side in the 1960s, and I-895 directly north in the early 1970s, Lawyers Hill remains remarkably intact.

SAVAGE

CM18 SAVAGE MILL

c. 1822 founded; later additions; 8600 Foundry St.

The Savage Manufacturing Company was founded in 1822 by the Williams Brothers at the site of a c. 1810 gristmill and takes its name from financial backer John Savage of Philadelphia. Located on the north bank of the Little Patuxent River, the complex included a stone textile mill, gristmill, and sawmill, all using waterpower from the river falls. By 1825, the textile mill was producing cotton duck, a heavy canvas used for ships sails, tents, and other purposes, and employing two hundred people, mainly women and children, as was typical in the textile industry. Baltimore dry goods merchant William H. Baldwin Jr. bought the operation in 1847. His family owned Savage Mill for the next hundred years, expanding the facility to increase production numerous times, such as the addition of a brick weaving shed in 1916. Production was converted to coal-generated electric power in 1918; the mill plant also provided electricity for the town of Savage. Textile production ceased in 1948, and after a short-lived Christmas ornament manufacturing endeavor in the early 1950s, the mill closed permanently. In the early 1970s, the mill complex was adapted for a restaurant, artist studios, and antique shops.

CM19 SAVAGE MILL VILLAGE

Early 19th–early 20th centuries. Bounded by the Little Patuxent River and Foundry, Baltimore, and Fair sts.

Savage Mill Village was a paternalistic company town typical of the textile industry, with workers renting houses built nearby from their employer. The mill village is arranged on a roughly five-by-three block grid of streets just north of the mill. Extant housing ranges from semidetached brick houses likely built in the 1830s to typical 1920s bungalows on the east side of the neighborhood. The early semidetached worker houses at 9040, 9050, and 9060 Washington Street are six bays wide, with the entrances at the end bays and a shared central chimney. The building at 9078 Washington has six narrow bays with entrances paired at the center, and smaller variants are at 9051–9053 and 9063–9065 Baltimore Street. Later semidetached house variations include the shed-roofed, Italianate-inspired 9114–9115 Baltimore Street and the wood, shared-porch houses on the 8400 block of Commercial Street. Single-family wood houses built in the third quarter of the nineteenth century are found on the 8900 block of Baltimore Street.

A large, late-nineteenth-century house with a mansard roof sits on a spacious lot at 8502 Fair Street. Typical of the hierarchy of mill towns, this impressive structure housed the Savage Mill manager, while the owner's house (9110 Washington), dubbed The Mansion, was used as a summer house by the Baldwins. Built between 1859 and 1878, this Italianate dwelling features a cupola on its hipped roof.

The former company store and post office is a two-and-a-half-story brick building at 8520 Commercial, and the two-story brick Masonic lodge (1897; 9140 Wash-ington) was built by the company. Carroll Baldwin Memorial Hall (9035 Foundry Street), a rubble stone one-story community building, was erected in 1921 in memory of the longtime Savage Manufacturing Company director. Unlike communities associated with larger mills in Baltimore City, Savage Mill village remained a company town until after World War II, with the mill company providing electricity, sewerage, and other municipal functions. Today it is an unincorporated town in Howard County.

CM20 BOLLMAN SUSPENSION TRUSS BRIDGE

1869, Wendel Bollman, engineer. Spanning Little Patuxent River near the junction of Foundry St. and Gorman Rd.

This 160-foot-long, two-span, through-truss bridge next to Savage Mill is thought to be the only remaining example of the Bollman bridge design critical to the development of the railroad in the mid-nineteenth century. Baltimore engineer Wendel Bollman patented his design in 1852 for a uniquely strong composite bridge truss structure of cast and wrought iron. The thicker cast-iron members worked in compression while the thinner wrought-iron ones worked in tension to create a hybrid system combining elements of a suspension bridge and a rigid truss. The Bollman suspension truss offered the durability of a metal bridge while still being relatively inexpensive and easy to build, making it the first all-iron bridge to be adopted and widely used by a railroad. Bollman's first bridge using this method was actually built here in Savage for the B&O Railroad spanning the Little Patuxent River in 1850. However, the current structure was fabricated in 1869 and moved from the main railroad line to the small spur line serving Savage Mill in 1888. It sits on granite abutments with a single mid-river granite pier.

Between 1850 and 1875 more than a hundred Bollman suspension truss bridges were built for the B&O and other railroads. While many remained in service into the twentieth century, the design was later supplanted by bridges that could carry heavier loads. In recognition of its importance to railroad history and its rare survival, this bridge was designated the first National Historic Civil Engineering Landmark by the American Society of Civil Engineers in 1966 and a National Historic Landmark in 2000.

GLENWOOD

CM21 ST. ANDREW'S EPISCOPAL CHURCH (UNION CHAPEL)

1833; 1980s restored. 2892 Roxbury Mills Rd.

This building served as a nondenominational meetinghouse accommodating six different faiths, as well as meetings of the general community. It was used predominately by the local Methodists, who represented one-half of its original trustees. As characteristic of such chapels, it is an unpretentious building. Built of rough-cast stone, it features dual entrances and a central tripartite window on both stories, and a projecting chancel to the rear contains a similar window in stained glass. The interior encompasses a typical meetinghouse plan consisting of an open space occupied by nonfixed pews, surrounded on three sides by a gallery, and a chancel with a raised platform and simple lectern. The space has plain plaster walls, splayed window reveals without surrounds, and simple ceiling medallions. Abandoned by the 1950s, Union Chapel was restored in the 1980s and currently serves an Episcopal congregation.

BALTIMORE COUNTY

TOWSON

CM22 BALTIMORE COUNTY COURTHOUSE

1854–1855, Dixon and Dixon; 1910 additions, Baldwin and Pennington; 1925 addition, Pennington and Pennington; 1958 addition. 400 Washington Ave.

Designed by a prominent Baltimore architectural firm, this Greek Revival courthouse is in a style then popular for civic architecture. The warm hue and quarry-faced texture of the ashlar limestone building provides an interesting contrast to the lighter, smoother marble pedimented portico, with its fluted Doric columns and a triglyph-and-metope entablature. The stone came from the quarries at Hampton (see CM27), as did the inspiration for the octagonal cupola that crowns the building. Originally flanked by two bays, additional bays sen-

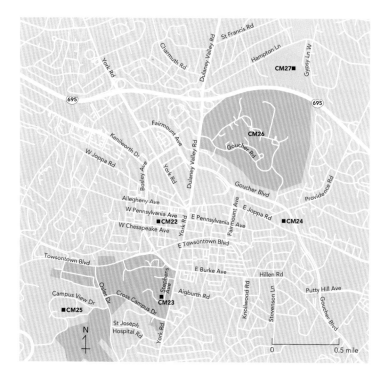

sitive to the original design and materials were added later. Their plain pilasters, entablature, and pediments mirror those of the original building, although differentiated by smooth stone. A wing added in 1925 to the center of the rear facade was later raised and extended. The H-plan was finally realized in 1958 with a massive two-story addition abutting the rear wing. To the front of the courthouse is a public square, and to its west across the plaza is the Baltimore County Courts Building (1975–1977), a Brutalist design by Paul L. Goudreau.

Dixon and Dixon also designed the Italianate Baltimore County Jail (1855; 222 Courthouse Square) built of irregularly coursed limestone with a central tower. Along the square at 101 Chesapeake Avenue is the classical, two-story ashlar limestone U.S. Post Office (1937, Louis A. Simon, Supervising Architect of the U.S. Treasury).

A Works Progress Administration project, the interior boasts the five-panel mural, *History of Transportation* (1939), painted by Russian immigrant artist Nicolai Cikovsky.

CM23 STEPHENS HALL, TOWSON STATE UNIVERSITY
1915, Parker, Thomas and Rice. 7900 Stephens Ave.

This distinctive Jacobean Revival building was one of two first erected on the new suburban campus of Baltimore's State Normal School, now Towson State University. It served as the classroom and administration building, concurrent with the similar Newell Hall dormitory. Referencing the architecture of such English universities as Oxford and Cambridge, the style was popularly adopted by American universities during the late nineteenth and early twentieth centuries. It is now the university's perform-

Left: Baltimore County Courthouse (**CM22**). **Right:** Baltimore County Public Safety Building (**CM24**).

ing arts building. The campus has greatly expanded since 1915, most recently to include a modern state-of-the-art Science Complex (2018–2020) featuring a multistory atrium, created by Cannon-Design.

CM24 BALTIMORE COUNTY PUBLIC SAFETY BUILDING
1972, Peterson and Brickbauer. 700 E. Joppa Rd.

Built for Maryland Blue Cross–Blue Shield health insurance company, this bold mirrored glass cube served as its headquarters until 1989. The design by Peterson and Brickbauer, best known for Baltimore-Washington International (BWI) Thurgood Marshall Airport (WS90), places the main eleven-story tower on a verdant green lawn with a semicircular recessed drive and concrete base of subterranean parking. A dramatic red-glazed brick heating, ventilation, and air conditioning (HVAC) tower sits in the foreground of the site, reflected in the glass wall of the tower and consistent with Brickbauer's later use of red-glazed tile walls at BWI. After Blue Cross–Blue Shield relocated in 1989, Baltimore County purchased the building and its approximately seven-acre site to house its Public Safety Department.

CM25 SHEPPARD-PRATT HOSPITAL
1860 gatehouse, Dixon and Dixon; 1862–1891 hospital, Calvert Vaux; many later additions. 6501 N. Charles St.

Founded over 150 years ago on a bucolic campus north of Baltimore, Sheppard-Pratt Hospital was on the forefront of humane treatment for the mentally ill. The private hospital began with Baltimore Quaker merchant Moses Sheppard's bequest "to carry forward and improve the ameliorated system of treatment of the insane, irrespective of expense." Upon his death in 1857 nearly $600,000 was given to establish the Sheppard Asylum. The first building erected was a stone Gothic Revival gatehouse built in 1860. While Baltimore architects Thomas and James Dixon designed the gatehouse, the commission for the hospital was given to New York City architect Calvert Vaux, widely known for his design of Central Park. Vaux's design called for an east and west building with a courtyard between for the separate housing of male and female patients. Mirror images of each other, each side-by-side red brick building was 360 feet long and ornamented with towers and dormers. It took almost thirty years for Vaux's buildings to be completed as funds were made available from the interest on Sheppard's trust.

Although of the same hospital reform impulse as the Kirkbride Plan mental asylums built in the nineteenth century, the private status and drawn-out period of construction make Sheppard-Pratt's design more singular than the model promoted by Dr. Kirkbride. The first patients received in 1891 were housed in small private rooms and cared for by individual attendants. Another prominent Quaker philanthropist, Enoch Pratt, the originator of Baltimore's free library system, pledged over $1 million for patient care and construction of additional buildings in 1896. Many buildings have been added to the Sheppard-Pratt campus over the decades, including a sympathetic 1971 structure filling the courtyard between Vaux's buildings. However, the original buildings here represent remarkably intact examples of late-nineteenth-century hospital design.

CM26 GOUCHER COLLEGE

1938–1963, Moore and Hutchins; later additions. 1021 Dulaney Valley Dr.

Founded in 1855 as a women's college by Baltimore's Lovely Lane Methodist Church (BC102), Goucher was outgrowing its city campus by the early twentieth century. The more than four-hundred-acre site of the former Epsom estate north of downtown Towson was purchased in 1921. In 1938 an invitational competition was held, with approval of the AIA Baltimore Chapter, for a campus master plan and library. The New York City firm of Moore and Hutchins was selected, and they served as lead architects until the mid-1950s, designing about nine buildings and guiding the development of the new campus. Their master plan moved away from a traditional quadrangle to informal functional nodes linked by pedestrian pathways. Distinctly modern, the Goucher College buildings designed under Moore and Hutchins have low horizontal lines and prominent use of local gneiss stone and other natural building materials such as wood and slate.

Their first building on the new campus was Mary Fisher Hall, built in 1941–1942 to meet the urgent need for student housing. The College Center (now Dorsey Center), built in 1961–1963 after designs by Pietro Belluschi with Rogers, Taliaferro and Lamb, expands the Moore and Hutchins architectural vocabulary with a structurally expressive approach. The Dorsey Center is a two-part complex constructed of structural steel, local stone, wood, and copper with a theater/music building joined to an administrative building by a breezeway. Also noteworthy is the Haebler Memorial Chapel (1961–1963), the last building on campus by Moore and Hutchins. In 1957 landscape architect Hideo Sasaki was hired to guide campus planning during the construction of I-695, the Baltimore Beltway, which forms the north border of the campus. Now a coeducational institution, the original core of

Goucher College's Towson campus offers an elegant and understated study in midcentury design along with sympathetic newer additions.

CM27 HAMPTON (HAMPTON NATIONAL HISTORIC SITE)
1783–1790. 535 Hampton Ln.

For over 150 years the home of the prominent Ridgely family, Hampton is among the largest and most elaborate post–Revolutionary War houses in Maryland, if not the country. The massively scaled late-Georgian house encompasses a three-story, two-pile, central-passage main block flanked by hyphenated wings to form a five-part composition. The design was a collaboration between original owner Captain Charles Ridgely and master carpenter-builder Jehu Howell. It is built of rubble stone quarried on-site with a stuccoed finish scored to resemble ashlar believed to be original to the house. Its octagonal cupola likewise represents an early domestic use, providing extensive vistas of the landscaped gardens. The exterior is indicative of the most refined Georgian houses comprising identical central pavilions with two-story pedimented porticos at both carriage and garden facades,

ornamented slab chimneys, a Palladian window in the pediments, and Chippendale railings on the porticos. To one side of the broad central passage are drawing and music rooms, and to the other, dining and sitting rooms flanking the stair hall; the pantry and kitchen are in one hyphenated wing and an office and laundry in the other.

At its height, Hampton encompassed 25,000 acres, with terraced formal gardens, walks and paths, and outbuildings that include an orangery and greenhouse for the cultivation of the estate's flowers, shrubs, and exotic trees. The Home Farm, unusually sited in full view of the house and likely dating to the Ridgely's original acquisition in 1745, includes an early Chesapeake house, three stone two-family slave quarters, log quarters, and accompanying farm buildings.

Acquired by the National Park Service in 1948, it was the first property designated a National Historic Site for architectural significance, and it is important for its association with the Ridgely family, merchants, ironmasters, planters, privateers, and politicians who made substantial contributions to the development of Baltimore.

MIDDLE RIVER

Middle River was a vital manufacturing center during World War II due to the expansion of the pioneering Glenn L. Martin Aircraft Company, which founded its operations here in 1928. With the outbreak of war in Europe, Middle River rapidly became a defense boomtown. Between 1939 and 1943, the number of Martin employees surged from 3,000 to 52,000. The small town, with 161 residents in 1939, and its local building community were unprepared and unequipped to house the massive influx of newcomers. The Martin Company began the expansion of the town's residential facilities and called on the federal government to continue. In 1941, the Maryland State Planning Commission hired Hale Walker, planner for Greenbelt for the Farm Security Administration (CR16), and Irving C. Root of the National Park Service to prepare a master plan for Middle River. Their plan incorporated many Garden City features already started by the Martin Company housing—pedestrian paths to playgrounds and schools, curving residential streets separated from the new dual highways of Martin and Eastern boulevards, and neighborhood shopping centers.

Construction of single-family and semidetached houses began in the Victory Villa subdivision in 1942. Other surviving residential areas such as Aero Acres, with detached single-family houses, and Stansbury Estates garden apartments also were built as defense worker housing. Victory Villa Gardens built by the Farm Security Administration in 1943 (demolished 2005) included a thousand attached units in one-story wood multifamily dwellings arranged on curving streets named after Air Force bases and offering communal green space. Development of these wartime home-front projects transformed Middle River and represented the largest such effort in the greater Baltimore-Washington region, foreshadowing the industrial decentralization and large-scale suburban development to come in the postwar decades. Although somewhat altered and under redevelopment pressure, Middle River still offers an outstanding collection of World War II–era national defense resources in its buildings, land-use patterns, and community institutions.

CM28 GLENN L. MARTIN AIRCRAFT COMPANY PLANT NO. 2/MIDDLE RIVER DEPOT
1941, Albert Kahn and Associates. 2800 Eastern Blvd.

The Martin company worked repeatedly with the innovative Detroit architectural and engineering firm of Albert Kahn and Associates. His Plant No. 1 in Middle River was started in 1928. However, it was a series of expansions built in anticipation of World War II, including Plant

No. 2, that emerged as landmarks in modern industrial engineering. Plant No. 2's iconic status was further assured by Mies van der Rohe's use of an interior photograph for his hypothetical "Concert Hall" design from 1942.

In 1937 Kahn designed a new Assembly Building for Plant No. 1. Using parallel-chord roof trusses adapted from bridge technology, the Assembly Building offered an unobstructed 300 × 450–foot interior for manufacturing aircraft at an unprecedented scale. Kahn designed an addition to Plant No. 1 in 1939. Plant No. 2, built in 1941 approximately one mile from Plant No. 1, repeated the successful design elements of Kahn's previous work for Martin Aircraft, including a 602 × 900–foot Assembly Building with parallel-chord bridge trusses. It was the first factory expansion funded by the federal government under the Emergency Plant Facilities Act. As such, the Army Air Corps leased the factory to the Martin Company for production of B-26 Marauders.

Plant No. 2 encloses over 1 million square feet of space. Kahn took advantage of the natural grade to provide a basement level, an unusual feature for an aircraft factory. Supported by ten concrete mushroom columns and open on three sides, the basement housed such manufacturing processes as creating parts and subassembly. The first-floor assembly areas have steel columns spaced 50 × 100 feet apart with a truss clearance of 22 feet. The 28-foot tall "high bay" at the west end of the Assembly Building accommodated final aircraft assembly with a 100 × 200–foot span. Massive telescoping cantilevered doors here allowed the assembled B-26 Marauders to be moved to the Paint Shop and then to the adjacent Pennsylvania Railroad siding for shipment. The complex also includes an administration building, oil house, boiler house, and drop hammer building.

Lockheed Martin continued manufacturing at a much-altered Plant No. 1 until 2010. Plant No. 2 survived remarkably intact, having been used for many years as a warehouse by the U.S. General Services Administration (GSA). The property was sold to private developers in 2006 and remains slated for mixed-use redevelopment that would retain the historic buildings.

CM29 VICTORY VILLA COMMUNITY CENTER
c. 1942. 404 Compass Rd.

Victory Villa Community Center is a remarkable surviving example of a government-sponsored wartime community building. It is prominently sited on the south edge of the Victory Villa subdivision and across Martin Boulevard from the Aero Acres subdivision. At first the government provided trailers for workers near the Glenn L. Martin Aircraft factory (CM28), but during 1942, 1,100 prefabricated plywood houses were built in the new neighborhood of Victory Villa by the Farm Security Administration. The project also included a school and community center.

The community center was intended to help build community identity for a large population of workers and their families from places as varied as northern cities and rural Appalachia. The building is divided into two sections—a two-story gymnasium/auditorium with a slightly arched roof and a perpendicular one-story wing housing offices and meeting rooms. It has a plain, modern appearance created using prefabricated rectangular wood siding panels and industrial metal sash windows. The center's interior is still remarkably intact, with original wood doors and composite panel walls. The stage is still in place in the auditorium/gymnasium, although there is now a drop ceiling between the first- and second-story levels. The center was located near a kindergarten building, administration building, and small commercial structures, reflecting the careful planning of community amenities for this defense worker boomtown.

CM30 BENGIES DRIVE-IN THEATER
1956, Jack K. Vogel; 1973 marquee. 3417 Eastern Blvd.

The last operating drive-in movie theater in Maryland has all the features associated with the type—illuminated sign at the roadside, ticket booths, an operations building including concession stand, restrooms, and a projection booth, and careful site planning including one-way lanes and parking along berms to facilitate views of the big screen. Its designer, architectural engineer Vogel, was a prolific designer of drive-ins. This drive-in, constructed and operated for decades by his brother Hank Vogel, was part of their small family-run theater chain of both indoor and drive-in theaters. Bengies is still owned and operated by the Vogel family.

DUNDALK

The unincorporated town of Dundalk sits just southeast of the city of Baltimore, adjacent to the massive Bethlehem Steel works at Sparrows Point. Prior to World War I, it was a small settlement mainly known for the McShane Bell Foundry established in 1856. It was owner Henry McShane who named the local depot of the Baltimore and Sparrows Point Railroad Dundalk after his birthplace in Ireland. In 1916 Bethlehem Steel purchased approximately a thousand acres of farmland near the McShane Foundry and formed a subsidiary, the Dundalk Company, to develop housing for its steel mill and shipyard workers. During World War I Dundalk became the site of the only two U.S. Shipping Board Emergency Fleet Corporation (EFC) projects in Maryland and a significant early example of a federal planned community embracing Garden City principles. Dundalk was one of a small handful of EFC projects to reach full development.

In 1918 Bethlehem Steel entered into an agreement with the EFC to develop the St. Helena and Dundalk projects. St. Helena was located on the west side of Dundalk Avenue and included 284 row houses for unmarried shipyard workers and a mess hall (now demolished) on gridplan streets. Directly east across Dundalk Avenue was the Dundalk project of 531 houses intended for families, now referred to as Old Dundalk. Baltimore architect Edward L. Palmer, known for his work with the Roland Park Company (see BC110), was hired to design the mix of row, semidetached, and detached houses arranged on curvilinear streets. In keeping with the Garden City model promoted by English planner Ebenezer Howard, Dundalk included communal green space and strategically placed commercial and school buildings to serve the residential community. Also consistent with the Garden City model, Dundalk buildings displayed one of Palmer's preferred designs—an Arts and Crafts movement interpretation of English vernacular.

The Armistice in November 1918 ended the EFC's short-lived foray into community building, although the Dundalk projects were far enough along that they were almost completed. By 1920, the EFC houses were sold to private owners or the Dundalk Company, under the management of former Roland Park Company president Edward H. Bouton. The artful designs and community planning, as well as the continued involvement of Palmer and Bouton, combined to give Dundalk a reputation as "the workingman's Roland Park."

CM31 DUNDALK BUILDING
1919, Edward L. Palmer. 19–39 Shipping Pl.

Like the groundbreaking Roland Park shopping center (see BC108) for that planned community, Dundalk included a neighborhood retail complex. The center was arranged around a town green—Veterans Park—along the east side of Dundalk Avenue. For the Dundalk Building, Palmer designed a "Tudorish" structure to house stores, EFC offices, a community hall, and apartments. With a steeply pitched slate roof, a variety of gables and dormers, and stucco walls with brick trim, the Dundalk Building continued the aesthetics of the surrounding houses.

Additional buildings added to the ensemble during the 1920s include a movie theater (1926, John Erying) at 1 Shipping Place, a combination fire/police station (1920, William Emory) at number 7, and the Dunleer (1929) and Dunkirk Buildings (1930) at 41–49 and 63–81 Shipping, respectively. These Colonial Revival variations on the Dundalk Building also contain stores, offices, and apartments. The Dundalk Company offices (4 Center Place) were housed in a one-story Colonial Revival building designed by Palmer in 1924. Located in Veterans Park and from 1958 used as a branch library for many years, this building now houses the Dundalk-Patapsco Neck Historical Society and Museum.

CM32 OLD DUNDALK RESIDENTIAL AREA
1918–1919, Edward L. Palmer. Bounded by Shipway, Eastship, Northship, Portship, and Sunship rds., Admiral Blvd. and Dundalk Ave.

The Emergency Fleet Corporation houses in Dundalk are hollow-tile construction with stuccoed exterior walls and slate roofs. Despite the budget limitations placed on Palmer, these houses have a harmonious Arts and Crafts character, with varying configurations and details. Old Dundalk includes row houses, semidetached (*pictured*), and detached houses designed by Palmer according to nine basic types, with differences in roof and porch form or plan. All the houses offer five or six rooms and are one-and-a-half-stories high, some with additional attic space. The widest street is Admiral Boulevard, which features spacious semidetached and detached houses on larger lots in the blocks closer to Veterans Park. The blocks north of Yorkship Square, at the crossing of Admiral and Midship Road, transition to primarily row houses. Other roads with vaguely nautical names such as Flagship, Kinship, and Township are narrower but lined with a similar variety of types, continuing the stylistic theme, some now altered with aluminum siding.

CATONSVILLE

Catonsville's development was enabled by the Ellicott Brothers construction of Frederick Road in 1787, providing access from their mills to Baltimore harbor. Charles Carroll was among those who owned land midway between; realizing the potential for development, he tasked his son-in-law and wealthy Baltimore merchant Richard Caton, who began with his own summer house (no longer extant). Lots were first platted between 1807 and 1810, with Caton's "Village" plan following in c. 1822. The community was situated on a broad ridge overlooking the scenic Patapsco River Valley, and by the mid-nineteenth century, wealthy Baltimoreans recognizing its virtues began building summer houses. Development increased once the community was accessible by a horsecar line between Catonsville and Baltimore built in 1862, followed by the Catonsville Short Line Railroad in 1884 and a streetcar line in the 1890s. By then Catonsville was becoming a year-round middle-class community, infilling with smaller foursquare and bungalow houses. Several well-recognized Baltimore builders, mostly of German descent, contributed to Catonsville's development, including Joseph M. Cone; H. J. Farber; John Hubner; William, John, and George Gerwig; James F. Nagle; L. R. Servary; and Maisel and Kern.

CM33 CATONSVILLE RESIDENTIAL NEIGHBORHOOD

c. 1880s–1930s. Roughly bounded by Edmondson Rd., and S. Rolling, Ridge, and Seminole rds.

This residential area encompasses romantic-style houses of the mid- to late nineteenth century, built for a professional class. Many were custom built or architect designed and sit on large lots along tree-lined streets. The first houses constituted local types such as the many front-facing L-configured houses with wraparound porch, employing a mix of Queen Anne, Colonial Revival, and Shingle Style characteristics. They include the George and Lizzie Wentz House (c. 1893; 35 Melvin), the Mamie Stiefel House (1908, Ehlers and Wagner; 14 Melvin), and 111 Melvin, and 20 N. Beaumont. Ehlers and Wagner also designed the marbleized, faux-ashlar stucco-finished Colonial Revival Lang House (c. 1909; 107 N. Beaumont). German immigrant builder John Hubner erected the large Queen Anne house for Siegfried and Minnie Mitchell (c. 1890; 100 N. Beechwood), run as a summer boardinghouse, and another for James and Margaret McDonough (1907; 121 Beechwood). L. R. Servary built a rambling Queen Anne house for physician Godefroy Grempler (1904; 128 N. Beechwood) and another at 202 N. Beechwood.

Later transitioning from Queen Anne to foursquare are houses such as that for James and Alice Haynes House (1909) at 115 N. Beaumont. A noteworthy Arts and Crafts house (1909; 117 N. Beaumont) was designed by architect Walter M. Gieske for his brother, tobacco dealer Hardy Gieske.

Exemplary Queen Anne and Shingle Style houses appear along Montrose Road, including numbers 1, 2, 11, 101, and 108. Of note is the Colonial Revival Gorman House (1906; 200 Montrose) designed by Joseph Evans Sperry and the early concrete Walter Brinkmann House (1908; 1301 Edmondson) designed by Wyatt and Nolting and modeled after Thomas Jefferson's Monticello.

OELLA

CM34 OELLA HISTORIC MILL TOWN

1809 founded. Oella Ave., from Frederick Rd. to Race Rd.

The industrial village of Oella was established by the Union Manufacturing Company to house its textile mill workers, later supplemented by housing for the Granite Hill Factory and its successor firm, W. J. Dickey Company. Oella encompasses approximately a hundred housing units dating from the early nineteenth through the early twentieth centuries, along with the last remaining mill, built in 1918. Preserved and rehabilitated, Oella is an intriguing residential community consisting mostly of semi-detached and other multi-unit dwellings set along the curving roads and hillsides of this picturesque, steep and densely wooded gorge of the Patapsco River.

Capitalizing on the success of nearby Ellicott's Mills, Union Manufacturing Company opened a textile mill here in 1808, building the "Stone Row" complex for its workers (871–881 Oella Avenue). Banked into the hillside, the random ashlar granite row features distinctive quoining and tiered galleries. The mill town so captured the imagination of architect Maximillian Godefroy that he created a drawing in 1812 that includes Stone Row.

By 1820, Union was the largest textile mill outside New England. To accommodate the growing workforce, Long Brick Row (c. 1850; 744–780 Oella; *pictured*) was erected. The visually compelling continuous row of two-story, two-bay row houses includes stone stoops, shared chimneys, and firewalls and is articulated to follow the curving contour of the roadway. Nearby three-story brick semidetached houses (1830–1840; 929–947 Oella) feature half-story windows in the third floor.

Granite Hill Factory was established in 1844, and while the mill buildings were destroyed in the devastating flood of 1868, the c. 1844 stone workers' houses survive (1200–1215 Oella). Overlooking the Patapsco River are three semidetached and two single houses, built of locally quarried granite with quoining and monolithic lintels. The two-and-a-half-story, three-bay units are set on high basements with elevated porches, with the semidetached units sharing a center brick chimney and rear kitchen ell.

The mill town was purchased in 1887 by W. J. Dickey Company, adding two-story, two-bay frame housing units (728–747 Oella) with Italianate details. Following a fire, a new mill (1918; 840 Oella) was built, and operations expanded to include woolen cloth, becoming the largest manufacturer in the South. The brick industrial building with large metal windows and entrance tower is banked along the Patapsco River and the old millrace, rising from four to six stories. Unable to compete with new synthetic fabrics, coupled with a devasting flood, the company was forced to close in 1972. Forming the Oella Company, William Dickey's grandson, Charles Wagandt, worked with architects, planners, and government officials to rehabilitate the houses while maintaining architectural integrity and ensuring former mill workers were not displaced. The mill was purchased separately and rehabilitated as loft apartments.

CM35 BENJAMIN BANNEKER HISTORICAL PARK (BENJAMIN BANNEKER CABIN AND JOSHUA HYNES HOUSE)
2009 cabin; c. 1849–1851 house. 318 and 310 Oella Ave.

To honor the memory and interpret the life of free African American almanac author, surveyor, farmer, and naturalist Benjamin Banneker, the county acquired the farmland purchased by his parents in 1737, and a replica of the log cabin (*pictured above*) in which Banneker lived much of his life was reconstructed by Oak Grove Restorations. Based on historical and archaeological investigations, the one-room cabin was built of old hewn chestnut logs with a stone foundation and a stone and brick end chimney. It has been sparsely furnished in a manner indicative of the era to reflect Banneker's humble circumstances. It was on this site that Banneker, largely self-taught, wrote his almanacs and famously corresponded with Thomas Jefferson on issues of slavery and racial equality. An accomplished mathematician, Banneker also undertook astrological observations and in 1791 was part of the survey team for the new federal city.

The hundred-acre Banneker farm was later acquired by Joshua Hynes, who built an imposing five-bay house of local ashlar granite. Its stone construction and subtle Greek Revival details, including a third half-story of frieze-band windows, sets it apart from other area farmhouses.

REISTERSTOWN

CM36 ST. MICHAEL'S CHURCH (HANNAH MORE CHAPEL)

1853–1854, John W. Priest; 1928 addition. 12025 Reisterstown Rd.

St. Michael's was built through the efforts of the Reverend Arthur John Rich, chaplain at the adjacent Hannah More Academy, an Episcopal girls' boarding school founded in 1838. With the construction of St. Michael's, students and local residents could move their worship services out of the school building and into a proper church. It served in this capacity for several decades until the construction of All Saints near the center of town (1891, Longfellow, Alden and Harlow; 208 E. Chatsworth Avenue). St. Michael's was closed and then reopened as a chapel for the school in 1908.

New York City architect Priest was a leading church designer, before his early death in 1859. He was a founding member of the New York Ecclesiological Society, which promoted the ideals of authentic medieval architecture for Episcopal churches and, with Richard Upjohn, was one of the founding members of the American Institute of Architects. His design for this small rural chapel exemplified his approach to Gothic Revival form, plan, and materials for parish churches and recalls the church designs published by Upjohn in *Rural Architecture* (1852). The board-and-batten church has steeply pitched roofs on the nave, entrance porch, and chancel and is modestly decorated with simple vergeboards and a bell cote. The entrance porch projects from the west side of the three-bay nave, and the lower three-bay-long chancel includes a shed roof sacristy on its east side. Originally two bays, the chancel was extended in 1928. Lancet windows and pointed-arched openings at the porch complete the textbook example of Gothic Revival.

The interior is similarly restrained and well detailed, with exposed principal rafter roof trusses between an oiled pine ceiling, oak pews arranged on either side of a central aisle, an oak altar rail dividing the chancel into choir and sanctuary, and a heavy oak altar pierced by a quatrefoil design on its sides. The stained and enameled glass windows were fabricated in Brooklyn by H. P. Bloor and Company at the direction of the architect. The church was deconsecrated in 1978 and acquired along with the adjacent Hannah More Academy (main building built 1858) by Baltimore County. Currently the campus is used as a special education school.

LUTHERVILLE-TIMONIUM

CM37 U.S. POST OFFICE (JOHN DEERE COMPANY BUILDING)
1966, Charles Lamb for RTKL Associates. 9600 Deereco Rd.

A decade after receiving the firm's first national attention for the design of the Girl Scout Lodge (WS77) at Camp Woodlands, Lamb enhanced his reputation as one of Maryland's most innovative modernists with this building for the John Deere Company. The American Institute of Architects recognized this project with a first-place award in 1967. The structurally daring warehouse features a swooping precast concrete roof supported by steel cables embedded into concrete anchors. The design allowed the 197,000-square-foot space to be open to accommodate production of large-scale industrial farm equipment. Blade-like battered concrete buttresses line the convex curve of the front of the building, with ribbon windows and floor slabs for offices suspended between. Used partially as a post office facility for Lutherville-Timonium since 1987, the structure now houses a variety of firms.

CM38 THE CLOISTERS (PARKER HOUSE)
1930–1932, Sumner A. Parker. 10440 Falls Rd.

Wealthy Baltimoreans Sumner and Dudrea Parker traveled extensively during the 1910s and 1920s, collecting medieval objects, art, and architectural fragments to be incorporated into their future country house.

The Parkers' city house was in the Mount Vernon neighborhood and inadequate to display the many collections that they stored in a warehouse after each trip. Sumner Parker was trained as an architect and engineer and for many decades served as president of Armstrong and Parker Co., a prominent Baltimore architectural ironwork firm responsible for ornamental balconies, fences, and gates throughout the city. He designed the house himself, incorporating steel beams and modern amenities into a fanciful medieval mode house. The steel beams helped support the weight of an unusual flagstone roof on exterior walls of rusticated Butler stone, a granite-like local stone prized for its unusual grey coloring with flecks of gold from quartz, mica, and other minerals.

In 1930 the Parkers began construction of their long-planned retreat on an approximately fifty-five-acre hilly and wooded parcel. The main elevation faces south and features two massive half-timbered gables acquired in France that dominate a not quite symmetrical composition. The rest of the exterior is a rich variety of forms and materials, with crenellated parapets, gargoyles, molded chimney caps, and diamond pane iron casement windows of varied shape and size. A one-story octagonal chapel structure extends from the house's west side, and a massive octagonal stair tower appears on the rear at the cloistered terrace.

The interior is packed with even more medieval decorative detail such as carved woodwork, plaster ceilings designed to resemble Gothic stone ribbed vaulting, and ornamental ironwork. Parker designed and his firm fabricated the four-story spiral stair railing at the center of the house, the library staircase bannister, and window grilles and balconies. Many of the interior doors and mantels are fifteenth- and sixteenth-century pieces collected by the Parkers in France and Italy. The Parkers also used windows, doors, and other features they salvaged from Glen Ellen, the Baltimore area's earliest Gothic Revival house designed by Ithiel Town and Alexander Jackson Davis in 1832 and demolished in 1929–1930.

Several rooms housed specialized collections the Parkers displayed to the public. On the first floor the library exhibited rare manuscripts among the exposed wood ceiling trusses and tall bookcases, and tapestries and paintings were displayed in the gallery, a tall, spacious room with heavy carved ceiling beams. Upstairs rooms were dedicated to dolls and dollhouses, and Dudrea Parker's family heirloom American colonial furniture and objects. Sumner Parker died in 1945 and Dudrea Parker willed the house and its contents to the City of Baltimore upon her death in 1972. It is currently an event venue managed by the Baltimore Office of Promotion and the Arts. Although a rare and eccentric accomplishment, the Cloisters speaks to the early-twentieth-century interest in handicraft and architectural authenticity popularized by the Arts and Crafts movement and the 1920s fashion for revival architecture, most commonly seen in movie palaces and luxury hotels, that created fantasy stage settings invoking a romantic past.

CM39 ROCKLAND MILL VILLAGE
c. 1806–1813. 2201 Old Court Rd.

Established by physician Thomas Johnson as a commercial gristmill and worker's village, Rockland speaks to the early industrial transformation of upper Baltimore, where the Jones Falls and its tributaries offered the prime location for water-powered mills. Their development was further facilitated by Oliver Evans's innovative 1784 system of internal elevators and conveyers that mechanized production and significantly reduced labor requirements, and by the construction of the Falls Turnpike for the transport of goods to Baltimore harbor. Rockland village was established along the turnpike the year after it was completed. The stone mill is banked into the hillside, retaining its waterwheel and remnants of the mill race. It was later converted to more lucrative cotton production, manufacturing printed calico fabric.

The village includes workers' row houses, a miller's house, tavern, gable-front general store, and blacksmith shop, all constructed of irregularly coursed stone. Built to attract workers to what was then a remote area, the row houses (c. 1820–1830) at 10106–10116 Falls Road form a continuous grouping of eight two- and three-story, two-bay units of four to six rooms each. Distinct from the workers' housing is the side-hall-plan miller's house (c. 1830; 10010 Falls).

A remnant of the farm upon which the village was built is the Chesapeake-style Turkey Cock Hall (c. 1730; 10131 Falls) that served as Johnson's residence. His son William Fell Johnson later hired David Carlisle to build the imposing Greek Revival Rockland house (1837; 10214 Falls) that sits adjacent to the town. Now a quaint suburban community, Rockland is among the few remaining examples of an intact mill village.

CARROLL COUNTY
WESTMINSTER

CM40 CARROLL COUNTY COURTHOUSE
c. 1838, James Shellman; 1882 additions, Thomas Dixon; 1935 addition, Buckler and Fenhagen. 43 N. Court St.

Named for distinguished Marylander Charles Carroll of Carroll-

ton, the oldest surviving signer of the Declaration of Independence who died in 1832, Carroll County was created in 1837 from portions of Baltimore and Frederick counties. The Carroll County Courthouse sits at the center of a modest courthouse square on

Top: Carroll County Almshouse and Farm Museum (**CM42**). **Bottom:** Union Mills Homestead (**CM43**).

land donated by Issac Shriver, who owned the inn and store at the intersection of Main Street and the newly created Court Street. Designed by Westminster's first mayor, James Shellman, the courthouse is a rather conservative rescaling of a typical center-hall domestic form. Some fashionable, yet quirky, Greek Revival features were added shortly after completion, including a two-story tetrastyle portico, an octagonal cupola, a box cornice, and door surrounds. The one-story additions to either side are from 1882; they were rebuilt and enlarged in 1935.

CM41 ASCENSION EPISCOPAL CHURCH
c. 1844, Robert Cary Long Jr. 23 N. Court St.

Prominent Baltimore architect Long Jr. conceived Ascension Episcopal according to the Ec-

clesiological Society's principles guiding Anglican church design in this period. The diminutive church is only four bays deep and has a small entrance vestibule at the gable end. Rubble stone laid in random ashlar coursing creates a lively exterior. A trefoil window over the entrance, stone bell cote at the roof peak, and lancet windows on the side and rear elevations all contribute to its picturesque Gothic Revival appearance. The interior is simply finished with white plaster walls and exposed wood rafters and scissor trusses.

CM42 CARROLL COUNTY ALMSHOUSE AND FARM MUSEUM
1852–1853. 500 S. Center St.

In 1965, Carroll County opened the first public farm museum in Maryland to celebrate the agricultural history of the region and in the process preserved the recently closed historic county almshouse. The county's tax commissioners were empowered in 1840 to borrow money "to be applied to the purchase of farm, and the creation of suitable buildings for the use of the poor." Finally erected in 1852, the Almshouse provided board and lodging for impoverished residents who, if able-bodied, were expected to work to earn their keep. The long brick almshouse forms the centerpiece of a complex of historic, reconstructed, and new buildings on approximately 140 acres on the outskirts of Westminster. The small casement windows in the attic story reveal the use of that space for living quarters, and a bell sits in a modest cupola on the ridge line. An additional two-story brick building perpendicular to the almshouse contained a summer kitchen, washhouse, bakehouse, and additional quarters. A steward and other staff lived on-site to supervise the residents. Other noteworthy buildings include a bank barn and a dairy ornamented by jigsawn bargeboards and an oversized finial at the peak of its pyramidal roof. Currently many of the buildings are used for demonstrations of historic crafts and trades.

CM43 UNION MILLS HOMESTEAD
1797; 1973–1983 restored. 3311 Littlestown Pike

A joint venture or "union" between brothers Andrew and David Shriver, Union Mills was the first industrial complex in the region and remains today one of the best preserved and documented. A self-sufficient enterprise situated along a main road between Baltimore and Pennsylvania, it encompassed a farm, house, saw- and gristmills, a tannery, and cooper, blacksmith, and wheelwright shops. The log, dogtrot house was built by Pennsylvania carpenter-joiner Henry Kohlstock to comprise two, two-story sections of a single room per floor—one section for each brother—connected by an open central passage and front porch. As the families grew, the house expanded to encompass twenty-three rooms that included a store, school, tavern, and post office.

The imposing mill is erected of bricks made on site, under the direction of millwright John Mong following the innovative, production-line system developed by Oliver Evans in 1784. After six generations of ownership, in 1964 the Shriver family formed the Union Mills Homestead Foundation, creating a museum of American rural culture. It was acquired by the county in 1970 and restored, returning the old mill to working order in 1983.

CM44 ST. MARY'S EVANGELICAL LUTHERAN CHURCH
1894–1895, John A. Dempwolf. 3978 Littlestown Pike

This stone Gothic Revival church sits on the site of houses of worship shared for well over a century by combined German Lutheran and German Reform congregations. A simple log structure built in 1762 was replaced in 1821 by a large brick meetinghouse. However, as both congregations continued to grow, they separated in 1893, with each building a new church. The Lutherans' elaborate and more mainstream church was designed by German-born Dempwolf of York, Pennsylvania, where he designed the first of many churches, St. John's German Lutheran (1874). St. Mary's features a corner tower with slate-shingled spire and an open belfry with Dempwolf's signature mark. A cross-gable section features a tripartite stained glass window to the front, with trefoil-arch pattern exposed framing resembling German timber-framed Fachwerk to the rear. The auditorium-style interior features a vaulted ceiling supported by exposed trusses.

TANEYTOWN

CM45 TREVANION

1817; 1855–1857. 1800 Trevanion Rd.

Trevanion represents the transformation of an early-nineteenth-century farmhouse into a fashionable villa combining elements of Italianate and Gothic Revival. Originating as a brick farmhouse built in the plain Pennsylvania folk tradition of the region, it was purchased in 1855 by William A. Dallas, who, with the help of brother-in-law Joshua Shorb, undertook its renovation. Dallas was a progressive farmer who practiced the latest innovations—undoubtedly desiring that the same ideals be applied to his residence. His picturesque villa incorporates design elements outlined in Andrew Jackson Downing's *The Architecture of Country Houses* (1850). The renovation included a central three-story tower, arcaded porch, projecting bays, and balconies. Dallas dubbed his rejuvenated farm *Trevanion*, a Welsh term meaning "the meeting of the streams," for its location near the confluence of Big Pipe Creek and Meadow Branch. It encompasses numerous outbuildings, many of which share decorative elements with the house, such as the brick summer kitchen and a cold storage building. A brick and stone structure is believed to have been a slave quarters.

UNIONTOWN

As a quintessential linear nineteenth-century agricultural village, Uniontown maintains an excellent state of preservation. Its development coincides with the 1808 completion of the Baltimore-Hagerstown Turnpike that forms its Main Street, with taverns such as the former Uniontown Hotel (1802, 1842 addition; 3477 Uniontown Road) among its earliest buildings. The town attracted a wide range of artisans and storekeepers, who combined their shop and residence under a single roof or attached section, a pattern still in evidence. Uniontown formed the social and commercial center for the area during the first half of the nineteenth century, acquiring a church, school, social and beneficial organizations, a savings bank, and a town newspaper. While its influence waned after being bypassed by the Western Maryland Railway in the 1850s, Uniontown continued to prosper as a local commercial center. Recognizing its importance as an intact rural village, Historic Uniontown was formed in 1971 to preserve its history and integrity.

CM46 DEVILBISS STORE AND HOUSE

c. 1815; 1859 additions. 3444 Uniontown Rd.

The grandest of the many house-and-store buildings in Uniontown was established by Harrison H. Weaver in 1859, becoming Devilbiss Store in 1908. Although sections of the building date to c. 1815, it was remodeled and expanded by Weaver to include the gable-front store with ornamental bargeboards, a form shared by other stores in Uniontown dating from the third quarter of the nineteenth century. Included among these is William Hiteshew's store and tavern (c. 1856; 3476 Uniontown) and the Oliver Hiteshew House and added furniture store with meeting hall above (c. 1809, 1878; 3463 Uniontown). Also noteworthy is the William Anders House and attached shed-roofed tailor shop with intact storefront (c. 1877; 3451 Uniontown).

CM47 JONAS CRUMBACKER HOUSE

c. 1811. 3423 Uniontown Rd.

The finest Federal-period residence in Uniontown is that of prominent local businessman and real estate speculator Jonas Crumbacker. The side-hall plan, two-story house with rear ell is distinguished by its elaborate frontispiece with semicircular fanlight, segmental-arched lintels, and cornice of modillions and diamond-patterns. It was later owned by physician Thomas Shreeve, who built the adjacent gable-front building as his office c. 1888.

Another Federal house of note is the handsome side-hall plan house (c. 1811, c. 1815 addition; 3400 Uniontown) built for John Hyder, postmaster, who operated the post office from the shed-roofed addition.

CM48 UNIONTOWN MUSEUM (UNIONTOWN BANK, CARROLL COUNTY SAVINGS BANK)

1907. 3424 Uniontown Rd.

This diminutive classical building was constructed as the Carroll County Savings Bank, established in 1871. The design is typical of small-town banks, featuring a shed roof with front parapet and brick construction with contrasting stone frontispiece and other details. The bank closed in 1979 but retains its original interiors and vault. It was donated to Historic Uniontown for use as a local history museum, further accommodated by a modern raised-seam metal-sheathed addition to the rear.

CM49 WEAVER-FOX HOUSE
1874–1875. 3411 Uniontown Rd.

This exuberant house was built by local carpenters for physician Jacob J. Weaver Jr. as a rural expression of the Italianate Villa. Its picturesque quality and detailing, while indicative of the era, was not common within rural communities. Weaver was a graduate of the University of Maryland Medical School, practicing in Uniontown from 1870 until 1887, when he turned to banking, serving as president of the Uniontown Bank (CM48). The house passed to daughter Florence Weaver Fox, remaining in the family until 1984.

Diagonally opposite is Weaver's father's house (1812; 1859, additions; 3406 Uniontown). In 1859, physician Jacob J. Weaver Sr. purchased a log house and expanded it with a gable-front addition, re-imagining it as a board-and-batten Gothic Revival cottage. The single-story wing to the opposing side is the office from which he and his son practiced medicine. A graduate of the University of Pennsylvania's medical school, Weaver Sr. practiced here from 1848 to 1880.

CM50 UNIONTOWN ACADEMY
1851. 3347 Uniontown Rd.

Uniontown Academy was established in 1810 as an English-speaking school in the town predominated by those of German descent. It represents the local interest in education and continued learning. The diminutive, three-bay brick building features a false-front stepped parapet with tripartite window, central entrance, and nine-over-six-light windows with rosette corner-block lintels. It served the local literary and debate society as the Clay Lyceum in the 1860s before being acquired by the newly formed public school system. It is now owned by Historic Uniontown.

UNION BRIDGE

Union Bridge is an industrial and commercial center for the area that began in the late eighteenth century as a market village established by English Quaker and German settlers to include a sawmill, nail factory, general store, and a few log houses. Substantive growth did not occur, however, until the coming of the Western Maryland Railway in 1862, after which its linear plan was expanded to the current grid, and most of its buildings were erected. Union Bridge is notable for the railway buildings, and for its exuberant late-nineteenth-century residences erected by local builders. The most significant buildings are along Main Street, with industrial development clustered around the railway to the east, and residences to the south.

CM51 WESTERN MARYLAND RAILWAY BUILDINGS
1902, Jackson C. Gott. 41 N. Main St.

Instrumental to the development of Union Bridge was the Western Maryland Railway (WMR) that arrived in Union Bridge in 1862. Replacing the original shop facilities, the current buildings comprise a separate brick passenger station and office building joined by a frame baggage room, breezeway, and bracketed sheltering overhang. Once completed, the office building became the new WMR headquarters, which was moved here from Baltimore as the railway progressed into Pennsylvania and West Virginia. The WMR was central to the economy of Carroll County, providing additional markets for its farm produce and manufactured goods. Light industries developed along its tracks, such as the extant c. 1883 grain elevator and the cement plant that began in 1910 as Tidewater Portland Cement Company (40 N. Main Street).

Gott's design for the station and office buildings reflects the fashion for classicism. They were built by local contractor and carpenter Joseph Wolfe and then-partner John Rakestraw, using the "best hard run of kiln Berlin Junction [Pennsylvania] bricks" and white Baltimore County limestone "free from blue streaks." As the railway reduced services to light freight only, the Western Maryland Railway Historical Society was formed in 1967, now maintaining a museum in the former office building.

CM52 JOSEPH WOLFE HOUSE
c. 1880, Joseph Wolfe. 101 S. Main St.

Union Bridge's exuberant late-nineteenth-century residences were designed and erected by a handful of local builders and likely informed by the many pattern books of the times. Among the most prolific was Joseph Wolfe, a carpenter-contractor and dealer in lumber, sash, and other wood building components. Of the many houses that he designed and erected, particularly noteworthy is the frame house with quoining resembling cut stone that he built for himself. Wolfe undoubtedly chose wood, instead of the brick prevalent along Main Street, to showcase the millwork produced in his carpentry shops. Built on a corner lot, the Wolfe House includes a secondary side entrance with porch.

It is one of many similarly styled houses in town distinguished by scalloped bargeboards, steep center gable with decorative cross-bracing and pendant, bracketed eaves, and porch with jigsawn detailing. These include the Norris House (1885; 103 S. Main), Peter Shriner House (1882; 9 S. Main), and the house at 33 W. Broadway, likely erected by Wolfe as well.

CM53 UNION BRIDGE BANKING AND TRUST BUILDING
1899, Joseph Wolfe. 18 N. Main St.

This is the most architecturally distinctive building in the business district, reflecting the importance of Union Bridge as a commercial center. The eclectic buff-brick and limestone building embraces a wide elliptical stone arch framing a recessed entrance, recessed balcony, pressed-metal cornice, and Flemish-gable wall dormers. Wolfe was assisted in its construction by local mason William Rickell. Bank-

ing in Union Bridge began with a private enterprise established by George P. Buckey c. 1883 that grew to form this institution. The building was intended to instill confidence through its superior design, which was hailed by the local paper as "one of the handsomest banking buildings to be found in any of the smaller towns in the State."

Also of note in the commercial district is the more traditional Anders and Lightner store building (1868; 2 S. Main) representing Union Bridge's initial railway-era boom. It is a two-story, brick building divided into two units with separate storefronts.

A combination town hall and firehouse was built by partners John M. Furney and William H. Morningstar (1884; 10 E. Broadway). The long-anticipated building filled the need for both public meeting space and an appropriate place to store the town's new Holloway Chemical Fire Engine. The first-floor fire house includes a three-cell lock-up, and on the second floor are a public hall and council chamber separated by a retractable partition to create flexible space.

LINWOOD

Linwood is an agricultural village developed during the last quarter of the nineteenth century, largely by the Englar family, descendants of Phillip Englar, a German Swiss immigrant who came to Maryland via Pennsylvania in 1764. Taking advantage of the Linwood Station of the Western Maryland Railway that arrived in 1868, his grandson, Josiah, established a grain elevator, warehouse complex, lumberyard, and coal and grocery businesses. Numerous distinctive brick houses were erected by the Englar family and others, many sharing similar features that suggest a skilled local builder.

Josiah Englar's house and the gable-front Englar and Son general store (1877; 419 McKinstrys Mill Road) still sits adjacent to the grain elevator (CM54). David F. Albaugh also ran a general store, incorporated within his handsome six-bay brick house (1876; 418 McKinstrys Mill), accessed through a side entrance. Similarly styled is the five-bay Washington Senseney House (1866; 429 McKinstrys Mill), and the Second Empire House (1886) with entrance tower at number 428 was built for Nathan Englar. Near the edge of town is the traditional five-bay farmhouse (1870; 432 McKinstrys Mill) built for Jonas Englar, along with a barn, smokehouse, and windmill. Also extant are the schoolhouse, Linwood Hall (1898; 525 McKinstrys Mill), and the Linwood Brethren Church (1905; 575 McKinstrys Mill). Just beyond, the Lantz-Hyde House at number 580, a V-notched log house with contrasting brick chinking, reflects the architectural traditions of the town's eighteenth-century German settlers.

CM54 LINWOOD GRAIN ELEVATOR
1882. 417 McKinstrys Mill Rd.

Built by Joseph Englar, this is one of the oldest extant buildings of its type in the country, heralded in its day as the finest grain elevator along the Western Maryland Railway. It was a tremendous boon to local farmers whose grain could now be processed, stored, and loaded directly into railroad cars for transport to Baltimore, an otherwise two-day wagon ride. It reflects the importance of grain production to the economy of Carroll County, then among the richest grain producers in the state. The two-and-a-half-story frame structure has a gable roof with a tall monitor, decorative exposed rafters, and distinctive framed window surrounds. The site includes a two-story office addition, warehouse and loading dock, and its original mill machinery, including the interior elevator.

NEW WINDSOR VICINITY

CM55 MCKINSTRY'S MILL
1844. 10999 McKinstrys Mill Rd.
The small settlement along Sam's Creek near the border between Carroll and Frederick counties is an intact survivor of a once common nineteenth-century development pattern in the grain-growing areas of Maryland. The McKinstry family owned an earlier gristmill on the site, which they replaced in 1844 with the current three-and-a-half-story rubble stone and frame building.

Miller Samuel McKinstry built his own center-hall house nearby in 1849. The grouping also includes the McKinstry homestead (c. 1825; 4504 Sam's Creek Road), a combination store and dwelling (1850; 1494 McKinstrys Mill), two other small houses, and a variety of associated outbuildings for domestic and agricultural purposes. McKinstry proudly included marble datestones with his initials on the mill, house, and store. Also noteworthy is a Warren pony-truss steel bridge that spans Sam's Creek. It was fabricated in 1908 by the York Bridge Company in York, Pennsylvania, and is the only surviving metal truss bridge in Carroll County.

CM56 ALBAUGH-DUVALL FARM
c. 1800; c. 1835, c. 1883 additions. 2709 Marston Rd.

This well-preserved example of an early-to-mid-nineteenth-century Carroll County farmstead encompasses an exceptional array of outbuildings that speak to the self-sufficient farm life of the period. As typical of the region, the original house is of log construction in a two-story, hall-parlor plan; a log kitchen was soon added to the east. The house was built by James Murray, who received a patent for the land in 1792. Log dwellings made up 90 percent of the housing stock in the county at that time, and log construction predominated late into the nineteenth century. Likely built by Abraham Albaugh, who purchased the farm in 1831, is the two-bay log section to the west end, introducing a formal parlor and a hall with an open stairway. A porch runs the length of the facade, with the walls underneath painted white to indicate a sanitary workspace. Later additions were made to the rear.

The amazingly intact complex of outbuildings encompasses a timber-framed forebay bank barn, wagon shed, blacksmith shop with stone forge, and storage shed with unusual pent sides. There is also a log smokehouse, stone washhouse, and root cellar. Once included was a lime kiln for the production of fertilizer, sawmill, stone icehouse, and corn cribs. The farm was purchased by Preston Duvall in 1896. A concrete block milking parlor and milk house were added in the 1940s and a frame loafing shed in 1955. The farm is still carefully maintained by the Duvall family.

CM57 SYKESVILLE B&O STATION

1883, E. Francis Baldwin. 7618 Main St.

In 1831 Sykesville became a key location along the B&O Railroad main line as it moved west out of Howard County from Ellicott's Mills to Point of Rocks. A substantial hotel built by town namesake James Sykes in 1836 on the Howard County side of the Patapsco River made Sykesville an important destination for the railroad tourist trade from Baltimore. The first station built by the B&O served for several decades until a devastating flood in 1868 destroyed it and most of the buildings on both sides of the river. In 1883 Sykesville received a fashionable new red brick Queen Anne train station designed by the B&O's chief architect, Baldwin. The station remained in service until the 1950s and since the 1990s has been adaptively used as a restaurant.

CM58 PATAPSCO DISTILLING COMPANY (JOHN MCDONALD AND CO. STORE)

1865; 1889 addition. 7609 Main St.

The stone store at 7609 Main Street was one of the few survivors of the 1868 flood. The two-story, five-bay building received a two-bay addition on the north. The building continued to be used as a general store into the 1930s. In 1939 it was sold to the Sykesville Volunteer Fire Department which added large doors on the south end to accommodate fire engines (since removed). In 1949, the property was sold to St. Barnabas Episcopal Church for use as a parish house for several decades. It was sitting unused until restored by the Patapsco Distilling Company for use as a production facility and tasting room opened in 2017.

CM59 MAIN STREET COMMERCIAL BUILDINGS

Late 19th to early 20th century. 7600 and 7500 blocks (west side) of Main St.

The core of Sykesville commercial district is Main Street north of the Patapsco River and the B&O railroad tracks, while its historic residential areas, with buildings dating from the late nineteenth century, are located on the surrounding hillsides. A two-block section of Main Street contains the most noteworthy commercial buildings, primarily built around the turn of the twentieth century. A group of two-story frame buildings at 7602–7608 Main share a cohesive storefront design with bay display windows, colored glass transoms, and a bracketed cornice between the first and second floors. At 7600 Main is the brick Colonial Revival former First National Bank (1907). The Warfield Building (1901; 7564 Main) is an orange brick Renaissance Revival design with monumental window bays.

CM60 HARFORD COUNTY COURTHOUSE

1858, J. Crawford Neilson; 1904 additions, John A. Dempwolf; c. 1981 addition. 38 S. Main St.

Harford County was created in 1774 from territory in eastern Baltimore County, and Bel Air was designated the county seat in 1782. Development here centered on the courthouse and approximately forty blocks along Main Street. After the first courthouse was destroyed by a fire in 1858, officials moved quickly to replace it, hiring Baltimore architect Neilson that same year. He designed a two-and-a-half-story red brick Italianate pile with round-arched openings and topped by a cupola. After the Civil War, Bel Air and Harford County grew substantially due to the construction of the Maryland and Pennsylvania Railroad, the burgeoning canning industry, which amplified the value of local agricultural production, and other financial interests. Regionally prolific architect Dempwolf of York, Pennsylvania, was hired in 1904 to design large additions that covered the front and rear of the Neilson courthouse, creating an I-shaped plan. Demp-

wolf's additions were distinct, but complementary, retaining the red brick of the earlier courthouse and shifting to a more Georgian appearance. A less complementary addition looming at the rear of the ensemble dates to 1981.

The commercial district along the sections of Office and Courtland streets flanking the courthouse include a representative assortment of small-scale offices, stores, and hotels built from the mid-nineteenth to the early twentieth century. Baltimore architect George Archer designed the Beaux-Arts classical former First National Bank Building (12 Office Street) in 1900. Unfortunately, his 1889 building for Harford National Bank was demolished for the 1980s courthouse addition. The Harford Mutual Building (1930; 18 Office) is a two-story office building with Colonial Revival details, including paired limestone pilasters, keystones, and cornice. Designed by John B. Hamme of York, Pennsylvania, it now serves as a county office. The building (1869) at 21 W. Courtland was constructed as newspaper offices for *The Harford Democrat*. It now has a Colonial Revival facade from a 1940 renovation by Alexander Shaw of Bel Air and Taylor and Fisher of Baltimore.

CM61 BEL AIR ARMORY

1915, John B. Hamme. 37 N. Main St.

Expansion and reorganization of the National Guard in the early twentieth century led to a spate of armory building throughout Maryland. This armory is a classic example of the type, with a castellated head house building of rusticated Port Deposit granite with octagonal turrets, similar to the ones built in Hyattsville (see CR21) and Elkton (ES14). Granite buttresses continue along the side elevations of the large gymnasium, or drill hall, to the rear.

CM62 BEL AIR HISTORICAL COLORED HIGH SCHOOL
1924. 205 S. Hays St.

This wood school building was constructed with plans and financial assistance from the Rosenwald Foundation initiative to improve educational facilities for Black students throughout the South. Opened as a grammar school in 1924, this building served as the only area high school for African American students from 1935 to 1951. Many jurisdictions in Maryland, including Harford County, maintained racially segregated school systems well into the mid-twentieth century. Prior to 1935, local Black students wishing to progress in their education had to pass an entrance exam and go to school in Baltimore, which had the only high school for African Americans in the state. The original three-room plan (two small classrooms on one side and a larger one on the other) was altered into small offices for county workers in 1975.

CM63 LIRIODENDRON
1898, Wyatt and Nolting; J. Kift and Son, landscape architects. 502 W. Gordon St.

Architectural historian Christopher Weeks contends in *An*

Architectural History of Harford County, Maryland that Liriodendron "symbolizes what might be called Harford's 'Country Place Era,' the years between the Civil War and World War I," when dozens of affluent Baltimore families built grand summer houses. Now adjacent to a residential subdivision of Bel Air, when constructed in 1898 for physician Howard Kelly and his large family, Liriodendron offered a green respite from their Baltimore house on Eutaw Place. Kelly was considered one of the greatest surgeons of his day, instrumental in the early success of The Johns Hopkins Hospital (BC77), and author of hundreds of books and articles. He moved to Baltimore from Philadelphia in 1889 to chair the obstetrics-gynecology department. A zealous reformer and self-improver who promoted temperance and pure food and drug laws, Kelly was also an avid naturalist, naming his estate Liriodendron for the Latin name of the tulip poplars throughout the property.

The Kellys hired the prolific Baltimore firm of Wyatt and Nolting to design their summer house after acquiring the nearly two-hundred-acre tract in 1897. Liriodendron is a sprawling Georgian-inspired villa, seven bays wide and two bays deep, with a terrace along its length, a highly decorated pedimented pavilion

at its center with monumental engaged Ionic columns, and a robust door surround. Cream glazed terra-cotta is used for the cornices and moldings and for the terrace's balustrades and urns. Spacious semicircular porches supported by stylized composite columns on each end of the main block provide additional exterior space for entertaining and respite.

The interior of the main block is divided nearly equally into three roughly square spaces—dining room, central hall, and parlor with connecting doors or wide archways allowing for excellent cross ventilation. A two-story rear ell contained well-appointed kitchens and service spaces. The Kelly family sold the house to Harford County in the 1970s, and it is operated by a nonprofit as a cultural and recreational center.

CM64 TUDOR HALL
c. 1847. 17 Tudor Ln.

Tudor Hall is an exceptionally fine example of picturesque pattern book architecture from the antebellum period. Popularized by the best-selling publication *Rural Residences* (1837) by Alexander Jackson Davis, this romantic vision of country living encouraged the construction of villas and cottages with fanciful Gothic or Italianate details. Davis's success inspired many imitations including William H. Ranlett's pattern book *The Architect,* published in 1847. Renowned Shakespearean actor Junius Brutus Booth purchased

a copy of *The Architect* and began building his country house on property he had owned since 1824. He chose a brick Gothic Revival design depicted on plates 44 and 45, "Parsonage in the Tudor Style." The design was characterized by a generous porch, a small decorative balcony, steeply pitched gables, clustered chimneys, and diamond-pane leaded glass windows. The house is one of Maryland's earliest examples of a picturesque Gothic Revival cottage.

Booth emigrated from England in 1821 and was famous for both his transatlantic theater career and unconventional personal life. Initially he lived in a whitewashed log cabin he had moved to his rural Harford County farm and embraced his role by encouraging his neighbors to call him "Farmer Booth." He lived at Tudor Hall with Mary Ann Holmes, his long-time mistress and later second wife, and their ten children. Two of their sons became prominent actors in their own right, Edwin Booth and John Wilkes Booth. Today, John Wilkes Booth is best known as President Lincoln's assassin, overshadowing the stage accomplishments of the family. Now on a smaller parcel of land surrounded by suburban development, Tudor Hall retains its romantic Gothic Revival appearance. A detached kitchen house was incorporated into the footprint of the main structure with infill additions dating to the late nineteenth century.

CM65 LADEW TOPIARY GARDENS
1930s–1970s. 3535 Jarrettsville Pike, 7 miles east of Monkton

Although the address for the Gardens is in Baltimore County, the gardens themselves lie across the county line in Harford County. Harry Ladew, a wealthy, self-taught gardener, hunt enthusiast, and artist, created the gardens after becoming captivated by the topiary gardens of England. Ladew foxhunted there during the winter season, spending time in aristocratic country houses and gardens. Seeking to create a similar environment at home, he purchased a farmstead adjacent to the Elkridge-Harford Hunt Club and began his decades-long quest to create one of the nation's most outstanding topiary gardens. The 22-acre site ranges from large-scale designed landscapes to intimate specialty gardens and "garden rooms," with a main axis extending 1,100 feet from the house's Terrace Garden, across the Great Bowl and Oval Pool, to the Temple of Venus garden folly. To the west are themed gardens and a croquet court, and to the north, the topiary Sculpture Garden. Running perpendicular is a cascading stream with aquatic plants and pond. The rear of the house overlooks the wildflower meadow, with the Hunt Scene topiary gardens to the south.

When acquired, the antiquated farmhouse consisted of a c. 1850 Greek Revival main block with a c. 1750 south wing. Famed interior decorators Billy Baldwin, Jean Levy, and Ruby Ross Wood led an extensive interior remodeling while architect James W. O'Connor designed a Colonial Revival hyphen and wing. The wing contains the widely admired Oval Library and the hyphen, the Elizabethan Room transplanted from England. In 1976, Ladew established an organization to maintain the site and open it to the public.

KINGSVILLE

CM66 JERUSALEM MILL
1769–1772. 2813 Jerusalem Rd.

Designed and built by miller David Lee and millwright Isaiah Linton, Jerusalem is the only remaining milling complex within this area erected during the era of early industrialization. Built to take advantage of the flour export trade through the port of Baltimore, Jeru-

salem Mill is indicative of the transformation occurring at the hands of early entrepreneurs during America's Industrial Revolution. Lee was a Quaker who migrated from Bucks County, Pennsylvania. By 1814, the site encompassed a flour mill, sawmill, blacksmith and coopers' shops, general store and post office, residences, and other support structures.

The mill is a massive heavy-timber-frame structure on a stone ground floor, with upper stories sheathed in board and batten and a steeply pitched gable roof with uncommon tiered dormers. While much of the interior framing and equipment date to the nineteenth century, it operated as a water-powered mill until 1961. It was then purchased by the Maryland Department of Natural Resources as part of Gunpowder Falls State Park. A restoration by the Friends of Jerusalem Mill began in 1987, providing a rare opportunity to view the workings of a self-sufficient mill village.

CM67 JERICHO COVERED BRIDGE
1865, Thomas F. Forsyth; 1937, 1982 renovations. 12228 Jericho Rd. over Little Gunpowder Falls

Jericho is one of only six extant covered bridges in Maryland and a good representation of the innovative Burr arch through truss, named for original designer Theodore Burr and first developed in 1804. The covered bridge came about during the era of timber-frame bridge construction in areas of extreme weather as a means of protecting the wood components from water damage caused by snow and rain. It has become a quintessential American structural form that enjoys broad appeal.

The Burr truss combines a parabolic arch to bear the load with a multiple king-post truss to keep the bridge rigid. The long arches to either side are sandwiched between king-post structures to create an extremely stable bridge. Burr was among the earliest and most prominent bridge builders in the country, and his truss was used frequently by local bridge builders such as Forsyth. The bridge was a boon to the local industries that had advocated for its construction, aiding in a more direct transport of goods. Despite renovations in 1937 and 1982, the bridge remains a significant example of its type.

JOPPA (JOPPATOWNE)

CM68 MCCOMAS INSTITUTE
1867. 1913 Singer Rd.

McComas Institute is a surviving example of a Freedmen's Bureau school built by the federal Bureau of Refugees, Freedmen, and Abandoned Lands created in 1865 as part of the War Department. It was charged with assisting new-

ly freed enslaved people in the southern states and the District of Columbia. As a slaveholding Union border state, Maryland was not included in the 1863 Emancipation Proclamation. Instead, slavery was outlawed on November 1, 1864, with the adoption of a new state constitution. In Maryland the Freedmen's Bureau was mainly involved with education and legal matters for both the formerly enslaved and the large free Black population. Constructed in 1867, McComas Institute was named for local abolitionist and tobacco merchant George McComas.

Across Maryland, Freedmen's Bureau schools provided new opportunities for public education in a segregated system that had limited facilities in this period. McComas was one of three Freedmen's Bureau schools built in Harford County and the most intact survivor. Berkley School (also known as Hosanna School) in Darlington, a two-story frame structure that included a church and community meeting rooms, was reconstructed in 2005 and now houses the Hosanna School Museum. Greenspring (or Hopewell)

School was burned in 1926, reputedly by the Ku Klux Klan.

McComas Institute is a long rectangular wood building with an entrance on the short gable end and a small bell cote over the entrance. The interior has wall-mounted chalkboards in the larger of the two rooms. When the Freedmen's Bureau was discontinued in 1872, McComas Institute became part of the Harford County Public School system. It continued to serve as a "colored" public school until it was closed around 1935. In later years the school was taken over and cared for by the neighboring Mount Zion Methodist Church. McComas Institute serves as a reminder of the complicated history of education for African American Marylanders in the immediate aftermath of the Civil War.

ABINGDON

CM69 ST. MARY'S
EPISCOPAL CHURCH

1849–1851, attributed to Niernsee and Neilson. 1 St. Mary's Church Rd.

The election of William R. Whittingham as the Episcopal bishop of the Maryland diocese in 1840 set off a wave of church building. An architecture enthusiast and believer in the theological and design principles of the Ecclesiological Society, Whittingham found

a kindred spirit in the Reverend William Brand, son of a New Orleans architect-builder. In 1849 Brand was tasked with creating a new parish in Harford County and building a church ultimately paid for by his wife Sophia Hall's wealthy and well-connected family. The design of St. Mary's has been attributed to the famed Baltimore firm of Niernsee and Neilson, but Brand himself appears to have had a close hand in its execution and ultimate appearance. A prototype can be found in a design published in the October 1849 issue of the *New York Ecclesiologist* for a "First Pointed Church."

As constructed, the church is robustly built with rubble stone walls edged by dressed Port Deposit granite. Brand insisted upon exposed roof timbers on the interior, which had Minton floor tiles imported from England and frescoes by German-born artist Johannes Oertel. Oertel also carved the lectern and pulpit. St. Mary's is also noteworthy as the only church in the United States to have a complete set of stained glass windows by William Butterfield, the celebrated English designer and Ecclesiologist; the windows depict events in the life of St. Mary. The church is similar to Grace Memorial Episcopal Church (1876, Theophilus Parsons Chandler Jr.; 1022 Main Street, Darlington), funded by physician and financier Daniel Clark Wharton Smith as a memorial to his father.

DARLINGTON AND VICINITY

CM70 SILVER FAMILY HOUSES
1853–1859, William H. Reasin. 337 Fox Rd., 3643 and 3646 Harmony Church Rd., and 521 Darlington Rd.

Already known for its picturesque landscape, by the mid-nineteenth century the Darlington area was appreciated for its architecture as well, beginning with the country houses built by the Silver family. The family's architectural legacy started with the purchase of Calvert Vaux's *Villas and Cottages* (1857). Equipped with inspiration, and with land and a stone quarry inherited from their grandfather, Benjamin, Jeremiah, Silas, and William Silver built an exceptional group of houses between 1853 and 1859. At least two of the houses were designed by Baltimore architect Reasin, a Harford County native who maintained his own country house here. Jeremiah Silver's classically inspired house (1853; 337 Fox Road) was the first that Reasin designed for the family. Benjamin Silver built the next house (1856; 3646 Harmony Church Road) in a striking similar pattern. Reasin was also responsible for physician Silas B. Silver's house (1859; 3643 Harmony Church), built in the Italianate mode, as was the house for William F. Silver (1857–1858; 521 Darlington Road). They were the first of many villa or country house retreats built in Harford County and designed by Baltimore- and Philadelphia-based architects.

CM71 CONOWINGO DAM AND HYDROELECTRIC PLANT
1926–1928, Stone and Webster. Spanning the Susquehanna River

Stretching across the Susquehanna River between Harford and Cecil counties, this hydroelectric dam greatly advanced access to electrical power in the surrounding rural area and is still one of the largest nonfederal dams in the United States. The Boston engineering firm of Stone and Webster was hired by Philadelphia Electric Company to design the medium-height, concrete masonry gravity dam and the associated powerhouse and substation. These structures exhibit simplified Art Deco

aesthetics that break from use of historicizing details. The dam includes the bridge carrying U.S. 1 across the river because an earlier bridge, as well as the original village of Conowingo, was inundated after its construction.

CM72 ROCK RUN MILL BUILDINGS, SUSQUEHANNA STATE PARK
1794–1805. 761 Stafford Rd.

Sitting along a remnant of the former Susquehanna and Tidewater Canal is the gristmill erected by John Stump. Stump was one of the richest businessmen in the county, owning thousands of acres of farmlands for grain production, as well as a shipping business. He erected this mill to take advantage of the region's lucrative flour trade, producing for both the local market and an international clientele, shipped through the port of Baltimore. Built of rubble stone reinforced by keystoned lintels and large quoins, the mill was powered by water provided by a millpond and dam on Rock

Run. Following Stump's death in 1816, his daughter Ann and her husband, physician John Archer Jr., took over production.

To transport their flour, a turnpike connecting Rock Run with Baltimore was completed by 1818, facilitated by the first bridge across the Susquehanna, built by the Stump-Archer family, operating as the Rock Run Bridge and Banking Company. Although the bridge no longer exists, the small, story-and-a-half toll house and keeper's residence still stands.

The Carter-Archer House was erected in 1804 for Stump's business partner, John Carter. One of the finest houses of its day in Harford County, the thirteen-room stone dwelling is perhaps the earliest example of a regional house type whereby the gable-roofed main block and wing are joined by a hip. Stump acquired the house, which also passed to Ann. The mill ceased operations in 1954, and the entire site was acquired by the state in 1960 as part of Susquehanna State Park.

Located at the head of the Chesapeake Bay and its confluence with the Susquehanna River, Havre de Grace was an important port town dating to 1695. It was then that the Maryland General Assembly granted permission to establish a ferry here at what was known as Susquehanna Lower Ferry. The ferry offered the most direct route between Baltimore and Philadelphia, and inns were established on either side of the river. The town was incorporated in 1785, portioned into lots, and renamed Havre de Grace by the Marquis de Lafayette, who likened it to the French harbor town of Le Havre. The town's French connection stems from the Revolutionary War era when generals Washington and Lafayette and others of the French army visited. In fact, the region was mapped and the city redesigned in 1799 by French engineer C. P. Hauducoeur, naming streets for American and French patriots Washington, Adams, Lafayette, Girard, and Bourbon, along with Revolution, Union, and Congress. His ambitious town plan, modeled after Philadelphia, optimistically set aside lots for such civic amenities as public squares, a college, hospital, almshouse, market house, and courthouse. Havre de Grace prospered from the shipping trade and, by the 1830s, from trade along the Susquehanna and Tidewater Canal (see CM79) and the railroad, and later from canning and fish processing. Most of the early buildings were destroyed by fires in 1775 and during the War of 1812; thus much of today's historic cityscape dates from the 1830s through 1880s. The commercial center lies near the waterfront, where industry has given way to luxury town houses, condominiums, and pleasure-boat marinas.

CM73 OLD ORDINARY
c. 1814. 100 St. John St.

This building was built as an ordinary, or tavern, by innkeeper and town commissioner George Bartol. Inns catering to travelers were among the earliest buildings erected in Havre de Grace. This inn faces the Susquehanna River and includes a two-story, wraparound gallery and a low-hipped roof, reminiscent of French Colonial architecture. It is one of two buildings in Havre de Grace that reflect the early influence of French inhabitants.

CM74 S. J. SENECA FACTORY AND WAREHOUSE
1878–1885. 210 St. John St.

Built as a fruit-canning and can-manufacturing plant operated by S. J. Seneca, the building harkens back to one of the town's most important industries. Up until World War II, farmers brought their produce for canning to this plant located on the waterfront, with a railroad spur to facilitate shipping. During the Spanish-American

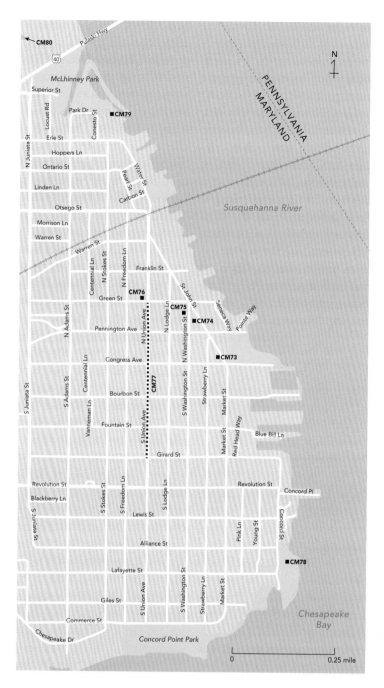

War, the factory produced Red Cross–brand canned goods for the U.S. government. Erected in phases, the early section is built of stone with a high basement reinforced with buttresses; an upper story of brick was later added, as was a long brick section with loading docks with a commercial street-front business entrance in the gable end.

CM75 ELIZABETH RODGERS HOUSE
c. 1780. 226 N. Washington St.

This is the only eighteenth-century building in Havre de Grace, having survived the burning of the town by the British during the War of 1812. It was the Federal-style town house of Elizabeth Rodgers, widow of John Rodgers, the owner and operator of two well-known taverns, one here (no longer extant) and the other, Rodgers Tavern (ES6), across the river in Perryville. They were the parents of Commodore John Rodgers Jr. of Sion Hill (CM80). While a common form in towns across Maryland, this two-and-a-half-story, three-bay Federal house is the only one of its type in Havre de Grace and the most stylish building in the commercial district.

CM76 AVERILHE-GOLDSBOROUGH HOUSE
c. 1801. 300 N. Union St.

This is one of the oldest houses in Havre de Grace, and its French Colonial characteristics reflect the heritage of its original owner, John Baptist Averilhe. Its square configuration with a slightly flared hipped roof and stucco-over-brick finish make it unique among the town's residential buildings. A central chimney provides a fireplace in each room of the side-hall plan house. Averilhe moved to Havre de Grace from Charleston, South Carolina. Indebted by the cost of construction, he was forced to sell the house in 1805. It was purchased in 1816 by wealthy merchant, town commissioner, and treasurer Howes Goldsborough and remained in his family until 1855.

CM77 UNION STREET HOUSES
c. 1838–1896. From the 200 block of N. Union St. to the 300 block of S. Union St.

Union Street was the fashionable address for the town's wealthy professionals and industrialists by the 1840s, remaining so throughout the nineteenth century. Greek Revival and exuberant Queen Anne and Italianate houses predominated along this pleasant tree-lined street. Among the early trendsetters is the physician Thomas Hopkins's Greek Revival house (c. 1838; 229 N. Union). Hopkins was a graduate of the University of Maryland medical school and served in the Maryland legislature. Built of Port Deposit rock-faced granite, the Spencer-Silver House (1896; 200 N. Union) is an eclectic Queen Anne, arguably the most elaborate in Havre de Grace. Reflecting the wealth of the town's maritime industries, it was built for John Spencer, the owner of a fish-packing plant, and was later the home of cannery owner Charles B. Silver. The eclectic Vandiver House (1886; 301 S. Union) was built for Murray Vandiver, a member of the Maryland House of Delegates and state treasurer. Blending Queen Anne with elements of the Stick Style is the house (c. 1888; 123 S. Union) built by Louis Vosbury, owner of a lumber and sash mill, for his son as a wedding present. Similar and equally appealing is the adjacent Carver House (c. 1888; 115 S. Union).

CM78 CONCORD POINT LIGHTHOUSE
1827, John Donahoo; 1979–1984 restored. 701 Concord St.

The twenty-six-foot-tall lighthouse at the junction of the Susquehanna River and the Chesapeake Bay is one of the first generation of conical stone Maryland lighthouses constructed by master lighthouse builder Donahoo, along with Piney Point (WS5) in St. Mary's County. Built of Port Deposit granite painted white, Concord Point had whale oil lamps when first activated, but after a series of upgrades received a fifth-order Fresnel lens in 1891. A keeper's house was built in 1827 and received a second floor in 1884. John O'Neill was hired as the first keeper, in recognition of his heroics in defending Havre de Grace from the British during the War of 1812. O'Neill descendants continued to serve in the job until the light was automated in 1918. The lighthouse was decommissioned in 1975, and the property was purchased by Friends of Concord Point Lighthouse. The keeper's house was thought to be lost, but it was still extant encased in later alterations at 714 Concord Street. The house was restored to its 1884 appearance by Friends of Concord Point Lighthouse and opened to the public in 2005.

de Grace with Wrightsville, Pennsylvania, and a network of interconnected canals extending through Maryland, Pennsylvania, Delaware, New York, and New Jersey. Crucial to the regional economy, the canal provided Havre de Grace exclusive access to goods within Pennsylvania's agricultural heartland. Its use declined with the coming of the railroads, however, and the canal ceased operations in 1900. While little of the canal remains, this section, along with the lock and lockhouse, has been preserved, and through it, the history of the canal interpreted.

The brick lockhouse sits along the dry-laid, hewn granite canal passage adjacent to a restored lock. More substantial than most lockhouses, it is a handsome Greek Revival building with a low-hipped roof and tripartite windows that flank entrances into the keeper's residence and the toll-collection office. A porch now shades the canal-facing front, beneath which the red brick walls are whitewashed. The site was given to the city in 1979 and restored in 1982.

CM79 SUSQUEHANNA MUSEUM OF HAVRE DE GRACE AT THE LOCK HOUSE
1840; 1979–1982 restored. 817 Conesteo St.

This site was built as part of the forty-five-mile Susquehanna and Tidewater Canal, linking Havre

CM80 SION HILL
c. 1787; c. 1810. 2026 Level Rd.

This is among the first and most elaborate country seats in Harford County, majestically situated with commanding views of

Havre de Grace and the Susquehanna River. It was built by English scholar John Ireland, who operated an academy for boys in the west wing. The next owner, merchant Gideon Denison, added terraced formal boxwood gardens. His daughter Minerva and her husband, Commodore John Rodgers, took up residence in 1806, adding the high-style interior woodwork. The symmetrical, three-part, classically inspired brick villa comprises a five-bay main block flanked by slope-roof wings that, while not common, appear in Isaac Ware's *Complete Body of Architecture* (1756). The interior encompasses private family rooms to the west of a central hall with formal rooms for entertaining to the east; referred to as the "winter" and "summer" dining rooms, they speak to the hospitality offered at Sion Hill. It was designated as a National Historic Landmark in 1990 for its association with Commodore Rodgers, known as the Father of the U.S. Navy, and six generations of his descendants, also distinguished naval officers.

CAPITAL REGION

Montgomery and Prince George's counties now form the Maryland suburbs adjoining Washington. In many ways, they followed parallel paths; both largely agricultural until the twentieth century, dependent from early settlement on tobacco cultivation, later benefiting from proximity to the U.S. government to underpin suburban communities and establish agencies within their borders. However, more southerly both geographically and in mindset, Prince George's County sustained enslavement-based tobacco plantations longer, reflected in its current wealth of former plantation houses. It is also significant today as one of the most prominent majority African American counties in the nation. Its tobacco legacy is attributed to a soil more conducive to tobacco growth and better access to navigable waterways, with six tobacco ports to Montgomery County's one. Abolitionist Quakers, the first settlers in Montgomery County, also made large-scale plantations dependent on enslaved labor less sustainable, resulting in more town development and dispersed populations. As ardent promoters of agricultural experimentation, Friends formed early agricultural societies resulting in a timelier move to less labor-intensive grain production.

Early European settlers to both counties were largely descendants of Maryland's first immigrant populations from the Chesapeake, migrating up the Patuxent River and its tributaries. Early buildings thus reflected the architectural traditions of the Chesapeake, embracing hall-parlor-plan frame and log dwellings at the center of a farmstead augmented by freestanding dependencies and outbuildings.

In Prince George's, early town development resulted from the designation of tobacco ports and inspection stations. Upper Marlboro witnessed the greatest growth, becoming the county seat in 1721, followed by Bladensburg, designated in the 1740s. With over half the county's population enslaved in 1750, a less fluid society resulted in stagnated population growth until the post–Civil War end to the plantation system. Meanwhile, by the 1820s iron works and textile mills developing around Laurel offered new economic opportunities.

Montgomery County's grain production and the growth of local mills created anchors for market town development, attracting trades related to agricultural processes as part of a progressive national trend. The county's only port was Georgetown, later annexed for the nation's capital. It fortuitously marked the southern terminus of the Chesapeake and Ohio Canal by the 1830s. Although quickly overshadowed by the Baltimore and Ohio Railroad, the canal passed through the county, facilitating the movement of agricultural goods and other commodities.

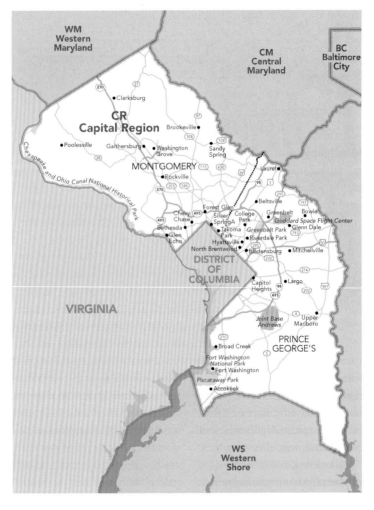

The two counties shared more post–Civil War. Prince George's, formerly the wealthiest tobacco-producing county in Maryland, witnessed a reversal of fortune as large plantations, no longer sustainable, were broken up into smaller farms. The formerly enslaved worked mostly as tenant farmers and sharecroppers aided by the Freedmen's Bureau. Tobacco remained the principal crop, although agricultural experimentation promised change, led by individuals such as Charles Benedict Calvert, who helped establish both the Department of Agriculture and the Maryland Agricultural College (University of Maryland; CR25), built on a portion of his Riversdale estate (CR22) beginning in 1856. In Montgomery County, free Black communities grew mostly around existing enclaves in towns such as Sandy Spring (see CR45).

Both counties benefited from the arrival of the B&O Railroad, in Prince George's County the Washington Branch and in Montgomery County the Metropolitan Branch. The B&O touted "hundreds of locations along the line" where "picturesque" suburban homes and bucolic surroundings offered "health, comfort, and happiness" within easy commute to the city. By the 1870s preexisting communities such as

Hyattsville and Rockville were further subdivided for building lots. The growth of the federal government facilitated by the passage of the Pendleton Civil Service Act in 1883 contributed to suburban development by establishing a stable workforce. In the 1880s, new communities were created, while hotels, resorts, and retreats gave refuge to Washingtonians seeking to escape the summer heat.

Rapid post–World War I growth generated concern leading to the 1927 creation of the bi-county Maryland–National Capital Park and Planning Commission (M-NCPPC), which regulated growth and established an extensive system of regional parks and scenic parkways. Growth continued even during the Great Depression with investment by President Franklin D. Roosevelt's New Deal era programs and experiments in affordable housing through prefabrication. Depression and wartime housing shortages witnessed the development of apartment complexes based on Garden City design principles backed by the Federal Housing Administration (FHA). Prefabrication characterized the 1950s and 1960s in communities with both noteworthy modern and more traditional housing developments.

After World War II, fear of nuclear attack on the capital accelerated the decentralization of federal agencies and military installations into the suburbs that began earlier with facilities such as the U.S. Department of Agriculture's Beltsville Agricultural Research Center (CR26) and Bethesda Naval Hospital (CR33). Both counties have since grown and expanded exponentially, once again generating concerns about unbridled development and urban sprawl. The opening of the Capital Beltway (I-495) in 1964 and the Metro subway system in 1976 further blurred the lines between city and suburb, facilitating the movement of workers into downtown Washington and solidifying this region's role as a bedroom community for the nation's capital.

PRINCE GEORGE'S COUNTY

UPPER MARLBORO

CR1 DARNALL'S CHANCE

c. 1742; c. 1858 renovated; 1986 restored. 14800 Governor Ogden Bowie Dr.

Darnall's Chance is a heavily restored early brick manor house, preserving Upper Marlboro's most significant landmark. One of the earliest substantial houses in the region, it was built as a five-bay, one-and-a-half-story dwelling of Flemish-bond brick with quoining, a central pavilion, paired flanking chimneys, and a jerkinhead roof. Exemplary of the period, the generous 55 × 35–foot house was described in 1760 as a four-room plan with broad center passage, a full cellar with kitchen, and a fireplace in each room. It was built for Scottish immigrant and prominent merchant James Wardrop on land once owned by Henry Darnall, a relative of the colonial proprietors, the Calvert family.

By the mid-nineteenth century, the house was remodeled as an Italianate Villa and raised to a full two stories; a stuccoed facade was applied. It was extensively restored by owners M-NCPPC in 1986, which reconstructed the original roof, chimneys, and leaded casement windows. The property includes a burial vault dating to c. 1775.

CR2 UPPER MARLBORO RESIDENTIAL DISTRICT

c. 1730. From Old Upper Marlboro Pike, to Old Crain Hwy., and Church and Elm sts.

This area encompasses houses spanning nearly two centuries, representing the evolution of domestic architecture in the county seat. Kingston (c. 1730, 1859; 5415 Old Crain Highway), the oldest dwelling, began as a one-and-a-half-story Chesapeake house built by merchant, planter, and county court justice David Craufurd. Succeeding generations also followed the Chesapeake vernacular. A modest two-story frame dwelling known as Content (c. 1787; 14518 Church Street) with back-to-back rooms sharing a gable-

end pent chimney was built for granddaughter Sarah Contee; and a frame hall-parlor dwelling later known as the Diggs-Sasscer House (c. 1826; 14507 Elm) was erected by Benjamin Hodges.

By midcentury all three houses were improved to reflect the latest architectural trends and accommodations. Kingston was remade in 1859 as a fashionable Gothic Revival cottage, Content received a side-hall addition, a two-story gallery (c. 1800), and a telescoping service wing (c. 1840), while attorney Daniel Carroll Diggs appended a two-story center-hall section embracing Greek Revival details to the Hodges house in the 1840s.

Kingston was later subdivided, paving the way for a new phase of development represented by the John H. Traband House (1894–1897; 14204 Old Marlboro Pike). The asymmetrical Queen Anne "six-room cottage" was designed by architect-builder Arthur Nicholson and carpenter B. Wesley Cranford of Upper Marlboro, likely inspired by pattern book designs. The district includes the Gothic Revival Trinity Episcopal Church (1845–1846; 14519 Church), built by William R. McNeal of Alexandria, Virginia, and designed by Baltimore architect Robert Cary Long Jr.

CLINTON

CR3 POPLAR HILL AT HIS LORDSHIP'S KINDNESS

1784–1786, James Hogan, Leonard Harbaugh. 7606 Woodyard Rd.

One of the most well-crafted five-part Georgian houses in

Maryland is Poplar Hill, built for Robert Darnall on land granted to his grandfather, Henry Darnall, by colonial proprietor Charles Calvert in 1703. According to Darnall ledgers, Hogan began the

design and construction, which was later assumed by Harbaugh, architect for Washington's War and Treasury buildings. The house is distinguished by Palladian detailing and specialized rooms, including a private Catholic chapel (now a library). A broad central hall with elaborate stairway is flanked by formal rooms with a perpendicular hall leading to the wings. Carriage and garden fronts present Palladian windows lighting the upper hall, with a pedimented central pavilion and Adamesque frontispiece to the carriage front. Also of note is its M-shaped roof construction used to span the double-pile plan with lighter timbers by transferring the load to the partition walls. Bisected laterally, when viewed from the front, the roof forms a low hip and central pediment, while the rear displays side-by-side hipped roofs. The property includes a terraced boxwood garden, family cemetery, and brick former slave building, smokehouse, washhouse, and privy. It is owned by a foundation intending to open it as a house museum.

CR4 WYOMING

Late 18th to early 19th centuries; 1817 kitchen; c. 1850 hyphen. 11530 Thrift Rd.

Wyoming displays characteristics emblematic of the Chesapeake region including a gambrel roof, pent chimneys, a timber frame with brick-nogged construction, and a telescoping configuration to incorporate a formerly separate kitchen building. The two-room-deep, gambrel-roofed main block provided a more sophisticated use of space than the typical hall-parlor house of the period, reflecting increasing social aspirations among wealthy families. A slightly asymmetrical center-passage plan allows for a larger parlor with a lit pent chimney closet that adjoins a small study. Originally separate, the kitchen building is dated through dendrochronology to 1817. It features the exposed timber framing and brick nogging also used in the main block. The kitchen was connected by a two-story frame hyphen.

Wyoming was erected by politician and tobacco planter Luke Marbury, who operated the tobacco inspection station in Piscataway. The name likely derived from Pennsylvania's picturesque Wyoming Valley, famously exalted in Thomas Campbell's 1809 epic poem *Gertrude of Wyoming*. The property is now operated as Wyoming Farm LLC, growing pawpaw and chestnut trees.

CR5 ST. JOHN'S CHURCH (ST. JOHN'S BROAD CREEK EPISCOPAL CHURCH)

1767–1768, Thomas Cleland, builder. 9801 Livingston Rd.

This fourth church on the site was erected for one of the thirty Anglican parishes established in Maryland in 1692, following the repeal of colonial proprietor Cecil Calvert's Act of Toleration. It is among Maryland's few extant colonial-era ecclesiastic buildings, located directly across the Potomac River from George Washington's Mount Vernon. Distinguished by its hipped roof with decorative flared eaves and west side entrance porch, the interior consists of a single space with a balcony at the west end. The church resembles St. James Herring Creek (1762; 5757 Solomons Island Road) in Lothian and All Hallows (c. 1727; 3600 Solomons Island Road) in Edgewater.

FORT WASHINGTON

CR6 FORT WASHINGTON NATIONAL PARK

1814–1824, T. Maurice, W. K. Armistead; 1840s remodeled; 1891–1896 additions. 13551 Fort Washington Rd.

Fort Washington was a key coastal defense location overlooking the Potomac River in the early years of the nation's capital. The first fort built in 1808 was destroyed by its own garrison in 1814 as British forces overtook and burned Washington during the War of 1812. Renamed Fort Washington after the first U.S. president, it was rebuilt between 1814 and 1824 and then remodeled in the 1840s. Prior to construction of the ring of Civil War forts around the capital, it served as Washington's main defense. Like many military installations, Fort Washington was altered and expanded many times over its decades of service. Most notable was implementation of the Endicott System starting in 1891, which added eight batteries with new concrete emplacements and rifled steel guns.

Fort Washington's role as harbor defense was short-lived, with the large guns removed before World War I and the fort used as a staging ground for troops shipping out to France. In the interwar years it housed the 3rd Battalion 12th Infantry, which functioned at the ceremonial unit for the Military District of Washington. The post was abandoned in 1939 and slated to be demolished for bridge and parkway construction. However, World War II delayed the transfer, and Fort Washington was quickly pressed into service as the Adjutant General School for officers. In 1946 Fort Washington became part of the National Park Service (NPS), which maintains and interprets its historic features, including the brick and stone fortification walls with a neoclassical stone portal, brick officers' quarters and barracks buildings flanking the parade ground, and a c. 1821 Commandant's House converted into a NPS visitor center.

CR7 HARD BARGAIN FARM
*1924–1927, Alice Ferguson. 2001
Bryan Point Rd.*

In 1922 artist Alice Ferguson purchased property along the Potomac River as a country retreat for herself and her husband, Henry Ferguson, a prominent U.S. Geological Survey scientist. Following Alice Ferguson's designs and vision, they soon began building a two-story Colonial Revival–influenced farmhouse on the hilltop, surrounded by outbuildings and gardens. Ferguson also developed a landscape plan that responded to the varied terrain of the site, including an entrance drive that winds through a steep, wooded ravine and opens to the meadows and gardens around the house with stunning views of the Potomac. Agricultural building complexes on the 130-acre parcel supported her development of a working farm.

Dubbed Hard Bargain Farm, the Fergusons' retreat hosted a group of regular visitors that included architect Charles Wagner and sculptor Lenore Thomas Straus. An avid amateur archaeologist, Ferguson directed her friends in digs along the riverbank that ultimately led to discovery of the Accokeek Creek site, one of the most important in the nation for understanding Native American societies of the East Coast. She was also instrumental in creating the surrounding Moyaone Reserve, a pioneering land conservation entity dedicated to environmental stewardship and preserving the viewshed across the river from Mount Vernon through low-density development and scenic easements. In 1957 the Accokeek Foundation was created by Moyaone Reserve residents and the Mount Vernon Ladies' Association to hold key pieces of viewshed land in public trust. Hard Bargain Farm is now an environmental center operated by the Alice Ferguson Foundation, with a portion of its original acreage comprising Piscataway Park.

CR8 WAGNER HOUSE
*1946–1951, Charles Wagner. 1910
Bryan Point Rd.*

Architect Wagner moved to the Washington area to work for the WPA, and starting in 1936 he was a frequent guest at Hard Bargain Farm (CR7). After World War II, Wagner and his wife Nancy became pioneer residents of the Moyaone Reserve, purchasing a twelve-acre lot and building their modernist house over a period of several years. The one-story Wagner House is an informal composition of five low-slung sections with board-and-batten or window walls and a butterfly roof with wide overhanging eaves. Construction started with a one-room guesthouse and carport and then proceeded with the main house, which consisted of a bedroom, bath, kitchen, and dining room. A "children's wing," added in 1950, included a playroom and bedroom cubbies for the four Wagner children. The living room with window walls completed the house in 1951. Wagner went on to design seventeen unpretentious but modern custom houses on the large forested lots of the Moyaone Reserve between 1946 and 1978. His aesthetic vision of clean lines and an intimate connection with the natural features of each lot perfectly meshed with the overall environmental goals of the community.

CAPITOL HEIGHTS

CR9 RIDGELEY SCHOOL
1927; c. 1940s addition; 2011 restored. 8507 Central Ave.

Ridgeley School is an excellent surviving example of a two-room Rosenwald school built for Black students during the 1920s. Philanthropist Julius Rosenwald, president of Sears, Roebuck and Company, established a fund in 1917 to address school inequality for Black children in racially segregated states. The Rosenwald Fund offered model plans for one-teacher, two-teacher, and larger school buildings with seed money toward construction. School districts had to provide the remainder of the costs, and each local Black community contributed cash or such in-kind contributions as building materials and labor. Rosenwald Schools were built in twenty Maryland counties, mainly between 1920 and 1928 for a total of 156 of the approximately 5,000 built in fifteen southern states.

Ridgeley School is a fine example of the two-room, two-teacher type most common in Maryland, with a small rear addition of the late 1940s. Two classrooms separated by a hall and cloakroom are each lit by a row of five large twelve-over-twelve windows, natural light being a key feature of the model plans. Prior to construction of the school, local Black students attended classes in a nearby church hall. The school closed after desegregation in 1954 but remained part of the county school system as a special education center and then county school bus administrative offices. Restored in 2011, the school now houses museum exhibits and is open to the public.

LARGO

CR10 MOUNT LUBENTIA
1798–1799. 603 Largo Rd.

One of the county's most notable Federal houses, Mount Lubentia is an imposing, nearly square building with a dormered hipped roof, recognized for its interior decorative detailing and asymmetrical plan. The latter features a center passage open to a stair hall with an open-well elliptical stair, located where otherwise would be the northeast room of a four-room plan. The considerable area given to these spaces and the size and appointments of the rooms reflect a refinement and sense of social awareness indicative of the more elite houses of the period. Separate parlors received guests and served the family, each with its own individual finishes, including richly carved mantels, crosseted surrounds, and decorative built-in cabinets. Mount Lubentia, Latin for "delight," was built for tobacco planter Dennis Magruder. It was one of only four houses built in the county during this period valued at the highest income bracket and the only one remaining substantially intact.

MITCHELLVILLE

CR11 NEWTON WHITE MANSION

1939, William Lawrence Bottomley; 1990s addition and renovations. 2708 Enterprise Rd.

This Colonial Revival house is an exceptional example of Maryland's twentieth-century estate architecture. Bottomley designed the house for the commanding officer of the USS *Enterprise,* Newton White Jr., as the centerpiece of a model dairy farm. Built of the Flemish-bond brick popular during the eighteenth century, it has an unusual curved hipped roof with flared eves, scrolled ridge rod, and clipped corner end chimneys. The facade is ornamented by a molded concrete frontispiece, diamond-shaped vents, and triglyph-and-medallion stringcourse. Whimsical details include porthole-like windows—perhaps a nod to White's naval career—and gateposts topped by a sculptural molded-brick rooster and a hen with chicks. In a modern twist on Maryland's five-part house, the main block is flanked by parapet-wall hyphens connecting to wings with roofs that mimic those of the main block, set behind curved walls connecting to freestanding dependencies. The farm was purchased by M-NCPPC in 1971 and is now an event venue and golf course. The extensive farm complex comprises a gambrel-roofed dairy barn and silo, fertilizer barn, tenant houses, stables, smokehouse, and corncrib.

CR12 BELAIR
1742–1746, Benjamin Tasker; c. 1914 wings, Delano and Aldrich. 12207 Tulip Grove Dr.
1907, Belair Stables. 2835 Belair Dr.

Built for Provincial Governor Samuel Ogle, this massive, seven-bay Georgian house remained the country estate of his descendants for four generations. The main block features pedimented central pavilions, a low-pitched hip-on-hip roof, glazed header brick facade, a galleted foundation, and a rear cryptoporticus. Benjamin Ogle, governor of Maryland from 1798 to 1801, was the second owner. Belair was purchased in 1898 by wealthy bachelor banker James T. Woodward, later passing to his nephew, lawyer and banker William Woodward, who was responsible for the flanking hyphenated wings. In the 1950s, the Belair estate was acquired by Levitt and Sons and developed into a residential community known as Belair at Bowie (CR13), using the house as offices. Once the residential development was completed, Belair served as Bowie's City Hall before being restored as a museum and event venue.

Since Samuel Ogle's time, Belair has been associated with horse breeding and thoroughbred horse racing, a popular Maryland pastime. The Woodward family continued the tradition with two Triple Crown winners. Befitting Belair's equestrian prominence is a 1907 stable (*pictured*) composed of a hip-roofed main block of local sandstone, with two perpendicular brick sheds to form a U-shaped structure with a central drive-through arch, living quarters, and carriage house. It was acquired by the City in 1969 and restored in 2001 as a horse-racing museum.

CR13 BELAIR AT BOWIE
1960–1970, Levitt and Sons. Roughly bounded by U.S. 50, MD 197, Race Track Rd., and MD 3

This is the fourth and final of the iconic megacommunities constructed by the famed Levitt firm following World War II. It was conceived as a smaller-scale version of other Levittowns. The company brought elite amenities to a broader audience with a comprehensively planned community encompassing nodes for education, recreation, worship, and shopping. Eight furnished display houses representing six models, were described by the *Washington Post* (October 1960) as "roomy, basically simple, well-planned, sturdy, and in the Levitt tradition of maximum living space per dollar—minus extras or frills."

To compete in the national capital region, Levitt architects employed traditional forms thought to attract middle-class families. A Cape Cod at 12420 Stonehaven Lane represents the least expensive model. The Rancher model, as at 12408 Stonehaven, met consumer demand for this most popular postwar house form. A more traditional two-story house at 12500 Swirl Lane represents the four-bedroom colonial model. Erected as an amenity was the Belair Bath and Tennis Club (Belair and Tulip Grove drives). As was their practice, Levitt restricted sales to white buyers, until the county's 1967 open housing law and the federal Fair Housing Act of 1968 compelled it otherwise.

CR14 BOWIE RAILROAD BUILDINGS
c. 1913 tower, waiting shed; c. 1930 freight and passenger building; 1993 restored. 8614 Chestnut Ave.

Rare surviving examples of a once commonplace small-scale railroad junction, these three frame structures served as the Pennsylvania Railroad's depot complex at the Washington and Popes Creek branches. The two-story interlocking tower housed the critical function of controlling all the signals and switches in the vicinity of the Bowie junction. The tower, a waiting shed, and a combination freight and passenger building were moved approximately fifty feet from the active Amtrak right-of-way and preserved by the City of Bowie as a small community museum highlighting the local role of the railroad.

GLENN DALE

CR15 DORSEY CHAPEL (BROOKLAND M.E. CHURCH)
1900; 1990s restored. 10704 Brookland Rd.

This rare surviving rural, turn-of-the-twentieth-century chapel was built by African American farmers who developed a community around the Good Samaritan Lodge, a freedmen's beneficial society. It was named for the first pastor, the Reverend A. B. Dorsey, who also presided over camp meetings held here. Inspired by Gothic Revival architecture, the chapel employs lancet windows and a steeply pitched gable-front roof with decorative shingling in the gable end. A dwindling congregation led to the chapel's closure in 1971, and for nearly two decades it was allowed to fall into disrepair. Recognized for its reflection of the cultural and religious heritage of the county's Black population, it was purchased by a friends' group and restored in the 1990s. M-NCPPC now operates it as a public museum.

GREENBELT

CR16 OLD GREENBELT

1935–1938, Hale Walker, planner, Douglas Ellington and Reginald J. Wadsworth, architects. Roughly bounded by Edmonston and Greenbelt rds., the Beltsville Agricultural Research Center, and the Baltimore-Washington Pkwy.

Of international importance, Greenbelt is an extraordinarily complete example of a "greenbelt town" planned and built by the federal government. Economist Rexford Guy Tugwell proposed developing model communities and resettling rural and urban families when appointed head of the Department of Agriculture's new Resettlement Administration (RA). Of the three pilot projects, Greenbelt is the least conventional in its planning and design and the most fully realized. Greenbelt exhibits the basic features of the ideals promoted by urban planner Clarence Stein and the Regional Planning Association of America (RPAA), including groupings of residential buildings with access to communal green space, main transportation arteries for automobiles pushed to the edges of pedestrian-oriented superblocks, and centrally placed nodes of community facilities.

At Greenbelt, planner Hale Walker created a crescent-shaped layout with a school, commercial center with movie theater, and recreation facilities clustered at the middle. Four-story apartment buildings were placed adjacent to this area, with groups of modest row houses beyond. The two main automobile axes, Crescent and Ridge roads, join at their north and south ends to form a continuous loop. Pedestrian paths leading from residential areas to community amenities were routed through underpasses to minimize the hazard of crossing streets. Attached houses in rows of two to eight units were situated to face communal courts on their "garden side." Services such as garages, parking lots, and trash bins were located around the outside of each grouping.

Greenbelt's architects designed a variety of simple, efficient structures inspired by Ernst May's avant-garde German housing estates, with contemporary streamlined flourishes. The row houses, available in two-, three-, or four-bedroom units, include a more traditional brick veneer gable-roofed model and a concrete block, flat roof variation (*pictured*). Bands of raised brick at the corners—now affectionately called "speed lines"—added visual interest at minimal cost. The Greenbelt Mu-

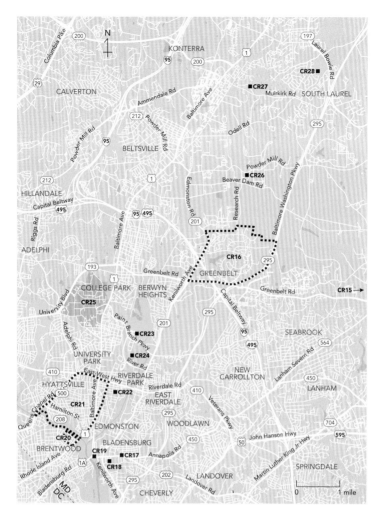

seum (10B Crescent Road) presents a representative two-bedroom, attached garage, concrete block unit as a house museum complete with the original Scandinavian modern furniture and electric appliances. The apartment buildings shared the streamlined look and materials of the concrete block houses and included large areas of glass block at the entrances.

The Moderne aesthetic extends to Greenbelt Center School (now Greenbelt Community Center; 15 Crescent) which features glass block, angular fluted fins, and curving corners. The stylized bas-reliefs by sculptor Lenore Thomas on the front elevation depict scenes representing the Preamble of the U.S. Constitution. The commercial area now known as the Roosevelt Center (107–131 Centerway) includes two streamlined concrete and brick veneer buildings housing shops, offices, and a movie theater flanking a plaza featuring Thomas's stylized *Mother and Child* sculpture. A pedestrian underpass provided access to the plaza from the residential areas on the other side of Crescent Road.

The original residents of Greenbelt were chosen for their limited means and willingness to create and join cooperative community organizations. Only white families were eligible. When the federal government decided to sell in 1952, residents formed a cooperative to purchase the original houses, some of the apartment buildings, and over a thousand additional wood units added as defense housing during 1941–1942. Later decades of development have expanded the city of Greenbelt, but the original New Deal community, now a National Historic Landmark district, maintains its cohesive plan and cooperative community structure.

BLADENSBURG

CR17 HILLTOP MANOR GARDEN APARTMENTS

1942–1943, Ross and Walton; J. H. Smalls and Son, landscape architects. 5302 Annapolis Rd.

Wartime expansion of the federal workforce inspired residential development in the Maryland suburbs. Hilltop Manor is a rare early example of defense housing in Prince George's County financed by the National Housing Act, particularly because it was intended to be permanent rather than the more common temporary construction. The established adjacent neighborhood, a new elementary school, and convenient access to the National Defense Highway (Annapolis Road) made Hilltop Manor attractive to young middle-class families. The 150-apartment complex consists of eight two- and three-story brick buildings situated around landscaped courtyards, paths, and driveways designed by a Washington firm. Combining FHA recommended types with rectangular or L-shaped plans helped maximize light and ventilation for each apartment. Designed by local architects, detailing included a fashionable combination of Colonial Revival and Moderne with alternating gable and flat roofs, and door surrounds with fluted pilasters. While the original steel casement windows have been replaced, the interior layout of the apartments has changed very little. Hilltop Manor is still serving families seeking affordable and conveniently located housing.

CR18 BOSTWICK

1746; c. 1793 addition; c. 1904 renovated. 3901 48th St.

Merchant Christopher Lowndes was one of the original town commissioners for the port of Bladensburg, established in 1742. A bustling official county inspection station and tobacco port during the eighteenth century, Bladensburg included a shipyard and ropewalk owned by Lowndes, waterfront wharves, a tannery, taverns, stores, and a number of houses. Lowndes's own house, called Bostock, or Bostwick, was likely built with his input on the design. The two-and-a-half-story, five-bay original section is symmetrical with a center passage and walls of Flemish-bond brick. Its steeply pitched roof was dated to fall 1745 through dendrochronology. The lower wing on the north side and the large and unusual buttress at the south end wall were probably added around 1793 by Benjamin Stoddard, the second owner.

By the second quarter of the nineteenth century, the port of Bladensburg was in decline, with the Anacostia River too silted in to accommodate large vessels and trade shifting to the port of Baltimore. Around 1904 owners Hettie Parker Kyner and James H. Kyner gave Bostwick and its landscape a Colonial Revival update, including new full-width porches, terraces, boxwood gardens, and updated agricultural buildings. Currently owned by the Town of Bladensburg, Bostwick is used by the University of Maryland's Graduate Program in Historic Preservation as a study site.

CR19 PEACE CROSS
1925, John J. Earley. 4500 Annapolis Rd.

The Prince George's County World War I memorial takes the striking form of a forty-foot tall Latin cross fashioned from exposed aggregate concrete panels. A local American Legion post sponsored the project and dedicated the memorial on July 12, 1925. Local concrete innovator Earley designed and constructed the memorial using his patented method of creating precast panels incorporating colorful exposed aggregate mosaics. Earley's concrete construction appears in projects around the country and in the Washington area at the Justice Department, Meridian Hill Park, and the Polychrome Houses (CR40). The Peace Cross, which features the American Legion symbol at its center, also served as the starting point of the new National Defense Highway between Bladensburg and Annapolis. The memorial was the subject of a 2019 U.S. Supreme Court decision allowing it to remain over the objections of the American Humanist Association, which filed a federal lawsuit objecting to the presence of religious symbolism on what is now public property.

NORTH BRENTWOOD

CR20 NORTH BRENTWOOD HISTORIC DISTRICT
1891 founded. Roughly bounded by 39th Pl., Rhode Island Ave., and Allison and Webster sts.

The first incorporated African American community in the county, North Brentwood was founded in 1891 by Captain Wallace A. Bartlett, a veteran commander of the U.S. Colored Troops and a federal employee. He purchased a large tract of farmland northeast of the city and platted the property into narrow lots. The flood-prone lots on the north side of the parcel were less expensive and sales there were directed to Black buyers, many indirectly associated with Bartlett through military service. North Brentwood, called Randalltown in its early years, became a thriving enclave for Black families who commuted to federal jobs in Washington. They were able to achieve the financial security of home ownership in a time when restrictive covenants in property deeds made many neighboring jurisdictions whites only.

The first houses in North Brentwood were wood I-houses and front gable structures, many built by members of the Randall family between 1892 and 1904. The row of front gable dwellings at 4504–4508 41st Avenue were common rural house forms adapted to small suburban lots. A surviving example of North Brentwood's earliest houses includes Peter Randall's at 4508 Rhode Island Avenue; he worked at the Government Printing Office.

The City and Suburban Electric Trolley line opened along Rhode Island Avenue in 1898. Like other streetcar suburb communities in the vicinity, North Brentwood experienced strong growth in the early twentieth century, with construction of house types such as bungalows, foursquares, and, later in the period, brick Cape Cods. Several churches are also present in this mainly residential community, such as the Gothic-influenced Brentwood AME Zion Church (1920; 4037 Webster Street). North Brentwood was officially incorporated in 1924, two years after the white community of Brentwood.

HYATTSVILLE

CR21 RESIDENTIAL, MUNICIPAL, AND COMMERCIAL BUILDINGS

1886 incorporated. Roughly bounded by the Northwest Branch, B&O railroad tracks, East–West Hwy., and Queens Chapel Rd.

The historic core of Hyattsville includes the residential and commercial areas flanking U.S. 1 and the former B&O railroad right-of-way of the Washington Branch. Hyattsville represents the evolution of a middle-class suburban enclave from railroad- to streetcar- to automobile-oriented development within the orbit of Washington.

The availability of stable nonpatronage federal jobs after passage of the Pendleton Civil Service Act in 1883 encouraged residential growth in such Maryland suburbs as Hyattsville. The earliest houses were clustered near the B&O line served by a handsome Queen Anne passenger station (now demolished). Hyattsville residents built in all the fashionable architectural modes including Queen Anne, Stick, Shingle, and Italianate in both high-style and vernacular interpretations, as illustrated by the large late-nineteenth-century houses on small lots along the 4100 block of Gallatin Street. The streetcar began serving Hyattsville in 1899 and suburban growth continued with the addition of foursquares and bungalows placed in new subdivisions to the north and west. Houses built by small builders using pattern books or kit houses from Sears, Montgomery Ward, or Aladdin were popular. Well-preserved examples of Sears houses include the Bellewood model at 5416 39th Avenue, the Kilbourne at 4219 Nicholson Street, and the Vallonia at 4212 Queenbury Road. Residential Hyattsville continued to reflect national trends, with construction of houses on lots that included garages or otherwise accommodated the now ubiquitous automobile.

The growth of automobile travel transformed Hyattsville and its main commercial thoroughfare, Baltimore Avenue (U.S. 1). Garages, car dealerships, and other automobile-related businesses sprang up, coexisting with older commercial structures such as the Hyattsville Hardware Co. (c. 1889; 5121–5123 Baltimore). A castellated stone armory (1918, Robert L. Harris; 5340 Baltimore) built for the Maryland National Guard signaled the growing importance of Hyattsville in northern Prince George's County. The New Deal brought a handsome Colonial Revival U.S. Post Office (1935, Louis A. Simon, Supervising Architect of the U.S. Treasury; 4325 Gallatin) that features murals, *Hyattsville Pastoral* (1938) by Eugene Kingman. In 1950 Lustine Chevrolet opened an eye-catching curved aluminum and glass-front showroom (F. Dano Jackley; *pictured*) at 5710 Baltimore that has been preserved amid a new town house development.

RIVERDALE PARK

CR22 RIVERSDALE
1801–1807. 4811 Riverdale Rd.
Riversdale stands out among many five-part plan houses in Maryland for its refined composition and details. It is also significant for its association with Rosalie Stier Calvert, whose letters provide vivid descriptions of life at Riversdale and her efforts to oversee completion of the house and grounds started by her father. Henri Joseph Stier was a Flemish Catholic financier and art collector who brought his family to Maryland in 1794 as they fled the violent aftermath of the French Revolution. In 1800 Stier purchased 729 acres of land, and construction on the two-story stuccoed brick house, unusual in the region, began in June 1801 with the east wing. The portico columns on both sides of the center block were carved from Aquia Creek, Virginia, sandstone, the same material used for major government buildings in Washington in this period.

Upon returning to Belgium in 1803 Stier gave the property to his youngest daughter, Rosalie, who had married prominent Maryland landowner George Calvert in 1799. Rosalie Calvert wrote often to her father while overseeing completion of the house, telling him about the progress and asking him to send furnishings and fixtures. She acknowledged her integration of European aesthetics into the house: "there is a lot of talk about our house, not because it is so splendid… [but] because of its distinctive style, and people always admire anything done by Europeans." Rather than a typical Georgian central hall, Riversdale has a small entrance on the north side that leads to a transverse hall. Three large rooms—dining, salon, drawing room—are arranged en suite across the south side of the main block. The most elaborate interior decoration appears in the salon, which has a triple-arch motif on each wall, including wood pilasters with delicate ornament and three triple-hung windows on the southern exposure.

Rosalie Calvert consulted with artist William Russell Birch of Philadelphia for landscape plans and began these improvements shortly after the house was completed. The grounds included formal gardens, an artificial lake, and terracing, a portion of which remains on the north side of the house. Only a two-story brick dependency, rebuilt c. 1820–1845 on the foundations of an earlier structure, remains of the many farm structures, outbuildings, and overseers and slave quarters once associated with Riversdale. Although most of the physical remnants of slavery are gone, a remarkable journal (now digitized and in the collection of the Smith-sonian Institution's Anacostia Museum) written by Adam Francis Plummer, an enslaved worker at Riversdale who remained as a paid foreman after Emancipation, provides rare insights into the lives of pre- and post-emancipation African Americans.

Son Charles Benedict Calvert retained the property after his parents' deaths. Calvert became known as a progressive farmer, and Riversdale was a showplace of modern agriculture in the mid-nineteenth century. He helped establish the Federal Bureau of Agriculture, later the Department of Agriculture, and the Maryland Agricultural College, now the University of Maryland, College Park (CR25). The Calvert heirs sold the estate in 1887 to developers who formed the Riverdale Park Company and used the house as their surveyor's office and headquarters until 1893. After serving as a boardinghouse, country club, and private residence to several U.S. senators, the property was sold to the Maryland-National Capital Park and Planning Commission (M-NCPPC) in 1949 and was restored in the 1980s as a house museum.

COLLEGE PARK

CR23 COLLEGE PARK AIRPORT AND AVIATION MUSEUM

1909 airport founded; 1998 museum, HOK Architects; 2014 operations building. 1909 Corporal Frank Scott Dr.

Established in 1909 as the Signal Corps flight school with in-struction by Wilbur Wright, this modest airfield has been in continuous operation ever since. Its military aviation career was short-lived, but the airport became integral to early civilian aviation, including such milestones as early commercial airmail service (1918) and controlled helicopter testing (1920–1924). The Bureau of Standards tested radio-controlled navigation here (1927–1935), another example of the presence of federal science and technology programs in the Maryland suburbs. The oldest surviving structure at the airport is the 1919 airmail hangar, and the newest is the Operations Building, opened in 2014. Also noteworthy is a c. 1918 concrete compass rose used by early aviators to calibrate their compasses to true north before taking off. The museum on-site is a Smithsonian affiliate with small aircraft on display and expansive window walls facing the runway.

CR24 NATIONAL OCEANIC AND ATMOSPHERIC ADMINISTRATION (NOAA) CENTER FOR WEATHER AND CLIMATE PREDICTION
2012, HOK Architects. 5830 University Research Ct.

Located in an otherwise conventional office park area, the NOAA Center is a gleaming, sculptural home for federal meteorologists and research scientists. The design combines three curved wings around a central five-story atrium. Large expanses of window wall on the largest wing are screened with brise soleil, while portions of the lower wings are sheathed with opaque masonry composite materials pierced by tall windows set at deliberately irregular angles. Environmentally sustainable features include a combination of green and membrane roofs, with a four-story waterfall collecting runoff into a cistern for site irrigation.

CR25 UNIVERSITY OF MARYLAND, COLLEGE PARK (MARYLAND AGRICULTURAL COLLEGE)
1856 founded. 3618 Campus Dr.

The flagship campus in the University of Maryland system has buildings ranging in age from the c. 1803 Rossborough Inn, which predates the university's founding, to the Iribe Computer Science building dedicated in 2019. Founded as the Maryland Agricultural College, the campus was established on land from founder C. B. Calvert's Riversdale (CR22) holdings. In 1865 the college became Maryland's land-grant educational institution and after 1887 included the Maryland Agricultural Experiment Station, which was housed at the Rossborough Inn.

A 1912 fire destroyed almost all the buildings on campus and set the stage for redevelopment of the university in its current Colonial Revival mode. The Baltimore firm of Flournoy and Flournoy was hired in 1918 to create a campus plan, the first of several between that year and 1931. In 1920 the institution was redesignated the University of Maryland, and major expansion commenced during the 1920s and 1930s. Heavy emphasis on red brick buildings with white stone or wood Colonial Revival decorative detailing, first recommended in the 1918 campus plan, characterized most of the construction on campus, from more elaborate Georgian Revival expressions such as Anne Arundel Hall (1937) to Moderne variations like Ritchie Coliseum (1932).

Rapid growth of the student body after World War II generated even more construction and expansion, with the focal point of campus shifting from the south hill, or Acropolis, to McKeldin Mall on the north. This nine-acre quadrangle, one of the largest in the United States, was lined with Colonial Revival academic buildings and anchored on the west by McKeldin Library (1958) and on the east by the Main Administration Building (c. 1944). Another 1950s variation on Colonial Revival was the Memorial Chapel (1952), which features a columned portico and tall steeple and was situated on the crest of the hill overlooking the lawns down to U.S. 1 and the horseshoe drive lined with fraternity houses.

Recently, new construction on campus has shifted dramatically away from adherence to Colonial Revival, starting with the School of Architecture Building (1971). The Clarice Smith Performing Arts Center is a sleek contemporary collection of auditoriums and exhibit and rehearsal spaces opened on the north edge of campus (2001, Moore Ruble Yudell in association with Ayers/Saint/Gross). The Brendan Iribe Center for Computer Sciences and Engineering (2019, HDR; *pictured*) is cantilevered on dramatic V-shaped supports and looms large next to the main Campus Drive entrance gate.

BELTSVILLE

CR26 LOG LODGE, BELTSVILLE AGRICULTURAL RESEARCH CENTER
1934–1937. 302 Log Lodge Rd.

In 1910 the Department of Agriculture began acquiring land in Prince George's County to create a new research center, and the Beltsville site was designated the National Agricultural Research Center in 1935. Four Civilian Conservation Corps (CCC) camps assigned to the Beltsville site and other New Deal funding supported expansion, with the research center growing to over 12,000 acres. CCC enrollees worked on numerous projects, eventually constructing 21 buildings and 79 miles of roads, trails, and bridges and completing major fencing, sewerage, drainage, and landscaping projects.

For the lodge, CCC enrollees used pine and white oak logs harvested on-site to build a rustic structure in the form of an oversized cabin with stone chimneys. The main interior space is one large room in the central block open to the roof trusses and featuring stone fireplaces at each end. The structure was used by the CCC for recreation until the onset of World War II. It served as a cafeteria from 1942 until 1985 and then as a visitor center and currently as a meeting space.

CR27 ABRAHAM HALL
1889, John W. Jackson, builder; 1991 restored. 7612 Old Muirkirk Rd.

This frame gable-front building was erected by the Benevolent Sons and Daughters of Abraham as Rebecca Lodge No. 6 to support the African American communities of Rossville and Muirkirk. Both were populated by freedmen employed at Muirkirk Iron Furnace, providing an opportunity for non-agricultural employment and the growth of a stable African American community. Constructed in the aftermath of the Civil War to assist newly emancipated enslaved people in becoming self-sufficient, Abraham Hall was an outgrowth of the federal Freedmen's Bureau, established in 1865. Builder John W. Jackson was also responsible for the construction of numerous houses in the community. The hall provided meeting, social, and religious event space; it served for over twenty-five years as a schoolhouse, later as a union hall, and then as a Jobs Corps center. It is one of two surviving in Prince George's County; the other is St. Mary's Beneficial Society Hall (1892) at 14825 Pratt Street in Upper Marlboro. While falling into disrepair by the 1970s, it was restored in 1991.

LAUREL

CR28 MONTPELIER
1783; 1794–1795 hyphens and wings. 9650 Muirkirk Rd.

Montpelier (*see p. 54*) is an exceptional example of Maryland's many five-part Georgian houses, begun with the main block to which was later appended hyphenated wings. Its extraordinary detailing has been compared to the work of William Buckland, and while postdating Buckland, his design for the Hammond-Harwood House (WS42) appears to have influenced Montpelier, including the unusual polygonal bay wings. The interior plan differs significantly, however, featuring a central hall and stairway, with ornate parlor and dining room at the front, and a family parlor and study to the rear. Perhaps as a nod to owner Richard Snowden's Quaker heritage, the latter rooms not intended for public view are devoid of the elaborate ornamentation that figures prominently in the others. Montpelier's landscape includes terracing, boxwood gardens, and a rare 1796 octagonal summerhouse or garden folly.

The Snowden family settled here c. 1690, receiving a sizable land grant from Maryland's colonial proprietor. Montpelier is the grandest of numerous family houses built on lands once encompassing over 27,000 acres in three counties. Through their tobacco plantations, ironworks, and textile mills, the Snowdens dominated the local economy for well over a century. Montpelier is now owned by M-NCPPC and open to the public.

CR29 OLD COURTHOUSE HISTORIC DISTRICT

1891–1940. Bounded by Maryland Ave., Courthouse Sq., and S. Washington and E. Jefferson sts.

The district encompasses what remains of the town's historic commercial and governmental center surrounding the Romanesque Revival Old Red Brick Courthouse (*pictured above*). The buildings face onto Rockville's former main street as a reminder of earlier patterns of growth, prior to its redevelopment as the first Maryland city to take advantage of federally sponsored urban renewal funding. Beginning in 1962, much of the historic downtown was demolished for a shopping mall. Closed by 1979, the downtown was once again reimagined in the late 1990s as part of a New Urbanism design scheme. The quiet of the old town is maintained in the area that surrounds the historic courthouse by a pedestrian mall and green space.

The courthouse (1891, Frank E. Davis; 29 Courthouse Square), the third marking Rockville as the seat of Montgomery County, is built of pressed brick with rock-faced Seneca sandstone trim and distinguished by its six-story entrance tower. A classical annex (1931, Delos H. Smith and Thomas H. Edwards) was created of Indiana limestone featuring a massive projecting pedimented Ionic portico, demonstrating the changes in architectural preferences that had occurred in the ensuing decades.

The First National Bank of Maryland, built as the Farmers' Banking and Trust Company (1930, Tilghman Moyer; 4 Courthouse Square) combines elements of classicism with Art Deco in a comprehensive design that includes elaborate interior décor as a means of attracting customers. The former U. S. Post Office (1938, R. Stanley-Brown; 2 W. Montgomery Avenue) is a Georgian Revival design, the only one of its kind in the county, erected as a Works Progress Administration (WPA) project. The hewn ashlar limestone building features a two-tiered hexagonal entrance tower and an interior mural titled *Sugarloaf Mountain* (1940) by Judson Smith, director of the Woodstock School of Painting.

The Beall-Dawson House (c. 1815; 103 W. Montgomery) is among the few extant buildings harkening back to the days when Rockville was coming into its own as county seat. The Federal side-hall plan house with telescoping service wing was built for Upton Beall, clerk of the Montgomery County Court. It was acquired by the Montgomery County Historical Society in 1960 to serve as its headquarters and is now a museum interpreting the lives of its original, upper-income residents and the enslaved African Americans who served them.

On the same property is the Stonestreet Museum of 19th Century Medicine. The one-room gable-front frame building ornamented with bargeboards and incised details served as the office where physician Edward Stonestreet practiced medicine from 1852 to 1903.

To the east at 98 Church Street is the exuberant Queen Anne railroad station (1873, E. Francis Baldwin) for the B&O Railroad's Metropolitan Branch that ran from Washington to Point of Rocks in Frederick County. Nearby, the former Wire Hardware (1895; 22 Baltimore Road) is the last of the nineteenth-century commercial buildings that once defined Rockville. Its cast-iron first-story shopfront is by George L. Mesker Iron Works of Evansville, Indiana.

CR30 NEW MARK COMMONS

1967–1973, Edmund Bennett, developer; Keyes, Lethbridge and Condon, architects. Roughly bounded by Maryland Ave., Argyle St., Monroe St., Tower Oaks, and I-270

New Mark Commons represents a fully realized planned community project for prolific Maryland builder Bennett and the local design firm Keyes, Lethbridge and Condon. Planned Unit Development (PUD) zoning implemented in the 1960s encouraged New Town cluster planning and common open space among more conventional suburbs. Here a variety of split-level "contemporary" ranch houses with expansive window areas and wide eaves were rendered with clean lines and modern materials, offering a second generation of modernist tract houses to the Washington-area consumer. The town house clusters (*pictured above*)

FEDERAL INFLUENCE IN MARYLAND

NASA Goddard Space Flight Center, Greenbelt

From the moment of its founding in 1790, the District of Columbia changed its Maryland neighbors. The federal city was created from Maryland and Virginia property ten miles square on either side of the Potomac River. In 1846–1847 the Virginia portion, including Alexandria, retroceded to the Commonwealth, leaving only the original Maryland territory to accommodate the national capital.

During the early nineteenth century Washington grew slowly, and even the close-by Maryland jurisdictions remained economically and socially distinct. Tremendous growth during the Civil War and its aftermath changed all that, particularly following the Pendleton Act of 1883, which mandated merit-based civil service rather than political spoils. The U.S. government also became a major employer of African Americans in a time of segregation. Development in

also sought a traditional scale translated into simple volumetric forms free of applied ornamentation. An artificial lake formed the centerpiece of the community, with staggered rows of town houses built on its concrete retaining walls, creating a sculptural effect. Developer and architects collaborated on several other modernist Montgomery County subdivisions such as Potomac Overlook (1956–1959) and Carderock Springs (1962–1966), with all their projects characterized by a careful attention to preserving natural features of the building site.

CR31 STRATHMORE HALL AND THE MUSIC CENTER AT STRATHMORE

1899–1901 house, Appleton P. Clark Jr.; 1914 additions and renovations, Charles Barton Keen. 10701 Rockville Pike

2001–2005 music hall, William Rawn and Associates; Grimm and Parker; Kirkegaard Associates, sound design. 5301 Tuckerman Ln.

Strathmore Hall is a distinguished example of early-twentieth-century country house architecture. One of Washington's most prominent and prolific architects of the period, Clark favored Georgian sources for his residential de-the adjacent Maryland suburbs was increasing driven by federal jobs and the availability of transportation such as railroads and streetcars.

As the designated federal city became more densely developed, federal agencies seeking space began moving out into Maryland and Virginia. An early example was the Department of Agriculture, which needed land for experimental fields and greenhouses as its mission was expanded at the turn of the twentieth century. New Deal expansion of the federal government both increased the demand for residential development and funded construction of new federal facilities in the greater capital region. The Beltsville Agricultural Research Center (**CR26**) was expanded, and the Bethesda vicinity of Montgomery County saw the establishment of Bethesda Naval Hospital (**CR33**), the new National Institutes of Health headquarters (1940), and the David Taylor Model Basin, an innovative naval ship testing facility built in 1938. World War II accelerated these trends, as housing and office space strained to accommodate the increased needs. Most famously, the Pentagon was constructed for the Department of Defense in Virginia, but all the Maryland military and civilian installations saw wartime expansion.

Threat of nuclear attack after the first Russian atomic bomb test in 1949 increased interest in decentralizing the operations of the federal government to reduce the value of Washington as a target and provide continuity of operations. Major new government campuses included the White Oak Naval Surface Warfare Center in Silver Spring (1954), the Atomic Energy Commission in Germantown (1957), NASA Goddard Space Flight Center in Greenbelt (1961), and the National Bureau of Standards in Gaithersburg (1966). Reaching farther into the Maryland hinterland required new road construction such as the Capital Beltway (I-495, completed 1964), and I-270 through Montgomery County, which emerged as a high-tech corridor for the military industrial complex.

signs, as exhibited in this house created for James F. Oyster as a nine-bedroom summer retreat. In 1908 new owner industrialist Charles Corby hired Philadelphia architect Keen to remodel and expand the house, adding the Flemish-bond brick facing and the north additions. At its height, the estate encompassed 400 acres and 21 outbuildings. In 1979, it was acquired by Montgomery County in the interest of creating an arts center.

Built on the grounds is a 1,976-seat concert hall and educational facility. Its architects worked with an acoustical designer to create a spectacular modern structure with exemplary sound quality. It is built of concrete with cream and gray limestone facing and a soaring 65-foot curtain wall of beveled glass with an undulating roofline and multifaceted sections such as the dramatic curved reception area. The concert hall features soaring ceilings, and paneling and other details carried out in light maple and birch, with a unique wall covering of brass metal fabric to provide both excellent acoustics and stunning aesthetic appeal.

CR32 ROBERT LLEWELLYN WRIGHT HOUSE

1953, 1957–1958, Frank Lloyd Wright; Lloyd Wright, landscape. 7927 Deepwell Dr.

Dramatically sited on a sloping lot along Cabin John Creek, this is one of a comparatively small number of Wright's "hemicycle" houses. Designed for the architect's youngest son, the house is composed of two intersecting hemicycles resulting in a football-shaped plan. A large rounded tower of concrete block pushes out from the arc of the approach elevation and rises above the broad fascia made up of overlapping boards of Philippine mahogany. Inside, a broad living-dining area extends across the rear with the kitchen and fireplace occupying the interior of the tower. The form and arrangement of the public spaces is in keeping with the Usonian concept that guided much of Wright's domestic design for middle-class households beginning in the 1930s.

CR33 WALTER REED NATIONAL MILITARY MEDICAL CENTER, BETHESDA NAVAL HOSPITAL

1939–1942, Paul P. Cret, consulting architect, Fredric W. Southworth, architect; c. 1960 addition. 8901 Rockville Pike

President Franklin Delano Roosevelt (FDR), a former secretary of the U.S. Navy and architecture enthusiast, took a personal interest in the design of a new naval hospital in the Maryland suburbs. After funds were appropriated in 1937, he helped choose its site near the new campus of the National Institutes of Health (NIH), which was under construction across Wisconsin Avenue. In contrast to the conventional NIH buildings, the hospital took the dramatic skyscraper form sketched by FDR on a piece of White House stationery and inspired by his visit to the Nebraska State Capitol.

Cret, who designed several federal buildings, refined FDR's

concept into a twenty-story tower with strong vertical lines of stacked window bays and a base of interconnected three- and four-story pavilions. Executed by a Navy Bureau of Docks and Yards architect, the reinforced concrete and structural steel building was clad with quartz-faced concrete panels that contrasted with the bronze window sash and serpentine spandrels of the stacked window bays. The elegant "Modern Classical" (Cret's term) hospital was placed in a bucolic, landscaped site.

When completed in 1942, the complex housed a five-hundred-bed hospital and training and research facilities, including a medical school, dental school, and the Naval Medical Research Institute. Now with additional wings added to the pavilions, the hospital provides medical care to each sitting president and many other dignitaries and navy personnel.

CR34 MONTGOMERY FARM WOMEN'S COOPERATIVE MARKET (BETHESDA WOMEN'S MARKET)
1932. 7155 Wisconsin Ave.

This building represents a beloved institution and a rare survivor of downtown Bethesda's post–World War I development. It was built as a marketplace where the farm women of Montgomery County could sell their local produce, dairy products, and canned and baked goods. Motivated by a desire to alleviate economic woes caused by the Great Depression, the women located their market within this wealthy suburb of Washington. They were part of the Home Demonstration Clubs, sponsored by the Extension Service of the University of Maryland in cooperation with Montgomery County and the U.S. Department of Agriculture. The plain, elongated, single-story frame building is distinguished by its hipped roof, central pavilion with elliptical opening and recessed entrance, and cheerful green-and-white striped metal awnings. The open-space market met with immediate success. It is among the few extant historic buildings in the ever-expanding downtown Bethesda, a late-nineteenth-century community that boomed in the post–World War I and II eras.

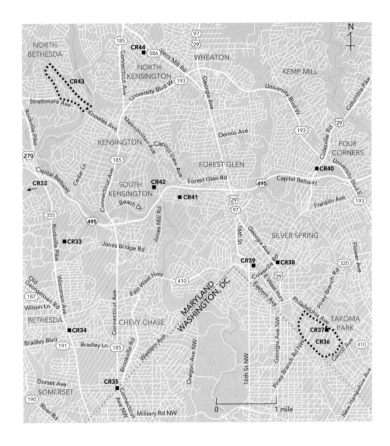

CHEVY CHASE

CR35 RESIDENTIAL BUILDINGS

1892–1930. Bounded by Grafton St., Cedar Pkwy., East–West Hwy., and Wisconsin and Western aves.

Chevy Chase was one of the first suburban communities in the area to capitalize on the speculative potential of careful and comprehensive planning. Forming the Chevy Chase Land Company in 1890, Francis G. Newlands engaged civil, sanitary, and structural engineers, as well as architects, landscape architects, and real estate agents, in the planning process. The community was strategically located adjacent to Washington to take advantage of its potential home-buying market, and the Rock Creek Railway

facilitated transportation to and from the city. The community is centered along a main thoroughfare (Connecticut Avenue) into Washington, with Chevy Chase Circle as the formal gateway. A verdant landscape design embraces the picturesque qualities of suburban planning and amenities such as the Village Hall, which contained a library (now the town hall) and a post office, and the Chevy Chase Club.

As an elite residential community, Chevy Chase was regulated by racial covenants and design guidelines controlled by the company's supervising architects, Leon Dessez and Lindley Johnson. They set the tone with such designs as the English Tudor house for Newlands

(c. 1893; 9 Chevy Chase Circle), the Queen Anne houses at 12 and 14 W. Kirke Street, and Dessez's own house (c. 1894) at 3 E. Irving Street. Prime examples of various styles include Colonial Revival (c. 1896, McKim, Mead and White; 11 W. Kirke); Tudor Revival (1929, Rodier and Kunzin; 25 W. Kirke); Spanish Revival (1916; 16 Primrose Street); classical (c. 1910; 102 E. Kirke); Arts and Crafts (c. 1892; 17 E. Kirke); and bungalow (1916; 34 W. Kirke). Among the many noted Washington architects represented are Edward W. Donn Jr. (1915; 18 W. Lenox Street), Arthur B. Heaton (1911; 17 Primrose, and 1924; 11 W. Lenox), Clarence L. Harding (1896; 6 E. Lenox), Reginald Geare (1920s; 4103 and 4106 Leland Street), Porter and Lockie (c. 1925; 5903 Connecticut), George Oakley Totten Jr. (c. 1910; 4201 Bradley Lane), Clarke Waggaman (10 E. Lenox), Harry Wardman (1920; 1 E. Kirke), and Waddy E. Wood (c. 1912; 8 Oxford Street and 15 E. Melrose)

TAKOMA PARK

CR36 HISTORIC DISTRICT

1883 founded. Bounded by the Washington City line, and Philadelphia, Takoma, and Ethan Allen aves.

This was the most successful of the many middle-class suburban communities that appeared along the fringes of Washington during the late nineteenth century. Its development was facilitated by the construction of the Metropolitan Branch of the B&O Railroad to provide ready access to downtown, and the job stability created by the enactment of the 1883 Civil Service Act. As the first suburban community in the county, it became the model for nearby Forrest Glen (1887), Capitol View (1887), and Woodside (1889). Established by New York congressman Benjamin Franklin Gilbert, Takoma Park was a speculative subdivision with lots laid out along meandering streets, offering a healthy alternative to city life for its middle-class home buyers. Promoted as "The Sylvan Suburb of the National Capital," Takoma Park encompassed both residential and commercial development. It met with such success that it was incorporated in 1890, with Gilbert as its mayor, and by 1913 it was the largest town in Montgomery County.

The historic district centers around commercial buildings along Ethan Allen and Carroll avenues, mostly early- to mid-twentieth-century buildings erected after a fire destroyed the downtown in 1893. It is surrounded by houses in an eclectic mix of turn-of-the-twentieth-century architectural styles, including Queen Anne, Shingle, and bungalow houses. Within easy commute to the city, Takoma Park offered the verdant surroundings indicative of country living, conjured by street names such as Maple, Cedar, Holly, and Tulip.

CR37 SEARS MAIL-ORDER BUNGALOWS
1928. 7418, 7420, and 7421 Cedar Ave.

Three Sears mail-order bungalows clustered together represent two of the most popular models offered, the Uriel/Conway and the Starlight. They were erected for Margaret Petty Hodge in the Petty Estate Subdivision of Takoma Park as an enticement to potential lot buyers. Takoma Park has among the highest number of Sears houses in the region, with the Uriel/Conway being the most popular model. The Uriel is identified by its cross-gable front that extends to provide cover for the inset front porch supported by battered columns set on stone piers. The slightly more diminutive Starlight features a hipped roof, inset porch, and clipped-gable dormer.

While pattern books were long popular, purchasing actual houses by mail was a phenomenon of the early twentieth century, with Sears being one of the largest suppliers, operating from 1908 to 1942. In total, the company offered 370 models. The house kits included everything from precut lumber and millwork to plumbing fixtures, lighting, and decorative features. They were made possible by the post–Civil War rise in such building technologies as balloon framing and wholesale dimensional lumber, increased railroad transport, and a growing middle class.

SILVER SPRING

CR38 SILVER THEATER AND SILVER SPRING SHOPPING CENTER
1936–1938, John Eberson; 1998–2004 theater restoration, Gensler; theater new construction, Smith-Group Architects; shopping center restoration and new construction. 8533–8575 Georgia Ave.

When this shopping center opened on October 27, 1938, the *Washington Post* covered the event with a twelve-page special section, and six thousand people attended the ceremony. The excitement was echoed in the flamboyant Art Deco design by a nationally famous theater architect. Based in New York City, Eberson was celebrated for his "atmospheric" movie palace designs in the 1920s, but starting in 1930 he developed a selection of more compact and economical theaters for Warner Brothers, including the Silver Theater. The complete project was the brainchild of realtor C. H. Hillegeist, and its construction inspired a commercial building boom in Silver Spring.

The U-shaped complex was sited in a "park and shop" configuration that placed parking at the front. Additional parking at the rear was originally linked via a shallow underpass. The stores in the shopping center were visually united by curved canopies and a stepped limestone parapet.

The attached theater portion was turned to face Colesville Road, with a marquee and sign of stacked neon letters spelling *SILVER* (now a replica). The thousand-seat auditorium has been somewhat altered to accommodate projection of modern movies but still conveys streamlined glamour. The stacked bands of cove lighting flanking the proscenium recall massive outstretched wings, and murals in niches along the side walls depict peacocks and exotic foliage. Saved from demolition after a lengthy preservation fight, the theater is now home to the American Film Institute and incorporates adjacent new construction with two theaters, offices, and exhibit space. The shopping center continues to serve as a commercial hub in downtown Silver Spring.

in the Washington area after World War II, the Falkland was a highly influential early prototype. This complex, located just north of the Washington city line, is noteworthy for being the first garden apartment complex in Maryland built with FHA financing, representing an early federal foray into affordable multifamily housing with communal outdoor space. Its construction was a response to the exponential growth of Montgomery County's population in the 1930s due to New Deal job opportunities in Washington.

The design of the Falkland complex was in keeping with early FHA guidance directing developers to follow natural topography and provide generous setbacks and landscaping. The existing stands of deciduous trees and a small stream were incorporated into the twenty-two-acre site plan by Justement. A Washington-based planner and designer, he created a handsome complex of two- or three-story Colonial Revival buildings containing a total of 479 apartments in several buildings set among winding paths with generous courtyards. While some portions of the complex have been demolished or altered, the Falkland still effectively represents a highly significant episode in the national development of low-scale, multifamily housing.

CR39 FALKLAND

1936–1938, William D. Blair, developer; Louis Justement, architect. 1545 N. Falkland Ln. and 8305 Falkland Ln.

While garden apartment construction became commonplace

CR40 POLYCHROME HOUSES

1934, John J. Earley, Basil Taylor, and J. Robie Kennedy. 9900 and 9904 Colesville Rd., and 9919, 9923 and 9925 Sutherland Rd.

The Polychrome Houses represent an unusually decorative attempt to produce sustainable and affordable prefabricated housing that combines master craftsmen Earley's artistic colored concrete mosaics with precast slab construction developed in partnership with engineer Basil Taylor. They are among many such experimental demonstration houses built around the nation's capital in the wake of the Great Depression. Each sought to derive cost savings from increased automation and utilize manufactured building materials to create a better, more innovative housing future. Through the patented "Earley Process" that combined exposed aggregate rock, ceramics, and vitreous enamels in a mix of concrete, Earley was able to create structures possessing innovative construction and artistic appeal. To overcome the stigma associated with prefabrication, Earley changed colors and patterns to achieve individuality. The thinness of the panels and simplicity of their on-site assembly revolutionized the use of concrete within the building industry. The design of "Polychrome [House] No. 1" as the prototype was undertaken in collaboration with architect J. Robie Kennedy Jr., who worked in the Office of the Supervising Architect of the Treasury, with Polychrome No. 2, built next door the following year. Three two-story Polychrome Houses were constructed to the rear along Sutherland Road in 1935–1936, identical in design but varying in color.

FOREST GLEN

CR41 NATIONAL PARK SEMINARY PAGODA
1905, Emily Elizabeth Holman(?). 2801 Linden Ln.

Likely modeled after the Toji Temple (796 AD) in Tyoko, Japan, this is the most academically designed and elaborate of the many buildings on the former campus of the National Park Seminary, an elite women's college preparatory school that operated between 1894 and 1942. The campus is located within a dramatic natural landscape that encompasses buildings that range from the classically inspired to the romantic and exotic, represented by eight whimsical sorority houses. Built between 1898 and 1904, they include the American Bungalow, Japanese Bungalow, Dutch Windmill, Swiss Chalet, Indian Mission, English Castle, and Colonial House. As a group they appear to offer a lesson in architectural history and an introduction to foreign exploration. They exemplify the eclecticism that defined the era, inspired by various turn-of-the-twentieth-century international exhibitions held in the United States.

Also extant is the former

Queen Anne Ye Forest Inn built to attract Washingtonians to the suburban community of Forest Glen, which became the main building for the school in 1894. Other noteworthy buildings include the attached single-story, stuccoed chapel (1898), the Odeon Theater (1907) with semicircular bay and Ionic portico, and the former gymnasium (1907) adorned by a Corinthian portico. The school was purchased in 1942 by the U.S. Army for veterans' rehabilitation as an annex to Walter Reed Army Hospital and, beginning in 2003, was remodeled as a residential community.

KENSINGTON

CR42 TEMPLE OF THE CHURCH OF JESUS CHRIST OF LATTER-DAY SAINTS
1974, Keith W. Wilcox. 9900 Stoneybrook Dr.

Travelers navigating the north side of the Capital Beltway (I-495) see the spires of a castle-like building that has inspired the graffiti "Surrender Dorothy" on a nearby railroad overpass. This soaring edifice was built by the Church of Jesus Christ of Latter-day Saints, commonly referred to as the Mormons, as their first temple located on the East Coast. Temple visitation is reserved for specialized religious rites such as sealings (marriages) and vicarious baptisms for deceased ancestors while regular worship and community gathering takes place in smaller chapels and meetinghouses. Businessman J. Willard Marriott, of the hotel chain, was instrumental in guiding construction of the temple in Montgomery County.

The Washington temple is a 160,000 square foot reinforced-concrete structure sheathed in gleaming Alabama white marble. The tallest of its six pointed spires is 280 feet high and topped by an 18-foot-tall statue of the angel Moroni, who the LDS believe will herald the second coming of Jesus Christ. This design pays homage to the flagship Salt Lake Temple in Utah, interpreting its six-spire form in a late-modern idiom. Only Mormons in good standing are allowed to enter the temple, but a visitor center on site welcomes the curious to examine a cutaway scale model.

CR43 GARRETT PARK
1887 established, William Saunders, landscape architect. Bounded by Strathmore and Kenilworth aves., Rock Creek, and the B&O Railroad

Garrett Park was established by the Metropolitan Investment and Building Company as a suburban community linked to Washington by the Metropolitan Branch of the B&O Railroad, a fact acknowledged by its naming for the railroad's president, John W. Garrett. The company boasted that

Garrett Park would be the Washington equivalent to New York's Tuxedo Park and erected model houses such as 4609 Waverly Avenue to set the tone. Laid out by a horticulturalist and landscape architect who was superintendent of grounds for the Agricultural Department, the plan called for winding, tree-lined "avenues" that, as a Scotsman, Saunders named for places from Sir Walter Scott's novels. Exuberant Queen Anne houses were built, along with a store and post office (4600 Rokeby Avenue) and an Episcopal church that now serves as town hall (1897; 10706 Kenilworth Avenue). Representative houses built c. 1887–1892 include the Mills-Abernathy, Brady-Stephenson, Talcott-Melville, and Herman Hollerith at 10909, 11018, 11112, and 11210 Kenilworth, respectively, and the Grace E. D. Sprigg (4710 Waverly Avenue) and J. C. Stoddard (4711 Waverly) houses.

Between 1924 and 1926, Maddux, Marshall, and Company built thirty-nine "Chevy Houses." These simple five-room cottages included the Sylvan, Roseland, and Woodbine models. Each came with an Atwater-Kent radio with an option for a garage with a Chevrolet automobile to complete the American Dream of the post–World War I era. The intent was to make homeownership possible for families of moderate means yet in a community built in "an environment fit for millionaires," referencing the earlier Queen Anne houses. Many appear along Clermont Road and Clermont Place, exemplified by the Kerr-Parsons House (4517 Clermont).

The post–World War II era witnessed the construction of a number of midcentury modern house types similarly intended to create innovative houses at low cost. Architect Alexander Richter designed twenty-five houses displaying the influences of Frank Lloyd Wright's Prairie Houses, such as those at 10708 and 10709 Weymouth Street. In 1954, Boston architect Albert C. Koch developed prefabricated Techbuilt Houses that utilize factory-built modular stressed-skin panels and a post-and-beam frame with nonloadbearing interior walls for design flexibility, sold in packaged kits, at, for example, 4709 Waverly Avenue.

CR44 HAMMOND WOOD
1949–1951, Charles M. Goodman. Bounded by Pendleton and College View drs., and Highview Ave.

Goodman's designs for the houses in the Hammond Wood development illustrate his innovative approach to residential design and development, creating affordable yet avant-garde housing set within a wooded suburban context and providing privacy and indoor-outdoor connections. Goodman was among the first to partner successfully with local developers (in this case, Paul Hammond and Paul I. Burman) to utilize modular plans and prefabricated standardized building components erected on site to maximize efficiency and lower costs. While not expansive, innovative open plans and unfolding spaces gave the illusion of spaciousness, including combined living-dining areas.

The house types encompass split-levels for sloping sites, one-story rectangular slab-on-grade (*pictured*), and larger two-story versions. The houses have simple massing, shallow-pitched gable roofs, and exterior walls that combine wood siding, brick, and floor-to-ceiling windows. Hammond Wood's fifty-eight houses were positioned on irregular lots circumscribed by the gently curving drives that respond to the topography and preexisting stands of trees.

Goodman later partnered with Bancroft Construction Company to develop a similar subdivision nearby, Rock Creek Woods (1958–1961), bounded by Spruell Drive, Rickover Road, and Ingersol Drive.

SANDY SPRING AND VICINITY

CR45 RELIGIOUS AND COMMERCIAL BUILDINGS

c. 1728 founded. Bounded by Olney–Sandy Spring, Norwood, and Brooke rds., and Meeting House Ln.

Sandy Spring, the county's oldest community, was founded c. 1728 by members of the Society of Friends and still maintains a vibrant Quaker presence. Early settlers James Brooke and John Thomas received land from father-in-law Richard Snowden, whose father was a Quaker dissenter and the recipient of a grant from Lord Baltimore. Their agrarian-based community encompassed a network of small plantations, tenanted farms, and mills situated near the headwaters of the Anacostia and Patuxent rivers. They engaged in experimental farming and established agricultural societies, making Sandy Spring one of the richest growing regions in the county. Life revolved around the meetinghouse (1817; 17715 Meeting House Lane; *pictured*), a Federal-period Flemish-bond brick building reflecting Friends' Plain-style building traditions. Built by the Thomas family of master builders, it follows the prototypical form for American Friends meetinghouses with dual entrances for men and women. The property includes a burying ground dating to 1754 and the adjacent frame Community House or Lyceum erected in 1858–1859 to serve as a lecture hall and meeting place. Past the log-constructed Quaker farmstead Harewood (1794) is the freshwater spring that gave the community its name, and the woods beyond that were part of the Friends' Underground Railroad network, now an interpretive trail.

Baltimore architects Ghequiere and May designed Colonial Revival brick buildings for Sandy Spring Bank and the Mutual Fire Insurance Company—institutions that reflect Friends progressive economic and social agenda—and the Cedars (1901; 1601 Olney–Sand Spring Road) for insurance company secretary-treasurer Allen Farquhar. More recently, architects Miche Booz and Thomas Bucci designed the Sandy Spring Museum (1996–2007; 17901 Bentley Road) as a multipart building delineated by function to resemble local buildings such as the meetinghouse.

A free Black settlement dating from the late eighteenth century, among the oldest in the state, is located along parts of Olney-Sandy Spring, Norwood, Brooke, and Chandlee Mill roads. Freed slaves were encouraged by Friends willingness to offer land and support for their own church and school, creating the largest of fourteen such enclaves that once existed in and around Sandy Spring. While most early houses have been replaced, the extant Hopkins House (c. 1900; 18470 Brooke) reflects those built by Black subsistence farmers. It now sits near the Slave Museum (1988; 18524 Brooke). The heart of the community is Sharp Street Methodist Church (1924; 1310 Olney-Sandy Spring), named for the "mother church" in Baltimore. A log church was first built c. 1822 with land and legally mandated oversight provided by Friends as the first independent Black organization in the county. The current church is the third on site. The adjacent two-story frame, gable-front Odd Fellows Hall (c. 1920) provided support services while serving as a social hall. This lodge was part of an Odd Fellows order established for African Americans founded in Baltimore in 1843.

CR46 THOMAS FAMILY HOUSES
c. 1748–c. 1806. 17107 and 17530 New Hampshire Ave., and 17201 and 16501 Norwood Rd.

Over the course of a half-century, the Quaker Thomas family built four well-crafted brick houses—Clifton, Cherry Grove, Norwood, and Woodlawn—that together demonstrate evolving architectural trends in this region c. 1748 to c. 1805. Clifton (c. 1748) at 17107 New Hampshire, one of the oldest extant houses in the county, is a refined example of the early Chesapeake house that speaks to the migration of settlers inland. It exhibits the gambrel roof that first appeared in Maryland about 1740 and a sophisticated three-room-and-passage plan, popular among the planter class. It reflects the transition between the early Chesapeake hall-parlor plan and the later Georgian center-passage plan. It encompasses a wide entrance hall and two-run stairway with heavy balustrade and a study to the rear, adjoining parlor and dining room to the opposing side, and a telescoping service wing. Period details include full-height paneled walls, corner fireplaces with bolection surrounds, and decorative corner cabinets.

Cherry Grove (c. 1784; 17530 New Hampshire) was built by John Thomas's son Richard following a fire that destroyed the earlier house. Unlike his father's

Chesapeake house, Richard erected a full two-story brick house in the Georgian mode, with updated gauged jack-arch lintels and a distinctive belt course. However, the three-room-and-passage plan and interior details harken back to Clifton, including a near-identical stairway, wood-paneled walls, fireplace surrounds, and built-in cabinets. The originally separate kitchen was joined by a hyphen to form a similar telescoping wing.

While Richard Thomas was rebuilding Cherry Grove, he was erecting the Georgian Norwood (c. 1784; 17201 Norwood) for his eldest son Samuel. Exhibiting significant differences, it embraces Georgian symmetry in a typical five-bay facade and double-pile, center-passage plan. It was expanded in 1867 to encompass a two-story service wing to one side and such improvements as enlarged windows (also installed at Cherry Grove) and an entrance with an elliptical fanlight and sidelights. It is worth noting that Norwood later became the home of Philip E. Thomas, Samuel's cousin and the first president of the B&O Railroad, for whom the Thomas Viaduct (CM15) was named.

Built for Samuel Thomas Jr., Woodlawn (c. 1806; 16501 Norwood) is similar in appearance to Norwood, encompassing a two-story, five-bay brick house with Federal-period features original to the design, such as the frontispiece with an elliptical fanlight and enlarged windows and a side service wing. Woodlawn includes an 1854 log slave house and a stone barn (CR47).

CR47 WOODLAWN BARN
1832. 16501 Norwood Rd.

Built by local stonemason Isaac Holland for physician and farmer William Pennell Palmer, the barn is among the most substantial and well-appointed agricultural buildings in the county. It was erected in the tradition of the Pennsylvania barn, which enjoyed a heyday between 1790 and 1840, spreading to neighboring states and eventually diffusing westward. Now a ubiquitous part of the nation's agricultural landscape, it resulted from the consolidation of earlier assemblages of smaller outbuildings into one large multifunctional structure; Woodlawn Barn includes livestock stabling, threshing floor, hay storage, granary, corn crib, and root cellar under one roof. It is banked into the hillside to provide direct access to stabling from the lower side and to the threshing floor from the upper side. Woodlawn is of the less typical three-story, stone-arched, forebay type introduced by the Quaker farmers of Chester County, Pennsylvania, from which Palmer, also a Quaker, originated.

The barn is a manifestation of the rise in scientific approaches to agriculture instituted by Sandy Spring farmers. As a member of the Enterprise Farmer's Club, Palmer was among those who adopted innovations such as the use of guano, lime, and plaster fertilizers, crop rotation, and grain production. The barn now features interpretive exhibits that tell the story of Sandy Spring's local agricultural practices, its Quaker and free Black communities, and their involvement in the Underground Railroad.

CR48 OAKLEY CABIN AFRICAN AMERICAN MUSEUM AND PARK
c. 1780. 3610 Brookeville Rd., Olney

This modest log dwelling, now the centerpiece of the Oakley Cabin African American Museum and Park, interprets Reconstruction-era rural Black life. It was built of hewn chestnut logs held by dovetail joints and encompasses a stone foundation and end chimney. The interior is partitioned into two rooms with an open-hearth fireplace and a loft above. The structure likely stood by 1783, when records indicate the existence of "two small log dwelling houses" on Richard Brooke's Oakley Farm. Possibly it was an overseer's house or Brooke's own residence prior to the construction of Oakley's main house (now gone). It was occupied by free Blacks post–Civil War and continued to be inhabited by Black residents until 1976, when acquired by M-NCPPC and later restored.

BROOKEVILLE

CR49 RESIDENTIAL AND EDUCATIONAL BUILDINGS
c. 1798 founded. Market and North sts., and High St. from Market to Church sts.

Coexisting with Sandy Spring's rural agrarian landscape is the former market town of Brookeville, encompassing mills powered by a tributary of the Patuxent. Its establishment reflected the social and economic transformation of rural communities that occurred nationwide during the post–Revolutionary War period. By 1813, Brookeville included two mills, a tan yard, stores, a post office, a blacksmith shop, a school, and fourteen houses. Expanding during the nineteenth century, by 1880 it boasted the third largest population in Montgomery County. Now a quiet residential community, it encompasses a range of building styles nestled within an idyllic, rolling landscape.

Noteworthy is the Madison House (c. 1798; 205 Market Street), a Federal-style two-story brick residence with a wing that housed the town's first store and post office. The name references its role as refuge to President James Madison during the War of 1812 British invasion of Washington. The neighboring Italianate house (c. 1850; 207 Market) was built for physician Artemus Riggs, encompassing his brick office to the rear. A Federal side-hall-plan brick house (c. 1801; 307 Market) was built for the town's blacksmith. David Newlin's simple, one-room and loft stone house (c. 1800; 318 Market), later significantly enlarged, sat adjacent to his former mill.

Built c. 1800 to attract skilled workers are three hall-parlor cottages, banked into the hillsides to provide a ground-level kitchen, with the formal room on the main level and loft above. The cottage (203 Market) erected for Richard Thomas's millhand is of stone while the other two cottages, (198 and 313 Market), are of frame and log construction, respectively.

The stone Brookeville Academy (c. 1810; 5 High Street), built as a boys' private school, is now the community meeting hall, and the quintessential one-room Brookeville Public School House (c. 1865; North Street) is one of the only original seventy frame schoolhouses in Montgomery County by 1880 to survive.

CR50 OAKS II
c. 1797, 1805; 1980s restored. 5815 Riggs Rd.

This distinctive gambrel-roofed house is a preserved early hall-parlor plan dwelling built of logs by the Riggs family, who migrated here from the Chesapeake, bringing the region's architectural traditions with them. It encompasses an unusual upper story, accessed via a winder stair, whereby a wide hall runs the length of the front with small bedchambers lined along the rear, lit from both sides by dormer windows. A log kitchen with open-hearth fireplace was soon appended. The parlor retains its paneled walls and similar open-hearth fireplace. Used for storing hay for nearly a century prior to its restoration, it is among Maryland's few such houses to retain its modest original plan and configuration.

GAITHERSBURG

CR51 AGRICULTURAL HISTORY FARM PARK (MAGRUDER-BUSSARD FARMSTEAD)
1900–1910. 18400 Muncaster Mill Rd.

This turn-of-the-twentieth-century farm complex encompasses a quintessential vernacular farm-house (*pictured*), frame bank barn, log smokehouse, double corncrib, and frame silo. The dwelling form, comprised of a two-and-a-half-story, five-bay, center-passage house with central cross-gable peak and front porch, appeared throughout the region from the mid-nineteenth through the early twentieth centuries. This particularly striking example includes an octagonal bay window, a side wing once used as a kitchen (predating the existing house), and a later, rear kitchen ell. The property was settled as a tobacco plantation by the locally prominent

Magruder family, who owned it from 1734 to 1888. The next owner, Thaddeus Bussard, erected most of the extant buildings, including the c. 1895 bank barn. The family transferred the property to M-NCPPC in 1971. Recognizing its integrity and potential for conveying life on a farmstead of the period, it was established as the Agricultural History Farm Park.

CR52 KENTLANDS
1988–2001, Andres Duany and Elizabeth Plater-Zyberk (DPZ). Bounded by Great Seneca Hwy., Quince Orchard and Darnestown rds., and Inspiration Ln.

Kentlands is considered the second major and first nonresort community in the United States to embody the tenets of neotraditional town planning known as New Urbanism. It was developed by a Montgomery County residential builder, Joseph Alfandre, in conjunction with Duany and Plater-Zyberk (DPZ), established leaders in neotraditional town planning with Seaside, Florida.

Principal characteristics of New Urbanism featured at Kentlands include walkability, mix of residential types for visual interest and a heterogeneous demographic, and commercial and recreational facilities. Referencing historical forms and styles, many houses have front porches and rear parking. This approach represented a break with typical suburban zoning and development in favor of replicating older patterns.

The first models opened in 1990, encompassing detached single-family houses, town houses, condominiums, and rental apartments designed to suit the metropolitan area's preference for colonial imagery. In 1996, a retail and commercial area was developed centered on a new Market Square. Largely complete, Kentlands includes approximately 1,800 dwellings in eleven distinct neighborhoods, an elementary school, three commercial areas, and recreation facilities.

WASHINGTON GROVE

CR53 RELIGIOUS AND RESIDENTIAL BUILDINGS
1874 founded. Bounded by Center St., Chestnut Rd, McCauley St., and Grove Rd.

The opening of the B&O Metropolitan Branch in 1873 brought a group of United Methodist clergy from Washington to hold summer revival meetings. Attracted to the healthy rural setting with plentiful trees and water, they purchased a 268-acre site and laid out a campground of seven avenues radiating from a circle containing an open-sided wood tabernacle (demolished). Association shares sold to congregants allowed them to pitch tents and, eventually, build small wood cottages.

The characteristic Washington Grove cottage has Carpenter Gothic features, including a steeply pitched roof, board-and-batten siding, and decorative bargeboards. Excellent examples such as 15 The Circle (*pictured*), 105 and 213 Grove Avenue, and 303 First Avenue vary somewhat in detail and plan but share a steep front gable, wide porches, and decorative details. Many of the cottages are on a standard 50 × 150–foot lot with front porches close to the still pedestrian-only avenues.

Orientation toward pedestrian walkways is a distinctive characteristic of Washington Grove's houses that extends beyond the first radial avenues to an alternating grid of roads and walkways to the south toward the railroad. McCathran Hall (1902; 300 Grove), an octagonal wood structure, was built as an indoor chapel and to accommodate Chautauqua meetings; it gradually became the town hall. Now a year-round community, the town of Washington Grove was incorporated in 1937 after the Washington Grove Camp Meeting Association was disbanded.

CLARKSBURG

CR54 COMSAT LABORATORIES

1968–1969, DMJM with Cesar Pelli, partner in charge; Lester Collins, landscape architect; 1981–1982 addition, HOK. 22300 Comsat Dr.

COMSAT is the premier example of a mid-twentieth-century corporate suburban campus in Maryland, with additional international significance through its function as a groundbreaking public-private entity in the development of artificial satellite communications for military and civilian applications. COMSAT, or Communications Satellite Corporation, was created by the Communications Satellite Act of 1962, and President John F. Kennedy personally picked its leaders as part of his space program initiative.

After a few years as a publicly traded corporation, COMSAT built a new laboratory facility along the I-270 corridor. Constructed as the Washington National Pike between 1953 and 1960 and connected to the Capital Beltway in 1964, this highway was emerging as a high-tech corridor through federal decentralization projects such as the relocation of the Atomic Energy Commission in 1957 and the National Bureau of Standards in 1966.

Pelli designed the laboratory to be seen from the highway, presenting a gleaming image of high-tech modernism set within a naturalistic 150-acre campus created by Collins with stands of native trees and manicured lawns. Pelli sheathed the building in an aluminum and glass skin that recalled an airplane, with glass catwalks connecting the various wings and presenting a unified facade to the highway. The north end of the main circulation spine with wings for offices and laboratories terminates in a dramatic glass-walled two-story exhibition pavil-ion. Additional original wings to the east included machine shops, maintenance areas, and a massive Environmental Test Laboratory warehouse where testing could simulate space conditions. In 1998 COMSAT merged with Lock-heed Martin, and operations at the Clarksburg building were discontinued. While a major preservation initiative raised awareness, the building does not have any protective historic designations and still awaits a new long-term tenant to assure its survival.

POOLESVILLE AND VICINITY

CR55 CHESAPEAKE AND OHIO CANAL LOCK 24 AND SENECA CREEK AQUEDUCT
c. 1829–1830. Milepost 22.8 at end of Riley's Lock Rd.

Following the Potomac River, the canal provided a navigable waterway for the transport of goods and a link to emerging markets in the west. Clustered here are Lock 24, an aqueduct, and a lockkeeper's house, all constructed of distinctive, locally quarried Seneca sandstone, known for its warm red color, strength, and durability. Lock 24 and the aqueduct are integrated to form a single structure built of massive stone blocks.

The first of eleven aqueducts built along the canal between 1829 and 1832, it was the northern terminus of the first section, opened in 1830.

Adjacent is Riley's lockkeeper's house (1829; *pictured above*), named for the keeper who resided here with his family from 1890 until 1924, when the canal ceased operation. Likewise built of rough-cut Seneca sandstone, it has distinctive quoining and slab lintels and sills and is banked into the hillside with a basement kitchen.

Remnants of the Seneca Stone Cutting Mill sit near the canal

THE I-95 CORRIDOR

I-95 JFK toll plaza in Cecil County, December 9, 1963

Much has been written about the transformation wrought on the American landscape and social patterns by the interstate highway system since its creation in 1956. The construction of I-95 on the East Coast is perhaps the most important example, transforming rural outposts into bedroom communities and creating a series of sprawling metropolitan areas where there was once a clearer demarcation between city and country. This impact is particularly evident in Maryland, where I-95 travels northeast to southwest through Cecil, Harford, Baltimore, Howard, and Prince George's counties. The section between the Delaware border and Baltimore officially opened in November 1963. In 1960, Harford County had a population of 77,000 residents; by 2010 the population was 245,000. The independent city of Baltimore saw a related decline, shrinking from 939,000 to 621,000 residents in the same period. These fundamental demographic shifts exacerbated racial inequalities in housing and opportunity and would not have been possible without major highway construction such as I-95 and its many connector routes.

The massive volume of traffic moving along I-95 also feeds into the associated beltways around the two major cities in the region— I-695/895 in Baltimore and I-495 in Washington. I-95 between the two beltways was completed in 1971, further supplanting other roads such as U.S. 1 and the Baltimore-Washington Parkway and the railroad as routes for local commuters and through-travelers between Baltimore and Washington. As commercial and residential sprawl has swallowed up historic landscapes and districts along the I-95 corridor, the general result has been an overwhelmingly generic collection of commercial strips, office parks, town houses, and so-called McMansions. While justly criticized by many designers, planners, and environmentalists as ugly and unsustainable, it is these contemporary landscapes generated by construction of I-95 that define suburban life for many Maryland residents and form a major economic engine for the region.

---

towpath, including the massive seventy-foot-long east and thirty-foot south walls of cut sandstone, and the stone sluice that fed water diverted from the canal to power the machine turbines. It was built in two sections, beginning c. 1830, and operated until 1900.

CR56 SENECA SCHOOLHOUSE

1866. 16800 River Rd.

Built of Seneca sandstone, this is among the earliest and one of only three extant one-room schoolhouses in Montgomery County, constructed following the establishment of a statewide public education system in 1860. It was built according to specifications developed by national public education advocate Horace Mann that appeared in his 1848 publication *School Architecture,* through plans provided by the state superintendent of public instruction. It is the only one of the eighty-three public schoolhouses in the county in 1880 to be built of stone. Although school operations were generally funded by the state, many rural schools were constructed though private donation. This one was erected by Seneca (grist) Mill owner Upton Darby. The gable-front main block and vestibule are built of rough-cut Seneca sandstone with quoining. The restored interior includes two-person desks, a long bench from which children recited their lessons, a teacher's desk, blackboards, and a coal-burning stove for heat. It is available for tours, meetings, and events.

CR57 SENECA STORE AND UPTON DARBY HOUSE
1901 store; c. 1855 house. 16315 and 16401 Old River Rd.

This building typifies the rural stores built in the region around the turn of the twentieth century. It was erected for Frederick Allnutt, who purchased property from the Darby family that included the adjacent house. The gable-front frame building is shaded by a porch and maintains its interior built-in shelving. The Allnutt family operated the store until 1965, when it was sold to Raymond Poole. Renamed Poole's General Store, it catered to the local agricultural and equestrian community, selling feed and other specialized goods. When it closed in 2010, it was the oldest general store in continuous operation in the county and remains one of the few extant (including the 1910 Darby Store; 19801 Darnestown Road and the c. 1860 Holland Store; 16400 Layhill Road, all three owned by M-NCPPC). It is now protected by a preservation easement.

Adjacent is the frame storekeeper's house erected by Seneca Mill owner Upton Darby. It is typical of the rural two-story, five-bay houses of the period, enhanced by a jigsawn ornamented front porch.

CR58 ROCKLANDS FARM WINERY (ROCKLANDS FARM)
1870. 14531 Montevideo Rd.

Representing the many local houses erected of Seneca sandstone, Rocklands is distinguished by its Italianate Villa styling, made popular through period pattern books. The symmetrical building has a low hipped roof, widow's walk with cut-out balustrade and bracketed cornice, tall sash windows, and ornamented entrance porch. The coursed stone walls include a datestone that names original owner, Benoni Allnutt. A regional accommodation is the side wing with two-level galleries. In his *History of Western Maryland* (1879), John Scharf describes Rockland as "a model and handsomely improved farm" and the house as "one of the finest in the county… not only a handsome architectural specimen, but [it] embodies all the comforts and conveniences that improved skill and refined taste could suggest." Included is a board-and-batten bank barn resting on a cut sandstone foundation, pass-through granary, sandstone dairy, log meat house, and tenant house. The property is now home to Rocklands Farm Winery.

CR59 GLENSTONE

2006 gallery, Charles Gwathmey; PWP Landscape Architecture; 2018 the Pavilions, Thomas Phifer. 12100 Glen Rd., Potomac

Glenstone combines minimalist modern architecture, contemporary art, and nature in a serene and engaging environment described by the American Institute of Architects award committee as "a virtuoso display of design and detail, and a poetic integration of art, architecture and landscape." The site's original gallery and the Pavilions display art of the post–World War II era with 230 acres of winding paths and trails that traverse meadows, woodlands, and streams with the occasional sculpture. Set in a meadow of native grasses and perennial flowers, the buildings were inspired by such sites as Ryoanji, a Zen temple in Kyoto, Japan. They form a cluster of cube-like structures of varying size made from large blocks of poured concrete, lit by glass clerestories, and connected by walkways of solid glass held with steel mullions and surrounded by the Water Court. The collection includes over 1,300 works of art representing more than 200 noted artists of the twentieth and twenty-first centuries.

GLEN ECHO

CR60 CHESAPEAKE AND OHIO CANAL, LOCK, AND LOCKHOUSE 22

1829–1831. Milepost 19.63

The Potomac River Valley in western Maryland had been identified as a viable transportation corridor by the Potomac Canal Company, chartered in 1784 and first led by George Washington. Renewed interest in developing a canal along the Potomac led to formal establishment of the Chesapeake and Ohio Canal Company, which hired several men with Erie Canal experience and began construction in July 1828. Difficulties in obtaining rights-of-way, labor shortages, and challenging terrain slowed work, but by 1839, 134 miles had been completed. When the canal was officially completed in 1850, it had already been superseded by the newer technology of the B&O Railroad. Nevertheless, the canal was profitable for brief periods in the nineteenth century as it was used to transport goods, lime, stone, and coal from western Maryland to Washington.

The canal consisted of the canal prism with a berm on one side to provide a stable slope and a towpath on the other for the horse or mule to pull the boat along the canal. To overcome the 610-foot difference in elevation between

Georgetown and Cumberland, 74 lift locks were needed to raise or lower boats. Four generations of locks have been identified along the canal, with Lock 22 and its accompanying lockhouse representing the initial 1828 design specifications, here constructed of local Seneca red sandstone. Lockhouse 22, which housed the lock-keeper and his family, also was built using the standard specifications developed by the canal company. The simple one-and-a-half-story side gable structure has whitewashed gray and red Seneca sandstone walls.

CR61 GLEN ECHO PARK
1891 established; 1911–1940s additions. 7300 MacArthur Blvd.

Glen Echo Park, first developed as a residential community by Edward and Edwin Baltzley, combines a bucolic natural landscape with an eclectic mix of late-nineteenth-century and early- to mid-twentieth-century buildings that reflect changing trends in educational, recreational, and amusement activities. Its alluring landscape, perched on a verdant bluff overlooking the Potomac River, has captured the imagination of Washingtonians for over a century. In that time, Glen Echo evolved from a suburban retreat to Chautauqua, to trolley line amusement park, to national park, remnants of which are all still embedded in the landscape.

Glen Echo's heyday came in 1911 when it was developed as an amusement park for the trolley line linking Washington with its outlying suburbs. Such end-of-the-line attractions were fairly common, crediting trolley companies with the development of the amusement park as an American institution. Parks such as Glen Echo, among the few surviving, were enabled by a national increase in leisure time and disposable income and the rise of thrill-seeking rides. Conversely, post–World War II changes in entertainment trends contributed to their decline. Glen Echo ceased operation in 1968 following civil rights protests challenging its racial segregation. It was transferred to the National Park Service in 1970 and now operates as a recreation and arts center.

The park preserves many of the iconic features of amusement parks and other reminders of its early days. The Chautauqua's stone tower designed by Victor Mindeleff as a grand entrance still stands, as does the trolley's "Yellow [car] Barn." Also extant is the streamlined entrance canopy (*pictured*) designed by Philadelphia architect Edward Schoeppe, the penny arcade, shooting gallery, popcorn concession, and bumper car and "Cuddle Up" rides. The only operational ride is the rare surviving 1922 carousel manufactured by the William H. Dentzel Company of Philadelphia. It is housed within a Shingle Style pavilion with a dual-pitched bell-shaped roof and contains fifty-two carved wooden animals created by one of the nation's most skilled carousel carvers, Dan-iel C. Muller. Also functioning is its Wurlitzer 165 Military Band organ.

A park anchor is the 1933 Spanish Ballroom, also designed by Schoeppe. Fueled by Big Band, swing, and jazz music, dance halls became all the rage between the two World Wars. They represented the democratization of dances originally the domain of debutante and society balls. Spanish-influenced elements include a stuccoed facade, faux vigas, and a tile roof, along with Art Deco zigzagged balustrades and pylons. The two-story ballroom includes a mezzanine-level viewing promenade. Patrons danced to live music performed by Dave McWilliams and his orchestra, and other celebrity Big Band and jazz ensembles. A year-round dance season still draws crowds.

CR62 CLARA BARTON HOUSE
1891, Julian B. Hubbell. 5801 Oxford Rd.

This house was erected for the founder of the American Red Cross by Baltzley Brothers with-in their planned residential community (see CR61) and Glen Echo Chautauqua. Hoping to attract a wealthy and cultured clientele, they believed an association with Clara Barton and the Red Cross would lend credibility to their endeavor. Under Barton's direction, amateur architect, Red Cross physician, and close confident Julian B. Hubbell laid out an adaptable multipurpose space. It was used primarily as a warehouse until 1897, when Barton took up permanent residence, relocating the organization's headquarters. As a multifunctional building, the house is an unusual design that encompassed an open two-and-a-half-story central gallery and rooms divided by flexible, frame partition walls. Ornamented with medieval castle-like stone towers to blend with the Chautauqua buildings, the massive rectangular edifice was constructed from wood salvaged from the buildings that sheltered victims of the 1889 Johnston Flood. It has operated as a National Park Service house museum since 1974.

⫸ ⫷

WESTERN
MOUNTAINS

Encompassing Frederick, Washington, Allegany, and Garrett counties, western Maryland is distinguished by the peaks and valleys of the Appalachian Plateau, Blue Ridge Mountains, and Piedmont foothills. Nearly a century passed from the time of Maryland's first European settlement in the Chesapeake before Charles Calvert opened this mountainous "backcountry" in 1729. Lacking serviceable roads and sufficient population, the inland areas remained largely unsettled by Europeans. Moreover, with its rocky outcroppings and open fields devoid of timber, the region was mistakenly thought unfarmable, referred to as "the barrens." Making his own foray in 1744, however, Receiver General Daniel Dulany proclaimed that it "equals, if does not exceed any in America for natural advantages" including "rich soil for planting." He quickly acquired tracts along the Monocacy River and Antietam Creek valleys and on behalf of Calvert offered farms of 100 to 300 acres to Scots-Irish and German settlers from Pennsylvania. As further enticement, in 1745 Dulany laid out "Frederick Town" as a market center. By 1748, it was the largest city in the state and the seat of newly formed Frederick County.

Unlike Chesapeake tobacco planters, the German settlers were grain farmers, praised for their sober industry and orderly farm-steads, recognizable by their central-chimney stone and log houses and bank barns. Merchant gristmills processing grain for export were built, numbering eighty by 1798. Wagon roads connected Frederick to Baltimore via the Baltimore Turnpike that became part of the National Road, pushing settlement westward while providing a corridor for the development of market towns and stage stops catering to travelers and drovers hauling goods.

Boundary disputes motivated Calvert to lay claim to lands even farther west. In 1741, Dulany sent agents into the mountains to fa-cilitate settlement west of the Potomac. In 1754, Fort Cumberland offered a frontier outpost and staging point for military maneuvers during the French and Indian War. The area west of Fort Cumberland was opened in 1774, offering land as enticement for military service. When Allegany County was set off from Washington in 1789, Cum-berland became the county seat. German, Scots-Irish, and French be-gan migrating from Frederick County. Development was bolstered by arrival of the National Road in 1811, the Baltimore and Ohio (B&O) Railroad in 1842, and the Chesapeake and Ohio Canal in 1850. These

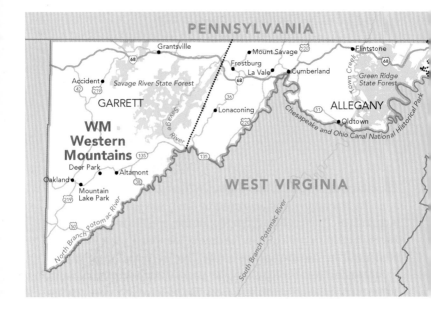

transportation networks further opened the region to settlement and to the extraction of iron and its greatest commodity, coal.

Coal deposits were identified in the Georges Creek region as early as 1810, and by the 1840s mining gained momentum. As part of the Great Appalachian coal fields extending from northern Pennsylvania to central Alabama, western Maryland was fast becoming one of the nation's principal coal producers. Paternalistic company towns were created, populated largely by Irish immigrants. Iron manufacture and brickmaking contributed to economic development. Coal production peaked in 1907, declining into the 1930s, when most of the deep mines closed.

In contrast, the area farther west that became Garrett County in 1872 was agricultural, with grain as its greatest commodity. Settlements sprang up along the National Road, offering inns and hotels, and around the gristmills at the heart of farming communities. Sawmills were likewise established, facilitating the transformation from log settler cabins to plank and balloon-frame houses. The B&O gave impetus for Garrett County's formation. Oakland was laid out as its future county seat in 1849 in anticipation of the railroad's arrival in 1851, naming the county for its president, John W. Garrett. Garrett encouraged resort development in the new county to promote use of his railroad, touting the fresh mountain air and scenic beauty. Garrett County continued the tradition of outdoor recreation in the twentieth century. Deep Creek Lake, created from a hydroelectric dam project in 1925, became a major boating destination, while state parks and resorts provide year-round recreational opportunities, including hiking and skiing in the "Maryland Alps."

Meanwhile, by 1850 Frederick was second only to Baltimore in wealth, with light industries such as tanning, glassmaking, brickmaking, distilling, and brewing now thriving along with milling. But west-

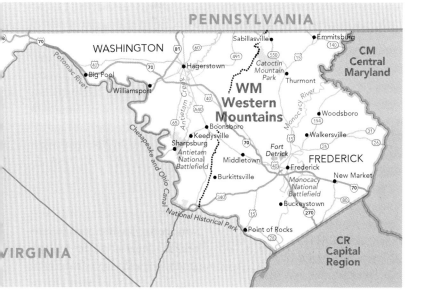

ern Maryland's industrial focus soon shifted to Hagerstown, a railroad hub and manufacturing center known for products such as furniture and organs. The Civil War greatly impacted the region, with Confederate incursions and major battles fought in such places as Antietam/ Sharpsburg and Monocacy. Struggling to recover in the aftermath, farmers diversified in order to compete with grain-producing regions in the Midwest, while industry and emancipation drew laborers away. Agricultural lime production helped increase yields, but by c. 1900 dairy farming had taken hold, spurred by innovations in milk processing.

Post–World War II construction of the Eisenhower Defense Highway (I-70 and I-270) begun in 1956 facilitated suburban development while making the area more commutable to jobs in Baltimore and Washington. Since then, farms have increasingly given way to suburban sprawl. Frederick is currently the second largest city in Maryland and witnessing the revitalization of its historic downtown. Farther west, cities such as Hagerstown and Cumberland still suffer from deindustrialization, seeking to reinvigorate their once powerful economies. Outdoor recreation and tourism related to the region's Civil War history are now the major economic drivers in the mountain counties of western Maryland.

FREDERICK COUNTY
FREDERICK

Since its establishment in 1745, Frederick has been one of Maryland's most important towns. It rose from western outpost to inland market center and county seat within a few short years, settled largely by

German and Scots-Irish immigrants. Its development was enabled by early roadways that cross at the center of its city grid and commercial area: the north–south road from Georgetown to Pennsylvania, and the east–west road from Baltimore that became the National Road. Although bypassed by the Chesapeake and Ohio Canal, it enjoyed a spur line to the Baltimore and Ohio Railroad by the mid-nineteenth century. Even once usurped by Hagerstown as regional industrial leader, Frederick maintained its prominence as the region's municipal, financial, and commercial epicenter, and remains the area's most prosperous town.

WM1 COURT SQUARE AND FREDERICK CITY HALL (FREDERICK COUNTY COURTHOUSE)

1785 Court Square; 1862–1864, Thomas Dixon. Bounded by N. Court, W. Church, Record, and Council sts.

Erected as the Frederick County Courthouse after an 1861 fire destroyed the original 1785 Georgian courthouse, the building became the city hall when a new courthouse (100 W. Patrick Street) was built in 1982. When completed in 1864, the courthouse signaled the transformation of Frederick from industrial hub to civic epicenter, followed by other public buildings such as a city hall and market house (1873; 124 N. Market Street). Reflecting the latest architectural trends, the two-story building with a tall central pavilion and a cupola encompasses Italianate design reserved for Frederick's best commercial, civic, and residential buildings. It was erected of manufactured pressed brick forming inset panels and decorative corbels.

The building is situated in Court Square, created c. 1785 as a civic center. The square's gentrification into a fashionable residential address was sparked by the 1810 removal of the associated jail and offices and the construction of its first upscale residences. Local architect-builder Andrew McCleery constructed paired three-story Federal houses (1817; 103 and 105 Council) replete with elliptical transom and Frederick "top-hat" dormers for industrialist John McPherson. Paired Greek Revival houses (111 and 113 Record) of equal sophistication were completed the same year, followed by the Federal Richard Potts House (1818, Robert Mills; 100 N. Court).

WM2 FREDERICK BUSINESS DISTRICT

c. 1790 to present. Market St. between 4th and All Saints sts., and Patrick St. from Court to Carroll sts.

The commercial heart of Frederick is the district along the intersecting Market and Patrick streets, segments of the early roads through Frederick. While few of the first-period log buildings erected by German settlers remain, still extant are Federal

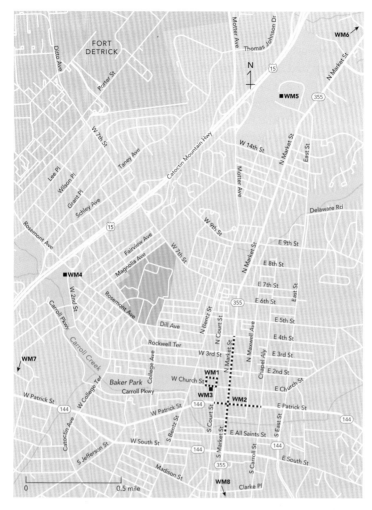

buildings dating from the 1790s through the 1840s. They are identified by their two-story, gable-roofed configurations, Flemish-bond brick, and Federal detailing. Many in the commercial area typically combined a house and shop, recognized by the decorative entrances into the residential section with storefront display windows added later, such as 209–211 (*pictured*), 217–219, and 306–308 N. Market. The shophouse pattern continued into the late nineteenth century with such examples as 332–334 Market, built of pressed brick with stone and terra-cotta details.

Today's commercial street-scapes are mostly composed of buildings from the post–Civil War recovery through the early twentieth century in various popular styles. Among the earliest Italianate buildings is the Baltimore and Ohio passenger station (1854; 100 S. Market) and the distinctive former City Hall and Market House (1873; 124 N. Market). Italianate soon dominated the commercial streetscape, featuring ornamental cast-iron drip-mold lintels, bracketed cornices, and elongated windows, exemplified by 48–52, 104–106, and 108–110 Market.

Richardsonian Romanesque is exemplified by Hendrickson

Dry Goods (42–44 N. Market), designed by German-born John A. Dempwolf, and the Benjamin Rosenour and Sons Mercantile Building (c. 1885; 37 N. Market), once one of the largest businesses of its type in the region. The now-commercial Romanesque Revival Houck House (1891; 228 N. Market) was designed by Dempwolf for Ezra Houck Jr., a wealthy landowner and businessman from an early German family, with the initials of progenitors Ezra and Catherine Houck in the family crest over the entrance and the faces of his daughters flanking the doorway. The elaborate Gomber Building (c. 1895; 36 S. Market) features a full cast-iron facade, manufactured by Mesker Brothers of St. Louis.

The twentieth century is represented by such Classical Revival buildings as the Mutual Insurance Company building (c. 1924; 112–114 N. Market), and Citizens Bank (1909, John A. Dempwolf; 2 S. Market). The bank is the most noteworthy of three banks erected at the "Square Corner" intersection of Market and Patrick streets, signifying Frederick's financial dominance. The Tivoli Theater (1927; 20 W. Patrick) was designed by John J. Zink, a Baltimore architect specializing in Moderne movie theaters, and built to accommodate both silent movies and live stage. Also noteworthy is the United Fire Company building (1848, 1905; 77–79 S. Market).

More eclectic buildings of note are the former Harris and Fuller Wholesale House (16–18 E. Patrick) exemplifying the period use of terra-cotta and pressed metal. The Rosenstock Building (c. 1900; 5–7 E. Patrick) that housed Joseph Rosenstock's clothing business features a grid of geometric spandrels and piers, bay windows, and classical cornice. Francis Scott Key Hotel (1923; 17–19 W. Patrick) was the city's first large-scale, luxury hotel, built on the site of earlier inns and marking a new era in hospitality. Its construction was sponsored by civic leaders to attract wealthy tourists.

The Ideal Car Company showroom (c. 1911; 112 E. Patrick) is more typical of early-twentieth-century commercial buildings with its parapet roofline and large plate-glass windows. The concrete Hardey Building (1936; 154 N. Market) is one of the few inspired by Art Deco. More recent is the modern courthouse and plaza, built by CAM Construction and completed in 1982. Incorporating rehabilitation of the adjacent late-eighteenth-century houses of political dignitaries John Hanson and Phillip Thomas (108 and 110 W. Patrick) was a nod to the town's early heritage. Carroll Creek Park (1970s–2016), a linear-designed landscape oriented along a canal that crosses under Market Street, was created as a flood control project to protect the historic downtown; it offers pedestrian paths, bridges, and a small, open-air amphitheater for performances.

WM3 ALL SAINTS EPISCOPAL CHURCH AND PARISH HALL
1856, Richard Upjohn; Andrew McCleery, master builder. 106 W. Church St.

Designed by nationally renowned Upjohn and erected by McCleery, this Gothic Revival church reflects Frederick's emergence as a refined urban center. It was one of eight significant churches enlarged or rebuilt during the mid-nineteenth century in an apparent competition among local congregations for the most sophisticated design. According to historian Diane Shaw in *Perspectives in Vernacular Architecture* (1995), church construction played a critical role in the architectural transformation of Frederick from small town to urban center. Likewise, the selection of Upjohn, perhaps the nation's foremost proponent of Gothic Revival, heralds an enlightened perspective beyond this once-rural community. Its prominence as a city landmark was further guaranteed by its location in an area newly defined by upscale residences, facing Court Square (WM1).

In its restrained yet archetypal interpretation of Gothic Revival, asymmetry, and attention to proportion and scaling, All Saints is quintessential Upjohn. Defining features include its steeply pitched roof, buttresses, lancet bays, entrance tower, and soaring octagonal spire. The interior features an open truss-work ceiling and side aisles separated by pointed-arched arcades.

The earlier church (1813–1814; 23 N. Court), now the parish hall, lies just around the corner. It was built by Henry McCleery, the father of the new church's builder, Andrew McCleery. The finely detailed classical building is distinguished by its pedimented gable front, Palladian windows, semicircular transoms, and stuccoed finish.

WM4 SCHIFFERSTADT
c. 1758, Elias Bruner; 1866–1867 kitchen. 1110 Rosemont St.

Schifferstadt is an exceptional surviving example of colonial-era German architecture. The stone main block was constructed by Bruner, who immigrated to America in 1729 from Germany and settled on land purchased in 1746 near the newly established town of Frederick. Schifferstadt has a distinctive *durchgangigen* or center-hall arrangement of interior spaces, one of the principal German plan types used in the American colonies. Traditionally interpreted as Anglo-influenced, *durchgangigen* houses are now understood to be part of the regularization of German domestic design against a broader ethos of gentility in the eighteenth century. The symmetry of Schifferstadt departs from the typical off-center entrance, conforming instead to contemporary Georgian convention. The central wishbone chimney, *Liegender Stuhl* (leaning truss system), vaulted cellar, stone kitchen window sink, decorative hardware, *Stroh Lehm* (mud and straw) paling insulation, and five-plate jamb stove, however, are fully characteristic of German architecture. Despite alterations and additions such as the two-story brick kitchen wing, Schifferstadt offers an unusual level of insight into an important immigrant group in the nation's early history. The house is currently operated as a museum.

WM5 ROSE HILL
c. 1789–1792; 1845–1853 renovated. 1611 N. Market St.

Home of noted political dignitaries Thomas Johnson and John Grahame, Rose Hill combines classical and Greek Revival with vernacular traditions particular to the region. Likely part of mid-nineteenth-century renovations is the impressive two-story pedimented portico, while regional elements include its plainer service wing with beehive oven and Frederick "top-hat" dormers. Johnson was the first elected governor of Maryland and an associate justice of the U.S. Supreme Court. Rose Hill was built for his daughter Ann and her husband John Grahame and is where Johnson spent his retirement years. Grahame was a major in the Frederick County Militia and served in the Maryland legislature. Rose Hill is one of the few such stately, classically inspired houses in the area, along with Prospect Hall (c. 1810; 889 Butterfly Lane), the country home of John McPherson of Catoctin Iron Works. McPherson, who married Ann's niece, purchased Rose Hill in 1833 ensuring Ann's continued residence once widowed. Later owners, local businessman John Wilson and his wife Ann, undertook the Greek Revival renovations. The building served as an inn and tearoom on the tourist route to Gettysburg in the 1930s, and in 1968 was purchased as part of the county park system and opened for tours. Outbuildings include the c. 1746 log house built by settler Hans Peter Hoffman, a laundry and meat house, icehouse, and dairy barn.

WM6 BEATTY-CRAMER HOUSE
1748; 1855. 9010 Liberty Rd.

Highly unusual for Maryland is this house built for Thomas Beatty following the building traditions familiar to his Dutch wife, Maria Jensen. The original two-room, single-pile section exhibits the heavy timber, transverse "H-bent" construction emblematic of Netherlandic framing, featuring two posts connected by a tie-beam to form an H-shape. The timber framing of the exterior walls is infilled with brick nogging (originally left exposed), while the horizontal planks forming the interior partition wall have earthen infill known as "Dutch biscuit." Evidence exists of a former Dutch tripartite arrangement of windows on the facade and a split-level or "Opkamer" plan. The east parlor was formerly about 2.5-feet higher that the west kitchen, with a cellar underneath the parlor accessed via the kitchen. The west room was raised to meet the east when the V-notched log addition was made to the west end. Also noteworthy is a rear curtain wall that preserves the original cornice, incorporating such reused scantling as first-period roof rafters. A two-story banked springhouse (c. 1782) features a spring-fed trough and a hood for a traditional Dutch jambless cooking fireplace on the lower level and a finished room above, possibly used to house one of the Beatty's eleven enslaved workers.

Thomas and Maria Beatty came from Ulster County, New York, to

Frederick, where Thomas's mother and siblings had previously settled. The property remained in the Beatty family until 1797. In 1855 it was purchased by farmer Jeremiah Henry Cramer, who built the log section. The house, although abandoned since 1985, remains structurally sound, and there is hope for its rehabilitation by its current owner, the Frederick County Landmarks Foundation.

WM7 GEORGE WIDRICK HOUSE
Second quarter of the 19th century.
5346 Ballenger Creek Pike

This house is a richly crafted example of a regionally distinctive domestic building form characterized by its side-attached, two-story kitchen wing with tiered inset porches. Although wings with double porches appear frequently throughout the Cumberland Valley, they customarily appear as a perpendicular rear ell. Influenced by the building traditions of German settlers from Pennsylvania, this form emerged in the central and western regions of the state, generally built between 1820 and 1860. Federal detailing and exceptional workmanship both inside and out set the Widrick House apart from others like it. The house embraces a side hall and double-parlor plan, and the wing encompasses a kitchen with a large cooking fireplace and a for-mal dining room. Widrick was of German descent, likely a retired Frederick merchant. In recognition of its architectural value, the house was preserved when the property was acquired by the county in 2010 as part of Ballenger Creek Park.

WM8 GAMBRILL HOUSE
c. 1872. 4801 Urbana Pike

James Gambrill, owner of the successful Araby Mill and later Frederick City Mill, chose a Second Empire design with mansard roofs and eave and porch brackets for his palatial new house south of the Monocacy River. The rear ell service wing has a simple two-story porch along its side, in keeping with local tradition. The main block of the house was generously appointed for entertaining with a double parlor, library, and dining room on the first floor and a ballroom with stage on the third.

The Gambrill House included such modern amenities as a coal furnace, hot and cold running water, sewage disposal, wall-mounted gas lamps, and a gas stove. A cistern still located behind the house stored water pumped from a nearby spring and delivered it to the house via a gravity system. Noteworthy interior decoration includes Italian marble fireplace mantels carved with fruit and flowers, heavy turned and carved newel post, and walnut balustrade between the first and third floors at the center-hall stair. The house is now occupied as offices for the National Park Service Historic Preservation Training Center, and the property is part of Monocacy National Battlefield.

WM9 MAIN STREET, NEW
MARKET
*1793–c. 1850. Main St. from
N. Federal St. to Emory Alley*

New Market was founded in 1793
by speculators William Plummer
and Nicholas Hall as a market
town and stage stop, capitalizing on the overland trade via
the newly established Baltimore
Turnpike to Frederick (later the
National Road), situated a day's
wagon ride away. The founders' intent is manifested by the
town's linear plan; 165-foot-long
parcels combine "front" lots that
line the turnpike or main street
with adjoining "back" lots along
the wide alleys where stables,
wagon stands, and carriage houses developed. New Market soon
boasted a nail and button factory, blacksmith shops, a tannery,
a distillery, dry goods stores, inns,
and taverns.

Its buildings date largely from
the early to mid-nineteenth century, are constructed of brick,
and reflect Federal, Greek Revival, and other popular styles.
Many combine a residence with
a commercial venture, indicative
of the small towns within this region. The most sophisticated is
5 W. Main (1803–1815), once the

National Hotel and Stage Office,
and later a general store and post
office. Others include the former
George Burgess house and attached grocery store (c. 1850; 18 E.
Main) and the regional gable and
half hip-roofed building (c. 1858;
1 W. Main) with a second-floor
residence. Utz Mercantile (1881;
26 W. Main), with a fully glazed
storefront, is one of the few continuously operating businesses.

Early log houses built by town-
founder William Plummer are a
one-room house (c. 1798; 37 W.
Main), now a rear wing, built
for his aunt, and his own house
(c. 1790s) at 51 W. Main. The distinctive federal period inn (c. 1793;
8 W. Main) was the town's first.
Erected for innkeeper John Rob-
erts, it was raised to three stories
in the mid-nineteenth century,
operating as E. T. Hilton's Hotel.
Representative of Federal houses is the imposing brick house
flanked by wings (c. 1793; 14 W.
Main), once the home and office of
physician Belt Brashear. In 1936,
it had the distinction of housing
New Market's first antique shop,
launching a period when it was
known as the "Antiques Capital of
Maryland."

BUCKEYSTOWN

WM10 DANIEL BAKER
HOUSE
c. 1866. 3619 Buckeystown Pike

This unincorporated crossroads
village south of Frederick takes its
name from John Buckey's stone

tavern (c. 1795) at 3624 Buckeystown Pike. The community once
housed such industries as a tannery, a cannery, and a brickyard.
It was primarily the Baker family
who generated Buckeystown's

economic growth through their various business ventures. Today its quiet residential character highlights several fine houses built by the Bakers in the second half of the nineteenth century. Patriarch Daniel Baker's large brick house was built around 1866 on expansive property that once included his brickyards. His son John Baker built a highly fashionable wood Queen Anne house (1896; 3503 Buckeystown) complete with fish scale shingle decoration and a corner tower topped by a bell-shaped roof. Another son, Daniel Baker Jr., lived in a more modest two-story frame cross-gable I-house said to have been built by his father around 1880 (3504 Buckeystown Pike).

The small-scale commercial buildings at the crossroads include McKinna's Store (1890; 7110 Michaels Mill Road), Delashmutt's Store (3532 Buckeystown), a c. 1815 stone building converted into a gas station in the 1930s, and William Baker's Queen Anne office (c. 1896) at 3604 Buckeystown. The village also has two areas of worker housing formerly for employees of the Thomas Brickyard and Buckeystown Cannery. Houses on Buckingham Lane include front-gable houses built c. 1900 on the southeast side by a local carpenter and two-story brick houses on the north. The predominantly Black worker housing settlement on Michaels Mill Road was generally occupied by domestic workers and laborers living in a variety of older structures including some early log dwellings.

POINT OF ROCKS

WM11 POINT OF ROCKS B&O RAILROAD STATION
1873–1875, E. Francis Baldwin. 3800 Clay St.

Marking the end of the Baltimore and Ohio's Metropolitan Branch from Washington, this picturesque station is located at its intersection with the main line to Baltimore. The branch provided a corridor for development that made possible the establishment of suburban and summer resort communities in Montgomery County, beginning in the last quarter of the nineteenth century. Its exuberant High Victorian Gothic design marks it as one of the most distinctive of Baldwin's numerous station designs. Combined with the nearby Chesapeake and Ohio Canal that fueled the early development of the town, the station was part of an important regional transportation hub, offering both passenger and freight service; it remains part of a significant commuter route into Washington.

Lying at the base of South Mountain is Burkittsville, a quintessential nineteenth-century western Maryland crossroads town. It was created in the early nineteenth century, providing needed services for the local agricultural community, and even today remains surrounded by farmlands. Neighbors Henry Burkitt and Joshua Harley sought to take advantage of their location at the intersection of two primary thoroughfares that included Gapland Road, one of the few mountain crossings. Burkitt commissioned a town survey c. 1829, and Harley opened the first general merchandise store and post office combined with a residence, still remarkably intact (c. 1820; 2 W. Main Street). Bearing striking similarity is the former house and tavern (c. 1815; 1 W. Main) that catered to early travelers before operating as a residence and general store from c. 1840 to the early 1980s.

The town included a wide range of light industries along its outskirts. Michael Weiner purchased the tannery established by Joshua Harley, adding blacksmith, cooper, wheelwright, pottery, and carpentry shops. Only a section of the brick and stone tannery office remains, now at the center of 111 W. Main, and Weiner's Federal-period house (1846; 109 W. Main). Reverend Emmanuel Slifer operated a tailor shop in the small building adjacent to his house (c. 1821, c. 1845; 1 and 3 E. Main), and Casper Pfeiffer had a cobbler shop attached to his house (c. 1859; 200 E. Main). Behind George Ennis's distinctive stone house is a log building, likely his blacksmith shop (c. 1805; 198 E. Main). German roots are manifested by the town's German Reformed Church (1830–1831, 1860) at 3 E. Main and the German Lutheran Church (1859) at number 5. The former is now home to the South Mountain Heritage Society.

Post–Civil War, such picturesque houses were erected as that of house carpenter Thomas Karn (c. 1873; 105 W. Main), and two brick Italianate-influenced houses (c. 1870; 100 W. Main and 3 E. Main), as well as St. Johns Chapel (1896) and Rectory (c. 1870) at 101 W. Main.

Industry died out in the post–World War II era and by the end of the century, commercial development had as well, leaving Burkittsville a primarily residential community, yet retaining its character and vibrancy. Burkittsville is also significant as the scene of the September 1862 Civil War Battle of South Mountain.

WM12 DAVID ARNOLD HOUSE
c. 1795; 1873 addition. 108 Gapland Rd.

This stone farmhouse represents an intriguing rural domestic building form particular to central and western Maryland and south-central Pennsylvania that appeared during the second and third quarters of the nineteenth century. The single-pile, gable-roof main block and wing, forming an L-shaped configuration, are joined at the corner with a hip. The gable-and-hipped roof creates the illusion of a much bigger house, when viewed from

Left: David Arnold House (**WM12**). **Right:** War Correspondents Memorial Arch (**WM13**).

that perspective, while presenting formal and service entrance facades visible from the street. This dwelling type was often erected during a single building campaign, but the Arnold House is the result of a later addition to the original hall-parlor house likely built by Burkittsville's founder Joshua Harley. Contributing to its picturesque quality is its coursed rubble stone construction with quoining, extensive porches, and siting within a lush, rolling landscape with stone walls and a whitewashed stone spring house with a finished room above. The farm was the site of the second wave of a Union attack upon Confederate forces at the Battle of South Mountain on September 14, 1862; the bodies of many of the dead are said to be buried in the surrounding fields.

WM13 WAR CORRESPONDENTS MEMORIAL ARCH

1896, George Alfred Townsend. Gapland Rd. at Arnoldtown Rd. in Gathland State Park

Civil War journalist and novelist George Alfred Townsend, who wrote under the pen name "Gath,"

acquired land on South Mountain in 1884 to create a retreat. Parts of the September 1862 Battle of South Mountain, the first major Civil War clash in Maryland, were fought on this property. One of the most unusual constructions Townsend built on his estate over the next decade was a fifty-foot-high memorial arch dedicated to war correspondents killed in combat. The polychrome materials, horseshoe arch, and crenellations across the top suggest popular interpretations of medieval architecture. The lively, asymmetrical composition includes a fifty-five-foot-tall tower with a large niche containing a zinc sculpture of Mercury, the messenger god. Two tablets on the back of the arch list the names of 157 journalists and artists, both northern and southern, collected by Townsend. The property was acquired by the State of Maryland to be Gathland State Park in 1949, and two surviving Townsend buildings have been restored. The War Correspondents Memorial Arch had been transferred to the War Department in 1904 and is administered by Antietam National Battlefield.

Founded in 1767, Middletown is located in the fertile valley between Frederick and Boonsboro, and like many towns in western Maryland, it owes its genesis to an advantageous position along trade routes. However, it was the opening of the interurban electric railway from Frederick that shaped Middletown's growth starting in 1896. Large houses designed in a variety of popular late-nineteenth-century architectural modes, many used as boardinghouses for travelers, were built on newly subdivided lots in a former orchard along E. Main Street, particularly in the 300 and 400 block. The wide setback here is a remnant of the interurban right of way. Bypassed by the new U.S. 40 between Frederick and Hagerstown in 1936 and further placed off the beaten track by construction of I-70 in the 1960s, Middletown is now a bedroom community that retains much of its historic commercial and housing stock.

WM14 BUILDINGS ON WEST MAIN STREET
Mid-19th century–mid-20th century. 12–305 W. Main St.

The commercial area of Main Street has a characteristic mix of early structures located close to the road and altered later. The now stucco-covered building at 12–14 W. Main is a good example of a mid-nineteenth-century log and frame structure with twentieth-century alterations, such as a neon sign for Main's Ice Cream and a c. 1930 addition at the rear for an ice cream plant. The Middletown Valley Historical Society (305 W. Main) is quartered in a restored c. 1840 stone three-bay side-hall building. Perhaps the most visually dominant building in Middletown is Zion Lutheran Church (1859; 107 W. Main) built to serve the many German families in the surrounding farms. The massive Greek Revival church was pressed into service as a military hospital in 1862 to 1863.

WALKERSVILLE

WM15 HERITAGE FARM PARK (HARRIS FARM)
1855. 9236 Devilbiss Bridge Rd.

Encompassing a spacious brick house and several outbuildings that illustrate the period of grain and livestock farming is this farmstead that belonged to a prosperous farmer and two-term member of the Maryland House of Delegates. The construction date is established by a datestone in the house's gable end that includes the initials of original owners Henry Ross Harris and Clarissa Harris. Greek Revival architectural influence is expressed in the transom-light entablature, entrance portico, and small upper-story frieze-band windows, while local building traditions are manifested in the perpendicular ell with two-story inset galleries. Outbuildings include a combination summer kitchen and smokehouse, a brick bank barn with patterned ventilators, and a drive-through corn crib. The property remained in the family until 1932. It was purchased by the town commissioners in 1986 and opened to the public as part of Heritage Farm Park.

WM16 FOUNTAIN ROCK LIME COMPANY
1872 kilns; early-20th-century dwellings. 8511 Nature Center Pl.

This former limestone quarry and kiln complex was developed by retired farmer Adam Diehl, who sought to take advantage of the limestone outcroppings on his property, just as the Frederick Branch of the Pennsylvania Railroad was established to provide easy transport. Lime and other fertilizers were introduced to increase agricultural yields. Spurred by competition to the local grain industry by emerging Midwestern markets, Frederick County became the largest lime-producing region in the state. Fountain Rock operated from 1872 to 1955 and is now a county park. Extant is much of the original eight-pot kiln (*pictured*), banked to provide ready access to the top and bottom openings into which coal fuel was fed and burned lime collected, respectively. Adjacent are the remnants of the lime crusher, sorting shed, limestone quarry, and railroad spur. Also extant are several company-built employee houses, a combination of simple two-story, three-bay log and balloon-frame dwellings. Fountain Rock is among the few extant of the many lime kilns that once operated in the region, commercially and on individual farms.

WOODSBORO

WM17 WOOD MILL FARM
c. 1770; 1830s outbuildings and renovations; 1950s, 1989 restored. 11210 Cash Smith Rd.

This Georgian house is exceptional as a colonial-era survivor and as a sophisticated, substantial brick dwelling, erected in an era of log construction. Its symmetrical five-bay, Flemish-bond brick facade with molded-brick water table, stringcourse, modillioned cornice, hipped roof, and interior end chimneys are classic Georgian. The house was built for John Wood Jr. following his marriage to Ann Reed in 1769. His father John Wood relocated here from Cecil County when this area was still largely unsettled territory. Seeking new opportunities, Wood Sr. was the great-grandson of Augustine Herrman, a merchant and surveyor for Lord Baltimore, and thus considered a gentleman of some standing. Augustine had been compensated with the vast Bohemia plantation. John Jr. was similarly influential, commanding the Frederick Battalion of the Maryland Militia and establishing the nearby town of Woodberry (now Woodsboro). He purchased the property from John Ridout of Annapolis, who, like many, had acquired it as a warrant for investment purposes. The house and farm were later upgraded, including the construction of the brick Pennsylvania bank barn with patterned brick ventilators. The single-story stone kitchen is a rehabilitation of the original, undertaken as part of the latest restoration.

JOHNSVILLE

WM18 HOPEWELL FARM
1818; 1966 addition. 14122 Pearre Rd., 4 miles east of Johnsville

In the same family for over two hundred years, Hopewell Farm consists of the gable-and-hipped-roof house particular to the region, a formal landscaped garden, and a full complement of outbuildings. The house has a symmetrical facade, Flemish-bond brickwork, and an elliptical-arched entrance, and it faces a terraced garden and boxwood allée. The main block possessed formal parlors with exceptional woodwork, while the wing encompassed dining and breakfast rooms, and the basement contained the original kitchen. An isolated guestroom housed an itinerant Methodist minister. Resembling a gambrel-roofed Chesapeake house, the 1966 addition was erected to preserve the integrity of the house while introducing modern amenities. A row of outbuildings includes a dairy, smokehouse, frame privy, carriage house, workshop, and bake house.

Hopewell was built for James and Mary Clemson, whose initials appear in the chimney date-stone and are silhouetted in the north parlor mantel. Their granddaughter Ann and her husband Oliver H. Pearre later renovated the farm, adding the barn and an innovative water system that fed fresh water from a meadow spring through the house to the dairy and barn. Originally raising grain, the farm switched to dairy production c. 1922.

EMMITSBURG

WM19 NATIONAL SHRINE OF SAINT ELIZABETH ANN SETON
c. 1750 Stone House; 1810 White House; c. 1840 mortuary chapel and cemetery; 1962–1965 basilica, Maguolo and Quick. 339 S. Seton Ave.

This basilica and shrine are dedicated to the first American-born person elevated to sainthood by the Roman Catholic Church. Born in New York City, Elizabeth Ann Seton converted to Catholicism and moved to Emmitsburg in 1809 after her husband's death. Here she founded the Sisters of Charity of St. Joseph, the first religious women's community in

what then constituted the United States (an earlier one was in New Orleans), and St. Joseph's Academy, a pioneer in Catholic education. Located adjacent to the shrine property, the former St. Joseph's campus is now the Department of Homeland Security National Emergency Training Center (closed to the public); the National Fallen Firefighters Memorial Park is also located nearby

The grounds of the shrine include the c. 1750 Stone House that served as the first home of the Sisters of Charity, and the White House, Mother Seton's first purpose-built structure with its earliest section dating to 1810. A walled cemetery for the sisters includes a diminutive c. 1840 Gothic Revival brick mortuary chapel with a tall central spire. The Latin cross plan basilica (*pictured above*) is a Byzantine-inspired design with tile roofs, a dome with a drum and narrow clerestory windows over the crossing, and colorful mosaics and marble throughout the interior. It was constructed at the time of Mother Seton's beatification to accommodate large groups of visitors to the site; she was elevated to sainthood by Pope Paul VI in 1975. The National Shrine Grotto of Our Lady of Lourdes, one of the oldest American replicas of the French site, is located off U.S. 15 South at 16330 Grotto Road.

SABILLASVILLE

WM20 TIPAHATO
1906. 17130 Raven Rock Rd.
This summer house commands expansive views from a nine-acre site near the summit of South Mountain. The Western Maryland Railway promoted resort development in this section of the Blue Ridge starting with the establishment of Pen Mar Park in 1878. Nearby Washington County seasonal communities of Highfield and Cascade received regular train service from Baltimore, attracting both day excursions and wealthy city dwellers building summer homes. In 1906 Baltimorean Katherine

Taylor purchased this property and proceeded to build a sizeable summer residence. The house sits on a high basement and is constructed with local rubble stone for the first story and shingled frame above. The interior has spacious entertaining rooms, including a dining room and parlor arranged around a skylit central hall. Although unconfirmed, the architect may have been Taylor's nephew Henry S. Taylor White, a partner in the Baltimore firm of Mottu and White, who inherited the property in 1940.

THURMONT

WM21 CATOCTIN FURNACE
1774–1904. 12607–12714 Catoctin Furnace Rd.

The former company town of Catoctin Furnace is illustrative of the iron industry that developed in this area. The first of three furnaces was erected in 1774 and two more in the 1850s, including the now preserved "Isabella." Representative stone, log, and frame workers' housing remain, including a stone cottage now serving as the Museum of the Iron Worker (c. 1820; 12610 Catoctin Furnace), and the only remaining two-story log house (c.1810, c. 1830; 12607 Catoctin Furnace). The log house once inhabited by the town's collier is now a museum and interpretative center. Both buildings are operated by the Catoctin Furnace Historical Society. Among the items produced here were iron tools, household utensils, and stoves, and its labor force included African American blacksmiths and forge men. Also extant is Fraley's General Store (c. 1900; 12625 Catoctin Furnace). The furnace complex was established by Thomas Johnson of Rose Hill (WM5) and his brothers, James, Roger, and Baker. Operations ceased in 1903.

WM22 CATOCTIN MOUNTAIN PARK (CATOCTIN RECREATIONAL DEMONSTRATION AREA)
1936–1938. 14707 Park Central Rd.

The cabin camp facilities at Catoctin Mountain Park are a product of the New Deal and a tour de force of rustic National Park Service (NPS) architecture. The NPS's Recreational Demonstration Administration (RDA) program reclaimed barren land to create recreation areas for city dwellers; Catoctin was the only RDA in Maryland. Here the cabin camps, associated trails, and outdoor recreation facilities were designed to bring the character-building benefits of group camping to underprivileged children from Baltimore and vicinity. Social service agencies could rent the camp facilities and provide an organized program of sleep-away camp activities in addition to room and board.

The three cabin camps—Misty Mount, Greentop, and Hi-Catoctin—were constructed by relief workers employed through the Works Progress Administration (WPA). Each camp included a cluster of central buildings around a dining hall and multiple cabin units. Camp Misty Mount's buildings arranged along a linear road on a steeply sloping site were leased to the YMCA and YWCA. Camp Greentop (*pictured*) was planned for use by the Baltimore-based Maryland League for Crippled Children. Placed on a much flatter site, the buildings were more closely spaced around a loop road, and many had access ramps. Providing recreational facilities for disabled children was unusual among the RDAs. However, despite lobbying by prominent African Americans leaders, Catoctin did not provide facilities for disabled Black children, and the entire project remained exclusively white.

Typical of the rustic aesthetic being developed at this time by the NPS and others, camp buildings at Catoctin featured local stone, V-notched chestnut logs with concrete chinking, and ac-cents of waney-edged siding with an unfinished edge maintaining the irregular line of the original tree. In 1938 NPS consulting architect Albert Good produced a three-volume edition entitled *Park and Recreation Structures,* which included several Catoctin examples. The informal layout of the administrative cluster and cabin units also reflected the latest thinking regarding organized camp planning and programming to emphasis the natural topography and outdoor play.

The intention was that all forty-six recreation areas be turned over to state or municipal agencies after their completion. Catoctin had a unique fate. In 1942, Camp No. 3, Hi-Catoctin, was subsumed into FDR's presidential retreat Shangri-La, now known as Camp David. By 1954 the original land of Catoctin RDA was divided between three entities. Approximately 5,700 acres, including Camps Misty Mount and Greentop, remained part of the NPS and were incorporated into Catoctin Mountain Park. The southern portion, including about 4,400 acres, became Cunningham Falls State Park.

WASHINGTON COUNTY
HAGERSTOWN AND VICINITY

Since its designation as the county seat in 1776, Hagerstown's position along major roads and the Baltimore and Ohio, Western Maryland, Norfolk and Western, and Cumberland Valley railroads have made it a regional economic center for both western Maryland and nearby parts of Pennsylvania and West Virginia. Although it grew steadily through the nineteenth century, it was manufacturing that launched Hagerstown ahead of Cumberland and Frederick to be the largest city

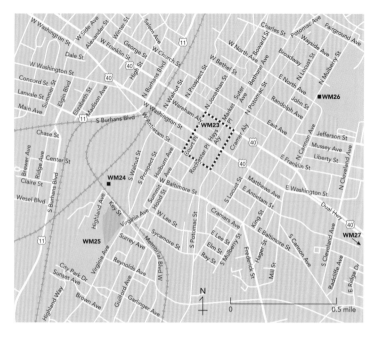

in western Maryland during the early twentieth century. The city's diverse economy included thriving machine shops, steam railroad repair, furniture and organ building, flour mills, and the production of knit goods. Residential development, both upscale and modest, flourished in a growing ring of neighborhoods spreading out from downtown, such as S. Prospect Street, Potomac-Broadway, City Park, Oak Hill, and Jonathan Street (after c. 1900 the Black neighborhood). Like other industrial cities, the economic downturn of the Great Depression and twentieth-century deindustrialization created economic challenges for Hagerstown.

WM23 PUBLIC SQUARE AND DOWNTOWN

Late 19th–early 20th century.
Bounded by Summit Ave./Jonathan St., Franklin, Potomac, and Antietam sts.

The neighborhood around the intersection of Washington and Potomac streets at the Hagerstown Public Square represents the city's commercial core and its exponential growth around the turn of the twentieth century. Washington Street is also U.S. 40, or the former National Road, as it travels through downtown Hagerstown, and Potomac Street is MD 65. Most of the prominent buildings now near this key historic crossroads date from around 1880 to 1930. However, the western anchor for this area is the Washington County Courthouse (1872; 95 W. Washington), a red brick Second Empire building designed by the Philadelphia firm of Sims and Sims. Another key institutional building is the former Washington County Free Library (1901–1902, Bruce Price; 21 Summit), a diminutive Beaux-Arts classical building.

At the public square, the six-story Ramacciotti Professional Arts Building (1936–1937; 1–3 S. Potomac; *pictured*) stands as Hagerstown's most substantial office tower. It was designed by Hagerstown architect Amos J. Klinkhart using a restrained Art Deco idiom for client Domenico Ramacciotti, an Italian immigrant with a produce wholesale business in Hagerstown. Klinkhart also designed the vaguely Colonial Revival Hagerstown City Hall a few years later (1939–1940; 1 E. Franklin).

Several commercial hotel buildings built to serve railroad and automobile travelers are still extant although repurposed for new uses, including the Hotel Dagmar (1910; c. 1929 two upper floors; 50 Summit), an eight-story reinforced concrete structure with simplified Renaissance Revival details; Hamilton Hotel (1880s; 90–96 W. Washington); Colonial Hotel (c. 1910; 57–59 S. Potomac), and the ten-story Colonial Revival Alexander Hotel (1927–1929; 3 E. Washington) on the public square. The elaborate terra-cotta facade of the Colonial Theater (1914; 12–14 S. Potomac) by local architect Harry E. Yessler marks the downtown entertainment district, although the interior has been extensively altered and occupied by a church since the 1970s.

WM24 JONATHAN HAGER HOUSE AND MUSEUM
c. 1740, Jonathan Hager; c. 1745; c. 1944–1954 restored. 19 Key St.

The Hager House is built of random limestone in a traditional four-room, central-chimney German vernacular form referred to as a *Flurkuchenhaus*. Entrance was originally directly into the kitchen, or *Kuche*, with its large cooking fireplace and stair to the upper floors, behind which was originally a smaller storage room and to the other side are the larger *Stube*, or stove room used as a parlor, and a narrow rear *Kammer*, or master bedroom. Also typically German, the house is banked and set on a raised basement over a stream-fed spring to provide running water and cold food storage; and it features mud and straw insulation, original woodwork, paneled walls, and built-in cabinets.

The house is also significant as the home of the town's founder, John Hager, a German immigrant who received a land grant in 1739. In 1762, he laid out a plan for the town that in 1776 became the seat of Washington County. A farmer, miller, and fur trader, Hager gave encouragement to other settlers by opening his house as a trading post. He sold the house in 1745 to Jacob Rohrer, who raised it to a full two stories. It was acquired by the Washington County Historical Society in 1944, restored, given to the City of Hagerstown in 1954, and opened to the public in 1962. A stone museum building housing artifacts discovered during archaeological investigations of the Hager House now sits to the rear.

WM25 HAGERSTOWN CITY PARK

1928–1930s, George Burnap; 1931 museum, Hyde and Shepard. Bounded by City Park Dr., Key St., and Virginia Ave.

Hagerstown Park was created in response to the national urban park and City Beautiful movements and to a period of unprecedented commercial and industrial growth within Hagerstown. Reclaimed land formerly used by light industries was transformed into a picturesque retreat and civic center. Between 1890 and 1930, Hagerstown was the second-largest manufacturing center in Maryland, tripling in population. The area was redeveloped as an upper-middle-class residential neighborhood and 105-acre urban park, while retaining the Greek Revival house (1845) and mill-race as the last remnants of the former Heyser Farm and mill site. Burnap's design featured a spring-fed lake, meandering paths, stone walls, terracing, rustic pavilions, and a classical stuccoed-frame bandshell. Decorative iron gateways mark formal entrances along Virginia Avenue, across from the exuberant Colonial Revival and Queen Anne residences.

Serving as part of the park's civic function, the Beaux-Arts classical Washington County Museum of Fine Arts overlooks the park's lake. A gift to the city from artist William Henry Singer Jr. and his wife, Anna, the museum includes works ranging from nineteenth- and early-twentieth-century American artists to European Old Masters.

WM26 WASHINGTON COUNTY FAIRGROUNDS, ENTRANCE PAVILION AND KEEPER'S RESIDENCE

c. 1890–1910. 412 N Mulberry St.

Among the most intriguing buildings in Hagerstown is the Classical Revival fairgrounds entrance pavilion and attached keeper's residence and offices of the Agricultural and Mechanical Association of Washington County. The association celebrated its twenty-fifth anniversary with the dedication of this sixty-five-acre fairgrounds. Representing the agricultural, industrial, and transportation center of the region, the Great Hagerstown Fair quickly developed a reputation as one of the largest in the eastern United States. Agricultural fairs had been at the heart of

rural America since the early nineteenth century and were a popular draw for large towns. This entrance pavilion stands as a tribute to Washington County's agricultural heyday. It is distinguished by fluted, two-story cast-iron columns that support a modillioned cornice and parapet with a pressed metal sign identifying the association. Appended to one end is the gable-front superintendent's residence connected by a hyphen to the similarly styled offices. Also extant is an extensive 114-unit stock shed, an open, shed-roofed wood structure with exposed rafters, supported by king-post truss posts.

WM27 DOUB'S MILL
Late 18th–early 19th century. 20512 Beaver Creek Rd.

This small, pastoral historic district on the outskirts of Hagers-town features a group of native limestone buildings clustered around Doub's Mill. Now rare, this type of small crossroad settlement focused on a gristmill operation used to be the economic driver for Washington County and the surrounding areas starting in the eighteenth century. The mill is a two-and-a-half-story coursed stone structure on the east bank of Beaver Creek. A two-story limestone dwelling nearby dates to c. 1794, and another two-story, three-bay stone house dates to 1811. The district also includes a one-story outbuilding with the date 1782 inscribed on one stone, a small stone tenant house from the early nineteenth century, a large stone-end bank barn with frame gables, and other farm buildings near the intersection of Cool Hollow and Beaver Creek rds.

BOONSBORO

WM28 INN BOONSBORO
1796; late-19th-century addition. 1 N. Main St.

The founding date of the small Washington County town of Boonsboro is usually identified as 1792, when brothers William and George Boone, cousins of the fa-

mous Daniel Boone, sold the first building lot on subdivided land along the wagon road between Frederick and Hagerstown at the crossroads to Sharpsburg. One of the town's earliest commercial buildings is this one at the northeast corner of the "square" or the U.S. 40 and MD 34 crossroad. The original two-story 1796 stone inn includes a late-nineteenth-century brick expansion to the rear, unified under a slate mansard roof and with a two-story porch.

Subsequent development of various turnpikes and the National Road in the early nineteenth century continued Boonsboro's growth as an important node in the movement of goods and people between Baltimore and western Maryland. Indica-

tive of the linear development typical along the National Road, Main Street (now Alternate U.S. 40) still includes many early-nineteenth-century buildings with later porches and additions that combined commercial and residential use. The former U.S. Hotel (1811; 2 S. Main) was built by physician Ezra Slifer and briefly used as his residence. The retail establishment at 14 S. Main is housed in c. 1802 log building; similarly, the brick building (1821) at 2–6 N. Main has been altered by two early-twentieth-century storefront windows. Boonsboro's prosperity has remained linked to road transportation, shifting to automobile travel in the twentieth century with the construction of U.S. 40, MD 68, and I-70.

KEEDYSVILLE

WM29 RESIDENTIAL AND COMMERCIAL BUILDINGS

1760s–1880s. Main St. from Park Ln. to Alley 10

Keedysville was established by German immigrants as a market town for the local milling industry, situated at the intersection of the Sharpsburg to Boonsboro Turnpike (MD 34) and the Frederick to Williamsport (Keedysville) Road. A section of old Keedysville Road remains intact, as do the connecting, c. 1830 stone arch bridges over Little Antietam Creek. The town began with Jacob Hess's house and mill in 1768, soon followed by nearby Hitt (Pry), Nichodemus, Eakles, and Orndorff mills. Early buildings are of indigenous log and stone construction, reflecting the Ger-

manic traditions of its settlers, including the brick, dual-entrance, gable-and-hip roofed Eversole House (c. 1850; 3 S. Main); the Hess House (c. 1768; 17 S. Main), with its typical three-room plan and a c. 1810 addition; furniture-maker William Carr's asymmetrical stone house (c. 1854; 38 S. Main); and butcher George Snively's stone house (c. 1845; 50 S. Main), with dual entrances into the guest parlor and family kitchen.

The town was renamed for the Keedy family when incorporated in 1873, with the arrival of the Washington County Branch of the Baltimore and Ohio Railroad. The Wyand House Hotel (c. 1874; 2 N. Main St.) was then erected on the town square to accommodate travelers. Picturesque late-nineteenth-century dwell- ings reflect the town's heyday, exhibiting features particular to Keedysville, such as steeply pitched central gables with jig- sawn trim and facades with a bay window to one side only, as at the Hoffman House (c. 1880; 56 S. Main). Many combine a house and business, such as the J. Thom- as house and store (c. 1870; 39 S. Main), and the Wyand house and store (1862; 5 N. Main) that occu- pies the square's northwest corner.

SHARPSBURG

Sharpsburg is best known as the site of the bloodiest battle of the Civil War (in terms of the most casualties in a single day) and the first major engagement on Union soil, fought in 1862. However, Sharpsburg was founded nearly a century prior, in 1763, and by the time of the war it was a thriving commercial center, supporting the local agricul- tural community and with trade and transportation via the nearby Chesapeake and Ohio Canal. The gridded town plan developed by founder Joseph Chapline called for setbacks to form a town square at its crossroads, now occupied by the Masonic Hall and former Kretzer's Market (1887; 100 E. Main Street) and by the Sharpsburg Library and Town Hall (1911; 106 E. Main) built by the International Order of Red Men (IORM).

Most of the early buildings were constructed of logs (hidden under siding), including at least thirty-five extant houses along Main Street. Sharpsburg's architectural highlights include a number of early cut- stone Georgian houses, such as the story-and-a-half William Good House (c. 1780; 107 E. Main), Piper House (1792–1804; 200 E. Main); Kretzer Homestead (c. 1790; 128 E. Main); and the William Chapline House (1789; 109 W. Main). Brick Federal houses followed, represented by the Grove-Delauney House (c. 1820; 100 W. Main). A number of houses are combined with a commercial function, such as that of physician Joseph C. Hays (c. 1823), set back along the town square at 105 W. Main. The wing included his medical office, later a dry goods store and, in 1920, was remodeled as Sharpsburg Bank. Also note- worthy is the Jacob Highbarger House (c. 1832; 201 W. Main), a Greek Revival–influenced limestone house and attached shop built by house carpenter Jacob Highbarger. His shop is a rare example of exposed hewn log construction with corner posts and diagonal bracing.

WM30 TOLSON'S CHAPEL
1866–1867. 111 E. High St.
An African American Methodist congregation built this log and frame church in the immediate aftermath of the Civil War. In 1860, 10 percent of the population of Washington County was Black, with just under half enslaved. The congregation for Tolson's Chapel included both the formerly en- slaved and long-time free Black people. Recognizing the dire need for education, a teacher was hired,

and the chapel used as a school for many decades, as public education opportunities for African Americans continued to be lacking. Starting in 2002, Friends of Tolson's Chapel restored the building and its adjacent cemetery, both designated a National Historic Landmark in 2021.

WM31 ANTIETAM NATIONAL BATTLEFIELD
1890 preservation plan; 1896, 1909 observation tower; 1962 Visitor Center, William Cramp Sheetz Jr. and NPS EDOC. 5831 Dunker Church Rd.

The Battle of Antietam took place on September 17, 1862, amid the agricultural landscape around Sharpsburg. Although the military outcome was technically a draw, Union troops successfully turned back the Confederate incursion into the north and created a political turning point in the Civil War. With generally positive news from Sharpsburg, President Abraham Lincoln proceeded to release the Emancipation Proclamation, which declared all enslaved people in rebelling states freed on January 1, 1863. Notably, this did not include the enslaved in Maryland, which remained with the Union and did not free its slaves until late 1864.

Starting in 1890 the U.S. War Department instituted a preservation and tourism plan for the battlefield. Much of the surrounding land remained in private hands, while the federal government acquired narrow rights-of-way to build a series of tour roads and provide access to key landmarks such as Dunker Church, Lower Bridge (Burnside's Bridge), and the "Bloody Lane." The "Antietam Plan" approach to battlefield preservation was in contrast to the major land acquisition that took place a few years earlier for Gettysburg and Chickamauga battlefields. Intended to be more cost effective while still fulfilling memorialization goals, this approach focused on purchasing narrow strips of land at key areas and leaving the surrounding property in private hands, on the assumption that it would remain agricultural indefinitely. It creates a distinctive tourist landscape of narrow one-way roads through the battlefield. The "Antietam Plan" of minimal land acquisition guided creation of a number of Civil War battlefield parks founded in the early twentieth century such as Appomattox, Petersburg, and Fredericksburg and Spotsylvania County in Virginia.

In addition to moving visitors through the landscape on tour roads, the War Department sought to create elevated vantage points for panoramic views of the battlefield, usually cast-iron observation towers. The substantial 60-foot limestone tower for Antietam (*pictured*) was located next to the infamous "Bloody Lane" battle landmark, a sunken farm lane that became the site of heavy Confederate casualties during a flanking maneuver by the Union troops. Local contractor Jacob Snyder built the original open platform version of the tower, and the pyramidal tile roof was added in 1909.

Visitors to Antietam Battlefield, including Civil War veterans, tourists, and military recruits taking part in training exercises, used the observation tower to experience a bird's-eye view of the landscape. In 1933, Antietam and all the War Department national military parks were transferred to the National Park Service. This section of the battlefield was again reaffirmed as a key focal point in 1962 when the National Park Service built a new visitor center nearby as part of the Mission 66 park infrastructure improvement initiative. The elegant modernist visitor center includes fieldstone walls and an observation platform offering sweeping views of the remarkably preserved battlefield landscape.

WM32 SHERRICK HOUSE
c. 1830. 18108 Burnside Bridge Rd.
The Sherrick House combines period architectural trends with local building traditions. Its five-bay facade and steeply pitched hipped roof identify it as late Georgian, while the emergent Greek Revival is seen in its Doric entrance portico, full-transom entablature, and interior details. Regional flavor is manifested by its double gallery and unusual combination gable-and-hipped roofline. It is one of several like it in Sharpsburg, including the Philip Pry House (1844; 18906 Shepherdstown Pike), Mt. Airy (1862; 17201 Shepherdstown), Remsburg (c. 1863; 6216 Sharpsburg), and Mumma Farmhouse (1863; 5923 Mumma Lane). Sherrick House has a formal front entrance and an informal entrance on the gallery side. Here, the house is banked into the hillside to accommodate a ground-level kitchen above a cellar through which flows a spring for cold food storage. It was built for prosperous farmer Joseph Sherrick and his wife Sarah, who abandoned it during the Civil War for use by Union and Confederate forces as a hospital for the wounded. A brick summer kitchen with half-story loft and remnants of a barn that burned in 1983 sit to the rear. Sherrick House is now owned by the National Park Service as part of Antietam National Battlefield.

WM33 CHESAPEAKE AND OHIO CANAL, CUSHWA WAREHOUSE

c. 1800. 205 W. Potomac St. (Milepost 99.6)

The large two-story brick and frame warehouse at Cushwa's Basin predates construction of the canal. When the canal was completed, the basin created here was one of the few places where a boat could turn around, and so Victor Cushwa put a brick addition onto his frame flour and feed warehouse to accommodate the increased business. Williamsport became a busy port for canal traffic, with many boats lining Cushwa's Basin waiting to unload or load. The Cushwa family dealt in coal, brick, iron, cement, and plaster for many years. Coal was transported inland from here to Hagerstown via the Western Maryland Railroad. The warehouse, painted with "Cushwa's Brick Coal" on the gable end facing the basin, was acquired by the National Park Service in the 1970s. Currently it serves as a visitor's center for C&O Canal Historical Park and a popular access point for the towpath.

WM34 CHESAPEAKE AND OHIO CANAL, CONOCOCHEAGUE CREEK AQUEDUCT

1834–1835, Thomas F. Purcell, engineer. Milepost 99.80

The Conococheague Creek Aqueduct was one of the eleven masonry aqueducts needed to carry the Chesapeake and Ohio Canal over tributaries of the Potomac River. Resident engineer Purcell designed the aqueduct to span Conococheague Creek, and it was built by Michael Byrne and Company using limestone taken from the nearby High Rock Quarry. Because it was built near the prominent canal port of Williamsport, this aqueduct was the most ornate. The 210-foot span is achieved with three arches sheathed with ashlar masonry, and the downstream face of the aqueduct has classical pilasters with capitals at each pier. However, in 1920 the upstream section collapsed due to flooding and was rebuilt in timber. In 2019, a restoration effort, including a new wood upstream face, allowed the aqueduct to be rewatered, making it the first functioning aqueduct on the canal since 1924.

BIG POOL

WM35 FORT FREDERICK STATE PARK

1756–1757; 1934–1937, Washington Reed Jr.; 1975 barracks reconstructed. 11100 Fort Frederick Rd.

Governor Horatio Sharpe requested that monies be appropriated in 1756 to build a substantial square fort with diamond-shaped bastions at each corner to protect the frontier settlers in western Maryland. A stone fort of this ambition was very unusual for the period, especially in such a remote location. Fort Frederick was never used in battle but did periodically garrison troops, house prisoners of war, and provide shel-

ter to local inhabitants from the French and Indian War through the Civil War. By the early twentieth century, the fort walls were in partial ruin, purportedly with some sections still at full height. As reconstructed, the walls are nearly eighteen feet high at their tallest point and consist of three layers of stone, with rubble sandwiched between the outer walls of coursed limestone.

Today Fort Frederick State Park tells the story of the Civilian Conservation Corps (CCC) as much as the original military use. After acquisition to be Maryland's first state park in 1922, the National Park Service assisted with archaeological and archival research. CCC Camp SP-1 began work in 1934 conducting archaeological digs and stabilizing and rebuilding the fort walls, as well as constructing a picnic area and state park administration and service buildings with squared logs and rustic stone chimneys. Using the stone foundations uncovered during the CCC period, two log 200-men barracks (*one pictured above*) facing each other across the parade ground were reconstructed as a Bicentennial project in 1975.

ALLEGANY COUNTY
CUMBERLAND

Founded as Fort Cumberland in 1754 and at the time the westernmost outpost of the British colonies, Cumberland became the county seat of newly created Allegany County in 1789. Its topography and location at the confluence of the Potomac River and Wills Creek made it a major transportation hub. Proximity to the Georges Creek coal mines encouraged industrial growth and residential development for the city, which was incorporated in 1834 and became Maryland's second-largest city by the mid-nineteenth century. Although surpassed by Hagerstown as a regional manufacturing center in the early twentieth century, Cumberland continued to be an important locale for steel, iron, glass, brick, and other manufacturing. The Great Depression and then deindustrialization drastically altered Cumberland's fortunes, as did the loss of historic buildings through urban renewal efforts and the construction of I-68 through the city. The fine quality of surviving historic neighborhoods and buildings are a testament to Cumberland's prosperity in the nineteenth and early twentieth centuries.

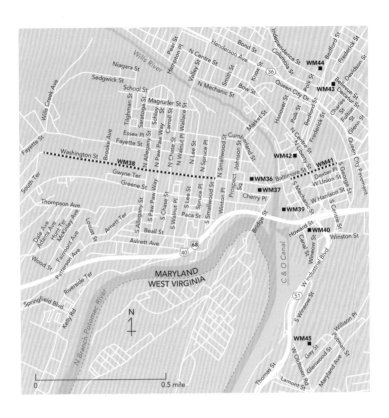

WM36 ALLEGANY COUNTY
COURTHOUSE
*1893–1894, Wright Butler; 1916,
1925 additions. 27 Washington St.*

The six-block stretch of prominent Washington Street comprises some of Cumberland's most significant civic, religious, and residential architecture, including the courthouse, one of Cumberland's most recognized

landmarks. It is a large lavishly ornamented polychromatic design using red brick, stone trim, terra-cotta, and banded red and gray slate. This outstanding Richardsonian Romanesque civic building is a testament to the city's industrial prosperity, designed by a native son. The asymmetrically placed tower is the most striking feature, while the rich Romanesque detailing is a wonderful expression of the civic pride that characterized late-nineteenth-century America. The interior, with its oak wainscoting and open stairway, ornamented tile floors, and stained glass windows, is typical of the period. Early-twentieth-century additions, sensitive in materials and details, flank the building and are set back from the principal facade. To the rear is a complementary, eclectic two-story brick building with parapet end walls and cross-gambrel roof erected as the sheriff's office and jail, now serving as law offices.

WM37 EMMANUEL EPISCOPAL CHURCH AND PARISH HALL

1849–1851, John Notman; c. 1902–1903 Parish Hall, Bruce Price. 16 Washington St.

The most prominent religious building on Washington Street is this church, designed by one of the most important and versatile architects of the antebellum period. Notman's design for Emmanuel Episcopal was ecclesiologically correct, supporting the High Church liturgy advocated by Britain's Oxford Movement. Along with Richard Upjohn, Notman of Philadelphia was the most sought-after designer of such churches.

While simpler than Notman's designs in Philadelphia and Pittsburgh, Emmanuel shares key elements such as stone construction, lancet openings, a large multistage tower and spire, timber roof carried on decorative hammer beams, and defined chancel. It differs in its use of prominent transepts that establish visual grounding for the building's lofty site and separate seating for enslaved and free African American congregants. The Parish Hall, connected via an arcaded passage, was added by Price, who spent his childhood in Cumberland and whose family was among the congregation. In 1905–1906, Louis Comfort Tiffany furnished designs for a new high altar and reredos, altar cross, candelabra, and stained glass windows.

WM38 WASHINGTON STREET RESIDENTIAL AREA

1850–1920. 200–600 blocks Washington St.

Washington Street features an exceptional array of mid-nineteenth- to early-twentieth-century houses, the majority of which maintain high integrity. Along with their verdant surroundings, they provide a rich residential streetscape. It was home to Cumberland's leading citizens including political and judicial representatives, industrialists, engineers, and civic and commercial leaders. Likewise, many houses represent the work of noted local and nationally recognized architects, representing Cumberland's heyday, when the city was the second largest in the state next to Baltimore and an important center of transportation and industry.

Numerous revival styles are represented, such as the Romanesque Revival house (c. 1880; 103–105 Washington) designed by Bruce Price and the Greek Revival house (1845; 201 Washington) built for M. E. Hazlehurst. Second Empire is exemplified by circuit court judge Albert Doub's house (1869; 403 Washington) and attorney Ferdinand Williams's house (1873; 535 Washington). Noteworthy

Queen Anne houses include one designed by George Sansbury (1890; 615 Washington) and others by Wright Butler at 400 (1890) and 412 (1905; *pictured*) Washington. Colonial Revival is well represented by the house designed by New York City architect Edward S. Childs for steel industrialist Walter J. Muncaster (c. 1912; 532 Washington), and the house designed by Herman Schneider for attorney Robert Henderson (1890s; 519 Washington). Italianate is perhaps best exemplified by banker Jonathan Magruder's house (1855; 515 Washington), later owned by George Henderson, superintendent of Cumberland Coal and Iron Company, and the Lucius M. Sheperd house (c. 1875; 508 Washington). Finally, the striking eclectic, stuccoed house (1924) at 531 Washington, with faux thatch roof was designed by Robert Holt Hutchins for Attorney General Thomas B. Finan.

WM39 WESTERN MARYLAND RAILWAY STATION
1913, C. M. Anderson; 1996–2000 restored. 13 Canal St.

Since the unfortunate demolition of the 1871 Baltimore and Ohio Railroad's Queen City Hotel and Station in 1972, this is the only remaining train depot in a city that prospered as a major railway transportation hub. The Western Maryland Railway (WMR) was formed in 1853 to rival the B&O, which arrived in Cumberland in 1852. The WMR ran north and west from Baltimore along the Pennsylvania border yet failed to reach Cumberland until 1906. With limited passenger service, it

hauled coal and freight between West Virginia and Baltimore with a line to Connellsville, Pennsylvania. Known as "Wild Mary," the rail line earned a reputation for extremely fast, efficient, and high-quality service.

The expansive three-story building housed both station and company offices, banked into the hillside, with the covered train platform to the west and business offices to the east. In 1968 it was acquired by the Chessie System (which owned the B&O and the C&O Canal) but closed in 1976. It was rehabilitated as the headquarters of the Canal Place Preservation Authority and the Western Maryland Scenic Railroad. A steam-powered, engine-driven train makes daily runs from here to Frostburg. Sited at the northern terminus of the C&O Canal, the station also welcomes hikers along the towpath as part of the Canal Place Heritage Area created in 1993.

WM40 FOOTER'S DYE WORKS
1906; 2015–2017 renovated. 2 Howard St.

Once part of a sprawling early-twentieth-century industrial complex, the preserved and adapted Footer's Dye Works building represents Cumberland's past lively manufacturing sector. Thomas Footer established his company in Cumberland in 1870. Footer's was a major cleaning and dyeing operation in the Mid-Atlantic, with branch offices in Baltimore, Pittsburgh, and Philadelphia. By the turn of the twentieth century lack of room for expansion at the original site motivated Footer and his sons to build a new complex near the C&O Canal terminus. The company closed after declaring bankruptcy in 1936 due to the Great Depression and an industry shift to favor new dry-cleaning methods over steam cleaning.

The four-story twenty-bay-long brick structure is only two bays wide at its gable ends, with corbeled cornices, belt courses, and quoins adding decoration. Massive painted signs on the west gable end declaring "Footer's Dye Works America's Greatest" were repainted as part of the renovation. In 1997 when the Canal Place Preservation and Development Authority purchased the property, most of the complex had been demolished. The preserved building sits near the Canal Place fairgrounds, the restored Western Maryland Railway Station (WM39), and the C&O Canal National Historical Park. Renovated using federal and state historic preservation tax credits, Footer's Dye Works now houses residential units on the upper floors and offices and retail, including a brew pub, on the lower. A one-story sawtooth roof addition at the south elevation suggests the original demolished in 2009.

WM41 BALTIMORE STREET COMMERCIAL BUILDINGS AND PEDESTRIAN MALL
c. 1875–1978. Baltimore St. between George and Mechanic sts.

Downtown Cumberland's main commercial thoroughfare, Balti-more Street, was converted into a pedestrian mall in 1978 in an urban renewal effort to revitalize the shopping district. Still lined with many of the city's finest commercial structures, the street encapsulates decades of architectural progress financed by Cumberland's commercial success. The east end of the pedestrian mall at George Street features former department stores including Schwarzenbach's (1911, Wright Butler; 128 Baltimore) and Rosenbaum's (c. 1900, John S. Seibert; 118 Baltimore). Each facade employs distinctive materials, with orange brick Romanesque decoration for Rosenbaum's and large areas of glazing framed by elegant copper spandrels and cornices for Schwarzenbach's,

The short block between Liberty and Centre streets has two of Cumberland's most prominent banks. The Liberty Trust Bank (c. 1910; 81 Baltimore), one of the tallest buildings in the vicinity at seven stories, was designed by local architect Wright Butler. Next door the Romanesque Revival Second National Bank (1880s; 71 Baltimore) is a tour-de-force of carved brownstone detail and orange brick, standing in contrast to the more reserved red brick Liberty Trust. Designed by Cumberland native Bruce Price at the height of his career as a celebrated New York City–based architect, the three-story facade employs a lively stylized floral decorative scheme at the openings and gable roof parapet.

Several buildings were stylishly updated with ground-level storefronts in the mid-twentieth century. The former YMCA building (1893–1910; 145 Baltimore) was converted into the Peskin's shoe and clothing store in 1940, complete with a new recessed ground-floor display area, limestone panels on the ground floor, and neon signs. The retail front of the former Cumberland Arms Hotel (1917) at 10 N. Liberty Street, now an apartment building, has a mid-twentieth-century storefront modernization with glass curved at its corners and black Vitrolite. The former Spear's Jewelry shop (c. 1940) in one of the hotel's storefronts at 62 Baltimore features an Art Deco recessed storefront renovation topped by a shell-like zigzag cove ceiling. Another impressive Art Deco building is the Embassy Theater (c. 1932–1933; 49 Baltimore), designed as a motion picture theater by architects Hodgens and Hills of Philadelphia.

WM42 CUMBERLAND CITY HALL
1911–1912, Holmboe and Lafferty, with Wright Butler. 76 Frederick St.

City Hall sits at the center of Cumberland's downtown public building complex and replaced an earlier structure that burned in 1910. The building was designed by the prolific Clarksburg, West Virginia, firm of Holmboe and Lafferty with Butler supervising construction. Curved corners appear at the two irregular sides of the lot, and paired fluted pilasters frame the round-arched opening at the central bay of each elevation; otherwise the exteriors have plain walls with simple cornices and balustrades. Plans for a grander two-story dome were reduced due to budget concerns, but

the interior is centered around a columned rotunda painted with murals by Gertrude du Brau. The murals depict scenes from the early history of Cumberland, including George Washington's military service.

Nearby at 35 Fredrick is the classical Public Safety Building, formerly the U.S. Courthouse and Post Office (1902–1904, James Knox Taylor, Supervising Architect of the U.S. Treasury) and the Colonial Revival Bell Tower Building (24 Frederick), built c. 1884 as a police station house and jail.

WM43 METROPOLITAN AME CHURCH
1892. 309 Frederick St.

This congregation was established in 1847 when the free Black worshippers at Centre Street Methodist Episcopal Church decided after many years of being segregated in the balcony that it was time to build their own sanctuary. A simple brick building was erected by 1848 and enlarged twice during the 1870s to accommodate a growing post-emancipation membership. In 1892 the current brick church replaced the earlier structure. It follows the common Methodist plan comprised of a worship space on the second floor of a gable-front building with meeting spaces below. The interior is plain, with three sections of curved pews facing the altar. Metropolitan AME is part of the Decatur Heights National Register Historic District, an early neighborhood in northeast Cumberland that gradually became predominantly African American. In addition to many vernacular houses, the district includes the former Carver School (1921; 340–344 Frederick), the designated Black regional high school until desegregation of local schools in 1955.

WM44 TOWN CLOCK CHURCH (GERMAN EVANGELICAL LUTHERAN CHURCH)
1848–1849, Harry Schmenner; John Hassel, builder. 312 Bedford St.

This relatively austere, classical church was built by German Lutherans to accommodate the influx of German settlers to Cumberland during the mid-nineteenth century. Originally part of the St. Paul's congregation, this group separated in order to maintain sermons in their native German. The town donated the land and offered a clock to the first of two German religious faiths competing to erect new edifices, lending the church its name. Legend has it that the Lutherans won because the women of the congregation provided torches to enable construction into the night. The church's prominence within the city skyline is established by its hilltop location and soaring four-part tower that encompasses the clock, belfry, and spire. The church was designed by a member of the congregation. The interior comprises a narthex, nave, and raised chancel, with a balcony that features one of the oldest working Opus No. 36 Moller organs extant.

WM45 KLOTS MILL LOFTS (KLOTS THROWING MILL)
1902–1903, Lansing C. Holden Sr; 2010–2011 renovated. 917 Gay St.

Located in south Cumberland in a residential neighborhood of small workers' houses, Klots Throwing Mill is a surviving example of the once-prevalent industrial presence in the city. Built as a silk-thread spinning mill employing mainly women, as was typical in the textile industry, the Cumberland plant was one of two owned by the company in Maryland. The second in Lonaconing was built in 1907 and still stands, albeit in ruined condition. The two-story, brick and timber frame Cumberland mill housed silk vaults and soaking facilities in the basement, offices on the first floor, and drying rooms on the second. Behind a firewall the larger windows and double-gable roof demarcate the production areas, which had machinery shafting in the basement, spinning on the first floor, and winding and doubling on the second. New York City architect and businessman Lansing C. Holden Sr. was the architect for a one-story 1909 repair shop addition on the south (demolished), and the National Register nomination attributes the rest of the mill to him.

The Klots Mill was adjacent to

the main B&O line with its own spur line, which facilitated delivery of raw materials and fuel for the steam boilers and shipping of completed product. Additional Klots mills were located in Pennsylvania, Virginia, and Massachusetts, for a total of fourteen plants and six thousand employees during the company's heyday in the late 1920s. Klots went into bankruptcy in 1932, and the mill was used to manufacture a variety of fabrics in later decades. Textile production halted in 1972, and the building was used for storage until conversion into low-to-moderate-income loft apartments.

OLDTOWN

WM46 MICHAEL CRESAP HOUSE

c. 1764; c. 1781 addition. 19015 Opessa St.

This house is significant for its early regional architecture and its association with noted frontiersman Michael Cresap. Oldtown was created in 1741 as a pioneering village and trading post by Cresap's father, Thomas, to help establish Maryland's claim to the region, operating under directions from Lord Baltimore's agent, Daniel Dulany. Located near an abandoned Shawnee village along the Nemacolin Trail (now a protected archaeological site), it was then the only settlement in Maryland west of the Potomac River. Michael Cresap was a noteworthy pioneer in his own right, clearing land and building roads to encourage settlement. He was captain of the first Maryland troops to join General Washington in a campaign against the French to maintain hold of the region. George Washington recorded his visit to this house in his diary.

In the German tradition, the house is built of indigenous stone and banked into the hillside over a spring to provide water and cold food storage. It contains two rooms per floor with a winding staircase rising from basement to attic. A nonconnecting brick section was later appended. The house was saved from demolition by the Reverend Irvin Allen, who purchased it in 1961, restoring it as a museum. It sits just north of the Chesapeake and Ohio Canal, Canal Lock 70, and a lockkeeper's house (c. 1849 canal, c. 1900 house).

WM47 OLDTOWN TOLL BRIDGE

1937–1938. Greenspring Rd. across the Potomac River

Just beyond the C&O Canal is the Potomac River and a toll bridge providing ready access to Greensprings, West Virginia. It was built by Melvin R. Carpenter, a tie inspector for the B&O Railroad who was motivated by the need to make regular trips into Greensprings that would otherwise require a ferry or a car ride to the nearest bridge 15 miles away. The 200-foot-long, 10-foot-wide bridge is built of steel beams resting on concrete pilings and carrying a roadbed of oak planks custom-made at a local sawmill. A toll booth still collects a fee for use; it is the only privately owned toll bridge in the state.

WM48 CHESAPEAKE AND OHIO CANAL, PAW PAW TUNNEL

1836–1841, 1848–1850, Ellwood Morris and C. B. Fisk, engineers. Milepost 155

One of the major engineering feats of the Chesapeake and Ohio Canal, and of its time, was the construction of the 3,118-foot-long Paw Paw Tunnel to avoid a 6-mile stretch of arduous terrain. The tunnel's construction, begun in 1836, involved excavating from the north and south portals, as well as drilling four vertical 8-foot-diameter shafts from above for ventilation and removal of spoils. Work ceased in 1841 and did not resume until November 1848, with new contractors. Paw Paw Tunnel has a 24-foot-wide opening with portals framed by limestone entablatures and is composed of a brick-lined barrel arch with a 12-foot radius. A 4-foot-wide brick towpath runs along one side of the canal bed. This impressive passageway is still used by bicyclists and hikers on the towpath.

FLINTSTONE

WM49 BREAKNECK VALLEY

Mid-18th to early 20th centuries. Breakneck Rd. NE, from Messick Hollow Ln. NE to Murley's Branch Rd. NE

Breakneck Valley forms a near-pristine landscape of family farms built within a rolling, picturesque vale flanked by mountain ridges offering spectacular views. The landscape reflects the survival and ongoing use of a pioneering agricultural settlement begun during the last quarter of the eighteenth century. The farms were established by English, Scots-Irish, and French settlers, most of whom migrated from Frederick County, growing wheat, oats, potatoes, and corn. The early houses were of log construction, with the majority now of timber frame, dating from the early to mid-nineteenth century. They were built in a local vernacular to encompass two-story, gable-roof configurations with stone foundations and chimneys, front porches, and rear ells with double galleries. Typical is the oldest remaining log house, the Captain George Robinette House (c. 1790) at 18300 Messick Hollow Lane NE. The Henry A. Jamison House (c. 1842; 10300 Murley's Branch Road NE) is a small log dwelling with a later timber frame section, and the Moses Robinette House (c. 1835; 18300 Breakneck Road NE) is notably of plank construction. More stylish and of brick construction are the Greek Revival–influenced George Tanner Robinette House (c. 1845; 11507 W. Wilson Road NE) and the five-bay classically styled

Rose Hill Farm house (c. 1845; 12301 W. Wilson NE) built by Jeremiah Berry. Balloon-frame, L-shaped farmhouses appeared during the late nineteenth century, of which the Summerfield Hinkle house (1902; Murley's Branch at Breakneck) is the most intact and elaborate. The farms likewise comprise noteworthy barns, summer kitchens, and other outbuildings.

LA VALE

WM50 LA VALE TOLL GATE HOUSE

1835–1836; 1960s restored. 14302 National Hwy. (Alternate U.S. 40)

The La Vale Toll Gate House is a surviving example of an early tollhouse built along the National Road, the first federally built highway, constructed between 1811 and 1818. Controversy about use of federal funds and growing competition from the B&O Railroad and C&O Canal prompted the federal government to turn the National Road over to the respective states in the early 1830s. Maryland accepted its portion in 1835; it then quickly established a toll rate schedule and began building tollhouses. Located approximately six miles west of Cumberland, this one was the first erected by the state.

The road gradually fell into disrepair as toll revenue fell short and railroad transportation became dominant in the region. The State of Maryland turned the road over to the relevant counties in 1878. In 1925 portions of the National Road, including the section in La Vale, were incorporated into the construction of U.S. 40. The Toll Gate House was preserved and restored in the late 1960s, becoming a rare survivor of its type. The seven-sided building features a distinctive two-story polygonal section with more conventional one-story wings extending from the rear and side. Tollhouses in the Pennsylvania section of the National Road exhibit a similar polygonal form, differentiating these small-scale public buildings from their domestic neighbors.

MOUNT SAVAGE

WM51 UNION MINING COMPANY BUILDING

c. 1910. 15905 Foundry Row NW

Erected to house the Mount Savage offices of the Union Mining

Company, this building is among the finest examples of the distinctive glazed brick for which the town was known. It is also one of the few tangible remnants of the once-thriving industries responsible for the establishment of Mount Savage. The building features a mix of multishaded brick with belt course and water table and such distinctive features as a large Syrian-arched entranceway and low pyramidal roof with eyebrow dormer. A rich deposit of mineral fire clay was first discovered here in 1839. The Mount Savage Fire Brick Works started production in 1841, making bricks for blast smelting and other such purposes. Incorporated as the Union Mining Company in 1864, it was engaged in brickmaking as well as coal mining; it operated as the Mount Savage Refractories Company from 1944. Although limited refractory brick production continues, the building was donated to the Mount Savage Historical Society in 2008.

seen in industrial buildings of this region, featuring Renaissance-inspired motifs and multishaded, locally produced brick, with contrasting brick jack-arch lintels and faux frieze-band windows under a modillioned cornice. Train service was discontinued in the 1940s, and the building was acquired by the Mount Savage Refractories Company. Just beyond it are two one-story stone structures built as the railroad's machine and carpenter shops, and the glazed-brick powerhouse, oil house, and blacksmith shop. The office building is now being used as a storage facility.

WM52 CUMBERLAND AND PENNSYLVANIA RAILROAD COMPANY OFFICE BUILDING
1901. Northwest of 15905 Foundry Row NW on a dirt road

By the mid-nineteenth century, Mount Savage was the center of a railroad operation run by the Cumberland and Pennsylvania that included transport of both industrial goods and passengers, with trains arriving and departing eight times a day for Cumberland and Piedmont. This building was erected as their Mount Savage headquarters. It displays a level of ornamentation not often

WM53 OLD ROW MUSEUM
c. 1842. 12911 Old Row Rd.

This is the only remaining of twenty-two, plank-constructed semidetached units built by the Maryland and New York Iron and Coal Company to house the Irish laborers brought here to work. Housing was a significant element of company paternalism, necessitated by the fact that Mount Savage and other industrial towns like it in Allegany County were developed in isolation, established specifically to exploit the region's natural resources. Vertical-plank construction was once common to western Maryland and southwestern Pennsylvania as an easy and effective mode of construction. Heavy planks running the height of the building were pegged or nailed to the sills, eliminating the need for complex joinery, studs, and cross-bracing. This unit is now a rare survivor, among the earliest uses of plank construction in the region. It sits on a raised stone basement, banked to conform to the hilly terrain, with entrances at the ground-level kitchen and to either side of the first story, where porches run the length of the facade, sharing a massive central chimney.

The duplex faces Jennings Run and the remnants of the company's iron furnace complex. The first heavy wrought-iron rails produced in America were manufactured here in 1844–1846, linking the town to Cumberland and facilitating its industrial development. It was later the site of the Mount Savage Refractories firebrick yard. The museum interprets the history of the town's industries and worker life.

WM54 THE CASTLE

c. 1870; 1909 additions. 15925 Mt. Savage Rd.

Built for Alexander Thompson, physician for the Mount Savage Iron Works, this house was expanded by Andrew Ramsey, general manager of the Mount Savage Enameled Brick Company. Ramsey trained in the pottery, brick, and enamel brick works of England before immigrating to Mount Savage in 1895. Here he developed a method for firing and glazing brick used in the production of Mount Savage's specialized enameled brick, which appeared throughout the country, including the New York City subways. In 1909, novelty brick and tile was used to construct the house's verandas and porches, and the house was raised and a wing added to incorporate a kitchen, sunken library, and skylit ballroom. While no longer produced, Ramsay's enameled brick can still be seen in the Mullaney Brothers Five-and-Dime Store (c. 1910; 12708 Cobblestone Road) and the former P. A. Fannon Variety Store (c. 1910; 15615 Main Street).

FROSTBURG

WM55 MAIN STREET BUILDINGS

1890s–1950s. Main St. (Alternative U.S. 40) between Water and Depot sts.

Frostburg was settled in 1812 by the Frost family, who in 1817 laid out a gridded town plan in anticipation of the arrival of the National Road in 1818. Although begun as a tavern and stagecoach stop, it grew as the commercial center of the Georges Creek Coal Region and later as a college town. Mining began in the area about 1810, gaining momentum by midcentury. From 1850 to 1910, Georges Creek was one of the richest coal mining regions in the nation. The Frostburg Coal Company was established here in 1845 and by 1900 was absorbed by the Consolidation Coal Company, among the largest in the nation. Aided by

the ironmaking and brickmaking industries, the town's most prosperous years were 1880 to 1920. Unlike most towns in the coal region, Frostburg was not built as a company town, and by the late nineteenth century it attracted tourists seeking fresh mountain air, with accommodations such as the eclectic Gunter Hotel (1897, J. N. Campbell; 11 W. Main; *pictured above*).

Main Street consists mostly of early- to mid-twentieth-century brick commercial buildings erected following a devastating fire in 1917, with stone detailing, banded windows, and ornamental brick and pressed-metal cornices. Exemplary of these are the former Durst Furniture Store (1919; 2 E. Main), Betz Grocery (1919; 4 E. Main), and Prichard's Hardware (1919; 6 E. Main). Of those that survived the fire, noteworthy is John U. Paul's Hall (1876; 20 E. Main), later the Lyric Theater; the Classical Revival Frostburg National Bank (1910; 2 W. Main); and the Colonial Revival brick U.S. Post Office (1912; James Knox Taylor, Supervising Architect of

the U.S. Treasury) at 37 W. Main, with full-height round-arched windows. A modern insertion in this street is the enameled-brick former Hafer Furniture Building (c. 1930; 23–25 E. Main). On the Frost homestead site is the Gothic Revival St. Michael's Catholic Church (1868; 44 E. Main), the Rectory (1871), and the Ursuline Sisters convent (1906).

The greatest driver of Frostburg's economy today is Frostburg State University, which began as State Normal School No. 2, in the Renaissance Revival Old Main building (1899; 65 E. College Avenue).

WM56 BORDEN MINES SUPERINTENDENT'S HOUSE
c. 1850. 18201 Mount Savage Rd. NW

Albert C. Greene, superintendent of the Borden Mining Company from 1850 to 1882, lived in this Italian Villa just north of Frostburg. Greene's residence emphasized the labor hierarchy of the surrounding coal-mining community, with the fine house on a hill occupied by upper management.

The L-shaped plan of the house is arranged around a three-story entrance and stair hall tower at the center, topped by a pyramidal roof with bracketed eaves. The house departed from local building traditions to follow, with minor variations in plan and elevation, Design XXII "Villa in the Italian Style" published in A. J. Downing's widely popular architectural pattern book *The Architecture of Country Houses* (1850).

Greene successfully managed the Borden Mining Company through the economic and labor turmoil of the Civil War and its aftermath, making it one of the most successful coal mining operations in the region. The Borden family chartered the company in 1846 to supply coal for their varied manufacturing interests in Fall River, Massachusetts. Greene had moved from Rhode Island to manage the Borden mines, which transported coal primarily via the C&O Canal to the port in Alexandria, Virginia. Thus, the fashionable superintendent's house signifies the presence of national business and transportation interests in Allegany County.

LONACONING

WM57 OLD STONE HOUSE
1790, John Van Buskirk. 15519 Old Coney Cemetery Rd.

This is one of the oldest positively dated houses in the region and among the few built of stone during a period when most domestic buildings were of crude log construction. Like many in this mountainous region, the house is banked into the hillside on a raised basement to include a ground-level kitchen entrance with the primary entrance to the street-level front. The house is built of irregularly coursed stone with decorative lintels, quoining, and interior end chimneys. It follows a traditional German three-room plan with a large room with fireplace and enclosed stair adjoining two smaller rooms with a shared chimney.

Owner John Van Buskirk was an early settler to the region, possibly one of many to receive land in exchange for military service. In 1843, he opened his house to a Redemptorist priest from Baltimore, Father John Neumann, who offered in-home Catholic Mass to German immigrant farmers and miners. The house sits on the extension of the old Legislative Road, the primary early route between Frostburg and Lonaconing.

WM58 LONACONING IRON FURNACE
1837–1839; 1976 restored. Furnace Park, E. Main St. at Bridge St.

Emblematic of the significance this region once held in the nation's iron industry is its only remaining iron furnace. Known historically as George's Creek Coal and Iron Company Furnace No. 1, it was the first furnace in the country to successfully demonstrate the use of coke and raw bituminous coal to fuel iron production. Smelting and casting began here in 1839, producing goods such as stoves, agricultural implements, machine parts, and dowels for the C&O Canal's lock walls. In 1845, it was leased to German-born engineer Christian E. Detmold, who developed a method of using furnace gases to heat the blast, producing about 2,500 tons of pig iron per year. Depletion in iron ore deposits caused operations to cease in 1856. Nonetheless, it provided the model for others in western Maryland.

Along with Mount Savage and Frostburg, Lonaconing formed the center of iron production in Allegany County. In fact, the presence of the iron furnace was the basis for its establishment as a company town, which now proudly displays the restored structure within a community park. The fifty-foot tall cut stone and brick furnace is set against a hillside retaining wall to facilitate the loading of ore and coal from the top into the firebrick-walled furnace chamber. Molten iron was discharged through the alcove at its base, while the flanking tunnels provided access to the furnaces, steam engines, boilers, and air compressors.

Adjacent is the unusually decorative Georges Creek Coal and Iron Company Office Building (c. 1840; 7–9 Park Street) that originally housed offices and boarded miners. It is significant as one of the earliest mining-related structures in the region, built for one of its first company towns, established in 1837.

GARRETT COUNTY

OAKLAND

WM59 GARRETT COUNTY COURTHOUSE
1907–1908, James Riely Gordon. 3 E. Alder St.

By the turn of the twentieth century Garrett County had outgrown its original 1877 courthouse. The county commissioners purchased an elevated site at the center of town for the new courthouse and invited five architectural firms to submit designs. After his selection as a finalist, Gordon, then working with the firm of Tracy and Swartwout in New York City, convinced the courthouse committee that his plan could be achieved for under $70,000, and he won the commission.

Gordon's extensive experience with courthouse design likely encouraged the committee to select him. Before relocating to New York City in 1902, Gordon worked in Texas, where he designed sixteen courthouses, mainly Richardsonian Romanesque in style, a specialty he continued in the early twentieth century for courthouse commissions in several states before shifting to a Beaux-Arts classical approach. The approved design for Garrett County Courthouse falls into the latter group of courthouses. Here the Indiana limestone and buff-colored pressed brick building is arranged around a domed rotunda at the crossing of its cruciform plan. The long rear wing of the courthouse was banked into the hillside on the east. The original terraces and stair leading to the main entrance were removed for the c. 1977 construction of county offices and a new jail; the roof of this structure now forms a plaza in front of the courthouse. Inside the rotunda the otherwise plain plastered dome interior is pierced by a ring of oval skylights draped with glazed terra-cotta festoons.

WM60 BALTIMORE AND OHIO RAILROAD STATION
1884, Baldwin and Pennington. 117 E. Liberty St.

This is one of the most exuberant of the B&O's many stations designed by the company's principal architects, responsible for over a hundred stations. Oakland is one of the first and most decorative surviving examples of their Queen Anne designs. Architecturally fashionable stations such as this were integral to the company's resort development, which was strongly promoted by the company's president, John W. Garrett. Primarily intended to link Baltimore with the Ohio River and the growing trade in the west, the B&O proved a significant boost to suburbanization and tourism, with several resort and religious revival communities emerging within proximity of the line. As an indication of how vital the railroad was to the development of the county, it was named for its president. Oakland was surveyed in 1849 in anticipation of the railroad's arrival in 1851, and it became the seat of Garrett County when it was established in 1872. This exceptionally well-preserved station is now a public museum and education center.

MOUNTAIN LAKE PARK

WM61 MOUNTAIN LAKE PARK RESORT BUILDINGS

1881–c. 1920. Roughly bounded by the B&O Railroad tracks, Youghiogheny Dr., Oakland Ave., and D St.

Mountain Lake Park was established as a "Mountain Chautauqua" and summer resort made possible by the extension of the B&O Railroad into western Maryland. It is the best preserved of numerous such resort communities,

located on a high plateau known as The Glades. The resort was laid out by landscape architect and civil engineer Augustus Faul, who was the superintendent of Druid Hill Park (BC101) in Baltimore from 1863 to c. 1890 and who developed the park's first comprehensive plan in 1870. A grid plan is intersected by curvilinear roads conforming to the contours of the land, a picturesque scheme accentuating Mountain Lake Park's peaceful rural seclusion. It was founded by Methodist ministers who sought to create a blending of religious revivalism and cultural and educational activities enhanced by fresh mountain air. The Chautauqua operated for nearly sixty years as one of most important centers of religious and cultural activity in the state. The last Chautauqua was held in 1941, when Mountain Lake Park became a purely residential community. Many of the structures associated with the Chautauqua have been lost, yet extant are the tabernacle (1882; 600 Spruce Street) and the eight-sided ticket office (1900; 301 G Street).

There are over two hundred extant Queen Anne and Gothic Revival cottages indicative of the resort architecture of the period, exhibiting irregular massing, towers, board-and-batten and clapboard walls, fish scale shingles, wraparound porches, and bargeboards. Among the most exuberant examples of Gothic Revival houses, all built roughly between 1881 and 1910, are those at 502 Allegheny Drive, the board-and-batten cottage at 25 G Street, the houses at 113 and 201 I Street, 412 Dave Turney Street, and 309 M Street. Representative examples of Queen Anne are at 22 G and 912 Allegheny; and of Colonial Revival at 105 and 113 G.

DEER PARK

WM62 PENNINGTON COTTAGE

c. 1889, Baldwin and Pennington. 65 Deer Park Hotel Rd.

In 1873, B&O Railroad president John Garrett opened the Deer Park Hotel designed by E. Francis Baldwin (c. 1942 demolished), drawing seasonal visitors to the area. Deer Park became the first and most exclusive resort in the region. Garrett had been advocating for development of summer resorts along B&O lines in western Maryland since the 1860s, but progress was delayed by the Civil War. The scenic beauty and healthful climate of southern Garrett County attracted visitors from Baltimore and such other major cities as Washington and Philadelphia. Deer Park especially drew many dignitaries during its late-nineteenth-century hey-

day, including President Grover Cleveland, who honeymooned in cottage number 2 in 1886.

While the hotel, railroad station, and resort amenities such as tennis courts and a golf course are no longer extant, a handful of cottages in popular Queen Anne or Shingle Style modes remain along a curving drive and speak to Deer Park's history. Nineteenth-century resort hotel proprietors commonly sold lots for construction of personal cottages, but surviving examples of this pattern are rare.

One of the most impressive survivors is Pennington Cottage, designed by and for architect Josias Pennington. Along with senior partner Baldwin, Pennington's firm designed many buildings for the B&O Railroad, including the hotel and cottages at Deer Park.

Pennington Cottage stands three stories on a raised stone foundation, with a tall gambrel roof, wraparound porch, and shingled siding. The surviving Deer Park cottages, while designed for summer leisure, convey the formal lifestyle and status of their late-nineteenth-century residents with their impressive scale, elevated siting, and fashionable ornament. The local springs supplied the pools at the hotel and also drinking water for B&O passengers; later acquisition of this operation led to use of the Deer Park town name as a bottled water brand.

ALTAMONT

WM63 OUR FATHER'S HOUSE
1933–1934. MD 135 at Old Wilson Rd.

This log building, a rustic interpretation of the once ubiquitous rural parish church, was built to serve summer residents and vacationers from Deep Creek Lake. The land and timber for the church were donated by seasonal residents and built by local farmers and B&O Railroad workers. Used by both groups, the church is referred to as "God's outpost in the Allegheny Mountains." It is built of dark-stained saddle-notched chestnut logs with heavy, contrasting white chinking. The gable-front nave adjoins a rear chancel and tower with such rustic touches as gable-front door hoods held by brackets and cross-bracing and a stone chimney. The interior consists of a single, sparsely decorated room with bench seating for forty. There is no running water or heating, and it is still dependent on an outhouse for the convenience of its worshippers.

ACCIDENT

WM64 KAESE MILL
1868, Henry August Kaese. 373 Fish Hatchery Rd.

Kaese Mill, built by a miller who emigrated from Germany, is now a rare survivor of the once-plentiful gristmills erected in Garrett County between the 1860s and the 1920s. With a large portion of the county's residents engaged in grain farming, mills served as a necessary component of the local economy and as the focal point for town development. Of the two dozen mills that once stood in nearby towns, only this mill and Stanton's Mill (WM69) still stand.

Kaese Mill is a gabled-front, frame, water-powered mill, banked into the hillside along Bear Creek, where the wood flume and millrace are still extant. Its original wood overshot wheel was replaced c. 1900 by an iron wheel manufactured by the Fitz Water Wheel Company of Hanover, Pennsylvania. This mill was the last fully operational water-powered gristmill in Maryland, remaining in use by Kaese's descendants until recent decades. The interior amazingly retains its nineteenth- and early-twentieth-century milling equipment including stone burrs, steel rollers, sifters, grain chutes, hoppers, and scale. As a center of economic and social activity in this sparsely populated, self-sustaining agrarian community, Kaese Mill also served as the local post office, meeting place, and exchange point for bartered goods.

WM65 JAMES DRANE LOG HOUSE

c. 1798; c. 1810 addition; 1991–1994 restored. Old Cemetery Rd., 0.1 miles north of Accident Bittinger Rd.

Built by the area's first permanent settler, this log house is likely the oldest standing structure in Gar-rett County and is emblematic of western Maryland's pioneering era. As a frontier cabin, it was erected when the rutted Brad-dock Road built in 1755 to facilitate military maneuvers was the only overland route. The town of Accident was surveyed for Lord Baltimore in 1774, yet the area remained largely unsettled until the 1840s influx of Germans. Easily and quickly erected from indigenous materials, log dwellings comprised most of the housing in this region prior to the mid-nineteenth century. Drane's house is constructed of hewn logs held by V-notch joints combined with later heavy timber framing. Also common was its two-room, hall-parlor plan, to which was later appended a separate kitchen and stone end chimney. Drane was a farmer from Prince George's County who attempted to introduce tobacco culture to the area, purchasing the property from his brother-in-law, Colonel William Lamar, in 1798. The house was purchased by the Town of Accident in 1987 as a landmark in the early history of western Maryland, restored, and, beginning in 1994, opened by appointment. James and his wife Pricilla are buried in the adjacent cemetery.

GRANTSVILLE

WM66 CASSELMAN INN

c. 1842. 113 Main St.

The Casselman Inn is one of the most intact survivors of the numerous inns that once appeared along the National Road through western Maryland. Still functioning as a restaurant and inn, this two-and-a-half-story brick structure has a double-pile, center-hall plan expanded with a dining room/kitchen ell to the rear. Other extant former National Road inns and taverns that survive but have been altered to various degrees include the Four Mile House (c. 1840; 520 Old U.S. 40) in La Vale, the Flintstone Hotel (c. 1807; 21998 Old U.S. 40), also in Allegany County, Hagan's Tavern (c. 1830; 5018A Old U.S. 40) in Frederick County, and the Tomlinson Inn (c. 1818; 12871 Old U.S. 40) on the outskirts of Grantsville.

WM67 CASSELMAN BRIDGE
1813. 10240 U.S. 40 Alternate (National Pike) in Casselman River Bridge State Park

Casselman Bridge represents the technical achievements required to complete the National Road between Cumberland and the Ohio River during the early National period. Rugged terrain presented a significant challenge to the transport of goods and the early commercial development of this mountainous region. A signature engineering achievement of its day, the bridge was the largest single-arch stone span in the United States at the time of its completion, stretching 48 feet between abutments. The total span of nearly 360 feet brought the National Road across the Casselman River in what is now Garrett County.

Portions of the old National Road became the right-of-way for U.S. 40 in 1925, but the Casselman Bridge was by-passed entirely after 1933. Small sections of the original road are preserved as part of Casselman River Bridge State Park. Wilson's Bridge (1819; Silas Harry builder; Independence Road), another more typical early National Road stone arch bridge with five spans, has been preserved as a small park where it crosses Conococheague Creek seven miles west of Hagerstown.

WM68 PENN ALPS INN AND SPRUCE FOREST ARTISAN VILLAGE
c. 1818; late 19th century altered; c. 1957. 125–177 Casselman Rd.

This mid-twentieth-century roadside attraction along U.S. 40 began as an early-nineteenth-century log dwelling later used as a tavern and inn. The inn was modified in the late nineteenth century into a two-and-a-half-story structure with Italianate detailing. This section faces old U.S. 40 (now Casselman Road) to the north and is still partially visible embedded within the various twentieth-century commercial additions.

Around 1957 Dr. Alta Schrock left her job as a biology professor and acquired the property to develop the Penn Alps Restaurant and craft store and the adjacent Spruce Forest Artisan Village. A March 15, 1964, *New York Times* article enthused that "the handiwork one finds here, plus the low prices and the unspoiled, uncluttered mountain scenery, makes one wonder if Penn Alps is part of the modern world." While committed to the preservation of traditional regional handicrafts through the nonprofit Penn-Alps Association, Schrock shrewdly expanded her operation over the decades, using the restaurant and festivals as a draw.

The adjacent village of around a dozen log and frame buildings was created gradually by building cabins from historic materials and techniques or moving historic structures to the site. It provides workshops for a variety of artisans creating traditional crafts such as baskets, pottery, and bird carvings. One of the first structures, the log Winterberg House (1820), was moved from nearby Grantsville in 1967 to become a demonstration studio for spinning and weaving. One of the oldest structures on-site is the Markley House (c. 1775) a two-story log house disassembled and rebuilt at Spruce Village in the late 1980s. Bear Hill School, a frame one-room schoolhouse in service from 1913 to 1952, was moved from Jennings, Maryland, in 1994 to become a woodturning shop.

WM69 STANTON'S MILL
c. 1859; c. 1900 addition. 84 Casselman Rd.

Some portions of an original 1797 foundation survive within the current mill rebuilt c. 1859 as a heavy timber-frame building on a coursed sandstone foundation. This five-bay section was expanded c. 1900 by a two-bay frame addition. The mill was still in operation until 1994, making it one of the longest continuously operating mills in Maryland. In 2002 the Penn Alps Association entered into an agreement with a Kentucky miller to restore and reopen the mill. A reproduction high breastshot waterwheel was installed, but the historic milling equipment is largely operated by electricity. Stanton Mill's products are sold at the Penn Alps store (see WM68).

WM70 NEW GERMANY STATE PARK
1936–1939. 349 Headquarters Ln.

Civilian Conservation Corps Camp S-52 built one of Maryland's earliest state parks on farmland acquired through Resettlement Administration funding. Maryland state officials generally were slow to embrace the New Deal but welcomed the forestry and recreation work performed by CCC enrollees. Dedicated July 1, 1939, New Germany State Park offered a campground, a superintendent's residence and park office, ten log cabins, and picnic shelters, all executed in the rustic manner popularized by the National Park Service. The log cabins with stone chimneys and foundations are arranged in a deliberately informal manner along a road at the south end of the lake. The lake at New Germany was a remnant of the Swauger family's nineteenth-century saw- and gristmill operation that originally dammed Poplar Lick Run. A few late-nineteenth- and early- twentieth-century wood buildings from the former village of New Germany are still extant in the park, including a former doctor's office and a school.

The undertaking of this book was significantly enhanced by the wealth of resources available through the Maryland Historical Trust (MHT), the state's historic preservation office. First and foremost are the online databases of the Maryland Inventory of Historic Properties forms (https://mht.maryland.gov/mihp/) and Maryland's digitized collection of National Register of Historic Places and National Historic Landmarks nominations (https://mht.maryland.gov/nr/). This includes numerous multiproperty nominations that provide context for themes such as tobacco barns, National Road inns, maritime resources, Baltimore's cast-iron buildings, and Rosenwald schools (https://mht.maryland.gov/nr/NRMPSList.aspx). In addition, MHT's extensive research library includes vertical files on select sites, searchable online at http://m30014.eos-intl.net/M30014/OPAC/index.aspx. As well as a long practice of funding individual county architectural histories and survey results that were extremely valuable, MHT undertook preliminary identification of sites for inclusion in the Maryland BUS volume including draft entries for select counties.

Other major statewide institutions with essential research collections include the Maryland State Archives, with significant primary records such as land records, historic maps, and special collections relating to Maryland history and searchable through an online finding aid (http://aomol.msa.maryland.gov/html/index.html). The Maryland Center for History and Culture (formerly the Maryland Historical Society) in Baltimore has an extensive research library and archive, with online resources available at https://www.mdhistory.org/online-resources/. The organization's journal, *Maryland Historical Magazine* (https://www.mdhistory.org/publications/maryland-historical-magazine-online/) was a valuable resource for many topics and sites.

In Baltimore, the Baltimore Architecture Foundation collections were instrumental in learning about and representing many of Maryland's foremost architects, particularly their Architect Biographies (http://baltimorearchitecture.org/2016/11/10/architect-biographies/). The Enoch Pratt Free Library is another Baltimore-based institution with important statewide history collections housed at the Central Branch, including those in the Maryland and Special Collections departments (https://www.prattlibrary.org/locations/central). The Baltimore City Archives is accessible through an online index of resources (https://msa.maryland.gov/bca/research-at-the-baltimore-city-archives/the-historiography-of-baltimore-city/ii-city-of-neighborhoods-1850-1950/index.html). The City of Baltimore's Commission for Historical and Architectural Preservation (CHAP), founded in 1964, maintains records on local historic districts, among other topics. For African American history in Baltimore the Baltimore Civil

Rights Heritage website is a useful source (https://baltimoreheritage .github.io/civil-rights-heritage/1885-1929/).

Outside of Baltimore, county historical societies or preservation offices provided resources and unpublished records unavailable elsewhere, as did some municipalities. The City of Frederick funded thematic architectural, agricultural, and industrial contexts particularly useful in evaluating and selecting numerous sites in the Western Mountain chapter (https://www.cityoffrederickmd.gov/Document Center/View/495/History-of-Architecture?bidId=).

At the federal level Maryland encompasses thirteen Heritage Areas that highlight publicly accessible historic sites considered for inclusion in the book (https://mht.maryland.gov/heritageareas.shtml). The Harriet Tubman Underground Railroad National Historical Park includes sites important to African American history (https:// www.nps.gov/hatu/index.htm). Finally, the records of the Historic American Buildings Survey, Historic American Engineering Record, and Historic American Landscapes Survey of the National Park Service, and its online Library of Congress Collection (http://www.loc .gov/pictures/collection/hh/) offer almost ninety years of survey and documentation in Maryland.

African American Historic and Cultural Resources in Prince George's County, Maryland. Upper Marlboro: Maryland–National Capital Park and Planning Commission, February 2012.

Alexander, Robert L. "Architecture and Aristocracy: The Cosmopolitan Style of Latrobe and Godefroy." *Maryland Historical Magazine* 56, no. 3 (Fall 1962): 229–43.

Baker, Nancy T. "Annapolis, Maryland 1695–1730." *Maryland Historical Magazine* 81, no. 3 (Fall 1986): 191–209.

Beirne, D. Randall. "Hampden-Woodbury: The Mill Village in an Urban Setting." *Maryland Historical Magazine* 100, no. 4 (Winter 2005): 446–67.

Bergengren, Charles. "Pennsylvania German House Forms." In *Architecture and Landscape of the Pennsylvania Germans, 1720–1920,* edited by Nancy van Dolsen, 23–46. Harrisburg, Pa.: The Vernacular Architecture Forum, 2004.

Blumgart, Pamela James, ed.

At the Head of the Bay: A Cultural and Architectural History of Cecil County, Maryland. Elkton, Md.: Cecil Historical Trust, Inc.; Crownsville: Maryland Historical Trust Press, 1996.

Bodenstein, William G. "St. Michaels, Maryland: An 18th-Century Speculative Development." *Maryland Historical Magazine* 8, no. 3 (Fall 1985): 228–39.

Bourne, Michael O. *Historic Houses of Kent County: An Architectural History, 1642–1860.* Chestertown, Md.: Historical Society of Kent County, 1998.

———. *Inventory of Historic Sites in Caroline County.* Annapolis: Maryland Historical Trust, 1980.

Bourne, Michael, Orlando Ridout V, Paul Touart, and Donna Ware. *Architecture and Change in the Chesapeake: A Field Tour on the Eastern and Western Shores.* Newark, Del.: Vernacular Architecture Forum; Crownsville: Maryland Historical Trust Press, 1998.

Breihan, Jack. "Necessary Vision:

Community Planning in Wartime." *Maryland Humanities* 71 (November 1998): 11–14.

Brewington, B. V. *Chesapeake Bay.* New York: Bonanza Books and Cornell Maritime Press, 1953.

——. *Chesapeake Bay Sailing Craft.* Calvert Marine Museum and Chesapeake Bay Maritime Museum. Portland, Maine: Anthoensen Press, 1986.

Brown, C. Christopher. *The Road to Jim Crow: The African American Struggle on Maryland's Eastern Shore, 1860–1915.* Baltimore: Maryland Historical Society, 2016.

Brugger, Robert J. *Maryland, a Middle Temperament, 1634–1980.* Baltimore: Johns Hopkins University Press and Maryland Historical Society, 1988.

Carr, Lois B. "The Metropolis of Maryland: A Comment on Town Development along the Tobacco Coast." *Maryland Historical Magazine* 69, no. 2 (Summer 1974): 124–45.

Carroll, Kenneth L. "Religious Influence on the Manumission of Slaves in Caroline, Dorchester, and Talbot Counties." *Maryland Historical Magazine* 56, no. 2 (1961): 182–83, 190.

Carson, Cary. "The 'Virginia House' in Maryland." *Maryland Historical Magazine* 69, no. 2 (Summer 1974): 146–68.

Carson, Cary, and Carl R. Lounsbury, eds. *The Chesapeake House: Architectural Investigation by Colonial Williamsburg.* Chapel Hill: University of North Carolina Press, in association with Colonial Williamsburg Foundation, 2013.

Chalfant, Randolph W., and Charles Belfoure. *Niernsee and Neilson, Architects of Baltimore: Two Careers on the Edge of the Future.* Baltimore: Baltimore Architecture Foundation, 2006.

Cronin, William B. *The Disappearing Islands of the Chesapeake.* Baltimore: Johns Hopkins University Press, 2005.

de Gast, Robert. *The Lighthouses of the Chesapeake.* Baltimore: Johns Hopkins University Press, 1973.

Dilts, James D. *The Great Road: The Building of the Baltimore and Ohio, the Nation's First Railroad, 1828–1853.* Stanford, Calif.: Stanford University Press, 1993.

Dodds, Richard J. *Solomons Island & Vicinity: An Illustrated History and Walking Tour.* Solomons, Md.: Calvert Marine Museum, 1995.

Dodds, Richard J., and Robert J. Hurry. *It Ain't Like It Was Then: The Seafood Packing Industry of Southern Maryland.* Solomons, Md.: Calvert Marine Museum, 2006.

Dodds, Richard J., and Pete Lesher, eds. *A Heritage in Wood: The Chesapeake Bay Maritime Museum's Small Craft Collection.* St. Michaels, Md.: Chesapeake Bay Maritime Museum, 1992.

Dorsey, John, and James D. Dilts. *A Guide to Baltimore Architecture.* 3rd ed. Centreville, Md.: Tidewater Publishers, 1997.

Downing, A. J. *Architecture of Country Houses.* New York: Dover, 1969, reprint.

Dudley, William S. *Maritime Maryland: A History.* Baltimore: Johns Hopkins University Press, 2010.

Ellis, Clifton. "Close Quarters: Master and Slave Space in Eighteenth-Century Annapolis." In *Slavery in the City: Architecture and Landscapes of Urban Slavery in North America,* edited by Clifton Ellis and Rebecca Ginsburg, 69–86. Charlottesville: University of Virginia Press, 2017.

Emory, Frederic. *Queen Anne's County, Maryland.* Queenstown, Md.: Queen Anne Press, 1981.

Farquhar, Roger Brooke. *Old Homes and History of Montgomery County, Maryland.* Brookeville, Md.: American History Research Associates, 1962.

Fee, Elizabeth, Linda Shopes, and Linda Zeidman, eds. *The Baltimore Book: New Views of Local*

History. Philadelphia: Temple University Press, 1991.

Fields, Barbara Jeanne. *Slavery and Freedom on the Middle Ground: Maryland during the Nineteenth Century.* New Haven, Conn.: Yale University Press, 1987.

Fly, Everett, and La Barbara Wigfall Fly. *Northeastern Montgomery County, Blacks Oral History Study.* Entourage, Inc. Rockville, Md.: Montgomery County Department of Housing and Community Development, 1983.

Forman, Henry Chandlee. *Early Manor and Plantation Houses of Maryland.* 2nd. ed. Baltimore: Bodine and Associates, 1982.

Fuke, Richard Paul. "Planters, Apprenticeship, and Forced Labor: The Black Family under Pressure in Post-Emancipation Maryland." *Agricultural History* 62, no. 4 (Autumn 1988): 57–60.

Getty, Joe. *Carroll's Heritage: Essays on the Architecture of a Piedmont Maryland County.* Westminster, Md.: Carroll County Commissioners and Historical Society of Carroll County, 1987.

Gibbons, Sheila J. Arenstam, and Robert J. Nicholls. "Island Abandonment and Sea-Level Rise: An Historical Analog from the Chesapeake Bay, USA." *Global Environmental Change* 16, no. 1 (February 2006): 40–47.

Gournay, Isabelle. "Context Essay—Modern Movement in Maryland (Draft)." N.d. http://mahdc.org/ma/wp-content/uploads/2017/02/Historic-Context-Modern-Movement-in-Maryland.pdf.

Harvey, Katherine A. "The Lonaconing Journals: The Founding of a Coal and Iron Community, 1837–1840." *Transactions of the American Philosophical Society* 67, no. 2 (1977): 1–78.

Hayward, Mary Ellen. *Baltimore's Alley Houses: Homes for Working People since the 1780s.* Baltimore: Johns Hopkins University Press, 2008.

Hayward, Mary Ellen, and Charles Belfoure. *The Baltimore Rowhouse.* New York: Princeton Architectural Press, 1999.

Hayward, Mary Ellen, and Frank R. Shivers Jr., eds. *The Architecture of Baltimore: An Illustrated History.* Baltimore: Johns Hopkins University Press, 2004.

Headley, Robert K. *Motion Picture Exhibition in Baltimore: An Illustrated History and Directory of Theaters, 1895–2004.* Jefferson, N.C.: McFarland, 2006.

Holland, Celia. *Old Homes and Families of Howard County, Maryland.* [Catonsville, Md.]: C. M. Holland, 1987.

Holland, F. Ross. *Maryland Lighthouses of the Chesapeake Bay.* Crownsville: Maryland Historical Trust Press, 1997.

Johnson, Paula J., ed. *Working the Water: The Commercial Fisheries of Maryland's Patuxent River.* Charlottesville: University Press of Virginia, 1988.

Kapsch, Robert J. *Canals.* New York: W. W. Norton, 2004.

Kelly, Clare Lise. *Montgomery Modern: Modern Architecture in Montgomery County, Maryland, 1930–1979.* Silver Spring: Maryland–National Capital Park and Planning Commission, 2015.

King, Julia, Christine Arnold-Lourie, and Susan Shaffer. *Pathways to History: Charles County, Maryland, 1658–2008.* Mount Victoria, Md.: Smallwood Foundation, 2008.

Kotarba, Kathleen G., and W. Edward Leon, eds. *Baltimore City's Designated Landmark List, 2003.* Baltimore: Commission for Historical and Architectural Preservation, Department of Housing and Community Development, 2003.

Kytle, Elizabeth. *Home on the Canal.* Baltimore: Johns Hopkins University Press, 1996.

Ladew, Marilynn. *Bel Air: An Architectural and Cultural History,*

1782–1945. Bel Air, Md.: Town of Bel Air, 1995.

Lane, Mills. *Architecture of the Old South: Maryland*. New York: Abbeville Press, 1991.

Lavoie, Catherine, and Marcia Miller, eds. *A Shared Heritage: Urban and Rural Experience on the Banks of the Potomac; A Field Guide for the Western Shore of Maryland*. Crownsville: Vernacular Architecture Forum and Maryland Historical Trust Press, 2018.

Legler, Dixie, and Carol M. Highsmith. *Historic Bridges of Maryland*. Crownsville: Maryland Department of Transportation State Highway Administration and Maryland Historical Trust Press, 2002.

Longstreth, Richard, ed. *Housing Washington: Two Centuries of Residential Development and Planning in the National Capital Area*. Chicago: Center for American Places at Columbia College, 2010.

MacMaster, Richard, and Ray Eldon Hiebert. *A Grateful Remembrance: The Story of Montgomery County, Maryland, 1776–1976*. Rockville, Md.: Montgomery County Government and the Montgomery County Historical Society, 1996.

Maryland Historical Trust. *Inventory of Historic Sites in Calvert County, Charles County, and St. Mary's County*. Annapolis: Maryland Historical Trust, 1973, repr. 1980.

Maryland National Park and Planning Commission, Historic American Buildings Survey, Historic American Engineering Record, National Park Service. *Landmarks of Prince George's County*. With architectural photographs by Jack E. Boucher. Baltimore: Johns Hopkins University Press, 1993.

Maryland State Road Commission. *A History of Road Building in Maryland*. Baltimore: State Roads Commission of Maryland, 1958.

McDaniel, George W. "Voices from the Past: Black Builders and Their Buildings." In *Three Centuries of Maryland Architecture: A Selection of Presentations Made at the 11th Annual Conference of the Maryland Historic Trust*, 86–87. [Crownsville]: Maryland Historical Trust Press, 1982.

McGrain, John W. *From Pig Iron to Cotton Duck: A History of Manufacturing Villages in Baltimore County*. Vol. 1. Towson, Md.: Baltimore County Library, 1985.

McWilliams, Jane Wilson. *Annapolis, City on the Severn: A History*. Baltimore: Johns Hopkins University Press; Crownsville: Maryland Historical Trust Press, 2011.

Menard, Russell R. "The Maryland Slave Population, 1658 to 1730: A Demographic Profile of Blacks in Four Counties." *William and Mary Quarterly* 32, no. 1 (1975): 29–54.

Messner, William. "A Certain Kind of Freedom: Black Agency in Talbot County, 1870–1910." *Maryland Historical Magazine* 114, no. 2 (Fall/Winter 2019): 187–201.

Miller, Marcia, and Orlando Ridout V, eds. *Architecture in Annapolis: A Field Guide*. Crownsville: Vernacular Architecture Forum and Maryland Historical Trust, 1998.

Olson, Sherry H. *Baltimore: The Building of an American City*. Revised and expanded Bicentennial Edition. Baltimore: Johns Hopkins University Press, 1997.

Pennington, James W. C. "The Fugitive Blacksmith, 1849." In *Great Slave Narratives*, selected and introduced by Arna Bontemps, 193–268. Boston: Beacon Press, 1969.

Porter, Frank W., III. "From Backcountry to County: The Delayed Settlement of Western Maryland." *Maryland Histori-*

cal Magazine 70, no. 4 (Winter 1975): 329–49.

Raitz, Karl, ed. *A Guide to the National Road*. Baltimore: Johns Hopkins University Press, 1996.

Ranzetta, Kirk E. *I'm Goin' Down County; An Architectural Journey through St. Mary's County*. Crownsville: Maryland Historical Trust, 2010.

Reed, Paula S., and Associates. "Mid-Maryland: An Agricultural History and Historic Context." Frederick, Md.: Catoctin Center for Regional Studies, 2003.

Reps, John W. *Tidewater Towns: City Planning in Colonial Virginia and Maryland*. Williamsburg, Va.: Colonial Williamsburg Foundation with University Press of Virginia, 1972.

Ridout, Orlando IV. *Building the James Brice House, 1767–1774*. Annapolis: Maryland State Archives, 2013.

Rivoire, J. Richard. *Homeplaces: Traditional Domestic Architecture of Charles County*. La Plata: Southern Maryland Studies Center, Charles County Community College, 1990.

Rountree, Helen C., Wayne E. Clark, and Ken Mountford. *John Smith's Chesapeake Voyages, 1607–1609*. Charlottesville: University of Virginia Press, 2007.

Seng, Joseph F. *Back When: The Story of Historic New Market, Maryland*. Westminster, Md.: Heritage Books, 2005.

Sharp, Henry K. *America's First Factory Town: The Industrial Revolution in Maryland's Patapsco River Valley*. Baltimore: Chesapeake Book Company, 2017.

———. *The Patapsco River Valley: Cradle of the Industrial Revolution in Maryland*. Baltimore: Maryland Historical Society, 2001.

Shaw, Diane. "Building and Urban Identity: The Clustered Spires of Frederick, Maryland." In *Gender, Class, and Shelter: Perspectives in Vernacular Architecture V,* edited by Elizabeth Collins Cromley

and Carter L. Hudgins, 55–69. Knoxville: University of Tennessee Press, 1995.

Stover, John F. *History of the Baltimore and Ohio Railroad*. West Lafayette, Ind.: Purdue University Press, 1987.

Striner, Richard, and Melissa Blair. *Washington and Baltimore Art Deco: A Design History of Neighboring Cities*. Baltimore: Johns Hopkins University Press, 2014.

Sween, Jane C. *Montgomery County: Two Centuries of Change*. Woodland Hills, Calif.: Windsor, 1984.

Touart, Paul Baker. *Along the Seaboard Side: The Architectural History of Worcester County, Maryland*. Snow Hill, Md.: Worcester County Commissioners, 1994.

———. *At the Crossroads: An Architectural History of Wicomico County*. Crownsville: Maryland Historical Trust Press, 2008.

———. *Somerset: An Architectural History*. Annapolis: Maryland Historical Trust, 1990.

Unrau, Harlan D. *Historic Resource Study: Chesapeake & Ohio Canal*. Prepared by Karen M. Gray. Hagerstown, Md.: U.S. Dept. of Interior, National Park Service, Chesapeake & Ohio Canal National Historical Park, 2007.

Virta, Alan. *Prince George's County: A Pictorial History*. Prince George's County Chamber of Commerce. Virginia Beach, Va.: Donning, 1984.

Ware, Donna. *Anne Arundel's Legacy: The Historic Properties of Anne Arundel County*. Annapolis: Office of Planning and Zoning, Anne Arundel County, 1990.

Ware, Donna M., et al. *Green Glades and Sooty Gob Piles: The Maryland Coal Region's Industrial and Architectural Past*. Crownsville: Maryland Historical Trust, 1991.

Warner, William W. *Beautiful Swimmers: Watermen, Crabs, and the Chesapeake Bay*. 2nd ed. Boston: Little, Brown, 1994.

Warren, Marion E., and Michael P. McCarthy. *The Living City: Baltimore's Charles Center and Inner Harbor Development*. Baltimore: Maryland Historical Society, 2002.

Weeks, Christopher. *An Architectural History of Harford County, Maryland*. Baltimore: Johns Hopkins University Press, 1996.

——, ed. *Between the Nanticoke and the Choptank: An Architectural History of Dorchester County, Maryland*. Baltimore: Johns Hopkins University Press and Maryland Historical Trust, 1984.

——. *The Building of Westminster in Maryland: A Socio-architectural Account of Westminster's First 250 Years, Including an Illustrated Inventory of Over 200 Historic Structures*. Annapolis: Fishergate, 1978.

——. *Where Land and Water Intertwine: An Architectural History of Talbot County, Maryland*. Baltimore: Johns Hopkins University Press and Maryland Historical Trust, 1984.

Westmont, V. Camille, Dennis J. Pogue, Melissa Butler, and Elizabeth Totten. "The Rossborough Inn on the University of Maryland Campus: Two Centuries of Change." *Maryland Historical Magazine* 114, no. 2 (Fall/Winter 2019): 153–85.

Zembala, Dennis M., ed. *Baltimore: Industrial Gateway of the Chesapeake Bay*. Baltimore: Baltimore Museum of Industry, 1995.

Zucker, Kevin. "Falls and Stream Valleys: Frederick Law Olmsted and the Parks of Baltimore." *Maryland Historical Magazine* 90, no. 1 (Spring 1995): 72–96.

⇛ ILLUSTRATION CREDITS ⇚

CMH-LC Carol M. Highsmith Archive, Prints and Photographs Division, Library of Congress
HABS Historic American Buildings Survey, Prints and Photographs Division, Library of Congress, Washington, D.C.
HAER Historic American Engineering Record, Prints and Photographs Division, Library of Congress, Washington, D.C.
MHT Maryland Historical Trust

Photographs not otherwise credited are by Lisa Pfueller Davidson and Catherine C. Lavoie.

Maps by Nat Case, INCase, LLC.

FRONT MATTER AND INTRODUCTION

Page x, HABS, Renee Bieretz, photographer; page xiv, Willie Graham, photographer; page 2, photograph by A. Aubrey Bodine (Image 14-027); page 5, Geography and Map Division, Library of Congress, Washington, D.C. (Item G3880 1670.H4); page 6, photograph by A. Aubrey Bodine (Image 15-068); page 7, courtesy of the B&O Railroad Museum; pages 8–9, Panoramic Photographs, Prints and Photographs Division, Library of Congress, Washington, D.C. (Items LC-USZ62-45070, LC-USZ62-45071, LC-USZ62-45072); page 11, photograph by A. Aubrey Bodine (Image 29-148); page 13, photograph by A. Aubrey Bodine (Image 25-011); page 15, The Miriam and Ira D. Wallach Division of Art, Prints and Photographs, New York Public Library; page 16, Prints and Photographs Division, Library of Congress, Washington, D.C. (Item LC-DIG-pga-08152); page 17, HABS, James W. Rosenthal, photographer

WESTERN SHORE

Page 20, HABS, Justin R. Scalera, photographer; WS19 Willie Graham, photographer; WS21 CMH-LC; WS36 HABS, Justin R. Scalera, photographer; WS40, WS42 HABS, Jarob J. Ortiz, photographer; page 54, HABS, Jack E. Boucher, photographer; WS47, WS49, WS52, WS56, WS57 HABS, Jarob J. Ortiz, photographer; WS59, WS60, WS62, WS71, WS73, WS75 HABS, Justin R. Scalera, photographer; WS80 CMH-LC; WS86 MHT

EASTERN SHORE

ES10 Christopher Marston, photographer; ES33 CMH-LC; ES36 HABS, Renee Bieretz, photographer; ES40, ES46 Willie Graham, photographer; ES48 James A. Jacobs, photographer; page 116, HAER, Mark Harrell, photographer; page 119, photograph by baldeaglebluff, CC BY SA2.0

BALTIMORE CITY

BC1 HABS, Jarob J. Ortiz, photographer; BC7 CMH-LC; BC13 HABS, Jarob J. Ortiz, photographer; BC20 HABS, James W. Rosenthal, photographer; BC25, BC27, BC28 HABS, Justin R. Scalera, photographer; BC29, BC31, BC33, BC35, BC39 HABS, Jarob J. Ortiz, photographer; BC42 HABS, James W. Rosenthal, photographer; BC45, BC47, BC50, BC53, BC54 HABS, Justin R. Scalera, photographer; BC57 CMH-LC; BC64, BC71 HABS, Justin R. Scalera, photographer; BC76 photograph by Smallbones, CC0 1.0; BC79 CMH-LC; BC84, BC87, BC88, BC99 HABS, Justin R. Scalera, photographer; BC112 photograph by John Margolies, John Margolies Roadside America photograph archive (1972–2008), Library of Congress, Prints and Photographs Division, Washington, D.C. (Item LC-DIG-mrg-00459); BC114 HABS, James W. Rosenthal, photographer

CENTRAL MARYLAND

CM1, CM2, CM6, CM34 HABS, Jarob J. Ortiz, photographer; CM38 HABS, James W. Rosenthal, photographer; CM45 Mark Mones, photographer; CM80 MHT, Christopher Weeks, photographer

CAPITAL REGION

Page 306, National Archives, Still Picture Branch; CR41 HABS, Jack E. Boucher, photographer; CR42 CMH-LC; page 325, State of Maryland, Maryland Transportation Authority, all rights reserved; CR62 CMH-LC

WESTERN MOUNTAINS

WM2, WM4, WM7 HABS, Justin R. Scalera, photographer; WM13 CMH-LC; WM23, WM24, WM26 HABS, Justin R. Scalera, photographer; WM38 Chris Stevens, photographer

BACK MATTER

Page 380, HABS, Jarob J. Ortiz, photographer; pages 388, 426, HABS, Justin R. Scalera, photographer

☇ INDEX ☇

Note: Properties named for individuals or families with a given surname are indexed in the form *surname (first name)*. For buildings or structures of the following types, please see these grouped entries: airports; almshouses; apartments and condominiums; aquariums; aqueducts; art galleries; arts centers; automobile dealerships; banks; barns; bridges; bungalows; campgrounds; canals; cemeteries; Chesapeake houses; churches, chapels, and cathedrals; city halls; clubhouses; colleges and universities; commercial buildings; community centers; cottages; courthouses; cultural centers; dams; dance halls; double houses; duplex houses; fairgrounds; farms; fire stations; five-part Palladian houses; forts and military installations; gardens; gas stations; grain elevators; historic districts; hospitals; hotels, inns, and motels; house museums; industrial buildings; iron furnaces; jails and prisons; libraries; lighthouses; lockhouses; log buildings; Masonic buildings; mills; mixed-use developments; monasteries and convents; monuments and memorials; movie theaters; museums; national battlefields; national parks; office buildings; parks and squares; pedestrian malls; planned communities; plantations; post offices; public buildings; public housing; public utilities; Quaker meetinghouses; railroads; railroad stations; recreational facilities; rectories; residential districts; resorts; restaurants; roads and highways; Rosenwald schools; row houses; school buildings; scientific facilities; shopping centers; shotgun houses; slave houses; social halls; sports facilities; state parks; synagogues; taverns; theaters and concert halls; tobacco barns; tobacco warehouses; toll gate houses; towers; transportation facilities; tunnels; visitors' centers; YMCA buildings; zoos. Page numbers in **boldface** refer to illustrations (listed by building names and under specific architects/firms and styles).

Abell House, Avondale, Solomons, 41
Abingdon, 275–76
abolitionism, 10, 84, 125, 127, 227, 283
Academy House (Bratt House), Oxford, 120
Accident, 376–77
Accokeek, 289–90
Acton Hall, Annapolis, 68–69, **69**, 70
Adamesque style, 55, 59, 72, 170, 180, 215, 287
Adams, William, 70
Adams-Kilty House, Annapolis, **70**, 70
AECOM, 76
African American residents and history: abolitionism, 10, 84, 125, 127, 227, 283; Abraham Hall, Beltsville, 303; African Academy, Baltimore City, 227; Baltimore City, 10, 150, 153; Banneker (Benjamin) Cabin, Oella, **255**, 255–56; Beall-Dawson House, Rockville, 305; Bel Air Historical Colored High School, 271; Benning Road Historic District, Galesville, 81–82; Black life and culture, 10–12; Buckeystown, 341; Butler (William) House, Annapolis, **71**, 71–72; Catoctin Furnace, Thurmont, 348; Catoctin Recreational Demonstration Area, Thurmont,

349; Christ Rock United Methodist Church, Cambridge, 126; Cottman House, Princess Anne, 137; Decatur Heights National Register Historic District, Cumberland, 364–65; Dorsey Chapel (Brookland M.E. Church), Glenn Dale, **293**, 293–94; Frederick Douglass, 12, 68, 78–79, 111, 114, 139, 196; Drayden African American Schoolhouse, 25; Eastern Shore, 12, 84–86; Emancipation Proclamation, 11, 274, 356; Emmanuel Episcopal Church, Cumberland, 361; federal government employment, 11, 298, 306; Fleet Street residential district, Annapolis, 62–63; Freedmen's Bureau, 11, 274, 275, 284, 303; "Half-House" row houses, Baltimore City, 201–2; Henry's (Colored) Hotel, Ocean City, **148**, 148; Highland Beach, 78–79; Hughes African American Methodist congregation, Bucktown, 128; Lewis Museum of Maryland and African American History, Baltimore City, **192**, 192; Main Street buildings, Annapolis, 65; Thurgood Marshall, 49–50, 83, 139, 211; Maryland Commission on African American History and Cul-

African American residents and history (*continued*)
ture, 68; Maynard-Burgess House, Annapolis, 70–71; McComas Institute, Joppa, 274–75; Metropolitan AME Church, Cumberland, 364–65; Metropolitan United Methodist Church, Princess Anne, **137,** 137–38; Morgan State University, 220–21; Mount Moriah Church (Banneker-Douglass Museum), Annapolis, 68; North Brentwood Historic District, 297–98; Oakley Cabin African American Museum and Park, Sandy Spring vicinity, 320; Odd Fellows Lodge, Sandy Spring, 318; Orchard Street United Methodist Church, Baltimore City, **211,** 211; Otterbein neighborhood, Baltimore City, 201; oyster shucking, 40, 81; Peale Center for Baltimore History and Architecture (Peale's Baltimore Museum), 181; Pine Street neighborhood, Cambridge, **124,** 124–25; Prince George's County, 283, 284; Prince Hall Grand Lodge, Baltimore City, 211; Ridgeley School, Capitol Heights, 290; Riversdale, Riverdale Park, 300; Rock School (Stanley Institute Museum), Cambridge, 126; St. Francis Xavier Roman Catholic Church and Newtown Manor, Leonardtown, 27; Sandy Spring, 284, 318; Tolson's Chapel, Sharpsburg, 355–56; Harriet Tubman, 12, 84, 103, 121, 122, 127, 128; Underground Railroad, 10, 84, 103, 121, 127, 227, 317, 320; University of Maryland Eastern Shore, Princess Anne, 138–39; Webb (James) Cabin, Harmony, **103,** 103; Western Shore, 21. *See also* free Black residents and history; Rosenwald schools; segregation; slave houses

agriculture: Agricultural History Farm Park (Magruder-Bussard Farmstead), Gaithersburg, **321,** 321–22; Breakneck Valley, Flintstone, 367–68; Carroll County Almshouse and Farm Museum, Westminster, **260,** 260–61; Washington County Fairgrounds, Hagerstown, 352–53. *See also* barns; dairy farming; farms; grain elevators; plantations; tobacco

airports: Baltimore-Washington International (BWI) Thurgood Marshall Airport, Linthicum, 83, 246; College Park Airport and Aviation Museum, 300–301

Aladdin houses, 13, 299

Albaugh (David F.) House, Linwood, 267

Alexander, Robert E., 58

Alfandre, Joseph, 322

Allegany County, 359–73; Courthouse, **360,** 360–61; in Maryland counties map, xvi; in Western Mountains, 331; –, map, 332

Almodington, Oriole, **140,** 140

almshouses: Carroll County Almshouse (Farm Museum), Westminster, **260,** 260–61; London Town Publik House, Woodland Beach, 80; Waterloo, Princess Anne, 139

Altamont, 376

amusement parks: Glen Echo Park, **328,** 328–29

"Anchors Away" (song), 70

Anders (William) House, Uniontown, 263

Anderson, C. M., 362

Anderson, Joseph Horatio, **20, 49,** 49, **76,** 76

Andrews (James) House, Annapolis, 55–56

Annapolis, 46–77; maps, 48, 64; architectural ascendancy, 15; Baltimore City overtakes, 48, 150; as capital of Maryland, 46, 66; Church Circle, 47, 65, 66, 67; colonial-era buildings, 1; Historic District, 16, 48, 49, 58; in Maryland topographical map, 3; origins, 46; residential architecture, 13, 47; sea-level rise, 119; State Circle, 47, 49, 50, 58, 59; tobacco, 21, 46, 47; town planning, 46, 47, 49, 66; view of (1800), **15**

Annapolis Plan, 47; Brice (James) House, Annapolis, 51; Brice (John II) House, Annapolis, 52; Carroll (Charles) House, Annapolis, 73; Hammond-Harwood House, Annapolis, 53; Ogle Hall, Annapolis, 56; Ratcliffe Manor, Easton, 113; Ridout (John) House, Annapolis, 72; Ridout Row, Annapolis, 72–73; Scott (Upton) House, Annapolis, 73–74; Wye House and Plantation, Copperville, 114

Anne Arundel County, 46–83; Courthouse, 68; gambling, 32; in Maryland counties map, xvi; recreational waterfront communities, 22; tobacco, 21; in Western Shore, 21; –, map, 22

"Antietam Plan," 356

apartments and condominiums: Belt's Landing Condominiums, Baltimore City, 193–94; Crop Ayre, Ocean City, 147; Falkland, Silver Spring, 313; Highfield House, Baltimore City,

217, 217; Hilltop Manor Garden Apartments, Bladensburg, 296; Klots Mill Lofts, Cumberland, 365–66; National Can Company, Baltimore City, **196**, 197; Rombro Building, Baltimore City, 173; Waverley Terrace, Baltimore City, **205**, 205

aquariums: Baltimore National Aquarium, 183, **184, 388**

aqueducts: Chesapeake and Ohio Canal, Conococheague Creek Aqueduct, Williamsport vicinity, 358; Seneca Creek Aqueduct, Poolesville, 324

Archer, George, 158, 270

Armagh, Elkridge, 241

Armistead, W. K., 288

armories: Bel Air Armory, 270–71; Dahlgren Hall, U.S. Naval Academy, Annapolis, 61; Elkton Armory, **93**, 93–94; Hyattsville Armory, 299. *See also* forts and military installations

Armstrong, Helen Maitland, 162

Armstrong and Parker Co., 258

Arnold (David) House, Burkittsville, 342–43, **343**

Art Deco style, 14, 107, 131, 142, 161, 165, 169, **178**, 178, **196**, 197, **221**, 221, **277**, 277, 304, **312**, 312, 329, 336, **350**, 351, 364. *See also* Art Moderne style

art galleries: Glenstone, Potomac, 327; Key (Francis Scott) Auditorium and Mellon Hall, St. John's College, Annapolis, 58; Maryland Institute College of Art (MICA), Baltimore City, 210; Peabody Institute, Baltimore City, 157; Peale Center for Baltimore History and Architecture (Peale's Baltimore Museum), 181. *See also* museums

Art Moderne style, 169, 295, 296, 302

Arts and Crafts style, 59, 219, 220, 252, 253, 254, 258, 311

arts centers: Church Hill Theater, 107; France-Merrick Performing Arts Center, Baltimore City, **171**, 172; Glen Echo Park, 328; Mar-Va Theater, Pocomoke City, 142; The Music Center at Strathmore, Rockville, 306–7; Smith (Clarice) Performing Arts Center, University of Maryland, College Park, 302

artworks and sculptures: Bank of America (Baltimore Trust Building), 178; Battle Monument, Baltimore City, **176**, 176; Carter Memorial Church (St. Peter the Apostle Church), Baltimore City, 204; Cecil County World War I monument, Elkton, 94; Christ Episcopal Church, Cambridge, 123; The Cloisters (Parker House), Lutherville-Timonium, 257–58; Columbia New Town, **237**, 238; Cumberland City Hall, 364; Douglass (Frederick) statue, Easton, 111; Emmanuel Episcopal Church, Cumberland, 361; Evergreen House, Baltimore City, 218; First Unitarian Church, Baltimore City, 160; Hutzler's Department Store, Baltimore City, 169; Maryland State House, Annapolis, 49; Mitchell (Clarence M., Jr.) Courthouse (Baltimore City Courthouse), 176–78; National Shrine Grotto of Our Lady of Lourdes, Emmitsburg, 347; National Shrine of Saint Elizabeth Ann Seton, Emmitsburg, 347; Old Greenbelt, 295; Pennsylvania Station, Baltimore City, 207; St. Alphonsus Church, Baltimore City, 162; St. Anne's Episcopal Church, Annapolis, 66; St. Mary's Episcopal Church, Abingdon, 276; St. Michael's Church (Hannah More Chapel), Reisterstown, 257; St. Paul's Episcopal Church, Baltimore City, 162; St. Peter's Catholic Church, Queenstown, 108; Temple Oheb Shalom, Baltimore City, 224; U.S. Post Office, Ellicott City, 232; U.S. Post Office, Hyattsville, 299; U.S. Post Office, Rockville, 304; U.S. Post Office, Towson, 245; Visionary Art Museum, sculpture garden, Baltimore City, 185–86; War Correspondents Memorial Arch, Burkittsville, **343**, 343; Washington Monument, Baltimore City, **153**, 153–54. *See also* monuments and memorials

Asbury, Francis, 131

automobile dealerships: Ellicott City Motor service garage and showroom, 232; Ideal Car Company, Frederick, 336; Lustine Chevrolet, Hyattsville, **298**, 299

Averilhe-Goldsborough House, Havre de Grace, 280

Aydelotte (John S.) House, Snow Hill, 145

Ayers/Saint/Gross Architects, 42, 207–8, 221, 302

Bachelor's Hope, Chaptico, **28**, 28–29

Baetjer, Edward B., 222

Baker (Daniel) House, Buckeystown, 340–41

Baker (Daniel, Jr.) House, Buckeystown, 341

Baker (John) House, Buckeystown, 341

Baldwin, Billy, 273

Baldwin, E. Francis, **160**, 160, 161, **193**, 193, 199, 202, 233, 269, 305, **341**, 341, 375. *See also* Baldwin and Pennington

Baldwin and Pennington, 16, 49, 57–58, 169, **171**, 183, 209, 244, **246, 374**, 374, 375–76, **380**

Baltimore, Cecil Calvert, 2nd Lord, 1, 33, 47, 96, 236, 247, 345

Baltimore, Charles Calvert, 3rd Lord, 73, 109

Baltimore, Charles Calvert, 5th Lord, 90, 331, 366

Baltimore City, 150–227; map, 151; African American residents and history, 10, 150, 153; Annapolis surpassed by, 48, 150; bird's-eye view (1872), **16**; boatbuilding, 116; Central Business District East, 176–81; —, map, 177; Central Business District West, 165–76; —, map, 166; East Baltimore/Old Town/Fell's Point, 188–98; —, map, 189; Federal Hill and Locust Point, 185–87; —, map, 182; fire of 1904, 152, 172, 178, 179, 209; Homesteading Program, 17, 152, 188, 201; industrial development, 4, 7, 8–10, 150; Inner Harbor area, **8–9**, 10, 17, 153, 181–85; —, map, 182; in Maryland regions map, xvi; in Maryland topographical map, 3; Mount Vernon and environs, 153–65; —, map, 152; National Road, 7, 150; nineteenth-century buildings, 1, 150–51; North Baltimore and Jones Falls Valley, 218–27; —, map, 213; North Charles Street and environs, 213–18; —, map, 213; Northwest Baltimore/Bolton Hill, 207–13; —, map, 208; population decline, 325; railroads, 150, 228–29; row houses, **13**, 13, 17, 151–52; Sharp-Leadenhall neighborhood, 202; Southwest Baltimore, 199–207; —, map, 200; trained architects, 15–16

Baltimore County, 244–59; in Central Maryland, 228; —, map 229; Cockeysville (Beaver Dam) marble, 229; Courthouse, 244–45, **246**; interstate highway system, 325; in Maryland counties map, xvi; Public Safety Building, Towson, **246**, 246; summer homes, 229

Baltimore and Ohio (B&O) Railroad. *See* railroads

Baltzley Brothers, 328, 329

banks: Bank of America (Baltimore Trust Building), **178**, 178; Bank of Somerset, Princess Anne, 134; Carroll County Savings Bank (Uniontown Bank; Uniontown Museum), 263–64; Cecil Bank, Elkton, 93; Centreville National Bank, 106; Citizens Bank, Frederick, 336; Commercial National Bank, Snow Hill, 144; Continental Trust Building (One South Calvert Building), Baltimore City, 178–79; Eutaw Savings Bank of Baltimore (Baltimore Equitable Society), 172–73; Exchange and Savings Bank, Berlin, 146; Farmers Bank of Maryland (Reynolds Tavern), Annapolis, 67; First National Bank, Bel Air, 270; First National Bank, Berlin, 146; First National Bank, Sykesville, 269; First National Bank of Maryland, Rockville, 304; Frostburg National Bank, 371; Liberty Trust Bank, Cumberland, 363; Mercantile Bank and Trust Building, Baltimore City, 167; Mercantile Bank of Southern Maryland, Leonardtown, 26–27; Mercantile Safe Deposit and Trust Building, Baltimore City, 170, 179; Old Patapsco National Bank of Maryland, Ellicott City, 233; Old Tome Bank, Port Deposit, 88–89; Oxford Bank, 121; Peoples Bank of Somerset, Princess Anne, 134–35; People's National Bank (Law Office), Denton, 101–2; Queen Anne National Bank (Centreville Town Hall), 105–6; Sandy Spring Bank, 318; Savings Bank of Baltimore, **167**, 167–68; Second National Bank, Cumberland, 363; Sharpsburg Bank, 355; Union Bridge Banking and Trust Building, 266; Washington Trust Company, Ellicott City, 233; Workingmen's Building and Loan Association, Annapolis, 62

Banneker, Benjamin, 68, 255, 256; Cabin, Oella, 12, **255**, 255–56

Barber, Thomas P., 123

Barnes, James, 54

Barnes (Francis) House, Princess Anne, 136

barns: bank barns, 241, 261, 268, 321, 322, 327, 331, 345, 346, 353; Carroll County Farm Museum, Westminster, 261; Pennsylvania barns, 319; Point Farm, St. Leonard, 42, 43; Ratcliffe Manor, Easton, 113; White (Newton) House, Mitchellville, 291; Woodlawn Barn, Sandy Spring vicinity, **319**, 319–20. *See also* tobacco barns

Barrister (Charles Carroll) House, Annapolis, 63

Barrowclif, Edward, 110

Bartlett, Hayward and Company, 155

Bartlett, Robbins and Company, 157, 173, 174

Barton (Clara) House, Glen Echo, **329,** 329–30

Baskt, Léon, 218

battlefields. *See* national battlefields

Baughman, Frederick, 165

Bay Ridge, 79

Beall-Dawson House, Rockville, 304–5

Beatty-Cramer House, Frederick, 338–39

Beaux-Arts, 60, 89, 138, 154, 164, 168, 173, 177, 194–95, **207,** 207, 214, 216, 233, 270, 351, 352, 374

Beckford, Princess Anne, 133, 137

Behnisch Architekten, 207–8

Bel Air, 229, 270–72

Belair at Bowie, **292,** 292

Bel Alton, 33–34

Bellevue, 118

Belluschi, Pietro, 16, **208,** 208–9, **222,** 222–23, 247

Beltsville, 302–3; map, 295

Benedict, 38–39

Bennett, Edmund, 14, **305,** 305

Berge, Edward, 165

Bergel, Henry, 160

Berlin, 146

Berry, Jeremiah, 368

Bethesda, 308–9; map, 310

Betterton, 86, 100

Bevan, T. Horatio, 165

Big Pool, 358–59

Billings, John Shaw, 197–98

Birch, William Russell, 300

Bishop, William, 62

Bishop (George W.) House, Snow Hill, 145

Black, John Nelson, 91

Bladen, Thomas, 57

Bladensburg, 283, 296–97; map, 295

Blair, William D., 313

Bloor (H. P.) and Company, 257

boats, ships, and boatyards: boatbuilding, 2, 5, 21, 41, 75, 114–15, 116–17; bugeyes, 39, 74, 116, 117; Captain Carter's fishing shanty, **101,** 101, 117; Chance Boatyard, Annapolis, 74–75; Maryland economy, 2; pungeys, 117; Rock Hall Marine Railway, 100–101; St. Michaels, 114; skipjacks, **6,** 74, **116,** 117; tugboat *Baltimore,* 186; USS *Constellation,* 182, 183. *See also* shipbuilding; steamboats

Bodouva (William Nicholas) + Associates, 83

Bollman, Wendel, 202, **243,** 243–44

Boonsboro, 353–54

Booth, E. Wilson, 138

Booth, John Wilkes, 37, 272

Booth, Junius Brutus, 272

Booz, Miche, 318

Borden Mines Superintendent's House, Frostburg, 371–72

Bordley-Randall House, Annapolis, 51, 59, 67

Boring and Tilton, 89

Bostwick, Bladensburg, **296,** 296–97

Boswell-Compton House, Port Tobacco, 34

Bottomley, William Lawrence, **291,** 291

Boulton, Richard, 30

Bouton, Edwin H., 218, 220, 252

Bowen (George T.) House, Highland Beach, 79

Bower, Lewis and Thrower, 214, 215

Bowie, James, 30

Bowie, 292–93

Bowland, William, **136,** 136, 137

Brady (Henry H.) House, Chesapeake City, 95

Brady-Stephenson House, Kensington, 316

Brand, William, 275

Brashear (Belt) House, New Market, 340

Brauns, Henry, 192

Breeden, Richard, 41

Brice (James) House, Annapolis, 50–51, 74

Brice (John II) House, Annapolis, 52, 56

Brickbauer, Charles, 83, 210. *See also* Peterson and Brickbauer

bridges: Bollman Suspension Truss Bridge, Savage, **243,** 243–44; Burnside's Bridge, Antietam, Sharpsburg, 356; Carrollton Viaduct, Baltimore City, 206–7, 240; Casselman Bridge, Grantsville vicinity, **378,** 378; Conowingo Dam and Hydroelectric Plant, Darlington vicinity, 277; Gilpin's Falls Covered Bridge, North East, **91,** 91–92; Hatem (Thomas J. Memorial) Bridge, Havre de Grace, 8; iron railroad bridges, 202; Jericho Covered Bridge, Kingsville, 92, 274; Lane (William Preston, Jr.) Memorial Bridge (Chesapeake Bay Bridge), 8, 76–77, **77,** 86, 100, 147; Little Antietam Creek bridges, Keedysville, 354; Nice (Governor Harry W.) Bridge, Newburg, 8, 31; Oldtown Toll Bridge, 366–67; Pocomoke City Bridge, 141; Snow Hill Bridge, 143; Thomas Viaduct, Elkridge, 233, 239–40, **240,** 241; Warren ponytruss bridge over Sam's Creek, New Windsor vicinity, 268; Wilson's Bridge, Hagerstown vicinity, 378

Brinkley (Joseph B.) House, Princess Anne, 136

Brinkmann (Walter) House, Catonsville, 254

Broad Creek, 288

Brome-Howard House, St. Mary's City, 24
Brookeville, 320–21
Brown, David, 133
Brown, Gustavus Richard, 35, 37
Brown, J. Benjamin, 124
Brown, William, **73**, 73–74, **79**, 79–80
Brown (Mercer) House, Rising Sun, 12, **87**, 87
brownstone, 155, 157–58, 164, 172, 174, 205, 363
Bruff, William H., 115
Bruff-Mansfield House, St. Michaels, 114
Bruner, Elias, **337**, 337–38
Brutalism, 156–57, 166, 245
Bryantown, 37
Bucci, Thomas, 318
Buckeystown, 340–41
Buckland, William, 15, **52**, 52–53, 53–55, **76**, 76, 303
Buckler and Fenhagen, 164, **231**, 231, 259
Bucktown, 128
bungalows: Avondale, Solomons, 41; Chevy Chase, 311; Hyattsville, 298; North Brentwood Historic District, 298; Ocean City, 147; Takoma Park, 312; Walker Cottage, Ocean City, 149
Burbage-Brock House, Elkton, 93
Burch, John Wood, 56
Burch House, Port Tobacco, 34
Burck, Henry, 190
Burgess, Willis, 71
Burgess (George) House, New Market, 340
Burgett, Harvey, 95
Burkittsville, 342–43
Burman, Paul I., 316
Burnap, George, 352
Burnham, Daniel, 177, 178–79
Burns (Russell) and Company, 179
Burr, Theodore, 91, 92, 274
Bushwood, 28
Butler, Wright, **360**, 360–61, **361**, 362, 363, 364
Butler (William) House, Annapolis, **71**, 71–72
Butterfield, William, 276
Butz, E. M., 130–31
Byrd, Harry Clifton, 138
Byrd, Richard, 125
Byrne (Michael) and Company, 358

Cabot and Chandler, 197–98
Callahan (Thomas) House, Annapolis, 62
Calvert, Cecil. *See* Baltimore, Cecil Calvert, 2nd Lord
Calvert, Charles, 3rd Lord Baltimore. *See* Baltimore, Charles Calvert, 3rd Lord
Calvert, Charles, 5th Lord Baltimore. *See* Baltimore, Charles Calvert, 5th Lord
Calvert, Charles Benedict, 284, 286, 300, 301
Calvert, Rosalie Stier, 299–300
Calvert, 87
Calvert County, 39–46; gambling, 32; in Maryland counties map, xvi; recreational waterfront communities, 22; tobacco, 11, 21; in Western Shore, 21; –, map, 22
Camalier, Vincent, 24
Cambridge, 84, 86, 121–26; map, 121
Cambridge Seven Associates, 183, **184**, **388**
CAM Construction, 336
Campbell, J. N., **371**, 371
Camp David, Thurmont, 349
campgrounds: Catoctin Mountain Park, Thurmont, **348**, 348–49; Girl Scout Lodge at Camp Woodlands, Annapolis vicinity, 75, 257; Washington Grove, 322
canals: Chesapeake and Delaware Canal, 7, 94–95, 96; Chesapeake and Ohio (C&O) Canal, 6–7, 283, 324–25, 327–28, 331, 341, 355, 358, 362, 363, 366, 367, 368, 372, 373; Susquehanna Canal, 87; Susquehanna and Tidewater Canal, 7, 278, **281**, 281. *See also* lockhouses
Cape Cod houses, 292, 298
Capellano, Antonio, 160, 162, 176
Capital Region, 283–330; map, 284; in Maryland regions map, xvi
Capitol Heights, 290
Carlisle, David, 259
Carnegie, Andrew, 209–10
Caroline County, 101–4; Courthouse, 101; in Eastern Shore, 84; –, map, 85; in Maryland counties map, xvi
Carpenter, Melville R., 366
Carpenter Gothic style, 82, 225, **322**, 323
Carrère and Hastings, 154, 177, 216
Carr (William) House, Keedysville, 354
Carroll, Charles, Jr., **215**, 215
Carroll, Charles, of Carrollton: Carroll County, 259; Carroll Mansion (Caton House), Baltimore City, 191–92; Carrollton Hall (Folly Quarter), Ellicott City, **235**, 236–37; Catonsville, 253; Doughoregan Manor, Ellicott City, 236; Green (Jonas) House, Annapolis, 69; Homewood, Baltimore City, 215; House, Annapolis, 73
Carroll, Charles, the Barrister, 205

Carroll, Charles, the Settler, 73, 237

Carroll, John, 34, 160

Carroll County, 259–69; Almshouse (Farm Museum), Westminster, **260,** 260–61; in Central Maryland, 228; —, map, 229; Courthouse, 259–60; in Maryland counties map, xvi

Carroll Mansion (Caton House), Baltimore City, 191–92

Carrollton Hall (Folly Quarter), Ellicott City, **235,** 236–37

Carson, Charles L., 16, 161, 172, 210, 217

Carter-Archer House, Darlington vicinity, 277

Carver House, Havre de Grace, 280

Cassell, Charles E., **122,** 122–23, 169–70, 220–21, 233

cast iron, 105, 106, 151, 155, 157, 158, 162, 168, 170, 200, 207, 240, 243, 335, 353, 356

cast-iron fronts: Abell Building, Baltimore City, **171,** 173; Alberti, Brink and Company Building, Baltimore City, 174; Baltimore City, 9; Bohemia Avenue buildings, Chesapeake City, 95; Gomber Building, Frederick, 336; Main Street buildings, Annapolis, 66; Maryland Avenue commercial buildings, Annapolis, 59; Rombro Building, Baltimore City, 173; Wire Hardware, Rockville, 305

Castle, The, Mount Savage, 370

Castro, Alex, 185–86, **187**

cathedrals. *See* churches, chapels, and cathedrals

Caton (Richard) House, Baltimore City, 191–92

Catonsville, 13, 229, 253–54

Cecil, John T., 25

Cecil County, 86–97; Courthouse, 92–93; in Eastern Shore, 84; —, map, 85; interstate highway system, 325; in Maryland counties map, xvi

Cedars, Sandy Spring, 318

cemeteries: Christ Episcopal Church, Cambridge, 123; Green Mount Cemetery, **163,** 164–65; National Shrine of Saint Elizabeth Ann Seton, Emmitsburg, 347; St. Anne's Episcopal Church, Annapolis, 66

Central Maryland, 228–82; map, 229; in Maryland regions map, xvi; railroads, 7, 228–29

Centreville, 105–7

Chanceford, Snow Hill, 145–46

Chandlee, Benjamin, 87

Chandler, Theophilus Parsons, Jr., 276

Channing, William Ellery, 160

Chapline (William) House, Sharpsburg, 355

Chaptico, 28–29

Charles County, 30–39; gambling, 32; in Maryland counties map, xvi; tobacco, 11, 21; in Western Shore, 21; —, map, 22

Charlestown, 84, 90–91, 92

Charlotte Hall, 30–31

Chase, Jeremiah Townley, 53, 54

Chase, Samuel, 54

Chase-Lloyd House, Annapolis, 53–55, 67, 70

Chautauqua, 323, 328, 329, 330, 374–75

Chermayeff, Peter, 183, **184, 388**

Chermayeff, Sollogub and Poole, 183, **184, 388**

Cherry Grove, Sandy Spring, 33, 318–19

Chesapeake Bay: boatbuilding, 116–17; Chesapeake Bay Maritime Museum, St. Michaels, 115, **116,** 116–17; Chesapeake culture, 4–5; climate change, sea-level rise and, 119; Lane (William Preston, Jr.) Memorial Bridge (Chesapeake Bay Bridge), 8, 76–77, **77,** 86, 100, 147

Chesapeake Beach, 7, 22, 45–46

Chesapeake City, 94–96

Chesapeake houses, 32–33; Annapolis, 47, 52; Belmont Manor, Elkridge, 240–41; Brice (John II) House, Annapolis, 52; Carroll (Charles) House, Annapolis, 73; Clifton, Sandy Spring, 33, 318; Cornhill Street buildings, Annapolis, 62; Craufurd (David) House, Upper Marlboro, 286; Cray House, Stevensville, 109–10; Glebe House, Princess Anne, 136–37; Grahame House, Lower Marlboro, 45; Green (Jonas) House, Annapolis, 69; Hancock's Resolution, Pasadena, **78,** 78; Hogshead, Annapolis, 33, **63,** 63; Holly Hill, Friendship, 82–83; Home Farm, Hampton, Towson, 248; Hopewell Farm, Johnsville, 346; La Grange, LaPlata, **36,** 36–37; Maidstone, Owings, **32,** 33, 46; Maxwell Hall, Benedict, 38–39; Morgan Hill Farm, Lusby, 42; Oaks II, Brookeville, 321, **321;** Ocean Hall, Bushwood, 28; Paca House, Charlestown, 90; Pemberton Hall, Salisbury, 33, 132–33; plantations, 21; Red Lyon Tavern (Black's Store), Charlestown, 91; Sarum, Charlotte Hall, **30,** 30–31; Sotterley, Hollywood, 30; Stagg Hall, Port Tobacco, **35,** 35; Turkey Cock Hall, Rockland, 259; Wyoming, Clinton, 33, 387

Chestertown, 12, 84, 97–99

Chevy Chase, 14, 310–11; map, 310

"Chevy Houses," 316
Chicago School, 178
Childs, Edward S., 362
Chimney House, Port Tobacco, 34
Cho, Diane, 185, **187**
Cho Benn Holback + Associates, **198**, 198
Cho Wilkes Benn, 200
Christman Company, 49
Church Creek, 127
churches, chapels, and cathedrals: All Hallows, Edgewater, 288; All Saints Church, Easton, 116; All Saints Church, Reisterstown, 256; All Saints Episcopal Church and Parish Hall, Frederick, 336–37; Ascension Episcopal Church, Westminster, 260; Basilica of the Assumption, Baltimore City, 2, **160**, 160–61, 222; Bethel African Methodist Episcopal Church, Cambridge, 125; Brentwood AME Zion Church, North Brentwood, 298; Carter Memorial Church (St. Peter the Apostle Church), Baltimore City, 203–4; Cathedral of Mary Our Queen, Baltimore City, 222; Christ Church, Stevensville, **109**, 109; Christ Church, West River, 82; Christ Episcopal Church, Cambridge, **122**, 122–23; Christ Episcopal Church, St. Michaels, 115–16; Christ Rock United Methodist Church, Cambridge, 126; Church of the Redeemer, Baltimore City, **222**, 222–23; Dorsey Chapel (Brookland M.E. Church), Glenn Dale, **293**, 293–94; Emmanuel Episcopal Church, Cumberland, 361; Faith Community Church (Asbury United Methodist Church), Salisbury, 131; First and Franklin Presbyterian Church (First Presbyterian Church) and Manse, Baltimore City, 158–59, 235; First Unitarian Church, Baltimore City, **159**, 159–60; German Lutheran Church, Burkittsville, 342; German Reformed Church, Burkittsville, 342; Grace Memorial Episcopal Church, Darlington, 276; Haebler Memorial Chapel, Goucher College, Towson, 247; Historic Little Wedding Chapel (Burbage-Brock House), Elkton, 93; Lovely Lane Methodist Church, Baltimore City, 164, 213–14; Linwood Brethren Church, 267; Memorial Chapel, University of Maryland, College Park, 302; Metropolitan AME Church, Cumberland, 364–65; Metropolitan United Methodist Church, Princess Anne, **137**, 137–38; Most Precious Blood

Catholic Church, Betterton, 100; Mount Moriah Church (Banneker-Douglass Museum), Annapolis, 68; Mount Vernon Place United Methodist Church, Baltimore City, **158**, 158; Mount Washington Presbyterian Church, Baltimore City, 225; National Park Seminary chapel, Forest Glen, 315; National Shrine of Saint Elizabeth Ann Seton, Emmitsburg, 346–47; **347**; Old Bohemia Church (St. Francis Xavier Church), Warwick, 96–97, 108; Old Otterbein Evangelical United Brethren Church, Baltimore City, 201; Orchard Street United Methodist Church, Baltimore City, **211**, 211; Our Father's House, Altamont, **376**, 376; St. Alphonsus Church, Baltimore City, 162–63; St. Andrew's Episcopal Church (Union Chapel), Glenwood, 244; St. Anne's Episcopal Church, Annapolis, 47, 54, **65**, 66; St. Christopher's-By-The-Sea, Gibson Island, 77–78; St. Francis Xavier Roman Catholic Church, Leonardtown, **27**, 27, 108; St. Ignatius Roman Catholic Church, Bel Alton, 34; St. James Herring Creek, Lothian, 288; St. John's Chapel, Burkittsville, 342; St. John's Church (Broad Creek Episcopal Church), 288; St. John's Episcopal Church, Ellicott City, 234–35, **235**; St. Luke's Episcopal Church, Church Hill, 107; St. Mary's Episcopal Church, Abingdon, **275**, 275–76; St. Mary's Evangelical Lutheran Church, Westminster, 261–62; St. Mary's Seminary Chapel, Baltimore City, 211–12; St. Michael's Catholic Church, Frostburg, 371; St. Michael's Church (Hannah More Chapel), Reisterstown, 256–57; St. Paul's By the Sea, Ocean City, 147; St. Paul's Episcopal Church, Baltimore City, 162; St. Peter's Catholic Church, Queenstown, 108; Sharp Street Methodist Church, Sandy Spring, 318; Temple of the Church of Jesus Christ of Latter-day Saints, Kensington, **315**, 315; Tolson's Chapel, Sharpsburg, 355–56; Tome Memorial United Methodist Church, Port Deposit, 88; Town Clock Church (German Evangelical Lutheran Church), Cumberland, **365**, 365; Trinity Episcopal Church, Upper Marlboro, 286; Trinity Methodist Episcopal Church, Bucktown, 128; University Baptist Church, Baltimore City, 214; University

Memorial Chapel, Morgan State University, Baltimore City, 220–21; U.S. Naval Academy chapel, Annapolis, 61; Waugh Chapel United Methodist Church, Cambridge, 124, 125; Whitehaven United Methodist Church, 133; Zion Lutheran Church, Baltimore City, 211; Zion Lutheran Church, Middletown, 344. *See also* Quaker meetinghouses; rectories

Church Hill, 107

Churchman, Amassa, 87

Churchman (John) House, Rising Sun, 87

Cikovsky, Nicolai, 245

City Beautiful movement, 153, 154, 178, 207, 352

city halls: Baltimore City Hall, **180,** 180–81; Bowie, 292; Centreville Town Hall, 105–6; Chevy Chase Village Hall, 310; Church Hill Town Hall, 107; Cumberland City Hall, 364; Elkton Town Hall, 93; Engine House and City Hall, Annapolis, 65; Frederick City Hall, 334, 335; Hagerstown City Hall, 351; McCathran Hall, Washington Grove, 323; Port Deposit Town Hall, 89; Sharpsburg Library and Town Hall, 355; Union Bridge, 266

Civilian Conservation Corps (CCC), 302, 359, 379

Civil War, 10, 85, 127, 359; Battle of Antietam (Sharpsburg), 333, 343, 355, 356–57; Battle of Monocacy, 333, 339; Battle of South Mountain, 342, 343

Claiborne, William, 109

Clark, Appleton P., 306–7

Clark, Joseph, **20, 49,** 49, **57,** 57

Clark (John) House, Chesapeake City, 95

Clarksburg, 323–24

Classical Revival style, 165, 192, 220, 336, 352, **353,** 371

classicism, 14–15, 53, 56, 60, 121, 161, **167,** 167–68, 170, 172, 180, **214,** 214–15, 263, 311, 337, 338, **365,** 365, 368. *See also* Beaux-Arts; Classical Revival style; Federal style; Greek Revival style; neoclassicism

Clay, Henry, 62

Cleland, Thomas, 288

Cleveland, Grover, 375

Clifton, Sandy Spring, 33, 318, 319

climate change, 119

Clinton, 286–87

Cloisters, The (Parker House), Lutherville-Timonium, **257,** 257–59

Cloverfields, Queenstown, **108,** 108–9

clubhouses: Baltimore County Club,

Baltimore City, 219; Belair Bath and Tennis Club, Bowie, 293; Gibson Island buildings, 77; South River Club, 80

coal, 4, 332, 358, 370–72

Coale, Griffith Baily, 178

Cochran, Alexander, 211

Cochran, Stephenson and Donkervoet, 209, 234–35, **235**

Coleman, Elwood F., 107

College Park, 300–302; map, 295

colleges and universities: College of Medicine of Maryland, Davidge Hall, Baltimore City, 151, **175,** 175–76; Frostburg State University, 371; Goucher College, Towson, 247–48; Johns Hopkins University, Gilman Hall—Homewood Campus, Baltimore City, 216–17; Maryland Institute College of Art (MICA), Baltimore City, 207, **209,** 209–10; Morgan State University, Baltimore City, 42, 138, 220–21; Towson State University, Stephens Hall, 245–46; University of Baltimore, Angelos (John and Frances) Law Center and Student Center, 207–8; University of Maryland Baltimore, 172; University of Maryland Eastern Shore, Princess Anne, 138–39; U.S. Naval Academy, Annapolis, 48, 56, **60,** 60–62; Washington College, Middle Hall, Chestertown, 98–99, **99.** *See also* St. John's College, Annapolis; University of Maryland, College Park

Collegiate Gothic style, 221, 245

Collins, Lester, 323

Collins (Jackson) House, Centreville, 106

Collins (Joseph Edward) House, Ocean City, 147

Colmary (Abraham L.) House, Chesapeake City, 95

Colonial Revival style, 14, 16, 30, 31, 43, 48, 55, 66–67, 68, 69, 98, 101, 122, 124, 126, 134, 138, 142, 143, 144, 147, **179,** 179–80, 218, 220, 232, 241, 252, 254, 269, 270, 273, 289, **291,** 291, 297, 299, 301–2, 311, 313, 317–18, 351, 352, 362, 364, 371, 375

Columbia, 237–38

commercial buildings: Anders and Lightner store, Union Bridge, 266; Annapolis Cornhill Street buildings, 62; Annapolis Main Street buildings, 64–66, **65;** Annapolis Maryland Avenue commercial buildings, 59; ASA Building, Baltimore City, 174; Benson (James) Building, St. Michaels, 115; Betz Grocery, Frost-

commercial buildings (*continued*)
burg, 371; Black's Store (Red Lyon Tavern), Charlestown, 91; Bouchelle (Byron) store, Chesapeake City, 95; Buckeystown, 341; Bucktown Store, 128; Caplan's department store, Ellicott City, 232; Cecil's Old Mill and Cecil's Country Store, Great Mills, **24**, 24–25; Chesapeake City Bohemia Avenue buildings, 95; Cohn Store Building, Princess Anne, 134; Columbia Mall, 238; Cumberland Baltimore Street commercial buildings and pedestrian mall, 363–64; Delashmutt's Store, Buckeystown, 341; Devilbiss Store and House, Uniontown, **263**, 263; Durst Furniture Store, Frostburg, 371; Ellicott City, 232, **235**; Englar and Son general store, Linwood, 267; Fannon (P. A.) Variety Store, Mount Savage, 370; Fraley's General Store, Thurmont, 348; Franklin and Jones General Store, Annapolis, 65; Franklin Hall, Chesapeake City, 95; Frederick business district, **334**, 334–36; Frostburg Main Street buildings, 370–71, **371**; Gomber Building, Frederick, 336; Goodman (Aaron L.) Building, Annapolis, 66; Goodman's clothing store, Snow Hill, 144; Hafer Furniture Building, Frostburg, 371; Hagerstown Public Square and Downtown, 350–51; Hardey Building, Frederick, 336; Harley store and post office, Burkittsville, 342; Harris and Fuller Wholesale House, Frederick, 336; Hayes Drug Store, Cambridge, 125; Hendrickson Dry Goods, Frederick, 335–36; Hiteshaw (William) store and tavern, Uniontown, 263; Hollins Market, Baltimore City, **204**, 204–5; Hutzler's Department Store, Baltimore City, 169, **171**, **380**; Hyattsville, 299; Hyattsville Hardware, 299; Long (Littleton) store, Princess Anne, 136; Maggio Fruit Company, Annapolis, 65; McDonald (John) and Co. Store (Patapsco Distilling Company), Sykesville, **269**, 269; McKinna's Store, Buckeystown, 341; Middletown West Main Street, 344; Montgomery Farm Women's Cooperative Market (Bethesda Women's Market), 309; Mullaney Brothers Five-and-Dime Store, Mount Savage, 370; New Market Main Street, 340; Oxford Mews commercial block, 120–21; Ozmon's store, Centreville, 107; Phillips Hardware, Cambridge, 124; Pritchard's

Hardware, Frostburg, 371; Reed (J. M.) Store, Chesapeake City, 95; Rees Hardware Store, Chesapeake City, 95; Roosevelt Center, Greenbelt, 295; Rosenbaum's department store, Cumberland, 363; Rosenour (Benjamin) and Sons Mercantile Building, Frederick, 336; Rosenstock Building, Frederick, 336; Sandy Spring, 318; Schwarzenbach's department store, Cumberland, 363; Seneca Store (Poole's General Store), Poolesville, 326; Shannahan and Wrightson Hardware Company, Easton, 111–12; Snow Hill business district, 144; Spear's Jewelry shop, Cumberland, 364; Stam Hall, Chestertown, 97; Stevens Hardware, Annapolis, 66; Stewart's Department Store (Posner Building), Baltimore City, 169–70; Sturgis Building, Snow Hill, 144; Sykesville Main Street, 269; Taylor's department store, Ellicott City, 232; Timmons (Charles B.) Furniture Store, Snow Hill, 144; Utz Mercantile, New Market, 340; Warfield Building, Sykesville, 269; Wire Hardware, Rockville, 305. *See also* automobile dealerships; banks; gas stations; hotels, inns, and motels; restaurants; shopping centers; taverns

community centers: Baldwin (Carroll) Memorial Hall, Savage Mill Village, 243; Brookeville, 321; Flippo (Joseph R.) Community House, Port Republic, 44; Galesville Rosenwald School, 82; Greenbelt Community Center, **xii**, 295; Lawyers Hill, Elkridge, **241**, 241; The McKim Center (The McKim Free School), Baltimore City, 188–89, 190; Sandy Spring Lyceum, 317; Victory Villa Community Center, Middle River, 250–51

Condit, J. R., 66
Cone, Joseph M., 253
Congdon, Henry M., 115–16
Conklin and Rossant, 166
Conrey, Thomas, 95; House, Chesapeake City, 95
Content, Upper Marlboro, 286
convents. *See* monasteries and convents
Cook, Walter, 216
Cooper, James, 118
Cooper (Alex) House, Tilghman Island, 118
Cooper (Thomas) House, Salisbury, 132
Copperville, 113–14
Corddry (W. D.) House, Snow Hill, 143
Costen House, Pocomoke City, 142
cottages: Charlestown, 90; concrete

row houses, Baltimore City, 219; Deer Park, 375–76; Edgevale Park, 220; Epping Forest and Sherwood Forest, Crownsville, 22; Evergreen Knoll Cottages, Betterton, 100; Lift-A-Latch, Elkridge, 241–42; Mountain Lake Park, 375; Ocean City, 147; Pennington Cottage, Deer Park, 375–76; Randall Court houses, Annapolis, 59; Thomas (Richard) House, Brookeville, 321; Tolson (Warren) Cottage, Piney Point, 26; Traband House, Upper Marlboro, 286; Tudor Hall, Bel Air, 272; Walker Cottage, Ocean City, 149; Washington Grove, **322,** 323; Weaver (Jacob J., Sr.) House, Uniontown, 264

Cottingham (Peter D.) House, Snow Hill, 145

Cottman House, Princess Anne, 137

cotton duck, 225, 226, 242

courthouses: Allegany County Courthouse, **360,** 360–61; Anne Arundel County Courthouse, 68; Baltimore County Courthouse, 244–45, **246;** Baltimore County Courts Building, 245; Caroline County Courthouse, 101; Carroll County Courthouse, 259–60; Cecil County Courthouse, 92–93; Dorchester County Courthouse, **122,** 122; Frederick County Courthouse, 334, 336; Frederick County Courthouse (former; now Frederick City Hall), 334; Garrett County Courthouse, 373–74; Harford County Courthouse, **270,** 270; Howard County Courthouse, **231,** 231–32; Kent County Courthouse, 97; Mitchell (Clarence M., Jr.) Courthouse (Baltimore City Courthouse), 176–78; Old Montgomery County Courthouse, **304,** 304; Queen Anne's County Courthouse, **105,** 105; Somerset County Courthouse, 134–35; Talbot County Courthouse, 111; U.S. Courthouse and Post Office (Public Safety Building), Cumberland, 364; U.S. Post Office and Courthouse, Baltimore City, 177; Washington County Courthouse, 351; Wicomico County Courthouse, 130–31; Worcester County Courthouse, 143

Covarrubius, Miguel, 218

covenants. *See* restrictive covenants

crabbing: boatbuilding, 116; Cambridge, 121–22; Chesapeake Bay, 5; crab pickers in Crisfield, **11;** Western Shore, 21

Craftsman style, 143. *See also* Arts and Crafts style

Craik, James, 36–37

Cram, Goodhue and Ferguson, 61

Cranford, B. Wesley, 286

Craufurd (David) House, Upper Marlboro, 286

Crawford, Leon W., 124

Cray House, Stevensville, 109–10

Creagh, Patrick, 50, **57,** 57, 205–6

Cresap (Michael) House, Oldtown, **366,** 366

Cret, Paul, 308–9, **309**

Crisfield, **11,** 86, 140–41

Crisp, Herbert G., **23,** 23

Cross Street Partners, 126

cruck construction, 28

Crumbacker (Jonas) House, Uniontown, 263

Culp, A. M., 98

cultural centers: Peabody Institute, Baltimore City, 151, 154–55, **157,** 157

Cumberland, 359–66; map, 360; as county seat, 331, 359; deindustrialization, 333, 359; industry, 9, 359; in Maryland topographical map, 3

Custom House, Chestertown, 97, **98,** 98

dairy farming: Hopewell Farm, Johnsville, 346; Point Farm, St. Leonard, 43; Ratcliffe Manor, Easton, 113; Western Mountains, 333; White (Newton) Mansion, Mitchellville, 291

dams: Conowingo Dam and Hydroelectric Plant, Darlington vicinity, 276–77, **277**

dance halls: Spanish Ballroom, Glen Echo Park, 329

Daniels, Howard, **212,** 212

Darby, Upton, 326; House, Poolesville, 326

Darlington, 275, 276–77

Darnall's Chance, Upper Marlboro, **285,** 285–86

Davis, Alexander Jackson, 258, 272

Davis, Frank E., 16, 134–35, **211,** 211, **304,** 304

Davis, Henry R., 134–35

Davis, Phineas, 202

Davis, Bowen and Friedel, 141

Day, Robert, 41

De Anna, Peter, 232

Deavour, John, 80

Deer Park, 7, 375–76

defense housing, 296

Delano and Aldrich, 154, **156,** 156, 292

Delaware Peninsula, 84, 119

Delorme, Philibert, 160, 175

Dempwolf, John A., 261–62, **270,** 270, 336

Dennis, John, 137

Denny, John, 110

Denton, 101–2
Denton House, Chestertown, 97
Dentzel (William H.) Company, 329
Design Collective, 183
Dessez, Leon, 310; House, Chevy Chase, 311
Devilbiss Store and House, Uniontown, **263**, 263
Diggs-Sasscer House, Upper Marlboro, 286
Dixon, James, 225. *See also* Dixon and Dixon
Dixon, Thomas, 93, 158, **205**, 205, 225, 259, 334. *See also* Dixon and Carson; Dixon and Davis; Dixon and Dixon
Dixon and Carson, **158**, 158
Dixon and Davis, 93
Dixon and Dixon, 16, 244–45, **246**, 246
DMJM, 83, 323
Dodson (Captain) House, St. Michaels, 117
dogtrot houses, 261
domes: Baltimore City Hall, **180**, 181; Basilica of the Assumption, Baltimore City, **160**, 160; Cumberland City Hall, 364; Davidge Hall, Baltimore City, **175**, 175; Eutaw Place Temple (Prince Hall Grand Lodge), Baltimore City, 211; First Unitarian Church, Baltimore City, 159, 160; Garrett County Courthouse, Oakland, 374; Lovely Lane Methodist Church, Baltimore City, 214; Maryland State House, Annapolis, **20**, **49**, 49; National Shrine of Saint Elizabeth Ann Seton, Emmitsburg, **347**, 347; Pennsylvania Station, Baltimore City, 207; U.S. Naval Academy chapel, Annapolis, 61; Walters Art Museum, Baltimore City, 156
Donahoo, John, **25**, 25, 280–81
Donn, Edward W., Jr., 311
Dorchester County, 121–30; Courthouse, **122**, 122; in Eastern Shore, 84; —, map, 85; in Maryland counties map, xvi
Doub (Albert) House, Cumberland, 361
double houses: Ship Caulkers' houses, Baltimore City, 196–97. *See also* duplex houses
Doughoregan Manor, Ellicott City, 236
Douglass, Charles, **78**, 78–79
Douglass, Frederick, 12, 68, 78–79, 111, 114, 139, 196
Douglass, Haley, 79
Douglass Summer House, Highland Beach, **78**, 78–79
Downing, Andrew Jackson, 102–3, 262, 372
DPZ, 322

Drane (James) Log House, Accident, 12, **377**, 377
Drayden, 25
Duany, Andres, 14, 322
du Brau, Gertrude, 364
Duff, Simon, **57**, 57
Duke, Roland, 27
Dulany, Daniel, 74, 331, 366
Dundalk, 230, 251–53
duplex houses: Benning Road Historic District, Galesville, 81; Brome-Howard Slave House, St. Mary's City, 24; Old Row Museum, Mount Savage, 369–70; Randall (Alexander) Duplex, Annapolis, 58
du Pont, William, Jr., 94
Durand et Compagnie, 156
durchgangigen (center-hall arrangement), 337
"Dutch biscuit," 338

Eagle House, St. Michaels, 117
Earley, John J., 297, 313–14
Eastern Shore, 84–149; map, 85; African American residents and history, 12, 84, 86; canneries, 9, 12, 85; Chesapeake houses, 32; grain production, 2, 11, 84; in Maryland regions map, xvi; railroads, 7, 85–86, 134; Southern Tidewater traditions, 1, 84
Eastern Shore Land Conservancy, 126
Eastlake style, 99, 107
Easton, 110–13; early commerce, 84; industrial expansion, 86; residential architecture, 12, 111
Eberson, John, **312**, 312–13
Ecclesiological Movement, 123, 235, 256, 260, 275
Edmunds, James R., Jr., **23**, 23, 169
Edwards, Robert, **215**, 215
Edwards, Thomas H., 304
Edwards, William, **215**, 215
Egyptian motifs, 165, 176
Ehlers and Wagner, 254
Elkridge, 238–42
Elkridge Landing, 228, 239
Elkton, 92–94; as county seat, 90, 92; industrial expansion, 86; as Wedding Capital, 92, 93
Ellicott City (Ellicott's Mills), 230–37; maps, 231, 234; Baltimore and Ohio Railroad, 6, 202, 207; Ellicott family, 189, 228, 230; founding, 228; as mill town, 230, 231; quarries, 229, 233; railroads, 228, 230, 232, 233; summer houses, 229
Ellicott (George) House, Ellicott City, 231
Ellington, Douglas, **xii**, **294**, 294
Elmonte, Ellicott City, 235–36

Emancipation Proclamation, 11, 274, 356

Emergency Fleet Corporation, 251, 252

Emmitsburg, 346–47

Emory, William, 252

enameled brick, 370, 371

Englar (John) House, Linwood, 267

Englar (Jonas) House, Linwood, 267

Englar (Nathan) House, Linwood, 267

Ennis (George) House, Burkittsville, 342

Epping Forest, 22

Epstein (A.) and Sons, 183

Erying, John, 252

Esham House, Ocean City, 147

Evans, Oliver, 104, 259, 261

Evergreen House, Baltimore City, 217–18

Eversole House, Keedysville, 354

Exeter, Federalsburg, 104

fairgrounds: Washington County Fairgrounds, Entrance Pavilion and Keeper's Residence, Hagerstown, 352–53, **353**

false-plate construction, 29, 33, 108, 110

Farber, H. J., 253

farms: Albaugh-Duvall Farm, New Windsor vicinity, **268,** 268; Breakneck Valley houses, Flintstone vicinity, 367–68; Elmonte, Ellicott City, 235–36; Hancock's Resolution, Pasadena, **78,** 78; Hard Bargain Farm, Accokeek, 289; Harewood, Sandy Spring, 317; Harris Farm (Heritage Farm Park), Walkersville, 344–45; Home Farm, Hampton, Towson, 248; Hopewell Farm, Johnsville, 346; Magruder-Bussard Farmstead (Agricultural History Farm Park), Gaithersburg, **321,** 321–22; Morgan Hill Farm, Lusby, **41,** 41–42; Point Farm, St. Leonard, 42, 43; Riversdale, Riverdale Park, 300; Rocklands Farm (Rocklands Farm Winery), Poolesville, 326–27; Southern Maryland tobacco farm, **2;** Trevanion, Taneytown, 262; White (Newton) Mansion, Mitchellville, 291; Wood Mill Farm, Woodsboro, 345–46. *See also* agriculture; barns; dairy farming; tobacco barns

Farrow (William H.) House, Snow Hill, 145

Faul, Augustus, **212,** 212, 374

Federal Housing Administration (FHA), 285, 296, 313

federal influence in Maryland, 306–7

Federalsburg, 104

Federal style, 12, 31, 65, 87, 104, 114, **131,** 131–32, 133, **135,** 135, 136, 137, 144–45, 170, 180, 191, 196, 215, 227, 263, 279–80, 290–91, **317,** 317, 319, 320, 334, 335, 339, 340, 342, 355

Fell, Edward, 192–93

Fentner, Louis, 178

Ferguson, Alice, 289

Finan (Thomas B.) House, Cumberland, 362

fire stations: Ellicott City Firehouse, 232, **235;** Engine House and City Hall, Annapolis, 65; firehouse, Ellicott City, 232; Union Bridge, 266; United Fire Company, Frederick, 336; Waterwitch Hook and Ladder Fire Station No. 1, Annapolis, 50

Fisher Architecture, 147

fishing: Betterton ark, 100; boatbuilding, 116; Captain Carter's fishing shanty, **101,** 101; Chance Boatyard, Annapolis, 74; Charlestown, 90; Eastern Shore, 84; Maryland economy, 2; St. Michaels, 114; Western Shore, 21. *See also* crabbing; oystering

Fisk, C. B., 367

five-part Palladian houses, 54–55; Annapolis, 47; Brice (James) House, Annapolis, 50–51; Hammond-Harwood House, Annapolis, **52,** 52–53, 55; Homewood, Baltimore, 55, **215,** 215–16; Montpelier, Laurel, **54,** 55, 303; Mount Clare, Baltimore City, 205–6; Paca (William) House, Annapolis, **51,** 51–52; Poplar Hill at His Lordship's Kindness, Clinton, 286–87, **287;** residential Maryland, 13; Riversdale, Riverdale Park, 55, 299–300; Talbot County Courthouse, Easton, 111; Teackle Mansion, Princess Anne, **135,** 135; Tulip Hill, Harwood, 55, 80–81, **81;** Whitehall, Annapolis, **76,** 76; White (Newton) Mansion, Mitchellville, **291,** 291

Flagg, Ernest, **60,** 60–61

Flintstone, 367–68

flour milling: Baltimore City, 9, 150; Central Maryland, 228; Doub's Mill, Hagerstown vicinity, 353; Eastern Shore, 84; Elkton, 92; Ellicott City, 230, 231; Hagerstown, 350; Jerusalem Mill, Kingsville, **273,** 273–74; Kaese Mill, Accident, 376–77; Mount Vernon Mills No. 1, 2, and 3, 226; Princess Anne, 134; Rock Run Mill Buildings, Darlington vicinity, 277; Western Mountains, 331

Flournoy and Flournoy, 301

Flurkuchenhaus (four-room, central-chimney German house form), 351

Footner, Hulbert, 92

Forest Glen, 314–15; map, 310

Forman, Henry Chandlee, 63

Formstone, 206

Forsyth, Thomas F., 274

forts and military installations: Aberdeen Proving Ground, 229; Edgewood Arsenal, 229; federal influence in Maryland, 307; Fort Cumberland, 331, 359; Fort Frederick, Big Pool vicinity, 358–59, **359**; Fort McHenry National Monument and Historic Shrine, Baltimore City, **187**, 187; Fort Washington National Park, 288; Naval Air Station Patuxent River, 23, 26, 41. *See also* armories

Fort Washington, 288

Foster, George, 51

foursquare houses, 241, 253, 254, 298

Fowler, Laurence Hall, 50, 66–67, 215, 217–18, 220

Fowler, Orson S., 225

Frainie Brothers & Haighley, 26

Frederick, George A., 16, **171,** 173, **180,** 180–81, **204,** 204–5, **212,** 212–13

Frederick, 333–39; map, 335; establishment, 2, 331; industries, 332–33; in Maryland topographical map, 3; residential architecture, 12; revitalization, 333

Frederick County, 333–49; Courthouse (Frederick City Hall), 334; in Maryland counties map, xvi; in Western Mountains, 331; —, map, 333

Freedmen's Bureau, 11, 274, 275, 284, 303

free Black residents and history, 10–12, 71, 81, 84, 103, 125, 150, 211, 275, 284, 318, 320, 355, 364–65

Freelon Group, **192,** 192

French Colonial style, **278,** 278, 280

French Renaissance Revival style, 164, **180,** 180–81, 220

Friendship, 82–83

Friz, Clyde N., **161,** 161

Frohman, Philip Hubert, 37

Frostburg, 362, 370–72

Furney, John M., 266

Gaithersburg, 321–22

Galesville, 21, 81–82

galleting, 51, 78, 233

Galloway, Samuel, 80, 81

gambling, 32–33

Gambrill, Horatio, 226

Gambrill House, Frederick, 339

Garden City planning, 223, 249, 251, 252, 285, 294–96

gardens: Bolton Square Commons, Baltimore City, 210; Ladew Topiary Gardens, Monkton vicinity, **273,** 273; Mount Vernon Place,

Baltimore City, 154; Paca (William) House, Annapolis, 52; Poplar Hill at His Lordships Kindness, Clinton, 287; Preston Gardens, Baltimore City, 177–78; Rawlings (Howard P.) Conservatory and Botanic Gardens, Baltimore City, **212,** 212–13; Ridout (John) House, Annapolis, 72; Rose Hill, Port Tobacco, 35–36; Scott (Upton) House, Annapolis, 74

garden suburbs, 14, 218, 219. *See also* planned communities

Gardner and Matthews, 172

Garrett, John W., 315, 332, 374, 375

Garrett County, 373–79; Courthouse, 373–74; in Maryland counties map, xvi; outdoor recreation, 332; in Western Mountains, 331; —, map, 332

Garrett-Jacobs House, Baltimore City, 155

Gassaway, Nicholas, 80

gas stations: Hurst Brothers Service Station, Vienna, **129,** 129

Geare, Reginald, 311

Gehry, Frank, 238

Gelbach, George, Jr., 224–25

Gensler, **312,** 312

Georgetown, 283

Georgian Revival style, 58, 194–95, 216, 230, 304

Georgian style, 2, 12, 13, 23, 27, 28, 35, **36,** 36, 39, 46, 47, 48, 50, 51, 52, 53, 55, 56, 57–58, 63, 66, 69, 72, 73, **73,** 73–74, 79, 79–80, 80–81, **81,** 89, 96, 98, 99, 111, **112,** 112–13, 114, 129–30, 137, 140, 145, 162, 170, 181, 194, 201, 206, 221, 236, **248,** 248, **271,** 271–72, 286–87, **287,** 292, 302, 303, 318, 319, 345, 355, 357. *See also* Georgian Revival style

German house plans: Cresap (Michael) House, Oldtown, **366,** 366; Hager (Jonathan) House and Museum, Hagerstown, **351,** 351–52, **426;** Keedysville houses (Eversole, Hess, Carr, Snively), 354; Old Stone House, Lonaconing, 372; Schifferstadt, Frederick, **337,** 337–38; Widrick (George) House, Frederick, **339,** 339

German residents and history: American Brewery (The Weinberg [Harry and Jeanette] Building), Baltimore City, 9–10, **198,** 198; architectural influence, 1, 12; Brewers' Exchange, Baltimore City, 168–69, **171;** Burkittsville, 342; Catonsville, 253; Frederick business district, 334, 336; Hansa Haus, Baltimore City, **167,** 167; New Germany State Park, Grantsville vicinity, 379; Old Bohemia Church (St. Francis Xavier

Church), Warwick, 97; Old Otter-bein Evangelical United Brethren Church, Baltimore City, 201; St. Alphonsus Church, Baltimore City, 162–63; St. Mary's Evangelical Lutheran Church, Westminster, 261–62; Town Clock Church (German Evangelical Lutheran Church), Cumberland, **365,** 365; Uniontown Academy, 264; Western Mountains, 331; Zion Lutheran Church, Middletown, 344

Gerry House, Port Deposit, 88

Gerwig, George, 253

Gerwig, John, 253

Gerwig, William, 234, 253

Ghequiere, T. Buckler, 233

Ghequiere and May, 317–18

Gibbs, James, 53, 57, 160

Gibson Island, 77–78

Gieske, Walter M., 254

Gieske (Hardy) House, Catonsville, 254

Gilbert, Benjamin Franklin, 311

Gillis-Grier House, Salisbury, 132

Gilpin, Samuel, 91

Gingerbread House, St. Michaels, 114

Girard Engineering, **178,** 178

Glebe House, Princess Anne, **136,** 136–37

Glen Echo, 327–30

Glen Ellen (demolished), Towson, 258

Glenn Dale, 293–94

Glenwood, 244

Glidden, Edward H., 180, 220

Godefroy, Maximilian, 15, **159,** 159–60, **176,** 176, 211–12, 255

Goldsborough, Charles, 124

Goldsborough-Phelps House, Cambridge, 123–24

Good, Albert, 349

Good (William) House, Sharpsburg, 355

Goodman, Charles M., 14, 16, **316,** 316–17

Gordon, James Riely, 373–74

Gorman House, Catonsville, 254

Gothic Revival style, 13, 15, 66, 68, 99, 108, **137,** 137–38, 145, 147, 156, 158–59, 162, **163,** 165, 211, 222, 225, 232, 235, 236, 256, 258, 260, 261–62, 264, 272, 286, **293,** 293, 296, 336–37, 347, 371, 375. *See also* High Victorian Gothic style

Gothic styles. *See* Carpenter Gothic style; Collegiate Gothic style; Gothic Revival style; High Victorian Gothic style; Venetian Gothic style

Gott, Jackson C., 131, 143, 145, 173, **265,** 265

Goudreau, Paul L., 245

Graham, John, 225

Grahame House, Lower Marlboro, 45

Graham-Hughes House, Baltimore City, 158

grain elevators: Linwood Grain Elevator, **267,** 267; Union Bridge, 265

Granite, 229

granite, Port Deposit, 88, 92, 115, 131, 214, 271, 275, 280–81

Grantsville, 377–79

Gravatt, G. Flippo, 44

Gray, John B., 44

Great Mills, 24–25

Greek Revival style, 15, 24, 46, 55–56, 57, 65, 98, 99, 104, 120, 132, 136, 144–45, 154, 155, 177, **190,** 190, 203, 230, **231,** 231–32, 236, 244–45, **246,** 256, 259, 260, 273, 280, **281,** 281, 286, 334, 338, 340, 344, 352, 355, 357, 361, 367

Greek Temple form, **167,** 167–68, 188, **190,** 190, 215

Greely, Rose, 42, 43

Green, Anne, 69

Greenbelt, 294–96; map, 295; as greenbelt town, 14, 294; NASA Goddard Space Flight Center, **306,** 307; planner for, 249, 294

greenbelt towns, 14, 294

Green (Jonas) House, Annapolis, 69

Greiner (J. E.) Company, 8, 76–77, **77,** 141, 143

Grempler (Godefroy) House, Catonsville, 254

Grieves (James R.) Associates, 155

Grimm and Parker, 306

Gropius, Walter, 16, **224,** 224

ground-rent system, 203

Grove-Delauney House, Sharpsburg, 355

Gunts, Edward, 192

Gwathmey, Charles, 327

GWWO Architects, **127,** 127, 187

Habre de Venture at Thomas Stone National Historic Site, Port Tobacco, 36

Hackerman House (Thomas-Jencks-Gladding House), Baltimore City, 155–56

Hager (Jonathan) House, Hagerstown, 12, **351,** 351–52, **426**

Hagerstown and vicinity, 349–53; map, 350; deindustrialization, 333; establishment, 2; manufacturing, 9, 333, 334, 349–50, 352, 359; in Maryland topographical map, 3; railroads, 229, 333, 349

hall-parlor plan: Albaugh-Duvall farmhouse, New Windsor vicinity, **268,** 268; Almodington, Oriole, 140; Annapolis Plan versus, 52; Arnold (David) House, Burkittsville, 343; Brookeville, 321; Burch House, Port Tobacco, 34; Capital Region, 283;

hall-parlor plan (*continued*)
Chesapeake houses, 33; Clifton, Sandy Spring, 318; Cloverfields, Queenstown, 108; Cray House, Stevensville, 110; Drane (James) Log House, Accident, 377; Exeter, Federalsburg, 104; Green (Jonas) House, Annapolis, 69; Hogshead, Annapolis, 63; Holly Hill, Friendship, 82; Maidstone, Owings, 46; Oaks II, Brookeville, 321; **321;** Old Treasury Building, Annapolis, 50; Paca House, Charlestown, 90; Pemberton Hall, Salisbury, 132–33; Sarum, Charlotte Hall, 31; Sotterley, Hollywood, 30; Tidewater houses, 12; Venables (Seth D.) House (Simplicity), Princess Anne, 136; Whitehaven Hotel, 133

Hamme, John B., 270–71
Hammersley, William, 28
Hammond, John, 68–69
Hammond, Matthias, 53, 69, 74
Hammond, Paul, 316
Hammond-Harwood House, Annapolis, **52,** 52–53, 55, 67, 69, 70, 74, 303
Hampton, Towson, **248,** 248–49
Hancock's Resolution, Pasadena, **78,** 78
Handsell, Vienna, **129,** 129–30
Handy, Isaac, 132
Hanson (John) House, Frederick, 336
Harbaugh, Leonard, 286–87, **287**
Harding, Clarence L., 311
Hardy, Levin, 131
Hardy Holzman Pfeiffer Associates, 172
Harford County, 270–82; canneries, 9, 270; in Central Maryland, 228; —, map, 229; Courthouse, **270,** 270; interstate highway system, 325; in Maryland counties map, xvi; military facilities, 230; quarries, 229; summer homes, 229
Hargis House, Snow Hill, 145
Harmony, 103
Harper, Robert Goodloe, 215
Harper House, Centreville, **x, 106,** 106
Harris, Robert L., 26–27, 299
Harris, Samuel, **231,** 231
Harrison, Joseph, 115
Harrison, Richard, 83
Harrison, Samuel, 83
Harrison (John) House, St. Michaels, 114
Harvey, Thomas, 51
Harwood, Hester Loockerman, 53
Harwood, Lucy and Hester Ann, 53
Harwood, Richard and Frances, 53
Harwood, 80–81
Hassel, John, **365,** 365
Hasson, John, 91

Hathaway, Andrew A., 113
Hauducoeur, C. P., 278
Havre de Grace, 278–82; map, 279; deep-water port, 228, 278; Maritime Museum, 117; in Maryland topographical map, 3; Perryville ferry, 89
Hayman (Charles H.) House, Princess Anne, 134
Haynes (James and Alice) House, Catonsville, 254
Hays (Joseph C.) House, Sharpsburg, 355
Hayward, Bartlett and Company, 179, 200
Hazlehurst (M. E.) House, Cumberland, 361
"H-bent" construction, 338
HDR, **301,** 302
Heaton, Arthur B., 311
Heiner, Elias, 224–25
Hellmuth, Obata and Kassabaum (HOK), 199, 221. *See also* HOK Architects
Henderson (Robert) House, Cumberland, 362
Henry, Charles, 148
Henry (J. F.) House, Cambridge, 125
Hensley, Philemon, 108
Herrman, Augustine, 96–97, 345; *Map of Virginia and Maryland,* 4, **5**
Hess House, Keedysville, 354
Hicks, Thomas, 85
Higgins House, St. Michaels, 117
Highbarger (Jacob) House, Sharpsburg, 355
Highland Beach, 22, 78–79
High Victorian Gothic style, 115, **122,** 123, 130–31, **158,** 158, 173, 190, **341,** 341
highways. *See* roads and highways
Hill and Thompson, 106
Hillegeist, C. H., 313
Hinkle (Summerfield) House, Flintstone vicinity, 368
historic districts: Annapolis Historic District, 49, 58; Benning Road Historic District, Galesville, 81–82; Chestertown old town district, 97; Decatur Heights National Register Historic District, Cumberland, 364–65; Doub's Mill, Hagerstown vicinity, 353; Easton, 111; Fell's Point Historic District, Baltimore City, 192–93; Hyattsville, 298–99; Maryland, 1, 16; Newtown Historic District, Salisbury, 132; North Brentwood Historic District, 297–98; Old Courthouse Historic District, Rockville, **304,** 304–5; Oxford, 118, 120–21; Takoma Park, **311,** 311

Hiteshaw (Oliver) House, Uniontown, 263

Hodge (Margaret Perry) House, Takoma Park, 312

Hodgens and Hills, 364

Hodges, Benjamin, 286

Hodgkins, Thomas Brooke, 70

Hoffman House, Keedysville, 355

Hogan, James, 286–87, **287**

Hogg, John W., 217

Hogshead, Annapolis, 33, **63**, 63

Hohne (Christopher) House, Annapolis, 62

HOK Architects, 300, 301

HOK Sport, **199**, 199–200

Holden, Lansing C., Sr., 365–66

Holland Island, **119**, 119

Hollerith (Herman) House, Kensington, 316

Holliday, Benjamin, 62

Hollingsworth, Zebulon, 91

Hollyday, Henry, 113

Holly Hill, Friendship, 82–83

Hollywood, 29–30

Holman, Emily Elizabeth, **314**, 314

Holmboe and Lafferty, 364

Home Demonstration Clubs, 309

Homewood, Baltimore City, 55, **215**, 215–16

Hooper, William E., 226

Hopkins, Henry Powell, 50, 66–67

Hopkins, Johns, 151, 165, 189, 198

Hopkins House, Sandy Spring, 318

Hopkins (Thomas) House, Havre de Grace, 280

horse racing: Belair, Bowie, **292**, 292; Fair Hill Racetrack, Elkton, 94

hospitals: The Johns Hopkins Hospital, Baltimore City, 151, 158, 170, 197–98, 271; Walter Reed National Military Center, Bethesda Naval Hospital, 285, 308–9, **309**; Sheppard-Pratt Hospital, Towson, 246–47

hotels, inns, and motels: Alexander Hotel, Hagerstown, 351; Atlantic Hotel, Berlin, 146; Baltimore Hyatt Regency, 183; Bayard House Hotel, Chesapeake City, 95; Belvedere Hotel, Baltimore City, 164, 168; Casselman Inn, Grantsville, 377–78; Colonial Hotel, Hagerstown, 351; Cumberland Arms Hotel, Cumberland, 364; Fell's Point Recreational Pier, Baltimore City, 195; Flintstone Hotel, 378; Four Mile House, La Vale, 378; Gunter Hotel, Frostburg, **371**, 371; Hamilton Hotel, Hagerstown, 351; Henry's (Colored) Hotel, Ocean City, **148**, 148; Hilton (E. T.) Hotel, New Market, 340; Hotel Dagmar, Hagerstown, 351; Howard House Hotel, Ellicott City, 232; Hyatt Place, Ocean City, 147; The Inn at Henderson's Wharf, Baltimore City, **193**, 193–94; Inn Boonsboro, **353**, 353–54; Key (Francis Scott) Hotel, Frederick, 336; Lord Baltimore Hotel, Baltimore City, 168, **171**; Madison Beach Motel, Ocean City, 149; Maryland Inn, Annapolis, **65**, 65; Morris (Robert) Inn, Oxford, **120**, 120; National Hotel and Stage Office, New Market, 340; on National Road, 377–78; Ocean City, 147; The Old Inn, St. Michaels, **115**, 115; (Old) Patapsco Hotel, Ellicott City, 232; Penn Alps Inn, Grantsville, 378; Railroad Hotel, Ellicott City, 232; revival architectures, 259; Sea Breeze Inn (Sea Breeze Motel), Ocean City, **148**, 148–49; Shine Inn Motel, Newburg, 31–33; Sun Tan Motel, Ocean City, 149; Tomlinson Inn, Grantsville, 378; Uniontown Hotel, 262; U.S. Hotel, Boonsboro, 354; Washington Hotel, Princess Anne, 133–34; Whitehaven Hotel, **133**, 133; Wyand House Hotel, Keedysville, 354; Ye Forest Inn, Forest Glen, 315

Houck House, Frederick, 336

house museums: Barton (Clara) House, Glen Echo, **329**, 329–30; Beall-Dawson House, Rockville, 304–5; Brice (James) House, Annapolis, 50–51; Carroll (Charles) House, Annapolis, 73; Carroll Mansion (Caton House), Baltimore City, 191; Costen House, Pocomoke City, 142; Cresap (Michael) House, Oldtown, **366**, 366; Darnall's Chance, Upper Marlboro, **285**, 285–86; Evergreen House, Baltimore City, 217–18; Exeter, Federalsburg, 104; Greenbelt Museum, **294**, 294–96; Habre de Venture, Port Tobacco, 36; Hager (Jonathan) House and Museum, Hagerstown, **351**, 351–52, **426**; Hammond-Harwood House, Annapolis, **52**, 52–53; Hancock's Resolution, Pasadena, **78**, 78; Handsell, Vienna, **129**, 129–30; Homewood, Baltimore City, **215**, 215–16; Irish Railroad Workers Museum, Baltimore City, **203**, 203; Maxwell Hall, Benedict, 38–39; Montpelier, Laurel, **54**, 303; Mount Clare, Baltimore City, 205–6; Mudd (Dr. Samuel A.) House, Bryantown, **37**, 37; Oakland Manor, Columbia, 238; Oakley Cabin African American Museum and Park, Olney, 320; Old Jail Museum, Leonardtown, 26; Old Row Museum, Mount Savage, **369**, 369–70; Paca (William) House, Annapolis, **51**, 51–52; Pemberton

house museums (*continued*)
Hall, Salisbury, 132–33; Poe (Edgar Allan) House, Baltimore City, 204; Poplar Hill, Salisbury, **131**, 131–32; Ridgeley School, Capitol Heights, 290; Riversdale, Riverdale Park, 299–300; Rodgers Tavern Museum, Perryville, **89**, 89; Rose Hill, Frederick, 338; Schifferstadt, Frederick, **337**, 337–38; Shiplap House, Annapolis, **63**, 63–64; Sotterley, Hollywood, **29**, 29–30; Stonestreet Museum, Rockville, 305; Susquehanna Museum of Havre de Grace at the Lock House, **281**, 281; Teackle Mansion, Princess Anne, **135**, 135; Tilghman Waterman's Museum, Tilghman Island, **118**, 118; Tobacco Prise Warehouse, Annapolis, 64; Tucker House, Centreville, 106; Tudor Hall, Bel Air, 272; Webb (James) Cabin, Harmony, **103**, 103; Wright's Chance, Centreville, 106

Houston, Charles Hamilton, 139
Howard, Ebenezer, 252
Howard, William K., 188–89
Howard County, 230–44; in Central Maryland, 228; —, map, 229; Courthouse, **231**, 231–32; interstate highway system, 325; in Maryland counties map, xvi; population increase, 325
Hubbell, Julian B., **329**, 329–30
Hubner, John, 253, 254
Hughes, Langston, 79
Hughes, W. V., 130
Hughesville, 21, 38
Humphreys (Cathell and Isabella Huston) House, Salisbury, 132
Hutchins, Robert Holt, 362
Hyattsville, 13, 285, 298–99; map, 295
Hyde and Shepard, 352
Hyder (John) House, Uniontown, 263
Hynes (Joshua) House, Oella, 256

I-95: corridor, 8, 229, 325; JFK toll plaza, **325**
I-houses, 41, 104, 142, 298, 341
Indiantown, Vienna, **129**, 129–30
industrial buildings: Abell Building, Baltimore City, **171**, 173; Alberti, Brink and Company Building, Baltimore City, 174; American Brewery (The Weinberg [Harry and Jeanette] Building), Baltimore City, 9–10, **198**, 198; Baltimore and Ohio railroad shops (Baltimore and Ohio Transportation Museum), Baltimore City, **202**, 202–3; Baltimore and Ohio Railroad warehouse, Camden Yards, Baltimore City, 199; Balti-

more Shot Tower (Phoenix Shot Tower), 10, **190**, 190–91; Belt's Wharf Warehouse, Baltimore City, 193–94; Bond Street Wharf Building, Baltimore City, **195**, 195; Brown's Wharf Warehouses, Baltimore City, 195; Chance Boatyard, Annapolis, 74–75; Chesapeake and Delaware Canal Pumphouse Museum, Chesapeake City, **96**, 96; Corddry Lumber Warehouse, Snow Hill, **143**, 143; Cushwa Warehouse, Williamsport, 358; Deere (John) Company Building (U.S. Post Office), Lutherville-Timonium, **257**, 257; Domino Sugar Factory, Baltimore City, 186, **187**; Duncan Brothers Garage (Delmarva Discovery Center), Pocomoke City, 141–42; Footer's Dye Works, Cumberland, **362**, 362–63; Fountain Rock Lime Company, Walkersville, **345**, 345; Heiser Building, Baltimore City, 173; Krug (G.) and Son Ironworks, Baltimore City, 170, **171**; Levering and Company Coffee Warehouse, Baltimore City, 195; Lore (J. C.) Oyster House, Solomons, **40**, 40–41; Martin (Glenn L.) Aircraft Company Plant No. 2/Middle River Depot, 230, 249–50; National Can Company, Baltimore City, 9, **196**, 197; Patapsco Distilling Company (McDonald [John] and Co. Store), Sykesville, **269**, 269; Phillips Packing Co., Plant F, Cambridge, **125**, 125–26; Platt (S. B.) and Co. Oyster Packing (Baltimore Museum of Industry), 186; Rombro Building, Baltimore City, 173; Rosenfeld Building, Baltimore City, 173; Seneca (S. J.) Factory and Warehouse, Havre de Grace, 278–79; Strauss Building, Baltimore City, 173; Ward Brothers Workshop, Crisfield, **140**, 140–41; West Denton Warehouse and Wharf, 102. *See also* iron furnaces; mills; shipbuilding; tobacco warehouses
inns. *See* hotels, inns, and motels; taverns
International Style, 147, 167
iron furnaces: Baltimore City, 9; Catoctin Furnace, Thurmont, 348; Elkridge Furnace complex, 228, 238–39; Lonaconing Iron Furnace, **372**, 372–73; Maryland and New York Iron and Coal Company furnace complex, Mount Savage, 369; Muirkirk Iron Furnace, 303
Irvin (Levin T. H.) House, Princess Anne, 136
Italianate style, 13, 60, 65–66, **71**, 71–

72, 97, 98, 102, 122, 129, 132, 134, 136, 142, **155,** 155, **156,** 156, **171,** 173, 196, 200, **204,** 204–5, **205,** 205, 210, 212, 217, 226, 232, 235, 241, 242, 243, 245, 255, 262, 276, 280, **285,** 286, 298, 320, 326, 334, 335, 342, 362, 378
Italian Renaissance Revival style, 220

Jackley, F. Dano, **298,** 299
Jackson, John W., 303
Jacobean Revival style, 220, 245
Jacobean style, **23,** 23
Jacobson, Hugh Newell, 16, 210
jails and prisons: Baltimore County Jail, Towson, 245; Cumberland, 364; Howard County Jail, Ellicott City, 232
James, Richard, 109
Jamison (Henry A.) House, Flintstone vicinity, 367
Jefferson, Thomas, 53, 225, 254, 256
Jencks, Francis H., 189
Jenkins (Ann) House, Snow Hill, 146
Johansen, John, 166
Johnson, George H., 174
Johnson, Joseph G., **91,** 91
Johnson, Lindley, 310
Johnsville, 346
Jones, Wrightson, 115
Jones Town, 150
Joppa (Joppatowne), 274–75
Jory, Hubert G., 232
Jung/Brannen Associates, **208,** 208–9
Justement, Louis, 313

Kaese, Henry August, 376–77
Kahn (Albert) and Associates, 249–50
Kallmann, McKinnell and Wood, 156
Karn (Thomas) House, Burkittsville, 342
Karsner (William C.) House, Chesapeake City, 95
Keedysville, 354–55
Keen, Charles Barton, 306-7
Kellogg Bridge Company, 157
Kelly, Howard, 271
Kemp, Joseph F., 172–73, 200
Kennard, John A., 97
Kennedy, J. Robie, Jr., 313–14
Kensington, 315–17; map, 310
Kent County, 97–101; Courthouse, 97; in Eastern Shore, 84; –, map, 85; in Maryland counties map, xvi
Kepes, Gyorgy, 224
Keplinger, Michael, 215
Kerr-Parsons House, Kensington, 316
Kessler, George, 218
Key, Francis Scott, 58
Keyes, Lethbridge and Condon, 16, **305,** 305–6

Kift (J.) and Son, **271,** 271
Kilty, William, 70
Kingman, Eugene, 299
Kingston, Upper Marlboro, 286
Kingsville, 273–74
Kirkbride Plan, 247
Kirkegaard Associates, 306
Kirk (Elisha) House, Rising Sun, 87
kit houses. *See* mail-order houses
Kliment Hasbland, 216
Klinkhart, Amos J., **350,** 351
Knight, L. Albert, 206
Knight (William and Elizabeth) House, Rising Sun, 87
Koch, Albert C., 316
Kohlstock, Henry, 261
Kohn Pederson Fox, 221
Koubek, Vlastimi, 184
Kretzer Homestead, Sharpsburg, 355

Labadists, 96–97
Laboriere House, Baltimore City, 224
La Cité Development, 204
La Farge, John, 177
La Grange, LaPlata, **36,** 36–37
Laing, John, 232
Lamb, Charles, 75, **257,** 257. *See also* Rogers, Taliaferro and Lamb; RTKL Associates
Lamb, Thomas, **171,** 172
Lamdin, William D., 220
Lantz-Hyde House, Linwood, 267
Lang House, Catonsville, 254
Langrell, Frank, 104
LaPlata, 21, 36–37
Larew, Abraham, 238
Largo, 290–91
Latrobe, Benjamin Henry, 15, 96, **160,** 160-61, 215, 236, 237
Latrobe, Benjamin Henry, Jr., **163,** 164-65, 239–40, **240**
Latrobe, Charles H., **196,** 197
Laurel, 283, 303; map, 295
Lauretum, Chestertown, **99,** 99
La Vale, 368
Layman (Firman) House, Chesapeake City, 95
Leavitt, Sheldon, **224,** 224
Lecates (William) House, Princess Anne, 136
Lee, David, 273, 274
Leonardtown, 21, 26–27
Levin/Brown Architects, **224,** 224
Levitt and Sons, 14, 292–93
Levy, Jean, 273
Lewin, Lewis, 46
Lewis, Abraham, 104
Lewis, Albert W., 199
Lewis, James K.: House, Vienna, 129; Wharf House, Vienna, **128,** 128–29

libraries: The Cloisters (Parker House), Lutherville-Timonium, 258; Mc-Keldin Library, University of Maryland, College Park, 302; Peabody Institute, Baltimore City, **157,** 157; Pratt (Enoch) Free Library Central Building, Baltimore City, 151, **161,** 161; Richardson (Earl S.) Library, Morgan State University, Baltimore City, 221; Sharpsburg Library and Town Hall, 355; Washington County Free Library, Hagerstown, 351

Liegender Stuhl (leaning truss system), 337

Lift-A-Latch, Elkridge, 241–42

lighthouses: Concord Point Lighthouse, Havre de Grace, 280–81; Cove Point Lighthouse, Calvert County, 25; Drum Point Lighthouse, Solomons, **iv, 39,** 39–40, 76; Hooper Strait Lighthouse, St. Michaels, 40, 76, 117; Piney Point Lighthouse, **25,** 25–26, 76; screw-pile, **iv, 39,** 39–40, 75–76, 117, 183; Seven Foot Knoll Lighthouse, Baltimore City, 40, 183; Thomas Point Shoal Light Station, Annapolis vicinity, 40, 75–76; Turkey Point Lighthouse, Cecil County, 25

lime, 333, 345

Lind, Edmund G., 16, **65,** 66, **99,** 99, 154, **157,** 157, 158–59

Linden, Prince Frederick, 44

Linthicum, 83

Linton, Isaiah, 273

Linwood, 266–67

Liriodendron, Bel Air, **271,** 271–72

Little Hill House, Elkridge, 241

Lloyd, Edward, IV, 55, 110

Lloyd, James, 206–7

lockhouses: Chesapeake and Ohio Canal, Lock, and Lockhouse 22, Glen Echo, 327–28; Chesapeake and Ohio Canal Lock 24, Poolesville, **324,** 324–25; Chesapeake and Ohio Canal, Canal Lock 70, Oldtown, 366; Susquehanna Museum of Havre de Grace at the Lock House, **281,** 281

log buildings: African American, 11; Albaugh-Duvall Farm, New Windsor vicinity, 268; Banneker (Benjamin) Cabin, Oella, **255,** 255–56; Beatty-Cramer House, Frederick, 339; Bond-Simms barn complex, Hollywood, 29; Boonsboro, 354; Breakneck Valley houses, Flintstone vicinity, 367; Brown (Mercer) House, Rising Sun, 87; Capital Region, 283; Catoctin Furnace, Thurmont, 348; Catoctin Mountain Park,

Thurmont, **348,** 349; Cray House, Stevensville, 109; Drane (James) Log House, Accident, 12, **377,** 377; early housing stock, 12, 14; Ennis (George) House, Burkittsville, 342; Flippo (Joseph P.) Community House, Port Republic, 44; Frederick, 334; Harewood, Sandy Spring, 317; Log Lodge, Beltsville Agricultural Research Center, 302–3; New Germany State Park, Grantsville vicinity, 379; New Market Main Street, 340; Oakley Cabin, Sandy Spring vicinity, 12, 320; Oaks II, Brookeville, 321, **321;** Our Father's House, Altamont, **376,** 376; preservation, 17; Red Lyon Tavern, Charlestown, 91; Rose Hill outbuildings, Frederick, 338; Sharpsburg, 355; slave houses, 42, 319; Webb (James) Cabin, Harmony, 12, **103,** 103; Western Mountains, 331; Winterberg House, Spruce Forest Artisan Village, 379; Woodlawn log slave house, Sandy Spring, 319

Lonaconing, 365, 372–73

London Town, 21

Long, Louis L., 157

Long, Robert Cary, Jr., 15, 162–63, **163,** 164–65, **190,** 190, 203–4, 231, 233, 260, 286

Long, Robert Cary, Sr., 15, 159, **175,** 175–76, 181

Longfellow, Alden and Harlow, 256

Long (Littleton) House, Princess Anne, 136

Long (Robert) House, Baltimore City, 194

Lore, Joseph, Sr., 40

Lowell, Guy, 220

Lower Marlboro, 21, 45

Lusby, 41–42

Lutherville-Timonium, 257–59

Lynes, Phillip, 26

MacAlpine, Ellicott City, 234

Mackall, McGill, 178

Madison House, Brookeville, 320

Maginnis, Walsh and Kennedy, 222

Magruder (Jonathan) House, Cumberland, 362

Maguolo and Quick, 346, **347**

Maidstone, Owings, **32,** 33, 46

mail-order houses, 13, 299, 312

Main, Charles T., 186, **187**

Maisel and Kern, 253

Malone and Williams, 92, 130, 131

Mann, Horace, 326

Mansion, The, Savage Mill Village, 243

Marcotte (L.) and Company, 156

maritime culture and trade, 4–5, 100, 107, 115, 116-17, 118, 128-29, 192.

See also boats, ships, and boatyards; fishing; crabbing; oystering; seafood processing; wharfs

Markley House, Spruce Forest Artisan Village, Grantsville, 379

Marshall, Joseph M., **59,** 59

Marshall, Thurgood, 49–50, 83, 139, 211

Maryland: map of geographical features, 3; map of regions/counties covered by volume, xvi. *See also specific regions, counties, cities, and towns by name*

Maryland Archaeological Conservation Laboratory, 21, 22–23, 42, 43

Maryland Gazette (newspaper), 69

Maryland–National Capital Park and Planning Commission (M-NCPPC), 285, 291, 294, 300, 303, 320, 322, 326

Maryland Toleration Act (1649), 1, 46, 123, 288

Mason (David W.) House, Port Republic, **43,** 43–44

Masonic buildings: Masonic Hall, Sharpsburg, 355; Masonic Hall and Opera House, Annapolis, **59,** 59–60; Masonic lodge, Savage Mill Village, 243; Masonic Lodge, Snow Hill, 144; Masonic lodge (Law Office), Denton, 102; Prince Hall Grand Lodge, Baltimore City, 210–11; Temple of the Scottish Rite, Baltimore City, 214

Matthews, Mother Bernardina, 37

Matthews, George, 189–90

Matthews, Henry, 65

Maurice, T., 288

Maxwell Hall, Benedict, 38–39

Maybury, Beriah, 62

Maycroft, Elkridge, 241

Mayer Studio, 204

Maynard, John T. and Maria, 71

Maynard-Burgess House, Annapolis, 70–71

McCartney, John, 233, 239, **240**

McCleery, Andrew, 334, 336–37

McCleery, Henry, 337

McClenahan (John) House, Port Deposit, 89

McDonough (James and Margaret) House, Catonsville, 254

McKim, John, 188–89

McKim (Catherine) House, Baltimore City, 163

McKim, Mead and White, 16, 155, **163,** 164, 213–14, 311

McKinstry (Samuel) House, New Windsor vicinity, 268

McLaughlin, Andrew, 232, 233

McMansions, 325

McMillan Plan, 60

McNeal, William R., 286

McPherson (John) House, Frederick, 334

memorials. *See* monuments and memorials

Memory Lane, Williston, 102–3

Mendez, Antonio Tobias, 49–50

Merchant (William) House, St. Michaels, 114

Merrick, Samuel V., **96,** 96

Mesick, Cohen, Wilson, and Baker, 49

Mesker Brothers, 336

Mesker (George L.) Iron Works, 95, 305

midcentury modern style, 210, 316

Middle River, 230, 249–51

Middletown, 344

Mies van der Rohe, Ludwig, 16, **17,** 165–66, **217,** 217, 250

military installations. *See* forts and military installations

Miller (Decatur) Row House, Baltimore City, **155,** 155

Mills, Robert, 15, 68, **153,** 153–55, 181, 334

mills: Baltimore City, 8–9, 10; Cecil's Old Mill and Cecil's Country Store, Great Mills, **24,** 24–25; Central Maryland, 228; Dickey (W. J.) Company, Oella, 255; Doub's Mill, Hagerstown vicinity, 353; Jerusalem Mill, Kingsville, 228, **273,** 273–74; Jones Falls Valley mills, Baltimore City, 225; Kaese Mill, Accident, 376–77; Keedysville, 354; Klots Throwing Mill (Klots Mill Lofts), Cumberland, 365–66; Linchester Mill, Preston, **103,** 103–4; McKinstry's Mill, New Windsor vicinity, 228, 267–68; Mount Vernon Mills No. 1, 2, and 3, 10, 226, 227; Mount Washington Mill, Baltimore City, 10, 224, 225–26; Rockland mill village, 228, 259; Rock Run Mill Buildings, Darlington vicinity, 277; Savage Mill, 242, 243; Stanton's Mill, Grantsville, 376, 379; Union Mill (Druid Mill), Baltimore City, 10, **226,** 226; Union Mills Homestead, Westminster, 228, **260,** 261; Williston Mill and Miller's House, Preston, 104; Wye Mill, Wye Mills, 110. *See also* flour milling

Mills-Abernathy House, Kensington, 316

minimalism, 210, 327

Mitchell, Alexander, 76

Mitchell (Siegfried and Minnie) House, Catonsville, 254

Mitchellville, 291

mixed-use developments: Center/West, Baltimore City, 204; Columbus Center, Baltimore City, 183; Bromo Seltzer Arts Tower (Emerson mixed-use developments (*continued*) Bromo-Seltzer Tower), Baltimore City, 10, **174**, 174–75; Footer's Dye Works, Cumberland, 363; Harborplace at Inner Harbor, Baltimore City, 182–83, **184**, 184–85; Martin (Glenn L.) Aircraft Company, Middle River, 250; Mount Vernon Mills No. 1, 2, and 3, 226; One Charles Center, Baltimore City, 165–66; Pratt Street Power Plant, Baltimore City, 183; Savage Mill, 242; Union Mill (Druid Mill), Baltimore City, **226**, 226

Moderne style. *See* Art Moderne style

modernism, **xii**, 14, 58, 75, 78, 165–66, 192, 204, 208, 210, 215, **217**, 217, 222, 223, 247, 257, **289**, 289–90, **294**, 294–95, 306, **316**, 316–17, 355. *See also* Art Deco style; Art Moderne style; Brutalism; International Style; midcentury modern style

monasteries and convents: Mount Carmel Monastery, LaPlata, 37; National Shrine of Saint Elizabeth Ann Seton, Emmitsburg, 346–47; Ursuline Sisters convent, Frostburg, 371

Monkton vicinity, 273

Monroe (William) House, Annapolis, 62

Montgomery County, 304–30; Baltimore and Ohio Railroad, 284; in Capital Region, 283; —, map, 284; market town development, 283; in Maryland counties map, xvi; Old County Courthouse, **304**, 304; Quaker agricultural societies, 283, 317

Montgomery Ward houses, 299

Montpelier, Laurel, **54**, 55, 303

monuments and memorials: Baltimore City, 151; Battle Monument, Baltimore City, 154, **176**, 176, 177; Cecil County World War I monument, Elkton, 94; Confederate monument, Easton, 111; Fort McHenry National Monument and Historic Shrine, Baltimore City, **187**, 187; Marshall (Thurgood) monument, Maryland State House, Annapolis, 49–50; National Fallen Firefighters Memorial Park, Emmitsburg, 347; Otterbein (Reverend Philip Wilhelm) monument, Baltimore City, 201; Peace Cross (World War I memorial), Bladensburg, 297; War Correspondents Memorial Arch, Burkittsville, **343**, 343; Washington Monument, Baltimore City, **153**, 153–54, 229; World War I memorial, Leonardtown, 26

Moore and Hutchins, 247

Moore Ruble Yudell, 302

Moorish style, 169, 190, 211, 213

Morningstar, William H., 266

Morris, Ellwood, 367

Morris, James Rownd, 145

Morris, Robert (businessman), 120

Morris, Robert (writer), 76, 113

motels. *See* hotels, inns, and motels

Mottu and White, 220, 233, 348

Mountain Lake Park, 7, 374–75

Mt. Airy, Sharpsburg vicinity, 357

Mount Clare, Baltimore City, 205–6

Mount Ida, Ellicott City, 233

Mount Lubentia, Largo, 290–91

Mount Republican, Newburg, 31

Mount Savage, 368–70

movie theaters: Bengies Drive-In Theater, Middle River, 251; Church Hill Theatre, 107; Colonial Theater, Hagerstown, 351; Dundalk, 252; Embassy Theater, Cumberland, 364; Greenbelt Theater, 294, 295; Hippodrome Theater at the France-Merrick Performing Arts Center, Baltimore City, **171**, 172; Mar-Va Theater, Pocomoke City, **142**, 142; Senator Theater, Baltimore City, **221**, 221; Silver Theater, Silver Spring, **312**, 312–13; Tivoli Theater, Frederick, 336

Moyer, Tilghman, 304

Mudd (Dr. Samuel A.) House, Bryantown, **37**, 37

Muller, Daniel C., 329

Mumma Farmhouse, Sharpsburg vicinity, 357

Muncaster (Walter J.) House, Cumberland, 362

murals. *See* artworks and sculptures

Murchison, Kenneth M., **207**, 207

Murphy and Dittenhaufer, 208

Murray, Donald Gaines, 138–39

Murray, James, 69

Murray (William) House, Chestertown, 97

museums: American Visionary Art Museum, Baltimore City, 185–86, **187**; Baltimore and Ohio Ellicott City Station Museum, 233–34, **235**; Baltimore and Ohio Transportation Museum, Baltimore City, **202**, 202–3; Baltimore Museum of Art, 36, **214**, 214–15; Baltimore Museum of Industry, 9, 186; Baltimore Shot Tower (Phoenix Shot Tower), 191; Banneker-Douglass Museum, Annapolis, 68; Belair Stables Museum, Bowie, 292; Betterton Heritage Museum, 100; Calvert Marine Museum, Solomons, 39, 40, 117; Carroll

County Farm Museum, Westminster, **260,** 260–61; Chesapeake and Delaware Canal Pumphouse Museum, Chesapeake City, **96,** 96; Chesapeake Bay Maritime Museum, St. Michaels, 115, **116,** 116–17; Chesapeake Beach Railway Museum, 45–46; College Park Airport and Aviation Museum, 301; Delmarva Discovery Center, Pocomoke City, 141–42; Dundalk-Patapsco Neck Historical Society and Museum, 252; Havre de Grace Maritime Museum, 117; Jewish Museum of Maryland, Baltimore City, 190; Krug (G.) and Son Ironworks and Museum, Baltimore City, 170, **171;** Lewis Museum of Maryland and African American History, Baltimore City, **192,** 192; Maryland Institute College of Art (MICA), Baltimore City, 210; Maryland Science Center, Baltimore City, 182; Museum of the Iron Worker, Thurmont, 348; Oxford Museum, 120; Peale Center for Baltimore History and Architecture (Peale's Baltimore Museum), 151, 181; Sandy Spring Museum, 318; Slave Museum, Sandy Spring, 318; Union Mills Homestead, Westminster, 261; Uniontown Museum, 263–64; U.S. Lifesaving Station and Guardhouse, Ocean City, 147–48, **148;** Walters Art Museum, Baltimore City, 155, **156,** 156–57; Ward Museum of Waterfowl Art, Salisbury University, 141; Washington County Museum of Fine Arts, Hagerstown, 352; Western Maryland Railway Historical Society Museum, Union Mills, 265; Wye Mill, Wye Mills, 110. *See also* house museums

Nagle, James F., 253
national battlefields: Antietam National Battlefield, 343, **356,** 356–57; Fort McHenry National Monument and Historic Shrine, Baltimore City, **187,** 187; Gambrill House, Monocacy National Battlefield, Frederick, 339
national historic sites: Barton (Clara) House (National Historic Site), Glen Echo, **329,** 329–30; Hampton National Historic Site, Towson, **248,** 248–49; Stone (Thomas) National Historic Site, Port Tobacco, 36
national parks: Catoctin Mountain Park, Thurmont, **348,** 348–49; Chesapeake & Ohio Canal (National Historical Park), 6–7, **324,** 324–25, 327–28, 358, 362–63, 366, 367; Fort

Washington National Park, 288; Glen Echo Park, **328,** 328–29; Mission 66 initiative, 187, 357; Tubman (Harriet) Underground Railroad Visitor Center, Church Creek, **127,** 127

Native American residents and history: Accokeek Creek finds, 289; boatbuilding, 116; Cresap (Michael) House, Oldtown, 366; Eastern Shore, 4, 84; longhouse, Handsell, Vienna, **129,** 130; Nause-Waiwash Longhouse (Trinity Methodist Episcopal Church), Bucktown, 128; Patterson (Jefferson) Park, St. Leonard, 42; Port Tobacco, 34; Snow Hill, 142; Western Shore, 4, 23

Neilson, J. Crawford, **105,** 105, 106, 123, **157,** 157, **270,** 270. *See also* Niernsee and Neilson

neoclassicism, 15, 76, **159,** 159–60, **160,** 160–61, **175,** 175, 181, **235,** 236–37

Néo-Grec style, 173

Neutra and Alexander, **58,** 58

Newburg, 31–33

Newlands, Francis G., 310; House, Chevy Chase, 310–11

Newlin (David) House, Brookeville, 320

New Market, 340

Newtown Manor, Leonardtown, 27

New Towns, 14, 237, 305

New Urbanism, 14, 304, 322

New Windsor vicinity, 267–68

Nichols, John, 104, 225

Nicholson, Arthur, 286

Nicholson, Francis, 47, 62, 66

Niernsee, John R., **160,** 160, 161. *See also* Niernsee and Neilson

Niernsee and Neilson, 16, 154, **155,** 155–56, 164, 200, **275,** 275

Noke, William, 53

Norris House, Union Bridge, 266

North Brentwood, 13, 297–98; map, 295

North East, 91–92

Norwood, Sandy Spring, 319

Notman, John, 361

Nottingham Lots, 86, 87

NPS EDOC, 356

Oakland, 332, 373–74

Oakland estate, Baltimore City, 215

Oakland Manor, Columbia, 238

Oakley Cabin, Sandy Spring vicinity, 12, 320

Oaks II, Brookeville, 321, **321**

Ocean City, 7, 86, 147–49

Ocean Hall, Bushwood, 28

O'Connor, James W., 273

Oella, 228, 231, 254–56

Oertel, Johannes, 276
office buildings: Brewers' Exchange, Baltimore City, 168–69, **171;** Bromo Seltzer Arts Tower (Emerson Bromo-Seltzer Tower), Baltimore City, 10, **174,** 174–75; Canton House, Baltimore City, **179,** 179–80; Charles Center South, Baltimore City, 166; Court Row, Chestertown, 97; Cumberland and Pennsylvania Railroad Company, Mount Savage, 369; Furness House, Baltimore City, 180; Georges Creek Coal and Iron Company Office Building, Lonaconing, 373; Hansa Haus, Baltimore City, **167,** 167; Harford Mutual Building, Bel Air, 270; James Senate Office Building, Annapolis, 66–67; Lawyers' Row, Ellicott City, 232; Lewis (James K.) Wharf House, Vienna, **128,** 128–29; Mutual Insurance Company building, Frederick, 336; One Charles Center, Baltimore City, **17,** 165–66, 182; Ramacciotti Professional Arts Building, Hagerstown, **350,** 351; Sun Life Building, Baltimore City, 167; Transamerica Tower (United States Fidelity and Guaranty [USF&G] Building; Legg Mason Building), Baltimore City, 182, 184; Two Charles Center, Baltimore City, 166; Union Mining Company Building, Mount Savage, **368,** 368–69; Wootton (Henry) Law Office, Ellicott City, 232; World Trade Center, Baltimore City, 182, 184
Ogle, Samuel, 56, 292
Ogle Hall, Annapolis, 56
Okie, R. Brognard, 241–42
Old Stone House, Lonaconing, 372
Oldtown, 366–67
Olmsted, Frederick Law, 89, 154
Olmsted, Frederick Law, Jr., 219, 220
Olmsted Brothers, 77, 153, 205–6, 213, 218
"Opkamer" plan, 338
orangeries, 114, 248
Oriole, 140
Otterbein, Philip Wilhelm, 201
Owens, Jonas, 91
Owings, 33, 46
Owings Mill, 228
Oxford, 118, 120–21
Oxford Movement, 361
oystering: Avondale, Solomons, 41; Benning Road Historic District, Galesville, 81; boatbuilding, 116, 117; Calvert Marine Museum, Solomons, 39; Cambridge, 121, 125; Chesapeake Bay, 5, **6;** Lore (J. C.) Oyster House, Solomons, **40,** 40–41; National

Can Company, Baltimore City, 197; Platt (S. B.) and Co. Oyster Packing (Baltimore Museum of Industry), 9, 186; St. Michaels, 114, 115; Western Shore, 21
Ozmon, John H., 107

Paca, John, 90
Paca, William, 51, 90; House, Annapolis, **51,** 51–52, 74
Paca House, Charlestown, 90
Pain, William, 215
Palladianism, 13, **28,** 28, 35, 36, 47, 51, 52, 53, 54–55, 72, 98, 113, 114, 132, 162, 206, 241, 248, 287, 337. *See also* five-part Palladian houses
Palmer, Edward L., 219–20, **252,** 252–53
Parker, Carey Mulholland, 42
Parker, Dudrea, 257, 258
Parker, Sumner A., **257,** 257–58
Parker and Thomas, 164, **167,** 167–68
Parker House (The Cloisters), Lutherville-Timonium, **257,** 257–59
Parker, Thomas and Rice, 77, **167,** 167, 216, 245–46
Park Hall, Salisbury, 132
Parkinson, J. L., 148
parks and squares: Baltimore City, 153; Belmont Manor historic park, Elkridge, 240–41; Carroll Creek Park, Frederick, 336; Carroll Park, Baltimore City, 206; Court Square, Frederick, 334; Druid Hill Park, Baltimore City, 210, **212,** 212–13; Edgevale Park, 220; Franklin Square, Baltimore City, 205; Hagerstown City Park, 352; Hagerstown Public Square, 350–51; Heritage Farm Park, Walkersville, 344–45; Leonardtown, 26; Mount Vernon Place, Baltimore City, 154–55; Oakley Cabin African American Museum and Park, Sandy Spring vicinity, 320; Patterson (Jefferson) Park, St. Leonard, 42; Patterson Park Observatory, Baltimore City, **196,** 197; Queen Anne's County Courthouse, Centreville, 105; Western Shore, 22. *See also* national parks; state parks
Pasadena, 78
Patapsco Bridge and Ironworks, 159
pattern books, 13, 14, 15, 47, 53, 55, 126, 215, 218, 262, 272, 312, 326, 372
Patterson, Jefferson, 42
Patterson, Mary Breckenridge (Marvin), 42, 43
Payne House, Snow Hill, 145
Payne (George S.) House, Snow Hill, 145
Peale, Charles Willson, 52, 181
Peaslee, Horace, **23,** 23, 42, 43

pedestrian malls: Baltimore Street commercial buildings and pedestrian mall, Cumberland, 363–64; Old Courthouse Historic District, Rockville, 304

Pei (I. M.) and Partners, 16, 184

Pell and Corbett, **209**, 209–10

Pelli, Cesar, 323–24

Pemberton Hall, Salisbury, 33, 132–33

Pendleton Civil Service Act (1883), 285, 298, 306, 311

Penn, William, 86

Pennington, James, 11–12

Pennington, Josias, 375–76. *See also* Baldwin and Pennington

Pennington, Pleasants, 199

Pennington and Pennington, 244, **246**

Perryville, 89

Peterson and Brickbauer, 83, 167, **246, 246**

Phifer, Thomas, 327

Phillips, Albanus, 125; House, Cambridge, 124

Phillips, Levi, 125; House, Cambridge, 124

Phoenix Iron Company, 157

picturesque architecture and landscape, 41, 59, 82, 99, 122, 163, 197, 212, 229, 236, 254, 260, 262, 264, 272, 276, 284, 287, 310, 341, 342, 343, 352, 367, 374

Pietsch, Theodore Wells, 194–95

Piney Point, 25–26

Piper House, Sharpsburg, 355

Pippins (R. K.) and Sons, 99

Plain style (Quaker), 2, 87, 112, 317

planned communities, 13–14; Chevy Chase, 14, 310–11; Coldspring Newtown, Baltimore City, 14, **223**, 223; Columbia New Town, 14, **237**, 237–38; Dundalk, 230, 251–53; Gibson Island, 77–78; Greenbelt, **294**, 294–96; Guilford, Baltimore City, 220; Kentlands, Gaithersburg, 14, 322; Middle River, 230, 249–51; Mountain Lake Park, 374–75; New Mark Commons, Rockville, 14, **305**, 305–6; Roland Park, Baltimore City, 13–14, **218**, 218–19; Washington Grove, **322**, 322–23. *See also* garden suburbs; greenbelt towns; New Towns; New Urbanism

plank construction, 30, 91, 106, 109, 239, 332, 367, 369–70

plantations: Almodington, Oriole, 140; Annapolis, 46; Brome-Howard House and slave house, St. Mary's City, 24; Doughoregan Manor, Ellicott City, 236; Magruder-Bussard Farmstead (Agricultural History Farm Park), Gaithersburg, **321**, 321–22; Montpelier, Laurel, **54**, 55, 303;

Morgan Hill Farm, Lusby, 41–42; Mount Clare, Baltimore City, 205–6; Mount Republican, Newburg, 31; Old Bohemia Church (St. Francis Xavier Church), Warwick, 96; Poplar Hill at His Lordship's Kindness, Clinton, 286–87, **287;** Prince George's County, 283, 284; Ratcliffe Manor, Easton, **112**, 112–13; Riversdale, Riverdale Park, 299–300; St. Francis Xavier Roman Catholic Church and Newtown Manor, Leonardtown, 27; Sarum, Charlotte Hall, **30**, 30–31; Sotterley, Hollywood, **30**, 29–30; Spray (Godiah) Tobacco Plantation, St. Mary's City, 24; tobacco, 2, 11, 21, 46, 283; Tulip Hill, Harwood, 80–81; Waterloo, Princess Anne, 139; Western Shore, 21; Wye House and Plantation, Copperville, **113**, 113–14. *See also* slave houses

Plater, George, II, 30

Plater-Zyberk, Elizabeth, 14, 322

Platt, Charles, 155

Plummer, Adam Francis, 300

Plummer, William, 340; House, New Market, 340

Pocomoke City, 141–42

Poe, Edgar Allan: grave, 204; House, Baltimore City, 204

Point of Rocks, 341

Polychrome Houses, Silver Spring, 297, 313–14

Poole, Bobby C., 183, **184, 388**

Poolesville and vicinity, 324–27

Pope, John Russell, 16, 154, 155, **214,** 214–15, 220

Poplar Hill, Salisbury, **131**, 131–32

Poplar Hill at His Lordship's Kindness, Clinton, 286–87, **287**

Port Deposit, 87–89

Porter and Lockie, 311

Port Republic, 43–44

Port Tobacco, 21, 34–36

Post, George B., 168

post-in-the-ground construction, 29, 30, 31, 32

post offices: U.S. Courthouse and Post Office (Public Safety Building), Cumberland, 364; U.S. Post Office, Annapolis, **65**, 67; U.S. Post Office, Ellicott City, 232; U.S. Post Office, Frostburg, 371; U.S. Post Office, Hyattsville, 299; U.S. Post Office (Deere [John] Company Building), Lutherville-Timonium, **257**, 258; U.S. Post Office, Rockville, 304; U.S. Post Office, Towson, 245; U.S. Post Office and Courthouse, Baltimore City, 177

Potts (Richard) House, Frederick, 334

Powell (Samuel) House, Ellicott City, 233

Pratt, Enoch, 161, 165, 247; Free Library Central Building, Baltimore City, 151, **161**, 161

prefabricated buildings, 14, 197, 250, 251, 314, 316

preservation: Annapolis, 48; Antietam National Battlefield, Sharpsburg, 356; Baltimore City, 16–17, 152; Baltimore Shot Tower (Phoenix Shot Tower), **190**, 191; Banneker (Benjamin) Cabin, Oella, **255**, 255–56; Bostwick, Bladensburg, 297; Camden Yards, Baltimore City, 199; Footer's Dye Works, Cumberland, **362**, 362–63; Homestead Row Houses, Baltimore City, **188**, 188; Long (Robert) House, Baltimore City, 194; Maryland's preservation ethic, 16; Mount Moriah Church (Banneker-Douglass Museum), Annapolis, 68; Mount Royal B&O Station, Baltimore City, 209; Moyaone Reserve, Accokeek, 289–90; Oaks II, Brookeville, 321, **321**; Old Treasury Building, Annapolis, 50; Otterbein neighborhood, Baltimore City, 201; Seneca Store (Poole's General Store), Poolesville, 326; Statehouse and Historic St. Mary's City, **23**, 23–24; Uniontown, 263

Preston, 103–4

Price, Bruce, 351, 361, 363

Price, Henry, 65

Price, Robert, 106

Priest, John W., 256

Prince Frederick, 21–22, 44

Prince George's County, 285–303; African American residents and history, 283, 284; Baltimore and Ohio Railroad, 284; in Capital Region, 283; –, map, 284; interstate highway system, 325; in Maryland counties map, xvi; tobacco, 11, 283, 284

Princess Anne, 12, 84, 133–39; map, 134

prisons. *See* jails and prisons

Prospect Hall, Frederick, 338

Pry (Philip) House, Sharpsburg vicinity, 357

public buildings: Baltimore County Public Safety Building, Towson, **246**, 246; James Senate Office Building, Annapolis, 66–67; Maryland State House, Annapolis, **20**, 47, **49**, 49–50; Old Custom House, Vienna, **128**, 128–29; Old Maryland State House, St. Mary's City, **23**, 23; Old Treasury Building, Annapolis, 50; Oxford Custom House, 118; Public Safety Building, Cumberland, 364; U.S. Lifesaving Station and Guardhouse, Ocean City, 147–48, **148**. *See also* city halls; courthouses; fire stations; jails and prisons; post offices

public housing: Poe Homes, Baltimore City, 204

public utilities: Eastern Avenue Pumping Station, Baltimore City, 192; Pratt Street Power Plant, Baltimore City, 183

public works. *See* aqueducts; bridges; dams; lighthouses; tunnels

Pugin, A. W. N., 162

Purcell, Thomas F., 358

Pusey (W. P.) and Sons, 135

PWP Landscape Architecture, 327

Quaker meetinghouses: East Nottingham Friends Meeting House, Rising Sun, 86–87; Old Town Friends Meeting House (Aisquith Street Meeting House), Baltimore City, 189–90; Sandy Spring, **317**, 317; Third Haven Friends Meeting House, Easton, **xiv**, **112**, 112

quarries, 88, 229

Queen Anne's County, 105–10; Courthouse, **105**, 105; in Eastern Shore, 84; –, map, 85; in Maryland counties map, xvi

Queen Anne Style, 13, 41, 56, **58**, 58, 69, 70, 89, 99, 106, 132, 134, 145, **163**, 163, 202, 219, 225, 233, 241, 254, 269, 280, 286, 298, 305, 311, 315, 316, 341, 352, 362, **374**, 374, 375

Queenstown, 105, 108–9

Quinn Evans Architects, **116**, 116–17

railroads: Baltimore and Ohio (B&O) Railroad, 2, **7**, 7, 150, 193, 199, 200, 202–3, 206–7, 209, 228, 230, 232, 233, 239–40, 241, 243–44, 269, 284, 298, 305, 311, 315, 319, 322, 327, 331, 332, 334, 341, 349, 354, 362, 366, 368, 374, 375, 376; Baltimore and Sparrows Point Railroad, 251; Baltimore and Susquehanna Railroad, 224; Baltimore, Chesapeake, and Atlantic Railway, 116; Baltimore City, 2, 150, 228–29; Berlin, 146; Bollman truss bridges, 243, 244; Bowie railroad buildings, 293; Cambridge, 121; Catonsville Short Line Railroad, 253; Central Maryland, 7, 228–29; Cumberland and Pennsylvania Railroad, 369; Delaware and Chesapeake Railroad, 118; Dorchester and Delaware Railroad, 121, 125; Eastern Shore, 7, 85–86, 134; elevated, 219; Ellicott City, 228, 230, 232, 233; Hagerstown, 229, 333,

349; interurban electric railway from Frederick, 344; Kent County Railroad, 97; Leonardtown, 26; Maryland and Delaware Railroad, 111, 118; Maryland and Pennsylvania (Ma&Pa) Railroad, 229, 270; Ocean City, 7, 147; oyster industry, 40; Pennsylvania Railroad, 7, 207, 250, 293, 345; Rock Creek Railway, 310; Rock Hall Marine Railway, 100–101; Salisbury, 123, 130; Snow Hill, 143; suburbanization, 13; Washington and Chesapeake Beach Railway, 45; water transport supplanted by, 5, 6; Western Maryland Railway (WMR), 7, 207, 228, 263, 264, 265, 266, 267, 347, 349, 358, 362; Western Maryland Scenic Railroad, 362; Western Shore, 21

railroad stations: Baltimore and Ohio passenger station, Frederick, 335; Baltimore and Ohio Railroad Station (Baltimore and Ohio Ellicott City Station Museum), 232, 233–34, **235;** Baltimore and Ohio Railroad Station, Oakland, **374,** 374; Camden Station, Baltimore City, 200; Chesapeake Beach Railway Museum, 45–46; Mount Clare Station (Baltimore and Ohio Transportation Museum), Baltimore City, **202,** 202–3; Mount Royal B&O Station, Baltimore City, 209; Pennsylvania Station, Baltimore City, **207,** 207; Point of Rocks B&O Railroad Station, **341,** 341; Rockville Baltimore and Ohio Railroad station, 305; Sykesville B&O Station, 269; Western Maryland Railway buildings, Union Bridge, **265,** 265; Western Maryland Railway Station, Cumberland, 362

Rakestraw, John, 265

Ramsay, Andrew, 370

Randall, Alexander: Duplex, **58,** 58–59; Randall Court houses, Annapolis, 59

Randall (Peter) House, North Brentwood, 298

Ranlett, William H., 272

Ratcliffe Manor, Easton, **112,** 112–13, 140

Rathburn, Annie E., 44

Rational House plan, 237

Rawlings, John, 49, 54, **76,** 76

Rawn (William) and Associates, 306

Reasin, William H., **190,** 190, 276

Recreational Demonstration Administration, 348–49

recreational facilities: Fell's Point Recreational Pier, Baltimore City, 194–95. *See also* amusement parks; dance halls; fairgrounds; sports facilities

rectories: Carter Memorial Church (St. Peter the Apostle Church) Rectory, Baltimore City, 203; Emmanuel Episcopal Church Parish Hall, Cumberland, 361; St. John's Chapel Rectory, Burkittsville, 342; St. Paul's Episcopal Church, Baltimore City, 162

Reed, Washington, Jr., 358

Reisterstown, 256–57

Remsburg, Sharpsburg vicinity, 357

Renaissance Revival style, 155, 157, 168, 169, 172, 174, 177, **209,** 209–10, 220, 269, 351, 371

residential districts: Avondale, Solomons, 41; Belair at Bowie, 14, 292–93; Benning Road Historic District, Galesville, 81–82; Bolton Square Commons, Baltimore City, 210; Buckeystown, 341; Captain's Houses, Centreville, **107,** 107; Catonsville residential neighborhood, 253–54; Chevy Chase, 310–11; Coldspring Newtown, Baltimore City, 14, **223,** 223; Columbia New Town, 14, **237,** 237–38; Cornhill Street buildings, Annapolis, 62; Eastport, Annapolis, 74; Fleet Street, Annapolis, 62–63; Garrett Park, Kensington, 315–16; Gibson Island buildings, 77–78; Glen Echo Park, 328; Guilford, Baltimore City, 14, 219, 220; Hagerstown City Park, 352; Hammond Wood, Kensington, 14, **316,** 316–17; Homeland, Baltimore City, 219; Hyattsville, 298–99; Kentlands, Gaithersburg, 14, 322; Lawyers Hill, Elkridge, 229, 241–42; Main Street, Ellicott City, 233; Mountain Lake Park, 375; Mount Vernon Place, Baltimore City, 154–55, 219; Mount Washington residential area buildings, Baltimore City, 224–25; New Mark Commons, Rockville, 14, **305,** 305–6; Newtown, Salisbury, 132; North Brentwood Historic District, 297–98; Oella historic mill town, **254,** 254–55; Old Dundalk residential area, **252,** 252–53; Old Greenbelt, **xii, 294,** 294–96; Old Row Museum, Mount Savage, **369,** 369–70; Otterbein neighborhood, Baltimore City, 201; Pine Street neighborhood, Cambridge, **124,** 124–25; Randall Court houses, Annapolis, 59; Rockland mill village, 259; Roland Park, Baltimore City, 13–14, **218,** 218–19; St. Helena project, Dundalk, 251; Savage Mill Village, 242–43; Scientists' Cliffs, Port Republic, 12, 44; Snow Hill residential area, 144–45; Stone Hill, Bal-

residential districts (*continued*)
timore City, 226, 227; Union Street
houses, Havre de Grace, 280; Upper
Marlboro residential district, 286;
Victory Villa subdivision, Middle
River, 249, 250; Washington Street
buildings, Cumberland, **361**, 361–62;
Waverley Terrace, Baltimore City,
155, **205**, 205. *See also* garden cities;
planned communities; row houses

resorts: Baltimore and Ohio Railroad
and, 7, 374, 375; Betterton, 86, 100;
Chesapeake Beach, 45; Deer Park,
375–76; Eastern Shore, 86; Garrett
County, 332; Mountain Lake Park
resort buildings, 374–75; Ocean
City, 147; Piney Point, 26

restaurants: Coffee House, Annapolis,
65; Duke's Fountain Bar Restaurant,
Leonardtown, 27; Reynolds Tavern,
Annapolis, 67; Sykesville B&O
Station, 269

restrictive covenants, 218, 219, 293,
298, 310

Revett, Nicholas, 188

revival styles: Cloisters, The (Parker
House), Lutherville-Timonium,
258–59; Druid Hill Park, Baltimore
City, 212; Guilford, Baltimore City,
220; Newtown Historic District,
Salisbury, 132; Washington Street
buildings, Cumberland, 361. *See also
specific styles by name*

Reynolds, Elijah, 98, **99**

Reynolds, William, 67

Richardson (Samuel) House, Snow
Hill, 145

Richardsonian Romanesque style, **163**,
164, 173, 179, 335–36, **360**, 360–61,
373

Richter, Alexander, 316

Ridgely House, Annapolis, 62

Ridout, Hester Ann Chase, 54

Ridout, John, 346; House, Annapolis,
72, 74

Ridout Row, Annapolis, **72**, 72–73

Ridout, Molly, 49

Riggs (Artemus) House, Brookeville,
320

Rinehart, William R., 66, 165

Rising Sun, 86–87

Riverdale Park, 299–300; map, 295

Riversdale, Riverdale Park, 55, 284,
299–300

roads and highways: Baltimore
and Frederick Turnpike, 230,
331, 340; Baltimore Beltway, 247;
Baltimore City, 17, 153; Baltimore-
Hagerstown Turnpike, 262;
Baltimore-Washington Parkway,
8, 325; Braddock Road, 377; Capital
Beltway (I-495), 8, 285, 307, 315, 323,

325; Eisenhower Defense Highway
(I-70), 333; Falls Turnpike, 227, 259;
Frederick, 334; Frederick Road, 253;
Gapland Road, 342; I-95 corridor,
8, 229, **325**, 325; improved roads
movement, 7–8; Inner Harbor area,
Baltimore City, 181–82; interstate
highway system, 8, 325, 333; Legislative Road, 372; National Defense
Highway (MD-202), 296, 297; National Road, 6, 7, 150, 331, 332, 333,
340, 350, 354, 368, 370, 377–78; Post
Road between Philadelphia and
Annapolis, 90; Rock Run–Baltimore
turnpike, 277; U.S. 1, 8, 277, 298, 299,
302, 325; U.S. 40, 7, 8, 344, 350, 354,
368, 370, 378; Washington National
Pike, 323; Western Mountains, 331;
Western Shore, 21

roadside attractions: Penn Alps Inn
and Spruce Forest Artisan Village,
Grantsville, 378–79

Robbins, James B., 104

Robeson, Paul, 79

Robinette (Captain George) House,
Flintstone vicinity, 367

Robinette (George Tanner) House,
Flintstone vicinity, 367

Robinette (Moses) House, Flintstone
vicinity, 367

Robins, Albert, 120

Roche, Michael, 157

Rock Hall, 100–101

Rockland, 259

Rockville, 285, 304–7

Rococo style, 76, 109

Rodgers, John, Jr., 280, 282

Rodgers (Elizabeth) House, Havre de
Grace, 279–80

Rodier and Kunzin, 311

Rogers and Taliaferro, 75. *See also*
Rogers, Taliaferro and Lamb; RTKL
Associates

Rogers, Taliaferro and Lamb, **222**, 222,
247. *See also* RTKL Associates

Romanesque Revival style, 88, 169,
209, 210, **304**, 304, 336, 361, 363. *See
also* Richardsonian Romanesque
style

Romanesque style, 66, 131, 162, 211,
214, 235. *See also* Romanesque
Revival style

Rookwood Pottery, 207

Roosevelt, Franklin D. (FDR), 308, 349

Root, Irving C., 249

Rose Hill, Frederick, 338

Rose Hill, Port Tobacco, 35–36, 37

Rose Hill Farm house, Flintstone
vicinity, 368

Rosenwald, Julius, 82, 271, 290

Rosenwald schools: Bel Air Historical
Colored High School, 271; Galesville

Rosenwald School, 81–82; Ridgeley School, Capitol Heights, 290
Ross, Frank, 121
Ross and Walton, 296
Roth (Emory) and Sons, 167
Rouse, James, 14, 182, 185, 230, **237,** 237
Rouse Company, **184,** 184–85, 237–38
row houses, 188, 201, 203, 204; African American residents and history, 12; Baltimore City, **13,** 13, 17, 151–52; Belvidere Terrace, Baltimore City, **163,** 163; Bolton Square Commons, Baltimore City, 210; Brownstone Row, Baltimore City, 157–58; Canby Place, Baltimore City, 205; concrete row houses, Baltimore City, 219–20; "daylight" plan, 219–20; Douglass Place, Baltimore City, **196,** 196; Fell's Point Historic District, Baltimore City, 193; Fleet Street, Annapolis, 62; "Half-House" row houses, Baltimore City, 201–2; Hamilton Street Row Houses, Baltimore City, 159; Homestead Row Houses, Baltimore City, **188,** 188; Irish railroad workers' row houses, Baltimore City, **203,** 203; marble for, 229; Miller (Decatur) Row House, Baltimore City, **155,** 155; Oella historic mill town, **254,** 254–55; Old Dundalk residential area, 253; Old Greenbelt, 294; Otterbein neighborhood, Baltimore City, 201; Pascault Row, Baltimore City, 170, 172; Poe (Edgar Allan) House, Baltimore City, 204; Ridout Row, Annapolis, **72,** 72; Rockland mill village, 259; St. Helena project, Dundalk, 251; Shakespeare Street Row Houses, Baltimore City, 195–96; Ship Caulkers' Houses, Fell's Point, 196–97; Tonge Row, Ellicott City, 233; Waverley Terrace, Baltimore City, 155, **205,** 205; Wilkens Avenue Row Houses, Baltimore City, 206
Rowles, Hezekiah, 87
RTKL Associates, 16, 75, 166, 183, **192,** 192, **195,** 195, **199,** 199, 209, 210, 222, **257,** 257

Sabillasville, 347–48
Safdie, Moshe, 14, 16, **223,** 223
St. Clair (Cyrus) House, Cambridge, 125
St. John's College, Annapolis: Key (Francis Scott) Auditorium and Mellon Hall, **58,** 58; McDowell Hall, 48, **57,** 57–58; McKeldin Planetarium, 58
St. Leonard, 42–43
St. Mary's City, 4, 23–24, 47, 66
St. Mary's County, 23–30; gambling, 32; in Maryland counties map, xvi; Naval Air Station Patuxent River, 23, 26; tobacco, 11, 21; in Western Shore, 21; –, map, 22
St. Michaels, 114–17
St. Thomas Manor, Bel Alton, 33–34
Salisbury, 86, 130–33; in Maryland topographical map, 3
Salter, John, **112,** 112
Sandy Spring and vicinity, 284, 317–20
Sansbury, George, 362
Sarum, Charlotte Hall, **30,** 30–31
Sasaki, 221
Sasaki, Hideo, 247
Saunders, William, 315–16
Savage, 228, 242–44
Sawyer, Gertrude, 42–43
Scarff, John, 181
Schamu Machowski + Patterson, 172
Scharf, John, 326
Schifferstadt, Frederick, **337,** 337–38
Schmenner, Harry, **365,** 365
Schneider, Herman, 362
Schoeppe, Edward, **328,** 329
school buildings: African Academy, Baltimore City, 227; Bear Hill School, Spruce Forest Artisan Village, Grantsville, 379; Berkley (Hosanna) School, Darlington, 275; Brookeville Academy, 321; Brookeville Public School House, 321; Carver School, Cumberland, 365; Chestertown Public School, 98; Drayden African American Schoolhouse, 25; Greenbelt Center School (Greenbelt Community Center), **xii,** 295; Hog Island School, Preston, 104; Linwood Hall, 267; Maryland Military Academy, 118, 120; McComas Institute, Joppa, 274–75; The McKim Free School (The McKim Center), Baltimore City, 188–89; More (Hannah) Academy, Reisterstown, 254, 255; Mount Washington Female College, Baltimore City, 225; National Park Seminary Pagoda, Forest Glen, **314,** 314–15; Patapsco Female Institute, Ellicott City, 231, 233; Rock School (Stanley Institute Museum), Cambridge, 126; Roland Park Country Day School, Baltimore City, 219; St. Joseph's Academy, Emmitsburg, 347; Seneca Schoolhouse, Poolesville, 325–26; Tolson's Chapel, Sharpsburg, 356; Tome Institute, Port Deposit, 89; Tome School for Boys, Port Deposit, 89; Uniontown Academy, 264; Whitehaven Schoolhouse, 133. *See also* Rosenwald schools
Schrock, Alta, 378–79

Schuler, Hans, 165
scientific facilities: Beltsville Agricultural Research Center, 285, 302–3, 307; COMSAT Laboratories, Clarksburg, 323–24; Iribe (Brendan) Center for Computer Sciences and Engineering, University of Maryland, College Park, **301**, 302; NASA Goddard Space Flight Center, Greenbelt, **306**, 307; National Oceanic and Atmospheric Administration (NOAA) Center for Weather and Climate Prediction, College Park, 301
Scott (Upton) House, Annapolis, **73**, 73–74
sculptures. *See* artworks and sculptures
seafood processing, 7, 9, **11**, 21, 40, 41, 81, 85, 115, 116, 121–22, 124, 125–26, 150, 186. *See also* fishing; crabbing; oystering
sea-level rise, 119
Second Empire style, 95, 97, 132, **180**, 180–81, 224, 232, 267, 339, 351, 361
segregation, 11; Baltimore City, 150, 153, 211; Cambridge, 122; Chesapeake houses' dependencies, 33; Druid Hill Park, Baltimore City, 213; Eastern Shore, 86; educational, 25, 82, 138–39, 221, 271, 275, 290; Emmanuel Episcopal Church, Cumberland, 361; Galesville, 81; Glen Echo Park, 328; Henry's (Colored) Hotel, Ocean City, 148; housing, 12, 153, 293, 295–96, 298; Mar-Va Theater, Pocomoke City, 142; Metropolitan AME Church, Cumberland, 364; Poe Homes, Baltimore City, 204; post–Civil War Maryland, 10, 11; Pratt (Enoch) Free Library, Baltimore City, 161; Roland Park, Baltimore City, 218, 219; war memorials, 94
Seibert, John S., 363
Seneca sandstone, 57, 304, 324, 325, 326, 328
Senseney (Washington) House, Linwood, 267
Servary, L. R., 253, 254
Seton, Saint Elizabeth Ann, 346–47
Seward (Daniel O.) House, Cambridge, **124**, 125
Sharpe, Horatio, 47, 72, 74
Sharpsburg, 355–57
Shaw, Alexander, 270
Shaw, Diane, 337
Sheetz, William Cramp, Jr., 356
Shellman, James, 259–60
Shelton, Herbert R., 23
Sheperd (Lucius M.) House, Cumberland, 362

Shepley, Bullfinch, Richardson and Abbott, 156
Sheppard, Moses, 165, 189, 246
Sherrick House, Sharpsburg vicinity, **357**, 357
Sherwood Forest, 22
Shingle Style, 59, 69, 219, 241, 254, 298, 311, 329, 375
shipbuilding: Baltimore City, 150; cotton duck for, 225, 242; Fell's Point Historic District, Baltimore City, 192–93; Oxford, 118. *See also* boats, ships, and boatyards
Shiplap House, Annapolis, **63**, 63–64
Shipley, Charles, **203**, 203, **205**, 205
shopping centers: Dundalk Building, 252; Harbor Place, Baltimore City, 184–85; Roland Park, Baltimore City, **218**, 219; Silver Spring Shopping Center, **312**, 312–13
shotgun houses: Avondale, Solomons, 41
Shriner (Peter) House, Union Bridge, 266
sidebars: The Chesapeake House, 32–33; Climate Change, Sea-Level Rise, and the Chesapeake Bay, 119; Federal Influence in Maryland, 306–7; The Five-Part Palladian House, 54–55; The I-95 Corridor, 325; Maryland Wood Boatbuilding, 116–17
Sill, Howard, 220
Silver Family Houses, Darlington, 276
Silver Spring, 312–14; map, 310
Simon, Louis A., 67, 245, 299
Simplicity (Venables [Seth D.] House), Princess Anne, 135–36
Sims and Sims, 351
Singer, William Henry, Jr., 352
Sion Hill, Havre de Grace, 280, **281**, 281–82
slave houses: Beatty-Cramer springhouse, Frederick, 338; Brome-Howard House and slave house, St. Mary's City, 24; Chesapeake houses and, 33; few remain, 11; Hampton, Towson, 248; Morgan Hill Farm, Lusby, 42; Riversdale, Riverdale Park, 300; Sotterley, Hollywood, 30; Trevanion, Taneytown, 262; Woodlawn log slave house, Sandy Spring, 319; Wye House and Plantation, Copperville, 114
Slye, Gerrard, 28
Small, Jacob, Jr., 15, 233–34, **235**
Small, Jacob, Sr., 201
Small, William F., 15, 170, 181, 188–89, 191, **235**, 236–37
Smalls (J. H.) and Son, 296
Smith, Delos H., 304
Smith, Edward, **63**, 63

Smith, John, 4, 34, 84
Smith, Judson, 304
Smith and May, **178,** 178, **179,** 179–80
Smith-Group Architects, **312,** 312
Smith (George Washington Purnell) House, Snow Hill, 145
Smith (Governor John Walter) House, Snow Hill, 145
Smith Island, 86, 119
Snively (George) House, Keedysville, 354
Snow Hill, 84, 142–46; map, 144
Snyder, Jacob, 357
social halls: Abraham Hall, Beltsville, 303; Fell's Point Recreational Pier, Baltimore City, 194–95; Hollins Market, Baltimore City, 204–5; Odd Fellows Hall, Sandy Spring, 318; Odd Fellows Lodge, Easton, 111; St. Mary's Beneficial Society Hall, Upper Marlboro, 303. *See also* Masonic buildings
Solomons, 39–41
Somerset County, 133–41; Courthouse, 134–35; in Eastern Shore, 84; —, map, 85; in Maryland counties map, xvi
Sotterley, Hollywood, **29,** 29–30
South River, 80
Southworth, Fredric W., 308–9, **309**
Spanish Revival style, 311
Sparrows Point, 9, 230, 251
Spear, Joseph, **199,** 199–200
Spencer-Silver House, Havre de Grace, 280
Sperry, Joseph Evans, **159,** 159, 168–69, **171, 174,** 174–75, 210–11, 216, 254. *See also* Wyatt and Sperry
sports facilities: Fair Hill Racetrack, Elkton, 94; Hot Sox Negro League Baseball field, Galesville, 81; Memorial Stadium (demolished), Baltimore City, 199; Oriole Park at Camden Yards, Baltimore City, 17, **199,** 199–200; Ravens stadium, Baltimore City, 200. *See also* horse racing
Sprigg (Grace E. D.) House, Kensington, 316
squares. *See* parks and squares
stadiums. *See* sports facilities
Stagg Hall, Port Tobacco, **35,** 35
stained glass. *See* artworks and sculptures
Stam (Colin F.) House, Chestertown, 97
Stanley, Ezekiel, 126
Stanley-Brown, R., 304
Starkweather, Norris G., 16, 158–59, 234–35, **235,** 235–36
Star-Spangled Flag House, Baltimore City, 191

state parks: Casselman River Bridge State Park, Grantsville vicinity, 378; Cunningham Falls State Park, Thurmont, 349; Fort Frederick State Park, Big Pool vicinity, 358–59, **359;** Garrett County, 332; Gathland State Park, Burkittsville, 343; Greenwell State Park, Hollywood, 29; Gunpowder Falls State Park, Kingsville, 274; New Germany State Park, Grantsville vicinity, 379; Susquehanna State Park, Darlington vicinity, 277; Tubman (Harriet) Underground Railroad State Park Visitor Center, Church Creek, **127,** 127
steamboats: Betterton, 100; Cambridge, 121; Chestertown, 97; Eastern Shore, 84, 86; Leonardtown, 26; Piney Point Lighthouse, 25; St. Michaels, 115; trucks replace, 141, 143; Western Shore, 21, 22, 45
Steele (Captain [John]) House, Baltimore City, 194
Stein, Clarence, 294
Stephenson, William, 56
Stevensville, 109–10
Stick Style, 106, 108, 212, 225, 280, 298
Stiefel (Mamie) House, Catonsville, 254
Stoddard, Benjamin, 297
Stoddard (J. C.) House, Kensington, 316
Stoddart, William L., 168, **171**
Stokes, Granville, 148
Stoll, Charles, **198,** 198
Stone, Edward Durell, 182
Stone, Thomas, 36
Stone, William F., Jr., **122,** 122
Stone and Webster, 276–77, **277**
Strathmore Hall, Rockville, 306–7
streetcars: Baltimore City, 152, 210, 212; Catonsville, 253; Glen Echo Park, 328, 329; Hyattsville, 298; North Brentwood Historic District, 298; suburbanization, 13
Stroh Lehm (mud and straw), 337
Strong house, Gibson Island, 78
Struever Bros. Eccles and Rouse, 126
Stuart, H. M., 97
Stuart, James, 188
StudioEIS, 49
STV Group, 83
Sullivan, Louis H., 174
sustainable design, 208, 301, 314
Swanston, Rebecca, 185–86, **187**
Sykesville, 228, 229, 269
Symington, W. Stuart, 77
synagogues: Baltimore Hebrew Congregation Synagogue, 210; B'nai Israel Synagogue, Baltimore City, 190; Eutaw Place Temple (Prince Hall Grand Lodge), Baltimore City,

synagogues (*continued*)
210–11, 224; Lloyd Street Synagogue, Baltimore City, **190**, 190, 204; Temple Oheb Shalom, Baltimore City, **224**, 224

TAC (The Architects Collaborative), **224**, 224
Takoma Park, 311–12; map, 310
Talbot County, 110–21; Courthouse, 111; in Eastern Shore, 84; —, map, 85; in Maryland counties map, xvi; sea-level rise, 119
Talcott-Melville House, Kensington, 316
Taneytown, 262
Tasker, Benjamin, 292
taverns: Brewster Tavern, Annapolis, 62; Cross Keys Tavern, Rising Sun, 87; Hagan's Tavern, Frederick County, 378; Harp and Crown tavern (Shiplap House), Annapolis, 63; Harrison (Joseph) tavern, St. Michaels, 115; Indian Queen Tavern, Charlestown, **90**, 90–91; Kings' Arms Tavern, Annapolis, 62; London Town Publik House, Woodland Beach, 73, **79**, 79–80; Middletown Tavern, Annapolis, 66; Old Ordinary, Havre de Grace, **278**, 278; Red Lyon Tavern (Black's Store), Charlestown, 91; Reynolds Tavern, Annapolis, 67; Rodgers Tavern Museum, Perryville, **89**, 89, 280; White Swan Tavern, Chestertown, 97
Taylor, Basil, 313–14
Taylor, James Knox, **65**, 67, 364, 371
Taylor and Fisher, **178**, 178, 270
Taylor (Captain James F.) House, Chestertown, 98
Teackle Mansion, Princess Anne, 133, **135**, 135, 136, 137
Techbuilt Houses, 316
telescoping plan: Beall-Dawson House, Rockville, 305; Boswell-Compton House, Port Tobacco, 34; Brome-Howard House, St. Mary's City, 24; Cherry Grove, Sandy Spring, 319; Chesapeake houses, 12; Clifton, Sandy Spring, 318; Content, Upper Marlboro, 286; Farrow (William H.) House, Snow Hill, 145; Mount Republican, Newburg, 31; Mudd (Dr. Samuel A.) House, Bryantown, **37**, 37; Wyoming, Clinton, 33, 387
Tenthouse Creek Village, 81
terra-cotta: Abell Building, Baltimore City, 173; Allegany County Courthouse, 360; ASA Building, Baltimore City, 174; Belvidere Terrace, Baltimore City, 163;

Brewers' Exchange, Baltimore City, 169; Colonial Theater, Hagerstown, 351; Frederick business district, 335, 336; Garrett County Courthouse, Oakland, 374; The Johns Hopkins Hospital, Baltimore City, 198; Liriodendron, Bel Air, 272; Mercantile Safe Deposit and Trust Building, Baltimore City, 179; One South Calvert Building (Continental Trust Building), Baltimore City, 178; Rombro Building, Baltimore City, 173; Stewart's Department Store (Posner Building), Baltimore City, 169; U.S. Naval Academy, Annapolis, 61; Washington Trust Company, Ellicott City, 233
Terrell, Robert and Mary Church, 79
theaters and concert halls: Baskt Theater, Evergreen, Baltimore City, 217–18; Chesapeake Shakespeare Company theater, Baltimore City, 179; Church Hill Theatre, 107; Colonial Theater, Hagerstown, 351; Elkton Opera House (Cecil Bank), 93; Hippodrome Theater at the France-Merrick Performing Arts Center, Baltimore City, **171**, 172; Key (Francis Scott) Auditorium and Mellon Hall, St. John's College, Annapolis, 58; Lyric Theater, Frostburg, 371; Mar-Va Theater, Pocomoke City, **142**, 142; Masonic Hall and Opera House, Annapolis, **59**, 59–60; Mechanic (Morris A.) Theater (demolished), Baltimore City, 166; Meyerhoff (Joseph) Symphony Hall, Baltimore City, **208**, 208–9; Odeon Theater, Forest Glen, 315. *See also* movie theaters
Thomas, Lenore, 289, 295
Thomas, Philip E., 240, 319
Thomas Family Houses, Sandy Spring, 33, 318–19
Thomas (J.) House, Keedysville, 355
Thomas (Phillip) House, Frederick, 336
Thomas (Richard) House, Brookeville, 321
Thomas-Jencks-Gladding House (Hackerman House), Baltimore City, 155–56
Thompson, Benjamin, **184**, 184–85
Thurmont, 348–49
Tiffany, Louis Comfort, 361
Tiffany Studios, 123, 156, 160, 162, 164
Tilghman Island, 118
Tilton, Edward, 221
Tilton and Githens, **161**, 161
Tilton House, Annapolis, 70
Timanus, Charles, Jr., **231**, 231–32
Timonium. *See* Lutherville-Timonium
Tipahato, Sabillasville, 347–48
tobacco: Annapolis, 21, 46, 47; Brome-

Howard House and slave house, St. Mary's City, 24; Calvert County, 11, 21; Cambridge, 121; Capital Region, 283; Charles County, 11, 21; Chesapeake Bay, 4; Doughoregan Manor, Ellicott City, 236; Drane (James) Log House, Accident, 377; Eastern Shore, 84; Hancock's Resolution, Pasadena, **78,** 78; Lower Marlboro, 45; Magruder-Bussard Farmstead (Agricultural History Farm Park), Gaithersburg, **321,** 321–22; Mount Republican, Newburg, 31; plantations, 2, 21, 46, 283; Port Tobacco, 21, 34; Prince George's County, 11, 283, 284; St. Mary's County, 11, 21; St. Francis Xavier Roman Catholic Church and Newtown Manor, Leonardtown, 27; Southern Maryland farm, **2;** Western Shore, 11, 21–22. *See also* tobacco barns; tobacco warehouses

tobacco barns: Bond-Simms barn complex, Hollywood, 29; Maidstone, Owings, 46; Morgan Hill Farm, Lusby, **41,** 42; Sarum, Charlotte Hall, 31; Western Shore, 21

tobacco warehouses: Henderson's Wharf B&O Tobacco Warehouse (The Inn at Henderson's Wharf), Baltimore City, **193,** 193; Hughesville tobacco warehouses, **38,** 38; Main Street buildings, Annapolis, 66; Tobacco Prise Warehouse, Annapolis, 64

toll gate houses: La Vale Toll Gate House, **368,** 368; Oldtown toll booth, 367

Tolson (Warren) Cottage, Piney Point, 26

Tome, Jacob, 88–89

"top-hat" dormers, 334, 338

Totten, George Oakley, Jr., 311

Touart, Paul, 139

tourism: Antietam National Battlefield, Sharpsburg, 356–57; Baltimore and Ohio (B&O) Railroad and, 7, 374; Berlin, 146; Betterton, 100; Cambridge, 122; Eastern Shore, 86; Frostburg, 371; Inner Harbor redevelopment, Baltimore City, 10, 181–83, 185; Ocean City, 86, 147; St. Michaels, 115; Sykesville, 269; Western Maryland Railway Station, Cumberland, 362; Western Mountains, 333. *See also* resorts

towers: Allegany County Courthouse, **360,** 360; Antietam National Battlefield, Sharpsburg, **356,** 356–57; Baltimore Shot Tower (Phoenix Shot Tower), 10, **190,** 190–91; Bromo Seltzer Arts Tower (Emerson Bromo-Seltzer Tower), Baltimore City, 10, **174,** 174–75; Christ Episcopal Church, Cambridge, **122,** 123; Lovely Lane Methodist Church, Baltimore City, 213–14; Mount Royal B&O Station, Baltimore City, 209; St. Paul's Episcopal Church, Baltimore City, 162; Town Clock Church (German Evangelical Lutheran Church), Cumberland, **365,** 365; U.S. Lifesaving Station and Guardhouse, Ocean City, 148

Town, Ithiel, 258

Towne, John T., **96,** 96

Townsend, George Alfred, **343,** 343

Towson, 229, 244–49; map, 245

Towson and Steuart, 154

Traband (John H.) House, Upper Marlboro, 286

Tracy and Swartwout, 373

transportation facilities, 5–8; Tome carriage house, Port Deposit, 88, **88.** *See also* airports; canals; lockhouses; railroad stations; roads and highways; toll gate houses

Trevanion, Taneytown, **262,** 262

Trotter, James, 80

Trowbridge, Alexander B., 78

Tubman, Harriet, 12, 84, 103, 121, 122, 127, 128; Underground Railroad Visitor Center, Church Creek, **127,** 127

Tucker House, Centreville, 106

Tudor Hall, Bel Air, 272

Tudor Hall, Leonardtown, 26, 29

Tudor Revival style, **218,** 219, 220, 311

Tugwell, Rexford Guy, 294

Tulip Hill, Harwood, 55, 80–81, **81**

tunnels: Chesapeake and Ohio Canal, Paw Paw Tunnel, Oldtown vicinity, 367

Turkey Cock Hall, Rockland, 259

Turnbull, Bayard, 220

Tyson, Elisha, 189; House, Baltimore City, **227,** 227

Underground Railroad, 10, 84, 103, 121, 127, 227, 317, 320

Union Bridge, 228, 264–66

Uniontown, 262–64

universities. *See* colleges and universities

University of Maryland, College Park, 301–2; Arundel (Anne) Hall, 302; Bostwick House, Bladensburg, 297; establishment as Maryland Agricultural College, 284, 300, 301; Iribe (Brendan) Center for Computer Sciences and Engineering, **301,** 302; McKeldin Library, 302; McKeldin Mall, 302; Memorial Chapel, 302; Ritchie Coliseum, 302; Rossborough Inn, 301; Smith (Clarice) Performing Arts Center, 302

Upjohn, Richard, 82, **122,** 122, 162, 256, 336–37, 361
Upper Marlboro, 283, 285–86, 303
urban renewal: Baltimore City Homesteading Program, 17, 152, 188, 201; Baltimore Street commercial buildings and pedestrian mall, Cumberland, 363; Bolton Square Commons, Baltimore City, 210; Cumberland, 359; Inner Harbor redevelopment, Baltimore City, 181–83; Old Courthouse Historic District, Rockville, 304; One Charles Center, Baltimore City, 165–66; Otterbein neighborhood, Baltimore City, 201; Poe (Edgar Allan) House, Baltimore City, 204; Sun Life Building, Baltimore City, 167
URS Corporation, 83

Vail House, Avondale, Solomons, 41
Van Buskirk, John, 372
Vandiver (Murray) House, Havre de Grace, 280
Vansant, Stanley F., 101
Van Sweringen, Garrett, 24
Variety Iron Works, 173
Vaux, Calvert, 246–47, 276
Veazey, John, 90
Venables (Seth D.) House (Simplicity), Princess Anne, 135–36
Venetian Gothic style, 174
Vickers, Harrison W., 99
Vickers (George) House, Ocean City, 147
Vienna, 128–30
visitors' centers: Antietam National Battlefield, Sharpsburg, 357; Baltimore Visitor Center, 183; Fort McHenry National Monument and Historic Shrine, Baltimore City, 187; Fort Washington National Park, 288; Tubman (Harriet) Underground Railroad Visitor Center, Church Creek, **127,** 127
Vogel, Jack K., 251
Vosbury (Louis) House, Havre de Grace, 280
Voysey, Charles F. A., 220

Waddell (Commodore [James Iredell]) House, 56
Wadsworth, Reginald J., **xii, 294,** 294
Waggaman, Clarke, 311
Waggaman, Henry, 139
Wagner, Charles, 289, 290; House, Accokeek, **289,** 289–90
Waite (John G.) Associates, 160
Walker, Hale, 249, **294,** 294
Walker Cottage, Ocean City, 149
Walker (Alexander) House, Ellicott City, 233

Walkersville, 344–45
Wallace, Charles, 62
Walters, Henry, 156, 165
Ward, Lemuel, Jr., 140–41
Ward, Steve, 140–41
Wardman, Harry, 311
Ware, Isaac, 51, 282
Warnecke (John Carl) and Associates, 60–62
Warwick, 96–97
Washington, Booker T., 79
Washington, George, 49, 89, 99, 153–54, 278, 288, 327, 364, 366
Washington County, 349–59; Courthouse, 351; in Maryland counties map, xvi; in Western Mountains, 331; —, map, 333
Washington Grove, 322–23
Waterloo, Princess Anne, 139
Waters, Joseph R., 138
Watkins, James, 114
Weaver-Fox House, Uniontown, 264
Weaver (Jacob J., Sr.) House, Uniontown, 264
Webb (James) Cabin, Harmony, 12, **103,** 103
Webster, S. L., 104
Weeks, Christopher, 271
Weiner (Michael) House, Burkittsville, 342
Welch, Winthrop A., 216
Wentz (George and Lizzie) House, Catonsville, 254
Western Mountains, 331–79; map, 332–33; in Maryland regions map, xvi
Western Shore, 21–83; map, 22; Chesapeake houses, 32; in Maryland regions map, xvi; recreational waterfront communities, 22; Southern Tidewater traditions, 1; tobacco, 11, 21–22
Westminster, 228, 259–62
Westphal, Walter, 206
West River, 82
Wetmore, James A., 177
wharfs, 26, 90, 96, 98, 102, 107, 118, 128, 193–94, 195; communities, 21, 28, 45
White, Andrew, 33
White, Henry S. Taylor, 348. *See also* Mottu and White
White, Stanford, 154, **163,** 164, 214. *See also* McKim, Mead and White
Whitehall, Annapolis, **76,** 76
Whitehaven, 86, 133
White (Newton) Mansion, Mitchellville, 55, **291,** 291
Whiteside, Henry, 76
Whiting Turner Contracting, 117
Whittingham, William R., 275
W-houses, **118,** 118

Wicomico County, 130–33; Court-
house, 130–31; in Eastern Shore, 84;
—, map, 85; in Maryland counties
map, xvi
Widehall, Chestertown, 97
Widrick (George) House, Frederick,
339, 339
Wight, Rezin, 170
Wilcox, Keith W., **315**, 315
Williams, Henry and Georgeanna, 44
Williams (Ferdinand) House, Cumber-
land, 361
Williamsport, 358
Willis, John Arthur, 102
Williston, 102–3
Willson, Jacob C., 104
Wilson, Henry, 191; House, Galesville,
81
Wilson, John Appleton, 16, 49
Wilson and Wilson, **163**, 163
Winans, Ross (grandfather), 165, 202
Winans, Ross (grandson), 165; House,
Baltimore City, **163**, 164
Winterberg House, Spruce Forest
Artisan Village, 379
Winterbottom, W. Grason, 124, 125
Wolfe, Joseph, 265, 266; House, Union
Bridge, 265–66
women residents and history: Clara
Barton, 329–30; Rosalie Stier
Calvert, 299–300; Alice Ferguson,
289; Anne Green, 69; Montgomery
Farm Women's Cooperative Market
(Bethesda Women's Market), 309;
Mount Washington Female College,
Baltimore City, 225; National Park
Seminary, Forest Glen, 314–15;
Patapsco Female Institute, Ellicott
City, 231, 233; Point Farm, St.
Leonard, 42–43; Rosie Riveters of
Eastport, 74; Alta Schrock, 378–79;
Saint Elizabeth Ann Seton, 346–47;
Sisters of Charity of St. Joseph,
346–47
Wood, Ruby Ross, 273

Wood, Waddy E., 311
Woodbury Cotton Duck Company,
226
Woodland Beach, 79–80
Woodlawn, Sandy Spring, 319
Woodsboro, 345–46
Worcester County, 141–49; Court-
house, 143; in Eastern Shore, 84;
—, map, 85; in Maryland counties
map, xvi
worker housing, 47, 124–25, 225, 227,
232–33, 242–43, 249, 251, 254–55,
259, 341, 348, 369–70
Works Progress Administration
(WPA), 139, 304, 349
Wren, Christopher, 67, 160, 201
Wright, Frank Lloyd, 78, **308**, 308, 316
Wright, Lloyd, **308**, 308
Wright, Russel, 63
Wright's Chance, Centreville, 106
Wright (Robert Llewellyn) House,
Bethesda, **308**, 308
Wyand House, Keedysville, 355
Wyatt and Nolting, 176–77, 205, 216,
218, 219, 254, **271**, 271–72
Wyatt and Sperry, 16, **163**, 163, 179
Wye House and Plantation, Copper-
ville, **113**, 113–14, 135, 145
Wye Mills, 110
Wyoming, Clinton, 12, 33, 387

Yates, Theophilus, 31
Yessler, Harry E., 351
YMCA buildings: Baltimore Street
commercial buildings and pedes-
trian mall, Cumberland, 363–64
York Bridge Company, 268

Zeidler, Eberhard, 183
Ziger/Snead, 58, 67, 210
Zimmerman (Charles) House, Annapolis, 70
Zink, John J., **221**, 221, 336
zoos: Maryland Zoo, Baltimore City,
170, 212

BUILDINGS OF THE UNITED STATES is a series of books on American architecture compiled and written on a state-by-state basis. The primary objective of the series is to identify and celebrate the rich cultural, economic, and geographical diversity of the United States as it is reflected in the architecture of each state. The series has been commissioned by the Society of Architectural Historians, an organization dedicated to the study, interpretation, and preservation of the built environment throughout the world.

PUBLISHED BY THE UNIVERSITY OF VIRGINIA PRESS

Buildings of Arkansas, Cyrus A. Sutherland and contributors (2017)

Buildings of Delaware, W. Barksdale Maynard (2008)

Buildings of Hawaii, Don J. Hibbard (2011)

Buildings of Maryland, Lisa Pfueller Davidson and Catherine C. Lavoie (2022)

Buildings of Massachusetts: Metropolitan Boston, Keith N. Morgan, with Richard M. Candee, Naomi Miller, Roger G. Reed, and contributors (2009)

Buildings of Michigan (revised edition), Kathryn Bishop Eckert (2012)

Buildings of Mississippi, Jennifer V. O. Baughn and Michael W. Fazio, with Mary Warren Miller (2020)

Buildings of North Dakota, Steve C. Martens and Ronald L. M. Ramsay (2014)

Buildings of Pennsylvania: Philadelphia and Eastern Pennsylvania, George E. Thomas, with Patricia Likos Ricci, Richard J. Webster, Lawrence M. Newman, Robert Janosov, and Bruce Thomas (2011)

Buildings of Pennsylvania: Pittsburgh and Western Pennsylvania, Lu Donnelly, H. David Brumble IV, and Franklin Toker (2010)

Buildings of Texas: Central, South, and Gulf Coast, Gerald Moorhead, with James W. Steely, W. Dwayne Jones, Anna Mod, John C. Ferguson, Cheryl Caldwell Ferguson, Mario L. Sánchez, and Stephen Fox (2013)

Buildings of Texas: East, North Central, Panhandle and South Plains, and West, Gerald Moorhead, with James W. Steely, Willis C. Winters, Mark Gunderson, Jay C. Henry, and Joel Warren Barna (2019)

Buildings of Vermont, Glenn M. Andres and Curtis B. Johnson, with contributions by Chester H. Liebs (2013)

Buildings of Virginia: Valley, Piedmont, Southside, and Southwest, Anne Carter Lee and contributors (2014)

Buildings of Wisconsin, Marsha Weisiger and contributors (2016)

SAH/BUS CITY GUIDE

Buildings of New Orleans, Karen Kingsley and Lake Douglas (2018)

Buildings of Savannah, Robin B. Williams, with David Gobel, Patrick Haughey, Daves Rossell, and Karl Schuler (2015)

PUBLISHED BY THE SOCIETY OF ARCHITECTURAL HISTORIANS AND THE CENTER FOR AMERICAN PLACES

Buildings of Pittsburgh, Franklin Toker (2007)

PUBLISHED BY OXFORD UNIVERSITY PRESS

Buildings of Alaska, Alison K. Hoagland (1993)

Buildings of Colorado, Thomas J. Noel (1997)

Buildings of the District of Columbia, Pamela Scott and Antoinette J. Lee (1993)

Buildings of Iowa, David Gebhard and Gerald Mansheim (1993)

Buildings of Louisiana, Karen Kingsley (2003)

Buildings of Michigan, Kathryn Bishop Eckert (1993)

Buildings of Nevada, Julie Nicoletta, with photographs by Bret Morgan (2000)

Buildings of Rhode Island, William H. Jordy; Richard Onorato and William McKenzie Woodward, contributing editors (2004)

Buildings of Virginia: Tidewater and Piedmont, Richard Guy Wilson and contributors (2002)

Buildings of West Virginia, S. Allen Chambers Jr. (2004)

◀ Jonathan Hager House and Museum (WM24), Hagerstown